The Ultimate Mediterranean Diet Cookbook For Beginners

Discover An Easy Guide To Keep Fit, And ***1300+*** *Healthy, Tested, And Easy Meal Prep Recipes. With A*

4-Week Meal Plan

To Change Your Eating Lifestyle.

By

Jemma Zannina

TABLE OF CONTENTS

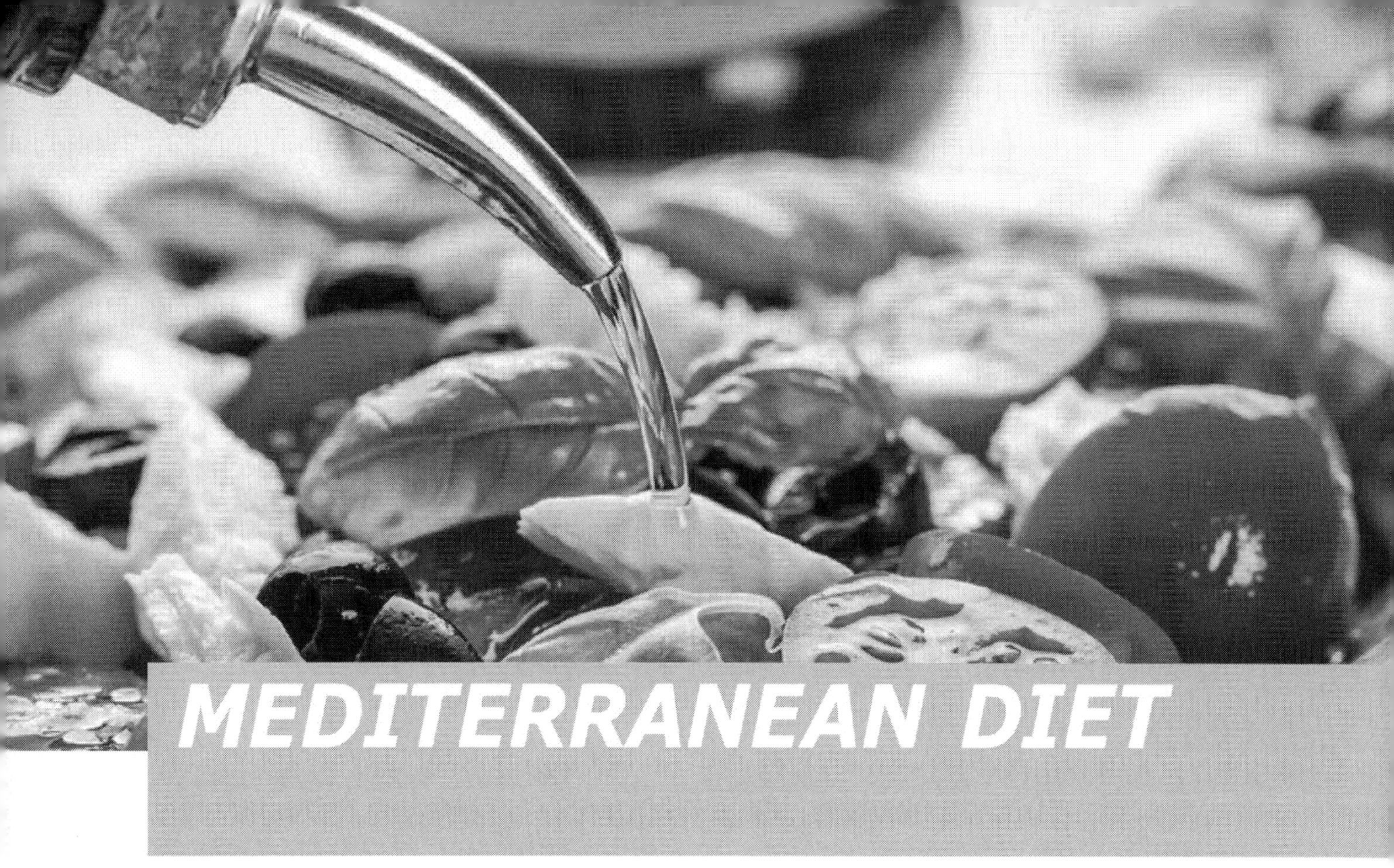

MEDITERRANEAN DIET

The Mediterranean diet is a dietary pattern that is very rich in plant foods, including fresh fruit and vegetables and lots of plant protein.

In addition to fruits and vegetables, which can be eaten as part of the Mediterranean diet, this diet is rich in low-fat dairy products, such as cottage cheese and yogurt, lean meat, fish and poultry, olive oil, and nuts.

People eating the Mediterranean diet tend to have less heart disease, less obesity, better lipid levels, lower blood pressure, fewer signs of diabetes, and more years of good health.

These health benefits result from the many plant foods in this diet, such as fiber-rich whole grains, beans, nuts, berries, and some vegetables and fruits. Studies have shown that individuals with a Mediterranean diet, who eat lots of fish and veggies and limit meat and dairy, have a much lower risk of death and have a much lower risk of developing heart disease and diabetes.

Health Benefits of The Mediterranean Diet

The Mediterranean diet has been found to reduce the risk of cardiovascular disease by about 30 percent. A newer study found that it can reduce the risk of cancer and Alzheimer's by 40 percent.

It helps to prevent colorectal cancer. This diet may lower the risk of colorectal cancer by reducing harmful inflammation-causing bacteria in the intestines.

- It may reduce the risk of Type 2 diabetes by lowering insulin levels. People following a Mediterranean diet have lower insulin levels than those who don't follow it, lowering blood sugar levels.
- It may lower the risk of heart disease by lowering blood pressure and cholesterol levels.
- It may lower the risk of Alzheimer's disease by decreasing inflammation in the brain.
- It may help the prevention and treatment of some types of cancer. It may lower the risk of breast cancer, ovarian cancer, and colon cancer. It may also reduce the risk of lung cancer.
- It may help prevent osteoporosis and osteoarthritis.

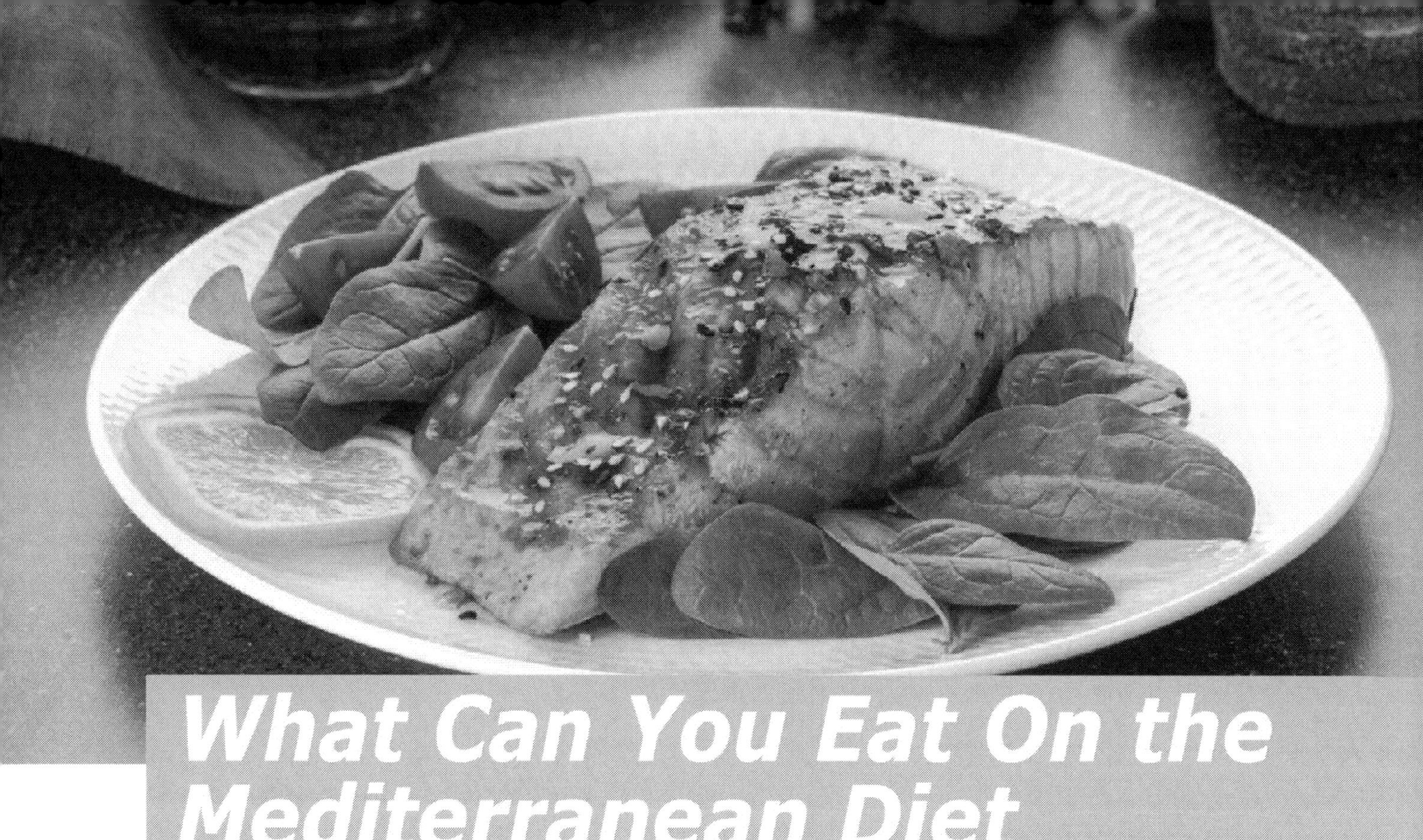

What Can You Eat On the Mediterranean Diet

The diet offers flexibility. You can eat as much as you want of the Mediterranean diet foods as long as they are in moderation. One good way to stay within the Mediterranean diet is to stick with the foods linked to the best benefits and fruits and vegetables, which have numerous health benefits. This is the best way to limit the intake of foods like red meat, eggs, fried foods, and sweets, which are not part of the Mediterranean diet.

Here are the nine foods to eat most on the Mediterranean diet:

- Almonds: The nutrient-rich almonds are a good source of heart-healthy omega-3 fatty acids. They are also a good source of magnesium, which is essential for regulating blood sugar, controlling cholesterol levels, and preventing high blood pressure.

- Artichokes: Full of vitamins C and K, magnesium, and fiber, artichokes are a perfect choice for a healthy, fiber-rich, heart-healthy diet. They can help reduce your risk for cardiovascular disease and can also prevent atherosclerosis in the arteries.

- Spinach: Contains antioxidants that can help reduce your risk of heart disease and may lower the risk of stroke.

- Nectarines and grapes: Both fruits are rich in vitamin C and potassium, which can help reduce your risk of blood clots and help lower blood pressure.

- Avocados: Avocados contain heart-healthy monounsaturated fat that can help prevent bad cholesterol from accumulating in your arteries.

- Pomegranates: A pomegranate has 8 grams of fiber in it, which can help regulate blood sugar. Pomegranates also contain bromelain, a protein with powerful antibacterial and anticancer properties.

- Figs: Figs are known to aid digestion, relieve constipation, aid with hypertension, lower blood pressure, and are high in potassium. Also high in fiber and low in calories, the fruit can help control weight.

- Walnuts: Almonds are a rich source of omega-3 fatty acids and fiber, but walnuts are higher in heart-healthy fats and lower in calories. They can help lower bad cholesterol and may help prevent coronary artery disease. They can also help reduce the risk of stroke.

- *Flaxseed: Flaxseed is high in omega-3 fatty acids, which are effective for preventing heart disease. Flaxseed can help lower LDL (bad) cholesterol levels.*

And don't forget to get your potassium fixed with watermelon, which has more potassium than a banana.

Workout for Starting A Mediterranean Diet

It is essential to start the Mediterranean diet to keep it healthy for a long time. It is advisable to change your eating habits to ensure you follow a Mediterranean diet. The first thing to do is to get rid of the food groups that are unhealthy in the Mediterranean diet, such as pizza, chips, and French fries. Healthy food choices should replace these unhealthy foods.

Good sources of plant protein include legumes, tofu, quinoa, nuts, and beans. High-fiber foods, such as whole-grain foods, fruits, and vegetables, should also be replaced by other choices.

Your diet should include lots of healthy fats, such as olive oil, avocado, salmon, nuts, and seeds. Every day, the Mediterranean diet should contain around 3 grams of monounsaturated fats, such as olive oil.

The Mediterranean diet should have no more than 600 milligrams of sodium a day. The Mediterranean diet should contain 30 grams of fiber a day, which is one-quarter of a cup. The fiber in the diet promotes the proper development of your digestive system, which helps to keep you feeling fuller for longer.

Fruits and vegetables are high in antioxidants, good for your immune system, and help prevent cancer and heart disease. The Mediterranean diet should include a variety of fruits and vegetables, such as:

- Fruits
- Vegetables
- Beans
- Whole grains
- Nuts
- Avocado

Some exercise should also accompany the Mediterranean diet. Some simple exercises can help you develop cardiovascular endurance and balance.

It is advisable to complete some aerobic exercise three to four times a week. Cardio exercise is the type of exercise that increases the amount of oxygen your body can absorb. The benefits of the Mediterranean diet also apply to weight loss, combining regular exercise, eating fruits and vegetables, and consuming high-fiber foods may help you reduce your weight.

As you make the Mediterranean diet a part of your life, you can adopt healthier eating habits and increase overall health.

HOW TO MAKE THE MEDITERRANEAN DIET WORK

- The Mediterranean diet is perfect for weight management. The Mediterranean diet helps make your body feel lighter and more energetic for people who have a weight problem.
- The Mediterranean diet is perfect for heart health. The extra fat and calorie content of this diet make it a good choice for heart health.
- The Mediterranean diet is good for arthritis. This diet promotes a healthy joint.
- The Mediterranean diet is good for the prevention of lung cancer.
- The Mediterranean diet is good for the prevention and treatment of prostate cancer.

The Mediterranean Diet And Stomach Cancer

A Mediterranean diet is excellent for cancer prevention because the diet's extra fat and calorie content make it a good choice for preventing stomach cancer.

Stomach cancer is prevalent in America and Europe, and Mediterranean diets have been shown to lower the incidence of stomach cancer.

Mediterranean diets help reduce the risk of stomach cancer by increasing the amount of polyunsaturated fat.

As polyunsaturated fat is metabolized to unhealthy cholesterol, consuming the right amount is essential to prevent the formation of heart disease.

Foods like macadamia nuts, soybeans, and olive oil are exceptionally high in polyunsaturated fat.

Fruit and vegetables are high in monounsaturated fat, which may help prevent stomach cancer. As well as the Mediterranean diet, healthy weight control and regular exercise may also reduce the risk of stomach cancer.

The Mediterranean Diet And Alzheimer's

Increased consumption of fruits and vegetables may reduce the risk of Alzheimer's disease, a type of dementia. Research has shown that people who eat more fruits and vegetables are less likely to develop dementia.

A Mediterranean diet also provides a host of other nutrients, including:

- Antioxidants
- Vitamin C
- Omega 3
- Magnesium
- Potassium
- Zinc

There are many other ways the Mediterranean diet may help protect against a wide range of illnesses and diseases. However, it would be best if you still made an individual assessment of your health and lifestyle.

There is no easy, quick fix, but the Mediterranean diet can significantly contribute to your health.

The Mediterranean Diet And Heart Attack

The Mediterranean diet can lower your risk of a heart attack or stroke by 25 to 35 percent.

The Mediterranean diet has been shown to lower the risk of heart attack, stroke, and certain types of cancer.

As there is a Mediterranean diet, these healthy living habits can be passed down to the next generation.

Ways to Follow the Mediterranean Diet

Consuming plenty of fruits and vegetables, and other fiber-rich foods is one of the keys to eating a healthy diet.

Mediterranean Diet For Weight Loss

It's no secret that losing weight is a healthy way to achieve improved health and improved physical functioning. It's also a simple way to have a positive effect on your quality of life. The Mediterranean diet is excellent for helping you lose weight because it involves eating more fish and vegetables than is typically considered appropriate for weight loss. The health benefits of eating healthy food are well-documented.

The Mediterranean diet can help you achieve optimal weight loss by following below steps.

Focus on proteins - as an indication of the Mediterranean diet, choose lean protein sources. For example, grilled salmon, grass-fed meat, chicken, and eggs are high in protein.

As an indication of the Mediterranean diet, choose lean protein sources. For example, grilled salmon, grass-fed meat, chicken, and eggs are high in protein. Limit carbohydrates - eat your carbohydrate foods in moderation. This means limiting your intake of white bread and white rice.

Mediterranean Diet In Children

Parents and caregivers need to speak with a physician before introducing the Mediterranean diet into a child's diet. It is imperative to talk with your doctor about your child's diet and a diagnosis of food allergies or intolerances.

Your child's doctor may be able to offer tips on a diet that may work best for your child. Healthy changes to your child's diet may be best if they:

- Is planning to have children or may become pregnant.
- Is allergic to food such as dairy or eggs.
- Is lactose intolerant.
- Lacks iron or vitamin B12.
- Has celiac disease or gluten sensitivity.
- May have sleep problems.
- Has a gluten allergy.
- Is allergic to nut products such as almonds, walnuts, or pecans.
- Is allergic to peanuts, tree nuts, or shellfish.
- Is allergic to latex.
- Has a food allergy to meat, such as peanuts or soybeans.

Consulting with a dietitian is also recommended to ensure the appropriate dosage and routine of food and supplements needed to support good health.

Here are some general guidelines:

- Introduce foods slowly and only a tiny amount at first.
- Eat at least 3 to 4 meals per day, and increase the number of meals if necessary.
- Limit the number of calories that your child is eating at each meal.
- Limit the intake of food from foods with saturated fats.
- *Limit intake of foods containing sugar as much as possible, and keep fruits and vegetables as an option at each meal.*
- *Limit intake of alcohol, caffeine, and alcohol-containing drinks, and use tea or coffee with no sweetener.*

HOW EXACTLY DOES THE MEDITERRANEAN DIET WORK

The Mediterranean diet was not intended to be a weight-loss method. There is no official method to follow because it was not formed but simply an eating style in an area that evolved gradually over generations. However, it is popular because it is a well-rounded, non-restrictive approach to eating. Two of the five so-called blue zones — locations where people live longer lives and have lower illness rates — are in Mediterranean cities (Ikaria in Greece and Sardinia in Italy).

It's important to note that there are many variations of the Mediterranean diet, and the technique itself can be tricky to implement and follow. Regardless of what you call it, the Mediterranean diet is a diet that shares many similar components. For example, you might find yourself limiting or eliminating the consumption of meat and dairy products, avoiding processed foods, eating more vegetables, and consuming extra fruit and fiber, as well as using olive oil as your primary source of fat and reducing the consumption of sugar and salt.

In a nutshell, the core principles of the Mediterranean diet can be broken down

Optimum nutrition - eating foods that provide the body with all of the essential nutrients that it needs.

- Eating foods that provide the body with all of the essential nutrients that it needs. Quality over quantity - choosing a healthy, balanced diet that minimizes the consumption of meats, dairy products, grains, and processed foods.
- Choose a healthy, balanced diet that minimizes the consumption of meats, dairy products, grains, and processed foods. Healthy lifestyle - the Mediterranean diet is a lifestyle that is based on the principle of eating healthfully, taking proper precautions with physical activity, and staying active.
- The Mediterranean diet is a lifestyle based on the principle of eating healthfully, taking proper precautions with physical activity, and staying active. Sustained attention to detail - the Mediterranean diet is a strict guideline. It can be challenging to do it perfectly, so it's recommended to make small changes and never feel you are failing at the diet altogether.

The idea of the Mediterranean diet is to eat healthfully by eating healthfully. However, it's not a strict diet, so you can modify the way you eat by removing particular food groups or just eating an extra portion of your usual servings.

Ways To Increase Your Health And Prevent Disease

The following tips will help you stay healthy.

- Drink water with lemon and lime or with cucumber or mint.
- Eat meals at least 2 hours after you wake up.
- Get 8 hours of sleep per night.
- Exercise 30 minutes or more per day.
- Control high blood pressure.
- Manage high cholesterol.
- Maintain a healthy weight.
- Get regular mammograms, colonoscopies, and mammography.
- Remove or reduce your family's long-term intake of salt and sugar.

- Eat Mediterranean-style eating to improve your cholesterol, blood pressure, and triglycerides.
- Consume a variety of proteins such as fish, poultry, eggs, and legumes.

If you would like to start eating healthier foods, it is best to do it gradually. Avoid a sudden change in your diet and try to make a gradual transition to a healthier lifestyle.

Incorporating the Mediterranean diet into your lifestyle and making other healthy lifestyle changes, such as exercise, can help you become healthier.

How Can I Apply The Mediterranean Diet To My Daily Life?

There are several ways to incorporate some of the recommended components of the Mediterranean diet into your everyday life. You can start with a few easy food swaps that can help incorporate many of these healthy habits into your lifestyle. These will be significant but doable ways to reduce the risk of heart disease, as well as improve your overall health.

Blueberries

Blueberries have been linked to a lower risk of heart disease and stroke. They can help reduce your risk by keeping your blood vessels healthy. In the United States, low blueberry consumption has been linked to high blood pressure, high cholesterol, and heart disease. Eating a little more than two cups of blueberries can reduce your blood pressure and cholesterol by two-thirds.

Fatty fish

Eating omega-3 fatty acids helps promote a healthy heart. Many Americans don't eat enough of the fats we need in our diet. You can make a lot of progress to ensure you're getting enough of the fats you need by incorporating fatty fish, such as salmon, trout, mackerel, and sardines.

Whole grains

Whole grains contain a wealth of nutrients and are an excellent source of fiber. They also contain anti-inflammatory properties. These properties help improve your heart health and help prevent inflammatory diseases, such as heart disease and diabetes.

Reaching for your broccoli is a no-brainer.

One of the best ways to ensure you get your recommended servings of fruit and vegetables in your diet is to make them part of the smoothies and other drinks you drink throughout the day. They're easy to take with you, and they're a good source of heart-healthy nutrients. You can even make your own by blending your veggies. This can be fun and convenient. It makes the most of the vegetables that you have on hand.

Consider adding whole grains to your diet by using quinoa, bulgur, millet, and barley. There's a huge variety of whole grains available to use.

Difference Between Dash Diet and Mediterranean Diet

DASH Diet		Mediterranean Diet	
Food Group	Daily Servings	Food Group	Daily Serving
Whole grains Vegetables Fruits Dairy, low-fat or non-fat	7-8 4-5 4-5 2-3	Whole grains, Vegetables, Fruits, seeds, olive oil, beans, nuts, legumes	Base every meal on these foods
Lean meals, poultry, fish	2 or fewer	Fish, seafood	Eat at least twice a week
Nuts, seeds, dry beans	4-5 per week	Poultry, eggs, yogurt, cheese	Eat moderate portions daily to weekly
Fats and oils	2-3	Red meats processed meats	<2 servings/week <2 servings/week
Sweets	5 per week	Sweets	<1 serving/week

MEASUREMENT CONVERSIONS

US STANDARD	US STANDARD (OUNCES)	METRIC (APPROXIMATE)
2 tablespoons	1 fl. oz.	30 mL
1/4 cup	2 fl. oz.	60 mL
1/2 cup	4 fl. oz.	120 mL
1 cup	8 fl. oz.	240 mL
1 1/2 cups	12 fl. oz.	355 mL
2 cups or 1 pint	16 fl. oz.	475 mL
4 cups or 1 quart	32 fl. oz.	1 L
1 gallon	128 fl. oz.	4 L

Oven Temperatures

FAHRENHEIT (F)	CELSIUS (C) (APPROXIMATE)
250° F	120° C
300° F	150° C
325° F	165° C
350° F	180° C
375° F	190° C
400° F	200° C
425° F	220° C
450° F	230° C

VolumeEquivalent(Dry)

US STANDARD	METRIC (APPROXIMATE)
1/8 teaspon	0.5 mL
1/4 teaspon	1 mL
1/2 teaspon	2 mL
3/4 teaspon	4 mL
1 teaspon	5 mL
1 tablespon	15 mL
1/4 cup	59 mL
1/3 cup	79 mL
1/2 cup	118 mL
2/3 cup	156 mL
3/4 cup	177 mL
1 cup	235 mL
2 cups or 1 pint	475 mL
3 cups	700 mL
4 cups or 1 quart	1 L
1/2 gallon	2 L
1 gallon	4 L

BREAKFAST

1) Breakfast Tostadas

Ingredients

- ½ white onion, diced
- 1 tomato, chopped
- 1 cucumber, chopped
- 1 tablespoon fresh cilantro, chopped
- ½ jalapeno pepper, chopped
- 1 tablespoon lime juice
- 6 corn tortillas
- 1 tablespoon canola oil
- 2 oz Cheddar cheese, shredded
- ½ cup white beans, canned, drained
- 6 eggs
- ½ teaspoon butter
- ½ teaspoon Sea salt

DIRECTIONS: Servings: 6|Preparation time: 6 Minutes

Make Pico de Gallo:

- ✓ To the salad container, mix together diced white onion, tomato, cucumber, fresh cilantro, and jalapeno pepper.
- ✓ Add lime juice and a ½ tablespoon of canola oil. Mix the mixture well. Pico de Gallo is cooked.
- ✓ Then, Switch on the oven, preheat it setting its temperature to 390F.
- ✓ Line the tray with baking paper.
- ✓ Arrange the corn tortillas on the paper and brush with canola oil from both sides.
- ✓ Bake the tortillas until they start to be crunchy.
- ✓ Chill the cooked crunchy tortillas well.
- ✓ Meanwhile, toss the butter into the skillet.
- ✓ Crack the eggs into the melted butter, then sprinkle them using sea salt.
- ✓ Fry the eggs until the egg whites become cooked. For 3-5 minutes over medium heat.
- ✓ Mash the beans until you get a puree texture.
- ✓ Spread the bean puree on the corn tortillas.
- ✓ Add fried eggs.
- ✓ Top the eggs with Pico de Gallo and then shredded Cheddar cheese.

NUTRITION Calories 246 | Fat 11.1g | Fiber 4.7g | Carbs 24.5g | Protein 13.7g

2) Raspberry Pudding

Ingredients

- ½ cup raspberries
- 2 teaspoons maple syrup
- 1 ½ cup Plain yogurt
- ¼ teaspoon ground cardamom
- 1/3 cup Chia seeds, dried

Directions: Servings: 2

Preparation time: 30 minutes

- ✓ Mix up together Plain yogurt with maple syrup and ground cardamom.
- ✓ Add Chia seeds. Stir it gently.
- ✓ Put the yogurt to the serving glasses and top with the raspberries.
- ✓ Refrigerate the breakfast for at least 3 minutes or overnight.

NUTRITION Calories 303| Fat 11.2g| Fiber 11.8g| Carbs 33.2g| Protein 15.5g

3) Walnuts Yogurt Mix

Ingredients

- 2 and ½ cups Greek yogurt
- 1 and ½ cups walnuts, chopped
- 1 teaspoon vanilla extract
- ¾ cup honey
- 2 teaspoons cinnamon powder

DIRECTIONS: Servings: 6|Preparation time: 0 Minutes

- ✓ In a container, mix the yogurt and the walnuts and the rest of the ingredients, toss, divide into smaller containers and keep to the fridge for 10 minutes before serving for breakfast.

NUTRITION Calories 388| Fat 24.6g| Fiber 2.9g | Carbs 39.1g | Protein 10.2g

4) Mushroom Egg Casserole

Ingredients

- ½ cup mushrooms, chopped
- ½ yellow onion, diced
- 4 eggs, beaten
- 1 tablespoon coconut flakes
- ½ teaspoon chili pepper
- 1 oz Cheddar cheese, shredded
- 1 teaspoon canola oil

DIRECTIONS: Servings: 3|Preparation time: 25 minutes

- ✓ Pour canola oil into the skillet and preheat well.
- ✓ Add mushrooms and onion and roast for 5-8 minutes or until the vegetables are light brown.
- ✓ Transfer the cooked vegetables to the casserole mold.
- ✓ Add coconut flakes, chili pepper, and Cheddar cheese.
- ✓ Then add eggs and stir well.
- ✓ Bake the casserole for 15 minutes at 360F.

NUTRITION Calories 152| Fat 11.1 | Fiber 0.7| Carbs 3g | Protein 10.4g

5) Olive and Milk Bread

Ingredients

- 1 cup black olives, pitted, chopped

- *1 tablespoon olive oil*
- *½ teaspoon fresh yeast*
- *½ cup milk, preheated*
- *½ teaspoon salt*
- *1 teaspoon baking powder*
- *2 cup wheat flour, whole grain*
- *2 eggs, beaten*
- *1 teaspoon butter, melted*
- *1 teaspoon sugar*

DIRECTIONS: Servings: 6|Preparation time: 50 minutes

✓ *To the big container, combine together fresh yeast, sugar, and milk. Stir it until yeast is dissolved.*

✓ *Then add salt, baking powder, butter, and eggs. Stir the dough mixture until homogenous, and add 1 cup of wheat flour. Mix it up until smooth.*

✓ *Add olives and resting flour. Knead the non-sticky dough.*

✓ *Transfer the dough into the non-sticky dough mold.*

✓ *Bake the bread for 50 minutes at 350 F.*

✓ *Check if the bread is cooked using the toothpick. If it is dry, the bread is cooked.*

✓ *Remove the bread from the oven; allow to chill for 10-15 minutes.*

✓ *Remove it from the loaf mold*

✓ *Slice it and serve.*

NUTRITION Calories 238 | Fat 7.7g | Fiber 1.9 | Carbs 35.5g | Protein 7.2g

6) Blueberry and Vanilla Scones

Ingredients

- *½ cup almond flour*
- *3 manic eggs, beaten*
- *2 tsp baking powder*
- *½ cup stevia*
- *2 tsp vanilla extract, unsweetened*
- *¾ cup fresh raspberries*
- *1 tbsp olive oil*

DIRECTIONS: Servings:12Preparation time:20 minutes

✓ *Switch on the oven, preheat it setting its temperature to 375 °F*

✓ *Take a large container, add eggs and flour in it, stir in baking powder, stevia, and vanilla until combined, and then fold in berries until mixed.*

✓ *Take a baking dish and grease with oil, scoop the prepared batter on it with an ice cream scoop, bake all for 10 minutes until done.*

✓ *When done, transfer scones on a wire rack, cool them completely, and then serve.*

NUTRITION Calories 133 | Total Fat 8g| Total Carbs 4g | Protein 2g

7) Tahini Pine Nuts Toast

Ingredients

- *2 whole-wheat bread slices, toasted*
- *1 teaspoon water*
- *1 tablespoon tahini paste*
- *2 teaspoons feta cheese, crumbled*
- *Juice of ½ lemon*
- *2 teaspoons pine nuts*
- *A pinch of black pepper*

DIRECTIONS: Servings: 2 Preparation time: 0 minutes

✓ *In a container, mix the tahini and water and the lemon juice, whisk really well, and spread over the toasted bread slices.*

✓ *Top each serving with the resting ingredients and serve for breakfast.*

NUTRITION Calories 142 | Fat 7.6g | Fiber 2.7g | Carbs 13.7g | Protein 5.8g

8) Chili Scramble

Ingredients

- *3 tomatoes*
- *4 eggs*
- *¼ teaspoon of sea salt*
- *½ chili pepper, chopped*
- *1 tablespoon butter*
- *1 cup water for cooking*

DIRECTIONS: Servings: 4Preparation time: 15 minutes

✓ *Pour water into the saucepan, bring it to a boil.*

✓ *Then remove water from the heat and add tomatoes.*

✓ *Let the tomatoes stay in hot water for 2-3 minutes.*

✓ *Then, remove the tomatoes from the water and peel them.*

✓ *Place butter into the pan and melt it.*

✓ *Add chopped chili pepper and fry it for 3 minutes over medium heat.*

✓ *Then chop the peeled tomatoes and add them into the chili peppers.*

✓ *Cook the vegetables for 5 minutes over medium heat. Stir them from time to time.*

✓ *Then, add sea salt and crack then eggs.*

✓ *Stir (scramble) the eggs well with the help of the fork and cook them for 3 minutes over medium heat.*

NUTRITION Calories 105 | Fat 7.4g | Fiber 1.1g | Carbs 4g | Protein 6.4g

9) Pear Oatmeal

Ingredients

- *1 cup oatmeal*
- *1/3 cup milk*

- 1 pear, chopped
- 1 teaspoon vanilla extract
- 1 tablespoon Splenda
- 1 teaspoon butter
- ½ teaspoon ground cinnamon
- 1 egg, beaten

DIRECTIONS:Servings: 4Preparation time:25 minutes

- ✓ To the big container, mix up together oatmeal, milk, egg, vanilla extract, Splenda, and ground cinnamon.
- ✓ Melt butter, add it to the oatmeal mixture.
- ✓ Add chopped pear and stir it well.
- ✓ Transfer the mixture to the casserole mold and flatten gently. Cover it with foil and secure edges.
- ✓ Bake the oatmeal for 25-26 minutes at 350F.

NUTRITION Calories 151| Fat 3.9g| Fiber 3.3g| Carbs 23.6g| Protein 4.9g

10) Mediterranean Egg Casserole

Ingredients

- 1 ½ cups (6 ounces) feta cheese, crumbled
- 1 jar approximately (6 ounces) marinated artichoke hearts, drained well, coarsely chopped
- 10 eggs
- 2 cups milk, low-fat
- 2 cups fresh baby spinach, packed, coarsely chopped
- 6 cups whole-wheat baguette, cut into i-inch cubes
- 1 tablespoon garlic (about 4 cloves), finely chopped
- 1 tablespoon olive oil, extra-virgin
- ½ cup red bell pepper, chopped
- ½ cup Parmesan cheese, shredded
- ½ teaspoon pepper
- ½ teaspoon red pepper flakes
- ½ teaspoon salt
- 1/3 cup kalamata olives, pitted, halved
- ¼ cup red onion, chopped
- ¼ cup tomatoes (sun-dried) in oil, drained, chopped

DIRECTIONS: Servings: 8Preparation time: 50 minutes

- ✓ Preheat oven to 350 F.
- ✓ Grease a 9x13 baking dish with oil cooking spray.
- ✓ In an 8-inch non-stick pan over medium heat, heat the olive oil. Add the garlic, onions, and bell pepper; cook for about 3 minutes, frequently stirring, until slightly softened. Add the spinach; cook for about 1 minute or until starting to wilt.
- ✓ Layer half of the baguette cubes to the prepared baking dish, then 1 cup of the feta, 1/4 cup Parmesan, the bell pepper mix, artichokes, the olives, and the tomatoes. Top with the resting baguette cubes and then with the resting ½ cup of feta.
- ✓ In a large mixing container, whisk the eggs and the low-fat milk together. Beat to the pepper, salt, and pepper. Pour the mix over the bread layer to the baking dish, slightly pressing down. Sprinkle with the resting ¼ cup Parmesan.
- ✓ Bake until the center is set and the top is golden brown. Before serving, let stand for 15 minutes.

NUTRITION Calories 360, Fat 21g, Chol 270mg, Sodium 880mg, Carb 24g, Fiber 3g, Sugar 7g, Protein 20g

11) Paprika Salmon Toast

Ingredients

- 4 whole-grain bread slices
- 2 oz smoked salmon, sliced
- 2 teaspoons cream cheese
- 1 teaspoon fresh dill, chopped
- ½ teaspoon lemon juice
- ½ teaspoon paprika
- 4 lettuce leaves
- 1 cucumber, sliced

DIRECTIONS:Servings: 2 Preparation time: 3 minutes

- ✓ Toast the bread to the toaster (1-2 minutes totally).
- ✓ To the container, mix up together fresh dill, cream cheese, lemon juice, and paprika.
- ✓ Then spread the toasts with the cream cheese mixture.
- ✓ Slice the smoked salmon and place it on bread slices.
- ✓ Add sliced cucumber and lettuce leaves.
- ✓ Top the lettuce with resting bread toasts and pin it with the toothpick.

Nutrition Calories 202| Fat 4.7g | Fiber 5.1g | Carbs 31.5g | Protein 12.7g

12) Cheesy Olives Bread

Ingredients

- 4 cups whole-wheat flour
- 3 tablespoons oregano, chopped
- 2 teaspoons dry yeast
- ¼ cup olive oil
- 1 and ½ cups black olives, pitted and sliced
- 1 cup water
- ½ cup feta cheese, crumbled

DIRECTIONS:Servings: 10 Preparation time:30 minutes

- ✓ In a container, mix the flour and the water, the

yeast, and the oil, stir, and knead your dough very well.

- *Put the dough in a container, cover with plastic wrap and keep in a warm place for 1 hour.*
- *Divide the dough into 2 containers and stretch each ball really well.*
- *Add the rest of the ingredients to each ball and tuck them inside, well kneading the dough again.*
- *Flatten the balls a bit and leave them aside for 4 minutes more.*
- *Transfer the balls to a baking sheet lined with parchment paper, make a small slit in each, and bake at 425 degrees F for 30 minutes.*
- *Serve the bread as a Mediterranean breakfast.*

NUTRITION Calories 251| Fat 7.3g | Fiber 2.1g | Carbs 39.7g | Protein 6.7g

13) Mediterranean Freezer Breakfast Wraps

Ingredients

- *1 cup spinach leaves, fresh, chopped*
- *1 tablespoon water or low-fat milk*
- *½ teaspoon garlic-chipotle seasoning or your preferred seasoning*
- *4 eggs, beaten*
- *4 pieces (8-inch) whole-wheat tortillas*
- *4 tablespoons tomato chutney (or dried tomatoes, chopped or calmed tomatoes)*
- *4 tablespoons feta cheese, crumbled (or goat cheese)*
- *Optional: prosciutto, chopped or bacon, cooked, crumbled*
- *Salt and pepper to taste*

DIRECTIONS: Servings: 4| Preparation time: 3 minutes

- *In a bowl, whisk the eggs, water, or milk, and seasoning together.*
- *Heat a skillet with oil; pour the eggs and scramble for about 3-4 minutes, or until just cooked.*
- *Lay the tortillas on a clean surface; divide the eggs between them, arranging the scrambled eggs, and leave the tortilla edges free to fold later.*
- *Top the egg layer with about 1 tablespoon of cheese, 1 tablespoon of tomatoes, and 1/ 4 cup spinach. If using, layer with prosciutto or bacon.*
- *In a burrito style, roll up the tortillas, folding both of the ends to the process.*
- *In a panini maker or a clean skillet, cook for about 1 minute, turning once, until the tortilla wraps are crisp and brown; serve.*

Nutrition Calories 450 | Fat 15g | Sodium 280mg | Pot. 960mg | Carb 64g | Fiber 6g | Sugar 20g | Protein 17g

14) Milk Scones

Ingredients

- *½ cup wheat flour, whole grain*
- *1 teaspoon baking powder*
- *1 tablespoon butter, melted*
- *1 teaspoon vanilla extract*
- *1 egg, beaten*
- *¾ teaspoon salt*
- *3 tablespoons milk*
- *1 teaspoon vanilla sugar*

Directions: Servings: 4 Preparation time: 10 minutes

- *To the mixing container, combine together wheat flour, baking powder, butter, vanilla extract, and egg. Add salt and knead the soft and non-sticky dough. Add more flour if needed.*
- *Then make the log from the dough and cut it into triangles.*
- *Line the tray with baking paper.*
- *Arrange the dough triangles on the baking paper and transfer them to the preheat to the 360F oven.*
- *Cook the scones for 9-- 10 minutes or until they are light brown.*
- *Then chill the scones and brush with milk and sprinkle with vanilla sugar.*

NUTRITION Calories 112| Fat 4.4g | Fiber 0.5g | Carbs 14.3g | Protein 3.4g

15) Avocado Egg Scramble

Ingredients:

- *4 eggs, beaten*
- *1 white onion, diced*
- *1 Tbsp avocado oil*
- *1 avocado, finely chopped*
- *½ Tsp chili flakes*
- *1 oz Cheddar cheese, shredded*
- *½ Tsp salt*
- *1 Tbsp fresh parsley*

Direction: Preparation time: 8 minutes Cooking time: 15 minutes Servings: 4

- *Pour avocado oil into the skillet and bring it to a boil.*
- *Add diced onion, roast it until it is light brown.*
- *Mix up together chili flakes, beaten eggs, and salt.*
- *Coat the egg mixture over the cooked onion and cook the mixture for 1,30 minutes over medium heat.*
- *Scramble the eggs with the help of the fork; cook the eggs until they are solid but soft.*
- *Add chopped avocado and shredded cheese.*
- *Stir the scrambled well and transfer to the serving plates.*

✓ *Sprinkle the meal with fresh parsley.*
Nutrition: Calories 236, Fat 20.1, Fiber 4, Carbs 7.4, Protein 8.6

16) Breakfast Tostadas

Ingredients:

- ½ white onion, diced
- 1 tomato, chopped
- 1 cucumber, chopped
- 1 Tbsp fresh cilantro, chopped
- ½ jalapeno pepper, chopped
- 1 Tbsp lime juice
- 6 corn tortillas
- 1 Tbsp canola oil
- 2 oz Cheddar cheese, shredded
- ½ cup white beans, canned, drained
- 6 eggs
- ½ Tsp butter
- ½ Tsp Sea salt

Direction: Preparation time: 15 minutes Cooking time: 6 minutes Servings: 6

✓ *Make Pico de Galo: to the salad container, combine together diced white onion, tomato, cucumber, fresh cilantro, and jalapeno pepper.*

✓ *Then add lime juice and a ½ Tbsp of canola oil. Mix up the mixture well. Pico de Galo is cooked.*

✓ *After this, Switch on the oven, preheat it setting its temperature to 390F.*

✓ *Line the tray with baking paper.*

✓ *Pour the corn tortillas on the baking paper, brush with resting canola oil from both sides.*

✓ *Bake the tortillas for 10 minutes or until they start to be crunchy.*

✓ *Chill the cooked crunchy tortillas well.*

✓ *Meanwhile, toss the butter into the skillet*

✓ *Crack the eggs into the melted butter and sprinkle them with sea salt.*

✓ *Fry the eggs until whites become cooked. Approximately 3-5 minutes over medium heat.*

✓ *Mash the beans until you get a puree texture, then Spread them on the corn tortillas.*

✓ *Add a fried egg, then top them with Pico de Galo and shredded Cheddar cheese.*
Nutrition Calories 454 | Fat 15g | Chol 220mg | Sodium 280mg | Pot. 960mg | Carb 64g | Fiber 6g | Sugar 20g | Protein 17g

17) Parmesan Omelet

Ingredients:

- 1 Tbsp cream cheese
- 2 eggs, beaten
- ¼ Tsp paprika
- ½ Tsp dried oregano
- ¼ Tsp dried dill
- 1 oz Parmesan, grated
- 1 Tsp coconut oil

Direction: Preparation time: 5 minutes Cooking time: 10 minutes Servings: 2

✓ *Mix up together cream cheese with eggs, dried oregano, and dill.*

✓ *Place coconut oil into the skillet and heat it up until it coats all the skillet.*

✓ *Then pour the egg mixture into the skillet and flatten it.*

✓ *Add grated Parmesan and close the lid.*

✓ *Cook omelet for 10 minutes over low heat.*

✓ *Then transfer the cooked omelet to the serving plate and sprinkle with paprika.*
Nutrition: Calories 148, fat 11.5, fiber 0.3, carbs 1.4, protein 10.6

18) Meemen

Ingredients:

- 2 tomatoes, chopped
- 2 eggs, beaten
- 1 bell pepper, chopped
- 1 Tsp tomato paste
- ¼ cup of water
- 1 Tsp butter
- ½ white onion, diced
- ½ Tsp chili flakes
- 1/3 Tsp sea salt

Direction: Preparation time: 6 minutes Cooking time: 15 minutes Servings: 4

✓ *Pour batter into the pan and melt it.*

✓ *Add bell pepper and then cook it for 3 minutes over medium heat. Stir it from time to time.*

✓ *Add diced onion and cook it for 2 minutes more.*

✓ *Stir the vegetables and add tomatoes.*

✓ *Cook them for 5 minutes over medium-low heat.*

✓ *Then add water and tomato paste. Stir well.*

✓ *Add beaten eggs, chili flakes, and salt.*

✓ *Stir well and cook menemen for 4 minutes over medium-low heat.*

✓ *The cooked meal should be half runny.*
Nutrition: Calories 67, fat 3.4, fiber 1.5, carbs 6.4, protein 3.8

19) Watermelon Pizza

Ingredients:

- 9 oz watermelon slice
- 1 Tbsp Pomegranate sauce
- 2 oz Feta cheese, crumbled
- 1 Tbsp fresh cilantro, chopped

Direction: Preparation time: 10 minutes Servings: 2

✓ *Place the watermelon slice on the plate and sprinkle*

with crumbled Feta cheese.

- ✓ *Add fresh cilantro.*
- ✓ *After this, sprinkle the pizza with Pomegranate juice generously.*
- ✓ *Cut the pizza into servings.*

Nutrition: Calories 143, fat 6.2, fiber 0.6, carbs 18.4, protein 5.1

20) Ham Muffins

Ingredients:

- *3 oz ham, chopped*
- *4 eggs, beaten*
- *2 Tbsps coconut flour*
- *½ Tsp dried oregano*
- *¼ Tsp dried cilantro*
- *Cooking spray*

Direction: Preparation time: 10 minutes Cooking time: 15 minutes Servings: 4

- ✓ *Spray the muffin's molds with cooking spray from inside.*
- ✓ *To the container, mix up together beaten eggs, coconut flour, dried oregano, cilantro, and ham.*
- ✓ *When the liquid is homogenous, pour it into the prepared muffin molds.*
- ✓ *Bake the muffins for 15 minutes at 360F.*
- ✓ *Chill the cooked meal well, and only after this remove it from the molds.*

Nutrition:Calories 67, fat 3.4, fiber 1.5, carbs 6.4, protein 3.8

21) Morning Pizza with Sprouts

Ingredients:

- *½ cup wheat flour, whole grain*
- *2 Tbsps butter, softened*
- *¼ Tsp baking powder*
- *¾ Tsp salt*
- *5 oz chicken fillet, boiled*
- *2 oz Cheddar cheese, shredded*
- *1 Tsp tomato sauce*
- *1 oz bean sprouts*

Direction: Preparation time: 15 minutes Cooking time: 20 minutes Servings: 6

- ✓ *Make the pizza crust: mix up together wheat flour, butter, baking powder, and salt. Knead the soft and non-sticky dough. Add more wheat flour if needed.*
- ✓ *Leave the dough for 10 minutes to chill.*
- ✓ *Place the dough on the baking paper, and cover it with the second baking paper sheet.*
- ✓ *Roll up the dough with the rolling pin to get the round pizza crust.*
- ✓ *Remove the upper baking paper sheet.*
- ✓ *Transfer the pizza crust to the tray.*
- ✓ *Spread the crust with tomato sauce.*
- ✓ *Shred the chicken fillet and arrange it over the pizza crust.*
- ✓ *Add shredded Cheddar cheese.*
- ✓ *Bake pizza for 20 minutes at 355F.*
- ✓ *Then top the cooked pizza with bean sprouts and slice into the servings.*

Nutrition: Calories 157, fat 8.8, fiber 0.3, carbs 8.4, protein 10.5

22) Banana Quinoa

Ingredients:

- *1 cup quinoa*
- *2 cup milk*
- *1 Tsp vanilla extract*
- *1 Tsp honey*
- *2 bananas, sliced*
- *¼ Tsp ground cinnamon*

Direction: Preparation time: 10 minutes Cooking time: 12 minutes Servings: 4

- ✓ *Pour milk into the saucepan, add quinoa, and close the lid*
- ✓ *Cook it over medium heat for 12-13 minutes or until quinoa will absorb all liquid.*
- ✓ *Chill the quinoa for 10-15 minutes. Then place in the serving mason jars.*
- ✓ *Add honey, vanilla extract, and ground cinnamon.*
- ✓ *Stir well.*
- ✓ *Top quinoa with banana and stir it all before serving.*

Nutrition: Calories 270, fat 5.2, fiber 4.6, carbs 48.4, protein 10.7

23) Avocado Milk Shake

Ingredients:

- *1 avocado, peeled, pitted*
- *2 Tbsps of liquid honey*
- *½ Tsp vanilla extract*
- *½ cup heavy cream*
- *1 cup milk*
- *1/3 cup ice cubes*

Direction: Preparation time: 10 minutes Servings: 3

- ✓ *Chop the avocado and put it in the food processor.*
- ✓ *Add milk, liquid honey, vanilla extract, heavy cream, and ice cubes.*
- ✓ *Blend the mixture until it is smooth.*
- ✓ *Pour the cooked milkshake into the glasses.*

Nutrition: Calories 292, fat 22.1, fiber 4.5, carbs 22, protein 4.4

24) Egg Casserole with Paprika

Ingredients:

- *2 eggs, beaten*
- *1 chopped red bell pepper*

- *1 chili pepper, chopped*
- *½ red onion, diced*
- *1 Tsp canola oil*
- *½ Tsp salt*
- *1 Tsp paprika*
- *1 Tbsp fresh cilantro, chopped*
- *1 garlic clove, diced*
- *1 Tsp butter, softened*
- *¼ Tsp chili flakes*

Direction: Preparation time: 10 minutes Cooking time: 28 minutes Servings: 4

- ✓ *Brush the casserole mold with canola oil, then coat beaten eggs inside.*
- ✓ *After this, toss the butter into the skillet and melt it over medium heat.*
- ✓ *Add chili pepper and red bell pepper.*
- ✓ *Add red onion, cook the vegetables for 7-8 minutes over medium heat. Stir them from time to time.*
- ✓ *Transfer the vegetables to the casserole mold.*
- ✓ *Add cilantro, salt, paprika, diced garlic, and chili flakes. Stir with a spatula to get a homogenous mixture.*
- ✓ *Bake the casserole for 20-22 minutes at 355F in the oven*
- ✓ *Chill the meal and cut into servings. Transfer the casserole to the serving plates helping with the spatula.*

Nutrition: Calories 68, fat 4.5, fiber 1, carbs 4.4, protein 3.4

25) Cauliflower Fritters

Ingredients:

- *1 cup cauliflower, shredded*
- *1 egg, beaten*
- *1 Tbsp wheat flour, whole grain*
- *1 oz Parmesan, grated*
- *½ Tsp ground black pepper*
- *1 Tbsp canola oil*

Direction: Time to prepare: 10 minutes Time to cook: 10 minutes 2 servings

- ✓ *To the bowl, mix all together shredded cauliflower and egg.*
- ✓ *Add wheat flour, grated Parmesan, and black pepper.*
- ✓ *Stir the mixture using the fork until it is homogenous and smooth.*
- ✓ *Pour canola oil into the skillet, and bring it to a boil*
- ✓ *With the help of the fingertips, Make the fritters from the cauliflower mixture and transfer them to the hot oil.*
- ✓ *Roast the fritters for 4-5 minutes from each side over medium-low heat.*

Nutrition: Calories 167, fat 12.3, fiber 1.5, carbs 6.7, protein 8.8

26) Creamy Oatmeal with Figs

Ingredients:

- *2 cups oatmeal*
- *1 ½ cup milk*
- *1 Tbsp butter*
- *3 figs, chopped*
- *1 Tbsp honey*

Direction: Preparation time: 10 minutes Cooking time: 20 minutes Servings: 5

- ✓ *Pour milk into the saucepan*
- ✓ *Add oatmeal and close the lid.*
- ✓ *Cook the oatmeal for 14-15 minutes over medium-low heat.*
- ✓ *Add chopped figs and honey.*
- ✓ *Add butter and mix the oatmeal well.*
- ✓ *Cook it for 5 minutes more.*
- ✓ *Close the lid and let the breakfast rest for 10 minutes before serving.*

Nutrition: Calories 222, fat 6, fiber 4.4, carbs 36.5, protein 7.1

27) Baked Oatmeal with Cinnamon

Ingredients:

- *1 cup oatmeal*
- *1/3 cup milk*
- *1 pear, chopped*
- *1 teaspoon extract de Vanille*
- *1 Tbsp Splenda*
- *1 Tsp butter*
- *½ Tsp ground cinnamon*
- *1 egg, beaten*

Direction: Preparation time: 10 minutes Cooking time: 25 minutes Servings: 4

- ✓ *To the big container, mix up together oatmeal, milk, egg, vanilla extract, Splenda, and ground cinnamon.*
- ✓ *Melt butter and add it to the oatmeal mixture.*
- ✓ *Add chopped pear and stir it well.*
- ✓ *Transfer the oatmeal mixture to casserole mold and flatten gently. Cover it with foil and secure edges.*
- ✓ *Bake the oatmeal for 25-26 minutes at 350F.*

Nutrition: Calories 151, carbs 23.6, protein 4.9

28) Almond Chia Porridge

Ingredients:

- *3 cups organic almond milk*
- *1/3 cup chia seeds, dried*
- *1 Tsp vanilla extract*
- *1 Tbsp honey*
- *¼ Tsp ground cardamom*

Direction: Preparation time: 10 minutes Cooking

time: 30 minutes Servings: 4

- ✓ Pour almond milk into the saucepan and bring it to a boil
- ✓ Then chill the almond milk for appx. 10-15 minutes.
- ✓ Add vanilla extract, honey, and ground cardamom. Stir well.
- ✓ Add chia seeds and stir again.
- ✓ Close the lid let chia seeds soak the liquid for 22-25 minutes.
- ✓ Transfer the porridge into the serving ramekins.

Nutrition: Cal 150, fat 7.3, fiber 6.1, carbs 18, protein 3.7

29) Cocoa Oatmeal

Ingredients:

- 1 ½ cup oatmeal
- 1 Tbsp cocoa powder
- ½ cup heavy cream
- ¼ cup of water
- 1 Tsp vanilla extract
- 1 Tbsp butter
- 2 Tbsps Splenda

Direction: Preparation time: 10 minutes Cooking time: 15 minutes Servings: 2

- ✓ Mix all together oatmeal with cocoa powder and Splenda.
- ✓ Transfer the mixture into the saucepan.
- ✓ Add water, vanilla extract, heavy cream. Stir it gently using the spatula.
- ✓ Close the lid and cook it for 12-15 minutes over medium-low heat.
- ✓ Remove the cocoa oatmeal from the heat and add butter.
- ✓ Stir it well.

Nutrition: Calories 230, fat 10.6, fiber 3.5, carbs 28.1, protein 4.6

30) Cinnamon Roll Oats

Ingredients:

- ½ cup rolled oats
- 1 cup milk
- 1 Tsp vanilla extract
- 1 Tsp ground cinnamon
- 2 Tsp honey
- 2 Tbsps Plain yogurt
- 1 Tsp butter

Direction: Preparation time: 7 minutes Cooking time: 10 minutes Servings: 4

- ✓ Pour milk into the saucepan, then bring it to a boil.
- ✓ Add rolled oats and stir well.
- ✓ Close the lid and simmer the oats for 5 minutes over medium heat. The cooked oats will absorb all milk.
- ✓ Then add butter and stir the oats well.
- ✓ To the separated container, whisk together Plain yogurt with honey, cinnamon, and vanilla extract.
- ✓ Transfer the cooked oats to the serving containers.
- ✓ Top the oats with the yogurt mixture to the shape of the wheel.

Nutrition: Calories 243, fat 20.2, fiber 1, carbs 2.8, protein 13.3

31) Pumpkin Oatmeal with Spices

Ingredients:

- 2 cups oatmeal
- 1 cup of coconut milk
- 1 cup milk
- 1 Tsp Pumpkin pie spices
- 2 Tbsps pumpkin puree
- 1 Tbsp Honey
- ½ Tsp butter

Direction: Preparation time: 10 minutes Cooking time: 13 minutes Servings: 6

- ✓ Pour coconut milk and milk into the saucepan. Add butter and bring the liquid to a boil.
- ✓ Add oatmeal, stir well with the help of a spoon and close the lid.
- ✓ Simmer the oatmeal for 7 minutes over medium heat.
- ✓ Meanwhile, mix up together honey, pumpkin pie spices, and pumpkin puree.
- ✓ When the oatmeal is cooked, add pumpkin puree mixture and stir well.
- ✓ Transfer the cooked breakfast to the serving plates.

Nutrition: Cal 232, fat 12.5, fiber 3.8, carbs 26.2, pro 5.9

32) Zucchini Oats

Ingredients:

- 2 cups rolled oats
- 2 cups of water
- ½ Tsp salt
- 1 Tbsp butter
- 1 zucchini, grated
- ¼ Tsp ground ginger

Direction: Preparation time: 10 minutes Cooking time: 10 minutes Servings: 4

- ✓ Pour water into the saucepan.
- ✓ Add rolled oats, butter, and salt.
- ✓ Stir gently and start to cook the oats for 4 minutes over high heat.
- ✓ When the mixture starts to boil, add ground ginger and grated zucchini. Stir well.
- ✓ Cook the oats for 5 minutes more over medium-low heat.

Nutrition: Calories 189, fat 5.7, fiber 4.7, carbs 29.4,

33) Breakfast Spanakopita

Ingredients:

- 2 cups spinach
- 1 white onion, diced
- ½ cup fresh parsley
- 1 Tsp minced garlic
- 3 oz Feta cheese, crumbled
- 1 Tsp ground paprika
- 2 eggs, beaten
- 1/3 cup butter, melted
- 2 oz Phyllo dough

Direction: Preparation time: 12 minutes Cooking time: 1 Hour Servings: 4

- ✓ Separate Phyllo dough into 2 parts
- ✓ Brush the casserole mold with butter well and place 1 part of Phyllo dough inside.
- ✓ Brush its surface with butter too.
- ✓ Put the spinach and fresh parsley in the blender. Blend it until smooth and transfer to the mixing container.
- ✓ Add minced garlic, Feta cheese, ground paprika, eggs, and diced onion. Mix up well.
- ✓ Place the spinach mixture in the casserole mold and flatten it well.
- ✓ Cover the spinach mixture with resting Phyllo dough and pour resting butter over it.
- ✓ Bake spanakopita for 1 hour at 350F.
- ✓ Cut it into servings.

Nutrition: Calories 190, fat 15.4, fiber 1.1, carbs 8.4, protein 5.4

34) Quinoa Container

Ingredients:

- 1 sweet potato, peeled, chopped
- 1 tablespoon extra virgin olive oil
- ½ Tsp chili flakes
- ½ Tsp salt
- 1 cup quinoa
- 2 cups of water
- 1 Tsp butter
- 1 Tbsp fresh cilantro, chopped

Direction: Preparation time: 10 minutes Cooking time: 20 minutes Servings: 4

- ✓ Line the baking tray with parchment.
- ✓ Arrange the chopped sweet potato on the tray and sprinkle it with chili flakes, salt, and olive oil.
- ✓ Bake the potato for 20-22 minutes at 355F.
- ✓ Meanwhile, pour water into the saucepan.
- ✓ Add quinoa and cook it over medium heat for 7 minutes or until quinoa will absorb all liquid.
- ✓ Add butter to the cooked quinoa and stir well.
- ✓ Transfer it to the containers, add baked sweet potato and chopped cilantro.

Nutrition: Calories 221, fat 7.1, fiber 3.9, carbs 33.2, protein 6.6

35) Overnight Oats with Nuts

Ingredients:

- ½ cup oats
- 2 Tsp chia seeds, dried
- 1 Tbsp almond, chopped
- ½ Tsp walnuts, chopped
- 1 cup skim milk
- 2 Tsp honey
- ½ Tsp vanilla extract

Direction: Preparation time: 10 minutes Cooking time: 8 hours Servings: 2

- ✓ To the big container, mix up together chia seeds, oats, honey, and vanilla extract.
- ✓ Then add skim milk, walnuts, and almonds. Stir well.
- ✓ Transfer the prepared mixture into the mason jars and close with lids.
- ✓ Put the mason jars in the fridge and leave them overnight.
- ✓ Store the meal in the fridge for up to 2 days.

Nutrition: Calories 202, fat 5.4, fiber 4.9, carbs 29.4, protein 8.7

36) Poblano Fritatta

Ingredients:

- 5 eggs, beaten
- 1 poblano chile, chopped, raw
- 1 oz scallions, chopped
- 1/3 cup heavy cream
- ½ Tsp butter
- ½ Tsp salt
- ½ Tsp chili flakes
- 1 Tbsp fresh cilantro, chopped

Direction: Preparation time: 10 minutes Cooking time: 15 minutes Servings: 4

- ✓ Mix up together eggs with heavy cream and whisk until homogenous.
- ✓ Add chopped poblano chile, scallions, salt, chili flakes, and fresh cilantro.
- ✓ Toss butter into the skillet and melt it.
- ✓ Add egg mixture and flatten it into the skillet if needed.
- ✓ Close the lid and cook the frittata for 15 minutes over medium-low heat.
- ✓ When the frittata is cooked, it will be solid.

Nutrition: Calories 131, fat 10.4, fiber 0.2, carbs 1.3, protein 8.2

37) Mushroom-Egg Casserole

Ingredients:

- ½ cup mushrooms, chopped
- ½ yellow onion, diced
- 4 eggs, beaten
- 1 Tbsp coconut flakes
- ½ Tsp chili pepper
- 1 oz Cheddar cheese, shredded
- 1 Tsp canola oil

Direction: Preparation time: 7 minutes Cooking time: 25 minutes Servings: 3

✓ Pour canola oil into the skillet and preheat well.

✓ Add mushrooms and onion and roast for 5-8 minutes or until the vegetables are light brown.

✓ Transfer the cooked vegetables to the casserole mold.

✓ Add coconut flakes, chili pepper, and Cheddar cheese.

✓ Then add eggs and stir well.

✓ Bake the casserole for 15 minutes at 360F.

Nutrition: Calories 152, fat 11.1, fiber 0.7, carbs 3, protein 10.

38) Vegetable Breakfast Container

Ingredients:

- 1 cup sweet potatoes, peeled, chopped
- 1 russet potato, chopped
- 1 red onion, sliced
- 2 bell pepper, trimmed
- ½ Tsp garlic powder
- ¾ Tsp onion powder
- 1 tbsp of virgin olive oil
- 1 Tbsp Sriracha sauce
- 1 Tbsp coconut milk

Direction: Preparation time: 10 minutes Cooking time: 35 minutes Servings: 4

✓ Line the baking tray with baking paper.

✓ Place the chopped russet potato and sweet potato on the tray.

✓ Add onion, bell peppers, and sprinkle the vegetables with olive oil, onion powder, and garlic powder.

✓ Mix up the vegetables well with the help of the fingertips and transfer them to the preheated 360F oven.

✓ Bake the vegetables for 45 minutes.

✓ Meanwhile, make the sauce: mix up together Sriracha sauce and coconut milk.

✓ Transfer the cooked vegetables to the serving plates and sprinkle them with Sriracha sauce.

Nutrition: Calories 213, fat 7.2, fiber 4.8, carbs 34.6, protein 3.6

39) Breakfast Green Smoothie

Ingredients:

- 2 cups spinach
- 2 cups kale
- 1 cup bok choy
- 1 ½ cup organic almond milk
- 1 Tbsp almonds, chopped
- ½ cup of water

Direction: Preparation time: 7 minutes Servings: 2

✓ Place all to the blender and blend until you get a smooth mixture.

✓ Pour the smoothie into the serving glasses.

✓ Add ice cubes if desired.

Nutrition: Calories 107, fat 3.6, fiber 2.4, carbs 15.5, protein 4.8

40) Almonds Crusted Rack of Lamb with Rosemary

Ingredients:

- 1 garlic clove, minced
- ½ tablespoon of virgin olive oil
- salt and black pepper, freshly cracked
- ¾ lb rack of lamb
- 1 small organic egg
- 1 tbsp breadcrumbs
- 2 oz almonds, finely chopped
- ½ tbsp fresh rosemary, chopped

Direction: Preparation time: 10 minutes Cooking time: 35 minutes Servings: 2

✓ Switch on the oven and set its temperature to 350°F,

✓ Meanwhile, take a baking tray, grease it with oil, and set aside until required.

✓ Mix garlic, oil, salt, and freshly cracked black pepper in a container and coat the rack of lamb with this garlic, rub it on all sides.

✓ Crack the egg in a container, whisk it until blended, and set aside until required.

✓ Place breadcrumbs in another dish, add almonds and rosemary and stir until mixed.

✓ Dip the seasoned rack of lamb with egg, dredge with the almond mixture until evenly coated on all sides and then place it onto the prepared baking tray.

✓ When the oven has preheated, place the rack of lamb in it, and cook for 35 minutes until thoroughly cooked.

✓ When done, take out the baking tray, transfer the rack of lamb onto a dish, and serve straight away.

✓ For meal prep, cut the rack of lamb into pieces, evenly divide the lamb between two heatproof containers, close them with a lid and refrigerate for up to 3 days until ready to serve.

Nutrition: Calories 471, Total Fat 31.6g, Total Carbs

8.5g, Protein 39g, Sugar 1.5g, Sodium 1

41) Cheesy Eggs in Avocado

Ingredients:

- *1 medium avocado*
- *2 organic eggs*
- *¼ cup shredded cheddar cheese*
- *Salt and freshly cracked black pepper*
- *1 tbsp olive oil*

Direction: Preparation time: 20 minutes Cooking time: 15 minutes Servings: 2

- ✓ *Switch on the oven, preheat it setting its temperature to 425°F*
- ✓ *Meanwhile, prepare the avocados and for this, cut the avocado in half and remove its pit.*
- ✓ *Take two muffin tins, grease them with oil, and then add an avocado half into each tin.*
- ✓ *Crack an egg into each avocado half, season well with salt and freshly cracked black pepper, and then sprinkle cheese on top.*
- ✓ *When the oven has preheated, place the muffin tins in the oven and bake for 15 minutes until cooked.*
- ✓ *When done, take out the muffin tins, transfer the avocados baked organic eggs to a dish, and then serve them.*

Nutrition: Calories 210, Total Fat 16.6g, Total Carbs 6.4g, Protein 10.7g, Sugar 2.2g, Sodium 151mg

42) Bacon, Vegetable and Parmesan Combo

Ingredients:

- *2 slices of bacon, thick-cut*
- *½ tbsp mayonnaise*
- *½ of medium green bell pepper, deseeded, chopped*
- *1 scallion, chopped*
- *¼ cup grated Parmesan cheese*
- *1 tbsp olive oil*

Direction: Preparation time: 10 minutes Cooking time: 25 minutes Servings: 2

- ✓ *Switch on the oven, preheat it setting its temperature to 375°F*
- ✓ *Meanwhile, take a baking dish, grease it using oil, and add slices of bacon to it.*
- ✓ *Spread mayonnaise on top of the bacon, then top with bell peppers and scallions, sprinkle with Parmesan cheese, and bake for about 25 minutes until cooked thoroughly.*
- ✓ *When done, take out the baking dish and serve immediately.*
- ✓ *For meal prepping, wrap bacon in a plastic sheet and refrigerate for up to 2 days.*
- ✓ *When ready to eat, reheat bacon to the microwave and then serve.*

Nutrition: Calories 197, Total Fat 13.8g, Total Carbs 4.7g, Protein 14.3g, Sugar 1.9g, Sodium 662mg

43) Four-Cheese Zucchini Noodles with Basil Pesto

Ingredients:

- *4 cups zucchini noodles*
- *4 oz Mascarpone cheese*
- *1/8 cup Romano cheese*
- *2 tbsp grated parmesan cheese*
- *¼ tsp salt*
- *½ tsp cracked black pepper*
- *2 1/8 tsp ground nutmeg*
- *1/8 cup basil pesto*
- *½ cup shredded mozzarella cheese*
- *1 tbsp olive oil*

Direction: Preparation time: 10 minutes Cooking time: 15 minutes Servings: 2

- ✓ *Switch on the oven, preheat it setting its temperature to 400°F*
- ✓ *Meanwhile, place zucchini noodles in a heatproof container and microwave at high heat setting for 3 minutes, set aside until required.*
- ✓ *Take another heatproof container, add all cheeses in it, except for mozzarella, season with salt, black pepper, and nutmeg, and microwave at high heat setting for 1 minute until cheese has melted.*
- ✓ *Whisk the cheese mixture, add cooked zucchini noodles in it along with basil pesto and mozzarella cheese and fold until well mixed.*
- ✓ *Take a casserole dish, and grease it with oil, add zucchini noodles mixture in it, and then bake for 10 minutes until done.*
- ✓ *Serve straight away.*

Nutrition: Calories 139, Total Fat 9.7g, Total Carbs 3.3, Protein 10.2g, Sodium 419mg, Sugar 0.2g

44) Baked Eggs with Cheddar and Beef

Ingredients:

- *3 oz ground beef, cooked*
- *2 organic eggs*
- *2oz shredded cheddar cheese*
- *1 tbsp olive oil*

Direction: Preparation time: 10 minutes Cooking time: 20 minutes Servings: 2

- ✓ *Switch on the oven, preheat it setting its temperature to 390°F*
- ✓ *Take a baking dish, grease it with oil, add spread cooked beef to the bottom, then make two holes in it and crack an organic egg into each hole.*
- ✓ *Sprinkle cheese on top of beef and eggs and bake for 20 minutes until beef has cooked and eggs have set.*
- ✓ *When done, let baked eggs cool for 5 minutes and then serve straight away.*

- ✓ For meal prepping, wrap baked eggs in foil and refrigerate for up to two days.
- ✓ When ready to eat, reheat baked eggs to the microwave and then serve.

Nutrition: Calories 512, Total Fat 32.8g, Total Carbs 1.4g, Protein 51g, Sugar 1g, Sodium 531mg

45) Heavenly Egg Bake with Blackberry

Ingredients:

- Chopped rosemary
- 1 tsp lime zest
- ½ tsp salt
- ¼ tsp vanilla extract, unsweetened
- 1 tsp grated ginger
- 3 tbsp coconut flour
- 1 tbsp unsalted butter
- 5 organic eggs
- 1 tbsp olive oil
- ½ cup fresh blackberries
- Black pepper to taste

Direction: Preparation time: 10 minutes Cooking time: 15 minutes Servings: 4

- ✓ Switch on the oven, preheat it setting its temperature to 350°F
- ✓ Meanwhile, place ingredients in a blender, reserving the berries, and pulse for 2 to 3 minutes until well blended and smooth.
- ✓ Take four silicon muffin cups, grease them with oil, evenly distribute the blended batter to the cups, top with black pepper, and bake for 15 minutes until cooked through and the top has golden brown.
- ✓ When done, let blueberry egg bake cool to the muffin cups for 5 minutes, then take them out, and cool on a wire rack and then serve.
- ✓ For meal prepping, wrap each egg bake with aluminum foil, and freeze for up to 3 days.
- ✓ When ready to eat, reheat blueberry egg bake to the microwave and then serve.

Nutrition: Calories 144, Total Fat 10g, Total Carbs 2g, Protein 8.5g

46) Protein-Packed Blender Pancakes

Ingredients:

- 2 organic eggs
- 1 scoop protein powder
- Salt to taste
- ¼ tsp cinnamon
- 2oz cream cheese, softened
- 1 tsp unsalted butter

Direction: Preparation time: 5 minutes Cooking time: 10 minutes Servings: 1

- ✓ Crack the eggs in a blender, add resting ingredients except for butter, and pulse for 2 minutes until well combined and blended.
- ✓ Take a skillet pan, place it over medium heat, add butter and when it melts, pour in prepared batter, spread it evenly, and cook for 4 to 5 minutes per side until cooked through and golden brown.
- ✓ Serve straight away.

Nutrition: Calories 450, Total Fat 29g, Total Carbs 4g, Protein 41g

47) Blueberry and Vanilla Scones

Ingredients:

- 1½ cup almond flour
- 3 organic eggs, beaten
- 2 teaspoon baking powder
- ½ cup stevia
- 2 tsp vanilla extract, unsweetened
- ¾ cup fresh raspberries
- 1 tbsp olive oil

Direction: Preparation time: 10 minutes Cooking time: 10 minutes Servings: 12

- ✓ Switch on the oven, preheat it setting its temperature to 375 °F
- ✓ Take a large container, add flour and eggs in it, stir in baking powder, stevia, and vanilla until combined, and then fold in berries until mixed.
- ✓ Take a baking dish, grease it with oil, scoop the prepared batter on it with an ice cream scoop, bake for 10-11 minutes until done.
- ✓ When done, transfer scones on a wire rack, cool them thoroughly and then serve.

Nutrition: Calories 133, Total Fat 8g, Total Carbs 4g, Protein 2g

48) Healthy Blueberry and Coconut Smoothie

Ingredients:

- 1 cup fresh blueberries
- 1 tsp vanilla extract, unsweetened
  28 oz coconut milk, unsweetened
- 2 tbsp lemon juice

Direction: Preparation time: 5 minutes Cooking time: 0 minutes Servings: 2

- ✓ Add berries in a blender or food processor, then add the rest ingredients and pulse for 2 minutes until smooth and creamy.
- ✓ Pour the smoothie between two glasses and serve.

Nutrition: Calories 152, Total Fat 13.1g, Total Carbs 6.9g, Protein 1.5g, Sugar 4.5g, Sodium 1mg

49) Avocado and Eggs Breakfast Tacos

Ingredients:

- 4 organic eggs
- 1 tbsp unsalted butter
- 2 low-carb tortillas
- 2 tbsp mayonnaise
  4 sprigs of cilantro

- *½ of an avocado, sliced*
- *Seasoning with salt and black pepper to taste*
- *1 tbsp Tabasco sauce*

Direction: Preparation time: 10 minutes Cooking time: 13 minutes Servings: 2

- ✓ *Take a container, crack eggs in it and whisk well until smooth.*
- ✓ *Take a skillet pan, place it over medium heat, add butter and when it melts, pour in eggs, spread them evenly into the pan, and cook for 4 to 5 minutes until done.*
- ✓ *When done, transfer eggs to a plate and set aside until required.*
- ✓ *Add tortillas into the pan, cook for 2 to 3 minutes per side until warm through, and then transfer them onto a plate.*
- ✓ *Assemble tacos and for this, spread mayonnaise on the side of each tortilla, then distribute cooked eggs and top with cilantro and sliced avocado.*
- ✓ *Season with salt and black pepper, drizzle with tabasco sauce, and roll up the tortillas.*
- ✓ *Serve straight away or store in the refrigerator for up to 2 days until ready to eat.*

Nutrition: Calories 289, Total Fat 27g, Total Carbs 6g, Protein 7g

50) Delicious Frittata with Brie and Bacon

Ingredients:

- *4 slices of bacon*
- *4 organic eggs, beaten*
- *½ cup heavy cream*
- *Seasoning with salt and black pepper to taste*
- *4 oz brie, diced*
- *1 ½ cup of water*
- *1 tbsp olive oil*

Direction: Preparation time: 10 minutes Cooking time: 20 minutes Servings: 2

- ✓ *Switch on the instant pot, insert its inner pot, press the 'sauté' button, and when hot, add bacon slices and cook for 5 to 7 minutes until crispy.*
- ✓ *Then transfer bacon to a plate lined with paper towels to drain grease and set aside until required.*
- ✓ *Crack eggs in a container, add cream, season with salt and black pepper and whisk until combined.*
- ✓ *Chop the cooked bacon, add to the eggs along with brie and stir until mixed.*
- ✓ *Take a baking dish, and grease it using oil, pour into the egg mixture, and spread evenly.*
- ✓ *Carefully pour water into the instant pot, insert a trivet stand, place baking dish on it, shut with lid, press the 'manual' button, and cook the frittata for 20 minutes at a high-pressure setting.*
- ✓ *When the timer beeps, press the 'cancel' button, allow pressure to release naturally until the pressure valve drops, then open the lid and take out the baking dish.*
- ✓ *Wipe clean moisture on top of the frittata with a paper towel and let it cool completely.*
- ✓ *For meal prep, cut frittata into six slices, then place each slice in a plastic bag or airtight container and store in the refrigerator for up to three days or store in the freezer until ready to eat.*

Nutrition: Preparation time: 5 minutes Cooking time: 5 minutes Servings: 1

51) Awesome Coffee with Butter

Ingredients:

- *1 cup of water*
- *1 tbsp coconut oil*
- *1 tbsp unsalted butter*
- *2 tbsp coffee*

Direction: Preparation time: 5 minutes Cooking time: 5 minutes Servings: 1

- ✓ *Take a small pan, place it over medium heat, pour in water, and bring to a boil*
- ✓ *Then add resting ingredients, stir well, and cook until butter and oil have melted.*
- ✓ *Remove pan from heat, pass the coffee through a strainer, and serve immediately.*

Nutrition: Calories 230, Total Fat 25g, Total Carbs 0g, Protein 0g

52) Buttered Thyme Scallops

Ingredients:

- *¾ lb sea scallops*
- *½ tbsp fresh minced thyme*
- *Salt and black pepper, to taste*
- *1 tbsp unsalted butter, melted*
- *1 tbsp olive oil*

Direction: Preparation time: 10 minutes Cooking time: 5 minutes Servings: 2

- ✓ *Switch on the oven, preheat it setting its temperature to 390°F*
- ✓ *Take a large container, add all the ingredients in it and toss until well coated.*
- ✓ *Take a baking dish, grease it with oil, add prepared scallop mixture in it and bake for 5 minutes until thoroughly cooked.*
- ✓ *When done, take out the baking dish, then scallops cool for 5 minutes, and then serve.*
- ✓ *For meal prepping, transfer scallops into an airtight container and store them in the fridge for up to two days.*
- ✓ *When ready to eat, reheat scallops to the microwave until hot and then serve.*

Nutrition: Calories 202, Total Fat 7.1g, Total Carbs 4.4g, Protein 28.7g, Sugar 0g, Sodium 315mg

53) Cheesy Caprese Style Portobellos Mushrooms

Ingredients:

- *2 large caps of Portobello mushroom, gills removed*
- *4 tomatoes, halved*
- *Salt and black pepper, to taste*
- *¼ cup fresh basil*
- *4 tbsp olive oil*
- *¼ cup shredded Mozzarella cheese*

Direction: Preparation time: 5 minutes Cooking time: 15 minutes Servings: 2

✓ *Preheat the Oven setting it to 400°F*

✓ *Meanwhile, prepare mushrooms, and for this, brush them with olive oil and set them aside until required.*

✓ *Place tomatoes in a container, season with salt and black pepper, add basil, drizzle with oil and toss until mixed.*

✓ *Distribute cheese evenly to the bottom of each mushroom cap and then top with prepared tomato mixture.*

✓ *Take a baking sheet, line it with aluminum foil, place prepared mushrooms on it and bake for 15 minutes until thoroughly cooked.*

✓ *Serve straight away.*

Nutrition: Calories 315, Total Fat 29.2g, Total Carbs 14.2g, Protein 4.7g, Sugar 10.4g, Sodium 55mg

*54) **Persimmon Toast with Cream Cheese***

Ingredients:

- *2 slices whole-grain bread*
- *1 persimmon*
- *2 Tsp cream cheese*
- *1 Tsp honey*

Direction: Preparation time: 5 minutes Cooking time: 3 minutes Servings: 2

✓ *Toast the bread with the help of the toaster. You should get light brown bread slices.*

✓ *After this, slice persimmon.*

✓ *Spread the cream cheese on the toasted bread and top it with sliced persimmon.*

✓ *Then sprinkle very toast with honey.*

Nutrition: Cal 107, fat 2.2, , carbs 18.7, protein 4

*55) **Scrambled Eggs***

Ingredients:

- *1 Tbsp butter*
- *4 eggs*

Direction: Servings: 2 Preparation time: 25 mins

✓ *Combine together eggs, salt, and black pepper in a container and keep aside.*

✓ *Heat butter in a pan over medium-low heat and slowly add the whisked eggs.*

✓ *Stir the eggs continuously to the pan with the help of a fork for about 4 minutes.*

✓ *Dish out on a plate and serve immediately.*

✓ *You can refrigerate this scramble for about 2 days for meal prepping and reuse it by heating it in the microwave oven.*

Nutrition: Calories: 151 , Fat: 11.6g Carbohydrates: 0.7g Protein: 11.1g Sodium: 144mg Sugar: 0.7g

*56) **Bacon Veggies Combo***

Ingredients:

- *½ green bell pepper, seeded and chopped*
- *2 bacon slices*
- *¼ cup Parmesan Cheese*
- *½ Tbsp mayonnaise*
- *1 scallion, chopped*

Direction: Servings: 2 Preparation time: 35 mins

✓ *Switch on the oven, preheat it setting its temperature to 375 degrees F, and grease a baking dish.*

✓ *Place bacon slices on the baking dish and top with mayonnaise, bell peppers, scallions, and Parmesan Cheese.*

✓ *Bake for about 25 minutes.*

✓ *Dish out to serve immediately or refrigerate for about 2 days wrapped in a plastic sheet for meal prepping.*

Nutrition: Calories: 197 Fat: 13.8g Carbohydrates: 4.7g Protein: 14.3g Sugar: 1.9g Sodium: 662mg

*57) **Tofu with Mushrooms***

Ingredients:

- *1 cup fresh mushrooms, chopped finely*
- *1 block tofu, pressed and cubed into 1-inch pieces*
- *4 Tbsps butter*
- *Salt and black pepper, to taste*
- *4 Tbsps Parmesan cheese, shredded*

Direction: Servings: 2 Preparation time: 25 mins

✓ *Season the tofu with salt and pepper.*

✓ *Put butter and seasoned tofu in a pan and cook for about 5 minutes.*

✓ *Add mushrooms and Parmesan cheese and cook for another 5 minutes, stirring occasionally.*

✓ *Dish out and serve immediately or refrigerate for about 3 days wrapped in a foil for meal prepping and microwave it to serve again.*

Nutrition: Calories: 423 Fat: 37g Carbohydrates: 4g Protein: 23.1g Sugar: 0.9g Sodium: 691mg

*58) **Ham Spinach Ballet***

Ingredients:

- *4 Tsp cream*
- *¾ pound fresh baby spinach*
- *7-ounce ham, sliced*
- *Salt and black pepper, to taste*
- *1 Tbsp unsalted butter, melted*

Direction: Servings: 2Preparation time: 40 mins

- ✓ *Switch on the oven, preheat it setting its temperature to 360 degrees F., and grease 2 ramekins with butter.*
- ✓ *Put butter and spinach in a skillet and cook for about 3 minutes.*
- ✓ *Add cooked spinach to the ramekins and top with ham slices, cream, salt, and black pepper.*
- ✓ *Bake for about 25 minutes and dish out to serve hot.*
- ✓ *For meal prepping, you can refrigerate this ham spinach ballet for about 3 days wrapped in foil.*

Nutrition: Calories: 188 Fat: 12.5g Carbohydrates: 4.9g Protein: 14.6g Sugar: 0.3g Sodium: 1098mg

59) Creamy Parsley Soufflé

Ingredients:

- *2 fresh red chili peppers, chopped*
- *Salt, to taste*
- *4 eggs*
- *4 Tbsps light cream*
- *2 Tbsps fresh parsley, chopped*

Direction: Servings: 2Preparation time: 25 mins

- ✓ *Switch on the oven, preheat it setting its temperature to 375 degrees F, and grease 2 soufflé dishes.*
- ✓ *Combine all in a container and mix well.*
- ✓ *Put the mixture into prepared soufflé dishes and transfer in the oven.*
- ✓ *Cook for about 6 minutes and dish out to serve immediately.*
- ✓ *You can refrigerate this creamy parsley soufflé to the ramekins covered in foil for meal prepping for about 2-3 days.*

Nutrition: Calories: 108 Fat: 9g Carbohydrates: 1.1g Protein: 6g Sugar: 0.5g Sodium: 146mg

60) Vegetarian Three Cheese Quiche Stuffed Peppers

Ingredients:

- *2 large eggs*
- *¼ cup mozzarella, shredded*
- *1 medium bell peppers, sliced in half and seeds removed*
- *¼ cup ricotta cheese*
- *¼ cup grated Parmesan cheese*
- *½ Tsp garlic powder*
- *1/8 cup baby spinach leaves*
- *¼ Tsp dried parsley*
- *1 Tbsp Parmesan cheese to garnish*

Direction: Servings: 2Preparation time: 50 mins

- ✓ *Preheat oven to 375 degrees F.*
- ✓ *Blend all the cheeses, eggs, garlic powder, and parsley in a food processor and process until smooth.*
- ✓ *Pour the cheese mixture into each sliced bell pepper and top with spinach leaves.*
- ✓ *Stir with a fork, pushing them under the cheese mixture, and cover with foil.*
- ✓ *Bake for about 40 minutes and sprinkle with Parmesan cheese.*
- ✓ *Broil for about 5 minutes and dish out to serve.*

Nutrition: Calories: 157 Carbs: 7.3g Fats: 9g Proteins: 12.7g Sodium: 166mg Sugar: 3.7g

61) Spinach Artichoke Egg Casserole

Ingredients:

- *1/8 cup milk*
- *2.5-ounce frozen chopped spinach, thawed and drained well*
- *1/8 cup parmesan cheese*
- *1/8 cup onions, shaved*
- *¼ Tsp salt*
- *¼ Tsp crushed red pepper*
- *4 large eggs*
- *3.5-ounce artichoke hearts, drained*
- *¼ cup white cheddar, shredded*
- *1/8 cup ricotta cheese*
- *½ garlic clove, minced*
- *¼ Tsp dried thyme*

Direction: Servings: 2 Preparation time: 45 mins

- ✓ *Switch on the oven, preheat it setting its temperature to 350 degrees F, and grease a baking dish with nonstick cooking spray.*
- ✓ *Whisk eggs and milk together and add artichoke hearts and spinach.*
- ✓ *Mix well and stir in the rest of the ingredients, withholding the ricotta cheese.*
- ✓ *Coat the mixture into the baking dish and top evenly with ricotta cheese.*
- ✓ *Bake for about 30 minutes.*
- ✓ *Dish out and serve warm.*

Nutrition: Calories: 228 Carbs: 10.1g Fats: 13.3g Proteins: 19.1g Sodium: 571mg Sugar: 2.5g

62) Avocado Baked Eggs

Ingredients:

- *2 eggs*
- *1 medium-sized avocado, halved and pit removed*
- *¼ cup cheddar cheese, shredded*
- *Kosher salt and black pepper, to taste*

Direction: Servings: 2 Preparation time: 25 mins

- ✓ *Switch on the oven, preheat it setting its temperature to 425 degrees, and grease a muffin pan.*
- ✓ *Crack an egg into each half of the avocado and season with salt and black pepper.*

✓ *Top with cheddar cheese and transfer the muffin pan to the oven.*

✓ *Bake for about 15 minutes and dish out to serve.*

Nutrition: Calories: 210 Carbs: 6.4g Fats: 16.6g Proteins: 10.7g Sodium: 151mg Sugar: 2.2g

63) Cinnamon Faux-St Crunch Cereal

Ingredients:

- *¼ cup hulled hemp seeds*
- *½ Tbsp coconut oil*
- *¼ cup milled flax seed*
- *1 Tbsp ground cinnamon*
- *¼ cup apple juice*

Direction: Servings: 2Preparation time: 35 mins

✓ *Switch on the oven, preheat it setting its temperature to 300 degrees F, and line a cookie sheet with parchment paper.*

✓ *Put hemp seeds, flaxseed, and ground cinnamon in a food processor.*

✓ *Add coconut oil and apple juice and blend until smooth.*

✓ *Pour the mixture on the cookie sheet and transfer it to the oven.*

✓ *Bake for about 15 minutes and lower the temperature of the oven to 250 degrees F.*

✓ *Bake for another 10 minutes and dish out from the oven, turning it off.*

✓ *Cut into small squares and place in the turned-off oven.*

✓ *Place the cereal in the oven for 1 hour until it is crisp.*

✓ *Dish out and serve with unsweetened almond milk.*

Nutrition: Calories: 225 Carbs: 9.2g Fats: 18.5g Proteins: 9.8g Sodium: 1mg Sugar: 1.6g

64) Quick Keto McMuffins

Ingredients:

- *Muffins:*
- *¼ cup flax meal*
- *¼ cup almond flour*
- *¼ Tsp baking soda*
- *1 large egg, free-range or organic*
- *2 Tbsps water*
- *1 pinch salt*
- *2 Tbsps heavy whipping cream*
- *¼ cup cheddar cheese, grated*
- *Filling:*
- *1 Tbsp ghee*
- *2 slices cheddar cheese*
- *Salt and black pepper, to taste*
- *2 large eggs*
- *1 Tbsp butter*
- *1 Tsp Dijon mustard*

Direction: Servings: 2Preparation time: 15 mins

✓ *For Muffins:*

✓ *Mix all the dry ingredients for muffins in a small container and add egg, cream, cheese, and water.*

✓ *Combine well and pour in 2 single-serving ramekins.*

✓ *Microwave on high for about 90 seconds.*

✓ *For Filling:*

✓ *Fry the eggs on ghee and season with salt and black pepper.*

✓ *Cut the muffins in half and spread butter on the inside of each half.*

✓ *Top each buttered half with cheese slices, eggs, and Dijon mustard.*

✓ *Serve immediately.*

Nutrition: Calories: 299 Carbs: 8.8g Fats: 24.3g Proteins: 13g Sodium: 376mg Sugar: 0.4g

65) Keto Egg Fast Snickerdoodle Crepes

Ingredients:

- *For the crepes:*
- *5 oz cream cheese, softened*
- *6 eggs*
- *1 Tsp cinnamon*
- *Butter, for frying*
- *1 Tbsp Swerve*
- *For the filling:*
- *2 Tbsps granulated Swerve*
- *8 Tbsps butter, softened*
- *1 Tbsp cinnamon*

Direction: Servings: 2 Preparation time: 15 mins

✓ *For the crepes: Put all the ingredients together in a blender except the butter and process until smooth.*

✓ *Heat butter on medium heat in a nonstick pan and pour some batter into the pan.*

✓ *Cook for about 2 minutes, then flip and cook for 2 more minutes.*

✓ *Repeat with the resting mixture.*

✓ *Mix Swerve, butter, and cinnamon in a small container until combined.*

✓ *Spread this mixture onto the center of the crepe and serve rolled up.*

Nutrition: Calories: 543 Carbs: 8g Fats: 51.6g Proteins: 15.7g Sodium: 455mg Sugar: 0.9g

66) Cauliflower Hash Brown Breakfast Container

Ingredients:

- *1 Tbsp lemon juice*
- *1 egg*
- *1 avocado*

- *1 Tsp garlic powder*
- *2 Tbsp olive oil (extra virgin)*
- *2 oz mushrooms, sliced*
- *½ green onion, chopped*
- *¼ cup salsa*
- *¾ cup cauliflower rice*
- *½ small handful of baby spinach*
- *Salt and black pepper, to taste*

Direction: Servings: 2 Preparation time: 30 mins

- ✓ *Mash together avocado, lemon juice, garlic powder, salt, and black pepper in a small container.*
- ✓ *Whisk eggs, salt, and black pepper in a container and keep aside.*
- ✓ *Heat half of the olive oil over medium heat in a skillet and add mushrooms.*
- ✓ *Sauté for about 3 minutes and season with garlic powder, salt, and pepper.*
- ✓ *Sauté for about 2 minutes and dish out in a container.*
- ✓ *Add the rest of the olive oil, cauliflower, garlic powder, salt, and pepper.*
- ✓ *Sauté for about 5 minutes and dish out.*
- ✓ *Return the mushrooms into the skillet, add green onions and baby spinach.*
- ✓ *Sauté for about 30 seconds and add whisked eggs.*
- ✓ *Sauté for about 1 minute and scoop on the sautéed cauliflower hash browns.*
- ✓ *Top with salsa and mashed avocado and serve.*

Nutrition: Calories: 400 Carbs: 15.8g Fats: 36.7g Proteins: 8g Sodium: 288mg Sugar: 4.2g

67) Cheesy Thyme Waffles

Ingredients:

- *½ cup mozzarella cheese, finely shredded*
- *¼ cup Parmesan cheese*
- *¼ large head cauliflower*
- *½ cup collard greens*
- *1 large egg*
- *1 stalk green onion*
- *½ Tbsp olive oil*
- *½ tsp minced garlic*
- *¼ Tsp salt*
- *½ Tbsp sesame seed*
- *1 Tsp fresh thyme, chopped*
- *¼ Tsp ground black pepper*

Direction: Servings: 2 Preparation time: 15 mins

- ✓ *Put cauliflower, collard greens, spring onion, and thyme in a food processor and pulse until smooth.*
- ✓ *Dish out the mixture in a container and stir in the rest of the ingredients.*
- ✓ *Heat waffle iron and transfer the mixture evenly over the griddle.*
- ✓ *Cook until a waffle is formed and dish out in a serving platter.*

Nutrition: Calories: 144 Carbs: 8.5g Fats: 9.4g Proteins: 9.3g Sodium: 435mg Sugar: 3g

68) Baked Eggs and Asparagus with Parmesan

Ingredients:

- *4 eggs*
- *8 thick asparagus spears, cut into bite-sized pieces*
- *2 Tsp olive oil*
- *2 Tbsps Parmesan cheese*
- *Salt and black pepper, to taste*

Direction: Servings: 2 Preparation time: 30 mins

- ✓ *Switch on the oven, preheat it setting its temperature to 400 degrees F, and grease two gratin dishes with olive oil.*
- ✓ *Put half the asparagus into each gratin dish and place it in the oven.*
- ✓ *Roast for about 10 minutes and dish out the gratin dishes.*
- ✓ *Crack eggs over the asparagus and transfer into the oven.*
- ✓ *Bake for about 5 minutes and dish out the gratin dishes.*
- ✓ *Sprinkle with Parmesan cheese and put the dishes back in the oven.*
- ✓ *Bake for another 3 minutes and dish out to serve hot.*

Nutrition: Calories: 336 Carbs: 13.7g Fats: 19.4g Proteins: 28.1g Sodium: 2103mg Sugar: 4.7g

69) Low Carb Green Smoothie

Ingredients:

- *1/3 cup romaine lettuce*
- *1/3 tbsp scraped and sliced fresh ginger*
- *1½ cups filtered water*
- *1/8 cup fresh pineapple, chopped*
- *¾ Tbsp fresh parsley*
- *1/3 cup raw cucumber, peeled and sliced*
- *¼ Hass avocado*
- *¼ cup kiwi fruit, peeled and chopped*
- *1/3 Tbsp Swerve*

Direction: Servings: 2 Preparation time: 15 mins

- ✓ *Put all in a blender and blend until smooth.*
- ✓ *Pour into 2 serving glasses and serve chilled.*

Nutrition: Calories: 108 Carbs: 7.8g Fats: 8.9g Proteins: 1.6g Sodium: 4mg Sugar: 2.2g

70) Quinoa Fruit Salad

Ingredients:

- *For the Quinoa:*
- *1 cup quinoa*
- *2 cups water*
- *Pinch of salt*
- *3 Tbsps honey*
- *For the Honey Lime Dressing:*
- *Juice of 1 large lime*
- *2 Tbsps fresh mint, chopped*
- *For the fruit:*
- *1 1/2 cups blueberries*
- *1 1/2 cups strawberries*
- *1 1/2 cups chopped mango*
- *Extra chopped mint for garnish-optional*

Direction: Servings: 4 Preparation time: 25 mins

- ✓ *With a strainer, rinse the quinoa under cold water. Add quinoa, water, and salt to a medium saucepan and bring to a boil over medium heat. Boil for 4-5 minutes.*
- ✓ *Turn the heat to low and simmer until water is absorbed. Remove from heat and fluff with a fork. Let quinoa cool*
- ✓ *To make the Honey Lime Dressing:*
- ✓ *In a medium container, whisk the lime juice, honey, and mint together until combined. In a large container, Mix quinoa and fruits. Pour honey lime dressing over the fruit salad and mix until well combined.*
- ✓ *Garnish with mint, if you like. Serve at room temperature or chilled.*
- ✓ *Note: Use your favorite fruit for this salad. Blackberries, peaches, raspberries, pineapple, etc., are great options!*

Nutrition: Cal 308,1, Fat 18.2g, , Cholesterol 0mg, Total Carbohydrate 34.1g, Dietary Fiber 4.5g, Sugars 15.2g, Protein 4.4g

71) ***Baked Avocado Eggs***

Ingredients:

- *3 avocados, halved and seeded*
- *6 large eggs*
- *Kosher salt and black pepper to taste*
- *2 Tbsps fresh chives, chopped*

Direction: Servings: 4 Preparation time: 30 mins

- ✓ *Preheat oven to 400°F (200°C). Slice the avocados in half and remove the pits. Place the avocado halves on a baking sheet and scoop out some of the flesh to make a bigger hole. Crack one egg into each hole and season with salt and pepper.*
- ✓ *Choose your top and bake for 15 minutes or until the yolk achieves the appropriate texture. As desired, garnish with fresh herbs. Enjoy!*

Nutrition: Calories 249, Fat 19g, Carbs 9g, Fiber 5g, Sugar 0g, Protein 11g

72) ***Keto Breakfast Pizza***

Ingredients:

- *2 Tbsps coconut flour*
- *2 cups cauliflower, grated*
- *½ Tsp salt*
- *1 Tbsp psyllium husk powder*
- *4 eggs*
- *Toppings:*
- *Avocado*
- *Smoked Salmon*
- *Herbs*
- *Olive oil*
- *Spinach*

Direction: Servings: 6Preparation time: 30 mins

- ✓ *Switch on the oven, preheat it setting its temperature to 360 degrees F, and grease a pizza tray.*
- ✓ *Mix together all ingredients in a container, except toppings, and keep them aside.*
- ✓ *Pour the pizza dough onto the pan and mold it into an even pizza crust using your hands.*
- ✓ *Top the pizza with toppings and transfer in the oven.*
- ✓ *Bake for around 15-16 minutes until golden brown and remove from the oven to serve.*

Nutrition: Calories 454, Carbs 16g, Fat 31g, Protein 22g, Sodium 1325mg, Sugar 4.4g

73) ***Zucchini and Quinoa Pan***

Ingredients:

- *1 tablespoon of extra virgin olive oil*
- *2 garlic cloves, minced*
- *1 cup quinoa*
- *1 zucchini, roughly cubed*
- *2 Tbsps basil, chopped*
- *¼ cup green olives, pitted and chopped*
- *1 tomato, cubed*
- *½ cup feta cheese, crumbled*
- *2 cups water*
- *1 cup canned garbanzo beans, drained and rinsed*
- *A pinch of salt and black pepper*

Direction: Servings: 4 Preparation time: 20 Minutes

- ✓ *Heat up a pan with the oil over medium-high heat, add the garlic and quinoa, and brown for 3 minutes.*

✓ Add the water, zucchinis, salt, and pepper, toss, bring to a simmer, and cook for 15 minutes.

✓ Add resting ingredients, toss, divide everything between plates and serve for breakfast.

Nutrition: Calories 310, Fat 11g, Fiber 6g, Carbs 42g, Protein 11g

74) Peas Omelet

Ingredients:

- 4 oz green peas
- ¼ cup corn kernels
- 6 eggs, beaten
- ¼ cup heavy cream
- ½ Tsp of sea salt
- 1 red bell pepper, chopped
- 1 Tsp butter
- ½ Tsp paprika

Direction: Servings: 6Preparation time: 20 minutes

✓ Toss butter into the skillet and melt it.

✓ Add green peas, bell pepper, and corn kernels. Start to roast the vegetables over medium heat.

✓ Meanwhile, to the mixing container, whisk together eggs, heavy cream, sea salt, and paprika.

✓ Put the mixture over the roasted vegetables and stir well immediately.

✓ Close the lid and cook the omelet over medium-low heat for 15 minutes or until it is solid.

✓ Transfer the cooked omelet to the big plate and cut it into servings

Nutrition: Calories 113, Fat 7.1g, Fiber 1.5g, Carbs 6g, Protein 7.1g

75) Low Carb Green Smoothie

Ingredients:

- 1/ 3 cup romaine lettuce
- 1/3 tablespoon trimmed and sliced fresh ginger
- 1 ½ cups filtered water
- 1/8 cup fresh pineapple, chopped
- ¾ Tbsp fresh parsley
- 1/3 raw cucumber, peeled and sliced
- ¼ Hass avocado
- ¼ cup kiwi fruit, peeled and chopped
- 1/3 Tbsp Swerve

Direction: Servings: 2

Preparation time: 15 minutes

✓ Put all in a blender and blend until smooth.

✓ Pour into 2 serving glasses and serve chilled.

Nutrition: Calories: 108, Carbs: 7.8g, Fat: 8.9g, Protein: 1.6g, Sodium: 4 mg, Sugar: 2.2g

76) Vanilla Oats

Ingredients:

- ½ cup rolled oats
- 1 cup milk
- 1 Tsp vanilla extract
- 1 Tsp ground cinnamon
- 2 Tsp honey
- 2 Tbsps Plain yogurt
- 1 Tsp butter

Direction: Servings: 4 Preparation time: 10 Minutes

✓ Pour milk into the saucepan and bring it to a boil.

✓ Add rolled oats and stir well.

✓ Close the lid and simmer the oats for 5 minutes over medium heat. The cooked oats will absorb all milk.

✓ Then add butter and stir the oats well.

✓ To the separated container, whisk together Plain yogurt with honey, cinnamon, and vanilla extract.

✓ Transfer the cooked oats to the serving containers.

✓ Top the oats with the yogurt mixture to the shape of the wheel.

Nutrition: Calories 243, Fat 20.2, Fiber 1g, Carbs 2.8g, Protein 13.3g

77) Orzo and Veggie Containers

Ingredients:

- 2 and ½ 1 cup orzo (whole-wheat), cooked
- 14 ounces canned cannellini beans, drained and rinsed
- 1 yellow bell pepper, cubed
- 1 diced green bell pepper
- A pinch of salt and black pepper
- 3 tomatoes, cubed
- 1 red onion, chopped
- cup mint, chopped
- 2 cups feta cheese, crumbled
- 2 Tbsps olive oil
- ¼ cup lemon juice
- 1 Tbsp lemon zest, grated
- 1 cucumber, cubed
- 1 and ¼ cup peeled and diced kalamata olives
- 3 chopped cloves garlic

Direction: Servings: 4 Preparation time: 0 minutes

✓ In a salad container, combine the orzo with the beans, bell peppers, and the rest of the ingredients, toss, divide the mix between plates and serve for breakfast.

Nutrition: Calories 411, Fat 17g, Fiber 13g, Carbs 51g, Protein 14g

78) Spiced Chickpeas Containers

Ingredients:

- 15 ounces canned chickpeas, drained and rinsed
- ¼ Tsp cardamom, ground
- ½ Tsp cinnamon powder

- *1 and ½ Tsp turmeric powder*
- *1 Tsp coriander, ground*
- *Tbsp olive oil*
- *A pinch of salt and black pepper*
- *¾ cup Greek yogurt*
- *½ cup green olives pitted and halved*
- *½ cup cherry tomatoes halved*
- *1 cucumber, sliced*

Direction: Servings: 4 Preparation time: 30 minutes

- ✓ *Spread the chickpeas on a lined baking sheet, add the cardamom, cinnamon, turmeric, coriander, oil, salt, and pepper, toss and bake at 375 degrees F for 30 minutes.*
- ✓ *In a container, combine the roasted chickpeas with the rest of the ingredients, toss and serve for breakfast.*

Nutrition: Calories 519, Fat 34.5g, Fiber 13.3g, Carbs 49.8g, Protein 12g

79) ***Mediterranean Egg Feta Scramble***

Ingredients:

- *6 eggs*
- *¾ cup crumbled feta cheese*
- *2 Tbsps green onions, minced*
- *2 Tbsps red peppers, roasted, diced*
- *¼ Tsp kosher salt*
- *¼ Tsp garlic powder*
- *¼ cup Greek yogurt*
- *½ Tsp dry oregano*
- *½ Tsp dry basil*
- *1 Tsp olive oil*
- *A few cracks freshly ground black pepper*
- *Warm whole-wheat tortillas, optional*

Direction: Servings: 4 Preparation time: 15 minutes

- ✓ *Preheat a skillet over medium heat.*
- ✓ *In a container, whisk the eggs, sour cream, basil, oregano, garlic powder, salt, and pepper. Gently add the feta.*
- ✓ *When the skillet is hot, add the oil and then the egg mixture; allow the egg mix to set, then scrape the bottom of the pan to let the uncooked egg cook. Stir to the red peppers and the green onions.*
- ✓ *Continue cooking until the egg mixture is cooked to your preferred doneness. Serve immediately.*
- ✓ *If desired, sprinkle with extra feta and then wrap the scrambled eggs in tortillas.*

Nutrition: Calories 260, Fat 16g, Chol 350mg, Sodium 750mg, Pot. 190mg, Carb. 12g, Sugar 2g, Protein 16g

*80)**Fig with Ricotta Oatmeal***

Ingredients:

- *2 Tsp honey*
- *2 Tbsps ricotta cheese, part-skin*
- *2 Tbsps dried figs, chopped*
- *½ cup old-fashioned rolled oats*
- *1 Tbsp almonds, toasted, sliced*
- *1 cup water*
- *Pinch of salt*

Direction: Servings: 1Preparation time: 5 minutes

- ✓ *Put the water into a small saucepan and add the salt; bring to a boil.*
- ✓ *Stir to the oats and reduce heat to medium. Cook the oats for about 5 minutes, occasionally stirring, until most of the water is absorbed.*
- ✓ *Remove the pan from the heat, cover, and let stand for 2-3 minutes.*
- ✓ *Serve topped with the figs, almonds, ricotta, and a drizzle of honey*

Nutrition: Calories 315, Fat 8g, Chol. 10mg, Sodium 194mg, Pot. 359mg, Fiber 7g, Protein 10g

81) ***Raspberry Pudding***

Ingredients:

- *½ cup raspberries*
- *2 Tsp maple syrup*
- *1 ½ cup Plain yogurt*
- *¼ Tsp ground cardamom*
- *1/3 cup Chia seeds, dried*

Direction: Servings: 2Preparation time: 30 minutes

- ✓ *Mix up together Plain yogurt with maple syrup and ground cardamom.*
- ✓ *Add Chia seeds. Stir it gently.*
- ✓ *Put the yogurt to the serving glasses and top with the raspberries.*
- ✓ *Refrigerate the breakfast for at least 3 minutes or overnight.*

Nutrition: Calories 303, Fat 11.2g, Fiber 11.8g, Carbs 33.2g, Protein 15.5g

*82)**Walnuts Yogurt Mix***

Ingredients:

- *2 and ½ cups Greek yogurt*
- *1 and ½ cups walnuts, chopped*
- *1 Tsp vanilla extract*
- *¾ cup honey*
- *2 Tsp cinnamon powder*

Direction: Servings: 6 Preparation time: 0 Minutes

- ✓ *In a container, combine the yogurt with the walnuts and the rest of the ingredients, toss, divide into smaller containers and keep to the fridge for 10 minutes before serving for breakfast.*

Nutrition: Calories 388, Fat 24.6g, Fiber 2.9g, Carbs 39.1g, Protein 10.2g

83) Mushroom Egg Casserole

Ingredients:

- ½ cup mushrooms, chopped
- ½ yellow onion, diced
- 4 eggs, beaten
- 1 Tbsp coconut flakes
- ½ Tsp chili pepper
- 1 oz Cheddar cheese, shredded
- 1 Tsp canola oil

Direction: Servings: 3 Preparation time: 25 minutes

✓ Pour canola oil into the skillet and preheat well.

✓ Add mushrooms and onion and roast for 5-8 minutes or until the vegetables are light brown.

✓ Transfer the cooked vegetables to the casserole mold.

✓ Add coconut flakes, chili pepper, and Cheddar cheese.

✓ Then add eggs and stir well.

✓ Bake the casserole for 15 minutes at 360F.

Nutrition: Calories 152, Fat 11.1, Fiber 0.7, Carbs 3g, Protein 10.4g

84) Brown Rice Salad

Ingredients:

- 9 ounces brown rice, cooked
- 7 cups baby arugula
- 15 ounces canned garbanzo beans, drained and rinsed
- 4 ounces feta cheese, crumbled
- ¾ cup basil, chopped
- A pinch of salt and black pepper
- 2 Tbsps lemon juice
- ½ Tsp lemon zest, grated
- ½ cup olive oil

Direction: Servings: 4 Preparation time: 0 Minutes

✓ In a salad container, combine the brown rice with the arugula, the beans, and the rest of the ingredients, toss, and serve cold for breakfast.

Nutrition: Calories 473, Fat 22g, Fiber 7g, Carbs 53g, Protein 13g

85) Olive and Milk Bread

Ingredients:

- 1 cup black olives, pitted, chopped
- 1 Tbsp olive oil
- ½ Tsp fresh yeast
- ½ cup milk, preheated
- ½ Tsp salt
- 1 Tsp baking powder
- 2 cup wheat flour, whole grain
- 2 eggs, beaten
- 1 Tsp butter, melted
- 1 Tsp sugar

Direction: Servings: 6

Preparation time: 50 minutes

✓ To the big container, combine together fresh yeast, sugar, and milk. Stir it until yeast is dissolved.

✓ Then add salt, baking powder, butter, and eggs. Stir the dough mixture until homogenous, and add 1 cup of wheat flour. Mix it up until smooth.

✓ Add olives and resting flour. Knead the non-sticky dough.

✓ Transfer the dough into the non-sticky dough mold. Bake the bread for 50 minutes at 350 F.

✓ Check if the bread is cooked using the toothpick. If it is dry, the bread is cooked.

✓ Remove the bread from the oven, let it chill for 10-15 minutes.

✓ Remove it from the loaf mold, slice, and serve.

Nutrition: Calories 238, Fat 7.7g, Fiber 1.9, Carbs 35.5g, Protein 7.2g

86) Blueberry and Vanilla Scones

Ingredients:

- ½ cup almond flour
- 3 manic eggs, beaten
- 2 tsp baking powder
- ½ cup stevia
- 2 tsp vanilla extract, unsweetened
- ¾ cup fresh raspberries
- 1 tbsp olive oil

Direction: Servings: 12 Preparation time: 20 minutes

✓ Switch on the oven, preheat it setting its temperature to 375 °F

✓ Take a large container, add flour and eggs in it, stir in baking powder, stevia, and vanilla until combined, and then fold in berries until mixed.

✓ Take a baking dish, and then grease it with oil, scoop the prepared batter on it with an ice cream scoop and bake for 10 minutes until done.

✓ When done, transfer scones on a wire rack, cool them completely, and then serve.

Nutrition: 133 calories, 8 g total fat, 4 g total carbs, 2 g protein

87) Tahini Pine Nuts Toast

Ingredients:

- 2 whole-wheat bread slices, toasted
- 1 Tsp water
- 1 Tbsp tahini paste
- 2 Tsp feta cheese, crumbled
- Juice of ½ lemon

- 2 Tsp pine nuts
- A pinch of black pepper

Direction: Servings: 2Preparation time: 0 minutes

✓ In a container, mix the tahini with the water and the lemon juice, whisk really well, and spread over the toasted bread slices.

✓ Top each serving with the resting ingredients and serve for breakfast.

Nutrition: Calories 142, Fat 7.6g, Fiber 2.7g, Carbs 13.7g, Protein 5.8g

88)Chili Scramble

Ingredients:

- 3 tomatoes
- 4 eggs
- ¼ Tsp of sea salt
- ½ chili pepper, chopped
- 1 Tbsp butter
- 1 cup water for cooking

Direction: Servings: 4 Preparation time: 15 minutes

✓ Put water into the saucepan and bring it to a boil.

✓ Then remove water from the heat and add tomatoes.

✓ Let the tomatoes stay in hot water for 2-3 minutes.

✓ Then, remove the tomatoes from the water and peel them.

✓ Place butter into the pan and melt it.

✓ Add chopped chili pepper and fry it for 3 minutes over medium heat.

✓ Then chop the peeled tomatoes and add them into the chili peppers.

✓ Cook the vegetables for 5 minutes over medium heat. Stir them from time to time.

✓ Then, add sea salt and crack then eggs.

✓ Stir (scramble) the eggs well with the help of the fork and cook them for 3 minutes over medium heat.

Nutrition: Calories 105, Fat 7.4g, Fiber 1.1g, Carbs 4g, Protein 6.4g

89)Pear Oatmeal

Ingredients:

- 1 cup oatmeal
- 1/3 cup milk
- 1 pear, chopped
- 1 Tsp vanilla extract
- 1 Tbsp Splenda
- 1 Tsp butter
- ½ Tsp ground cinnamon
- 1 egg, beaten

Direction: Servings: 4Preparation time: 25 minutes

✓ To the big container, mix up together oatmeal, milk, egg, vanilla extract, Splenda, and ground cinnamon.

✓ Melt butter, add it to the oatmeal mixture.

✓ Then add chopped pear and stir it well.

✓ Coat the oatmeal mixture to the casserole mold and flatten gently. Cover it with foil and secure edges.

✓ Bake the oatmeal for 25-28 minutes at 350F.

Nutrition: Calories 151, Fat 3.9g, Fiber 3.3g, Carbs 23.6g, Protein 4.9g

90)Mediterranean Frittata

Ingredients:

- 9 large eggs, lightly beaten
- 8 kalamata olives, pitted, chopped
- ¼ cup olive oil
- 1/3 cup parmesan cheese, freshly grated
- 1/3 cup finely chopped fresh basil
- ½ Tsp salt
- ½ Tsp pepper
- ½ cup onion, chopped
- 1 sweet red pepper, diced
- 1 medium zucchini, cut to 1/2-inch cubes
- 1 package (4 ounces) feta cheese, crumbled

Direction: Servings: 6 Preparation time: 15 minutes

✓ In a 10-inch oven-proof skillet, heat the olive oil until hot. Add the olives, zucchini, red pepper, and onions, constantly stirring, until the vegetables are tender.

✓ In a container, mix the eggs, feta cheese, basil, salt, and pepper; pour into the skillet with vegetables. Adjust heat to medium-low, cover, and cook for some minutes, or until the egg mixture is almost set.

✓ Remove from the heat and sprinkle with the parmesan cheese. Transfer to the broiler.

✓ With the oven door partially open, broil 5 ½ from the source of heat for about 2-3 minutes or until the top is golden. Cut into wedges.

Nutrition: Calories 288.5, Fat 22.8g, Chol 301mg, Sodium 656 mg, Carb 5.6g, Fiber 1.2g, Sugar 3.3g, Protein 15.2g

91) Mediterranean Egg Casserole

Ingredients:

- 1 ½ cups (6 ounces) feta cheese, crumbled
- 1 jar (6 ounces) dried marinated artichoke hearts, roughly cut
- 10 eggs
- 2 cups milk, low-fat
- 2 cups of roughly chopped baby spinach
- 6 cups whole-wheat baguette, cut into i-inch cubes
- 1 Tbsp garlic (about 4 cloves), finely chopped
- 1 Tbsp extra-virgin olive oil

- *½ cup red bell pepper, chopped*
- *½ cup Parmesan cheese, shredded*
- *½ Tsp pepper*
- *½ Tsp red pepper flakes*
- *½ Tsp salt*
- *1/3 cup kalamata olives, pitted, halved*
- *¼ cup red onion, chopped*
- *¼ cup tomatoes (sun-dried) in oil, drained, chopped*

Direction: Servings: 8 Preparation time: 50 minutes

- ✓ *Preheat oven to 350 F.*
- ✓ *Grease a 9x13 inch baking dish with oil cooking spray.*
- ✓ *In an 8-inch non-stick pan over medium heat, heat the olive oil. Add the onions, garlic, and bell pepper; cook for about 3 minutes, frequently stirring, until slightly softened. Add the spinach; cook for about 1 minute or until starting to wilt.*
- ✓ *Layer half of the baguette cubes to the prepared baking dish, then 1 cup of the feta, 1/4 cup Parmesan, the bell pepper mix, artichokes, the olives, and the tomatoes. Top with the resting baguette cubes and then with the resting ½ cup of feta.*
  In a large mixing container, whisk the eggs and the low-fat milk together. Beat to the pepper, salt, and pepper. Pour the mix over the bread layer to the baking dish, slightly pressing down. Sprinkle with the resting ¼ cup Parmesan.
- ✓ *Bake for 40-45 mins, just until the middle is firm and lightly browned. Before serving, let stand for 15 minutes.*

Nutrition: Calories 360, Fat 21g, Chol 270mg, Sodium 880mg, Carb 24g, Fiber 3g, Sugar 7g, Protein 20g

92) Paprika Salmon Toast

Ingredients:

- *4 whole-grain bread slices*
- *2 oz smoked salmon, sliced*
- *2 Tsp cream cheese*
- *1 Tsp fresh dill, chopped*
- *½ Tsp lemon juice*
- *½ Tsp paprika*
- *4 lettuce leaves*
- *1 cucumber, sliced*

Direction: Servings: 2

Preparation time: 3 minutes

- ✓ *Toast the bread to the toaster (1-2 minutes totally).*
- ✓ *To the container, mix up together fresh dill, cream cheese, lemon juice, and paprika.*
- ✓ *Then spread the toasts with the cream cheese mixture.*
- ✓ *Slice the smoked salmon and place it on bread slices.*
- ✓ *Add sliced cucumber and lettuce leaves.*
- ✓ *Top the lettuce with resting bread toasts and pin it with the toothpick.*

Nutrition: Calories 202, Fat 4.7g, Fiber 5.1g, Carbs 31.5g, Protein 12.7g

93) Cheesy Olives Bread

Ingredients:

- *4 cups whole-wheat flour*
- *3 Tbsps oregano, chopped*
- *2 Tsp dry yeast*
- *¼ cup olive oil*
- *1 and ½ cups black olives, pitted and sliced*
- *1 cup water*
- *½ cup feta cheese, crumbled*

Direction: Servings: 10Preparation time: 30 minutes

- ✓ *In a bowl, mix the flour with the water, the yeast, and the oil, stir, and knead your dough very well.*
- ✓ *Put the dough in a container, cover with plastic wrap and keep in a warm place for 1 hour.*
- ✓ *Divide the dough into 2 containers and stretch each ball really well.*
- ✓ *Add the rest of the ingredients to each ball and tuck them inside, well kneading the dough again.*
- ✓ *Flatten the balls a bit and leave them aside for 4 minutes more.*
- ✓ *Transfer the balls to a baking sheet lined with parchment paper, make a small slit in each, and bake at 425 degrees F for 30 minutes.*
- ✓ *Serve the bread as a Mediterranean breakfast.*

Nutrition: Calories 251, Fat 7.3g, Fiber 2.1g, Carbs 39.7g, Protein 6.7g

94) Mediterranean Freezer Breakfast Wraps

Ingredients:

- *1 cup spinach leaves, fresh, chopped*
- *1 tbsp of low-fat milk or a tbsp of water*
- *½ Tsp garlic-chipotle seasoning or your preferred seasoning*
- *4 eggs, beaten*
- *4 whole-wheat tortillas (8-inch diameter)*
- *4 Tbsps tomato chutney (or dried tomatoes, chopped or calmed tomatoes)*
- *4 Tbsps feta cheese, crumbled (or goat cheese)*
- *Optional: prosciutto, chopped or bacon, cooked, crumbled*
- *Salt and pepper to taste*

Direction: Servings: 4 Preparation time: 3 minutes

- ✓ *In a mixing container, whisk the eggs, water, or*

milk, and seasoning together.

- ✓ *Heat a skillet with olive oil; pour the eggs and scramble for about 3-4 minutes, or until just cooked.*
- ✓ *Coat the tortillas on a clean surface; divide the eggs between them, arranging the scrambled eggs, and leave the tortilla edges free to fold later.*
- ✓ *Top the egg layer with about 1 Tbsp of cheese, 1 Tbsp of tomatoes, and 1/ 4 cup spinach. If using, layer with prosciutto or bacon.*
- ✓ *In a burrito style, roll up the tortillas, folding both of the ends to the process.*
- ✓ *In a panini maker or a clean skillet, cook for about 1 minute, turning once, until the tortilla wraps are crisp and brown; serve*

Nutrition: Calories 450, Fat 15g, Chol 220mg, Sodium 280mg, Pot. 960mg, Carb 64g, Fiber 6g, Sugar 20g, Protein 17g

*95) **Milk Scones***

Ingredients:

- *½ cup wheat flour, whole grain*
- *1 Tsp baking powder*
- *1 Tbsp butter, melted*
- *1 Tsp vanilla extract*
- *1 egg, beaten*
- *¾ Tsp salt*
- *3 Tbsps milk*
- *1 Tsp vanilla sugar*

Direction: Servings: 4 Preparation time: 10 minutes

- ✓ *To the mixing container, combine together wheat flour, baking powder, butter, vanilla extract, and egg. Add salt and knead the soft and non-sticky dough. Add more flour if needed.*
- ✓ *Then make the log from the dough and cut it into triangles.*
- ✓ *Line the tray with baking paper.*
- ✓ *Arrange the dough triangles on the baking paper and transfer them to the preheat to the 360F oven.*
- ✓ *Cook the scones until they are light brown.*
- ✓ *Then chill the scones and brush with milk and sprinkle with vanilla sugar.*

Nutrition: Calories 112, Fat 4.4g, Fiber 0.5g, Carbs 14.3g, Protein 3.4g

*96) **Herbed Eggs and Mushroom Mix***

Ingredients:

- *1 red onion, chopped*
- *1 bell pepper, chopped*
- *1 Tbsp tomato paste*
- *1/3 cup water*
- *½ Tsp of sea salt*
- *1 Tbsp butter*
- *1cup of finely sliced cremini mushrooms*
- *1 Tbsp fresh parsley*
- *1 Tbsp fresh dill*
- *1 Tsp dried thyme*
- *½ Tsp dried oregano*
- *½ Tsp paprika*
- *½ Tsp chili flakes*
- *½ Tsp garlic powder*
- *4 eggs*

Direction: Servings: 4 Preparation time: 20 minutes

- ✓ *Toss butter into the pan and melt it.*
- ✓ *Then add chopped mushrooms and bell pepper.*
- ✓ *Roast the vegetables for 5 minutes over medium heat.*
- ✓ *Then add onion and stir well.*
- ✓ *Sprinkle the ingredients with garlic powder, chili flakes, dried oregano, and dried thyme. Mix up well*
- ✓ *Then add tomato paste and water.*
- ✓ *Mix up the mixture until it is homogenous.*
- ✓ *Then add fresh parsley and dill.*
- ✓ *Cook the mixture for 5 minutes over medium-high heat with the closed lid.*
- ✓ *After this, stir the mixture with the help of the spatula well.*
- ✓ *Crack the eggs over the mixture and close the lid.*
- ✓ *Cook for 10 minutes over low heat.*

Nutrition: Calories 123, Fat 7.5g, Fiber 1.7g, Carbs 7.8, Protein 7.1g

*97) **Leeks and Eggs Muffins***

Ingredients:

- *3 eggs, whisked*
- *¼ cup baby spinach*
- *2 Tbsps leeks, chopped*
- *4 Tbsps parmesan, grated*
- *2 Tbsps almond milk*
- *Cooking spray*
- *1 small red bell pepper, chopped*
- *Season with salt and black pepper*
- *1 tomato, cubed*
- *2 Tbsps cheddar cheese, grated*

Direction: Servings: 2 Preparation time: 20 minutes

- ✓ *In a container, combine the eggs with the milk, salt, pepper, and the resting ingredients except for the cooking spray and whisk well.*
- ✓ *Grease a muffin tin with the cooking spray and divide the egg mixture in each muffin mould.*
- ✓ *Bake at 380 degrees F for no minutes and serve them for breakfast.*

Nutrition: Calories 308, Fat 19.4g, Fiber 1.7g, Carbs 8.7g, Protein 24.4g

98) Mango and Spinach Containers

Ingredients:

- 1 cup baby arugula
- 1 cup finely chopped fresh spinach
- 1 mango, peeled and cubed
- 1 cup strawberries, halved
- 1 tablespoon of hemp seeds
- 1 cucumber, sliced
- 1 Tbsp lime juice
- 1 Tbsp tahini paste
- 1 Tbsp water

Direction: Servings: 4 Preparation time: 0 minutes

✓ In a salad container, mix the arugula with the rest of the ingredients except the tahini and the water and toss.

✓ In a small container, combine the tahini with the water, whisk well, add to the salad, toss, divide into small containers and serve for breakfast.

Nutrition: Calories 211, Fat 4.5g, Fiber 6.5g, Carbs 10.2g, Protein 3.5g

99) Figs Oatmeal

Ingredients:

- 2 cups oatmeal
- 1 ½ cup milk
- 1 Tbsp butter
- 3 figs, chopped
- 1 Tbsp honey

Direction: Servings: 5 Preparation time: 20 minutes

✓ Put milk into the saucepan.

✓ Add oatmeal and close the lid.

✓ Cook the oatmeal for 15-17 minutes over medium-low heat.

✓ Then add chopped figs and honey.

✓ Add butter and mix up the oatmeal well.

✓ Cook it for 5 minutes more.

✓ Close the lid and let the cooked breakfast rest for 10 minutes before serving

Nutrition: Cal 222, Fat 6, Fiber 4.4g, carbs 36.5g, Pro 7.1g

100) Roasted Asparagus with Prosciutto and Poached Egg

Ingredients:

- 1 bunch fresh asparagus, trimmed
- 4 eggs
- 2 ounces minced prosciutto
- ½ lemon, zested and juiced
- 1 Tbsp olive oil
- 1 pinch salt
- 1 pinch ground black pepper
- 1 Tsp distilled white vinegar
- Ground black pepper

Direction: Servings: 4Preparation time: 25 minutes

✓ Preheat oven to 425F or 220C.

✓ In a baking dish, place the asparagus and drizzle with the extra-virgin olive oil.

✓ In a skillet, heat the oil over medium-low heat; add the prosciutto and cook for about 3-4 minutes, stirring until golden and rendered. Sprinkle over the asparagus to the baking dish and season with black pepper; toss to coat.

✓ Roast for 10 minutes, stir, return to the oven and continue roasting for 5 minutes or until the asparagus is tender but firm to the bite.

✓ Fill a large saucepan with about 2-3 inches of water; bring to a boil over high heat. Lower the heat and add the vinegar and a bit of salt when the water boils. Crack an egg into a small container, then gently slip the egg into the water. Repeat with the resting eggs. Poach the eggs for 4-5 min, or until the whites are crisp and the yolks are firm but not overcooked. Remove the eggs with a tilted spoon and place them on a warm dish after dabbing the spoon with a clean kitchen towel to remove any excess water.

✓ Drizzle the asparagus with the lemon juice and transfer divide between o plates. Top each asparagus bed with the o poached eggs, sprinkle with a pinch of lemon zest, and season with black pepper; serve.

Nutrition: Calories 163, Fat 12,3g, Chol 171mg, Sodium 273mg, Carb 4.4g, Fiber 1.9g, Protein 10.4g

101) Cream Olive Muffins

Ingredients:

- ½ cup quinoa, cooked
- 2 oz Feta cheese, crumbled
- 2 eggs, beaten
- 3 kalamata olives, chopped
- ¾ cup heavy cream
- 1 tomato, chopped
- 1 Tsp butter, softened
- 1 Tbsp wheat flour, whole grain
- ½ Tsp salt

Direction: Servings: 6 Preparation time: 20 minutes

✓ To the mixing container, whisk eggs and add Feta cheese.

✓ Then add chopped tomato and heavy cream.

✓ Then add wheat flour, salt, and quinoa.

✓ Then add kalamata olives and mix up the ingredients with the help of the spoon.

✓ Brush the muffin molds with the butter from inside.

✓ *Transfer the quinoa mixture to the muffin molds and flatten it with the help of the spatula or spoon if needed.*

✓ *Cook the muffins in the preheated 355F oven for 20 minutes.*

Nutrition: Calories 165, Fat 10.8g, Fiber 1.2g, Carbs 11.5g, Protein 5.8g

102) ***Veggie Quiche***

Ingredients:

- *½ cup of chopped solar-dried tomatoes*
- *1 prepared pie crust*
- *2 Tbsps avocado oil*
- *1 yellow onion, chopped*
- *2 garlic cloves, minced*
- *2 cups spinach, chopped*
- *1 minced red bell pepper*
- *¼ cup kalamata olives, pitted and sliced*
- *1 Tsp parsley flakes*
- *1 Tsp oregano, dried*
- *1/3 cup feta cheese, crumbled*
- *4 eggs, whisked*
- *1 and ½ cups almond milk*
- *1 cup cheddar cheese, shredded*
- *Season with salt and black pepper to perfection*

Direction: Servings: 8 Preparation time: 55 minutes

✓ *Heat up a pan with the oil over medium-high heat, add the garlic and onion and sauté for 3 minutes.*

✓ *Add the bell pepper and sauté for 3 minutes more.*

✓ *Add the olives, parsley, spinach, oregano, salt, pepper, and cook everything for some minutes.*

✓ *Add tomatoes and the cheese, toss and take off the heat.*

✓ *Arrange the pie crust on a pie plate, pour the spinach and tomatoes mix inside and spread.*

✓ *In a container, mix the eggs with salt, pepper, milk, and half of the cheese, whisk and pour over the mixture to the pie crust.*

✓ *Sprinkle the resting cheese on top and bake at 375 degrees F for 40 minutes.*

✓ *Cool the quiche down, slice, and serve for breakfast.*

Nutrition: Calories 211, Fat 14 4g, Fiber 1.4g, Carbs 12.5g, Protein 8.6g

103) ***Tuna and Cheese Bake***

Ingredients:

- *10 ounces canned tuna, drained and flaked*
- *4 eggs, whisked*
- *½ cup feta cheese, shredded*
- *1 Tbsp chives, chopped*
- *1 Tbsp parsley, chopped*
- *Salt and black pepper to the taste*
- *3 Tsp olive oil*

Direction: Servings: 4 Preparation time: 15 minutes

✓ *Grease a baking dish with the oil, add the tuna and the rest of the ingredients except the cheese, toss and bake at 370 degrees F for 15 minutes.*

✓ *Sprinkle the cheese on top, leave the mix aside for 5 minutes, slice, and serve for breakfast.*

Nutrition: Calories 283, Fat 14.2g, Fiber 5.6g, Carbs 12.1g, Protein 6.4g

104) ***Tomato and Cucumber Salad***

Ingredients:

- *3 tomatoes, chopped*
- *2 cucumbers, chopped*
- *1 red onion, sliced*
- *2 red bell peppers, chopped*
- *¼ cup fresh cilantro, chopped*
- *1 Tbsp capers*
- *1 oz whole-grain bread, chopped*
- *1 Tbsp canola oil*
- *½ Tsp minced garlic*
- *1 Tbsp Dijon mustard*
- *1 Tsp olive oil*
- *1 Tsp lime juice*

Direction: Servings: 4 Preparation time: 5 minutes

✓ *Coat canola oil into the skillet and bring it to a boil.*

✓ *Add chopped bread and roast it until crunchy (3-5 minutes).*

✓ *Meanwhile, to the salad container, combine together sliced red onion, cucumbers, tomatoes, bell peppers, cilantro, capers, and mix up gently.*

✓ *Make the dressing: mix up together lime juice, olive oil, Dijon mustard, and minced garlic.*

✓ *Put the dressing over the salad and stir it directly before serving*

Nutrition: Calories 136, Fat 5.7g, Fiber 4.1g, Carbs 20.2g, Protein 4.1g

105) ***Creamy Frittata***

Ingredients:

- *5 eggs, beaten*
- *1 poblano chile, chopped, raw*
- *1 oz scallions, chopped*
- *1/3 cup heavy cream*
- *½ Tsp butter*
- *½ Tsp salt*
- *½ Tsp chili flakes*
- *1 Tbsp fresh cilantro, chopped*

Direction: Servings: 4 Preparation time: 15 minutes

✓ *Mix up together eggs with heavy cream and whisk until homogenous.*

✓ Add chopped poblano chile, scallions, salt, chili flakes, and fresh cilantro.

✓ Toss butter into the skillet and melt it.

✓ Add egg mixture and flatten it into the skillet if needed.

✓ Close the lid and cook the frittata for 15 minutes over medium-low heat.

✓ When the frittata is cooked, it will be solid.

Nutrition: Calories 131, Fat 10.4g, Fiber 0.2g, Carbs 1.3g, Protein 8.2g

106) Dill, Havarti & Asparagus Frittata

Ingredients:

- 2 tsp minced fresh dill
- 4 oz Havarti cheese cubed
- 6 eggs, beaten welt
- Pepper and salt to taste
- 1 stalk green onions sliced (garnish)
- 3 tsp. olive oil
- 2/3 cup, cherry tomatoes diced
- 6-8 oz fresh asparagus, ends trimmed and cut into 1 ½-inch length

Direction: Servings: 4 Preparation time: 20 minutes

✓ Over the medium-high fire, place a large cast-iron pan and add oil when the oil is hot; stir-fry asparagus for 4 minutes.

✓ Add dill weed and tomatoes, cook for two minutes.

✓ Meanwhile, season eggs with pepper and salt. Beat well.

✓ Pour eggs over the tomatoes.

✓ Evenly spread cheese on top.

✓ Preheat broiler.

✓ Lower the fire to low, cover the pan and let it cook until the cheese on top has melted.

✓ Turn off the fire and transfer the pan to the oven; broil for 2-3 minutes or until the tops are browned.

✓ Remove from the oven, sprinkle sliced green onions.

✓ Serve, and enjoy.

Nutrition: Calories per service: 244, Protein: 16g; Carbs: 3.7g: Fat: 18.3g

107) Egg and Pepper Bake

Ingredients:

- 2 eggs, beaten
- 1 Crushed red bell pepper
- 1 chili pepper, chopped
- ½ red onion, diced
- 1 Tsp canola oil
- ½ Tsp salt
- 1 Tsp paprika
- 1 Tbsp fresh cilantro, chopped
- 1 garlic clove, diced
- 1 Tsp butter, softened
- ¼ Tsp chili flakes

Direction: Servings: 4 Preparation time: 28 minutes

✓ Brush the casserole mold with canola oil; put beaten eggs inside.

✓ Then toss the butter into the skillet and melt it over medium heat.

✓ Add chili pepper and red bell pepper.

✓ Then, add red onion, cook the vegetables for 7-8 minutes over medium heat. Stir them from time to time.

✓ Coat the vegetables to the casserole mold.

✓ Add salt, cilantro, diced garlic, paprika, and chili flakes. Stir gently with the help of a spatula to get a homogenous mixture.

✓ Bake the casserole at 355F in the oven.

✓ Chill the meal well, then cut into servings. Coat the casserole to the serving plates using the spatula.

Nutrition: Calories 68, Fat 4.5g, Fiber 1g, Carbs 4.4g, Protein 3.4g

108) Mediterranean Chicken Salad Pitas

Ingredients:

- 6 pieces (6-inch) whole-wheat pitas, cut into halves
- 6 slices (1/8-inch-thick) tomato, cut into halves
- 1 15-ounce can of saltless chickpeas (garbanzo beans) washed and drained
- 3 cups chicken, cooked, chopped
- 2 Tbsps lemon juice
- 12 Bibb lettuce leaves
- ¼ Tsp red pepper, crushed
- ¼ cup fresh cilantro, chopped
- ½ Tsp ground cumin
- ½ cup red onion, diced
- ½ cup (about 20 small) green olives, chopped, pitted
- 1 cup Greek yogurt, plain, whole-milk
- 1 cup (about 1 large) red bell pepper, chopped

Direction: Servings: 6Preparation time: 15 minutes

✓ In a small container, combine the yogurt, lemon juice, cumin, and red pepper; set aside.

✓ In a large mixing container, combine the chicken, red bell pepper, olives, red onion, cilantro, and chickpeas. Add the yogurt mixture into the chicken mixture; gently toss to coat.

✓ Line each pita half with 1 lettuce leaf and then with 1 tomato slice. Fill each pita half with ½ cup of the *chicken mixture.*

Nutrition: Calories 404, Fat 10.2g, Chol 66mg, Sodium 575mg, Carb 46.4g, Fiber 6g, Protein 33.6g

109) Raspberries and Yogurt Smoothie

Ingredients:

- 2 cups raspberries
- ½ cup Greek yogurt
- ½ cup almond milk
- ½ Tsp vanilla extract

Direction: Servings: 2 Preparation time: 0 minutes

✓ Mix the raspberries with the milk, vanilla, and yogurt In your blender, pulse well, divide into 2 glasses and serve for breakfast.

Nutrition: Calories 245, Fat 9.5g, Fiber 2.3g, Carbs 5.6g, Protein 1.6g

110) Farro Salad

Ingredients:

- 1 Tbsp olive oil
- a dash of black pepper and a bit of salt
- 1 bunch baby spinach, chopped
- 1 avocado, pitted, peeled, and chopped
- 1 garlic clove, minced
- 2 cups farro, already cooked
- ½ cup cherry tomatoes, cubed

Direction: Servings: 2Preparation time: 4 minutes

✓ Heat up a pan with the oil over medium heat, then put the spinach, and the rest of the ingredients, toss, cook for 4 minutes, divide into containers and serve.

Nutrition: Calories 157, Fat 13.7g, Fiber 5.5g, Carbs 8.6g, Protein 3.6g

111)Chili Avocado Scramble

Ingredients:

- 4 eggs, beaten
- 1 white onion, diced
- 1 Tbsp avocado oil
- 1 avocado, finely chopped
- ½ Tsp chili flakes
- 1 oz Cheddar cheese, shredded
- ½ Tsp salt
- 1 Tbsp fresh parsley

Direction: Servings: 4Preparation time: 15 minutes

✓ Pour avocado oil into the skillet, bring it to a boil.

✓ Add diced onion and roast it until it is light brown.

✓ Meanwhile, mix up together beaten eggs, chili flakes, and salt.

✓ Coat the egg mixture over the cooked onion, cook the mixture for 1 minute over medium heat.

✓ Then, scramble the eggs well with the fork or spatula. Cook the eggs until they are solid but soft.

✓ Then, add chopped avocado and shredded cheese.

✓ Stir well and transfer to the serving plates.

✓ Sprinkle the meal with fresh parsley.

Nutrition: Cal 236, Fat 20.1g, Carbs 7.4g, Pro 8.6g

112) Tapioca Pudding

Ingredients:

- ¼ cup pearl tapioca
- ¼ cup maple syrup
- 2 cups almond milk
- ½ cup coconut flesh, shredded
- 1 and ½ Tsp lemon juice

Direction: Servings: 3Preparation time: 15 minutes

✓ In a pan, combine the milk with the tapioca and the resting ingredients, bring to a simmer over medium heat and cook for 15-16 minutes.

✓ Divide the mix into containers, cool it down, and serve for breakfast.

Nutrition: Calories 361, Fat 28.5g, Fiber 2.7g, Carbs 28.3g, Protein 2.8g

113) Ricotta Tartine and Honey Roasted Cherry

Ingredients:

- 4 slices (1/2 inch thick) artisan bread, whole-grain
- 2 cups fresh cherries, pitted
- 2 Tsp extra-virgin olive oil
- ¼ cup slivered almonds, toasted
- 1 Tsp lemon zest
- 1 Tsp fresh thyme
- 1 Tbsp lemon juice
- 1 Tbsp honey, plus more for serving
- 1 cup ricotta cheese, part-skim
- Pinch of flaky sea salt (Maldon salt)
- Pinch of salt

Direction: Servings: 4 Preparation time: 15 minutes

✓ Preheat oven to 400F. Line a rimmed baking sheet with parchment paper; set aside.

✓ In a mixing container, toss the cherries with honey, oil, lemon juice, and salt. Transfer into a pan. Roast for 15-16 minutes, shaking the pan once or twice during roasting until the cherries are very soft and warm.

✓ Toast the bread. Top with the cheese, cherries, thyme, lemon zest, almonds, and season with sea salt. If desired, drizzle more honey.

Nutrition: Calories 320, Fat 13g, Carb 39g, Fiber 6g, Sugar 2g, Protein 15g

114) Mediterranean Breakfast Quiche

Ingredients:

- 11/2 cups all-purpose flour

- *1 tsp. dried oregano*
- *½ tsp. garlic powder*
- *2 tsp. salt*
- *5 TB. cold butter*
- *3 TB. vegetable shortening*
- *¼ cup ice water*
- *3 tablespoons of extra-virgin olive oil*
- *1 medium yellow onion, chopped*
- *1 TB. minced garlic*
- *4 stalks asparagus, chopped*
- *2 cups spinach, chopped*
- *4 large eggs*
- *½ cup heavy cream*
- *1 cup ricotta cheese*
- *1/3 cup grated Parmesan cheese*
- *1 tsp. paprika*
- *½ tsp. cayenne*
- *½ tsp. ground black pepper*
- *¼ cup fresh basil, chopped*
- *¼ cup fresh parsley, chopped*
- *1/3 cup sun-dried tomatoes, chopped*

Direction: Servings: 1/8 Quiche Preparation time: 1 Hour

- ✓ *In a food processor with a chopping blade, pulse 11/2 cups all-purpose flour, oregano, garlic powder, and ½ Tsp salt five times*
- ✓ *Put cold butter and vegetable shortening, pulse until mixture resembles coarse meal.*
- ✓ *While adding ice water, continue to pulse for 1 minute. Test dough if it holds together when you pinch it; it doesn't need any more water.*
- ✓ *If it doesn't come together, add 3 more Tbsps of cold water.*
- ✓ *Remove dough from the food processor, put it into a plastic bag, and form into a flat disc. Refrigerate for 3 minutes.*
- ✓ *Switch on the oven, preheat it setting its temperature to 400°F. Flour a rolling pin and your counter.*
- ✓ *Roll out dough to ¼ inch thickness. Fit dough into an 8-or 9-inch tart pan. Using a fork, slightly puncture the bottom of the piecrust. Bake for 14- 15 minutes. Remove from the oven and set aside.*
- ✓ *In a large skillet over medium heat, put extra-virgin olive oil, yellow onion, garlic, and asparagus, and sauté for 5 minutes.*
- ✓ *Add spinach, cook for 4 or 5 more minutes. Remove from heat and set aside.*
- ✓ *In a large container, whisk together eggs, heavy cream, and ricotta cheese.*
- ✓ *Add resting Tsp of salt, Parmesan cheese, paprika, cayenne, black pepper, basil, parsley, and sun-dried tomatoes, and stir to combine.*
- ✓ *Pour filling into the pie crust, and bake for 4 mins. Remove from the oven, let rest for no minutes before serving warm.*

Nutrition: Calories 346, Fat 19.4g, Protein 14.9g, Chol 34mg, Sodium 767mg, Pot 998mg

115) Feta and Eggs Mix

Ingredients:

- *4 eggs, beaten*
- *½ Tsp ground black pepper*
- *2 oz Feta, scrambled*
- *½ Tsp salt*
- *1 Tsp butter*
- *1 Tsp fresh parsley, chopped*

Direction: Servings: 4 Preparation time: 5 minutes

- ✓ *Melt butter into the skillet and add beaten eggs.*
- ✓ *Then add parsley, salt, and scrambled eggs. Cook the eggs for 1 minute over high heat.*
- ✓ *Add ground black pepper and scrambled eggs with the help of the fork.*
- ✓ *Cook the eggs for 3 minutes over medium-high heat.*

Nutrition: Calories 110, Fat 8.4g, Fiber 0.1g, Carbs 1.1g, Protein 7.6g

116) Betty Oats

Ingredients:

- *½ cup rolled oats*
- *1 cup almond milk*
- *¼ cup chia seeds*
- *A pinch of cinnamon powder*
- *2 Tsp honey*
- *1 cup berries, pureed*
- *1 Tbsp yogurt*

Direction: Servings: 2Preparation time: 0 minutes

- ✓ *In a container, combine the oats with the milk and the rest of the ingredients except the yogurt, toss, divide into containers, top with the yogurt and serve cold for breakfast.*

Nutrition: Calories 420, Fat 30.3g, Fiber 7.2g, Carbs 35.3g, Protein 6.4g

117) Avocado Chickpea Pizza

Ingredients:

- *1 and ¼ cups chickpea flour*
- *a dash of black pepper and salt*
- *1 and ¼ cups water*
- *2 Tbsps olive oil*
- *1 Tsp onion powder*
- *1 Tsp garlic, minced*
- *1 tomato, sliced*

- *1 avocado, peeled, pitted, and sliced*
- *2 ounces gouda, sliced*
- *¼ cup tomato sauce*
- *2 Tbsps green onions, chopped*

Direction: Servings: 2Preparation time: 20 minutes

- ✓ *In a container, mix the chickpea flour with salt, pepper, water, oil, onion powder, and garlic, stir well until you obtain a dough, knead a bit, put in a container, cover, and leave aside for no minutes.*
- ✓ *Transfer the dough to a clean surface, shape a bit circle, transfer it to a baking sheet lined with parchment paper, bake at 425 degrees F for 10 minutes.*
- ✓ *Spread the tomato sauce over the pizza, also spread the rest of the ingredients, and bake at 400 F for 10-11 minutes more.*
- ✓ *Cut and serve for breakfast.*

Nutrition: Calories 416, Fat 24.5g, Fiber 9.6g, Carbs 36.6g, Protein 15.4g

118) Pizza with Sprouts

Ingredients:

- *½ cup wheat flour, whole grain*
- *2 Tbsps butter, softened*
- *¼ Tsp baking powder*
- *¾ Tsp salt*
- *5 oz chicken fillet, boiled*
- *2 oz Cheddar cheese, shredded*
- *1 Tsp tomato sauce*
- *1 oz bean sprouts*

Direction: Servings: 6 Preparation time: 35 minutes

- ✓ *Make the pizza crust: mix wheat flour, baking powder, butter, and salt all together. Knead the soft and non-sticky dough. Add more wheat flour if needed.*
- ✓ *Leave the dough to chill. for 10 minutes*
- ✓ *Place the dough on the baking paper. Cover it with the second baking paper sheet.*
- ✓ *Roll up the dough with the rolling pin to get the round pizza crust.*
- ✓ *Remove the upper baking paper sheet.*
- ✓ *Transfer the pizza crust to the tray.*
- ✓ *Spread the crust with tomato sauce.*
- ✓ *Shred the chicken fillet, arranged it over the pizza crust.*
- ✓ *Add shredded Cheddar cheese.*
- ✓ *Bake pizza for 20 minutes at 355F.*
- ✓ *Then top the cooked pizza with bean sprouts, slice it into servings.*

Nutrition: Calories 157, Fat 8.8g, Fiber 0.3g, Carbs 8.4g, Protein 10.5g

119) Feta and Quinoa Egg Muffins

Ingredients:

- *8 eggs*
- *2 Tsp olive oil*
- *2 cups baby spinach, finely chopped*
- *¼ Tsp salt*
- *½ cup onion, finely chopped*
- *½ cup kalamata olives, chopped, pitted*
- *1 Tbsp fresh oregano, chopped*
- *1 cup quinoa*, cooked*
- *1 cup grape or cherry tomatoes, sliced or chopped*
- *1 cup feta cheese, crumbled*

Direction: Servings: 12Preparation time: 30 minutes

- ✓ *Preheat oven to 350F.*
- ✓ *Grease a 12 muffin with oil or place in silicone muffin holders on a baking sheet.*
- ✓ *Heat a skillet over medium heat. Add the olive oil. Add onions; sauté for about 2 minutes. Add the tomatoes, sauté for 1 minute more. Add the spinach; sauté for about 1 minute or until wilted. Turn the heat off.*
- ✓ *Stir to the olives and the oregano; set aside.*
- ✓ *Put the eggs in a container and whisk. Add the feta, quinoa, vegetable mixture, and salt; stir until well mixed. Divide the mixture evenly among the ready muffin tins or disposable cups. Bake for about 3 minutes or until the eggs are set and light golden brown.*
- ✓ *Cool for 5 minutes and then serve. You can eat these warm, chilled, or cold. To reheat leftovers, just microwave.*

Nutrition: Calories 120, Fat 3g, Carb 6g, Fiber 1g, Sugar 2g, Protein

120) Cauliflower Skillet

Ingredients:

- *1 cup cauliflower, chopped*
- *1 Tbsp olive oil*
- *½ red onion, diced*
- *1 Tbsp Plain yogurt*
- *½ Tsp ground black pepper*
- *1 Tsp dried cilantro*
- *1 Tsp dried oregano*
- *1 bell pepper, chopped*
- *1/ 3 cup milk*
- *½ Tsp Za'atar*
- *1 Tbsp lemon juice*
- *1 russet potato, chopped*

Direction: Servings: 5Preparation time: 25 minutes

- ✓ *Put olive oil into the skillet and preheat it.*
- ✓ *Add chopped russet potato and roast it for 5 minutes.*

- ✓ *Then, add cauliflower, ground black pepper, cilantro, oregano, and bell pepper.*
- ✓ *Roast the mixture for 10 minutes over medium heat. Then add milk, Za'atar, and Plain Yogurt. Stir it well.*
- ✓ *Saute the mixture for 10 minutes.*
- ✓ *Top the cooked meal with diced red onion and sprinkle with lemon juice.*
- ✓ *It is recommended to serve the breakfast hot.*

Nutrition: Calories 112, Fat 3.4g, Fiber 2.6g, Carbs 18.1g, Protein 3.1g

121) Cheese Pies

Ingredients:

- *7 OZ yufka dough/phyllo dough*
- *1 cup Cheddar cheese, shredded*
- *1 cup fresh cilantro, chopped*
- *2 eggs, beaten*
- *1 Tsp paprika*
- *¼ Tsp chili flakes*
- *½ Tsp salt*
- *2 Tbsps sour cream*
- *1 Tsp olive oil*

Direction: Servings: 6Preparation time: 20 minutes

- ✓ *To the mixing container, combine together sour cream, salt, chili flakes, paprika, and beaten eggs.*
- ✓ *Brush the springform pan with olive oil.*
- ✓ *Place ¼ part of all yufka dough into the pan and sprinkle it with ¼ part of the egg mixture.*
- ✓ *Add a ¼ cup of cheese and ¼ cup of cilantro.*
- ✓ *Cover the mixture with 1/3 part of the resting yufka dough and repeat all the steps again. You should get 4 layers.*
- ✓ *Cut the yufka mixture into 6 pies and bake at 360F for 20 minutes.*
- ✓ *The cooked pies should have a golden brown color.*

Nutrition: Calories 213, Fat 11.4g, Fiber 0.8g, Carbs 18.2g, Protein 9.1g

122) Spinach Pie

Ingredients:

- *2 cups spinach*
- *1 white onion, diced*
- *½ cup fresh parsley*
- *1 tablespoon of sliced garlic clove*
- *3 oz Feta cheese, crumbled*
- *1 Tsp ground paprika o eggs, beaten*
- *1/3 cup butter, melted*
- *2 oz Phyllo dough*

Direction: Servings: 6 Preparation time: 1 Hour

- ✓ *Separate Phyllo dough into 2 parts.*
- ✓ *Brush the casserole mold with butter well and place 1 part of Phyllo dough inside.*
- ✓ *Brush its surface with butter too.*
- ✓ *Put the spinach and fresh parsley in the blender. Blend it until smooth and transfer to the mixing container.*
- ✓ *Add minced garlic, Feta cheese, ground paprika, eggs, and diced onion. Mix up well.*
- ✓ *Place the spinach mixture in the casserole mold and flatten it well.*
- ✓ *Cover the spinach mixture with the resting Phyllo dough and pour the resting butter over it.*
- ✓ *Bake spanakopita for 1 hour at 350F.*
- ✓ *Cut it into servings.*

Nutrition: Calories 190, Fat 15.4g, Fiber 1.1g, Carbs 8.4g, Protein 5.4g

123) Bacon, Spinach and Tomato Sandwich

Ingredients:

- *2 whole-wheat bread slices, toasted*
- *1 Tbsp Dijon mustard*
- *3 bacon slices*
- *Salt and black pepper to the taste*
- *2 tomato slices*
- *¼ cup baby spinach*

Direction: Servings: 1 Preparation time: 0 minutes

- ✓ *Spread the mustard on each bread slice, divide the bacon and the rest of the ingredients on one slice, top with the other one, cut in half, and serve for breakfast*

Nutrition: Calories 246, Fat 11.2g, Fiber 4.5g, Carbs 17.5g, Protein 8.3g

124) Open-Face Egg and Bacon Sandwich

Ingredients:

- *¼ oz reduced-fat cheddar, shredded*
- *½ small jalapeno, thinly sliced*
- *½ whole-grain English muffin, split*
- *1 large organic egg*
- *1 thick slice of tomato*
- *1-piece turkey bacon*
- *2 thin slices of red onion*
- *4-5 sprigs of fresh cilantro*
- *Cooking spray*
- *Pepper to taste*

Direction: Servings: 1Preparation time: 20 minutes

- ✓ *On medium fire, place a skillet, cook bacon until crisp-tender, and set aside.*
- ✓ *To the same skillet, drain oils, and place ½ of English muffin and heat for at least a minute per side. Transfer muffin to a serving plate.*

- ✓ Coat the same skillet with cooking spray, fry an egg to the desired doneness. Once cooked, place the egg on top of the muffin.
- ✓ Add cilantro, tomato, onion, jalapeno, and bacon on top of the egg. Serve and enjoy

Nutrition: Cal 245, Carbs 24.7g, Protein 11.8g, Fat 11g

125) Artichokes and Cheese Omelet

Ingredients:

- 1 Tsp avocado oil
- 1 Tbsp almond milk
- 2 eggs, whisked
- A pinch of salt and black pepper
- 2 Tbsps tomato, cubed
- 2 Tbsps kalamata olives, pitted and sliced
- 1 artichoke heart, chopped
- 1 Tbsp tomato sauce
- 1 Tbsp feta cheese, crumbled

Direction: Servings: 1Preparation time: 8 minutes

- ✓ In a container, combine the eggs with the milk, salt, pepper, and the rest of the ingredients except the avocado oil and whisk well.
- ✓ Heat up a pan with the avocado oil over medium-high heat, add the omelet mix, spread into the pan, cook for 4 minutes, flip, cook for 4 minutes more, transfer to a plate, and serve.

Nutrition: Calories 303, Fat 17.7g, Fiber 9.9g, Carbs 21.9g, Protein 18.2g

126) Parmesan Omelet

Ingredients:

- 1 Tbsp cream cheese
- 2 eggs, beaten
- ¼ Tsp paprika
- ½ Tsp dried oregano
- ¼ Tsp dried dill
- 1 oz Parmesan, grated
- 1 Tsp coconut oil

Direction: Servings: 2Preparation time: 15 minutes

- ✓ Take cream cheese with eggs, dried oregano, dill, and Mix up together
- ✓ Put the coconut oil into the pan and heat it until it covers the entire pan.
- ✓ Then Coat the egg mixture into the skillet and flatten it.
- ✓ Add grated Parmesan and close the lid.
- ✓ Cook omelet for 10 minutes over low heat.
- ✓ Transfer the cooked omelet to the serving plate and sprinkle with paprika.

Nutrition: Calories 148, Fat 11.5g, Fiber 0.3g, Carbs 1.4g, Protein 10.6g

127) Blueberries Quinoa

Ingredients:

- 2 cups almond milk
- 2 cups quinoa, already cooked
- ½ Tsp cinnamon powder
- 1 Tbsp honey
- 1 cup blueberries
- ¼ cup walnuts, chopped

Direction: Servings: 4 Preparation time: 0 minutes

- ✓ In a container, mix the quinoa with the milk and the rest of the ingredients, toss, divide into smaller containers and serve for breakfast.

Nutrition: Calories 284, Fat 14.3g, Fiber 3.3g, Carbs 15.4g, Protein 4.4g

128) Creamy Chorizo Containers

Ingredients:

- 9 oz chorizo
- 1 Tbsp almond butter
- ½ cup corn kernels
- 2 tomato, chopped
- ¾ cup heavy cream
- 1 Tsp butter
- ¼ Tsp chili pepper
- 1 Tbsp dill, chopped

Direction: Servings: 4Preparation time: 15 minutes

- ✓ Chop the chorizo and place it into the skillet.
- ✓ Add almond butter and chili pepper.
- ✓ Roast the chorizo for 3 minutes.
- ✓ Then, add tomato and corn kernels.
- ✓ Add butter and chopped the dill. Mix up the mixture well. Cook for 2 minutes.
- ✓ Close the lid, simmer the meat for 10 minutes over low heat.
- ✓ Transfer the cooked meal into the serving containers.

Nutrition: Calories 422, Fat 36.2g, Fiber 1.2g, Carbs 7.3g, Protein 17.6g

129) Mediterranean Omelet

Ingredients:

- 2 teaspoons extra-virgin olive oil
- 2 TB. yellow onion, finely chopped
- 1 small clove garlic, minced
- ½ tsp. salt
- 1 cup fresh spinach, chopped
- ½ medium tomato, diced
- 2 large eggs
- 2 TB. whole or 2 percent milk
- 4 peeled and minced kalamata olives

- *½ tsp. ground black pepper*
- *3 TB. crumbled feta cheese*
- *1 TB. fresh parsley, finely chopped*

Direction: Servings: 1 Omelet Preparation time: 10 minutes

✓ *Add extra virgin olive oil in a nonstick pan over medium heat, and cook yellow onion and garlic for 2-3 minutes.*

✓ *Add spinach, salt, and tomato, and cook for 4 minutes.*

✓ *In a small container, whisk eggs adding whole milk.*

✓ *Add black pepper and kalamata olives to the pan, pour eggs over sautéed vegetables*

✓ *With a rubber spatula, slowly push down edges of eggs, letting raw egg form a new layer, and continue for about a minute*

✓ *Fold omelet in half, slide onto a plate. Top with feta cheese and fresh parsley, and serve warm*

Nutrition: Calories 117, Fat 2g, Protein 4g, Carbs 6g

130) ***Hummus and Tomato Sandwich***

Ingredients:

- *6 whole-grain bread slices*
- *1 tomato*
- *3 Cheddar cheese slices*
- *½ Tsp dried oregano*
- *1 Tsp green chili paste*
- *½ red onion, sliced*
- *1 Tsp lemon juice*
- *1 Tbsp hummus*
- *3 lettuce leaves*

Direction: Servings: 3 Preparation time:2 minutes

✓ *Slice tomato into 6 slices.*

✓ *To the shallow container, mix up together dried oregano, green chili paste, lemon juice, and hummus.*

✓ *Spread 3 bread slices with the chili paste mixture.*

✓ *Then, place the sliced tomatoes on them.*

✓ *Add sliced onion, Cheddar cheese, and lettuce leaves.*

✓ *Cover the lettuce leaves with the resting bread slices to get the sandwiches.*

✓ *Preheat the grill to 365F.*

✓ *Grill the sandwiches for 2 minutes.*

Nutrition: Calories 269, Fat 12.1g, Fiber 12.1g, Carbs 29.6g, Protein 13.9g

131) ***Sage Omelet***

Ingredients:

- *8 eggs, beaten*
- *6 oz Goat cheese, crumbled*
- *½ Tsp salt*
- *3 Tbsps sour cream*
- *1 Tsp butter*
- *½ Tsp canola oil*
- *¼ Tsp sage*
- *¼ Tsp dried oregano*
- *1 Tsp chives, chopped*

Direction: Servings: 8 Preparation time: 25 minutes

✓ *Put the butter into the skillet. Add canola oil and preheat the mixture until it is homogenous.*

✓ *Meanwhile, to the mixing container, combine together salt, sour cream, sage, dried oregano, and chives. Add eggs and stir the mixture carefully with the help of the spoon/fork.*
Pour the egg mixture into the skillet with butter-oil liquid.

✓ *Sprinkle the omelet with goat cheese and close the lid.*

✓ *Cook the breakfast for no minutes over the low heat. The cooked omelet should be solid.*

✓ *Slice it into the servings and transfer it to the plates.*

Nutrition: Calories 176, Fat 13.7g, fiber 0, Carbs 0, Protein 12.2g

132) ***Menemen***

Ingredients:

- *2 tomatoes, chopped*
- *2 eggs, beaten*
- *1 bell pepper, chopped*
- *1 Tsp tomato paste*
- *¼ cup of water*
- *1 Tsp butter*
- *½ white onion, diced*
- *½ Tsp chili flakes*
- *1/3 Tsp sea salt*

Direction: Servings: 4Preparation time: 15 minutes

✓ *Melt the butter in a pan and add bell pepper; cook it for 3 minutes over medium heat. Stir it from time to time.*

✓ *Add diced onion and cook it for a minute.*

✓ *Stir the vegetables and add tomatoes.*

✓ *Cook them for 4- 5 minutes over medium-low heat.*

✓ *Then add water and tomato paste. Stir well.*

✓ *Add beaten eggs, chili flakes, and salt.*

✓ *Stir well and cook menemen for 4 minutes over medium-low heat.*

✓ *The cooked meal should be half runny.*

Nutrition: Calories 67, Fat 3.4g, Fiber 1.5g, Carbs 6.4g, Protein 3.8g

133) ***Red Pepper and Artichoke Frittata***

Ingredients:

- *4 large eggs*
- *1 can (14-ounce) artichoke hearts, rinsed, coarsely chopped*
- *1 medium red bell pepper, diced*
- *1 Tsp dried oregano*
- *¼ cup Parmesan cheese, freshly grated*
- *¼ Tsp red pepper, crushed*
- *¼ Tsp salt, or to taste*
- *2 garlic cloves, minced*
- *2 Tsp extra-virgin olive oil, divided*
- *Freshly ground pepper to taste*

Direction: Servings: 2Preparation time: 15 minutes

- ✓ *In a 10-inch non-stick skillet, heat 1 Tsp of olive oil over medium heat. Add the bell pepper; cook for about 2 minutes or until tender. Add the garlic and the red pepper; cook for about 30 seconds, stirring.*
- ✓ *Transfer the mixture to a plate and wipe the skillet clean.*
- ✓ *In a medium mixing container, whisk the eggs. Stir to the artichokes, cheese, the bell pepper mixture, and season with salt and pepper. Place an oven rack 4 inches from the source of heat; preheat the broiler.*
- ✓ *Rush the skillet with the resting 1 Tsp olive oil and heat over medium heat. Coat the egg mixture into the skillet and turn it to distribute the yolks evenly. Reduce the heat to medium-low, cook for 3-4 minutes, raising the edges to allow the uncooked egg to flow below the frittata until the bottom is light brown.*
- ✓ *Transfer the pan into the broiler, cook for about 1 ½-2 ½ minutes, or until the top is set.*
- ✓ *Slide into a platter; cut into wedges, and serve.*

Nutrition: Calories 305, Carb 18g, Fiber 8g, Protein 21g

134) Stuffed Figs

Ingredients:

- *7 oz fresh figs*
- *1 Tbsp cream cheese*
- *½ Tsp walnuts, chopped*
- *4 bacon slices*
- *¼ Tsp paprika*
- *¼ Tsp salt*
- *½ Tsp canola oil*
- *½ Tsp honey*

Direction: Servings: 2 Preparation time: 25 minutes

- ✓ *Make the crosswise cuts in every fig.*
- ✓ *To the shallow container, mix up together cream cheese, walnuts, paprika, and salt.*
- ✓ *Fill the figs with cream cheese mixture and wrap them to the bacon.*
- ✓ *Secure the fruits with toothpicks and sprinkle with honey.*
- ✓ *Line the baking tray with baking paper.*
- ✓ *Place the prepared figs on the tray and sprinkle them with olive oil gently.*
- ✓ *Bake the figs for 15 minutes at 350F.*

Nutrition: Calories 299, Fat 19.4g, Fiber 2.3g, Carbs 16.7g, Protein 15.2g

135) Pumpkin Coconut Oatmeal

Ingredients:

- *2 cups oatmeal*
- *1 cup of coconut milk*
- *1 cup milk*
- *1 Tsp Pumpkin pie spices*
- *2 Tbsps pumpkin puree*
- *1 Tbsp Honey*
- *½ Tsp butter*

Direction: Servings: 6 Preparation time: 13 minutes

- ✓ *Pour coconut milk and milk into the saucepan. Add butter and bring the liquid to a boil.*
- ✓ *Add oatmeal, stir well with the help of a spoon and close the lid.*
- ✓ *Simmer the oatmeal for 7 minutes over medium heat.*
- ✓ *Meanwhile, mix up together honey, pumpkin pie spices, and pumpkin puree.*
- ✓ *When the oatmeal is cooked, add pumpkin puree mixture and stir well.*
- ✓ *Transfer the cooked breakfast to the serving plates.*

Nutrition: Calories 232, Fat 12.5g, Fiber 3.8g, Carbs 26.2g, Protein 5.9g

136) Mediterranean Crostini

Ingredients:

- *12 slices (1/3-inch thick) whole-wheat baguette, toasted*
- *Coarse salt and freshly ground pepper*
- *For the spread:*
- *1 can chieückpeas (15 ½ ounces), drained, rinsed*
- *¼ cup olive oil, extra-virgin*
- *1 Tbsp lemon juice, freshly squeezed*
- *1 small clove garlic, minced*
- *2 Tbsps olive oil, extra-virgin, divided*
- *2 Tbsps celery, finely diced, plus celery leaves for garnish*
- *8 large green olives, pitted, cut into 1/8-inch slivers*

Direction: Servings: 4 Preparation time: 15 minutes

- ✓ *In a food processor, mix the spread ingredients and season with salt and pepper; set aside.*
- ✓ *In a small mixing container, combine 1 Tbsp of*

olive oil and the resting ingredients. Season with salt and pepper. Set aside.

- ✓ *Divide the spread between the toasted baguette slices, top with the relish. Drizzle the resting Tbsp of olive oil over each and season with pepper. If desired, garnish with celery leaves. Serve immediately.*

Nutrition: Calories 603, Fat 3.7g, Carb 79.2g, Fiber 9.6g, Sugar 6.8g, Protein 19.1g

137) Quick Cream of Wheat

Ingredients:

- *4 cups whole milk*
- *½ cup farina*
- *½ tsp. salt*
- *3 TB. sugar*
- *3 TB. butter*
- *3 TB. pine nuts*

Direction: Servings: 1 Preparation time: 12 minutes

- ✓ *In a large saucepan over medium heat, bring whole milk to a simmer, cook for about 3-4 minutes. Do not allow milk to scorch.*
- ✓ *Whisk in farina, sugar, and salt, bring to a slight boil. Cook for 2-3 minutes, then reduces heat to low, cook for 3 more minutes. Stay close to the pan to avoid it doesn't boil over.*
- ✓ *Pour mixture into 4 containers, let cool for 4- 5 minutes*
- ✓ *In a small pan over low heat, start to cook butter, adding pine nuts for about 3 minutes or until pine nuts are lightly toasted.*
- ✓ *Evenly spoon butter and pine nuts over each container, and serve warm.*

Nutrition: Calories: 198 Fat: 12.5g Carbohydrates: 6.9g Protein: 14 g

138) Herbed Spinach Frittata

Ingredients:

- *5 eggs, beaten*
- *1 cup fresh spinach*
- *2 oz Parmesan, grated*
- *1/3 cup cherry tomatoes*
- *½ Tsp dried oregano*
- *1 Tsp dried thyme*
- *1 Tsp olive oil*

Direction: Servings: 4 Preparation time: 20 minutes

- ✓ *Chop the spinach into tiny pieces and or use a blender.*
- ✓ *Then combine together chopped spinach with eggs, dried oregano, and thyme.*
- ✓ *Add Parmesan and stir frittata mixture with the help of the fork.*
- ✓ *Brush the springform pan with olive oil and pour the egg mixture inside.*
- ✓ *Cut the cherry tomatoes into halves and place them over the egg mixture.*
- ✓ *Switch on the oven, preheat it setting its temperature to 360F.*
- ✓ *Bake the frittata until it is solid.*
- ✓ *Chill the cooked breakfast to room temperature and slice into servings.*

Nutrition: Calories 140, Fat 9.8g, Fiber 0.5g, Carbs 2.1g

139) Ham Spinach Ballet

Ingredients:

- *4 Tsp cream*
- *¼ pound fresh baby spinach*
- *7-Ounce ham, sliced*
- *Salt and black pepper to taste*
- *1 Tbsp unsalted butter, melted*

Direction: Servings: 2 Preparation time: 40 minutes

- ✓ *Switch on the oven, preheat it setting its temperature to 360 degrees F., and grease ramekins with butter.*
- ✓ *Put butter and spinach in a skillet and cook for about 3 minutes.*
- ✓ *Add cooked spinach to the ramekins and top with ham slices, cream, salt, and black pepper.*
- ✓ *Bake for about 25 minutes and dish out to serve hot.*
- ✓ *For meal propping, you can refrigerate this ham spinach ballet for about 3 days wrapped in foil.*

Nutrition: Calories: 188 Fat: 12.5g Carbohydrates: 4.9g Protein: 14.6g Sugar: 0.3g Sodium: 1098mg

140) Ham Muffins

Ingredients:

- *3 oz ham, chopped*
- *4 eggs, beaten*
- *2 Tbsp coconut flour*
- *½ Tsp dried oregano*
- *¼ Tsp dried cilantro*
- *Cooking spray*

Direction: Servings: 4 Preparation time: 25 minutes

- ✓ *Spray the muffin's molds with cooking spray from inside.*
- ✓ *To the container, mix up together beaten eggs, coconut flour, dried oregano, cilantro, and ham*
- ✓ *When the liquid is homogenous, pour in it the prepared muffin molds.*
- ✓ *Bake the muffins for 15 minutes at 360F*
- ✓ *Chill the cooked meal well, and only after this remove it from the molds.*

Nutrition: Calories 128, Fat 7.2g, Fiber 2.9g, Carbs 5.3g, Protein 10.1g

141) Banana Quinoa

Ingredients:

- 1 cup quinoa
- 2 cup milk
- 1 Tsp vanilla extract
- 1 Tsp honey
- 2 bananas, sliced
- ¼ Tsp ground cinnamon

Direction: Servings: 4 Preparation time: 22 minutes

✓ In a saucepan, Pour milk and quinoa.

✓ Close the lid, cook it over medium heat until quinoa absorbs all liquid.

✓ Then chill the quinoa for 15-20 minutes and place it in the serving mason jars.

✓ Add honey, vanilla extract, and ground cinnamon.

✓ Stir well.

✓ Top quinoa with banana, stir it before serving.

Nutrition: Calories 278, Fat 5.3g, Fiber 4.6g, Carbs 48 4g, Protein 10.7g

142) Quinoa Container

Ingredients:

- 1 sweet potato, peeled, chopped
- 1 tablespoon of extra virgin olive oil
- ½ Tsp chili flakes
- ½ Tsp salt
- 1 cup quinoa
- 2 cups of water
- 1 Tsp butter
- 1 Tbsp fresh cilantro, chopped

Direction: Servings: 4 Preparation time: 30 minutes

✓ Line the baking tray with parchment.

✓ Arrange the chopped sweet potato on the tray and sprinkle it with chili flakes, salt, and olive oil.

✓ Bake the sweet potato for no minutes at 355F.

✓ Meanwhile, pour water into the saucepan.

✓ Add quinoa and cook it over medium heat for 7 minutes or until quinoa will absorb all liquid.

✓ Add butter to the cooked quinoa and stir well.

✓ Transfer it to the containers, add baked sweet potato and chopped cilantro.

Nutrition: Calories 221, Fat 7.1g, Fiber 3.9g, Carbs 33.2g, Protein 6.6g

143) Almond Cream Cheese Bake

Ingredients:

- 1 cup cream cheese
- 4 Tbsps honey
- 1 oz almonds, chopped
- ½ Tsp vanilla extract
- 3 eggs, beaten
- 1 Tbsp semolina

Direction: Servings: 4 Preparation time: 2 Hours

✓ Put beaten eggs into the mixing container.

✓ Add cream cheese, semolina, and vanilla extract.

✓ Blend the mixture helping with the hand mixer until it is fluffy.

✓ Then add chopped almonds and mix up the mass well.

✓ Transfer the cream cheese mash to the non-sticky baking mold.

✓ Flatten the surface of the cream cheese mash well.

✓ Switch on the oven, preheat it setting its temperature to 325 F.

✓ Cook the breakfast for 2 hours.

✓ The meal is cooked when the surface of the mash is light brown. Chill

Nutrition: Calories 352, Fat 27.1g, Fiber 1g, Carbs 22.6g, Protein 10.4g

EGGS RECIPES

144) Breakfast Egg on Avocado

Ingredients:

- 1 tsp garlic powder
- 1/2 tsp sea salt
- 1/4 cup Parmesan cheese (shredded)
- 1/4 teaspoon of black pepper
- 3 medium avocados (cut in half, pitted, skin on)
- 6 medium eggs

Direction: Cooking Time: 15 minutes Servings: 6

- ✓ Prepare muffin tins and Switch on the oven, preheat it setting its temperature to 350oF.
- ✓ To ensure that the egg would fit inside the cavity of the avocado, lightly scrape off 1/3 of the meat.
- ✓ Coat avocado on muffin tin, ensuring that it faces with the top-up.
- ✓ Season each avocado with pepper, salt, and garlic powder.
- ✓ Add an egg on each avocado cavity, garnish tops with cheese.
- ✓ Bake until the egg white is set, around 15 minutes.
- ✓ Serve and enjoy.

Nutrition: Calories: 252; Protein: 14.0g; Carbs: 4.0g; Fat: 20.0g

145) Slow-Cooked Peppers Frittata

Ingredients:

- ½ cup almond milk
- 8 eggs, whisked
- Salt and black pepper to the taste
- 1 Tsp oregano, dried
- 1 and ½ cups roasted peppers, chopped
- ½ cup red onion, chopped
- 4 cups baby arugula
- 1 cup goat cheese, crumbled
- Cooking spray

Direction: Servings: 6 Preparation time: 3 Hours

- ✓ In a container, combine the eggs with salt, pepper, and oregano and whisk.
- ✓ Grease the slow cooker using the cooking spray, arrange the peppers and the resting ingredients inside, and pour the egg mixture over them.
- ✓ Set the lid on and cook on Low for 3 hours.
- ✓ Divide the frittata between plates and serve.

Nutrition: Calories 259, Fat 20.2g, Fiber 1g, Carbs 4.4g, Protein 16.3g

146) Breakfast Egg-Artichoke Casserole

Ingredients:

- 16 large eggs
- cleaned 14-ounce canned of artichoke hearts
- a 10-ounce box of thawed and well-drained frozen minced spinach
- 1 cup shredded white cheddar
- 1 garlic clove, minced
- 1 Tsp salt
- 1/2 cup parmesan cheese
- 1/2 cup ricotta cheese
- 1/2 Tsp dried thyme
- 1/2 Tsp crushed red pepper
- 1/4 cup milk
- 1/4 cup shaved onion

Direction: Cooking Time: 35 minutes Servings: 8

- ✓ Grease a 9x13-inch baking dish with cooking spray and Switch on the oven, preheat it setting its temperature to 350oF.
- ✓ In a large mixing container, add eggs and milk. Mix thoroughly.
- ✓ With a paper towel, squeeze out the excess moisture from the spinach leaves and add to the container of eggs
- ✓ Break the artichoke hearts Into small pieces, and separate the leaves. Add to the container of eggs.
- ✓ Except for the ricotta cheese, add resting ingredients to the container of eggs and mix thoroughly.
- ✓ Pour egg mixture into the dish.
- ✓ Evenly add ricotta cheese on top of the eggs, then put in the oven.
- ✓ Bake until eggs are set and don't jiggle when shook, about 35 minutes.
- ✓ Remove from the oven and evenly divide into suggested servings. Enjoy.

Nutrition: Calories: 302; Protein: 22.6g; Carbs: 10.8g; Fat: 18.7g

147) Brekky Egg-Potato Hash

Ingredients:

- 1 zucchini, diced
- 1/2 cup chicken broth
- ½ pound cooked chicken
- 1 Tbsp olive oil
- 4 ounces shrimp
- salt and ground black pepper to taste
- 1 large sweet potato, diced
- 2 eggs
- 1/4 tablespoon of cayenne pepper
- 2 Tsp garlic powder
- 1 cup fresh spinach (optional)

Direction: Cooking Time: 25 minutes Servings: 2,

- ✓ In a skillet, add olive oil.
- ✓ Fry the shrimp, cooked chicken, and sweet potato for 2 minutes.
- ✓ Add the cayenne pepper, garlic powder, and salt

and toss for 4 minutes.
- ✓ *Add the zucchini and toss for another 3 minutes.*
- ✓ *Whisk the eggs in a container and add them into the skillet.*
- ✓ *Season using salt and pepper. Cover with the lid.*
- ✓ *Cook for 1 minute, add the chicken broth.*
- ✓ *Cover and cook for another 8 minutes on high heat.*
- ✓ *Add the spinach and toss for 2 more minutes.*
- ✓ *Serve immediately.*

Nutrition: Calories: 190; Protein: 11.7g; Carbs: 2.9g; Fat: 12.3g

148) Cooked Beef Mushroom Egg

Ingredients:

- *¼ cup cooked beef, diced*
- *6 eggs*
- *4 mushrooms, diced*
- *Season with salt and pepper to perfection*
- *12 ounces spinach*
- *2 onions, chopped*
- *A dash of onion powder*
- *¼ green bell pepper, chopped*
- *A dash of garlic powder*

Direction: Cooking Time: 15 minutes Servings: 2

- ✓ *In a skillet, toss the beef for 3 minutes or until crispy.*
- ✓ *Take off the heat and add to a plate.*
- ✓ *Add the onion, bell pepper, and mushroom into the skillet.*
- ✓ *Add the rest of the ingredients.*
- ✓ *Toss for about 4 minutes.*
- ✓ *Return the beef into the skillet, toss for another minute.*
- ✓ *Serve hot.*

Nutrition: Calories: 213; Protein: 14.5g; Carbs: 3.4g; Fat: 15.7g

149) Curried Veggies and Poached Eggs

Ingredients:

- *4 large eggs*
- *½ tsp white vinegar*
- *1/8 teaspoon of smashed red pepper (optional)*
- *1 cup water*
- *1 14-oz canned chickpeas, drained*
- *2 medium zucchinis, diced*
- *½ lb sliced button mushrooms*
- *1 tbsp yellow curry powder*
- *2 cloves garlic, minced*
- *1 large onion, chopped*
- *2 tsp extra virgin olive oil*

Direction: Cooking Time: 45 minutes Servings: 4

- ✓ *On medium-high fire, Put a large saucepan and add oil*
- ✓ *Sauté onions around four to five minutes.*
- ✓ *Add garlic and continue sautéing for another minute.*
- ✓ *Add curry powder, cook and stir until fragrant, around two minutes.*
- ✓ *Add mushrooms, mix, cover, and cook for 7 to 8 minutes or until mushrooms are tender and have released their liquid.*
- ✓ *Add water, red pepper (optional), zucchini, and chickpeas. Mix well and bring to a boil.*
- ✓ *Once boiling, reduce fire to a simmer, cover, and cook zucchini around 15 - 20 minutes of simmering.*
- ✓ *In a small pot filled with 3-inches deep water, bring to a boil on a high fire.*
- ✓ *Once boiling, reduce fire to a simmer and add vinegar.*
- ✓ *Slowly add an egg, slipping it gently into the water. Allow simmering until egg is cooked, around 4 to 5 minutes.*
- ✓ *Remove the egg with a spoon and transfer it to a plate, one plate, one egg.*
- ✓ *Repeat the process with resting eggs.*
- ✓ *Once the veggies are cooked, divide evenly into 4 servings and place one serving per plate of an egg.*
- ✓ *Serve and enjoy.*

Nutrition: Calories: 215; Protein: 13.8g; Carbs: 20.6g; Fat: 9.4g

150) Dill and Tomato Frittata

Ingredients:

- *pepper and salt to taste*
- *1 tsp red pepper flakes*
- *2 garlic cloves, minced*
- *½ goat cheese, crumbled – optional*
- *2 tbsp fresh chives, chopped*
- *2 tbsp fresh dill, chopped*
- *4 tomatoes, diced*
- *8 eggs, whisked*
- *1 tsp coconut oil*

Direction: Cooking Time: 35 minutes Servings: 6

- ✓ *Grease a 9-inch round baking pan and preheat the oven to 325F.*
- ✓ *In a large container, mix well all ingredients and pour into prepped pan.*
- ✓ *Put into the oven and bake until middle is cooked through around 30-35 minutes.*
- ✓ *Remove from oven and garnish with more chives and dill.*

Nutrition: Calories: 210; Protein: 12.8g; Carbs: 20.2g; Fat: 8.2g

151) Dill, Havarti & Asparagus Frittata

Ingredients

- 2 tsp minced fresh dill
- 4-oz Havarti cheese cubed
- 6 eggs, beaten
- 1 stalk green onions sliced (garnish)
- 4 tsp. olive oil
- 2/3 cup cherry tomatoes, diced
- 6-8 oz fresh asparagus, ends trimmed, cut into 1 ½-inch length
- Pepper and salt to taste

Direction: Cooking Time: 20 minutes Servings: 4

- ✓ On medium-high, fire, place a large cast-iron pan and add oil once oil is hot, stir-fry asparagus for 4 minutes.
- ✓ Add dill weed and tomatoes and cook for two minutes.
- ✓ Meanwhile, season eggs with pepper and salt. Beat well.
- ✓ Pour eggs over the tomatoes.
- ✓ Evenly spread cheese on top.
- ✓ Preheat broiler.
- ✓ Lower the fire to low, cover the pan and let it cook for 10 minutes until the cheese on top has melted.
- ✓ Turn off the fire and transfer the pan to the oven and broil for 2 minutes or until tops are browned.
- ✓ Remove from the oven, add sliced green onions, serve.

Nutrition: Calories: 244; Protein: 16.0g; Carbs: 3.7g; Fat: 18.3g

152) Egg and Ham Breakfast Cup

Ingredients:

- 2 green onion bunch, chopped
- 12 eggs
- 6 thick pieces nitrate free ham

Direction: Cooking Time: 12 minutes Servings: 12

- ✓ Grease a 12-muffin tin and preheat the oven to 4000F.
- ✓ Add 2 hams per muffin compartment, press down to form a cup, and add egg in the middle. Repeat process to resting muffin compartments.
- ✓ Put to the oven and bake until eggs are cooked to desired doneness, around 10 to 12 minutes.
- ✓ To serve, garnish with chopped green onions.

Nutrition: Calories: 92; Protein: 7.3g; Carbs: 0.8g; Fat: 6.4g

153) Egg Muffin Sandwich

Ingredients:

- 1 large egg, free-range or organic
- 1/4 cup almond flour (25 g / 0.9 oz)
- 1/4 cup flaxseed meal (38 g / 1.3 oz)
- 1/4 cup grated cheddar cheese (28 g / 1 oz)
- 1/4 tsp baking soda
- 2 tbsp heavy whipping cream or coconut milk
- 2 tbsp water
- salt

Filing INGREDIENTS

- 2 tbsp cream cheese for spreading
- 1 tbsp ghee
- 1 tsp Dijon mustard
- Free-range or raw eggs (two large eggs)
- 2 slices cheddar cheese (56 g / 2 oz) or any firm cheese
- 1 cup greens (optional) (lettuce, kale, chard, spinach, watercress, etc.)
- Add a sprinkle of salt with pepper to satisfaction

Direction: Cooking Time: 10 minutes Servings: 2

- ✓ Make the Muffin: In a small mixing container, Combine flax meal, almond flour, baking soda, and salt. Stir in water, cream, and eggs. Mix Well
- ✓ Fold in cheese and evenly divide into two single-serve ramekins.
- ✓ Put it in the microwave and cook for 75 seconds.
- ✓ Make the filling: on medium, fire, place a small nonstick pan, heat ghee and cook the eggs to the desired doneness and Sprinkle with pepper and salt.
- ✓ To make the muffin sandwiches, slice the muffins in half, then spread cream cheese on one side, add mustard on the other side.
- ✓ Add egg and greens. Top with the other half of the muffin.
- ✓ Serve and enjoy.

Nutrition: Calories: 638; Protein: 26.5g; Carbs: 10.4g; Fat: 54.6g

154) Eggs Benedict and Artichoke Hearts

Ingredients:

- Salt and pepper to taste
- ¾ cup balsamic vinegar
- 4 artichoke hearts
- ¼ cup bacon, cooked
- 1 egg white
- 8 eggs
- 1 Tbsp lemon juice
- ¾ cup melted ghee or butter

Direction: Cooking Time: 30 minutes Servings: 2

- ✓ Line a baking sheet with parchment paper.

- ✓ *Switch on the oven, preheat it setting its temperature to 3750F.*
- ✓ *Cut the artichokes and remove the hearts. Coat the hearts in balsamic vinegar for 20 minutes. Set aside.*
- ✓ *Prepare the hollandaise sauce by using four eggs and separate the yolk from the white. Reserve the egg white for the artichoke hearts. Add the yolks and lemon juice and cook in a double boiler while constantly stirring to create a silky texture of the sauce. Add the oil and season with salt and pepper. Set aside.*
- ✓ *Remove the artichoke hearts from the balsamic vinegar marinade and place them on the cookie sheet. Brush the artichokes with the egg white and cook in the oven for 20 minutes.*
- ✓ *Poach the resting four eggs. Turn up the heat and let the water boil. Crack the eggs one at a time and cook for a minute before removing the egg.*
- ✓ *Assemble by layering the artichokes, bacon, and poached eggs.*
- ✓ *Pour over the hollandaise sauce.*
- ✓ *Serve with toasted bread.*

Nutrition: Calories: 640; Protein: 28.3g; Carbs: 36.0g; Fat: 42.5g

155) ***Eggs over Kale Hash***

Ingredients:

- *4 large eggs*
- *1 bunch chopped kale*
- *Dash of ground nutmeg*
- *2 sweet potatoes, cubed*
- *1 14.5-ounce of chicken broth*

Direction: Cooking Time: 20 minutes Servings: 4

- ✓ *Bring the chicken broth to a simmer in a large nonstick skillet; add the sweet potatoes and season lightly with salt and pepper. Add a dash of nutmeg to improve the flavor.*
- ✓ *Cook until the sweet potatoes become soft, around 10 minutes. Add kale and season with salt and pepper. Continue cooking for four minutes or until kale has wilted. Set aside.*
- ✓ *Using the same skillet, heat 1 Tbsp of olive oil over medium-high heat.*
- ✓ *Cook the eggs sunny side up until the whites become opaque and the yolks have set. Top the kale hash with the eggs. Serve immediately.*

Nutrition: Cal: 158; Protein: 9.8g; Carbs 18.5g; Fat: 5.6g

156) ***Eggs with Dill, Pepper, and Salmon***

Ingredients:

- *pepper and salt to taste*
- *1 tsp red pepper flakes*
- *2 garlic cloves, minced*
- *½ cup crumbled goat cheese*
- *2 tbsp fresh chives, chopped*
- *2 tbsp fresh dill, chopped*
- *4 tomatoes, diced*
- *8 eggs, whisked*
- *1 tsp coconut oil*

Direction: Cooking Time: 15 minutes Servings: 6

- ✓ *In a big container, whisk the eggs. Mix in pepper, salt, red pepper flakes, garlic, dill, and salmon.*
- ✓ *On low fire, place a nonstick fry pan and lightly grease with oil.*
- ✓ *Pour egg mixture and whisk around until cooked through to make scrambled eggs.*
- ✓ *Serve and enjoy topped with goat cheese.*

Nutrition: Calories: 141; Protein: 10.3g; Carbs: 6.7g; Fat: 8.5g

157) ***Fig and Walnut Skillet Frittata***

Ingredients:

- *1 cup figs, halved*
- *4 eggs, beaten*
- *1 Tsp cinnamon*
- *A pinch of salt*
- *2 Tbsps almond flour*
- *2 Tbsps coconut flour*
- *1 cup walnut, chopped*
- *2 Tbsps coconut oil*
- *1 Tsp cardamom*
- *6 Tbsps raw honey*

Direction: Cooking Time: 15 minutes Servings: 4,

- ✓ *In a mixing container, beat the eggs.*
- ✓ *Add the coconut flour, almond flour, cardamom, honey, salt, and cinnamon.*
- ✓ *Mix well. Heat the coconut oil in a skillet over medium heat.*
- ✓ *Add the egg mixture gently.*
- ✓ *Add the walnuts and figs on top.*
- ✓ *Cover and cook on medium-low heat for about 10 minutes.*
- ✓ *Serve hot with more honey on top.*

Nutrition: Calories: 221; Protein: 12.7g; Carbs: 5.9g; Fat: 16.3g

158) ***Frittata with Dill and Tomatoes***

Ingredients:

- *pepper and salt to taste*
- *1 tsp red pepper flakes*
- *2 garlic cloves, minced*
- *½ cup crumbled goat cheese – optional*
- *2 tbsp fresh chives, chopped*

- *2 tbsp fresh dill, chopped*
- *4 tomatoes, diced*
- *8 eggs, whisked*
- *1 tsp coconut oil*

Direction: Cooking Time: 35 minutes Servings: 4

- ✓ *Grease a 9-inch round baking pan and preheat the oven to 3250F.*
- ✓ *In a large container, mix well all ingredients and pour into prepped pan.*
- ✓ *Put into the oven and bake until middle is cooked through around 30-35 minutes.*
- ✓ *Remove from oven and garnish with more chives and dill.*

Nutrition: Calories: 309; Protein: 19.8g; Carbs: 8.0g; Fat: 22.0g

159) Italian Scrambled Eggs

Ingredients:

- *1 Tsp balsamic vinegar*
- *2 large eggs*
- *¼ Tsp rosemary, minced*
- *½ cup cherry tomatoes*
- *1 ½ cup kale, chopped*
- *½ Tsp olive oil*

Direction: Cooking Time: 7 minutes Servings: 1

- ✓ *Melt the olive oil in a skillet over medium-high heat.*
- ✓ *Sauté the kale and add rosemary and salt to taste. Add three Tbsps of water to prevent the kale from burning at the bottom of the pan and cook for three to four minutes.*
- ✓ *Add the tomatoes and stir.*
- ✓ *Push the vegetables on one side of the skillet and add the eggs—season with salt and pepper to taste.*
- ✓ *Scramble the eggs, then fold to the tomatoes and kales.*

Nutrition: Calories: 230; Protein: 16.4g; Carbs: 15.0g; Fat: 12.4g

160) Kale and Red Pepper Frittata

Ingredients:

- *Sprinkle of salt with a pinch of pepper to satisfaction*
- *½ cup almond milk*
- *8 large eggs*
- *2 cups kale, rinsed and chopped*
- *3 slices of crispy bacon, chopped*
- *1/3 cup onion, chopped*
- *½ cup red pepper, chopped*
- *1 Tbsp coconut oil*

Direction: Cooking Time: 23 minutes Servings: 4

- ✓ *Switch on the oven, preheat it setting its temperature to 3500F.*
- ✓ *In a medium container, combine the eggs and almond milk. Season with salt and pepper. Set aside.*
- ✓ *In a skillet, heat the coconut oil over medium flame and sauté the onions and red pepper for 3 minutes or until the onion is translucent. Add to the kale and cook for 5 minutes more.*
- ✓ *Add the eggs into the mixture and the bacon and cook for four minutes or until the edges start to set.*
- ✓ *Continue cooking the frittata in the oven for 15 minutes.*

Nutrition: Calories: 242; Protein: 16.5g; Carbs: 7.0g; Fat: 16.45g

161) Lettuce Stuffed with Eggs 'n Crab Meat

Ingredients:

- *24 butter lettuce leaves*
- *1 tsp dry mustard*
- *¼ cup finely chopped celery*
- *1 cup lump crabmeat, around 5 ounces*
- *3 tbsp plain Greek yogurt*
- *2 tablespoons of olive oil*
- *¼ tsp ground pepper*
- *8 large eggs*
- *½ tsp salt, divided*
- *1 tbsp fresh lemon juice, divided*
- *2 cups thinly sliced radishes*

Direction: Cooking Time: 10 minutes Servings: 8

- ✓ *In a medium container, mix ¼ tsp salt, 2 tsp. Juice and radishes. Cover and chill for half an hour.*
- ✓ *On a medium saucepan, place eggs and cover with water over an inch above the eggs. Bring the pan of water to a boil. Once boiling, reduce fire to a simmer and cook for ten minutes.*
- ✓ *Turn off fire, discard hot water and place eggs in an ice water bath to cool completely.*
- ✓ *Peel eggshells and slice eggs in half lengthwise, and remove the yolks.*
- ✓ *With a sieve on top of a container, place yolks and press through a sieve. Set aside a Tbsp of yolk.*
- ✓ *On resting container of yolks, add pepper, ¼ tsp salt, and 1 tsp juice. Mix well and as you are stirring, slowly add oil until well incorporated. Add yogurt, stir well to mix.*
- ✓ *Add mustard, celery, and crabmeat. Gently mix to combine. If needed, taste and adjust the seasoning of the filling.*
- ✓ *On a serving platter, arrange 3 lettuce in a fan for two egg slices. To make the egg whites sit flat, slice a bit of the bottom to make it flat. Evenly divide crab filling into egg white holes.*
- ✓ *Then evenly divide into eight servings the radish salad and add on the side of the eggs, on top of the lettuce leaves. Serve and enjoy.*

Nutrition: Calories: 121; Protein: 10.0g; Carbs: 1.6g; Fat: 8.3g

162) Mixed Greens and Ricotta Frittata

Ingredients:

- 1 tbsp pine nuts
- 1 clove garlic, chopped
- ¼ cup fresh mint leaves
- ¾ cup fresh parsley leaves
- 1 cup fresh basil leaves
- 8-oz part-skim ricotta
- 1 tablespoon of red wine vinegar
- ½ + 1/8 tsp ground black pepper, divided
- ½ tsp salt, divided
- 10 large eggs
- 1 lb chopped mixed greens
- Pinch of red pepper flakes
- 1 medium red onion, finely diced
- 1/3 cup + 2 tbsp olive oil, divided

Direction: Cooking Time: 35 minutes Servings: 8,

- ✓ Preheat oven to 350oF.
- ✓ On medium-high fire, place a nonstick skillet and heat 1 tbsp oil. Sauté onions until soft and translucent, around 4 minutes. Add half of greens and pepper flakes and sauté until tender and crisp, around 5 minutes. Remove cooked greens and place in the colander. Add resting uncooked greens in skillet and sauté until tender and crisp. When done, add to the colander. Allow cooked veggies to cool enough to handle, then squeeze dry and place in a container.
- ✓ Whisk well ¼ tsp pepper, ¼ tsp salt, Parmesan, and eggs in a large container.
- ✓ In a container of cooked vegetables, add 1/8 tsp pepper, ricotta, and vinegar. Mix thoroughly. Then pour into a container of eggs and mix well.
- ✓ On medium fire, place the same skillet used previously and heat 1 tbsp oil. Pour egg mixture and cook for 8 minutes or until sides are set. Turn off fire, place skillet inside the oven, and bake for 15 minutes or until the middle of frittata is set.
- ✓ Meanwhile, make the pesto by processing pine nuts, garlic, mint, parsley, and basil in a food processor until coarsely chopped. Add 1/3 cup oil and continue processing—season with resting pepper and salt. Process once again until thoroughly mixed.
- ✓ To serve, slice the frittata in 8 equal wedges and serve with a dollop of pesto.

Nutrition: Calories: 280; Protein: 14g; Carbs: 8g; Fat: 21.3g

163) Mushroom Tomato Frittata

Ingredients:

- ¼ cup mushroom, sliced
- 10 eggs
- 1 cup cherry tomatoes
- Salt
- Pepper
- 1 Tsp olive oil

Direction: Cooking Time: 8 minutes Servings: 8,

- ✓ Whisk the eggs in a container.
- ✓ Add the eggs to a skillet.
- ✓ Add the mushroom, cherry tomatoes and season using salt and pepper.
- ✓ Cover with lid and cook for about 5 to 8 minutes on low heat.

Nutrition: Calories: 190; Protein: 11.7g; Carbs: 2.9g; Fat: 12.3g

164) Mushroom, Spinach, and Turmeric Frittata

Ingredients:

- ½ tsp pepper
- ½ tsp salt
- 1 tsp turmeric
- 5-oz firm tofu
- 4 large eggs
- 6 large egg whites
- ¼ cup water
- 1 lb fresh spinach
- 6 cloves freshly chopped garlic
- 1 large onion, chopped
- 1 lb button mushrooms, sliced

Direction: Cooking Time: 35 minutes Servings: 6

- ✓ Grease a 10-inch nonstick and oven-proof skillet and preheat the oven to 350oF.
- ✓ Place skillet on medium-high fire and add mushrooms. Cook until golden brown.
- ✓ Add onions, cook until onions are tender.
- ✓ Add garlic, sauté for 30 seconds.
- ✓ Add water and spinach, cook, while covered until spinach is wilted, around 3 minutes.
- ✓ Remove lid, continue cooking until water is fully evaporated.
- ✓ In a blender, Pour the pureed pepper, salt, turmeric, tofu, eggs, and egg whites until smooth. Pour into the skillet once the liquid is fully evaporated.
- ✓ Pop skillet into oven and bake until the center is set around 25-30 minutes.
- ✓ Remove the skillet from the oven, let it stand for ten minutes before inverting and transferring to a serving plate.
- ✓ Cut into 6 wedges, serve and enjoy.

Nutrition: Calories: 166; Protein: 15.9g; Carbs: 12.2g; Fat: 6.0g

165) Paleo Almond Banana Pancakes

Ingredients:

- ¼ cup almond flour
- ½ Tsp ground cinnamon
- 3 eggs
- 1 banana, mashed
- 1 Tbsp almond butter
- 1 Tsp vanilla extract
- 1 Tsp olive oil
- Sliced banana to serve

Direction: Time to prepare: 10 minutes 3 servings

✓ Whisk the eggs in a mixing container until they become fluffy.

✓ In another container, mash the banana using a fork and add to the egg mixture.

✓ Add the vanilla, almond butter, cinnamon, and almond flour.

✓ Mix into a smooth batter.

✓ Heat the olive oil in a skillet.

✓ Add one spoonful of the batter and fry them from both sides.

✓ Keep doing these steps until you are done with all the batter.

✓ Add some sliced banana on top before serving.

Nutrition: Calories: 306; Protein: 14.4g; Carbs: 3.6g; Fat: 26.0g

166) Parmesan and Poached Eggs on Asparagus

Ingredients:

- 4 tbsp coarsely grated fresh Parmesan cheese, divided
- Freshly ground black pepper, to taste
- 2 tsp finely chopped fresh parsley
- 2 tablespoons of lemon juice
- 1 tbsp unsalted butter
- 1 garlic clove, chopped
- 1 tbsp extra virgin olive oil
- 2 bunches asparagus spears, trimmed around 40
- 1 tsp salt, divided
- 1 tsp white vinegar
- 8 large eggs

Direction: Cooking Time: 15 minutes Servings: 4

✓ Break eggs and place in one paper cup per egg. On medium-high fire, place a low-sided pan filled 3/4 with water. Add ½ tsp salt and vinegar into the water. Set aside.

✓ On medium-high fire, bring another pot of water to a boil. Once boiling, lower fire to a simmer and blanch asparagus until tender and crisp, around 3-4 minutes. Transfer asparagus to a serving platter and set aside.

✓ On medium fire, place a medium saucepan and heat olive oil. Once hot, for a minute, sauté garlic and turn off the fire. Add butter right away and swirl around the pan to melt. Add resting pepper, salt, parsley, and lemon juice and mix thoroughly. Add asparagus and toss to combine well with garlic butter sauce. Transfer to serving platter along with the sauce

✓ In a boiling pan of water, poach the eggs by slowly pouring eggs into the water and cooking for two minutes per egg. With a slotted spoon, remove the egg. To remove excess water, tap slotted spoon several times on kitchen towel and place on top of asparagus.

✓ To serve, top eggs with parmesan cheese and divide the asparagus into two and 2 eggs per plate. Serve and enjoy.

Nutrition: Calories: 256; Protein: 18g; Carbs: 8g; Fat: 16.9g

167) Scrambled Eggs with Feta 'n Mushrooms

Ingredients:

- Pepper to taste
- 2 tbsp feta cheese
- 1 whole egg
- 2 egg whites
- 1 cup fresh spinach, chopped
- ½ cup fresh mushrooms, sliced
- Cooking spray

Direction: Cooking Time: 6 minutes Servings: 1

✓ place a nonstick fry pan on medium-high fire and grease with cooking spray.

✓ Once hot, add spinach and mushrooms.

✓ Sauté, around 2-3 minutes.

✓ Meanwhile, whisk well egg, egg whites, and cheese in a container—season with pepper.

✓ Coat egg mixture into the pan, scramble until eggs are cooked through, around 3-4 minutes.

✓ Serve and enjoy with a piece of toast or brown rice.

Nutrition: Calories: 211; Protein: 18.6g; Carbs: 7.4g; Fat: 11.9g

168) Scrambled eggs with Smoked Salmon

Ingredients:

- 1 tbsp coconut oil
- Pepper and salt to taste
- 1/8 tsp red pepper flakes
- 1/8 tsp garlic powder
- 1 tbsp fresh dill, chopped finely
- 4 oz smoked salmon, torn apart
- 2 whole eggs + 1 egg yolk, whisked

Direction: Cooking Time: 8 minutes Servings: 1

- ✓ *In a big container, whisk the eggs. Mix in pepper, salt, red pepper flakes, garlic, dill, and salmon.*
- ✓ *On low fire, place a nonstick fry pan and lightly grease with oil.*
- ✓ *Pour egg mixture and whisk around until cooked through to make scrambled eggs, around 8 minutes on medium fire.*
- ✓ *Serve and enjoy.*

Nutrition: Calories: 366; Protein: 32.0; Carbs: 1.0g; Fat: 26.0g

169) Spiced Breakfast Casserole

Ingredients:

- *1 Tbsp nutritional yeast*
- *¼ cup water*
- *6 large eggs*
- *1 Tsp coriander*
- *1 Tsp cumin*
- *8 kale leaves, stems removed and torn into small pieces*
- *2 sausages, cooked and chopped*
- *1 large sweet potato, peeled and chopped*

Direction: Cooking Time: 35 minutes Servings: 6,

- ✓ *Switch on the oven, preheat it setting its temperature to 3750F.*
- ✓ *Grease an 8" x 8" baking pan with olive oil and set aside.*
- ✓ *Place sweet potatoes in a microwavable container and add ¼ cup water. Cook the chopped sweet potatoes in the microwave for three to five minutes. Drato, the excess water, then set aside.*
- ✓ *Fry in a skillet heated over a medium flame the sausage and cook until brown. Mix to the kale and cook until wilted.*
- ✓ *Add the coriander, cumin, and cooked sweet potatoes.*
- ✓ *In another container, mix together the eggs, water, and nutritional yeast. Add the vegetable and meat mixture into the container and mix completely.*
- ✓ *Place the mixture into the baking dish and make sure that the mixture is evenly distributed within the pan.*
- ✓ *Bake for 19 minutes or until the eggs are done.*
- ✓ *Slice into squares.*

Nutrition: Calories: 137; Protein: 10.1g; Carbs: 10.0g; Fat: 6.6g

170) Spinach, Mushroom and Sausage Frittata

Ingredients:

- *Sprinkle of salt and pinch of pepper to taste*
- *10 eggs*
- *½ small onion, chopped*
- *1 cup mushroom, sliced*
- *1 cup fresh spinach, chopped*
- *½ pound sausage, ground*
- *2 Tbsp coconut oil*

Direction: Cooking Time: 30 minutes Servings: 4,

- ✓ *Switch on the oven, preheat it setting its temperature to 3500F.*
- ✓ *Heat a skillet over medium-high flame, add the coconut oil.*
- ✓ *Sauté the onions until softened. Add to the sausage and cook for two minutes*
- ✓ *Add to the spinach and mushroom. Stir constantly until the spinach has wilted.*
- ✓ *Turn off the stove and distribute the vegetable mixture evenly.*
- ✓ *Pour to the beaten eggs and transfer to the oven.*
- ✓ *Cook for twenty minutes or until the eggs are completely cooked through.*

Nutrition: Calories: 383; Protein: 24.9g; Carbs: 8.6g; Fat: 27.6g

171) Tomato-Bacon Quiche

Ingredients:

- *¼ tsp black pepper*
- *¼ tsp salt*
- *¼ tsp ground mustard*
- *½ cup fresh spinach, chopped*
- *2/4 cups cauliflower, ground into rice*
- *5 slices nitrate-free bacon, cooked and chopped*
- *3 tbsp unsweetened plain almond milk*
- *½ cup organic white eggs*
- *5 eggs, beaten*
- *Zucchini Hash Crust:*
- *1/8 tsp sea salt*
- *1 tbsp butter*
- *1 tsp flax meal*
- *1 ½ tbsp coconut flour*
- *1 egg, beaten*
- *2 small to medium-sized organic zucchini, grated*

Direction: Cooking Time: 35-40 minutes Servings: 4-6,

- ✓ *Grease a pie dish and preheat the oven to 4000F.*
- ✓ *Grate zucchini, drain, and squeeze dry.*
- ✓ *In a container, add dry zucchini and resting crust ingredients and mix well.*
- ✓ *Place in the bottom of a pie plate and press down as if making a pie crust. Put to the oven and bake for 9 minutes.*
- ✓ *Meanwhile, whisk well black pepper, salt, mustard, almond milk, egg whites, and egg in a large mixing*

container.

- ✓ *Add bacon, spinach, and cauliflower rice. Mix well. Pour into baked zucchini crust, top with tomato slices.*
- ✓ *Pop back to the oven, bake for 28 minutes. If at 20 minutes baking time top is browning too much, cover with parchment paper for the remainder of cooking time.*
- ✓ *Once done cooking, remove from oven, let it stand for at least ten minutes.*
- ✓ *Slice into equal triangles, serve and enjoy.*

Nutrition: Calories: 154; Protein: 11.6g; Carbs: 3.4g; Fat: 10.3g

172) ***Your Standard Quiche***

Ingredients:

- *4 oz sliced Portobello mushrooms*
- *pepper and salt to taste*
- *½ tbsp dried basil*
- *½ tbsp dried parsley*
- *6 eggs, whisked*
- *¾ lb pork breakfast sausage*

Direction: Cooking Time: 45 minutes Servings: 6

- ✓ *Grease a 9-inch round pie plate or baking pan and preheat the oven to 3500F.*
- ✓ *On medium fire, place a nonstick fry pan and cook sausage. Stir fry until cooked as you break them into pieces. Discard excess oil once cooked.*
- ✓ *In a big container, whisk pepper, salt, basil, parsley, and eggs. Pour into prepped baking plate.*
- ✓ *Put into the oven and bake until middle is firm, around 30-35 minutes.*
- ✓ *Once done, remove from oven; let it stand for 10 minutes before slicing and serving.*

Nutrition: Calories: 283; Protein: 15.0g; Carbs: 3.2g; Fat: 23.3g

173) ***Zucchini Tomato Frittata***

Ingredients:

- *3 lbs tomatoes, thinly sliced crosswise*
- *¾ cup cheddar cheese, shredded*
- *¼ cup milk*
- *8 large eggs*
- *1 tbsp fresh thyme leaves*
- *3 zucchinis, cut into ¼-inch thick rounds*
- *1 onion, finely chopped*
- *1 tbsp olive oil*
- *Salt and pepper to taste*

Direction: Cooking Time: 30 minutes Servings: 8

- ✓ *Switch on the oven, preheat it setting its temperature to 425 degrees Fahrenheit.*
- ✓ *Prepare a nonstick skillet and heat it over medium heat.*
- ✓ *Sauté the zucchini, onion, and thyme. Cook and often stir for 8 to 10 minutes. Let the liquid into the pan evaporate, and season with salt and pepper to taste. Remove the skillet from heat.*
- ✓ *In a container, whisk the milk, cheese, eggs, salt, and pepper together. Over the zucchini into the skillet, sprinkle the beaten eggs. Lift the zucchini to allow the eggs to coat the pan. Arrange the tomato slices on top.*
- ✓ *Return into the skillet and heat to medium-low fire and cook until the sides are set or golden brown, around 7 minutes.*
- ✓ *Place the skillet inside the oven, cook for 10 to 15 minutes or until the center of the frittata is cooked through. To check if the egg is cooked through, insert a wooden skewer to the middle, and it should come out clean.*
- ✓ *Remove from the oven and loosen the frittata from the skillet. Serve warm.*

Nutrition: Calories: 175; Protein: 12.0g; Carbs: 13.6g; Fat: 8.1g

APPETIZER AND SNACKS RECIPES

174) Cucumber Cup Appetizers

Ingredients:

- 1 medium cucumber (about 8 ounces / 227 g, 8 to 9 inches long)
- ½ cup hummus (any flavor) or white bean dip
- 5 cherry tomatoes, sliced in half
- 2 Tbsps fresh basil, minced

Direction: Prep time: 5 minutes | Cook time: 0 minutes | Serves 2

✓ Slice the ends of the cucumber (about ½ inch from each side) and slice the cucumber into 1-inch pieces.

✓ With a paring knife or a spoon, scoop most of the seeds from the inside of each cucumber piece to make a cup, being careful not to cut all the way through.

✓ Fill each cucumber cup with about 1 Tbsp of hummus or bean dip.

✓ Top each with a cherry tomato half and a sprinkle of fresh minced basil.

Nutrition: calories: 135 | fat: 6g | protein: 6g | carbs: 16g | fiber: 5g | sodium: 242

175) Spiced Roasted Chickpeas

Ingredients:

- Seasoning Mix:
- ¾ Tsp cumin
- ½ Tsp coriander
- ½ Tsp salt
- ¼ Tsp freshly ground black pepper
- ¼ Tsp paprika
- ¼ Tsp cardamom
- ¼ Tsp cinnamon
- ¼ Tsp allspice
- Chickpeas: 1 (15-ounce / 425-g) can chickpeas, drained and rinsed
- 1 Tbsp olive oil
- ¼ Tsp salt

Direction: Prep time: 15 minutes | Cook time: 35 minutes | Serves 2

✓ Make the Seasoning Mix

✓ Combine the cumin, coriander, salt, freshly ground black pepper, paprika, cardamom, cinnamon, and allspice in a small container. Stir well to combine and set aside.

✓ Make the Chickpeas

✓ Preheat the oven setting its temperature to 400°F (205°C), and set the rack to the middle position. Line a baking sheet with parchment paper.

✓ Pat the rinsed chickpeas with paper towels or roll them in a clean kitchen towel to dry off any water.

✓ Place the chickpeas in a container and season them with olive oil and salt.

✓ Add the chickpeas to the lined baking sheet (reserve the container) and roast them for about 25 to 35 minutes, turning them over once or twice while cooking. Most should be light brown. Taste a couple to make sure they are slightly crisp.

✓ Place the roasted chickpeas back into the container and sprinkle them with the seasoning mix. Toss lightly to combine. Taste, and add additional salt if needed. Serve warm.

Nutrition: calories: 175 | fat: 15g | protein: 1,4g | carbs: 14g | fiber: 2g | sodium: 196mg

176) Apple Chips with Chocolate Tahini Sauce

Ingredients:

- 2 Tbsps tahini
- 1 Tbsp maple syrup
- 1 Tbsp unsweetened cocoa powder
- 1 to 2 Tbsps warm water (or more if needed)
- 2 medium apples
- 1 Tbsp roasted, salted sunflower seeds

Direction: Prep time: 10 minutes | Cook time: 0 minutes | Serves 2

✓ In a small container, mix together the tahini, maple syrup, and cocoa powder. Add warm water, a little at a time, until thin enough to drizzle. Do not microwave it to thin it, and it won't work.

✓ Slice the apples crosswise into round slices, and then cut each piece in half to make a chip.

✓ Lay the apple chips out on a plate and drizzle them with the chocolate tahini sauce.

✓ Sprinkle sunflower seeds over the apple chips.

Nutrition: calories: 261 | fat: 11g | protein: 5g | carbs: 43g | fiber: 8g | sodium: 21mg

177) Strawberry Caprese Skewers with Balsamic Glaze

Ingredients:

- ½ cup balsamic vinegar
- 16 whole, hulled strawberries
- 12 small basil leaves or 6 large leaves, halved
- 12 pieces of small Mozzarella balls

Direction: Prep time: 18 minutes | Cook time: 10 minutes | Serves 2

✓ To make the balsamic glaze, pour the balsamic vinegar into a small saucepan and bring it to a boil. Reduce the heat to medium-low and simmer until it's reduced by half and is thick enough to coat the back of a spoon.

✓ On each of the 4 wooden skewers, place a strawberry, a folded basil leaf, and a Mozzarella ball, repeating twice and adding a

✓ strawberry on end. (Each skewer should have 4 strawberries, 3 basil leaves, and 3 Mozzarella balls.)

✓ Drizzle 1 to 2 Tsp of balsamic glaze over the

skewers.
Nutrition: calories: 206 | fat: 10g | protein: 10g | carbs: 17g | fiber: 1g | sodium: 282mg

178) Labneh Vegetable Parfaits

Ingredients:

Labneh:

- *8 ounces (227 g) plain Greek yogurt (full-fat works best) Generous pinch salt*
- *1 Tsp za'atar seasoning*
- *1 Tsp freshly squeezed lemon juice Pinch lemon zest*

Parfaits:

- *½ cup peeled, chopped cucumber*
- *½ cup grated carrots*
- *½ cup cherry tomatoes halved*

Direction: Prep time: 15 minutes | Cook time: 0 minutes | Serves 2

- ✓ *Make the Labneh*
- ✓ *Line a strainer with cheesecloth and place it over a container.*
- ✓ *Stir together the Greek yogurt and salt and place them on the cheesecloth. Wrap it up and let it sit for 24 hours in the fridge.*
- ✓ *When ready, unwrap the labneh and place it into a clean container. Stir to the za'atar, lemon juice, and lemon zest.*
- ✓ *Make the Parfaits*
- ✓ *Divide the cucumber between two clear glasses.*
- ✓ *Top each portion of cucumber with about 3 Tbsps of labneh.*
- ✓ *Divide the carrots between the glasses.*
- ✓ *Top with another 3 Tbsps of the labneh.*
- ✓ *Top parfaits with the cherry tomatoes*

Nutrition: calories: 143 | fat: 7g | protein: 5g | carbs: 16g | fiber: 2g | sodium: 187mg

179) Rosemary and Honey Almonds

Ingredients:

- *1 cup raw, whole, shelled almonds*
- *1 Tbsp minced fresh rosemary*
- *¼ Tsp kosher or sea salt*
- *1 Tbsp honey*
- *Nonstick cooking spray*

Direction: Prep time: 8 minutes, Cook time: 10 minutes | Serves 6

- ✓ *In a large skillet over medium heat, mix the almonds, rosemary, and salt. Stir frequently for 1 minute.*
- ✓ *Drizzle to the honey and cook for 3 to 4 minutes, frequently stirring, until the almonds are coated and just starting to darken around the edges.*
- ✓ *Remove from the heat. Using a spatula, spread the almonds onto a pan coated with nonstick cooking spray. Cool for 10 minutes or so. Break up the almonds before serving.*

Nutrition: calories: 13 | fat: 1g | protein: 1g | carbs: 3g | fiber: 1g | sodium: 97mg

180) Pickled Turnips

Ingredients:

- *1 pound (454 g) turnips, washed well, peeled, and cut into 1-inch batons*
- *1 small beet, roasted, peeled, and cut into 1-inch batons*
- *2 garlic cloves, smashed*
- *1 Tsp dried Turkish oregano*
- *3 cups warm water*
- *½ cup red wine vinegar*
- *½ cup white vinegar*

Direction: Prep time: 5 minutes | Cook time: 0 minutes | Makes about 1 quart

- ✓ *In a jar, combine the turnips, beet, garlic, and oregano. Pour the water and vinegar over the vegetables, cover, then shake well and put it in the fridge.*
- ✓ *The turnips will be pickled after 1 hour.*

Nutrition: calories: 8 | fat: 0g | protein: 1g | carbs: 1g | fiber: 0g | sodium: 6mg

181) Garlic and Herb Marinated Artichokes

Ingredients:

- *2 (13¾-ounce / 390-g) cans artichoke hearts, drained and quartered*
- *¾ cup extra-virgin olive oil*
- *4 small garlic cloves, crushed with the back of a knife*
- *1 tbsp fresh rosemary leaves*
- *2 Tsp chopped fresh oregano or 1 Tsp dried oregano*
- *1 Tsp red pepper flakes (optional)*
- *1 Tsp salt*

Direction: Prep time: 10 minutes | Cook time: 0 minutes | Makes 2 cups

- ✓ *In a medium container, combine the artichoke hearts, olive oil, garlic, rosemary, oregano, red pepper flakes (if using), and salt. Toss to combine well.*
- ✓ *Store in an airtight glass container in the fridge and marinate for at least 24 hours before using. Store in the fridge for up to 2 weeks.*

Nutrition: calories: 275 | fat: 27g | protein: 4g|carbs: 11g

182) Balsamic Artichoke Antipasto

Ingredients:

- *1 (12-ounce / 340-g) jar roasted red peppers, drained, stemmed, and seeded*

- *8 artichoke hearts, either frozen (thawed) or jarred (drained)*
- *1 (16-ounce / 454-g) canned garbanzo beans, drained*
- *1 cup whole Kalamata olives, drained*
- *¼ cup balsamic vinegar*
- *½ Tsp salt*

Direction: Prep time: 5 minutes | Cook time: 0 minutes | Serves 4

- ✓ *Cut the peppers into ½-inch slices and put them into a large container.*
- ✓ *Cut the artichoke hearts into quarters, add them to the container.*
- ✓ *Add the garbanzo beans, olives, balsamic vinegar, and salt.*
- ✓ *Toss all the ingredients together. Serve chilled.*

Nutrition: calories: 281 | fat: 14g | protein: 7g | carbs: 30g | fiber: 9g | sodium: 1237mg

183) Mediterranean-Style Trail Mix

Ingredients:

- *1 cup roughly chopped unsalted walnuts*
- *½ cup roughly chopped salted almonds*
- *½ cup shelled salted pistachios*
- *½ cup roughly chopped apricots*
- *½ cup roughly chopped dates*
- *⅓ cup dried figs, sliced in half*

Direction: Prep time: 10 minutes | Cook time: 0 minutes | Serves 6

- ✓ *In a large zip-top bag, combine the walnuts, almonds, pistachios, apricots, dates, and figs and mix well.*

Nutrition: calories: 348 | fat: 23g | protein: 9g | carbs: 33g | fiber: 6g | sodium: 95mg

184) Savory Mediterranean Spiced Popcorn

Ingredients:

- *3 Tbsps extra-virgin olive oil*
- *¼ Tsp garlic powder*
- *¼ Tsp freshly ground black pepper*
- *¼ Tsp sea salt*
- *⅛ Tsp dried thyme*
- *⅛ Tsp dried oregano*
- *12 cups plain popped popcorn*

Direction: Prep time: 10 minutes | Cook time: 2 minutes | Serves 4 to 6

- ✓ *In a large skillet, heat the oil over medium heat until shimmering, and then add the garlic powder, pepper, salt, thyme, and oregano until fragrant.*
- ✓ *In a large container, drizzle the oil over the popcorn, toss, and serve.*

Nutrition: calories: 183 | fat: 12g | protein: 3g | carbs: 19g | fiber: 3g | sodium: 146mg

185) Turkish Spiced Mixed-Nuts

Ingredients:

- *1 Tbsp extra-virgin olive oil*
- *1 cup mixed nuts (walnuts, almonds, cashews, peanuts)*
- *2 Tbsps paprika*
- *1 Tbsp dried mint*
-
- *½ Tbsp ground cinnamon*
- *½ Tbsp kosher salt*
- *¼ Tbsp garlic powder*
- *¼ Tsp freshly ground black pepper*
- *⅛ Tbsp ground cumin*

Direction: Prep time: 10 minutes | Cook time: 5 minutes | Serves 4 to 6

- ✓ *In a small to a medium saucepan, heat the oil on low heat.*
- ✓ *Once the oil is warm, add the nuts, paprika, mint, cinnamon, salt, garlic powder, pepper, and cumin and stir continually until the spices are well incorporated with the nuts.*

Nutrition: calories: 204 | fat: 17g | protein: 6g | carbs: 10g | fiber: 3g | sodium: 874mg

186) Citrus-Thyme Chickpeas

Ingredients

- *2 Tsp extra-virgin olive oil*
- *1 (15-ounce / 425-g) can chickpeas, drained and rinsed*
- *¼ Tsp dried thyme or ½ Tsp chopped fresh thyme leaves*
- *⅛ Tsp kosher or sea salt*
- *½ Tsp zest of ½ orange*

Direction: Prep time: 5 minutes | Cook time: 23 minutes | Serves 4

- ✓ *Switch on the oven, preheat it to 450°F (235°C).*
- ✓ *Spread the chickpeas on a clean kitchen towel, rub gently until dry.*
- ✓ *Spread the chickpeas on a large, rimmed baking sheet. Drizzle with the oil, sprinkle with thyme and salt. With a Microplane or citrus zester, zest about half of the orange over the chickpeas. Mix well using your hands.*
- ✓ *Bake for 10 minutes, then open the oven, and give the baking sheet a quick shake using an oven mitt. (Do not remove the sheet from the oven.) Bake for 10 minutes more. Taste the chickpeas (carefully!). If they are golden but you think they could be a bit crunchier, bake for 3 minutes more before serving.*

Nutrition: calories: 97 | fat: 2g | protein: 5g | carbs: 14g | fiber: 4g | sodium: 232mg

187) Crispy Seedy Crackers

Ingredients:

- *1 cup almond flour*
- *1 Tbsp sesame seeds*
- *1 Tbsp flaxseed*
- *1 Tbsp chia seeds*
- *¼ Tsp baking soda*
- *¼ Tsp salt*
- *ground black pepper, to taste*
- *1 large egg, at room temperature*

Direction: Prep time: 10 minutes | Cook time: 10 minutes | Makes 24 crackers

- ✓ *Preheat the oven and set its temperature to 350°F (180°C).*
- ✓ *In a large container, combine the almond flour, sesame seeds, flaxseed, chia seeds, baking soda, salt, and pepper and stir well.*
- ✓ *In a small container, whisk the egg until well beaten. Add to the dry ingredients and stir well to mix and form the dough into a ball.*
- ✓ *Place one layer of parchment paper on your countertop and place the dough on top. Cover with a second layer of parchment and, using a rolling pin, roll the dough to ⅛-inch thickness, aiming for a rectangular shape.*
- ✓ *Cut the dough into 1-to 2-inch crackers and bake on parchment until crispy and slightly golden, 10 to 15 minutes, depending on thickness. Alternatively, you can bake the large rolled dough before cutting and break it into free-form crackers once baked and crispy.*
- ✓ *Store in an airtight container to the fridge for up to 1 week.*

Nutrition: calories: 119 | fat: 8g | protein: 5g | carbs: 4g | fiber: 2g | sodium: 242mg

188) Mediterranean Nutty Fat Bombs

Ingredients:

- *1 cup crumbled goat cheese*
- *4 Tbsps jarred pesto*
- *12 pitted Kalamata olives, finely chopped*

Direction: Prep time: 5 minutes | Cook time: 0 minutes | Makes 6 fat bombs

- ✓ *Combine the goat cheese, pesto, and olives in a medium container and mix well using a fork. Put in the fridge for at least 5 hours to harden.*
- ✓ *Using your hands, form the mixture into 6 balls, about ¾-inch diameter. The mixture will be sticky.*
- ✓ *Place the walnuts and rosemary in a small container and roll the goat cheese balls to the nut mixture to coat.*
- ✓ *Store the fat bombs in the fridge for up to 1 week or in the freezer for up to 1 month.*

Nutrition: calories: 166 | fat: 14g | protein: 5g | carbs: 4g | fiber: 1g | sodium: 337mg

189) Manchego Cheese Crackers

Ingredients:

- *4 Tbsps butter, at room temperature (optional)*
- *1 cup finely shredded Manchego cheese*
- *1 cup almond flour*
- *1 Tsp salt, divided*
- *¼ Tsp freshly ground black pepper*
- *1 large egg*

Direction: Prep time: 5 minutes | Cook time: 12 minutes | Makes 40 crackers

- ✓ *Using an electric mixer, cream together the butter (if desired) and shredded cheese until well combined and smooth.*
- ✓ *In a small container, combine the almond flour with ½ Tsp salt and pepper. Slowly add the almond flour mixture to the cheese, constantly mixing until the dough just comes together to form a ball.*
- ✓ *Transfer to a piece of parchment and roll into a cylinder log about 1½ inches thick. Wrap tightly and refrigerate for at least 1 hour.*
- ✓ *Switch on the oven, preheat it setting its temperature to 350°F (180°C)—line two silicone baking mats.*
- ✓ *To make the egg wash, whisk together the egg and resting ½ Tsp salt in a small container.*
- ✓ *Slice the refrigerated dough into small rounds, about ¼ inch thick, and place on the lined baking sheets.*
- ✓ *Brush the tops of the crackers with egg wash and bake until the crackers are golden and crispy, 12 to 15 minutes. Remove from the oven and allow to cool on a wire rack.*
- ✓ *Serve warm or, once fully cooled, store in an airtight container in the fridge for up to 1 week.*

Nutrition: calories: 243 | fat: 22g | protein: 7g | carbs: 2g | fiber: 1g | sodium: 792mg

190) Lemony Peanut Butter Hummus

Ingredients:

- *1 (15-ounce / 425-g) can chickpeas, drained, liquid reserved*
- *3 Tbsps freshly squeezed lemon juice (from about 1 large lemon)*
- *2 Tbsps peanut butter*
- *3 Tbsps extra-virgin olive oil, divided*
- *2 garlic cloves*
- *¼ Tsp kosher or sea salt (optional)*
- *Raw veggies or whole-grain crackers for serving (optional)*

Direction: Prep time: 10 minutes | Cook time: 0 minutes | Serves 6

- ✓ *In the food processor, combine the chickpeas and 2 Tbsps of the reserved chickpea liquid with the lemon juice, peanut butter, 2 Tbsps of oil, and the garlic. Process the mixture for 1 minute. Scrape down the sides of the container with a rubber spatula. Process for 1 more minute, or until smooth.*

- ✓ *Put in a serving container, drizzle with the resting 1 Tbsp of olive oil, sprinkle with the salt, if using, and serve with veggies or crackers, if desired.*

Nutrition: calories: 125 | fat: 5g | protein: 4g | carbs: 14g | fiber: 2g | sodium: 369mg

191) Light & Creamy Garlic Hummus

Ingredients:

- *1 1/2 cups dry chickpeas, rinsed*
- *2 1/2 tbsp fresh lemon juice*
- *1 tbsp garlic, minced*
- *1/2 cup tahini*
- *6 cups of water*
- *Pepper*
- *Salt*

Direction: Preparation Time: 10 minutes Cooking Time: 40 minutes Servings: 12

- ✓ *Add water and chickpeas into the instant pot.*
- ✓ *Seal pot with a lid and select manual, and set timer for 40 minutes.*
- ✓ *Once done, allow to release pressure naturally. Remove lid.*
- ✓ *Drain chickpeas well and reserved 1/2 cup chickpeas liquid.*
- ✓ *Transfer chickpeas, reserved liquid, lemon juice, garlic, tahini, pepper, and salt into the food processor and process until smooth.*
- ✓ *Serve and enjoy.*

Nutrition: Calories 152 Fat 6.9 g Carbohydrates 17.6 g Sugar 2.8 g Protein 6.6 g Cholesterol 0 mg

192) Perfect Queso

Ingredients:

- *1 lb ground beef*
- *32 oz Velveeta cheese, cut into cubes*
- *10 oz canned tomatoes, diced*
- *1 1/2 tbsp taco seasoning*
- *1 tsp chili powder*
- *1 onion, diced*
- *Pepper*
- *Salt*

Direction: Preparation Time: 10 minutes Cooking Time: 15 minutes Servings: 16

- ✓ *Set instant pot on sauté mode.*
- ✓ *Add meat, onion, taco seasoning, chili powder, pepper, and salt into the pot and cook until meat is no longer pink.*
- ✓ *Add tomatoes and stir well. Top with cheese, and do not stir.*
- ✓ *Seal pot with lid and cook on high for 4 minutes.*
- ✓ *Once done, release pressure using quick release. Remove lid.*
- ✓ *Stir everything well and serve.*

Nutrition: Calories 257 Fat 15.9 g Carbohydrates 10.2 g Sugar 4.9 g Protein 21 g Cholesterol 71 mg

193) Creamy Potato Spread

Ingredients:

- *1 lb sweet potatoes, peeled and chopped*
- *3/4 tbsp fresh chives, chopped*
- *1/2 tsp paprika*
- *1 tbsp garlic, minced*
- *1 cup tomato puree*
- *Pepper*
- *Salt*

Direction: Preparation Time: 10 minutes Cooking Time: 15 minutes Servings: 6

- ✓ *Add all ingredients except chives into the inner pot of the instant pot and stir well.*
- ✓ *Seal pot with lid, cook on high for 15 minutes.*
- ✓ *Once done, allow to release pressure naturally for 10-11 minutes, then release resting using quick release. Remove lid.*
- ✓ *Transfer instant pot sweet potato mixture into the food processor and process until smooth.*
- ✓ *Garnish with chives and serve.*

Nutrition: Calories 108 Fat 0.3 g Carbohydrates 25.4 g Sugar 2.4 g Protein 2 g Cholesterol 0 mg

194) Cucumber Tomato Okra Salsa

Ingredients:

- *1 lb tomatoes, chopped*
- *1/4 tsp red pepper flakes*
- *1/4 cup fresh lemon juice*
- *1 cucumber, chopped*
- *1 tbsp fresh oregano, chopped*
- *1 tbsp fresh basil, chopped*
- *1 tbsp olive oil*
- *1 onion, chopped*
- *1 tbsp garlic, chopped*
- *1 1/2 cups okra, chopped*
- *Pepper*
- *Salt*

Direction: Preparation Time: 10 minutes Cooking Time: 15 minutes Servings: 4

- ✓ *Add oil into the instant pot and set the pot on sauté mode.*
- ✓ *Add onion, garlic, pepper, and salt and sauté for 3 minutes.*
- ✓ *Add resting ingredients except for cucumber and stir well.*
- ✓ *Seal pot with lid and cook on high for 12 minutes.*

✓ Allow releasing pressure naturally for 10 minutes, then release resting using quick release. Remove lid.

✓ Once the salsa mixture is cool, then add cucumber and mix well.

✓ Serve and enjoy.

Nutrition: Calories 99 Fat 4.2 g Carbohydrates 14.3 g Sugar 6.4 g Protein 2.9 g Cholesterol 0 mg

195) Parmesan Potatoes

Ingredients:

- 2 lb potatoes, rinsed and cut into chunks
- 2 tbsp parmesan cheese, grated
- 2 tbsp olive oil
- 1/2 tsp parsley
- 1/2 tsp Italian seasoning
- 1 tsp garlic, minced
- 1 cup vegetable broth
- 1/2 tsp salt

Direction: Preparation Time: 10 minutes Cooking Time: 6 minutes Servings: 4

✓ Add all ingredients except cheese into the instant pot and stir well.

✓ Seal pot with lid and cook on high for 6 minutes.

✓ Once done, release pressure using quick release. Remove lid.

✓ Add parmesan cheese and stir until cheese is melted.

✓ Serve and enjoy.

Nutrition: Calories 237 Fat 8.3 g Carbohydrates 36.3 g Sugar 2.8 g Protein 5.9 g Cholesterol 2 mg

196) Creamy Artichoke Dip

Ingredients:

- 28 oz can artichoke hearts, drain and quartered
- 1 1/2 cups parmesan cheese, shredded
- 1 cup sour cream
- 1 cup mayonnaise
- 3.5 oz can green chilies
- 1 cup of water
- Pepper
- Salt

Direction: Preparation Time: 10 minutes Cooking Time: 5 minutes Servings: 8

✓ Add artichokes, water, and green chilies into the instant pot.

✓ Seal pot with the lid and select manual, set timer for 1 minute.

✓ Once done, release pressure using quick release. Remove lid. Drain excess water.

✓ Set instant pot on sauté mode. Add resting ingredients and stir well and cook until cheese is melted.

✓ Serve and enjoy.

Nutrition: Calories 262 Fat 7.6 g Carbohydrates 14.4 g Sugar 2.8 g Protein 8.4 g Cholesterol 32 mg

197) Homemade Salsa

Ingredients:

- 12 oz grape tomatoes, halved
- 1/4 cup fresh cilantro, chopped
- 1 fresh lime juice
- 28 oz tomatoes, crushed
- 1 tbsp garlic, minced
- 1 green bell pepper, chopped
- 1 red bell pepper, chopped
- 2 onions, chopped
- 6 whole tomatoes
- Salt

Direction: Preparation Time: 10 minutes Cooking Time: 5 minutes Servings: 8

✓ Add whole tomatoes into the instant pot and gently smash the tomatoes.

✓ Add resting ingredients except for cilantro, lime juice, and salt, and stir well.

✓ Seal pot with lid and cook on high for 5 minutes.

✓ Allow releasing pressure naturally for 11 minutes, then release resting using quick release. Remove lid.

✓ Add cilantro, lime juice, and salt and stir well.

✓ Serve and enjoy.

Nutrition: Calories 146 Fat 1.2 g Carbohydrates 33.2 g Sugar 4 g Protein 6.9 g Cholesterol 0 mg

198) Delicious Eggplant Caponata

Ingredients:

- 1 eggplant, cut into 1/2-inch chunks
- 1 lb tomatoes, diced
- 1/2 cup tomato puree
- 1/4 cup dates, chopped
- 2 tbsp vinegar
- 1/2 cup fresh parsley, chopped
- 2 celery stalks, chopped
- 1 small onion, chopped
- 2 zucchini, cut into 1/2-inch chunks
- Pepper
- Salt

Direction: Preparation Time: 10 minutes Cooking Time: 5 minutes Servings: 8

✓ Add all ingredients into the inner pot of the instant pot and stir well.

✓ Seal pot with lid and cook on high for 5 minutes.

✓ Once done, release pressure using quick release. Remove lid.

✓ Stir well and serve.

Nutrition: Calories 60 Fat 0.4 g Carbohydrates 14 g Sugar 8.8 g Protein 2.3 g Cholesterol 0.4 mg

199) Flavorful Roasted Baby Potatoes

Ingredients:

- *2 lbs baby potatoes, clean and cut in half*
- *1/2 cup vegetable stock*
- *1 tsp paprika*
- *3/4 tsp garlic powder*
- *1 tsp onion powder*
- *2 tsp Italian seasoning*
- *1 tbsp olive oil*
- *Pepper*
- *Salt*

Direction: Preparation Time: 10 minutes Cooking Time: 10 minutes Servings: 4

- ✓ *Add oil into the instant pot, set the pot on sauté mode.*
- ✓ *Add potatoes and sauté for 5 minutes. Add resting ingredients and stir well.*
- ✓ *Seal pot with lid and cook on high for 5 minutes.*
- ✓ *Once done, release pressure using quick release. Remove lid.*
- ✓ *Stir well and serve.*

Nutrition: Calories 175 Fat 4.5 g Carbohydrates 29.8 g Sugar 0.7 g Protein 6.1 g Cholesterol 2 mg

200) Perfect Italian Potatoes

Ingredients:

- *2 lbs baby potatoes, clean and cut in half*
- *3/4 cup vegetable broth*
- *6 oz Italian dry dressing mix*

Direction: Preparation Time: 10 minutes Cooking Time: 7 minutes Servings: 6

- ✓ *Add all ingredients into the inner pot of the instant pot and stir well.*
- ✓ *Seal pot with lid and cook on high for 7 minutes.*
- ✓ *Allow releasing pressure naturally for 3 minutes, then release resting using quick release. Remove lid.*
- ✓ *Stir well and serve.*

Nutrition: Calories 149 Fat 0.3 g Carbohydrates 41.6 g Sugar 11.4 g Protein 4.5 g Cholesterol 0 mg

201) Garlic Pinto Bean Dip

Ingredients:

- *1 cup dry pinto beans, rinsed*
- *1/2 tsp cumin*
- *1/2 cup salsa*
- *2 garlic cloves*
- *2 chipotle peppers in adobo sauce*
- *5 cups vegetable stock*
- *Pepper*
- *Salt*

Direction: Preparation Time: 10 minutes Cooking Time: 43 minutes Servings: 6

- ✓ *Add beans, stock, garlic, and chipotle peppers into the instant pot.*
- ✓ *Seal pot with lid and cook on high for 43 minutes.*
- ✓ *Once done, release pressure using quick release. Remove lid.*
- ✓ *Drain beans well and reserve 1/2 cup of stock.*
- ✓ *Transfer beans, reserve stock, and resting ingredients into the food processor and process until smooth.*
- ✓ *Serve and enjoy.*

Nutrition: Calories 129 Fat 0.9 g Carbohydrates 23 g Sugar 1.9 g Protein 8 g Cholesterol 2 mg

202) Creamy Eggplant Dip

Ingredients:

- *1 eggplant*
- *1/2 tsp paprika*
- *1 tbsp olive oil*
- *1 tbsp fresh lime juice*
- *2 tbsp tahini*
- *1 garlic clove*
- *1 cup of water*
- *Pepper*
- *Salt*

Direction: Preparation Time: 10 minutes Cooking Time: 20 minutes Servings: 4

- ✓ *Add water and eggplant into the instant pot.*
- ✓ *Seal pot with the lid and select manual, set timer for 20 minutes.*
- ✓ *Once done, release pressure using quick release. Remove lid.*
- ✓ *Drain eggplant and let it cool.*
- ✓ *Once the eggplant is cool, then remove eggplant skin and transfer eggplant flesh into the food processor.*
- ✓ *Add resting ingredients into the food processor and process until smooth.*
- ✓ *Serve and enjoy.*

Nutrition: Calories 108 Fat 7.8 g Carbohydrates 9.7 g Sugar 3.7 g Protein 2.5 g Cholesterol 0 mg

203) Jalapeno Chickpea Hummus

Ingredients:

- *1 cup dry chickpeas, soaked overnight, and drained*
- *1 tsp ground cumin*
- *1/4 cup jalapenos, diced*
- *1/2 cup fresh cilantro*
- *1 tbsp tahini*

- *1/2 cup olive oil*
- *Pepper*
- *Salt*

Direction: Preparation Time: 10 minutes Cooking Time: 25 minutes Servings: 4

- ✓ *Add chickpeas into the instant pot and cover with vegetable stock.*
- ✓ *Seal pot with lid and cook on high for 25 minutes.*
- ✓ *Once done, allow to release pressure naturally. Remove lid.*
- ✓ *Drain chickpeas well, transfer them into the food processor and resting ingredients, and process until smooth.*
- ✓ *Serve and enjoy.*

Nutrition: Calories 425 Fat 30.4 g Carbohydrates 31.8 g Sugar 5.6 g Protein 10.5 g Cholesterol 0 mg

204) Tasty Black Bean Dip

Ingredients:

- *2 cups dry black beans, soaked overnight, and drained*
- *1 1/2 cups cheese, shredded*
- *1 tsp dried oregano*
- *1 1/2 tsp chili powder*
- *2 cups tomatoes, chopped*
- *2 tbsp olive oil*
- *1 1/2 tbsp garlic, minced*
- *1 medium onion, sliced*
- *4 cups vegetable stock*
- *Pepper and Salt*

Direction: Preparation Time: 10 minutes Cooking Time: 18 minutes Servings: 6

- ✓ *Add all ingredients except cheese into the instant pot.*
- ✓ *Seal pot with lid and cook on high for 18 minutes.*
- ✓ *Once done, allow to release pressure naturally. Remove lid. Drain excess water.*
- ✓ *Add cheese and stir until cheese is melted.*
- ✓ *Blend bean mixture using an immersion blender until smooth.*
- ✓ *Serve and enjoy.*

Nutrition: Calories 402 Fat 15.3 g Carbohydrates 46.6 g Sugar 4.4 g Protein 22.2 g Cholesterol 30 mg

205) Healthy Kidney Bean Dip

Ingredients:

- *1 cup dry white kidney beans, soaked overnight, and drained*
- *1 tbsp fresh lemon juice*
- *2 tbsp water*
- *1/2 cup coconut yogurt*
- *1 roasted garlic clove*
- *1 tbsp olive oil*
- *1/4 tsp cayenne*
- *1 tsp dried parsley*
- *Pepper*
- *Salt*

Direction: Preparation Time: 10 minutes Cooking Time: 10 minutes Servings: 6

- ✓ *Add soaked beans and 1 3/4 cups of water into the instant pot.*
- ✓ *Seal pot with lid and cook on high for 10 minutes.*
- ✓ *Allow releasing pressure naturally. Remove lid.*
- ✓ *Drain beans well and transfer them into the food processor.*
- ✓ *Add resting ingredients into the food processor and process until smooth.*
- ✓ *Serve and enjoy.*

Nutrition: Calories 136 Fat 3.2 g Carbohydrates 20 g Sugar 2.1 g Protein 7.7 g Cholesterol 0 mg

206) Creamy Pepper Spread

Ingredients:

- *1 lb red bell peppers, chopped and remove seeds*
- *1 1/2 tbsp fresh basil*
- *1 tbsp olive oil*
- *1 tbsp fresh lime juice*
- *1 tsp garlic, minced*
- *Pepper*
- *Salt*

Direction: Preparation Time: 10 minutes Cooking Time: 15 minutes Servings: 4

- ✓ *Add all ingredients into the inner pot of the instant pot and stir well.*
- ✓ *Seal pot with lid and cook on high for 15 minutes.*
- ✓ *Once done, allow to release pressure naturally for 10 minutes, then release resting using quick release. Remove lid.*
- ✓ *Transfer bell pepper mixture into the food processor and process until smooth.*
- ✓ *Serve and enjoy.*

Nutrition: Calories 41 Fat 3.6 g Carbohydrates 3.5 g Sugar 1.7 g Protein 0.4 g Cholesterol 0 mg

207) Healthy Spinach Dip

Ingredients:

- *14 oz spinach*
- *2 tbsp fresh lime juice*
- *1 tbsp garlic, minced*
- *2 tbsp olive oil*
- *2 tbsp coconut cream*
- *Pepper*
- *Salt*

Direction: Preparation Time: 10 minutes Cooking Time: 8 minutes Servings: 4

- ✓ *Add all ingredients except coconut cream into the*

instant pot and stir well.

- ✓ *Seal pot with lid and cook on low pressure for 8 minutes.*
- ✓ *Allow releasing pressure for 5 minutes, then release resting using quick release. Remove lid.*
- ✓ *Add coconut cream and stir well and blend spinach mixture using a blender until smooth.*
- ✓ *Serve and enjoy.*

Nutrition: Calories 109 Fat 9.2 g Carbohydrates 6.6 g Sugar 1.1 g Protein 3.2 g Cholesterol 0 mg

208) Kidney Bean Spread

Ingredients:

- *1 lb dry kidney beans, soaked overnight and drained*
- *1 tsp garlic, minced*
- *2 tbsp olive oil*
- *1 tbsp fresh lemon juice*
- *1 tbsp paprika*
- *4 cups vegetable stock*
- *1/2 cup onion, chopped*
- *Pepper*
- *Salt*

Direction: Preparation Time: 10 minutes Cooking Time: 18 minutes Servings: 4

- ✓ *Add beans and stock into the instant pot.*
- ✓ *Seal pot with lid, cook on high for 18 minutes.*
- ✓ *Allow releasing pressure naturally. Remove lid.*
- ✓ *Drain beans well and reserve 1/2 cup stock.*
- ✓ *Transfer beans, reserve stock, and resting ingredients into the food processor and process until smooth.*
- ✓ *Serve and enjoy.*

Nutrition: Calories 461 Fat 8.6 g Carbohydrates 73 g Sugar 4 g Protein 26.4 g Cholesterol 0 mg

209) Tomato Cucumber Salsa

Ingredients:

- *1 cucumber, chopped*
- *1 1/2 lbs grape tomatoes, chopped*
- *1 tbsp fresh chives, chopped*
- *1 tbsp fresh parsley, chopped*
- *1 tbsp fresh basil, chopped*
- *2 onion, chopped*
- *1/4 cup vinegar*
- *2 tbsp olive oil*
- *1/4 cup vegetable stock*
- *2 chili peppers, chopped*
- *Pepper*
- *Salt*

Direction: Preparation Time: 10 minutes Cooking Time: 5 minutes Servings: 4

- ✓ *Add tomatoes, stock, and chili peppers into the instant pot and stir well.*
- ✓ *Seal pot with lid and cook on low pressure for 5 minutes.*
- ✓ *Allow releasing pressure for 5 minutes, then release resting using quick release. Remove lid.*
- ✓ *Transfer tomato mixture into the mixing container.*
- ✓ *Add resting ingredients into the container and mix well.*
- ✓ *Serve and enjoy.*

Nutrition: Calories 129 Fat 7.5 g Carbohydrates 15 g Sugar 8.3 g Protein 2.7 g Cholesterol 0 mg

210) Spicy Berry Dip

Ingredients:

- *10 oz cranberries*
- *1/4 cup fresh orange juice*
- *3/4 tsp paprika*
- *1/2 tsp chili powder*
- *1 tsp lemon zest*
- *1 tbsp lemon juice*

Direction: Preparation Time: 10 minutes Cooking Time: 15 minutes Servings: 4

- ✓ *Add all ingredients into the inner pot of the instant pot and stir well.*
- ✓ *Seal pot with lid and cook on high for 15 minutes.*
- ✓ *Once done, allow to release pressure naturally for 5 minutes, then release resting using quick release. Remove lid.*
- ✓ *Blend cranberry mixture using a blender until getting the desired consistency.*

Serve and enjoy.

Nutrition: Calories 49 Carbs 8.6 g Protein 0.3 g

211) Rosemary Cauliflower Dip

Ingredients:

- *1 lb cauliflower florets*
- *1 tbsp fresh parsley, chopped*
- *1/2 cup heavy cream*
- *1/2 cup vegetable stock*
- *1 tbsp garlic, minced*
- *1 tbsp rosemary, chopped*
- *1 tbsp olive oil*
- *1 onion, chopped*
- *Pepper*
- *Salt*

Direction: Preparation Time: 10 minutes Cooking Time: 15 minutes Servings: 4

- ✓ *Add oil into the instant pot and set the pot on sauté mode.*
- ✓ *Add onion and sauté for 5 minutes.*
- ✓ *Add resting ingredients except for the parsley and heavy cream and stir well.*

- ✓ Seal pot with lid and cook on high for 10 minutes.
- ✓ Once done, allow to release pressure naturally for 10 minutes, then release resting using quick release. Remove lid.
- ✓ Add cream and stir well—blend cauliflower mixture using an immersion blender until smooth.
- ✓ Garnish with parsley and serve.

Nutrition: Calories 128 Fat 9.4 g Carbohydrates 10.4 g Sugar 4 g Protein 3.1 g Cholesterol 21 mg

212) Tomato Olive Salsa

Ingredients:

- 2 cups olives, pitted and chopped
- 1/4 cup fresh parsley, chopped
- 1/4 cup fresh basil, chopped
- 2 tbsp green onion, chopped
- 1 cup grape tomatoes, halved
- 1 tbsp olive oil
- 1 tbsp vinegar
- Pepper
- Salt

Direction: Preparation Time: 10 minutes Cooking Time: 5 minutes Servings: 4

- ✓ Add all ingredients into the inner pot of the instant pot and stir well.
- ✓ Seal pot with lid and cook on high for 5 minutes.
- ✓ Allow releasing pressure for 5 minutes, then release resting using quick release. Remove lid.
- ✓ Stir well and serve.

Nutrition: Calories 119 Fat 10.8 g Carbohydrates 6.5 g Sugar 1.3 g Protein 1.2 g Cholesterol 0 mg

213) Easy Tomato Dip

Ingredients:

- 2 cups tomato puree
- 1/2 tsp ground cumin
- 1 tsp garlic, minced
- 1/4 cup vinegar
- 1 onion, chopped
- 1 tbsp olive oil
- Pepper
- Salt

Direction: Preparation Time: 10 minutes Cooking Time: 13 minutes Servings: 4

- ✓ Add oil into the instant pot, set the pot on sauté mode.
- ✓ Add onion and sauté for 3 minutes.
- ✓ Add resting ingredients and stir well.
- ✓ Seal pot with lid and cook on high for 10 minutes.
- ✓ Once done, allow to release pressure naturally for 10 minutes, then release resting using quick release. Remove lid.
- ✓ Blend tomato mixture until smooth.
- ✓ Serve and enjoy.

Nutrition: Calories 94 Fat 3.9 g Carbohydrates 14.3 g Sugar 7.3 g Protein 2.5 g Cholesterol 0 mg

214) Balsamic Bell Pepper Salsa

Ingredients:

- 2 red bell peppers, chopped and seeds removed
- 1 cup grape tomatoes, halved
- 1/2 tbsp cayenne
- 1 tbsp balsamic vinegar
- 2 cup vegetable broth
- 1/2 cup sour cream
- 1/2 tsp garlic powder
- 1/2 onion, chopped

Direction: Preparation Time: 10 minutes Cooking Time: 6 minutes Servings: 2

- ✓ Add all ingredients except cream into the instant pot and stir well.
- ✓ Seal pot with lid and cook on high for 6 minutes.
- ✓ Once done, release pressure using quick release. Remove lid.
- ✓ Add sour cream and stir well.
- ✓ Blend the salsa mixture using an immersion blender until smooth.
- ✓ Serve and enjoy.

Nutrition: Calories 235 Fat 14.2 g Carbohydrates 19.8 g Sugar 10.7 g Protein 9.2 g Cholesterol 25 mg

215) Spicy Chicken Dip

Ingredients:

- 1 lb chicken breast, skinless and boneless
- 1/2 cup sour cream
- 8 oz cheddar cheese, shredded
- 1/2 cup chicken stock
- 2 jalapeno pepper, sliced
- 8 oz cream cheese
- Pepper
- Salt

Direction: Preparation Time: 10 minutes Cooking Time: 15 minutes Servings: 10

- ✓ Add chicken, stock, jalapenos, and cream cheese into the instant pot.
- ✓ Seal pot with lid and cook on high for 12 minutes.
- ✓ Once done, release pressure using quick release. Remove lid.
- ✓ Shred chicken using a fork.
- ✓ Set pot on sauté mode. Add resting ingredients and stir well and cook until cheese is melted.
- ✓ Serve and enjoy.

Nutrition: Calories 248 Fat 19 g Carbohydrates 1.6 g Sugar 0.3 g Protein 17.4 g Cholesterol 83 mg

216) Slow-Cooked Cheesy Artichoke Dip

Ingredients:

- 10 oz artichoke hearts, drained and chopped
- 4 cups spinach, chopped
- 8 oz cream cheese
- 3 tbsp sour cream
- 1/4 cup mayonnaise
- 3/4 cup mozzarella cheese, shredded
- 1/4 cup parmesan cheese, grated
- 3 garlic cloves, minced
- 1/2 tsp dried parsley
- Pepper
- Salt

Direction: Preparation Time: 10 minutes Cooking Time: 60 minutes Servings: 6

- ✓ Add all ingredients into the pot of instant pot and stir well.
- ✓ Seal the pot with the lid, select slow cook mode, and set the timer for 60 minutes. Stir once while cooking.
- ✓ Serve and enjoy.

Nutrition: Calories 226 Fat 19.3 g Carbohydrates 7.5 g Sugar 1.2 g Protein 6.8 g Cholesterol 51 mg

217) Olive Eggplant Spread

Ingredients:

- 1 3/4 lbs eggplant, chopped
- 1/2 tbsp dried oregano
- 1/4 cup olives, pitted and chopped
- 1 tbsp tahini
- 1/4 cup fresh lime juice
- 1/2 cup water
- 2 garlic cloves
- 1/4 cup olive oil
- Salt

Direction: Preparation Time: 10 minutes Cooking Time: 8 minutes Servings: 12

- ✓ Add oil into the pot of instant pot and set the pot on sauté mode.
- ✓ Add eggplant and cook for 3-5 minutes. Turn off sauté mode.
- ✓ Add water and salt and stir well.
- ✓ Seal pot with lid and cook on high for 3 minutes.
- ✓ Once done, release pressure using quick release. Remove lid.
- ✓ Drain eggplant well and transfer into the food processor.
- ✓ Add resting ingredients into the food processor and process until smooth.
- ✓ Serve and enjoy.

Nutrition: Calories 65 Fat 5.3 g Carbohydrates 4.7 g Sugar 2 g Protein 0.9 g Cholesterol 0 mg

218) Pepper Tomato Eggplant Spread

Ingredients:

- 2 cups eggplant, chopped
- 1/4 cup vegetable broth
- 2 tbsp tomato paste
- 1/4 cup sun-dried tomatoes, minced
- 1 cup bell pepper, chopped
- 1 tsp garlic, minced
- 1 cup onion, chopped
- 3 tbsp olive oil
- Salt

Direction: Preparation Time: 10 minutes Cooking Time: 10 minutes Servings: 3

- ✓ Add oil into the pot of instant pot and set the pot on sauté mode.
- ✓ Add onion and sauté for 3 minutes.
- ✓ Add eggplant, bell pepper, and garlic and sauté for 2 minutes.
- ✓ Add resting ingredients and stir well.
- ✓ Seal pot with lid and cook on high for 5 minutes.
- ✓ Once done, release pressure using quick release. Remove lid.
- ✓ Lightly mash the eggplant mixture using a potato masher.
- ✓ Stir well and serve.

Nutrition: Calories 178 Fat 14.4 g Carbohydrates 12.8 g Sugar 7 g Protein 2.4 g Cholesterol 0 mg

219) Wrapped Plums

Ingredients:

- 2 ounces prosciutto, cut into 16 pieces
- 4 plums, quartered
- 1 Tbsp chives, chopped
- A pinch of red pepper flakes, crushed

Direction: Servings: 8Preparation time: 0 minutes

- ✓ Wrap each plum quarter in a prosciutto slice, Pour them all on a platter, sprinkle the chives and pepper flakes all over, and serve.

Nutrition:Cal 30,Fat 1g, Fiber 0,Carbs 4g,Protein 2g

220) Cucumber Tomato Okra Salsa

Ingredients:

- 1 lb tomatoes, chopped
- ¼ tsp red pepper flakes
- ¼ cup fresh lemon juice
- 1 cucumber, chopped
- 1 tbsp fresh oregano, chopped
- 1 tbsp olive oil
- 1 onion, chopped

- *1 tbsp garlic, chopped*
- *1 ½ cups okra, chopped*
- *Pepper*
- *Salt*

Direction: Servings: 4 Preparation time: 25 minutes

✓ *Add oil into the pot of the instant pot and set the pot on sauté mode.*

✓ *Add onion, garlic, pepper, and salt and sauté for 3 minutes.*

✓ *Add resting ingredients except for cucumber and stir well.*

✓ *Seal pot with lid and cook on high for 12 minutes.*

✓ *Allow to release pressure naturally for 10 minutes, then release resting using quick release. Remove lid.*

✓ *Once the salsa mixture is cool, then add cucumber and mix well.*

✓ *Serve and enjoy.*

Nutrition: Calories 99, Fat 4.2g, Carbs 14.3g, Sugar 6.4g, Protein 2.9g

221) ***Tomato Cream Cheese Spread***

Ingredients:

- *12 ounces cream cheese, soft*
- *1 big tomato, cubed*
- *¼ cup homemade mayonnaise*
- *2 garlic cloves, minced*
- *2 Tbsps red onion, chopped*
- *2 Tbsps lime juice*
- *Salt and black pepper to the taste*

Direction: Servings: 6 Preparation time: 0 minutes

✓ *In your blender, mix the cream cheese with the tomato and the rest of the ingredients. Divide into small cups and serve cold.*

Nutrition: Calories 204, Fat 6.7g, Fiber 1.4, Carbs 7.3g, Protein 4.5g

222) ***Italian Fries***

Ingredients:

- *1/3 cup baby red potatoes*
- *1 Tbsp Italian seasoning*
- *3 Tbsps canola oil*
- *1 Tsp turmeric*
- *½ Tsp of sea salt*
- *½ Tsp dried rosemary*
- *1 Tbsp dried dill*

Direction: Servings: 4 Preparation time: 40 minutes

✓ *Cut the red potatoes into the edges and transfer them to the big container.*

✓ *Sprinkle the vegetables with Italian seasoning, sea salt, turmeric, canola oil, dried rosemary, and dried dill.*

✓ *Shake the potato wedges carefully.*

✓ *Line the baking tray with baking paper.*

✓ *Place the potatoes wedges on the tray. Flatten it well to make one layer.*

✓ *Switch on the oven, preheat it setting its temperature to 375F.*

✓ *Place the tray with potatoes in the oven, bake for 40 minutes. Stir the potatoes using the spatula from time to time.*

✓ *The potato fries are cooked when they have crunchy edges.*

Nutrition: Calories 122, Fat 11.6g, Fiber 0.5g, Carbs 4.5g, Protein 0.6g

223) ***Garlic Pinto Bean Dip***

Ingredients:

- *1 cup dry pinto beans, rinsed*
- *½ tsp cumin*
- *½ cup salsa*
- *2 garlic cloves*
- *2 chipotle peppers in adobo sauce*
- *5 cups vegetable stock*
- *Pepper*
- *Salt*

Direction: Servings: 6 Preparation time: 53 minutes

✓ *Add beans, stock, garlic, and chipotle peppers into the instant pot.*

✓ *Seal pot with lid and cook on high for 43 minutes.*

✓ *Once done, release pressure using quick release. Remove lid.*

✓ *Drain beans well and reserve ½ cup of stock.*

✓ *Transfer beans, reserve stock, and resting ingredients into the food processor and process until smooth.*

✓ *Serve and enjoy*

Nutrition: Calories 129, Fat 0.9g, Carbs 23g, Sugar 1.9g, Protein 8g

224) ***Tempeh Snack***

Ingredients:

- *11 oz soy tempeh*
- *1 Tsp olive oil*
- *½ Tsp ground black pepper*
- *¼Tsp garlic powder*

Direction: Servings: 6 Preparation time: 8 minutes

✓ *Cut soy tempeh into the sticks*

✓ *Sprinkle every tempeh stick with garlic powder, black pepper, and olive oil.*

✓ *Preheat the grill to 375F.*

✓ *Place the tempeh sticks on the grill and cook for 4 minutes on each side. Cooking time depends on the size of the tempeh sticks.*

✓ *The cooked tempeh sticks will have a light brown*

Nutrition Cal 89, Fiber 3.6g, Carbs 10.2g,Protein6.5

225) Avocado Dip

Ingredients:

- *½ cup heavy cream*
- *1 green chili pepper, chopped*
- *Salt and pepper to the taste*
- *4 avocados, pitted, peeled, and chopped*
- *1 cup cilantro, chopped*
- *¼ cup lime juice*

Direction: Servings: 8 Preparation time: 0 minutes

- ✓ *In a blender, combine the cream with the avocados and the resting ingredients and pulse well.*
- ✓ *Divide the mix into containers and serve cold as a party dip.*

Nutrition: Calories 200, Fat 14.5g, Fiber 3.8g, Carbs 8.1g, Protein 7.6g

226) Savory Pita Chips

Ingredients:

- *3 Pitas*
- *¼ cup extra-Virgin olive oil*
- *¼ cup zaatar*

Direction: Servings: 1 Preparation time: 10 minutes

- ✓ *Switch on the oven, preheat it setting its temperature to 450°F.*
- ✓ *Cut pitas into 2-inch pieces and place them in a large container.*
- ✓ *Drizzle pitas with extra-virgin olive oil, sprinkle with za'atar, and toss to coat.*
- ✓ *Spread out pitas on a baking sheet, and bake for 8 minutes or until lightly browned and crunchy.*
- ✓ *Let pita chips cool before removing them from the baking sheet. Store in an airtight container for up to 1 month.*

Nutrition: Calories 82, Fat 1g, Protein 3g, Carbs 15g, Fiber 2g

227) Artichoke Skewers

Ingredients:

- *4 prosciutto slices*
- *4 artichoke hearts, canned*
- *4 kalamata olives*
- *4 cherry tomatoes*
- *¼ Tsp cayenne pepper*
- *¼ Tsp sunflower oil*

Direction: Servings: 4 Preparation time: 0 minutes

- ✓ *Skewer prosciutto slices, artichoke hearts, kalamata olives, and cherry tomatoes on the wooden skewers.*
- ✓ *Sprinkle antipasto skewers with sunflower oil and cayenne pepper.*

Nutrition: Calories 152, Fat 3.7g, Fiber 10.8g, Carbs 23.2g, Protein 11.1g

228) Mediterranean Polenta Cups Recipe

Ingredients:

- *1 cup yellow cornmeal*
- *1 garlic clove, minced*
- *½ Tsp fresh thyme, minced or ¼ Tsp dried thyme*
- *½ Tsp salt*
- *¼ cup feta cheese, crumbled*
- *¼ Tsp pepper*
- *2 Tbsps fresh basil, chopped*
- *4 cups water*
- *4 plum tomatoes, finely chopped*

Direction: Servings: 24 Preparation time: 5 minutes

- ✓ *In a saucepan, bring the water and the salt to a boil; reduce the heat to a gentle boil. Slowly whisk to the cornmeal; cook, stirring with a wooden spoon until the polenta is thick and pulls away cleanly from the sides of the pan. Remove from the heat; stir to the pepper and the thyme.*
- ✓ *Grease miniature muffin cups with cooking spray. Spoon a heaping Tbsp of the polenta mixture into each muffin cup.*
- ✓ *With the back of a spoon, make an indentation to the center of each; cover and chill until the mixture is set.*
- ✓ *Meanwhile, combine the feta cheese, tomatoes, garlic, and basil in a small-sized container.*
- ✓ *Unmold the chilled polenta cups; place them on an ungreased baking sheet. Tops each indentation with 1 heaping Tbsp of the feta mixture. Broil the cups 4 inches from the heat source for about 5 to 7 minutes, or until heated through.*

Nutrition: Calories 26, Chol. 1mg, Sodium 62mg, Carbs 5g, Fiber 1g, Protein 1g

229) Tomato Triangles

Ingredients:

- *6 corn tortillas*
- *1 Tbsp cream cheese*
- *1 Tbsp ricotta cheese*
- *½ Tsp minced garlic*
- *1 Tbsp fresh dill, chopped*
- *2 tomatoes, sliced*

Direction: Servings: 6 Preparation time: 0 minutes

- ✓ *Cut every tortilla into 2 triangles.*
- ✓ *Then mix up together cream cheese, ricotta cheese, minced garlic, and dill.*
- ✓ *Spread 6 triangles with cream cheese mixture.*
- ✓ *Then place the sliced tomato on them and cover with resting tortilla triangles.*

Nutrition: Calories 71, Fat 1.6g, Fiber 2,1g, Carbs 12.8g, Protein 2.3g

230) Balsamic Bell Pepper Salsa

Ingredients:

- 2 red bell peppers, chopped and seeds removed
- 1 cup grape tomatoes, halved
- ½tbsp cayenne
- 1 tbsp balsamic vinegar
- 2 cup vegetable broth
- ½ cup sour bream
- ½ onion, chopped
- ½ tsp garlic powder

Direction: Servings: 2 Preparation time: 16 minutes

- ✓ Add all ingredients except cream into the instant pot and stir well.
- ✓ Seal pot with lid and cook on high for 6 minutes.
- ✓ Once done, release pressure using quick release. Remove lid.
- ✓ Add sour cream and stir well.
- ✓ Blend the salsa mixture using an immersion blender until smooth.
- ✓ Serve and enjoy.

nutrition: Calories 236, Fat 14.2g, Carbs 19.8g, Sugar 10.7g, Protein 9.2g

231) Chili Mango and Watermelon Salsa

Ingredients:

- 1 red tomato, chopped
- Salt and black pepper to the taste
- 1 cup watermelon, seedless, peeled, and cubed
- 1 red onion, chopped
- 2 mangos, peeled and chopped
- 2 chili peppers, chopped
- ¼ cup cilantro, chopped
- 3 Tbsps lime juice
- Pita chips for serving

Direction: Servings: 12 Preparation time: 0 minutes

- ✓ In a container, mix the tomato with the watermelon and the rest of the ingredients except the pita chips and toss well.
- ✓ Divide the mix into small cups and serve with pita chips on the side.

Nutrition: Calories 62, Fat 4,7g, Fiber 1.3g, Carbs 3.9g, Protein 2.3g

232) Lavash Chips

Ingredients:

- 1 lavash sheet, whole grain
- 1 Tbsp canola oil
- 1 Tsp paprika
- ½ Tsp chili pepper
- ½ Tsp salt

Direction: Servings: 4 Preparation time: 10 minutes

- ✓ To the shallow container, whisk together canola oil, paprika, chili pepper, and salt.
- ✓ Then chop lavash sheet roughly (to the shape of chips).
- ✓ Sprinkle lavash chips with oil mixture and Pour into the tray to get one thin layer.
- ✓ Bake the lavash chips for 10-11 minutes at 365F. Flip them on another side from time to time to avoid burning.
- ✓ Cool the cooked chips well.

Nutrition: Calories 73, Fat 4g, Fiber 0,7g, Carbs 8.4g, Protein 1.6g

233) Homemade Salsa

Ingredients:

- 12 oz grape tomatoes, halved
- ¼ cup fresh cilantro, chopped
- 1 fresh lime juice
- 28 oz tomatoes, crushed
- 1 tbsp garlic, minced
- 1 green bell pepper, chopped
- 1 red bell pepper, chopped
- 2 onions, chopped
- 6 whole tomatoes
- Salt

Direction: Servings: 8 Preparation time: 5 minutes

- ✓ Add whole tomatoes into the instant pot and gently smash the tomatoes.
- ✓ Add resting ingredients except for cilantro, lime juice, and salt, and stir well.
- ✓ Seal pot with lid and cook on high for 5 minutes.
- ✓ Once done, allow to release pressure naturally for 10 minutes, then release resting using quick release. Remove lid.
- ✓ Add cilantro, lime juice, and salt and stir well.
- ✓ Serve and enjoy.

Nutrition: Calories 146, Fat 1.2g, Carbohydrates 33.2g, Sugar 4g, Protein 6.9g, Cholesterol 0 mg

234) Stuffed Zucchinis

Ingredients:

- 6 zucchinis, halved lengthwise and insides scooped out
- 2 garlic cloves, minced
- 2 Tbsps oregano, chopped
- Juice of 2 lemons
- Salt and black pepper to the taste
- 2 Tbsps olive oil
- 8 ounces feta cheese, crumbled

Direction: Servings: 6 Preparation time: 40 minutes

- ✓ Put the zucchini halves on a baking sheet lined with parchment paper, divide the cheese and the rest of the ingredients in each zucchini half, and bake at 450 degrees F for 40 minutes.
- ✓ Arrange the stuffed zucchinis on a platter and serve as an appetizer.

Nutrition: Calories 88, Fat 5g, Protein 8g, Carbs 6g, Fiber 2g

235) Yogurt Dip

Ingredients:

- 2 cups Greek yogurt
- 2 Tbsps pistachios, toasted and chopped
- A pinch of salt and white pepper
- 2 Tbsps mint, chopped
- 1 Tbsp kalamata olives, pitted and chopped
- ¼ cup za'atar spice
- ¼ cup pomegranate seeds
- 1/3 cup olive oil

Direction: Servings: 6 Preparation time: 0 minutes

- ✓ In a container, combine the yogurt with the pistachios and the rest of the ingredients, whisk well, divide into small cups, serve with pita chips on the side.

Nutrition: Calories 294, Fat 18g, Carbs 21g, Protein 10g

236) Popcorn-Pine Nut Mix

Ingredients:

- 1 Tbsp olive oil
- ½ cup pine nuts
- ½ Tsp Italian seasoning
- ¼ cup popcorn, white kernels, popped
- ¼ Tsp salt
- 2 Tbsps honey
- ½ lemon zest

Direction: Servings: 10 Preparation time: 10 minutes

- ✓ Place the popped corn in a medium container.
- ✓ In a dry pan or skillet over low heat, toast the pine nuts, frequently stirring for about 4 to 5 minutes, until fragrant and some begin to brown; remove from the heat.
- ✓ Stir the oil in; add honey, Italian seasoning, lemon zest, and salt. Stir to mix and pour over the popcorn; toss the ingredients to coat the popcorn kernels with the honey syrup.
- ✓ It's alright if most of the nuts sink to the container bottom.
- ✓ Let the mixture sit for about 2 minutes to allow the honey to cool and to set stickier.
- ✓ Transfer the contents of the container to a serving dish so that the nuts are on top. Stir gently and serve.

Nutrition: Calories 80, Fat 6g, pot. 60mg, Carbs. 5g, Fiber less than 1g, Sugar 4g, Protein 2g,

237) Zucchini Cakes

Ingredients:

- 1 zucchini, grated
- ¼ carrot, grated
- ¼ onion, minced
- 1 Tsp minced garlic
- 3 Tbsps coconut flour
- 1 Tsp Italian seasonings
- 1 egg, beaten
- 1 Tsp coconut oil

Direction: Servings: 4 Preparation time: 10 minutes

- ✓ To the mixing container, combine together grated zucchini, carrot, minced onion, and garlic.
- ✓ Add coconut flour, Italian seasoning, and egg.
- ✓ Stir the mass until homogenous.
- ✓ Heat up coconut oil into the skillet.
- ✓ Place the small zucchini fritters in the hot oil. Make them with the help of the spoon.
- ✓ Roast the zucchini fritters for 4 minutes from each side.

Nutrition: Calories 63, Fat 3.3g, Fiber 3g, Carbs 6.3g, Protein 3.3g

238) Parsley Nachos

Ingredients:

- 3 oz tortilla chips
- ¼ cup Greek yogurt
- 1 Tbsp fresh parsley, chopped
- ¼ Tsp minced garlic
- 2 kalamata olives, chopped
- 1 Tsp paprika
- ¼ Tsp ground thyme

Direction: Servings: 3 Preparation time: 0 minutes

- ✓ To the mixing container, mix up together Greek yogurt, parsley, minced garlic, olives, paprika, and thyme.
- ✓ Add tortilla chips and mix up gently.
- ✓ The snack should be served immediately.

Nutrition: Calories 81, Fat 1.6g, Fiber 2.2g, Carbs 13.1g, Protein 3.5g

239) Plum Wraps

Ingredients:

- 4 plums
- 4 prosciutto slices
- ¼ Tsp olive oil

Direction: Servings: 4 Preparation time: 10 minutes

- ✓ Switch on the oven, preheat it setting its temperature to 373F.

- ✓ *Wrap every plum in prosciutto slice and secure with a toothpick (if needed).*
- ✓ *Place the wrapped plums in the oven and bake for 10 minutes.*

Nutrition: Calories 62, Fat 2.2g, Fiber 0.9g, Carbs 8g, Protein 4.3g

240) Flavorful Roasted Baby Potatoes

Ingredients

- *2 lbs baby potatoes, clean and cut in half*
- *½ cup vegetable stock*
- *1 tsp paprika*
- *¾ tsp garlic powder*
- *1 tsp onion powder*
- *2 tsp Italian seasoning*
- *1 tbsp olive oil*
- *Pepper*
- *Salt*

DIRECTIONS: Servings: 4 Preparation time: 20 minutes

- ✓ *Add oil into the inner pot of the instant pot and set the pot on sauté mode.*
- ✓ *Add potatoes and sauté for 5 minutes. Add resting ingredients and stir well.*
- ✓ *Seal pot with lid and cook on high for 5 minutes.*
- ✓ *Once done, release pressure using quick release. Remove lid.*
- ✓ *Stir well and serve.*

Nutrition: Calorie 155, Fat 4.5g, Carbs 29.8g, Sugar 0.7g, Protein 6.1g

Beef pork and lamb Recipes

241) Pear Braised Pork

Ingredients

- 3 pounds pork shoulder
- 4 Pears, peeled and sliced
- 2 shallots, sliced
- 4 garlic cloves, minced
- 1 bay leaf
- 1 thyme spring
- ½ cup apple cider
- Salt and pepper to taste

DIRECTIONS: Servings: 10 Preparation time: 2 ¼ h

- ✓ Season the pork with salt and pepper.
- ✓ Combine the pears, shallots, garlic, bay leaf, thyme, and apple cider in a deep dish baking pan.
- ✓ Place the pork over the pears, then cover the pan with aluminum foil.
- ✓ Cook to the preheated oven at 330F for 2 hours. Serve the pork and the sauce fresh.

NUTRITION: Calories 455, Fat 29.3g, Protein 32.1g, Carbs 14.9g

242) Tasty Beef Stew

Ingredients

- 2 ½ lbs beef roast, cut into chunks
- 1 cup beef broth
- ½ cup balsamic vinegar
- 1 tbsp honey
- ½ tsp red pepper flakes
- 1 tbsp garlic, minced
- Pepper
- Salt

DIRECTIONS:Servings: 4 Preparation time: 30 minutes

- ✓ In the inner pot of the instant pot, combine all ingredients and stir well.
- ✓ Cook on high for 30 minutes after sealing the pot with a lid.
- ✓ Once done, allow to release pressure naturally. Remove lid.
- ✓ Stir well and serve.

Nutrition: **Calories 562, Fat 18g, Carbs 5.7g, Sugar 4.6g, Protein 87.5g, Cholesterol 253mg**

243) Pork And Sage Couscous

Ingredients

- 2 pounds pork loin boneless and sliced
- ¾ cup veggie stock
- 2 tablespoons olive oil
- ½ tablespoon chili powder
- 2 teaspoon sage, dried
- ½ tablespoon garlic powder
- Salt and black pepper to the taste
- 2 cups couscous, cooked

DIRECTIONS:Servings: 4 Preparation time: 7 Hours

- ✓ In a slow cooker, combine the pork with the stock and the other ingredients except for the couscous, put the lid on, and cook on low for 7 hours.
- ✓ Divide the mix between plates, add the couscous on the side, sprinkle the sage on top, and serve.

NUTRITION: **Calories 270, Fat 14.5g, Fiber 9g, Carbs 16.3g, Protein 14.3g**

244) Beef And Potatoes With Tahini Sauce

Ingredients

- ½ large yellow onion
- 1 lb. ground beef
- ½ tsp. salt
- ½ tsp. ground black pepper
- 6 small red potatoes, washed
- 3 TB. extra-virgin olive oil
- 2 cups plain Greek yogurt
- ¾ cup tahini paste
- 1½ cups water
- ¼ cup fresh lemon juice
- 1 TB. minced garlic
- ½ cup pine nuts

DIRECTIONS: Servings:1/6CasserolePreparation time:35minutes

- ✓ Switch on the oven, preheat it setting its temperature to 425°F.
- ✓ Blend the yellow onion for 30 seconds in a food processor with a chopping blade.
- ✓ Transfer onion to a large container. Mix in the beef, 1 teaspoon salt, and black pepper.
- ✓ Spread beef mixture evenly to the bottom of a 9-inch casserole dish, and bake for 20 minutes.
- ✓ Cut red potatoes into 1/4-inch-thick pieces, place in a container, and toss with 2 tablespoons extra-virgin olive oil and ½ teaspoon salt.
- ✓ Bake potatoes for 20 minutes after spreading them out on a baking pan.
- ✓ In a large container, combine Greek yogurt, tahini paste, water, lemon juice, garlic, and the resting 1 teaspoon salt.
- ✓ Take the beef and potatoes out of the oven and set them aside. Transfer the potatoes to the baking dish with a spatula. Bake for another 15 minutes after adding the yogurt sauce.
- ✓ In a small pan over low heat, heat the resting 1 tablespoon extra-virgin olive oil. Add pine nuts and toast for 1 or 2 minutes.
- ✓ Remove casserole dish from the oven, spoon pine nuts over the top and serve warm with brown rice.

NUTRITION ***Calories 342, Fat 11g, Protein 31g, Carbs 30g, Fiber 6g***

*245) **Spicy Beef Chili Verde***

Ingredients

- *½ lb beef stew meat, cut into cubes*
- *¼ tsp chili powder*
- *1 tbsp olive oil*
- *1 cup chicken broth*
- *1 Serrano pepper. chopped*
- *1 tsp garlic, minced*
- *1 small onion, chopped*
- *½ cup grape tomatoes, chopped*
- *½ cup tomatillos, chopped*
- *Pepper*
- *Salt*

DIRECTIONS:Servings: *2* ***Preparation time:23 minutes***

- ✓ *Set the instant pot to sauté mode and add the oil.*
- ✓ *Add garlic and onion and sauté for 3 minutes. Add resting ingredients and stir well.*
- ✓ *Cook on high for 20 minutes after sealing the pot with a lid. Once done, allow to release pressure naturally. Remove lid.*
- ✓ *Stir well and serve.*

Nutrition: ***Calories 317, Fat 15g, Carbs 6.4g, Sugar 2.6g, Protein 37g, Cholesterol 100mg***

*246) **Coriander Pork And Chickpeas Stew***

Ingredients

- *½ cup beef stock*
- *1 tablespoon ginger, grated*
- *1 teaspoon coriander. ground*
- *z teaspoons cumin, ground*
- *Salt and black pepper to the taste*
- *2 and ½ pounds pork stew meat, cubed*
- *28 ounces canned tomatoes, drained and chopped*
- *1 red onion, chopped*
- *4 garlic cloves, minced*
- *½ cup apricots, cut into quarters*
- *15 ounces canned chickpeas, drained*
- *1 tablespoon cilantro, chopped*

DIRECTIONS:Servings: *4* ***Preparation Time:*** *8 Hours*

- ✓ *In your slow cooker, combine the meat with the stock, ginger, and the rest of the ingredients except the cilantro and the chickpeas. Put the lid on, and cook on Low for 7 hours and 40 minutes.*
- ✓ *Add the cilantro and the chickpeas, cook the stew on low for 20 minutes more, divide into containers and serve.*

NUTRITION: ***Calories 283, Fat 11.9g, Fiber 4.5g, Carbs 28.8g, Protein 25.4g***

*247) **Beef And Grape Sauce***

Ingredients

- *1-pound beef sirloin*
- *1 teaspoon molasses*
- *1 tablespoon lemon zest, grated*
- *1 teaspoon soy sauce*
- *1 chili pepper, chopped*
- *¼ teaspoon fresh ginger, minced*
- *1 cup grape juice*
- *½ teaspoon salt*
- *1 tablespoon butter*

DIRECTIONS:Servings: *4* ***Preparation time:*** *25 minutes*

- ✓ *Sprinkle the beef sirloin with salt and minced ginger.*
- ✓ *Heat up the butter into the saucepan and add meat.*
- ✓ *Roast it for 5 minutes from each side over medium heat.*
- ✓ *After this, add soy sauce, chili pepper, and grape juice.*
- ✓ *Then add lemon zest and simmer the meat for 10 minutes.*
- ✓ *Add molasses and mix up meat well.*
- ✓ *Close the lid and cook meat for 5 minutes.*
- ✓ *Serve the cooked beef with grape juice sauce.*

NUTRITION: ***Calories 267, Fat 10g, Fiber 0.2g, Carbs 7.4g, Protein 34.9g***

*248) **Lamb And Tomato Sauce***

Ingredients

- *9 oz lamb shanks*
- *1 onion, diced*
- *1 carrot, diced*
- *1 tablespoon olive oil*
- *1 teaspoon salt*
- *1 teaspoon ground black pepper*
- *1 ½ cup chicken stock*
- *1 tablespoon tomato paste*

DIRECTIONS:Servings: *3* ***Preparation time:*** *55 minutes*

- ✓ *Sprinkle the lamb shanks with salt and ground black pepper.*
- ✓ *Heat up olive oil into the saucepan.*
- ✓ *Add lamb shanks and roast them for 5 minutes from each side.*
- ✓ *Transfer meat to the plate.*
- ✓ *After this, add onion and carrot to the saucepan.*
- ✓ *Roast the vegetables for 3 minutes.*

✓ Add tomato paste and mix up well.

✓ Then add chicken stock and bring the liquid to a boil.

✓ Add lamb shanks, stir well and close the lid.

✓ Cook the meat for 40 minutes over medium-low heat.

NUTRITION: Calories 232, Fat 11.3g, Fiber 1.7g, Carbs 7g, Protein 25g

249) Lamb And Sweet Onion Sauce

Ingredients

- 2 pounds lamb meat, cubed
- 1 tablespoon sweet paprika
- Salt and black pepper to the taste
- 1 and ½ cups veggie stock
- 4 garlic cloves, minced
- 2 tablespoons olive oil
- 1 pound sweet onion, chopped
- 1 cup balsamic vinegar

DIRECTIONS:Servings: 4 **Preparation time:** 40 minutes

✓ Heat up a pot with the oil over medium heat, add the onion, vinegar. Salt and pepper, stir and cook for 10 minutes.

✓ Add the meat and the rest of the ingredients. Toss, bring to a simmer, and cook over medium heat for 30 minutes.

✓ Divide the mix between plates and serve.

Nutrition: Calories 303, Fat 12.3g, Fiber 7g, Carbs 15g, Protein 17g

250) Pork And Mustard Shallots Mix

Ingredients

- 3 shallots, chopped
- 1 pound pork loin, cut into strips
- ½ cup veggie stock
- 2 tablespoons olive oil
- A pinch of salt and black pepper
- 2 teaspoons mustard
- 1 tablespoon parsley, chopped

DIRECTIONS:Servings: 4 **Preparation time:** 25 minutes

✓ Heat up a pan with the oil over medium-high heat, add the shallots and sauté for 5 minutes.

✓ Add the meat and cook for 10 minutes tossing it often.

✓ Toss in the remaining ingredients, cook for another 10 minutes, divide between plates, and serve right away.

NUTRITION: **Calories 296, Fat 12.5g, Fiber 9.3g, Carbs 13.3g, Protein 22.5g**

251) Ground Pork Salad

Ingredients

- 1 cup ground pork
- ½ onion, diced
- 4 bacon slices
- 1 teaspoon sesame oil
- 1 teaspoon butter
- 1 cup lettuce, chopped
- 1 tablespoon lemon juice
- 4 eggs, boiled
- ½ teaspoon salt
- 1 teaspoon chili pepper
- ¼ teaspoon liquid honey

DIRECTIONS:Servings: 8 **Preparation time:** 15 minutes

✓ Make burgers: to the mixing container, combine together ground pork, diced onion, salt, and chili pepper.

✓ Blake the medium size burgers.

✓ Melt butter into the skillet and add prepared burgers.

✓ Roast them for 5 minutes from each side over medium heat.

✓ When the burgers are cooked, chill them a little.

✓ Place the bacon into the skillet and roast it until golden brown. Then chill the bacon and chop it roughly.

✓ To the salad container, combine together chopped bacon, sesame oil, lettuce, lemon juice, and honey. Mix up salad well.

✓ Peel the eggs and cut them on the halves.

✓ Arrange the eggs and burgers over the salad. Don't mix salad anymore.

NUTRITION: **Calories 213, Fat 15.5g, Fiber 0.1g, Carbs 1.5g, Protein 16.5g**

252) . Beef And Dill Mushrooms

Ingredients

- 1 cup cremini mushrooms, sliced
- 4 oz beef loin, sliced onto the wedges
- 1 tablespoon olive oil
- 1 teaspoon dried oregano
- ½ cup of water
- ¼ cup cream
- 1 teaspoon tomato paste
- 1 teaspoon ground black pepper
- 1 teaspoon salt
- 1 tablespoon fresh dill, chopped

DIRECTIONS:Servings: 3 **Preparation time:** 35 minutes

✓ Into the saucepan, combine together olive oil and cremini mushrooms.

✓ Add dried oregano, ground black pepper, salt, and

dill. Mix up.

- ✓ *Cook the mushrooms for 2-3 minutes and add sliced beef loin.*
- ✓ *Cook the ingredients for 5 minutes over medium heat.*
- ✓ *After this, add cream, water, tomato paste, and mix up the meal*
- ✓ *Simmer the beef stroganoff for 25 minutes over medium heat*

Nutrition:* *Calories 196, Fat 11.8g, Fiber 0.8g, Carbs 3.5g, Protein 20g

253) Beef Pitas

Ingredients

- *1 ½ cup ground beef*
- *½ red onion, diced*
- *1 teaspoon minced garlic*
- *¼ cup fresh spinach, chopped*
- *1 teaspoon salt*
- *½ teaspoon chili pepper*
- *1 teaspoon dried oregano*
- *1 teaspoon fresh mint, chopped*
- *4 tablespoons Plain yogurt*
- *1 cucumber, grated*
- *½ teaspoon dill*
- *½ teaspoon garlic powder*
- *4 pitta bread*

***DIRECTIONS:Servings:* 4 *Preparation time:* 15 minutes**

- ✓ *To the mixing container, combine together ground beef, onion, minced garlic, spinach, salt, chili pepper, and dried oregano.*
- ✓ *Form the medium size balls from the meat mixture.*
- ✓ *Line the baking tray with baking paper and arrange the meatballs inside.*
- ✓ *Bake the meatballs for 15 minutes at 375F. Flip them on another side after 10 minutes of cooking.*
- ✓ *Meanwhile, make tzatziki: combine together fresh mint, yogurt, grated cucumber, dill, and garlic powder. Whisk the mixture for 1 minute.*
- ✓ *When the meatballs are cooked, place the over pitta bread and top with tzatziki.*

NUTRITION: Calorie 253, Fat 7g, Fiber 4g, Carbs 30g, Protein 16.3g

254) Lamb And Peanuts Mix

Ingredients

- *2 tablespoons lime juice*
- *1 tablespoon balsamic vinegar*
- *5 garlic cloves, minced*
- *2 tablespoons olive oil*
- *Salt and black pepper to the taste*
- *1 and ½ pound lamb meat, cubed*
- *3 tablespoons peanuts, toasted and chopped*
- *2 scallions, chopped*

DIRECTIONS: Servings: 4 Preparation time: 20 minutes

- ✓ *Cook the meat for 4 minutes on each side in a pan with the oil over medium-high heat.*
- ✓ *Add the scallions and the garlic and sauté for 2 minutes more.*
- ✓ *Toss in the remaining ingredients, cook for another 10 minutes, divide between plates, and serve right away.*

Nutrition: Calories 300, Fat 14.5g, Fiber 9g, Carbs 15.7g, Protein 17.5g

255) Cheddar Lamb And Zucchinis

Ingredients

- *1 pound lamb meat, cubed*
- *1 tablespoon avocado oil*
- *2 cups zucchinis, chopped*
- *½ cup red onion, chopped*
- *Salt and black pepper to the taste*
- *15 ounces canned roasted tomatoes, crushed*
- *¾ cup cheddar cheese, shredded*

***Directions: Servings:* 4 *Preparation Time:* 30 Minutes**

- ✓ *Heat up a pan with the oil over medium-high heat, add the meat and the onion, and brown for 5 minutes.*
- ✓ *Add the rest of the ingredients except the cheese, bring to a simmer and cook over medium heat for 20 minutes.*
- ✓ *Add the cheese, cook everything for 3 minutes more, divide between plates and serve.*

Nutrition:* *Calories 306, Fat 16.4g, Fiber 12.3g, Carbs 15.5g, Protein 18.5g

256) Fennel Pork

Ingredients

- *2 pork loin roast, trimmed and boneless*
- *Salt and black pepper to the taste*
- *3 garlic cloves. minced*
- *2 teaspoons fennel, around*
- *1 tablespoon fennel seeds*
- *2 teaspoons red pepper, crushed*
- *¼ cup olive oil*

***Directions: Servings:* 4 *Preparation Time:* 2 Hours**

- ✓ *In a roasting pan, combine the pork with salt, pepper, and the rest of the ingredients, toss, introduce to the oven and bake at 38 degrees F for 2 hours.*
- ✓ *Slice the roast, divide between plates and serve with a side salad.*

Nutrition:* *Calories 300, Fat 4g, Fiber 2g, Carbs 6g, Protein 15g

257) Lamb And Feta Artichokes

Ingredients

- *2 pounds lamb shoulder*
- *2 spring onions, chopped*
- *1 tablespoon olive oil*
- *3 Garlic cloves, minced*
- *1 tablespoon lemon juice*
- *Salt and black pepper to the taste*
- *1 and ½ cups veggie stock*
- *Six ounces canned artichoke hearts. drained and quartered*
- *½ cup feta cheese, crumbled*
- *2 tablespoons parsley, chopped*

Directions: Servings: *6* ***Preparation Time:*** *8 Hours*

- ✓ *Heat up a pan with the oil over medium-high heat, add the lamb, brown for 5 minutes, and transfer to your slow cooker.*
- ✓ *Add the rest of the ingredients except the parsley and the cheese, put the lid on, and cook on low for 8 hours.*
- ✓ *Add the cheese and the parsley, divide the mix between plates and serve.*

Nutrition:** **Calories 330, Fat 14.5g, Fiber 14.1g, Carbs 21.7g, Protein 17.5g

258) Lamb And Plums Mix

Ingredients

- *4 lamb shanks*
- *1 red onion, chopped*
- *2 tablespoons olive oil*
- *1 cup plums, pitted and halved*
- *1 tablespoon sweet paprika*
- *2 cups chicken stock*
- *Salt and pepper to the taste*

Directions: Servings: *4* ***Preparation Time:*** *6 Hours And 10 Minutes*

- ✓ *Heat up a pan with the oil over medium-high heat, add the lamb, brown for 5 minutes on each side, and transfer to your slot cooker.*
- ✓ *Add the rest of the ingredients, put the lid on, and cook on High for 6 hours.*
- ✓ *Divide the mix between plates and serve right away.*

Nutrition:** **Calories 295, Fat 13g, Fiber 9.7g, Carbs 15.7g, Protein 14.3g

259) Lamb And Mango Sauce

Ingredients

- *2 cups Greek yogurt*
- *1 cup mango, peeled and cubed*
- *1 yellow onion, chopped*
- *1/3 cup parsley, chopped*
- *1 pound lamb, cubed*
- *½ teaspoon red pepper Blakes*
- *Salt and black pepper to the taste*
- *2 tablespoons olive oil*
- *¼ teaspoon cinnamon powder*

Directions: Servings: *4* ***Preparation time:*** *1 Hour*

- ✓ *Heat up a pan with the oil over medium-high heat, add the meat, and brown for 5 minutes.*
- ✓ *Add the onion and sauté for 5 minutes more.*
- ✓ *Add the rest of the ingredients, toss, bring to a simmer and cook over medium heat for 45 minutes.*
- ✓ *Divide everything between plates and serve.*

Nutrition:** **Calories 300, Fat 15.3g, Fiber 9.1g, Carbs 15.8g, Protein 15.5g

260) Pork Chops And Cherries Mix

Ingredients

- *4 pork chops. boneless*
- *Salt and black pepper to the taste*
- *½ cup cranberry juice*
- *1 and ½ teaspoons spin mustard*
- *½ cup dark cherries pitted and halved*
- *Cooling spray*

Directions: Servings: 4 Preparation time: 12 minutes

- ✓ *Heat up a pan greased with the cooking spray over medium-high heat, add the pork chops, cook them for 5 minutes on each side, and divide between plates.*
- ✓ *Heat up the same pan over medium heat, add the cranberry juice and the rest of the ingredients, whisk, bring to a simmer, cook for 2 minutes, drizzle over the pork chops and serve.*

Nutrition:** **Calories 262g, Fat 8g, Fiber 1g, Carbs 16g, Protein 30g

261) Lambo And Barley Mix

Ingredients

- *2 tablespoons olive oil*
- *1 cup barley soaked overnight, drained, and rinsed*
- *1 pound lamb meat, cubed*
- *1 red onion, chopped*
- *4 garlic cloves, minced*
- *3 carrots, chopped*
- *6 tablespoons dill, chopped*
- *2 tablespoons tomato paste*
- *3 cups veggie stock*
- *A pinch of salt and black pepper*

Directions: Servings: *4* ***Preparation time:*** *8 Hours*

- ✓ *Heat up a pan with the oil over medium-high heat, add the meat, brown for 5 minutes on each side and transfer to your slot cooker*

- ✓ *Add the barley, the rest of the ingredients and put the lid on, and cook on low for 8 hours.*
- ✓ *Divide everything between plates and serve.*

***Nutrition:* Calories 292g, Fat 12g, Fiber 8.7g, Carbs 16.7, Protein 7.2g**

262) Cashew Beef Stir Fry

Ingredients

- *¼ cup coconut aminos*
- *1 ½ pound ground beef*
- *1 cup raw cashews*
- *1 green bell pepper, julienned*
- *1 red bell pepper, julienned*
- *1 small canned water chestnut, sliced*
- *1 onion, sliced*
- *1 tablespoon garlic, minced*
- *2 tablespoon ginger, grated*
- *2 teaspoon coconut oil*
- *Salt and pepper to taste*

***Directions: Servings:* 8 *Preparation Time:* 15 Minutes**

- ✓ *Add raw cashews to a skillet that has been heated over medium heat. Toast for a couple of minutes or until slightly brown. Set aside.*
- ✓ *To the same skillet, add the coconut oil and sauté the ground beef for 5 minutes or until brow.*
- ✓ *Add the garlic, ginger and season with coconut aminos. Stir for one minute before adding the onions, bell peppers, and water chestnuts. Cook until the vegetables are almost soft.*
- ✓ *Season with salt and pepper to taste.*
- ✓ *Add the toasted cashews last.*

***Nutrition:* Calories 325, Fat 22g, Carbs 12.4g, Protein 19g**

263) Lamb And Zucchini Mix

Ingredients

- *2 pounds lamb stew meat, cubed*
- *1 and ½ tablespoons avocado oil*
- *3 zucchinis, sliced*
- *1 brown onion, chopped*
- *3 garlic cloves, minced*
- *1 tablespoon thyme, dried*
- *2 teaspoons sage, dried*
- *1 cup chicken stock*
- *2 tablespoons tomato paste*

***Directions: Servings:* 4 *Preparation Time:* 4 Hours**

- ✓ *In a slow cooker, combine the lamb with the oil, zucchinis, and the rest of the ingredients, toss, put the lid on and cook on High for 4 hours.*
- ✓ *Divide the mix between plates and serve right away.*

***Nutrition:* Calories 270, Fat 14.5g, Fiber 10g, Carbs 20g, Protein 13.3g**

264) Pork And Green Beans Mix

Ingredients

- *1 cup ground pork*
- *1 sweet pepper, chopped*
- *1 oz green beans, chopped*
- *½ onion, sliced*
- *2 oz Parmesan, grated*
- *¼ cup chicken stock*
- *1 teaspoon olive oil*
- *½ teaspoon cayenne pepper*
- *1 teaspoon dried oregano*
- *½ teaspoon dried basil*
- *1 teaspoon paprika*
- *½ cup crushed tomatoes, canned*

Directions: Servings: 3 Preparation time: 35 minutes

- ✓ *Pour olive oil into the saucepan and heat it up.*
- ✓ *Add ground pork and cook it for 2 minutes.*
- ✓ *Then stir it carefully and sprinkle with cayenne pepper, dried oregano, dried basil, and paprika.*
- ✓ *Roast the meat for 5 minutes more and add green beans, sweet pepper, and sliced onion.*
- ✓ *Add chicken stock and crushed tomatoes.*
- ✓ *Mix up the ground pork and close the lid.*
- ✓ *Cook the meal for 20 minutes over medium heat. Stir it from time to time.*
- ✓ *Then sprinkle the bolognese meat with Parmesan and mix up well.*
- ✓ *Cook the meal for 5 minutes more.*

***Nutrition:* Calories 257, Fat 16.6g, Fiber 1.9g, Carbs 6.2g, Protein 20.9g**

265) Oregano And Pesto Lamb

Ingredients

- *2 pounds pork shoulder, boneless and cubed*
- *¼ cup olive oil*
- *2 teaspoons oregano, dried*
- *¼ cup lemon juice*
- *3 garlic cloves, minced*
- *2 teaspoons basil pesto*
- *Salt and black pepper to the taste*

Directions: Servings: 4 Preparation time: 25 minutes

- ✓ *Heat up a pan with the oil over medium-high heat, add the pork, and brown for 5 minutes.*
- ✓ *Add the rest of the ingredients, cook for 20 minutes more, tossing the mix from time to time, divide between plates and serve.*

***Nutrition:* Calories 297, Fat 14.5g, Fiber 9.3g, Carbs**

16.8g, Protein 22.2g

266) Chili Pork Meatballs

Ingredients

- *1 pound pork meat, ground*
- *½ cup parsley, chopped*
- *1 cup yellow onion, chopped*
- *4 garlic cloves, minced*
- *1 tablespoon ginger, grated*
- *1 Thai chili, chopped*
- *2 tablespoons olive oil*
- *1 cup veggie stock*
- *2 tablespoons sweet paprika*

***Directions:Servings:** 4 **Preparation time:** 20 minutes*

- ✓ *In a container, mix the pork with the other ingredients except for the oil, stock, and paprika, stir well and shape medium meatballs out of this mix.*
- ✓ *Heat up a pan with the oil over medium-high heat, add the meatballs and cook for 4 minutes on each side.*
- ✓ *Add the stock and the paprika, toss gently, simmer everything over medium heat for 12 minutes more. Divide into containers and serve.*

Nutrition: Cal 224, Fat 18g, Carbs 11.3g, Protein 14.4g

267) Square Meat Pies (Sfeeha)

Ingredients

- *1 large yellow onion*
- *2 large tomatoes*
- *One lb. ground beef*
- *¼ tsp. ground black pepper*
- *¼ tsp salt*
- *1 tsp. seven spices*
- *1 batch Multipurpose Dough*

Directions: Servings: 1 Preparation time: 20 minutes

- ✓ *Switch on the oven, preheat it setting its temperature to 425F.*
- ✓ *In a food processor with a chopping blade, pulse yellow onion and tomatoes for 30 seconds.*
- ✓ *Transfer tomato-onion mixture to a large container. Add beef, salt, black pepper, and seven spices and mix well.*
- ✓ *Form Multipurpose Dough into 18 balls and roll out to 4-inch circles. Spoon 2 tablespoons of meat mixture onto the center of each dough circle. Pinch together the two opposite sides of dough up to the meat mixture and pinch the opposite two sides together, forming a square. Place meat pies on a baking sheet and bake for 20 mins.*
- ✓ *Serve warm or at room temperature.*

Nutrition Cal 497, Fat 26g, Protein 34g, Carbs 38g, Fiber 9g

268) Lamb And Wine Sauce

Ingredients

- *2 tablespoons olive oil*
- *2 pounds leg of lamb, trimmed and sliced*
- *3 garlic cloves, chopped*
- *2 yellow onions, chopped*
- *3 cups veggie stock*
- *2 cups dry red wine*
- *2 tablespoons tomato paste*
- *4 tablespoons avocado oil*
- *1 teaspoon thyme, chopped*
- *Salt and black pepper to the taste*

Directions: Servings: 6 Preparation Time: 2 Hours And 40 Minutes

- ✓ *Heat up a pan with the oil over medium-high heat, add the meat, brown for 5 minutes on each side, and transfer to a roasting pan.*
- ✓ *Heat up the pan again over medium heat, add the avocado oil, add the onions and garlic and sauté for 5 minutes.*
- ✓ *Add the resting ingredients, stir, bring to a simmer and cook for 10 minutes.*
- ✓ *Pour the sauce over the meat, introduce the pan to the oven, and bake at 370 degrees F for 2 hours and 20 minutes.*
- ✓ *Divide onto plates and serve.*

Nutrition:** **Calories 273, Fat 21g, Fiber 11.1g, Carbs 16.2g, Protein 18g

269) Pork Meatloaf

Ingredients

- *1 red onion, chopped*
- *Cooling spray*
- *2 garlic cloves, minced*
- *2 pounds pork stem, ground*
- *1 cup almond milk*
- *¼ cup feta cheese, crumbled*
- *2 eggs, whisked*
- *1/3 cup kalamata olives, pitted and chopped*
- *4 tablespoons oregano, chopped*
- *Salt and black pepper to the taste*

Directions: Servings: 6 Preparation Time: 1 Hour And 20 Minutes

- ✓ *In a container, mix the meat with the onion, garlic, and the other ingredients except for the cooking spray, stir well, shape sour meatloaf, and put it in a loaf pan greased with a cooking spray.*
- ✓ *Bake the meatloaf at 370 degrees F for 1 hour and 20 minutes.*
- ✓ *Serve the meatloaf warm.*

***Nutrition:* Cal 350, Fat 23g, Fiber 1g, Carbs 17g, Protein 24g**

270) Lamb And Rice

Ingredients

- *1 tablespoon lime juice*
- *1 yellow onion, chopped*
- *1 pound lamb, cubed*
- *1-ounce avocado oil*
- *2 garlic cloves, minced*
- *Salt and black pepper to the taste*
- *2 cups veggie stock*
- *1 cup brown rice*
- *A handful of parsley, chopped*

Directions: Servings: 4 Preparation time: 1 Hour and 10 minutes

- ✓ *Heat up a pan with the avocado oil over medium-high heat, add the onion, stir and sauté for 5 minutes.*
- ✓ *Add the meat and brown for 5 minutes more.*
- ✓ *Add the rest of the ingredients except the parsley, bring to a simmer and cook over medium heat for 1 hour.*
- ✓ *Add the parsley, toss, divide everything between plates, and serve.*

***Nutrition:* Calories 302, Fat 13g, Fiber 10.7g, Carbs 15.7g, Protein 14.3g**

271) Italian Beef

Ingredients

- *1 lb ground beef*
- *1 tbsp olive oil*
- *½ cup mozzarella cheese, shredded*
- *½ cup tomato puree*
- *1 tsp basil*
- *1 tsp oregano*
- *½ onion, chopped*
- *1 carrot, chopped*
- *14 oz canned tomatoes, diced*
- *Pepper*
- *Salt*

Directions: Servings: 4 Preparation time: 35 minutes

- ✓ *Set the instant pot to sauté mode and add the oil.*
- ✓ *Add onion and sauté for 2 minutes.*
- ✓ *Add meat and sauté until bronzed.*
- ✓ *Add resting ingredients except for cheese and stir well.*
- ✓ *Seal pot with lid and cook on high for 35 minutes.*
- ✓ *Once done, release pressure using quick release. Remove lid.*
- ✓ *Add cheese and stir well and cook in sauté mode until cheese is melted.*
- ✓ *Serve and enjoy.*

***Nutrition:* Calorie 298, Fat 11.3g, Carbs 11g, Sugar 6.2g, Protein 37g, Chol 103mg**

272) Pork Chops And Peppercorns Mix

Ingredients

- *1 cup red onion, sliced*
- *1 tablespoon black peppercorns, crushed*
- *¼ cup veggie stock*
- *5 garlic cloves, minced*
- *A pinch of salt and black pepper*
- *2 tablespoons olive oil*
- *4 pork chops*

Directions: Servings: 4 Preparation time: 20 minutes

- ✓ *Heat up a pan with the oil over medium-high heat, add the pork chops, and brown for 4 minutes on each side.*
- ✓ *Add the onion and the garlic and cook for 2 minutes more.*
- ✓ *Add the rest of the ingredients, cook everything for 10 minutes, tossing the mix from time to time, divide between plates and serve.*

***Nutrition:* Calories 232, Fat 9.2g, Fiber 5.6g, Carbs 13.3g, Protein 24.2g**

273) Pork And Tomato Meatloaf

Ingredients

- *2 cups ground pork*
- *1 egg, beaten*
- *¼ cup crushed tomatoes*
- *1 teaspoon salt*
- *1 teaspoon ground black pepper*
- *1 oz Swiss cheese, grated*
- *1 teaspoon minced garlic*
- *1/3 onion, diced*
- *¼ cup black olives, chopped*
- *1 jalapeno pepper, chopped*
- *1 teaspoon dried basil*
- *Cooking spray*

Directions: Servings: 8 Preparation Time: 55 Minutes

- ✓ *Spray the loaf mold with cooking spray.*
- ✓ *Then combine together ground pork, egg, crushed tomatoes, salt, ground black pepper. Grated Swiss cheese, minced garlic, onion, olives, jalapeno pepper, and dried basil.*
- ✓ *Stir the mass until it is homogenous and transfer it to the prepared load mold.*
- ✓ *Flatten the surface of the meatloaf well and cover with foil.*
- ✓ *Bake the meatloaf for 40 minutes at 375F.*

- ✓ Then discard the foil and bake the meal for 15 minutes more.
- ✓ Chill the cooked meatloaf to room temperature, and then remove it from the loaf mold.
- ✓ Slice it on the servings.

Nutrition: Calories 263, Fat 18.3g, Fiber 0.6g, Carbs 1.9g, Protein 22g

274) Beef And Eggplant Moussaka

Ingredients

- 1 small eggplant, sliced
- 1 teaspoon olive oil
- ½ cup cream
- 1 egg, beaten
- 1 tablespoon wheat flour, whole grain
- 1 teaspoon cornstarch
- 3 oz Romano cheese, grated
- ½ cup ground beef
- ¼ teaspoon minced garlic
- 1 tablespoon Italian parsley, chopped
- 3 tablespoons tomato sauce
- ¾ teaspoon ground nutmeg

Directions: Servings: 3 **Preparation Time:** 50 Minutes

- ✓ Sprinkle the eggplants with olive oil and ground nutmeg and arrange them to the casserole mold in one layer.
- ✓ After this, place the ground beef into the skillet.
- ✓ Add minced garlic, Italian parsley, and ground nutmeg.
- ✓ Then add tomato sauce and mix up the mixture well.
- ✓ Roast it for 10 minutes over medium heat.
- ✓ Make the sauce: into the saucepan, whisk together cream with egg.
- ✓ Bring the liquid to a boil (simmer it constantly) and add wheat flour, cornstarch, and cheese. Stir well.
- ✓ Bring the liquid to a boil and stir till cheese is melted. Remove the sauce from the heat.
- ✓ Put the cooked ground beef over the eggplants and flatten well.
- ✓ Pour the cream sauce over the ground beef.
- ✓ Cover the meal with foil and secure the edges.
- ✓ Bake moussaka for 30 minutes at 365F.

Nutrition: Calories 270, Fat 16.1g, Fiber 5.9g, Carbs 15.4g, Protein 17.6g

275) Hearty Meat And Potatoes

Ingredients

- 1 lb. ground beef or lamb
- ¼ cup extra-Virgin olive oil
- 1 large yellow onion, chopped
- 5 large potatoes, peeled and cubed
- ½ tsp salt
- 1 TB. Seven spices
- ½ tsp. ground black pepper

DIRECTIONS: Servings: 2 Cups Preparation time: 30 minutes

- ✓ Brown beef for 5 minutes in a large 3-quart pot over medium heat, breaking up chunks with a wooden spoon.
- ✓ Cook for 5 minutes with extra-virgin olive oil and yellow onion.
- ✓ Toss in potatoes, salt, seven spices, and black pepper—cover and cook for a total of 10 minutes. Cook for another 10 minutes, tossing gently.
- ✓ Serve warm with a side of Greek yogurt.

Nutrition Calories 412, Fat 7g, Protein 19g, Carbs 81g, Fiber 9g

276) Ita Sandwiches

Ingredients

- 1 lb. ground beef
- 1 tsp. Salt
- ½ tsp. ground black pepper
- 1 tsp. seven spices
- 4 (6 or 7 in.) pitas

Directions: Servings: 1 Pita Sandwich Preparation time: 20 minutes

- ✓ Switch on the oven, preheat it setting its temperature to 400°F.
- ✓ In a medium container, combine beef, salt, black pepper, and seven spices.
- ✓ Place pitas on the counter and divide the beef mixture evenly among them, spreading beef to the edge of the pitas.
- ✓ Place pitas on a baking sheet and bake for 20 minutes.
- ✓ Serve warm with Greek yogurt.

Nutrition Calories 880, Fat 45g, Carbs 71g, Fiber 3g, Protein 47g

277) Lamb And Dill Apples

Ingredients

- 3 green apples, cored, peeled, and cubed
- Juice of 1 lemon
- 1 pound lamb stew meat, cubed
- 1 small bunch of dill, chopped
- 3 ounces heavy cream
- 2 tablespoon olive oil
- Salt and black pepper to the taste

Directions: Servings: 4 **Preparation Time:** 25 Minutes

- ✓ Heat up a pan with the oil over medium-high heat, add the lamb, and brown for 5 minutes.
- ✓ Add the rest of the ingredients, bring to a simmer and cook over medium heat for 20 minutes.

✓ Divide the mix between plates and serve.
Nutrition: Calories 328, Fat 16.7g, Fiber 10.5g, Carbs 21.6g, Protein 14.7g

278) Tomatoes And Carrots Pork Mix

Ingredients

- 2 tablespoons olive oil
- ½ cup chicken stock
- 1 tablespoon ginger, grated
- Salt and black pepper to the taste
- 2 and ½ pounds pork meat, roughly cubed
- 2 cups tomatoes, chopped
- 4 ounces carrots, chopped
- 1 tablespoon cilantro, chopped

Directions: Servings: 4

Preparation Time: 7 Hours

✓ In your slow cooker, combine the oil with the stock ginger and the rest of the ingredients, put the lid on, and cook on Low for 7 hours.

✓ Divide the mix between plates and serve.
NUTRITION: Calories 303, Fat 13g, Fiber 8.6g, Carbs 14.9g, Protein 10.8g

279) Greek Beef Meatballs

Ingredients

- 2 pounds ground beef
- 6 garlic cloves. minced
- 1 teaspoon dried mint
- 1 teaspoon dried oregano
- 1 shallot, finely chopped
- 1 carrot, grated
- 1 egg
- 1 tablespoon tomato paste
- 3 tablespoons chopped parsley
- Salt and pepper to taste

Directions: Servings: 8 Preparation Time: 1 Hour

✓ Combine all the ingredients in a container and mix well.

✓ Season with salt and pepper, then form small meatballs and place them in a baking tray lined with baking paper.

✓ Bake to the preheated oven at 350F for 25 minutes.

✓ Serve the meatballs warm and fresh.
NUTRITION: Calories 230, Fat 7.7g, Carbs 2.4g, Protein 35.5g

280) Moist Shredded Beef

Ingredients:

- 2 lbs beef chuck roast, cut into chunks
- 1/2 tbsp dried red pepper
- 1 tbsp Italian seasoning
- 1 tbsp garlic, minced
- 2 tbsp vinegar
- 14 oz canned fire-roasted tomatoes
- 1/2 cup bell pepper, chopped
- 1/2 cup carrots, chopped
- 1 cup onion, chopped
- 1 tsp salt

Direction: Preparation Time: 10 minutes Cooking Time: 20 minutes Servings: 8

✓ Set the instant pot to sauté mode and add all of the ingredients to the inner pot.

✓ Cook on high for 20 minutes after sealing the pot with a lid.

✓ Once done, release pressure using quick release. Remove lid.

✓ Shred the meat using a fork.

✓ Stir well and serve.
Nutrition: Calories 456 Fat 32.7 g Carbohydrates 7.7 g Sugar 4.1 g Protein 31 g Cholesterol 118 mg

281) Hearty Beef Ragu

Ingredients:

- 1 1/2 lbs beef steak, diced
- 1 1/2 cup beef stock
- 1 tbsp coconut amino
- 14 oz canned tomatoes, chopped
- 1/2 tsp ground cinnamon
- 1 tsp dried oregano
- 1 tsp dried thyme
- 1 tsp dried basil
- 1 tsp paprika
- 1 bay leaf
- 1 tbsp garlic, chopped
- 1/2 tsp cayenne pepper
- 1 celery stick, diced
- 1 carrot, diced
- 1 onion, diced
- 2 tbsp olive oil
- 1/4 tsp pepper
- 1 1/2 tsp sea salt

Direction: Preparation Time: 10 minutes Cooking Time: 50 minutes Servings: 4

✓ Set the instant pot to sauté mode and add the oil.

✓ Add celery, carrots, onion, and salt and sauté for 5 minutes.

✓ Add meat and resting ingredients and stir everything well.

✓ Cook on high for 30 minutes after sealing the pot with a lid.

✓ Allow 10 minutes for pressure to naturally release before releasing resting pressure with the quick release. Remove lid.

✓ Shred meat using a fork. Set pot on sauté mode and cook for 10 minutes. Stir every 2-3 minutes.

✓ Serve and enjoy.

Nutrition: Calories 435 Fat 18.1 g Carbohydrates 12.3 g Sugar 5.5 g Protein 54.4 g Cholesterol 152 mg

282) Dill Beef Brisket

Ingredients:

- 2 1/2 lbs beef brisket, cut into cubes
- 2 1/2 cups beef stock
- 2 tbsp dill, chopped
- 1 celery stalk, chopped
- 1 onion, sliced
- 1 tbsp garlic, minced
- Pepper
- Salt

Direction: Preparation Time: 10 minutes Cooking Time: 50 minutes Servings: 4

✓ In the inner pot of the instant pot, combine all ingredients and stir well.

✓ Seal pot with lid and cook on high for 50 minutes.

✓ Allow 10 minutes for pressure to naturally release before releasing resting pressure with the quick release. Remove lid.

✓ Serve and enjoy.

Nutrition: Calories 556 Fat 18.1 g Carbohydrates 4.3 g Sugar 1.3 g Protein 88.5 g Cholesterol 253 mg

283) Tasty Beef Stew

Ingredients:

- 2 1/2 lbs beef roast, cut into chunks
- 1 cup beef broth
- 1/2 cup balsamic vinegar
- 1 tbsp honey
- 1/2 tsp red pepper flakes
- 1 tbsp garlic, minced
- Pepper
- Salt

Direction: Preparation Time: 10 minutes Cooking Time: 30 minutes Servings: 4

✓ In the inner pot of the instant pot, combine all ingredients and stir well.

✓ Cook on high for 30 minutes after sealing the pot with a lid.

✓ Once done, allow to release pressure naturally. Remove lid.

✓ Stir well and serve.

Nutrition: Calories 562 Fat 18.1 g Carbohydrates 5.7 g Sugar 4.6 g Protein 87.4 g Cholesterol 253 mg

284) Flavorful Beef Bourguignon

Ingredients:

- 1 1/2 lbs beef chuck roast, cut into chunks
- 2/3 cup beef stock
- 2 tbsp fresh thyme
- 1 bay leaf
- 1 tsp garlic, minced
- 8 oz mushrooms, sliced
- 2 tbsp tomato paste
- 2/3 cup dry red wine
- 1 onion, sliced
- 4 carrots, cut into chunks
- 1 tbsp olive oil
- Pepper
- Salt

Direction: Preparation Time: 10 minutes Cooking Time: 20 minutes Servings: 4

✓ Set the instant pot to sauté mode and add the oil.

✓ Add meat and sauté until brown. Add onion and sauté until softened.

✓ Add resting ingredients and stir well.

✓ Seal pot with lid and cook on high for 12 minutes.

✓ Once done, allow to release pressure naturally. Remove lid.

✓ Stir well and serve.

Nutrition: Calories 744 Fat 51.3 g Carbohydrates 14.5 g Sugar 6.5 g Protein 48.1 g Cholesterol 175 mg

285) Delicious Beef Chili

Ingredients:

- 2 lbs ground beef
- 1 tsp olive oil
- 1 tsp garlic, minced
- 1 small onion, chopped
- 2 tbsp chili powder
- 1 tsp oregano
- 1/2 tsp thyme
- 28 oz canned tomatoes, crushed
- 2 cups beef stock
- 2 carrots, chopped
- 3 sweet potatoes, peeled and cubed
- Pepper
- Salt

Direction: Preparation Time: 10 minutes Cooking Time: 35 minutes Servings: 8

✓ Set the instant pot to sauté mode and add the oil.

✓ Add meat and cook until brown.

✓ Add resting ingredients and stir well.

✓ Seal pot with lid and cook on high for 35 minutes.

✓ Once done, allow to release pressure naturally. Remove lid.

✓ Stir well and serve.

Nutrition: Calories 302 Fat 8.2 g Carbohydrates 19.2 g Sugar 4.8 g Protein 37.1 g Cholesterol 101 mg

286) Rosemary Creamy Beef

Ingredients:

- *2 lbs beef stew meat, cubed*
- *2 tbsp fresh parsley, chopped*
- *1 tsp garlic, minced*
- *1/2 tsp dried rosemary*
- *1 tsp chili powder*
- *1 cup beef stock*
- *1 cup heavy cream*
- *1 onion, chopped*
- *1 tbsp olive oil*
- *Pepper*
- *Salt*

Direction: Preparation Time: 10 minutes Cooking Time: 40 minutes Servings: 4

- ✓ *Set the instant pot to sauté mode and add the oil.*
- ✓ *Add rosemary, garlic, onion, and chili powder and sauté for 5 minutes.*
- ✓ *Add meat and cook for 5 minutes.*
- ✓ *Add resting ingredients and stir well.*
- ✓ *Cook on high for 30 minutes after sealing the pot with a lid.*
- ✓ *Allow 10 minutes for pressure to naturally release before releasing resting pressure with the quick release. Remove lid.*
- ✓ *Serve and enjoy.*

Nutrition: Calories 574 Fat 29 g Carbohydrates 4.3 g Sugar 1.3 g Protein 70.6 g Cholesterol 244 mg

287) Spicy Beef Chili Verde

Ingredients:

- *1/2 lb beef stew meat, cut into cubes*
- *1/4 tsp chili powder*
- *1 tbsp olive oil*
- *1 cup chicken broth*
- *1 Serrano pepper, chopped*
- *1 tsp garlic, minced*
- *1 small onion, chopped*
- *1/4 cup grape tomatoes, chopped*
- *1/4 cup tomatillos, chopped*
- *Pepper*
- *Salt*

Direction: Preparation Time: 10 minutes Cooking Time: 23 minutes Servings: 2

- ✓ *Set the instant pot to sauté mode and add the oil.*
- ✓ *Add garlic and onion and sauté for 3 minutes.*
- ✓ *Add resting ingredients and stir well.*
- ✓ *Cook on high for 20 minutes after sealing the pot with a lid.*
- ✓ *Once done, allow to release pressure naturally. Remove lid.*
- ✓ *Stir well and serve.*

Nutrition: Calories 317 Fat 15.1 g Carbohydrates 6.4 g Sugar 2.6 g Protein 37.8 g Cholesterol 101 mg

288) Carrot Mushroom Beef Roast

Ingredients:

- *1 1/2 lbs beef roast*
- *1 tsp paprika*
- *1/4 tsp dried rosemary*
- *1 tsp garlic, minced*
- *1/2 lb mushrooms, sliced*
- *1/2 cup chicken stock*
- *2 carrots, sliced*
- *Pepper*
- *Salt*

Direction: Preparation Time: 10 minutes Cooking Time: 40 minutes Servings: 4

- ✓ *In the inner pot of the instant pot, combine all ingredients and stir well.*
- ✓ *Seal pot with lid and cook on high for 40 minutes.*
- ✓ *Allow 10 minutes for pressure to naturally release before releasing resting pressure with the quick release. Remove lid.*
- ✓ *Slice and serve.*

Nutrition: Calories 345 Fat 10.9 g Carbohydrates 5.6 g Sugar 2.6 g Protein 53.8 g Cholesterol 152 mg

289) Italian Beef Roast

Ingredients:

- *2 1/2 lbs beef roast, cut into chunks*
- *1 cup chicken broth*
- *1 cup red wine*
- *2 tbsp Italian seasoning*
- *2 tbsp olive oil*
- *1 bell pepper, chopped*
- *2 celery stalks, chopped*
- *1 tsp garlic, minced*
- *1 onion, sliced*
- *Pepper*
- *Salt*

Direction: Preparation Time: 10 minutes Cooking Time: 50 minutes Servings: 6

- ✓ *Set the instant pot to sauté mode and add the oil.*
- ✓ *Add the meat into the pot and sauté until brown.*
- ✓ *Add onion, bell pepper, and celery, and sauté for 5 minutes.*
- ✓ *Add resting ingredients and stir well.*
- ✓ *Seal pot with lid and cook on high for 40 minutes.*
- ✓ *Once done, allow to release pressure naturally.*

Remove lid.

- ✓ *Stir well and serve.*

Nutrition: Calories 460 Fat 18.2 g Carbohydrates 5.3 g Sugar 2.7 g Protein 58.7 g Cholesterol 172 mg

290) ***Thyme Beef Round Roast***

Ingredients:

- *4 lbs beef bottom round roast, cut into pieces*
- *2 tbsp honey*
- *5 fresh thyme sprigs*
- *2 cups red wine*
- *1 lb carrots, cut into chunks*
- *2 cups chicken broth*
- *6 garlic cloves, smashed*
- *1 onion, diced*
- *1/4 cup olive oil*
- *2 lbs potatoes, peeled and cut into chunks*
- *Pepper*
- *Salt*

Direction: Preparation Time: 10 minutes Cooking Time: 55 minutes Servings: 8

- ✓ *Add all ingredients except carrots and potatoes into the instant pot.*
- ✓ *Seal pot with lid and cook on high for 45 minutes.*
- ✓ *Once done, release pressure using quick release. Remove lid.*
- ✓ *Add carrots and potatoes and stir well.*
- ✓ *Seal pot again with lid and cook on high for 10 minutes.*
- ✓ *Once done, allow to release pressure naturally. Remove lid.*
- ✓ *Stir well and serve.*

Nutrition: Calories 648 Fat 21.7 g Carbohydrates 33.3 g Sugar 9.7 g Protein 67.1 g Cholesterol 200 mg

291) ***Jalapeno Beef Chili***

Ingredients:

- *1 lb ground beef*
- *1 tsp garlic powder*
- *1 jalapeno pepper, chopped*
- *1 tbsp ground cumin*
- *1 tbsp chili powder*
- *1 lb ground pork*
- *4 tomatillos, chopped*
- *1/2 onion, chopped*
- *5 oz tomato paste*
- *Pepper*
- *Salt*

Direction: Preparation Time: 10 minutes Cooking Time: 40 minutes Servings: 8

- ✓ *Set the instant pot to sauté mode and add the oil.*
- ✓ *Add beef and pork and cook until brown.*
- ✓ *Add resting ingredients and stir well.*
- ✓ *Seal pot with lid and cook on high for 35 minutes.*
- ✓ *Once done, allow to release pressure naturally. Remove lid.*
- ✓ *Stir well and serve.*

Nutrition: Calories 217 Fat 6.1 g Carbohydrates 6.2 g Sugar 2.7 g Protein 33.4 g Cholesterol 92 mg

292) ***Beef with Tomatoes***

Ingredients:

- *2 lb beef roast, sliced*
- *1 tbsp chives, chopped*
- *1 tsp garlic, minced*
- *1/2 tsp chili powder*
- *2 tbsp olive oil*
- *1 onion, chopped*
- *1 cup beef stock*
- *1 tbsp oregano, chopped*
- *1 cup tomatoes, chopped*
- *Pepper*
- *Salt*

Direction: Preparation Time: 10 minutes Cooking Time: 40 minutes Servings: 4

- ✓ *Set the instant pot to sauté mode and add the oil.*
- ✓ *Add garlic, onion, and chili powder, and sauté for 5 minutes.*
- ✓ *Add meat and cook for 5 minutes.*
- ✓ *Add resting ingredients and stir well.*
- ✓ *Cook on high for 30 minutes after sealing the pot with a lid.*
- ✓ *Allow 10 minutes for pressure to naturally release before releasing resting pressure with the quick release. Remove lid. Stir well and serve.*

Nutrition: Calories 511 Fat 21.6 g Carbohydrates 5.6 g Sugar 2.5 g Protein 70.4 g Cholesterol 203 mg

293) ***Tasty Beef Goulash***

Ingredients:

- *1/2 lb beef stew meat, cubed*
- *1 tbsp olive oil*
- *1/2 onion, chopped*
- *1/2 cup sun-dried tomatoes, chopped*
- *1/4 zucchini, chopped*
- *1/2 cabbage, sliced*
- *1 1/2 tbsp olive oil*
- *2 cups chicken broth*
- *Pepper*
- *Salt*

Direction: Preparation Time: 10 minutes Cooking Time: 30 minutes Servings: 2

- *Set the instant pot to sauté mode and add the oil.*
- *Add onion and sauté for 3-5 minutes.*
- *Add tomatoes and cook for 5 minutes.*
- *Add resting ingredients and stir well.*
- *Cook on high for 20 minutes after sealing the pot with a lid.*
- *Allow 10 minutes for pressure to naturally release before releasing resting pressure with the quick release. Remove lid.*
- *Stir well and serve.*

Nutrition: Calories 389 Fat 15.8 g Carbohydrates 19.3 g Sugar 10.7 g Protein 43.2 g Cholesterol 101

294) Beef & Beans

Ingredients:

- *1 1/2 lbs beef, cubed*
- *8 oz canned tomatoes, chopped*
- *8 oz red beans, soaked overnight, and rinsed*
- *1 tsp garlic, minced*
- *1 1/2 cups beef stock*
- *1/2 tsp chili powder*
- *1 tbsp paprika*
- *2 tbsp olive oil*
- *1 onion, chopped*
- *Pepper*
- *Salt*

Direction: Preparation Time: 10 minutes Cooking Time: 30 minutes Servings: 4

- *Set the instant pot to sauté mode and add the oil.*
- *Add meat and cook for 5 minutes.*
- *Add garlic and onion and sauté for 5 minutes.*
- *Add resting ingredients and stir well.*
- *Seal pot with lid and cook on high for 25 minutes.*
- *Once done, allow to release pressure naturally. Remove lid.*
- *Stir well and serve.*

Nutrition: Calories 604 Fat 18.7 g Carbohydrates 41.6 g Sugar 4.5 g Protein 66.6 g Cholesterol 152 mg

295) Delicious Ground Beef

Ingredients:

- *1 lb ground beef*
- *1 tbsp olive oil*
- *2 tbsp tomato paste*
- *1 cup chicken broth*
- *12 oz cheddar cheese, shredded*
- *1 tbsp Italian seasoning*
- *Pepper*
- *Salt*

Direction: Preparation Time: 10 minutes Cooking Time: 10 minutes Servings: 4

- *Set the instant pot to sauté mode and add the oil.*
- *Add meat and cook until browned.*
- *Add resting ingredients except for cheese and stir well.*
- *Seal pot with lid and cook on high for 7 minutes.*
- *Once done, release pressure using quick release. Remove lid.*
- *Add cheese and stir well and cook in sauté mode until cheese is melted.*
- *Serve and enjoy.*

Nutrition: Calories 610 Fat 40.2 g Carbohydrates 3.2 g Sugar 1.9 g Protein 57.2g Cholesterol 193 mg

296) Garlic Caper Beef Roast

Ingredients:

- *2 lbs beef roast, cubed*
- *1 tbsp fresh parsley, chopped*
- *1 tbsp capers, chopped*
- *1 tbsp garlic, minced*
- *1 cup chicken stock*
- *1/2 tsp dried rosemary*
- *1/2 tsp ground cumin*
- *1 onion, chopped*
- *1 tbsp olive oil*
- *Pepper*
- *Salt*

Direction: Preparation Time: 10 minutes Cooking Time: 40 minutes Servings: 4

- *Set the instant pot to sauté mode and add the oil.*
- *Add garlic and onion and sauté for 5 minutes.*
- *Add meat and cook until brown.*
- *Add resting ingredients and stir well.*
- *Cook on high for 30 minutes after sealing the pot with a lid.*
- *Once done, allow to release pressure naturally. Remove lid.*
- *Stir well and serve.*

Nutrition: Calories 470 Fat 17.9 g Carbohydrates 3.9 g Sugar 1.4 g Protein 69.5 g Cholesterol 203 mg

297) Cauliflower Tomato Beef

Ingredients:

- *1/2 lb beef stew meat, chopped*
- *1 tsp paprika*
- *1 tbsp balsamic vinegar*
- *1 celery stalk, chopped*
- *1/4 cup grape tomatoes, chopped*
- *1 onion, chopped*

- *1 tbsp olive oil*
- *1/4 cup cauliflower, chopped*
- *Pepper*
- *Salt*

Direction: Preparation Time: 10 minutes Cooking Time: 25 minutes Servings: 2

✓ *Set the instant pot to sauté mode and add the oil.*

✓ *Add meat and sauté for 5 minutes.*

✓ *Add resting ingredients and stir well.*

✓ *Cook on high for 20 minutes after sealing the pot with a lid.*

✓ *Once done, allow to release pressure naturally. Remove lid.*

✓ *Stir and serve.*

Nutrition: Calories 306 Fat 14.3 g Carbohydrates 7.6 g Sugar 3.5 g Protein 35.7 g Cholesterol 101 mg

298) Artichoke Beef Roast

Ingredients:

- *2 lbs beef roast, cubed*
- *1 tbsp garlic, minced*
- *1 onion, chopped*
- *1/2 tsp paprika*
- *1 tbsp parsley, chopped*
- *2 tomatoes, chopped*
- *1 tbsp capers, chopped*
- *10 oz canned artichokes, drained and chopped*
- *2 cups chicken stock*
- *1 tbsp olive oil*
- *Pepper*
- *Salt*

Direction: Preparation Time: 10 minutes Cooking Time: 45 minutes Servings: 6

✓ *Set the instant pot to sauté mode and add the oil.*

✓ *Add garlic and onion and sauté for 5 minutes.*

✓ *Add meat and cook until brown.*

✓ *Add resting ingredients and stir well.*

✓ *Seal pot with lid and cook on high for 35 minutes.*

✓ *Once done, allow to release pressure naturally. Remove lid.*

✓ *Serve and enjoy.*

Nutrition: Calories 344 Fat 12.2 g Carbohydrates 9.2 g Sugar 2.6 g Protein 48.4 g Cholesterol 135 mg

299) Italian Beef

Ingredients:

- *1 lb ground beef*
- *1 tbsp olive oil*
- *1/2 cup mozzarella cheese, shredded*
- *1/2 cup tomato puree*
- *1 tsp basil*
- *1 tsp oregano*
- *1/2 onion, chopped*
- *1 carrot, chopped*
- *14 oz canned tomatoes, diced*
- *Pepper*
- *Salt*

Direction: Preparation Time: 10 minutes Cooking Time: 35 minutes Servings: 4

✓ *Set the instant pot to sauté mode and add the oil.*

✓ *Add onion and sauté for 2 minutes.*

✓ *Add meat and sauté until browned.*

✓ *Add resting ingredients except for cheese and stir well.*

✓ *Seal pot with lid and cook on high for 35 minutes.*

✓ *Once done, release pressure using quick release. Remove lid.*

✓ *Add cheese and stir well and cook in sauté mode until cheese is melted.*

✓ *Serve and enjoy.*

Nutrition: Calories 297 Fat 11.3 g Carbohydrates 11.1 g Sugar 6.2 g Protein 37.1 g Cholesterol 103 mg

300) Greek Chuck Roast

Ingredients:

- *3 lbs beef chuck roast, boneless and cut into chunks*
- *1/2 tsp dried basil*
- *1 tsp oregano, chopped*
- *1 small onion, chopped*
- *1 cup tomatoes, diced*
- *2 cups chicken broth*
- *1 tbsp olive oil*
- *1 tbsp garlic, minced*
- *Pepper*
- *Salt*

Direction: Preparation Time: 10 minutes Cooking Time: 35 minutes Servings: 6

✓ *Set the instant pot to sauté mode and add the oil.*

✓ *Add onion and garlic and sauté for 3-5 minutes.*

✓ *Add meat and sauté for 5 minutes.*

✓ *Add resting ingredients and stir well.*

✓ *Seal pot with lid and cook on high for 25 minutes.*

✓ *Once done, allow to release pressure naturally. Remove lid.*

✓ *Serve and enjoy.*

Nutrition: Calories 869 Fat 66 g Carbohydrates 3.2 g Sugar 1.5 g Protein 61.5 g Cholesterol 234 mg

301) Beanless Beef Chili

Ingredients:

- *1 lb ground beef*
- *1/2 tsp dried rosemary*

- 1/2 tsp paprika
- 1 tsp garlic powder
- 1/2 tsp chili powder
- 1/2 cup chicken broth
- 1 cup heavy cream
- 1 tbsp olive oil
- 1 tsp garlic, minced
- 1 small onion, chopped
- 1 bell pepper, chopped
- 2 cups tomatoes, diced
- Pepper and Salt

Direction: Preparation Time: 10 minutes Cooking Time: 20 minutes Servings: 4

- ✓ Set the instant pot to sauté mode and add the oil.
- ✓ Add meat, bell pepper, and onion and sauté for 5 minutes.
- ✓ Add resting ingredients except for heavy cream and stir well.
- ✓ Seal pot with lid and cook on high for 5 minutes.
- ✓ Once done, release pressure using quick release. Remove lid.
- ✓ Add heavy cream and stir well and cook on sauté mode for 10 minutes.
- ✓ Serve and enjoy

Nutrition: Calories 387 Fat 22.2 g Carbohydrates 9.5 g Sugar 5 g Protein 37.2 g Cholesterol 142 mg

302) Sage Tomato Beef

Ingredients:

- 2 lbs beef stew meat, cubed
- 1/4 cup tomato paste
- 1 tsp garlic, minced
- 2 cups chicken stock
- 1 onion, chopped
- 2 tbsp olive oil
- 1 tbsp sage, chopped
- Pepper
- Salt

Direction: Preparation Time: 10 minutes Cooking Time: 40 minutes Servings: 4

- ✓ Set the instant pot to sauté mode and add the oil.
- ✓ Add garlic and onion and sauté for 5 minutes.
- ✓ Add meat and sauté for 5 minutes.
- ✓ Add resting ingredients and stir well.
- ✓ Cook on high for 30 minutes after sealing the pot with a lid.
- ✓ Once done, allow to release pressure naturally. Remove lid.
- ✓ Serve and enjoy.

Nutrition: Calories 515 Fat 21.5 g Carbohydrates 7 g Sugar 3.6 g Protein 70 g Cholesterol 203 mg

303) Rosemary Beef Eggplant

Ingredients:

- 1 lb beef stew meat, cubed
- 2 tbsp green onion, chopped
- 1/4 tsp red pepper flakes
- 1/2 tsp dried rosemary
- 1/2 tsp paprika
- 1 cup chicken stock
- 1 onion, chopped
- 1 eggplant, cubed
- 2 tbsp olive oil
- Pepper
- Salt

Direction: Preparation Time: 10 minutes Cooking Time: 30 minutes Servings: 4

- ✓ Set the instant pot to sauté mode and add the oil.
- ✓ Add meat and onion and sauté for 5 minutes.
- ✓ Add resting ingredients and stir well.
- ✓ Seal pot with lid and cook on high for 25 minutes.
- ✓ Once done, allow to release pressure naturally. Remove lid.
- ✓ Serve and enjoy.

Nutrition: Calories 315 Fat 14.5 g Carbohydrates 10 g Sugar 4.9 g Protein 36.1 g Cholesterol 101 mg

304) Lemon Basil Beef

Ingredients:

- 1 1/2 lb beef stew meat, cut into cubes
- 1/2 cup fresh basil, chopped
- 1/2 tsp dried thyme
- 2 cups chicken stock
- 1 tsp garlic, minced
- 2 tbsp lemon juice
- 1 onion, chopped
- 2 tbsp olive oil
- Pepper and Salt

Direction: Preparation Time: 10 minutes Cooking Time: 35 minutes Servings: 4

- ✓ Set the instant pot to sauté mode and add the oil.
- ✓ Add meat, garlic, and onion and sauté for 5 minutes.
- ✓ Add resting ingredients and stir well.
- ✓ Cook on high for 30 minutes after sealing the pot with a lid.
- ✓ Once done, allow to release pressure naturally. Remove lid.
- ✓ Serve and enjoy.

Nutrition: Calories 396 Fat 18 g Carbohydrates 3.5 g Sugar 1.7 g Protein 52.4 g Cholesterol 152 mg

305) Thyme Ginger Garlic Beef

Ingredients:

- 1 lb beef roast
- 2 whole cloves
- 1/2 tsp ginger, grated
- 1/2 cup beef stock
- 1/2 tsp garlic powder
- 1/2 tsp thyme
- 1/4 tsp pepper
- 1/4 tsp salt

Direction: Preparation Time: 10 minutes Cooking Time: 45 minutes Servings: 2

- ✓ Mix together ginger, cloves, thyme, garlic powder, pepper, and salt and rub over beef.
- ✓ Place meat into the instant pot. Pour stock around the meat.
- ✓ Seal pot with lid and cook on high for 45 minutes.
- ✓ Once done, release pressure using quick release. Remove lid.
- ✓ Shred meat using a fork and served.

Nutrition: Calories 452 Fat 15.7 g Carbohydrates 5.2 g Sugar 0.4 g Protein 70.1 g Cholesterol 203 mg

306) Beef Shavarma

Ingredients:

- 1/2 lb ground beef
- 1/4 tsp cinnamon
- 1/2 tsp dried oregano
- 1 cup cabbage, cut into strips
- 1/2 cup bell pepper, sliced
- 1/4 tsp ground coriander
- 1/4 tsp cumin
- 1/4 tsp cayenne pepper
- 1/4 tsp ground allspice
- 1/2 cup onion, chopped
- 1/2 tsp salt

Direction: Preparation Time: 10 minutes Cooking Time: 10 minutes Servings: 2

- ✓ Set instant pot on sauté mode.
- ✓ Add meat to the pot and sauté until brown.
- ✓ Add resting ingredients and stir well.
- ✓ Seal pot with lid and cook on high for 5 minutes.
- ✓ Once done, release pressure using quick release. Remove lid.
- ✓ Stir and serve.

Nutrition: Calories 245 Fat 7.4 g Carbohydrates 7.9 g Sugar 3.9 g Protein 35.6 g Cholesterol 101 mg

307) Beef Curry

Ingredients:

- 1/2 lb beef stew meat, cubed
- 1 bell pepper, sliced
- 1 cup beef stock
- 1 tbsp fresh ginger, grated
- 1/2 tsp ground cumin
- 1 tsp ground coriander
- 1/2 tsp cayenne pepper
- 1/2 cup sun-roasted tomatoes, diced
- 2 tbsp olive oil
- 1 tsp garlic, crushed
- 1 green chili pepper, chopped

Direction: Preparation Time: 10 minutes Cooking Time: 30 minutes Servings: 2

- ✓ Add all ingredients into the instant pot and stir well.
- ✓ Cook on high for 30 minutes after sealing the pot with a lid.
- ✓ Once done, allow to release pressure naturally. Remove lid.
- ✓ Serve and enjoy.

Nutrition: Calories 391 Fat 21.9 g Carbohydrates 11.6 g Sugar 5.8 g Protein 37.4 g Cholesterol 101 mg

308) Lamb Vegetable Soup

Ingredients:

- 1 ½ pound lamb shoulder, cubed
- 2 Tbsps olive oil
- 2 shallots, chopped
- 2 carrots. diced
- 2 celery stalks, diced
- ¼ Tsp grated finger
- 2 cups cauliflower florets
- ½ cup green peas
- 4 cups vegetable stock
- 6 cups water
- 1 thyme spring
- 1 oregano spring
- 1 basil spring
- Salt and pepper to taste
- 1 canned crushed tomatoes
- 2 Tbsps lemon juice

Direction: Preparation time:1 ½ Hour Servings: 8

- ✓ Heat the oil in a soup pot and stir to the lamb shoulder.
- ✓ Cook for some minutes on all sides, then add the water and stock.
- ✓ Cook for 40 minutes, then add the rest of the ingredients and season with salt and pepper.
- ✓ Continue cooking for another 20 minutes, then serve the soup fresh.

Nutrition: Calories 221, Fat 9,9g, Protein 25,7g, Carbs 6.5g

309) Spanish Meatball Soup

Ingredients:

- 2 Tbsps olive oil
- 1 onion, chopped
- 2 garlic cloves, chopped
- 2 red bell peppers, cored and diced
- 2 carrots. diced
- 1 celery stalk, diced
- 2 cups vegetable stock
- 6 cups enter
- 1 pound ground veal
- 1 egg
- 2 Tbsps chopped parsley
- 1 canned crushed tomatoes
- Salt and pepper to taste

Direction: Preparation time:1 Hour Servings: 8

- ✓ Heat the oil in a soup pot and stir to the onion, garlic, bell, peppers: carrots, celery stock, and water. Season with salt and pepper and bring to a boil.
- ✓ In the meantime, mix the veal, egg, and parsley in a container. Form small meatballs and place them in the boiling liquid.
- ✓ Add the tomatoes and adjust the taste with salt and pepper.
- ✓ Cook on low heat for 20 minutes.
- ✓ Serve the soup warm and fresh.

Nutrition: Calories 166, Fat 8.5g, Protein: 15.6g, Carbs 6.5g

310) Italian Meatball Soup

Ingredients:

- 4 cups chicken stock
- 4 cups water
- 1 shallot, chopped
- 2 red bell peppers, cored and diced
- 1 carrot, diced
- 1 celery stalk, diced
- 2 tomatoes, diced
- 1 cup tomato juice
- ½ Tsp dried oregano
- 1 Tsp dried basil
- 1 pound ground chicken
- 2 Tbsps white rice
- 1 lemon, juiced
- Salt and pepper to taste
- 2 Tbsps chopped parsley

Direction: Preparation time: 1 Hour **Servings:** 8

- ✓ Combine the stock, water, shallot, bell peppers, carrot, celery, tomatoes, tomato juice, oregano, and basil in a soup pot.
- ✓ Add salt and pepper to taste and cook for 10 minutes.
- ✓ Make the meatballs by mixing the chicken with rice and parsley.
- ✓ Form small meatballs and drop them into the hot soup.
- ✓ Continue cooking for another 15 minutes, then add the lemon
- ✓ Serve the soup right away.

Nutrition: Calories 150, Fat 4.7g, Protein 18g, Carbs 8.8g

311) Meat Cakes

Ingredients:

- 1 cup broccoli, shredded
- ½ cup ground pork
- 2 eggs, beaten
- 1 Tsp salt
- 1 Tbsp Italian seasonings
- 1 Tsp olive oil
- 3 Tbsps wheat flour, whole grain
- 1 Tbsp dried dill

Direction: Preparation time:10 minutes Servings: 4

- ✓ To the mixing container, combine together shredded broccoli and ground pork.
- ✓ Add salt, Italian seasoning, flour, and dried dill.
- ✓ Mix up the mixture until homogenous.
- ✓ Then add eggs and stir until smooth.
- ✓ Heat up olive oil into the skillet.
- ✓ With the help of the spoon, make latkes and place them in the hot oil.
- ✓ Roast the latkes for 4 minutes from each side over medium heat.
- ✓ The cooked latkes should have a light brown crust.
- ✓ Dry the latkes with paper towels if needed.

Nutrition: Calories 143, Fat 6g, Fiber 0.9g, Carbs 7g, Protein 15.1g

312) Braised Beef In Oregano-Tomato Sauce

Ingredients:

- 2 onions, chopped
- 3 celery stalks, diced
- 4 cloves garlic, minced
- 2 (28-ounce) cans of Italian-style stewed tomatoes
- 1 cup dry red vine
- 1 Tsp dried oregano
- 1 Tsp salt

- 3 pounds boneless beef chuck roast, cut into 1-1/2 -inch cubes
- ½ cup chopped fresh parsley
- ¼ cup vegetable oil
- ¾ Tsp black pepper

Direction: Preparation time:1 ½ Hour Servings: 12

- ✓ Place a pot on medium-high fire and heat for 2 minutes.
- ✓ Add oil and heat for another 2 minutes.
- ✓ Add beef and brown on all sides. Around 12 minutes.
- ✓ Add onions, celery, and garlic, and sauté for 5 minutes or until vegetables are tender. Add resting ingredients and bring to a boil.
- ✓ Reduce heat to low, cover, and simmer for 60 minutes or until beef is fork-tender.

Nutrition: Calories 285, Carbs 7.4g, Protein 31.7g, Fat 14.6g

313) Pork Chops And Herbed Tomato Sauce

Ingredients:

- 4 pork loin chops, boneless
- 6 tomatoes, peeled and crushed
- 3 Tbsps parsley, chopped
- 2 Tbsps olive oil
- ¼ cup kalamata olives pitted and halved
- 1 yellow onion, chopped
- 1 garlic clove, minced

Direction: Preparation time:10 minutes Servings: 4

- ✓ Heat up a pan with the oil over medium heat, add the pork chops, cook them for 3 minutes on each side, and divide between plates.
- ✓ Heat up the same pan again over medium heat, add the tomatoes, parsley, and the rest of the ingredients, whisk, simmer for 4 minutes, drizzle over the chops and serve.

Nutrition: Cal 334, Fat 17g, Fiber 2g, Carbs 12g, Protein 34g

314) Beef Shawarma

Ingredients:

- ½ lb ground beef
- ¼ tsp cinnamon
- ½ tsp dried oregano
- 1 cup cabbage, cut into strips
- ½ cup bell pepper, sliced
- ¼ tsp ground coriander
- ½ tsp cumin
- ¼ tsp cayenne pepper
- ¼ tsp ground allspice
- ½ cup onion, chopped
- ½ tsp salt

Direction: Preparation time:20 minutes Servings:2

- ✓ Set instant pot on sauté mode.
- ✓ Add meat to the pot and sauté until brown.
- ✓ Add resting ingredients and stir well.
- ✓ Seal pot with lid and cook on high for 5 minutes.
- ✓ Once done, release pressure using quick release. Remove lid.
- ✓ Stir and serve.

Nutrition: Calories 245, Fat 7.4g, Carbs 7.9g, Sugar 3.9g, Protein 35.6g, Cholesterol 101mg

315) Beef Brisket And Veggies

Ingredients:

- 3-pound beef brisket
- 1 carrot, peeled, chopped
- 1 onion, peeled
- 1 garlic clove, peeled
- 1 Tsp peppercorns
- 1 Tsp salt
- 1 Tsp ground black pepper
- ½ bay leaf
- ½ cup crushed tomatoes
- 3 cups of water
- 1 celery stalk, chopped

Direction: Preparation time: 4 Hours Servings:10

- ✓ Place the beef brisket into the saucepan.
- ✓ Add carrot, onion, garlic clove, peppercorns, salt, ground black pepper, bay leaf, crushed tomatoes, celery stalk, and water.
- ✓ Close the lid and bring the meat to a boil.
- ✓ Simmer the meat for 4 hours over medium heat.
- ✓ Serve the poached meat vegetables.

Nutrition: Calories 321, Fat 10.5g, Fiber 0.9g, Carbs 3g, Protein 50.4g

316) Hearty Beef Ragu

Ingredients:

- 1 ½ lb beef steak. Diced
- 1 ½ cup beef stock
- 1 tbsp coconut amino
- 14 oz canned tomatoes, chopped
- ½ tsp ground cinnamon
- 1 tsp dried oregano
- 1 tsp dried thyme
- 1 tsp dried basil
- 1 tsp paprika
- 1 bay leaf

- *1 tbsp garlic, chopped*
- *½ tsp cayenne pepper*
- *1 celery stick, diced*
- *1 carrot, diced*
- *1 onion, diced*
- *2 tbsp olive oil*
- *¼ tsp pepper*
- *1 ½ tsp sea salt*

Direction: Preparation time:1 hour Servings: 4

- ✓ *Set the instant pot to sauté mode and add the oil.*
- ✓ *Add celery, carrots, onion, and salt and sauté for 5 minutes.*
- ✓ *Add meat and resting ingredients and stir everything well.*
- ✓ *Cook on high for 30 minutes after sealing the pot with a lid.*
- ✓ *Allow 10 minutes for pressure to naturally release before releasing resting pressure with the quick release. Remove lid.*
- ✓ *Shred meat using a fork. Set pot on sauté mode and cook for 10 minutes. Stir every 2-3 minutes.*
- ✓ *Serve and enjoy.*

Nutrition: Calories 435, Fat 18.1g, Carbs 12.3g, Sugar 5.5g, Protein 54.4g, Cholesterol 152mg

317) Hot Pork Meatballs

Ingredients:

- *4 oz pork loin, grinded*
- *½ Tsp garlic powder*
- *¼ Tsp chili powder*
- *¼ Tsp cayenne pepper*
- *¼ Tsp ground black pepper*
- *¼ Tsp white pepper*
- *1 Tbsp water*
- *1 Tsp olive oil*

Direction: Preparation Time:10 minutes Servings:2

- ✓ *Mix up together garlic powder, cayenne pepper, ground black pepper, white pepper, and water.*
- ✓ *With the help of the fingertips, make the small meatballs.*
- ✓ *Heat up olive oil into the skillet.*
- ✓ *Range to the oil and cook for 10 minutes totally. Flip on another side from time to time.*

Nutrition: Calories 162, Fat 10.3g, Fiber 0.3g, Carbs 1g, Protein 15.7g

318) Beef And Zucchini Skillet

Ingredients:

- *2 oz ground beef*
- *½ onion, sliced*
- *½ bell pepper, sliced*
- *1 Tbsp butter*
- *½ Tsp salt*
- *1 Tbsp tomato sauce*
- *1 small zucchini, chopped*
- *½ Tsp dried oregano*

Direction: Preparation time:20 minutes Servings:2

- ✓ *Place the ground beef into the skillet.*
- ✓ *Add salt, butter, and dried oregano.*
- ✓ *Mix up the meat mixture and cook it for 10 minutes.*
- ✓ *After this, transfer the cooked ground beef to the container.*
- ✓ *Place zucchini, bell pepper, and onion into the skillet (where the ground meat was cooking) and roast the vegetables for 7 minutes over medium heat or until they are tender.*
- ✓ *Then add cooked ground beef and tomato sauce. Mix up well.*
- ✓ *Cook the beef toss for 2-3 minutes over medium heat.*

Nutrition: Calories 182, Fat 8.7g, Fiber 0.1g, Carbs 0.3g, Protein 24.1g

319) Meatloaf

Ingredients:

- *2 lbs ground beef*
- *2 eggs, lightly beaten*
- *¼ tsp dried basil*
- *3 tbsp olive oil*
- *½ tsp dried sage*
- *1 ½ tsp dried parsley*
- *1 tsp oregano*
- *1 tsp thyme*
- *1 tsp rosemary*
- *Pepper*
- *Salt*

Direction: Preparation time:35 minutes Servings: 6

- ✓ *Pour 1 ½ cups of water into the instant pot, then place the trivet to the pot.*
- ✓ *Spray loaf pan with cooking spray.*
- ✓ *Add all ingredients into the mixing container and mix until well combined.*
- ✓ *Transfer the meat mixture into the prepared loaf pan and place the loaf pan on top of the trivet to the pot.*
- ✓ *Seal pot with lid and cook on high for 35 minutes.*
- ✓ *Allow 10 minutes for pressure to naturally release before releasing resting pressure with the quick release. Remove lid.*
- ✓ *Serve and enjoy.*

Nutrition: Calories 365, Fat 18g, Carbs 0.7g, Sugar 0.1g, Protein 47.8g, Cholesterol 190mg

320) Tasty Lamb Ribs

Ingredients:

- 2 garlic cloves, minced
- ¼ cup shallot, chopped
- 2 Tbsps fish sauce
- ½ cup veggie stock
- 2 Tbsps olive oil
- 1 and ½ Tbsps lemon juice
- 1 tbsp coriander seeds, ground
- 1 Tbsp ginger, grated
- Salt and black pepper to the taste
- 2 pounds lamb ribs

Direction: Preparation time:2 Hours Servings:4

- ✓ In a roasting pan, combine the lamb with the garlic, shallots, and the rest of the ingredients, toss, introduce to the oven at 300 degrees F and cook for 2 hours.
- ✓ Divide the lamb between plates and serve with a side salad.

Nutrition: Calories 293, Fat 9.1g, Fiber 9.6g, Carbs 16.7g, Protein 2402g

321) Peas And Han Thick Soup

Ingredients:

- Pepper and salt to taste
- 1 lb. Ham, coarsely chopped
- 24 oz frozen sweet peas
- 4 cup ham stock
- ¼ cup white wine
- 1 carrot, chopped coarsely
- 1 onion, chopped coarsely
- 2 tbsp butter, divided

Direction: Preparation time:30 minutes Servings:4

- ✓ On a medium pot, heat oil. Sauté for 6 minutes the onion or until soft and translucent.
- ✓ Add wine and cook for 4 minutes or until nearly evaporated.
- ✓ Add ham stock and bring to a simmer and simmer continuously while covered for 4 minutes.
- ✓ Add peas and cook for 7 minutes or until tender.
- ✓ Meanwhile, in a nonstick fry pan, cook to a bronzed crisp the ham in 1 tbsp butter, around 6 minutes. Remove from fire and set aside.
- ✓ When peas are soft, transfer to a blender and puree. Return to pot, continue cooking while seasoning with pepper, salt, and ½ of crisped ham. Once the soup is to your desired taste, turn off the fire.
- ✓ Transfer to 4 serving containers and garnish evenly with crisped ham

Nutrition: Calories 403, Carbs: 32.5g, Protein 32.5g,

322) Beef Spread

Ingredients:

- 8 oz beef liver
- ½ onion, peeled
- ½ carrot, peeled
- ½ Tsp peppercorns
- 1 bay leaf
- ½ Tsp salt
- 1/3 cup water
- 1 Tsp ground black pepper

Direction: Preparation time:25 minutes Servings: 4

- ✓ Chop the beef liver and put it into the saucepan.
- ✓ Add onion, carrot, peppercorns, bay leaf, salt, and ground black pepper.
- ✓ Add water and close the lid.
- ✓ Boil the beef liver for 25 minutes or until all ingredients are tender.
- ✓ Transfer the cooked mixture to the blender and blend it until smooth.
- ✓ Then place the cooked pate in the serving container and flatten the surface of it.
- ✓ Refrigerate the pate for 20-30 minutes before serving.

Nutrition: Calories 109, Fat 2.7g, fiber 0.6g, Carbs 5.3g, Protein 15.3g

323) Pork Chops And Relish

Ingredients:

- 6 pork chops, boneless
- 7 ounces marinated artichoke hearts, chopped and their liquid reserved
- A pinch of salt and black pepper
- 1 Tsp hot pepper sauce
- 1 and ½ cups tomatoes, cubed
- 1 jalapeno pepper, chopped
- ½ cup roasted bell peppers, chopped
- ½ cup black olives, pitted and sliced

Direction: Preparation time:14 minutes Servings: 6

- ✓ In a container, mix the chops with the pepper sauce, reserved liquid from the artichokes, cover, and keep to the fridge for 15 minutes.
- ✓ Heat up a grill over medium-high heat, add the pork chops and cook for 7 minutes on each side.
- ✓ In a container, combine the artichokes with the peppers and the resting ingredients, toss, divide on top of the chops and serve.

Nutrition: Calories 215, Fat 6g, Fiber 1g, Carbs 6g, Protein 35g

324) Pork and Prunes Stew

Ingredients:

- *2 pounds pork tenderloin, cubed*
- *2 Tbsps olive oil*
- *1 Sweet onion, chopped*
- *4 garlic cloves, chopped*
- *2 carrots, diced*
- *2 celery stalks, chopped*
- *2 tomatoes, peeled and diced*
- *1 cup vegetable stock*
- *½ cup white wine*
- *1 pound prunes, pitted*
- *1 bay leaf*
- *1 thyme spring*
- *1 Tsp mustard seeds*
- *1 Tsp coriander seeds*
- *Salt and pepper to taste*

Direction: Preparation time:1 ¼ Hours Servings:8

- ✓ *In a deep dish baking pan, combine all the ingredients.*
- ✓ *Add salt and pepper to taste and cook to the preheated oven at 350F for 1 hour, adding more liquid as it cooks if needed.*
- ✓ *Serve and stew warm and fresh*

Nutrition: Calories 363, Fat 7.9g, Protein 31.7g, Carbs 41.4g

325) Pork And Rice Soup

Ingredients:

- *2 pounds pork stew meat, cubed*
- *A pinch of salt and black pepper*
- *6 cups water*
- *1 leek, sliced*
- *1 bay leaves*
- *1 carrot, sliced*
- *3 Tbsps olive oil*
- *1 cup white rice*
- *2 cups yellow onion, chopped*
- *½ cup lemon juice*
- *1 Tbsp cilantro, chopped*

Direction: Servings:4 Preparation time:7 Hours

- ✓ *In your slow cooker, combine the pork with the water and the rest of the ingredients except the cilantro, put the lid on, and cook on Low for 7 hours.*
- ✓ *Stir the soup, ladle it into containers, sprinkle the cilantro on top, and serve.*

Nutrition: Calories 300, Fat 15g, Fiber 7.6g, Carbs 17.4g, Protein 22.4g

326) Sage Pork And Beans Stew

Ingredients:

- *2 pounds pork stew meat, cubed*
- *2 Tbsps olive oil*
- *1 Sweet onion, chopped*
- *1 red bell pepper, chopped*
- *3 Garlic cloves, minced*
- *2 Tbsps sage, dried*
- *4 ounces canned white beans, drained*
- *1 cup beef stock*
- *2 zucchinis, chopped*
- *2 Tbsps tomato paste*
- *1 Tbsp cilantro, chopped*

Direction: Preparation time:4 Hours and 10 minutes Servings:4

- ✓ *Heat up a pan with the oil over medium-high heat, add the meat, brown for 10 minutes, and transfer to your slow cooker.*
- ✓ *Add the rest of the ingredients except the cilantro, put the lid on, and cook on High for 4 hours.*
- ✓ *Divide the stew into containers, sprinkle the cilantro on top, and serve*

Nutrition: Calories 423, Fat 15.4g, Fiber 9.6g, Carbs 2704g, Protein 43g

327) Pear Braised Pork

Ingredients:

- *3 pounds pork shoulder*
- *4 Pears, peeled and sliced*
- *2 shallots, sliced*
- *4 garlic cloves, minced*
- *1 bay leaf*
- *1 thyme spring*
- *½ cup apple cider*
- *Salt and pepper to taste*

Direction: Preparation time:2 ¼ hours Servings: 10

- ✓ *Season the pork with salt and pepper.*
- ✓ *Combine the pears, shallots, garlic, bay leaf, thyme, and apple cider in a deep dish baking pan.*
- ✓ *Place the pork over the pears, then cover the pan with aluminum foil.*
- ✓ *Cook to the preheated oven at 330F for 2 hours. Serve the pork and the sauce fresh.*

Nutrition: Calories 455, Fat 29.3g, Protein 32.1g, Carbs 14.9g

328) Beef And Potatoes With Tahini Sauce

Ingredients:

- *½ large yellow onion*
- *1 lb. ground beef*
- *½ tsp. salt*

- *½ tsp. ground black pepper*
- *6 small red potatoes, washed*
- *3 TB. extra-virgin olive oil*
- *2 cups plain Greek yogurt*
- *¾ cup tahini paste*
- *1½ cups water*
- *¼ cup fresh lemon juice*
- *1 TB. minced garlic*
- *½ cup pine nuts*

Direction: Preparation time:35 minutes Servings:1/6 Casserole

- ✓ *Switch on the oven, preheat it setting its temperature to 425°F.*
- ✓ *In a food processor fitted with a chopping blade, blend yellow onion for 30 seconds.*
- ✓ *Transfer onion to a large container. Add beef, 1 Tsp salt, black pepper, and mix well.*
- ✓ *Spread beef mixture evenly to the bottom of a 9-inch casserole dish, and bake for 20 minutes.*
- ✓ *Cut red potatoes into 1/4-inch-thick pieces, place in a container, and toss with 2 Tbsps extra-virgin olive oil and ½ Tsp salt.*
- ✓ *Spread potatoes on a baking sheet and bake for 20 minutes.*
- ✓ *In a large container, combine Greek yogurt, tahini paste, water, lemon juice, garlic, and the resting 1 Tsp salt.*
- ✓ *Remove beef mixture and potatoes from the oven. Using a spatula, transfer potatoes to the casserole dish. Pour yogurt sauce over the top and bake for 15 more minutes.*
- ✓ *In a small pan over low heat, heat the resting 1 Tbsp extra-virgin olive oil. Add pine nuts and toast for 1 or 2 minutes.*
- ✓ *Remove casserole dish from the oven, spoon pine nuts over the top and serve warm with brown rice.*

Nutrition: Calories 342, Fat 11g, Protein 31g, Carbs 30g, Fiber 6g

329) ***Coriander Pork And Chickpeas Stew***

Ingredients:

- *½ cup beef stock*
- *1 Tbsp ginger, grated*
- *1 Tsp coriander. ground*
- *z Tbsps cumin, ground*
- *Salt and black pepper to the taste*
- *2 and ½ pounds pork stew meat, cubed*
- *28 ounces canned tomatoes, drained and chopped*
- *1 red onion, chopped*
- *4 garlic cloves, minced*
- *½ cup apricots, cut into quarters*
- *15 ounces canned chickpeas, drained*
- *1 Tbsp cilantro, chopped*

Direction: Preparation Time:8 Hours Servings:4

- ✓ *In your slow cooker, combine the meat with the stock, ginger, and the rest of the ingredients except the cilantro and the chickpeas. Put the lid on, and cook on Low for 7 hours and 40 minutes.*
- ✓ *Add the cilantro and the chickpeas, cook the stew on low for 20 minutes more, divide into containers and serve.*

Nutrition: Calories 283, Fat 11.9g, Fiber 4.5g, Carbs 28.8g, Protein 25.4g

330) ***Yogurt-Marinated Pork Chops***

Ingredients:

- *6 pork chops*
- *1 cup plain yogurt*
- *1 mandarin, sliced*
- *2 garlic cloves, chopped*
- *1 red pepper, chopped*
- *Salt and pepper to taste*

Direction: Preparation time:2 Hours Servings:6

- ✓ *Season the pork with salt and pepper and mix it with the resting ingredients in a zip lock bag.*
- ✓ *Marinate for 1 ½ hour in the fridge.*
- ✓ *Heat a grill pan over medium flame and cook the pork chops on each side until browned.*
- ✓ *Serve the pork chops fresh and warm.*

Nutrition: Calories 293, Fat 20.4g, Protein 20.6g, Carbs 4.4g

331) ***Beef And Grape Sauce***

Ingredients:

- *1-pound beef sirloin*
- *1 Tsp molasses*
- *1 Tbsp lemon zest, grated*
- *1 Tsp soy sauce*
- *1 chili pepper, chopped*
- *¼ Tsp fresh ginger, minced*
- *1 cup grape juice*
- *½ Tsp salt*
- *1 Tbsp butter*

Direction: Preparation time:25 minutes Servings:4

- ✓ *Sprinkle the beef sirloin with salt and minced ginger.*
- ✓ *Heat up the butter into the saucepan and add meat.*
- ✓ *Roast it for 5 minutes from each side over medium heat.*
- ✓ *After this, add soy sauce, chili pepper, and grape juice.*
- ✓ *Then add lemon zest and simmer the meat for 10*

minutes.

- ✓ Add molasses and mix up meat well.
- ✓ Close the lid and cook meat for 5 minutes.
- ✓ Serve the cooked beef with grape juice sauce.

Nutrition: Calories 267, Fat 10g, Fiber 0.2g, Carbs 7.4g, Protein 34.9g

332) Lamb And Tomato Sauce

Ingredients:

- 9 oz lamb shanks
- 1 onion, diced
- 1 carrot, diced
- 1 Tbsp olive oil
- 1 Tsp salt
- 1 Tsp ground black pepper
- 1 ½ cup chicken stock
- 1 Tbsp tomato paste

Direction: Preparation time:55 minutes Servings:3

- ✓ Sprinkle the lamb shanks with salt and ground black pepper.
- ✓ Heat up olive oil into the saucepan.
- ✓ Add lamb shanks and roast them for 5 minutes from each side.
- ✓ Transfer meat to the plate.
- ✓ After this, add onion and carrot to the saucepan.
- ✓ Roast the vegetables for 3 minutes.
- ✓ Add tomato paste and mix up well.
- ✓ Then add chicken stock and bring the liquid to a boil.
- ✓ Add lamb shanks, stir well and close the lid.
- ✓ Cook the meat for 40 minutes over medium-low heat.

Nutrition: Calories 232, Fat 11.3g, Fiber 1.7g, Carbs 7g, Protein 25g

333) Lamb And Sweet Onion Sauce

Ingredients:

- 2 pounds lamb meat, cubed
- 1 Tbsp sweet paprika
- Salt and black pepper to the taste
- 1 and ½ cups veggie stock
- 4 garlic cloves, minced
- 2 Tbsps olive oil
- 1 pound sweet onion, chopped
- 1 cup balsamic vinegar

Direction: Servings: 4 Preparation time:40 minutes

- ✓ Heat up a pot with the oil over medium heat, add the onion, vinegar. Salt and pepper, stir and cook for 10 minutes.
- ✓ Add the meat and the rest of the ingredients. Toss, bring to a simmer, and cook over medium heat for 30 minutes.
- ✓ Divide the mix between plates and serve.

Nutrition: Calories 303, Carbs 15g, Protein 17g

334) Pork And Mustard Shallots Mix

Ingredients:

- 3 shallots, chopped
- 1 pound pork loin, cut into strips
- ½ cup veggie stock
- 2 Tbsps olive oil
- A pinch of salt and black pepper
- 2 Tbsps mustard
- 1 Tbsp parsley, chopped

Direction: Preparation time:25 minutes Servings: 4

- ✓ Heat up a pan with the oil over medium-high heat, add the shallots and sauté for 5 minutes.
- ✓ Add the meat and cook for 10 minutes tossing it often.
- ✓ Toss in the remaining ingredients, cook for another 10 minutes, divide between plates, and serve right away.

Nutrition: Cal 296, Fat 12.5g, Carbs 13.3g, Protein 22.5g

335) Basil And Shrimp Quinoa

Ingredients:

- 3 TB. extra-virgin olive oil
- 2 TB. minced garlic
- 1 cup fresh broccoli florets
- 3 stalk asparagus, chopped
- 4 cups chicken or vegetable broth
- ½ tsp. salt
- 1 tsp. ground black pepper
- 1 TB. lemon zest
- 2 cups red quinoa
- ½ cup fresh basil, chopped

Direction: Preparation time:20 minutes Servings:1

- ✓ ½ lb. medium raw shrimp (18 to 20), shells and veins removed
- ✓ In a 2-quart pot over low heat, heat extra-virgin olive oil. Add garlic and cook for 3 minutes.
- ✓ Increase heat to medium, add broccoli and asparagus and cook for 2 minutes.
- ✓ Add chicken broth, salt, black pepper, lemon zest, and bring to a boil. Stir in red quinoa, cover, and cook for 15 minutes.
- ✓ Fold in basil and shrimp, cover, and cook for 10 minutes.
- ✓ Remove from heat, fluff with a fork, cover, and set aside for 10 minutes. Serve warm.

Nutrition: Cal 128, Fat 12g, Fiber 6g, Protein 29g, Carbs 18g

336) Ground Pork Salad

Ingredients:

- *1 cup ground pork*
- *½ onion, diced*
- *4 bacon slices*
- *1 Tsp sesame oil*
- *1 Tsp butter*
- *1 cup lettuce, chopped*
- *1 Tbsp lemon juice*
- *4 eggs, boiled*
- *½ Tsp salt*
- *1 Tsp chili pepper*
- *¼ Tsp liquid honey*

Direction: Preparation time:15 minutes Servings:8

- ✓ *Make burgers: to the mixing container, combine together ground pork, diced onion, salt, and chili pepper.*
- ✓ *Blake the medium size burgers.*
- ✓ *Melt butter into the skillet and add prepared burgers.*
- ✓ *Roast them for 5 minutes from each side over medium heat.*
- ✓ *When the burgers are cooked, chill them a little.*
- ✓ *Place the bacon into the skillet and roast it until golden brown. Then chill the bacon and chop it roughly.*
- ✓ *To the salad container, combine together chopped bacon, sesame oil, lettuce, lemon juice, and honey. Mix up salad well.*
- ✓ *Peel the eggs and cut them on the halves.*
- ✓ *Arrange the eggs and burgers over the salad. Don't mix salad anymore.*

Nutrition: Calories 213, Fat 15.5g, Fiber 0.1g, Carbs 1.5g, Protein 16.5g

337) Beef Pitas

Ingredients:

- *1 ½ cup ground beef*
- *½ red onion, diced*
- *1 Tsp minced garlic*
- *¼ cup fresh spinach, chopped*
- *1 Tsp salt*
- *½ Tsp chili pepper*
- *1 Tsp dried oregano*
- *1 Tsp fresh mint, chopped*
- *4 Tbsps Plain yogurt*
- *1 cucumber, grated*
- *½ Tsp dill*
- *½ Tsp garlic powder*
- *4 pitta bread*

Direction: Preparation time:15 minutes Servings: 4

- ✓ *To the mixing container, combine together ground beef, onion, minced garlic, spinach, salt, chili pepper, and dried oregano.*
- ✓ *Prepare the medium size balls from the meat mixture.*
- ✓ *Line the baking tray with baking paper and arrange the meatballs inside.*
- ✓ *Bake the meatballs for 15 minutes at 375F. Flip them on another side after 10 minutes of cooking.*
- ✓ *Meanwhile, make tzatziki: combine together fresh mint, yogurt, grated cucumber, dill, and garlic powder. Whisk the mixture for 1 minute.*
- ✓ *When the meatballs are cooked, place the over pitta bread and top with tzatziki.*

Nutrition: Calorie 253, Fat 7g, Fiber 4g, Carbs 30g, Protein 16.3g

338) Mouth-Watering Lamb Stew

Ingredients:

- *½ cup golden raisins*
- *1 cup dates, cut in half*
- *1 cup dried figs, cut in half*
- *1 lb lamb shoulder, trimmed of fat and cut into 2-inch cubes*
- *1 onion, minced*
- *1 tbsp fresh coriander*
- *1 tbsp honey, optional*
- *1 tbsp olive oil*
- *1 tbsp Ras el Hanout*
- *2 cloves garlic, minced*
- *2 cups beef stock or lamb stock*
- *Pepper and salt to taste*
- *¼ tsp ground closes*
- *½ tsp ground black pepper*
- *1 tsp ground turmeric*
- *1 tsp ground nutmeg*
- *1 tsp ground allspice*
- *1 tsp ground cinnamon*
- *2 tsp ground mace*
- *2 tsp ground cardamom*
- *2 tsp ground ginger*
- *½ tsp anise seeds*
- *½ tsp ground cayenne pepper*

Direction: Servings: 4 Preparation time: 180 minutes

- ✓ *Preheat oven to 300F.*
- ✓ *In a small container, add all Ras el Hanout ingredients and mix thoroughly. Just get what the ingredients need and store resting in a tightly lidded spice jar.*

- ✓ *On high fire, place a heavy-bottomed medium pot and heat olive oil. Once hot, brown lamb pieces on each side for around 3 to 4 minutes.*
- ✓ *Lower fire to medium-high and add resting ingredients, except for the coriander.*
- ✓ *Mix well—season with pepper and salt to taste. Cover pot and bring to a boil.*
- ✓ *Once boiling, turn off the fire and pop the pot into the oven.*
- ✓ *Bake uncovered for 2 to 2.5 hours or until meat is fork-tender.*
- ✓ *Once the meat is tender, remove it from the oven.*
- ✓ *To serve, sprinkle fresh coriander and enjoy.*

Nutrition: Cal 633, Fat 21g, Carbs 78g, Protein 33g

339) Lamb And Peanuts Mix

Ingredients:

- *2 Tbsps lime juice*
- *1 Tbsp balsamic vinegar*
- *5 garlic cloves, minced*
- *2 Tbsps olive oil*
- *Salt and black pepper to the taste*
- *1 and ½ pound lamb meat, cubed*
- *3 Tbsps peanuts, toasted and chopped*
- *2 scallions, chopped*

Direction: Servings: 4 Preparation time: 20 minutes

- ✓ *Cook the meat for 4 minutes on each side in a pan with the oil over medium-high heat.*
- ✓ *Add the scallions and the garlic and sauté for 2 minutes more.*
- ✓ *Toss in the remaining ingredients, cook for another 10 minutes, divide between plates, and serve right away.*

Nutrition: Cal 300, Fat 14.5g, , Carbs 15.7g, Pro 17.5g

340) Cheddar Lamb And Zucchinis

Ingredients:

- *1 pound lamb meat, cubed*
- *1 Tbsp avocado oil*
- *2 cups zucchinis, chopped*
- *½ cup red onion, chopped*
- *Salt and black pepper to the taste*
- *15 ounces canned roasted tomatoes, crushed*
- *¾ cup cheddar cheese, shredded*

Direction: Servings: 4 Preparation time: 30 minutes

- ✓ *Heat up a pan with the oil over medium-high heat, add the meat and the onion, and brown for 5 minutes.*
- ✓ *Add the rest of the ingredients except the cheese, bring to a simmer and cook over medium heat for 20 minutes.*
- ✓ *Add the cheese, cook everything for 3 minutes more, divide between plates and serve.*

Nutrition: Calories 306, Fat 16.4g, Fiber 12.3g, Carbs 15.5g, Protein 18.5g

341) Fennel Pork

Ingredients:

- *2 pork loin roast, trimmed and boneless*
- *Salt and black pepper to the taste*
- *3 garlic cloves. minced*
- *2 Tbsps fennel, around*
- *1 Tbsp fennel seeds*
- *2 Tbsps red pepper, crushed*
- *¼ cup olive oil*

Direction: Servings: 4 Preparation time: 2 Hours

- ✓ *In a roasting pan, combine the pork with salt, pepper, and the rest of the ingredients, toss, introduce to the oven and bake at 38 degrees F for 2 hours.*
- ✓ *Slice the roast, divide between plates and serve with a side salad.*

Nutrition: Cal 300, Fat 4g, Fiber 2g, Carbs 6g, Pro 15g

342) Lamb And Feta Artichokes

Ingredients:

- *2 pounds lamb shoulder*
- *2 spring onions, chopped*
- *1 Tbsp olive oil*
- *3 Garlic cloves, minced*
- *1 Tbsp lemon juice*
- *Salt and black pepper to the taste*
- *1 and ½ cups veggie stock*
- *6 ounces canned artichoke hearts. drained and quartered*
- *½ cup feta cheese, crumbled*
- *2 Tbsps parsley, chopped*

Direction: Servings: 6 Preparation time: 8 Hours

- ✓ *Heat up a pan with the oil over medium-high heat, add the lamb, brown for 5 minutes, and transfer to your slow cooker.*
- ✓ *Add the rest of the ingredients except the parsley and the cheese, put the lid on, and cook on low for 8 hours.*
- ✓ *Add the cheese and the parsley, divide the mix between plates and serve.*

Nutrition: Cal 330, Fat 14.5g, Fiber 14.1g, Carbs 21.7g, Protein 17.5g

343) Lamb And Plums Mix

Ingredients:

- *4 lamb shanks*
- *1 red onion, chopped*

- *2 Tbsps olive oil*
- *1 cup plums, pitted and halved*
- *1 Tbsp sweet paprika*
- *2 cups chicken stock*
- *Salt and pepper to the taste*

Direction: Servings: 4 Preparation time: 6 Hours and 10 minutes

- ✓ *Heat up a pan with the oil over medium-high heat, add the lamb, brown for 5 minutes on each side, and transfer to your slow cooker.*
- ✓ *Add the rest of the ingredients, put the lid on, and cook on High for 6 hours.*
- ✓ *Divide the mix between plates and serve right away.*

Nutrition: Calories 295, Fat 13g, Fiber 9.7g, Carbs 15.7g, Protein 14.3g

344) Lamb And Mango Sauce

Ingredients:

- *2 cups Greek yogurt*
- *1 cup mango, peeled and cubed*
- *1 yellow onion, chopped*
- *1/3 cup parsley, chopped*
- *1 pound lamb, cubed*
- *½ Tsp red pepper Blakes*
- *Salt and black pepper to the taste*
- *2 Tbsps olive oil*
- *¼ Tsp cinnamon powder*

Direction: Servings: 4 Preparation time: 1 Hour

- ✓ *Heat up a pan with the oil over medium-high heat, add the meat, and brown for 5 minutes.*
- ✓ *Add the onion and sauté for 5 minutes more.*
- ✓ *Add the rest of the ingredients, toss, bring to a simmer and cook over medium heat for 45 minutes.*
- ✓ *Divide everything between plates and serve.*

Nutrition: Calories 300, Fat 15.3g, Fiber 9.1g, Carbs 15.8g, Protein 15.5

Poultry Recipes

345) Chicken Quinoa Pilaf

Ingredients

- *2 (8-oz) boneless, skinless chicken breasts, cut into ½-in. cubes*
- *3 TB. extra-virgin olive oil*
- *1 medium red onion, finely chopped*
- *1 TB. minced garlic*
- *1 (16-oz) can diced tomatoes, with juice*
- *2 cups water*
- *2 tsp. salt*
- *1 TB. dried oregano*
- *1 TB. turmeric*
- *1 tsp. paprika*
- *1 tsp. ground black pepper*
- *2 cups red or yellow quinoa*
- *½ cup fresh parsley, chopped*

DIRECTIONS: Servings: 1 Cup Preparation time: 35 minutes

- ✓ *In a large, 3-quart pot over medium heat, heat extra-virgin olive oil. Add chicken, and cook for 5 minutes.*
- ✓ *Add red onion and garlic, stir, and cook for 5 minutes.*
- ✓ *Add tomatoes with juice, water, salt, oregano, turmeric, paprika, and black pepper. Stir, and simmer for 5 minutes.*
- ✓ *Add red quinoa, and stir. Cover, reduce heat to low and cook for 20 minutes. Remove from heat.*
- ✓ *Fluff with a fork, cover again and let sit for 10 minutes.*
- ✓ *Serve warm.*

Nutrition Calories 306, Fat 6g, Protein 23g, Carbs 41g, Fiber 5g

346) Bulgur And Chicken Skillet

Ingredients

- *4 (6-oz) skinless, boneless chicken breasts*
- *1 tablespoon olive oil, divided*
- *1 cup thinly sliced red onion*
- *1 tablespoon thinly sliced garlic*
- *1 cup unsalted chicken stock*
- *1 tablespoon coarsely chopped fresh dill*
- *½ teaspoon freshly ground black pepper, divided*
- *½ cup uncooked bulgur*
- *2 teaspoons chopped fresh or ½ tsp. dried oregano*
- *4 cups chopped fresh kale (about 2 ½ oz.)*
- *½ cup thinly sliced bottled roasted red bell peppers*
- *2 ounces feta cheese, crumbled (about ½ cup)*
- *3/4 teaspoon kosher salt, divided*

DIRECTIONS: Servings: 4 Preparation time: 40 minutes

- ✓ *Place a cast-iron skillet on medium-high fire and heat for 5 minutes. Add oil and heat for 2 minutes.*
- ✓ *Season chicken with pepper and salt to taste.*
- ✓ *Brown chicken for 4 minutes per side and transfer to a plate.*
- ✓ *To the same skillet, sauté garlic and onion for 3 minutes. Stir in oregano and bulgur and toast for 2 minutes.*
- ✓ *Stir in kale and bell pepper, cook for 2 minutes. Pour in stock and season well with pepper and salt.*
- ✓ *Return chicken to skillet and turn off the fire. Pop in a preheated 400F oven and bake for 15 minutes.*
- ✓ *Remove from oven, fluff bulgur, and turn over chicken. Let it stand for 5 minutes.*
- ✓ *Serve and enjoy with a sprinkle of feta cheese.*

Nutrition Calories 369, Carbs 21g, Protein 45g, Fat 11g

347) Grilled Turkey With White Bean Mash

Ingredients

- *4 turkey breast fillets*
- *1 teaspoon chili powder*
- *1 teaspoon dried parsley*
- *Salt and pepper to taste*
- *2 cans white beans, drained*
- *4 garlic cloves, minced*
- *2 tablespoons lemon juice*
- *3 tablespoons olive oil*
- *2 sweet onions, sliced*
- *2 tablespoons tomato paste*

DIRECTIONS: Servings: 4 Preparation time: 45 minutes

- ✓ *Season the turkey with salt, pepper, and dried parsley.*
- ✓ *Heat a grill pan over medium flame and place the turkey on the grill. Cook on each side for 7 minutes.*
- ✓ *Combine the beans, garlic, lemon juice, salt, and pepper for the mash in a blender and pulse until well mixed and smooth.*
- ✓ *Heat the oil in a skillet and add the onions. Cook for 10 minutes until caramelized. Add the tomato paste and cook for 2 more minutes.*
- ✓ *Serve the grilled turkey with bean mash and caramelized onions.*

NUTRITION Cal 337, Fat 8.2g, Protein 21g, Carbs 47g

348) Vegetable Turkey Casserole

Ingredients

- *3 tablespoons olive oil*
- *2 pounds turkey breasts, cubed*
- *1 sweet onion, chopped*
- *3 carrots, sliced*
- *2 celery stalks, sliced*
- *2 garlic cloves, chopped*
- *½ teaspoon cumin powder*
- *½ teaspoon dried thyme*
- *2 cans diced tomatoes*
- *1 cup chicken stock*
- *1 bay leaf*
- *Salt and pepper to taste*

DIRECTIONS: Servings: 8 Preparation time: 1 ¼ Hour

- ✓ *Heat the oil in a deep heavy pot and stir to the turkey.*
- ✓ *Cook for 5 minutes until golden on all sides, then add the onion, carrot, celery, and garlic. Cook for 5 minutes, then add the rest of the ingredients.*
- ✓ *Season with salt and pepper and cook to the preheated oven at 350F for 40 minutes.*
- ✓ *Serve the casserole warm and fresh.*

NUTRITION Cal 186, Fat 7.3g, Protein 20g, Carbs 9.9g

349) ***Turkey Fritters And Sauce***

Ingredients

- *2 garlic cloves, minced*
- *1 egg*
- *1 red onion, chopped*
- *1 tablespoon olive oil*
- *¼ teaspoon red pepper flakes*
- *1 pound turkey meat, ground*
- *½ teaspoon oregano, dried*
- *Cooking spray*
- *For the sauce:*
- *1 cup Greek yogurt*
- *1 cucumber, chopped*
- *1 tablespoon olive oil*
- *¼ teaspoon garlic powder*
- *2 tablespoons lemon juice*
- *¼ cup parsley, chopped*

DIRECTIONS: Servings: 4 Preparation time: 30 minutes

- ✓ *Heat up a pan with 1 tablespoon oil over medium heat, add the onion and the garlic, sauté for 5 minutes, cool down and transfer to a container.*
- ✓ *Add the meat, turkey, oregano, and pepper flakes, stir and shape medium fritters out of this mix.*
- ✓ *Heat up another pan greased with cooking spray over medium-high heat, add the turkey fritters, and brow for 5 minutes on each side.*
- ✓ *Introduce the pan to the oven and bake the fritters at 375 degrees F for 15 minutes more.*
- ✓ *Meanwhile, mix the yogurt with the cucumber, oil, garlic powder, lemon juice, and parsley in a container and whisk really well.*
- ✓ *Divide the fritters between plates, spread the sauce all over, and serve for lunch.*

NUTRITION Calories 364, Fat 16.g, Fiber 5.5g, Carbs 26.8g, Protein 23g

350) ***Avocado And Turkey Mix Panini***

Ingredients

- *2 red peppers, roasted and sliced into strips*
- *¼ lb. thinly sliced mesquite smoked turkey breast*
- *1 cup whole fresh spinach leaves, divided*
- *2 slices provolone cheese*
- *1 tbsp olive oil, divided*
- *2 ciabatta rolls*
- *¼ cup mayonnaise*
- *½ ripe avocado*

DIRECTIONS: Servings: 2 Preparation time: 8 minutes

- ✓ *In a container, mash thoroughly together mayonnaise and avocado. Then preheat Panini press.*
- ✓ *Slice the bread rolls in half and spread olive oil on the insides of the bread. Then fill it with filling, layering them as you go: provolone, turkey breast, roasted red pepper, spinach leaves and spread the avocado mixture, and cover with the other bread slice.*
- ✓ *Place sandwich into the pan ini press and grill for 5 to 8 minutes until cheese has melted and bread is crisped and ridged.*

NUTRITION Calories 546, Carbs 31.9g, Protein 27.8g, Fat 34 8g

351) ***Paprika And Feta Cheese On Chicken Skillet***

Ingredients

- *¼ cup black olives, sliced in circles*
- *½ teaspoon coriander*
- *½ teaspoon paprika*
- *1 ½ cups diced tomatoes with the juice*
- *1 cup yellow onion, chopped*
- *1 teaspoon onion powder*
- *2 garlic cloves, peeled and minced*
- *2 lb. free-range organic boneless skinless chicken breasts*
- *2 tablespoons feta cheese*
- *2 tablespoons ghee or olive oil*

- *Crushed red pepper to taste*
- *Salt and black pepper to taste*

DIRECTIONS: Servings: 6 Preparation time: 35 minutes

- ✓ *Preheat oven to 400F.*
- ✓ *Place a cast-iron pan on medium-high fire and heat for 5 minutes. Add oil and heat for 2 minutes more.*
- ✓ *Meanwhile, mix well pepper, salt, crushed red pepper, paprika, coriander, and onion powder in a large dish. Add chicken and coat well in seasoning.*
- ✓ *Add chicken to pan and brown sides for 4 minutes per side. Increase fire to high.*
- ✓ *Stir in garlic and onions. Lower fire to medium and mix well.*
- ✓ *Pop pan in oven and bake for 15 minutes.*
- ✓ *Remove from oven, turn over chicken and let it stand for 5 minutes before serving.*

Nutrition Calories 232, Fat 8g, Carbs 5g, Protein 33g

352) Chicken Burgers With Brussel Sprouts Slaw

Ingredients

- *¼ cup apple, diced*
- *¼ cup green onion, diced*
- *½ avocado, cubed*
- *½ pound Brussels sprouts, shredded*
- *1 garlic clove, minced*
- *1 tablespoon Dijon mustard*
- *1/3 cup apple, sliced into strips*
- *1/8 teaspoon red pepper flakes, optional*
- *1-pound cooked ground chicken*
- *3 slices bacon, cooked and diced*
- *Salt and pepper to taste*

DIRECTIONS: Servings: 4 Preparation time: 15 minutes

- ✓ *In a mixing container, combine together chicken, green onion, Dijon mustard, garlic, apple, bacon, and pepper flakes. Season with salt and pepper to taste. Mix the ingredients, then form 4 burger patties.*
- ✓ *Heat a grill pan over a medium-high flame and grill the burgers. Cook for five minutes on the side. Set aside.*
- ✓ *In another container, toss the Brussels sprouts and apples.*
- ✓ *In a small pan, heat coconut oil and add the Brussels sprout mixture until everything is slightly wilted. Season with salt and pepper to taste.*
- ✓ *Serve burger patties with the Brussels sprouts slaw.*

NUTRITION Calories 325, Carbs 11.5g, Protein 32g

353) Chicken Wrap

Ingredients

- *2 whole wheat tortilla flatbreads*
- *6 chicken breast slices, skinless, boneless, cooked, and shredded*
- *A handful of baby spinach*
- *2 provolone cheese slices*
- *4 tomato slices*
- *10 kalamata olives, pitted and sliced*
- *1 red onion, sliced*
- *2 tablespoons roasted peppers, chopped*

DIRECTIONS: Servings: 2 Preparation time: 0 minutes

- ✓ *Arrange the tortillas on a working surface, and divide the chicken and the other ingredients on each.*
- ✓ *Roll the tortillas and serve them right away.*

NUTRITION Calories 190, Fat 6.8g, Fiber 3.5g, Carbs: 15g, Protein 6.6g

354) Carrots And Tomatoes Chicken

Ingredients:

- *2 pounds chicken breasts, skinless, boneless, and halved*
- *Salt and black pepper to the taste*
- *3 garlic cloves, minced*
- *3 tablespoons avocado oil*
- *2 shallots, chopped*
- *4 carrots, sliced*
- *3 tomatoes, chopped*
- *¼ cup chicken stock*
- *1 tablespoon Italian seasoning*
- *1 tablespoon parsley, chopped*

DIRECTIONS: Servings: 4 Preparation time: 1 Hour and 10 Minutes

- ✓ *Heat up a pan with the oil over medium-high heat, add the chicken, garlic, salt, and pepper, and brown for 3 minutes on each side.*
- ✓ *Add the rest of the ingredients except the parsley, bring to a simmer and cook over medium-low heat for 40 minutes.*
- ✓ *Add the parsley, divide the mix between plates and serve.*

NUTRITION Calories 309, Fat 12.4g, Fiber 11g, Carbs 23.8g, Protein 15g

355) Almond Chicken Bites

Ingredients

- *1-pound chicken fillet*
- *1 tablespoon potato starch*
- *½ teaspoon salt*
- *1 teaspoon paprika*
- *2 tablespoons wheat flour, whole grain*

- *1 egg, beaten*
- *1 tablespoon almond butter*

DIRECTIONS: Servings: 8 Preparation time: 5 minutes

- ✓ *Chop the chicken fillet on the small pieces and place it in the container.*
- ✓ *Add egg, salt, and potato starch. Mix up the chicken.*
- ✓ *Then mix up wheat flour and paprika.*
- ✓ *Then coat every chicken piece in a wheat flour mixture.*
- ✓ *Place almond butter into the skillet and heat it up.*
- ✓ *Add chicken popcorn and roast it for 5 minutes over medium heat.*
- ✓ *Dry the chicken popcorn with the help of a paper towel.*

NutritionCalories 141, Fat 6g, Fiber 0.4g, Carbs 3.3g, Protein 17.8

356) ***Butter Chicken Thighs***

Ingredients

- *1 teaspoon fennel seeds*
- *1 garlic clove, peeled*
- *1 tablespoon butter*
- *1 teaspoon coconut oil*
- *¼ teaspoon thyme*
- *½ teaspoon salt*
- *1 oz fennel bulb, chopped*
- *1 oz shallot, chopped*
- *4 chicken thighs, skinless, boneless*
- *1 teaspoon ground black pepper*

Directions: Servings: 4 Preparation time: 30 minutes

- ✓ *Rub the chicken thighs with ground black pepper.*
- ✓ *Into the skillet, mix up together butter and coconut oil.*
- ✓ *Add fennel seeds, garlic clove, thyme, salt, and shallot.*
- ✓ *Roast the mixture for 1 minute.*
- ✓ *Then add fennel bulb and chicken thighs.*
- ✓ *Roast the chicken thighs for 2 minutes from each side over high heat.*
- ✓ *Then transfer the skillet with chicken to the oven and cook the meal for 20 minutes at 360F.*

Nutrition Calories 324, Fat 15g, Fiber 0.6g, Carbs 2.6g, Protein 42.7g

357) ***Chicken And Olives Salsa***

Ingredients

- *2 tablespoon avocado oil*
- *4 chicken breast halves, skinless and boneless*
- *Salt and black pepper to the taste*
- *1 tablespoon sweet paprika*
- *1 red onion, chopped*
- *1 tablespoon balsamic vinegar*
- *2 tablespoons parsley, chopped*
- *1 avocado, peeled, pitted, and cubed*
- *2 tablespoons black olives, pitted and chopped*

DIRECTIONS: Servings: 4 Preparation time: 25 minutes

- ✓ *Heat up your grill over medium-high heat, add the chicken brushed with half of the oil and seasoned with paprika, salt, and pepper, cook for 7 minutes on each side, and divide between plates.*
- ✓ *Meanwhile, in a container, mix the onion with the rest of the ingredients and the resting oil, toss, add on top of the chicken and serve.*

NUTRITION Calories 289, Fat 12.4g, Fiber 9g, Carbs 23.8g, Protein 14g

358) ***Chicken Noodle Soup***

Ingredients

- *1 onion, minced*
- *1 rib celery, sliced*
- *3 cups chicken, shredded*
- *3 eggs, lightly beaten*
- *1 green onion for garnish*
- *2 tablespoons coconut oil*
- *1 carrot, peeled and thinly sliced*
- *2 teaspoons dried thyme*
- *2 ½ quarts homemade bone broth*
- *¼ cup fresh parsley, minced*
- *Salt and black pepper to taste*

DIRECTIONS: Servings: 6 Preparation time: 30 minutes

- ✓ *Heat coconut oil over medium-high heat in a large pot and add onions, carrots, and celery.*
- ✓ *Cook for about 4 minutes and stir to the bone broth, thyme, and chicken.*
- ✓ *Simmer for about 15 minutes and stir in parsley.*
- ✓ *Pour beaten eggs into the soup in a slow, steady stream.*
- ✓ *Remove soup from heat and let it stand for about 2 minutes.*
- ✓ *Season with salt and black pepper and dish out to serve.*

NUTRITION Calories 226, Carbs 3.5g, Fat 8.9g, Protein: 31.8g, Sodium 152mg, Sugar 1.6g

359) ***Green Chicken Enchilada Soup***

Ingredients

- *4 oz cream cheese, softened*
- *½ cup salsa verde*

- *1 cup cheddar cheese, shredded*
- *2 cups cooked chicken, shredded*
- *2 cups chicken stock*

DIRECTIONS: Servings: 5 Preparation time: 20 minutes

- ✓ *Put salsa verde, cheddar cheese, cream cheese, and chicken stock in an immersion blender and blend until smooth.*
- ✓ *Pour this mixture into a medium saucepan and cook for about 5 minutes on medium heat.*
- ✓ *Add the shredded chicken and cook for about 5 minutes.*
- ✓ *Garnish with additional shredded cheddar and serve hot.*

NUTRITION Calories 265, Carbs 2.2g, Fat 17.4g, Protein 24g, Sodium 686mg, Sugar 0.8g

360) Turkish Chicken Skewers

Ingredients

- *2 pounds chicken breasts, boneless skinless, cut into inch cubes*
- *2 tablespoons sumac spice for sprinkling*
- *2 lemons, thinly sliced for skewering*
- *For the marinade:*
- *5 cloves garlic*
- *2 Roma tomatoes*
- *1 lemon, juiced*
- *2 tablespoons olive oil*
- *¼ Cup yogurt*
- *¼ Cup total fresh cilantro and parsley leaves*
- *½ teaspoon salt*
- *½ teaspoon pepper*
- *½ teaspoon allspice*
- *1 teaspoon oregano*
- *1 teaspoon cinnamon*

DIRECTIONS: Servings: 4 Preparation time: 12 minutes

- ✓ *Switch on the oven, preheat it setting its temperature to 375F or a grill to medium-high heat.*
- ✓ *Put the marinade ingredients into a food processor; pulse until smooth.*
- ✓ *Toss the chicken with the marinade. Thread the chicken cubes in skewers, alternating with a thin slice of lemon between chicken cubes.*
- ✓ *Grill the skewers for about 3-5 minutes per side, covered.*
- ✓ *When cooked, sprinkle the skewers generously with the sumac.*
- ✓ *Serve with plenty of Aryan.*

NUTRITION Calories 303, Fat 11g, Fiber 2.5g, Sugar 2.5g, Carbs 8g, Protein 42.5g, Chol 134mg,

361) Slow-Cooked Chicken And Capers Mix

Ingredients

- *2 chicken breasts, skinless, boneless, and halved*
- *2 cups canned tomatoes, crushed*
- *2 garlic cloves, minced*
- *1 yellow onion, chopped*
- *2 cups chicken stock*
- *2 tablespoons capers, drained*
- *¼ cup rosemary, chopped*
- *Salt and black pepper to the taste*

DIRECTIONS: Servings: 4 Preparation time: 7 Hours

- ✓ *In your slow cooker, combine the chicken with the tomatoes, capers, and the rest of the ingredients. Put the lid on and cook on Low for 7 hours.*
- ✓ *Divide the mix between plates and serve.*

NUTRITION Calories 292, Fat 9.4g, Fiber 11.8g, Carbs 25g, Protein 36.4g

362) Chili Chicken Mix

Ingredients

- *2 pounds chicken thighs, skinless and boneless*
- *2 tablespoons olive oil*
- *2 cups yellow onion, chopped*
- *1 teaspoon onion powder*
- *1 teaspoon smoked paprika*
- *1 teaspoon chili pepper*
- *½ teaspoon coriander seeds, ground*
- *2 teaspoons oregano, dried*
- *2 teaspoon parsley flakes*
- *3 ounces canned tomatoes, chopped*
- *½ cup black olives pitted and halved*

DIRECTIONS: Servings: 4 Preparation time: 18 minutes

- ✓ *Set the instant pot on Sauté mode, add the oil, heat it up, add the onion, onion powder, and the rest of the ingredients except the tomatoes, olives, and the chicken, stir and sauté for 10 minutes.*
- ✓ *Add the chicken, tomatoes, and olives put the lid on, and cook on High for 8 minutes.*
- ✓ *Release the pressure naturally for 10 minutes, divide the mix into containers and serve.*

NUTRITION Cal 153, Fat 8g, Carbs 9g, Protein 12g

363) Ginger Duck Mix

Ingredients

- *4 duck legs, boneless*
- *4 Shallots, chopped*

- 2 tablespoons olive oil
- 1 tablespoon ginger, grated
- 2 tablespoons rosemary, chopped
- 1 cup chicken stock
- 1 tablespoon chives, chopped

DIRECTIONS:Servings: 4 Preparation time: 1 Hour and 50 minutes

✓ In a roasting pan, combine the duck legs with the shallots and the rest of the ingredients except the chives, toss, introduce to the oven at 250 degrees F and bake for 1 hour and 30 minutes.

✓ Divide the mix between plates, sprinkle the chives on top, and serve.

NutritionCalories 299, Fat 10g, Fiber 9g, Carbs 18g, Protein 17g

364) Duck And Orange Warm Salad

Ingredients

- 2 tablespoons balsamic vinegar
- 2 oranges, peeled and cut into segments
- 1 teaspoon orange zest, grated
- 1 tablespoon orange juice
- 3 shallot, minced
- 2 tablespoons olive oil
- Salt and black pepper to the taste
- 2 duck breasts, boneless and skin scored
- 2 cups baby arugula
- 2 tablespoons chives, chopped

DIRECTIONS: Servings:4 Preparation time: 25 minutes

✓ Heat up a pan with the oil over medium-high heat, add the duck breasts skin side down and brown for 5 minutes.

✓ Flip the duck, add the shallot and the other ingredients except for the arugula, orange and chives, and cook for 15 minutes more.

✓ Transfer the duck breasts to a cutting board, cool down, cut into strips, and put in a salad container.

✓ Add the resting ingredients, toss, and serve warm.

NutritionCalories 304, Fat 15.4g, Fiber 12.6, Carbs 25g, Protein 36.4g

365) Chicken Tacos

Ingredients

- 2 bread tortillas
- 1 teaspoon butter
- 2 teaspoons olive oil
- 1 teaspoon Taco seasoning
- 6 oz chicken breast, skinless, boneless, sliced
- 1/3 cup Cheddar cheese, shredded
- 1 bell pepper, cut on the wedges

Directions:Servings: 4 Preparation Time: 20 Minutes

✓ Pour 1 teaspoon of olive oil into the skillet and add chicken.

✓ Sprinkle the meat with Taco seasoning and mix up well.

✓ Roast chicken for 10 minutes over medium heat. Stir it from time to time.

✓ Then transfer the cooked chicken to the plate. s Add resting olive oil into the skillet.

✓ Then add bell pepper and roast it for 5 minutes. Stir it all the time.

✓ Mix up together bell pepper with chicken.

✓ Toss butter into the skillet and melt it.

✓ Put 1 tortilla into the skillet.

✓ Put Cheddar cheese on the tortilla and flatten it.

✓ Then add a chicken-pepper mixture and cover it with the second tortilla.

✓ Roast the quesadilla for 2 minutes from each side.

✓ Cut the cooked meal on the halves and transfer it to the serving plates.

NutritionCalories 194, Fat 8.3g, Fiber 0.6g, Carbs 16g, Protein 13g

366) Coriander And Coconut Chicken

Ingredients

- 2 pounds chicken thighs, skinless, boneless, and cubed
- 2 tablespoons olive oil
- Salt and black pepper to the taste
- 3 tablespoons coconut, shredded
- 1 and ½ teaspoons orange extract
- 1 tablespoon ginger, grated
- ¼ cup orange juice
- 2 tablespoons coriander, chopped
- 1 cup chicken stock
- ¼ teaspoon red pepper flakes

DIRECTIONS: Servings:4 Preparation time: 30 minutes

✓ Heat up a pan with the oil over medium-high heat, add the chicken, and brown for 4 minutes on each side.

✓ Add salt, pepper, and the rest of the ingredients, bring to a simmer and cook over medium heat for 20 minutes.

✓ Divide the mix between plates and serve hot.

NutritionCalories 297, Fat 14.4g, Fiber 9.6g, Carbs 22g, Protein 25g

367) Chicken Pilaf

Ingredients

- 4 tablespoons avocado oil

- *2 pounds chicken breasts, skinless, boneless, and cubed*
- *½ cup yellow onion, chopped*
- *4 garlic cloves, minced*
- *½ cup kalamata olives pitted*
- *½ cup tomatoes, cubed*
- *6 ounces baby spinach*
- *½ cup feta cheese, crumbled*
- *Pepper and Salt*
- *1 tablespoon marjoram, chopped*
- *1 tablespoon basil, chopped*
- *Juice of ½ lemon*
- *¼ cup pine nuts, toasted*

DIRECTIONS:Servings: 4 Preparation time: 30 minutes

- ✓ *Heat up a pot with 1 tablespoon avocado oil over medium-high heat, add the chicken, some salt, and pepper, brown for 5 minutes on each side, and transfer to a container.*
- ✓ *Heat up the pot again with the rest of the avocado oil over medium heat, add the onion and garlic and sauté for 3 minutes.*
- ✓ *Add the rice, the rest of the ingredients except the pine nuts, also return the chicken, toss, bring to a simmer and cook over medium heat for 20 minutes.*
- ✓ *Divide the mix between plates, top each serving with some pine nuts and serve*

NUTRITION Calories 282, Fat 12.5g, Fiber 8g, Carbs 21.5g, Protein 13.5g

368) Chicken And Black Beans

Ingredients

- *12 oz chicken breast, skinless, boneless, chopped*
- *1 tablespoon taco seasoning*
- *1 tablespoon nut oil*
- *½ teaspoon cayenne pepper*
- *½ teaspoon salt*
- *½ teaspoon garlic, chopped*
- *½ red onion, sliced*
- *1/3 cup black beans, canned, rinsed*
- *½ cup Mozzarella, shredded*

DIRECTIONS:Servings: 4 Preparation time: 20 minutes

- ✓ *Rub the chopped chicken breast with taco seasoning, salt, and cayenne pepper.*
- ✓ *Place the chicken into the skillet, add nut oil and roast it for 10 minutes over medium heat. Mix up the chicken pieces from time to time to avoid burning.*
- ✓ *After this, transfer the chicken to the plate.*
- ✓ *Add sliced onion and garlic into the skillet. Roast the vegetables for 5 minutes. Stir them constantly. Then add black beans and stir well. Cook the ingredients for 2 minutes.*
- ✓ *Add the chopped chicken and mix up well. Top the meal with Mozzarella cheese.*
- ✓ *Close the lid and cook the meal for 3 minutes.*

NutritionCalories 210, Fat 6.4g, Fiber 2.8g, Carbs 13.7, Protein 22.7g

369) Turkey And Chickpeas

Ingredients

- *2 tablespoons avocado oil*
- *1 big turkey breast, skinless, boneless, and roughly cubed*
- *Salt and black pepper to the taste*
- *1 red onion, chopped*
- *15 ounces canned chickpeas, drained and rinsed*
- *15 ounces canned tomatoes, chopped*
- *1 cup kalamata olives, pitted and halved*
- *2 tablespoons lime juice*
- *1 teaspoon oregano, dried*

DIRECTIONS: Servings: 4 Preparation time: 5 Hours

- ✓ *Heat up a pan with the oil over medium-high heat, add the meat and the onion, brown for 5 minutes, and transfer to a slow cooker.*
- ✓ *Add the rest of the ingredients, put the lid on, and cook high for 5 hours.*
- ✓ *Divide between plates and serve*

NUTRITION Calories 352, Fat 14.4, Fiber 11.8g, Carbs 25g, Protein 26.4g

370) Chicken And Mint Sauce

Ingredients

- *2 and ½ tablespoons olive oil*
- *2 pounds chicken breasts, skinless, boneless, and halved*
- *3 tablespoons garlic, minced*
- *2 tablespoons lemon juice*
- *1 tablespoon red wine vinegar*
- *1/3 cup Greek yogurt*
- *2 tablespoons mint, chopped*
- *A pinch of salt and black pepper*

DIRECTIONS:Servings: 4 Preparation time: 40 minutes

- ✓ *In a blender, combine the garlic with the lemon juice and the other ingredients except the oil and the chicken and pulse well.*
- ✓ *Heat up a pan with the oil over medium-high heat, add the chicken, and brown for 3 minutes on each side.*
- ✓ *Add the mint sauce, introduce it to the oven and bake everything a 370 degrees F for 25 minutes.*
- ✓ *Divide the mix between plates and serve.*

Nutrition Calories 278, Fat 12g, Fiber 11g, Carbs

18g, Protein 13.3g

371) Cardamom Chicken And Apricot Sauce

Ingredients

- Juice of 1/2 lemon
- zest of 1/2 lemon, grated
- 2 teaspoons cardamom, ground
- Salt and black pepper to the taste
- 2 chicken breasts, skinless, boneless, and halved
- 2 tablespoons olive oil
- 2 spring onions, chopped
- 2 tablespoons tomato paste
- 2 garlic cloves, minced
- 1 cup apricot juice
- ½ cup chicken stock
- ¼ cup cilantro, chopped

DIRECTIONS:Servings: 4 Preparation time: 7 Hours

- ✓ In your slow cooker, combine the chicken with the lemon juice, lemon zest, and the other ingredients except for the cilantro; toss, put the lid on, and cook on Low for 7 hours.
- ✓ Divide the mix between plates, sprinkle the cilantro on top, and serve.

NutritionCalories 323, Fat 12g, Fiber 11g, Carbs 24g, Protein 16.4g

372) Buttery Chicken Spread

Ingredients

- 8 oz chicken liver
- 3 tablespoon butter
- 1 white onion, chopped
- 1 bay leaf
- 1 teaspoon salt
- ½ teaspoon ground black pepper
- ½ cup of water

DIRECTIONS:Servings: 6 Preparation time: 20 minutes

- ✓ Place the chicken liver into the saucepan.
- ✓ Add onion, bay leaf, salt, ground black pepper, and water.
- ✓ Mix up the mixture and close the lid.
- ✓ Cook the liver mixture for 20 minutes over medium heat. Then transfer it to the blender and blend until smooth.
- ✓ Add butter and mix up until it is melted.
- ✓ Pour the pate mixture into the pate ramekin and refrigerate for 2 hours.

NutritionCalories 122, Fat 8.3g, Fiber 0.5g, Carbs 2g, Protein 9.5g

373) Chicken And Spinach Cakes

Ingredients

- 8 oz ground chicken
- 1 cup fresh spinach, blended
- 1 teaspoon minced onion
- ½ teaspoon salt
- 1 red bell pepper, grinded
- 1 egg, beaten
- 1 teaspoon ground black pepper
- 4 tablespoons Panko breadcrumbs

DIRECTIONS:Servings: 4 Preparation time: 15 minutes

- ✓ To the mixing container, mix up together ground chicken, blended spinach, minced garlic, salt, ground bell pepper, egg, and ground black pepper.
- ✓ When the chicken mixture is smooth, make 4 burgers from it and coat them in Panko breadcrumbs.
- ✓ Place the burgers to the non-stick baking dish or line the baking tray with baking paper.
- ✓ Bake the burgers for 15 minutes at 365F.
- ✓ Flip the chicken burgers on another side after 7 minutes of cooking.

NUTRITIONCalories 171, Fat 5.7g, Fiber 1.7g, Carbs 10.5g, Protein 19.4g

374) Chicken And Lemongrass Sauce

Ingredients

- 1 tablespoon dried dill
- 1 teaspoon butter, melted
- ½ teaspoon lemongrass
- ½ teaspoon cayenne pepper
- 1 teaspoon tomato sauce
- 3 tablespoons sour cream
- 1 teaspoon salt
- 10 oz chicken fillet, cubed

DIRECTIONS:Servings: 4 Preparation time: 20 minutes

- ✓ Make the sauce: into the saucepan, whisk together lemongrass, tomato sauce, sour cream, salt, and dried dill.
- ✓ Bring the sauce to a boil.
- ✓ Meanwhile, pour melted butter into the skillet.
- ✓ Add cubed chicken fillet and roast it for 5 minutes. Stir it from time to time.
- ✓ Then place the chicken cubes in the hot sauce.
- ✓ Close the lid and cook the meal for 10 minutes over low heat.

Nutrition Cal 166,Fat 8g,Fiber 0.2g,Carbs 1g,Pro 21

375) Paprika Chicken Wings

Ingredients

- *4 chicken wings, boneless*
- *1 tablespoon honey*
- *½ teaspoon paprika*
- *¼ teaspoon cayenne pepper*
- *¾ teaspoon ground black pepper*
- *1 tablespoon lemon juice*
- *½ teaspoon sunflower oil*

DIRECTIONS: Servings: 4 Preparation time: 8 minutes

- ✓ *Make the honey marinade: whisk together honey, paprika, cayenne pepper, ground black pepper, lemon juice, and sunflower oil.*
- ✓ *Then brush the chicken wings with marinade carefully.*
- ✓ *Preheat the grill to 385F.*
- ✓ *Place the chicken wings on the grill and cook them for 4 minutes from each side.*

NutritionCalories 26, Fat 0.8g, Fiber 0.3g, Carbs 5g, Protein 0.3g

376) Chicken And Parsley Sauce

Ingredients

- *1 cup ground chicken*
- *2 oz Parmesan, grated*
- *1 tablespoon olive oil*
- *2 tablespoons fresh parsley, chopped*
- *1 teaspoon chili pepper*
- *1 teaspoon paprika*
- *½ teaspoon dried oregano*
- *¼ teaspoon garlic, minced*
- *½ teaspoon dried thyme*
- *1/3 cup crushed tomatoes*

DIRECTIONS:Servings: 4 Preparation time: 25 minutes

- ✓ *Heat up olive oil into the skillet.*
- ✓ *Add ground chicken and sprinkle it with chili pepper, paprika, dried oregano, dried thyme, and parsley. Mix up well.*
- ✓ *Cook the chicken for 5 minutes and add crushed tomatoes. Mix up well.*
- ✓ *Close the lid and simmer the chicken mixture for 10 minutes over low heat.*
- ✓ *Then add grated Parmesan and mix up.*
- ✓ *Cook chicken bolognese for 5 minutes more over medium heat.*

NutritionCalories 154, Fat 9.3g, Carbs 3g, Protein 15.5g

377) Sage Turkey Mix

Ingredients

- *1 big turkey breast, skinless, boneless, and roughly cubed*
- *Juice of 1 lemon*
- *2 tablespoons avocado oil*
- *1 red onion, chopped*
- *2 tablespoons sage, chopped*
- *1 garlic clove, minced*
- *1 cup chicken stock*

DIRECTIONS:Servings: 4 Preparation time: 40 minutes

- ✓ *Heat up a pan with the avocado oil over medium-high heat, add the turkey, and brown for 3 minutes on each side.*
- ✓ *Add the rest of the ingredients, bring to a simmer and cook over medium heat for 35 minutes.*
- ✓ *Divide the mix between plates and serve with a side dish.*

NutritionCalories 382, Fat 12.6g, Fiber 9.6g, Carbs 16.6g, Protein 33g

378) Chipotle Turkey And Tomatoes

Ingredients

- *2 pounds cherry tomatoes, halved*
- *3 tablespoons olive oil*
- *1 red onion, roughly chopped*
- *1 big turkey breast, skinless, boneless, and sliced*
- *3 garlic cloves, chopped*
- *3 red chili peppers, chopped*
- *4 tablespoons chipotle paste*
- *Zest of ½ lemon, grated*
- *Juice of 1 lemon*
- *Salt and black pepper to the taste*
- *Handful coriander, chopped*

DIRECTIONS: Servings: 4 Preparation time: 1 Hour

- ✓ *Heat up a pan with the oil over medium-high heat, add the turkey slices, cook for 4 minutes on each side and transfer to a roasting pan.*
- ✓ *Heat up the pan again over medium-high heat, add the onion, garlic, and chili peppers and sauté for 2 minutes.*
- ✓ *Add the chipotle paste, sauté for 3 minutes more and pour over the turkey slices.*
- ✓ *Toss the turkey slices with the chipotle mix, also add the rest of the ingredients except the coriander, introduce them to the oven and bake at 400 degrees F for 45 minutes.*
- ✓ *Divide everything between plates, sprinkle the coriander on top, and serve.*

NutritionCalories 264, Fat 13g, Fiber 8.7g, Carbs 24g, Protein 33g

379) Curry Chicken, Artichokes And Olives

Ingredients

- *2 pounds chicken breasts, boneless, skinless, and cubed*
- *12 ounces canned artichoke hearts, drained*
- *1 cup chicken stock*
- *1 red onion, chopped*
- *1 tablespoon white wine vinegar*
- *1 cup kalamata olives, pitted and chopped*
- *1 tablespoon curry powder*
- *2 teaspoons basil, dried*
- *Salt and black pepper to the taste*
- *¼ cup rosemary, chopped*

Directions Servings: *6***Preparation time:** *7 Hours*

✓ *In your slow cooker, combine the chicken with the artichokes, olives, and the rest of the ingredients. Put the lid on, and cook on Low for 7 hours.*

✓ *Divide the mix between plates and serve hot.*

Nutrition Calories 275, Fat 12g, Fiber 7.6g, Carbs 19.7g, Protein 18.7g

380) Roasted Chicken

Ingredients

- *1 (5-lb) whole chicken*
- *1 TB. extra-virgin olive oil*
- *2 TB. minced garlic*
- *1 tsp. salt*
- *1 tsp. paprika*
- *1 tsp. black pepper*
- *1 tsp. ground coriander*
- *1 tsp. Seven spices*
- *½ tsp. ground cinnamon*
- *½ large lemon, cut in ½*
- *½ large yellow onion, cut in ½*
- *2 springs fresh rosemary*
- *2 sprigs of fresh thyme*
- *2 sprigs of fresh sage*
- *2 large carrots, cut into 1-in. pieces*
- *6 small red potatoes, washed and cut in ½*
- *4 cloves garlic*

Directions:Servings: *¼* **Chicken Preparation time:** *1* **Hour and 15 minutes**

✓ *Switch on the oven, preheat it setting its temperature to 450oF. Wash chicken and pat dry with paper towels. Place chicken in a roasting pan, and drizzle and then rub the chicken with extra-virgin olive oil.*

✓ *Combine garlic, salt, paprika, black pepper, coriander, seven spices, and cinnamon in a small container. Sprinkle and then rub the entire chicken with spice mixture to coat.*

✓ *Place ¼ lemon, ¼ yellow onion, 1 springs rosemary, 1 spring thyme, and 1 springs sage in the chicken cavity.*

✓ *Place resting rosemary, thyme, sage, lemon, and onion around the chicken in the roasting pan. Add carrots, red potatoes, and garlic cloves to the roasting pan.*

✓ *Roast for 15 minutes. Reduce temperature to 375°F, and roast for 1 more hour, basting chicken every 20 minutes.*

✓ *Let chicken rest for 15 minutes before serving.*

Nutrition Calories 405, Fat 23g, Protein 47g

381) Chicken And Celery Quinoa Mix

Ingredients

- *4 chicken things, skinless and boneless*
- *1 tablespoon olive oil*
- *Salt and black pepper to the taste*
- *2 celery stalks, chopped*
- *2 spring onions, chopped*
- *2 cups chicken stock*
- *½ cup cilantro, chopped*
- *½ cup quinoa*
- *1 teaspoon lime zest, grated*

DIRECTIONS:Servings: *4* **Preparation time: 50 minutes**

✓ *Heat up a pot with the oil over medium-high heat, add the chicken, and brown for 4 minutes on each side.*

✓ *Add the onion and the celery, stir and sauté everything for 5 minutes more.*

✓ *Add the rest of the ingredients, toss, bring to a simmer and cook over medium-low heat for 35 minutes.*

✓ *Divide everything between plates and serve.*

NutritionCalories 240, Fat 12.5,g Fiber 9.5g, Carbs 15.6g, Protein 34g

382) Creamy Chicken And Mushrooms

Ingredients

- *1 red onion, chopped*
- *1 tablespoon olive oil*
- *2 garlic cloves, minced*
- *2 carrots chopped*
- *Salt and black pepper to the taste*
- *1 tablespoon thyme, chopped*
- *1 and ½ cups chicken stock*
- *½ pound Bella mushrooms, sliced*
- *1 cup heavy cream*
- *2 chicken breasts, skinless, boneless, and cubed*
- *2 tablespoons chives, chopped*
- *1 tablespoon parsley, chopped*

DIRECTIONS:Servings: *4* **Preparation time: 30 minutes**

✓ *Heat up a Dutch oven with the oil over medium-*

high heat, add the onion and the garlic and sauté for 5 minutes.

- ✓ *Add the chicken and the mushrooms, and sauté for 10 minutes more.*
- ✓ *Add the rest of the ingredients except the chives and the parsley, bring to a simmer, and cook over medium heat for 15 minutes.*
- ✓ *Add the chives and parsley, divide the mix between plates and serve.*

NutritionCalories 275, Fat 12g, Fiber 10.6g, Carbs 26.7g, Protein 23.7g

383) Basil Turkey And Zucchinis

Ingredients

- *2 tablespoons avocado oil*
- *1 pound turkey breast, skinless, boneless, and sliced*
- *Salt and black pepper to the taste*
- *3 garlic cloves, minced*
- *2 zucchinis, sliced*
- *1 cup chicken stock*
- *¼ cup heavy cream*
- *2 tablespoons basil, chopped*

DIRECTIONS:Servings: 4 Preparation time: 1 Hour

- ✓ *Heat up a pot with the oil over medium-high heat, add the turkey, and brown for 5 minutes on each side.*
- ✓ *Add the garlic and cook everything for 1 minute.*
- ✓ *Add the rest of the ingredients except the basil, toss gently, bring to a simmer and cook over medium-low heat for 50 minutes.*
- ✓ *Add the basil, toss, divide the mix between plates and serve.*

NutritionCalories 262, Fat 9.8g, Fiber 12.2g, Carbs 25.8g, Protein 14.5g

384) Mediterranean Meatloaf

Ingredients

- *2 lb. ground chicken*
- *1/3 cup plain breadcrumbs*
- *½ tsp. salt*
- *1 tsp. garlic powder*
- *1 tsp. ground black pepper*
- *1 tsp. Paprika*
- *½ tsp. Dried oregano*
- *½ tsp. dried thyme*
- *2 TB. fresh basil, chopped*
- *2 TB. fresh Italian parsley, chopped*
- *1 large egg*
- *1 large carrot, shredded*
- *1 cup fresh or frozen green peas*
- *½ cup sun-dried tomatoes, chopped*
- *1 cup ketchup*

DIRECTIONS: Servings:1/8 LoafPreparation time: 45 minutes

- ✓ *Switch on the oven, preheat it setting its temperature to 400°F. Lightly coat all sides of a 9x5-inch loaf pan with olive oil spray.*
- ✓ *In a large container, combine chicken, breadcrumbs, salt, garlic powder, black pepper, paprika, oregano, thyme, basil, Italian parsley, egg, carrot, green peas, and sun-dried tomatoes.*
- ✓ *Transfer the chicken mixture to the prepared pan and even out the top. Cover the pan with a piece of aluminum foil, and bake for 40 minutes.*
- ✓ *After 40 minutes have passed, pour ketchup over top of the loaf and spread it out evenly. Bake for 5 more minutes.*
- ✓ *Remove meatloaf from the oven, and let rest for 10 minutes before slicing and serving warm.*

Nutrition Calories 390, Fat 18g, Protein 34g, Carbs 28g, Fiber 8g

385) Chicken And Mushroom Mix

Ingredients

- *9 oz chicken fillet, cubed*
- *1/3 cup cream*
- *¼ cup mushrooms, chopped*
- *1 teaspoon butter*
- *½ onion, diced*
- *½ teaspoon ground black pepper*
- *½ teaspoon salt*
- *1 teaspoon hot pepper*
- *1 teaspoon sunflower oil*

Directions:Servings: 2 Preparation time: 20 minutes

- ✓ *Sprinkle the chicken cubes with hot pepper and mix up.*
- ✓ *Pour sunflower oil into the skillet and roast chicken cubes for 5 minutes over medium heat. Stir them from time to time.*
- ✓ *Toss butter into the separated skillet and melt it.*
- ✓ *Add mushrooms and sprinkle them with salt and ground black pepper, then add the onion.*
- ✓ *Cook the vegetables for 10 minutes over low heat. Stir them with the help of Spatula every 3 minutes.*
- ✓ *Then add cream and bring to a boil.*
- ✓ *Add roasted chicken cubes and mix up well.*
- ✓ *Close the lid and simmer the meat for 5 minutes.*

NUTRITION Calories 213, Fat 10.7g, Fiber 0.5g, Carbs 3g, Protein 25g

386) Turkey and Cranberry Sauce

Ingredients:

- *1 cup chicken stock*

- *2 Tbsps avocado oil*
- *½ cup cranberry sauce*
- *1 big turkey breast, skinless, boneless, and sliced*
- *1 yellow onion, roughly chopped*
- *Salt and black pepper to the taste*

Preparation time: 10 minutes Cooking time: 50 minutes Servings: 4

✓ *Heat up a pan with the avocado oil over medium-high heat, add the onion and sauté for 5 minutes.*

✓ *Add the turkey and brown for 5 minutes more.*

✓ *Add the rest of the ingredients, toss, introduce to the oven at 350 degrees F and cook for 40 minutes*

Nutrition: Calories 382, fat 12.6, carbs 26.6, protein 17.6

387) Sage Turkey Mix

Ingredients:

- *1 big turkey breast, skinless, boneless, and roughly cubed*
- *Juice of 1 lemon*
- *2 Tbsps avocado oil*
- *1 red onion, chopped*
- *2 Tbsps sage, chopped*
- *1 garlic clove, minced*
- *1 cup chicken stock*

Direction: Preparation time: 10 minutes Cooking time: 40 minutes Servings: 4

✓ *Heat up a pan with the avocado oil over medium-high heat, add the turkey, and brown for 3 minutes on each side.*

✓ *Add the rest of the ingredients, bring to a simmer and cook over medium heat for 35 minutes.*

✓ *Divide the mix between plates and serve with a side dish.*

Nutrition: Calories 382, fat 12.6, fiber 9.6, carbs 16.6, protein 33.2

388) Turkey and Asparagus Mix

Ingredients:

- *1 bunch asparagus, trimmed and halved*
- *1 big turkey breast, skinless, boneless, and cut into strips*
- *1 Tsp basil, dried*
- *2 Tbsps olive oil*
- *A pinch of salt and black pepper*
- *½ cup tomato sauce*
- *1 Tbsp chives, chopped*

Direction: Preparation time: 10 minutes Cooking time: 30 minutes Servings: 4

✓ *Heat up a pan with the oil over medium-high heat, add the turkey, and brown for 4 minutes.*

✓ *Add the asparagus and the rest of the ingredients except the chives, bring to a simmer and cook over medium heat for 25 minutes.*

✓ *Add the chives, divide the mix between plates and serve.*

Nutrition: Calories 337, fat 21.2, fiber 10.2, carbs 21.4, protein 17.6

389) Herbed Almond Turkey

Ingredients:

- *1 big turkey breast, skinless, boneless, and cubed*
- *1 Tbsp olive oil*
- *½ cup chicken stock*
- *1 Tbsp basil, chopped*
- *1 Tbsp rosemary, chopped*
- *1 Tbsp oregano, chopped*
- *1 Tbsp parsley, chopped*
- *3 garlic cloves, minced*
- *½ cup almonds, toasted and chopped*
- *3 cups tomatoes, chopped*

Direction: Preparation time: 10 minutes Cooking time: 40 minutes Servings: 4

✓ *Heat up a pan with the oil over medium-high heat, add the turkey and the garlic, and brown for 5 minutes.*

✓ *Add the stock and the rest of the ingredients, bring to a simmer over medium heat and cook for 35 minutes.*

✓ *Divide the mix between plates and serve.*

Nutrition: Calories 297, fat 11.2, fiber 9.2, carbs 19.4, protein 23.6

390) Thyme Chicken and Potatoes

Ingredients:

- *1 Tbsp olive oil*
- *4 garlic cloves, minced*
- *A pinch of salt and black pepper*
- *2 Tsps thyme, dried*
- *12 small red potatoes, halved*
- *2 pounds chicken breast, skinless, boneless, and cubed*
- *1 cup red onion, sliced*
- *¾ cup chicken stock*
- *2 Tbsps basil, chopped*

Direction: Preparation time: 10 minutes Cooking time: 50 minutes Servings: 4

✓ *In a baking dish greased with the oil, add the potatoes, chicken, and the rest of the ingredients, toss a bit, introduce to the oven and bake at 400 degrees F for 50 minutes.*

✓ *Divide between plates and serve.*

Nutrition: Calories 281, fat 9.2, fiber 10.9, carbs 21.6, protein 13.6

391) Turkey, Artichokes, and Asparagus

Ingredients:

- 2 turkey breasts, boneless, skinless, and halved
- 3 Tbsps olive oil
- 1 and ½ pounds asparagus, trimmed and halved
- 1 cup chicken stock
- A pinch of salt and black pepper
- 1 cup canned artichoke hearts, drained
- ¼ cup kalamata olives, pitted and sliced
- 1 shallot, chopped
- 3 garlic cloves, minced
- 3 Tbsps dill, chopped

Direction: Preparation time: 10 minutes Cooking time: 30 minutes Servings: 4

- ✓ Heat up a pan with the oil over medium-high heat, add the turkey and the garlic, and brown for 4 minutes on each side.
- ✓ Add the asparagus, the stock, and the rest of the ingredients except the dill, bring to a simmer and cook over medium heat for 20 minutes.
- ✓ Add the dill, divide the mix between plates and serve.

Nutrition: Calories 291, fat 16, fiber 10.3, carbs 22.8, protein 34.5

392) Lemony Turkey and Pine Nuts

Ingredients:

- 2 turkey breasts, boneless, skinless, and halved
- A pinch of salt and black pepper
- 2 Tbsps avocado oil
- Juice of 2 lemons
- 1 Tbsp rosemary, chopped
- 3 garlic cloves, minced
- ¼ cup pine nuts, chopped
- 1 cup chicken stock

Direction: Preparation time: 10 minutes Cooking time: 30 minutes Servings: 4

- ✓ Heat up a pan with the oil over medium-high heat, add the garlic and the turkey, and brown for 4 minutes on each side.
- ✓ Add the rest of the ingredients, bring to a simmer and cook over medium heat for 20 minutes.
- ✓ Divide the mix between plates and serve with a side salad.

Nutrition: Calories 293, fat 12.4, fiber 9.3, carbs 17.8, protein 24.5

393) Yogurt Chicken and Red Onion Mix

Ingredients:

- 2 pounds chicken breast, skinless, boneless, and sliced
- 3 Tbsps olive oil
- ¼ cup Greek yogurt
- 2 garlic cloves, minced
- ½ Tsp onion powder
- A pinch of salt and black pepper
- 4 red onions, sliced

Direction: Preparation time: 10 minutes Cooking time: 30 minutes Servings: 4

- ✓ In a roasting pan, combine the chicken with the oil, the yogurt, and the other ingredients, introduce to the oven at 375 degrees F and bake for 30 minutes.
- ✓ Divide the chicken mix between plates and serve hot.

Nutrition: Calories 278, fat 15, fiber 9.2, carbs 15.1, protein 23.3

394) Chicken and Mint Sauce

Ingredients:

- 2 and ½ Tbsps olive oil
- 2 pounds chicken breasts, skinless, boneless, and halved
- 3 Tbsps garlic, minced
- 2 Tbsps lemon juice
- 1 Tbsp red wine vinegar
- 1/3 cup Greek yogurt
- 2 Tbsps mint, chopped
- A pinch of salt and black pepper

Direction: Preparation time: 10 minutes Cooking time: 30 minutes Servings: 4

- ✓ In a blender, combine the garlic with the lemon juice and the other ingredients except the oil and the chicken and pulse well.
- ✓ Heat up a pan with the oil over medium-high heat, add the chicken, and brown for 3 minutes on each side.
- ✓ Add the mint sauce, introduce it to the oven and bake everything at 370 degrees F for 25 minutes.
- ✓ Divide the mix between plates and serve.

Nutrition: Calories 278, fat 12, fiber 11.2, carbs 18.1, protein 13.3

395) Oregano Turkey and Peppers

Ingredients:

- 2 red bell peppers, cut into strips
- 2 green bell peppers, cut into strips
- 1 red onion, chopped
- 4 garlic cloves, minced
- ½ cup black olives, pitted and sliced
- 2 cups chicken stock
- 1 big turkey breast, skinless, boneless, and cut into strips
- 1 Tbsp oregano, chopped
- ½ cup cilantro, chopped

Direction: Preparation time: 10 minutes Cooking time: 1-hour Servings: 4

- ✓ *In a baking pan, combine the peppers with the turkey and the rest of the ingredients, toss, introduce to the oven at 400 degrees F, and roast for 1 hour.*
- ✓ *Divide everything between plates and serve.*

Nutrition: Calories 229, fat 8.9, fiber 8.2, carbs 17.8, protein 33.6

396) Chicken and Mustard Sauce

Ingredients:

- *1/3 cup mustard*
- *Salt and black pepper to the taste*
- *1 red onion, chopped*
- *1 Tbsp olive oil*
- *1 and ½ cups chicken stock*
- *4 chicken breasts, skinless, boneless, and halved*
- *¼ Tsp oregano, dried*

Direction: Preparation time: 10 minutes Cooking time: 26 minutes Servings: 4

- ✓ *Heat up a pan with the stock over medium heat, add the mustard, onion, salt, pepper, and oregano, whisk, bring to a simmer and cook for 8 minutes.*
- ✓ *Heat up a pan with the oil over medium-high heat, add the chicken, and brown for 3 minutes on each side.*
- ✓ *Add the chicken to the pan with the sauce, toss, simmer everything for 12 minutes more, divide between plates, and serve.*

Nutrition: Calories 247, fat 15.1, carbs 16.6, protein 26.1

397) Chicken and Sausage Mix

Ingredients:

- *2 zucchinis, cubed*
- *1 pound Italian sausage, cubed*
- *2 Tbsps olive oil*
- *1 red bell pepper, chopped*
- *1 red onion, sliced*
- *2 Tbsps garlic, minced*
- *2 chicken breasts, boneless, skinless, and halved*
- *Salt and black pepper to the taste*
- *½ cup chicken stock*
- *1 Tbsp balsamic vinegar*

Direction: Preparation time: 10 minutes Cooking time: 50 minutes Servings: 4

- ✓ *Heat up a pan with half of the oil over medium-high heat, add the sausages, brown for 3 minutes on each side, and transfer to a container.*
- ✓ *Heat up the pan again with the rest of the oil over medium-high heat, add the chicken and brown for 4 minutes on each side.*
- ✓ *Return the sausage, add the rest of the ingredients as well, bring to a simmer, introduce to the oven and bake at 400 degrees F for 30 minutes.*
- ✓ *Divide everything between plates and serve.*

Nutrition: Calories 293, fat 13.1, fiber 8.1, carbs 16.6, protein 26.1

398) Coriander and Coconut Chicken

Ingredients:

- *2 pounds chicken thighs, skinless, boneless, and cubed*
- *2 Tbsps olive oil*
- *Salt and black pepper to the taste*
- *3 Tbsps coconut flesh, shredded*
- *1 and ½ Tsps orange extract*
- *1 Tbsp ginger, grated*
- *¼ cup orange juice*
- *2 Tbsps coriander, chopped*
- *1 cup chicken stock*
- *¼ Tsp red pepper flakes*

Direction: Preparation time: 10 minutes Cooking time: 30 minutes Servings: 4

- ✓ *Heat up a pan with the oil over medium-high heat, add the chicken, and brown for 4 minutes on each side.*
- ✓ *Add salt, pepper, and the rest of the ingredients, bring to a simmer and cook over medium heat for 20 minutes.*
- ✓ *Divide the mix between plates and serve hot.*

Nutrition: Calories 297, fat 14.4, fiber 9.6, carbs 22, protein 25

399) Saffron Chicken Thighs and Green Beans

Ingredients:

- *2 pounds chicken thighs, boneless and skinless*
- *2 Tsps saffron powder*
- *1 pound green beans, trimmed and halved*
- *½ cup Greek yogurt*
- *Salt and black pepper to the taste*
- *1 Tbsp lime juice*
- *1 Tbsp dill, chopped*

Direction: Preparation time: 10 minutes Cooking time: 25 minutes Servings: 4

- ✓ *In a roasting pan, combine the chicken with the saffron, green beans, and the rest of the ingredients, toss a bit, introduce to the oven and bake at 400 degrees F for 25 minutes.*
- ✓ *Divide everything between plates and serve.*

Nutrition: Calories 274, fat 12.3, fiber 5.3, carbs 20.4, protein 14.3

400) Chicken and Olives Salsa

Ingredients:

- *2 Tbsp avocado oil*

- *4 chicken breast halves, skinless and boneless*
- *Salt and black pepper to the taste*
- *1 Tbsp sweet paprika*
- *1 red onion, chopped*
- *1 Tbsp balsamic vinegar*
- *2 Tbsps parsley, chopped*
- *1 avocado, peeled, pitted, and cubed*
- *2 Tbsps black olives, pitted and chopped*

Direction: Preparation time: 10 minutes Cooking time: 25 minutes Servings: 4

- ✓ *Heat up your grill over medium-high heat, add the chicken brushed with half of the oil and seasoned with paprika, salt, and pepper, cook for 7 minutes on each side, and divide between plates.*
- ✓ *Meanwhile, in a container, mix the onion with the rest of the ingredients and the resting oil, toss, add on top of the chicken and serve.*

Nutrition: Calories 289, fat 12.4, fiber 9.1, carbs 23.8, protein 14.3

401) ***Carrots and Tomatoes Chicken***

Ingredients:

- *2 pounds chicken breasts, skinless, boneless, and halved*
- *Salt and black pepper to the taste*
- *3 garlic cloves, minced*
- *3 Tbsps avocado oil*
- *2 shallots, chopped*
- *4 carrots, sliced*
- *3 tomatoes, chopped*
- *¼ cup chicken stock*
- *1 Tbsp Italian seasoning*
- *1 Tbsp parsley, chopped*

Direction: Preparation time: 10 minutes Cooking time: 1 hour and 10 minutes Servings: 4

- ✓ *Heat up a pan with the oil over medium-high heat, add the chicken, garlic, salt, and pepper, and brown for 3 minutes on each side.*
- ✓ *Add the rest of the ingredients except the parsley, bring to a simmer and cook over medium-low heat for 40 minutes.*
- ✓ *Add the parsley, divide the mix between plates and serve.*

Nutrition: Calories 309, fat 12.4, fiber 11.1, carbs 23.8, protein 15.3

402) ***Smoked and Hot Turkey Mix***

Ingredients:

- *1 red onion, sliced*
- *1 big turkey breast, skinless, boneless, and roughly cubed*
- *1 Tbsp smoked paprika*
- *2 chili peppers, chopped*
- *Salt and black pepper to the taste*
- *2 Tbsps olive oil*
- *½ cup chicken stock*
- *1 Tbsp parsley, chopped*
- *1 Tbsp cilantro, chopped*

Direction: Preparation time: 10 minutes Cooking time: 40 minutes Servings: 4

- ✓ *Grease a roasting pan with the oil, add the turkey, onion, paprika, and the rest of the ingredients, toss, introduce to the oven and bake at 425 degrees F for 40 minutes.*
- ✓ *Divide the mix between plates and serve right away*

Nutrition: Calories 310, fat 18.4, fiber 10.4, carbs 22.3, protein 33.4

403) ***Spicy Cumin Chicken***

Ingredients:

- *2 Tsps chili powder*
- *2 and ½ Tbsps olive oil*
- *Salt and black pepper to the taste*
- *1 and ½ Tsps garlic powder*
- *1 Tbsp smoked paprika*
- *½ cup chicken stock*
- *1 pound chicken breasts, skinless, boneless, and halved*
- *2 Tsps sherry vinegar*
- *2 Tsps hot sauce*
- *2 Tsps cumin, ground*
- *½ cup black olives, pitted and sliced*

Direction: Preparation time: 10 minutes Cooking time: 25 minutes Servings: 4

- ✓ *Heat up a pan with the oil over medium-high heat, add the chicken, and brown for 3 minutes on each side.*
- ✓ *Add the chili powder, salt, pepper, garlic powder, and paprika, toss and cook for 4 minutes more.*
- ✓ *Add the rest of the ingredients, toss, bring to a simmer and cook over medium heat for 15 minutes more.*
- ✓ *Divide the mix between plates and serve.*

Nutrition: Calories 230, fat 18.4, fiber 9.4, carbs 15.3, protein 13.4

404) ***Chicken with Artichokes and Beans***

Ingredients:

- *2 Tbsps olive oil*
- *2 chicken breasts, skinless, boneless, and halved*
- *Zest of 1 lemon, grated*
- *3 garlic cloves, crushed*
- *Juice of 1 lemon*

- *Salt and black pepper to the taste*
- *1 Tbsp thyme, chopped*
- *6 ounces canned artichokes hearts, drained*
- *1 cup canned fava beans, drained and rinsed*
- *1 cup chicken stock*
- *A pinch of cayenne pepper*
- *Salt and black pepper to the taste*

Direction: Preparation time: 10 minutes Cooking time: 40 minutes Servings: 4

- ✓ *Heat up a pan with the oil over medium-high heat, add chicken, and brown for 5 minutes.*
- ✓ *Add lemon juice, lemon zest, salt, pepper, and the rest of the ingredients, bring to a simmer, and cook over medium heat for 35 minutes.*
- ✓ *Divide the mix between plates and serve right away.*

Nutrition: Calories 291, fat 14.9, fiber 10.5, carbs 23.8, protein 24.2

405) Chicken and Olives Tapenade

Ingredients:

- *2 chicken breasts, boneless, skinless, and halved*
- *1 cup black olives, pitted*
- *½ cup olive oil*
- *Salt and black pepper to the taste*
- *½ cup mixed parsley, chopped*
- *½ cup rosemary, chopped*
- *Salt and black pepper to the taste*
- *4 garlic cloves, minced*
- *Juice of ½ lime*

Direction: Preparation time: 10 minutes Cooking time: 25 minutes Servings: 4

- ✓ *In a blender, combine the olives with half of the oil and the rest of the ingredients except the chicken and pulse well.*
- ✓ *Heat up a pan with the rest of the oil over medium-high heat, add the chicken, and brown for 4 minutes on each side.*
- ✓ *Add the olives, mix, and cook for 20 minutes more, tossing often.*

Nutrition: Calories 291, fat 12.9, fiber 8.5, carbs 15.8, protein 34.2

406) Spiced Chicken Meatballs

Ingredients:

- *1 pound chicken meat, ground*
- *1 Tbsp pine nuts, toasted and chopped*
- *1 egg, whisked*
- *2 Tsps turmeric powder*
- *2 garlic cloves, minced*
- *Salt and black pepper to the taste*
- *1 and ¼ cups heavy cream*
- *2 Tbsps olive oil*
- *¼ cup parsley, chopped*
- *1 Tbsp chives, chopped*

Direction: Preparation time: 10 minutes Cooking time: 20 minutes Servings: 4

- ✓ *In a container, combine the chicken with the pine nuts and the rest of the ingredients except the oil and the cream; stir well and shape medium meatballs out of this mix.*
- ✓ *Heat up a pan with the oil over medium-high heat, add the meatballs and cook them for 4 minutes on each side.*
- ✓ *Add the cream, toss gently, cook everything over medium heat for 10 minutes more, divide between plates and serve.*

Nutrition: Calories 283, fat 9.2, fiber 12.8, carbs 24.4, protein 34.5

407) Sesame Turkey Mix

Ingredients:

- *2 Tbsps avocado oil*
- *1 and ¼ cups chicken stock*
- *1 Tbsps sesame seeds, toasted*
- *Salt and black pepper to the taste*
- *1 big turkey breast, skinless, boneless, and sliced*
- *¼ cup parsley, chopped*
- *4 ounces feta cheese, crumbled*
- *¼ cup red onion, chopped*
- *1 Tbsp lemon juice*

Direction: Preparation time: 10 minutes Cooking time: 25 minutes Servings: 4

- ✓ *Heat up a pan with the oil over medium-high heat, add the meat, and brown for 4 minutes on each side.*
- ✓ *Add the rest of the ingredients except the cheese and the sesame seeds, bring everything to a simmer, and cook over medium heat for 15 minutes.*
- ✓ *Add the cheese, toss, divide the mix between plates, sprinkle the sesame seeds on top, and serve.*

Nutrition: Calories 283, fat 13.2, carbs 19.4, protein 24.5

408) Cardamom Chicken and Apricot Sauce

Ingredients:

- *Juice of ½ lemon*
- *Zest of ½ lemon, grated*
- *2 Tsps cardamom, ground*
- *Salt and black pepper to the taste*
- *2 chicken breasts, skinless, boneless, and halved*
- *2 Tbsps olive oil*
- *2 spring onions, chopped*

- *2 Tbsps tomato paste*
- *2 garlic cloves, minced*
- *1 cup apricot juice*
- *½ cup chicken stock*
- *¼ cup cilantro, chopped*

Direction: Preparation time: 10 minutes Cooking time: 7 hours Servings: 4

- ✓ *In your slow cooker, combine the chicken with the lemon juice, lemon zest, and the other ingredients except for the cilantro; toss, put the lid on, and cook on Low for 7 hours.*
- ✓ *Divide the mix between plates, sprinkle the cilantro on top, and serve.*

Nutrition: Calories 323, fat 12, fiber 11, carbs 23.8, protein 16.4

Fish and Seafood

Recipes

409) Lemon Swordfish

Ingredients

- 12 oz swordfish steaks (6 oz every fish steak)
- 1 teaspoon ground cumin
- 1 tablespoon lemon juice
- ¼ teaspoon salt
- 1 teaspoon olive oil

DIRECTIONS: Servings:2 Preparation time: 6 minute

✓ Sprinkle the fish steaks with ground cumin and salt from each side.

✓ Then drizzle the lemon juice over the steaks and massage them gently with the help of the fingertips.

✓ Preheat the grill to 395F.

✓ Brush every fish steak with olive oil and place it in the drill.

✓ Cook the swordfish for 3 minutes from each side.

NUTRITION Calories 289| Fat 1.5g | Fiber 0.1g | Carbs 0.6g | Protein 43.4g

410) Fish Tacos

Ingredients

- 4 tilapia fillets
- ¼ Cup fresh cilantro, chopped
- ¼ Cup fresh lime juice
- 2 tbsp paprika
- 1 tbsp olive oil
- Pepper
- Salt

DIRECTIONS: Servings:8Preparation time:18 minutes

✓ Pour 2 cups of water into the instant pot, then place the steamer rack to the pot.

✓ Place fish fillets on parchment paper.

✓ Season fish fillets with paprika, pepper, and salt and drizzle with oil and lime juice.

✓ Fold parchment paper around the fish fillets and place them on a steamer rack to the pot.

✓ Once done, release pressure using quick release. Remove lid.

✓ Remove fish packet from the pot and open it.

✓ Shred the fish with a fork and served.

Nutrition Calories 67 | Fat 2.5g | Carbs 1.1g | Sugar 0.2g | Protein 10.8g| Cholesterol 28mg

411) Cod Potato Soup

Ingredients

- 2 tablespoons olive oil
- 2 shallots, chopped
- 1 celery stalk, sliced
- 1 carrot, sliced
- 1 red bell pepper, cored and diced
- 2 garlic cloves, chopped
- 1 ½ pounds potatoes, peeled and cubed
- 1 cup diced tomatoes
- 1 bay leaf
- 1 thyme sprigs
- ½ teaspoon dried marjoram
- 2 cups chicken stock
- 6 cups water
- Salt and pepper to taste
- 4 cod fillets, cubed
- 2 tablespoons lemon juice

DIRECTIONS: Servings:8 Preparation time:1 Hour

✓ Heat the oil in a soup pot and stir to the shallots, celery, carrot, bell pepper, and garlic.

✓ Cook for 5 minutes, then stir to the potatoes, tomatoes, bay leaf, thyme, marjoram, stock, and water.

✓ Season with salt and pepper and cook on low heat for 20 minutes.

✓ Add the cod fillets and lemon juice and continue cooking for 5 additional minutes.

✓ Serve the soup warm and fresh.

Nutrition Calories 108 |Fat 3.9g |Protein 2.2g |Carbs 17g

412) Paprika Salmon And Green Beans

Ingredients

- ¼ cup olive oil
- ½ tablespoon onion powder
- ½ teaspoon bouillon powder
- ½ teaspoon cayenne pepper
- 1 tablespoon smoked paprika
- 1-pound green beans
- 2 teaspoon minced garlic
- 3 tablespoon fresh herbs
- 6 ounces of salmon steak
- Salt and pepper to taste

DIRECTIONS: Servings:3 Preparation time: 20 minutes

✓ Switch on the oven, preheat it setting its temperature to 400F.

✓ Grease a baking sheet and set it aside.

✓ Heat a skillet over medium-low heat and add the olive oil. Sauté the garlic smoked paprika, fresh herbs, cayenne pepper, and onion pot der. Stir for a minute, then let the mixture sit for 5 minutes. Set aside.

✓ Put the salmon steaks in a container and add salt and the paprika spice mixture. Rub to coat the salmon » ell.

✓ Place the salmon on the baking sheet and cook for

18 minutes.

- ✓ *Meanwhile, blanch the green beans in boiling enter with salt. Serve the beans with the salmon.*

NUTRITION Cal 945 | Fat 66.6 g |Protein 43g |Carbs 43g

413) Cucumber-Basil Salsa On Halibut Pouches

Ingredients

- *1 lime, thinly sliced into 8 pieces*
- *2 cups mustard greens, stems removed*
- *2 tsp olive oil*
- *4 -5 radishes trimmed and quartered*
- *4 -oz skinless halibut filets*
- *4 large fresh basil leaves*
- *Cayenne pepper to taste (optional)*
- *Pepper and salt to taste*
- *1 ½ cups diced cucumber*
- *1 ½ finely chopped fresh basil leaves*
- *2 tsp fresh lime juice*
- *Pepper and salt to taste*

DIRECTIONS: Servings: 4Preparation time: 17 minute

- ✓ *Preheat oven to 400F.*
- ✓ *Make four 15 X 12-inch rectangles to use as parchment papers. Fold the pieces in half lengthwise and place them on the table.*
- ✓ *Season halibut fillets with pepper, salt, and cayenne, if using cayenne.*
- ✓ *12 cup mustard greens should be placed just to the right of the fold, going lengthwise. In the center of the mustard greens, place a basil leaf and a lime slice. 14 radishes should be layered around the greens. Drizzle with 12 tablespoons of oil, season with pepper and salt, and top with a halibut fillet slice.*
- ✓ *Fold the parchment paper over your filling and crimp the edges of the parchment paper from one end to the other end, just like you would for a calzone. Pinch the crimped parchment paper's end to seal it.*
- ✓ *Repeat the process to the resting ingredients until you have 4 pieces of parchment paper filled with halibut and greens.*
- ✓ *Place pouches in a baking pan and bake in the oven until halibut is flaky, around 15 to 17 minut9S.*
- ✓ *Meanwhile, waiting for halibut pouches to cook, make your salsa by mixing all salsa ingredients in a medium container.*
- ✓ *When the halibut is done, take it out of the oven and make a tear in the top. Be cautious of the steam because it is extremely hot. Divide the salsa in half and spoon 14 tablespoons on top of the halibut through the slit you've made.*
- ✓ *Serve and enjoy.*

NUTRITION Calories 335 | Protein 20.2g | Fat 16.3g | Carbs 22g

414) Sardine Meatballs

Ingredients

- *11 oz sardines, canned, drained*
- *1/3 cup shallot, chopped*
- *1 teaspoon chili flakes*
- *½ teaspoon salt*
- *2 tablespoon wheat flour, whole grain*
- *1 egg. beaten*
- *1 tablespoon chives, chopped*
- *1 teaspoon olive oil*
- *1 teaspoon butter*

DIRECTIONS: Servings: 4|Preparation time: 10 minutes

- ✓ *Put the butter into the skillet and melt it.*
- ✓ *Add shallot and cook it until translucent.*
- ✓ *After this, transfer the shallot to the mixing container.*
- ✓ *Add sardines, chili flakes, salt, flour, egg, chives, and mix up until smooth with the help of the fork.*
- ✓ *Blake the medium size cakes and place them into the skillet.*
- ✓ *Add olive oil.*
- ✓ *Roast the fish cakes for 3 minutes from each side over medium heat.*
- ✓ *Dry the cooked fish cakes with a paper towel if needed and transfer them to the seeing plates.*

Nutrition Calories 221| Fat 12.2g | Fiber 0.1g | Carbs 5,4g| Protein 21.3g

415) Basil Tilapia

Ingredients

- *12 oz tilapia fillet*
- *2 oz Parmesan, grated*
- *1 tablespoon olive oil*
- *½ teaspoon ground black pepper*
- *1 cup fresh basil*
- *3 tablespoons avocado oil*
- *1 tablespoon pine nuts*
- *1 garlic clove, peeled*
- *¾ teaspoon white pepper*

DIRECTIONS: Servings: 3|Preparation time: 20 minutes

- ✓ *Make pesto sauce: blend the avocado oil, fresh basil, pine nuts, garlic clove, and white pepper until smooth.*
- ✓ *After this, cut the tilapia fillet into 3 servings.*
- ✓ *Sprinkle every fish serving with olive oil and ground black pepper.*
- ✓ *Roast the fillets over medium heat for 2 minutes*

from each side.

- ✓ *Meanwhile, line the baking tray with baking paper.*
- ✓ *Arrange the roasted tilapia fillets to the tray.*
- ✓ *Then top them with pesto and Parmesan.*
- ✓ *Bake the fish for 15 minutes at 365F.*

NUTRITION Calories 321 | Fat 17g | Fiber 1.2g | Carbs 4.4g| Protein 37.4g

416) Horseradish Cheesy Salmon Mix

Ingredients

- *2 ounces feta cheese, mumbled*
- *4 ounces cream cheese, soft*
- *3 tablespoons already prepared horseradish*
- *1 pound smoked salmon, skinless, boneless, and flaked*
- *2 teaspoons lime zest, grated*
- *1 red onion, chopped*
- *3 tablespoons chives, chopped*

DIRECTIONS: Servings: 8Preparation time: 1 Hour

- ✓ *In your food processor, mix cream cheese with horseradish, goat cheese, and lime zest and blend very well.*
- ✓ *In a container, combine the salmon with the rest of the ingredients, toss, and serve cold.*

Nutrition Calories 281 | Fat 17.9g | Fiber 1g | Carbs 4.2g | Protein 25g

417) Simple Lemon Clams

Ingredients

- *1 lb clams, clean*
- *1 tbsp fresh lemon juice*
- *1 lemon zest, grated*
- *1 onion, chopped*
- *½ cup fish stock*
- *Pepper*
- *Salt*

DIRECTIONS: Servings: 4Preparation time: 20 minutes

- ✓ *In the inner pot of the instant pot, combine all ingredients and stir well.*
- ✓ *Seal pot with lid and Cook on high for 10 minutes.*
- ✓ *Once done, release pressure using quick release. Remove lid.*
- ✓ *Serve and enjoy.*

NUTRITION Calories 76 | Fat 0.6g | Carbs 16.5g | Sugar 5.4 | Protein 1.8g | Cholesterol 0mg

418) Honey Halibut

Ingredients

- *1-pound halibut*
- *1 teaspoon lime zest*
- *½ teaspoon honey*
- *1 teaspoon olive oil*
- *½ teaspoon lime juice*
- *¼ teaspoon salt*
- *¼ teaspoon chili flakes*

DIRECTIONS: Servings: 3Preparation time: 15 minutes

- ✓ *Cut the fish on the sticks and sprinkle with salt and chili flakes.*
- ✓ *Whisk together lime zest, honey, olive oil, and lime juice.*
- ✓ *Brush the halibut sticks with the honey mixture from each side.*
- ✓ *Line the baking tray with baking paper and place the fish inside.*
- ✓ *Bake the halibut for 15 minutes at 375F. Flip the fish on another side after 7 minutes of cooking.*

Nutrition Calories 254 | Fat 19g | Fiber 0 | Carbs 0.7g | Protein 18.8g

419) Stuffed Mackerel

Ingredients

- *4 teaspoons capers. drained*
- *1-pound whole mackerel, peeled, trimmed*
- *1 teaspoon garlic powder*
- *½ teaspoon ground coriander*
- *½ teaspoon salt*
- *1 tablespoon lime juice*
- *¼ teaspoon chili flakes*
- *½ white onion. sliced*
- *4 teaspoons butter*
- *3 tablespoons water*

DIRECTIONS: Servings: 5Preparation time: 30 minutes

- ✓ *Rub the fish with salt, garlic powder, and chili flakes.*
- ✓ *Then sprinkle it with lime juice.*
- ✓ *Line the baking tray with parchment and arrange the fish inside.*
- ✓ *Fill the mackerel with capers and butter.*
- ✓ *Then sprinkle fish with water.*
- ✓ *Cover the fish with foil and secure the edges. Bake the mackerel for 30 minutes at 365F.*

NUTRITION Calories 262 | Fat 17.5g | Fiber 0.4g | Carbs 1.8g | Protein 25.5g

420) Healthy Carrot & Shrimp

Ingredients

- *1 lb shrimp, peeled and deveined*
- *1 tbsp chives, chopped*
- *1 onion, chopped*
- *1 tbsp olive oil*
- *1 cup fish stock*

- *1 cup carrots, sliced*
- *Pepper*
- *Salt*

***DIRECTIONS:Servings:** 4 **Preparation time:** 6 minutes*

- ✓ *Add oil into the inner pot of the instant pot and set the pot on sauté mode.*
- ✓ *Add onion and sauté for 2 minutes.*
- ✓ *Add shrimp and stir well.*
- ✓ *Add resting ingredients and stir well.*
- ✓ *Seal pot with lid and cook on high for 4 minutes.*
- ✓ *Once done, release pressure using quick release. Remove lid. Serve and enjoy.*

NUTRITION Calories 197| Fat 5.9g| Carbs 7g| Sugar 2.5g | Protein 27.7g| Cholesterol 239mg

421) ***Tomato Cod Mix***

Ingredients

- *1 teaspoon tomato paste*
- *1 teaspoon garlic, diced*
- *1 white onion, sliced*
- *1 jalapeno pepper, chopped*
- *1/3 cup chicken stock*
- *7 oz Spanish cod fillet*
- *1 teaspoon paprika*
- *1 teaspoon salt*

Directions: Servings: 2Preparation time: 5.5 Hours

- ✓ *Pour chicken stock into the saucepan.*
- ✓ *Add tomato paste and mix up the liquid until homogenous.*
- ✓ *Add garlic, onion, jalapeno pepper, paprika, and salt.*
- ✓ *Bring the liquid to a boil and then simmer it.*
- ✓ *Chop the cod fillet and add it to the tomato liquid.*
- ✓ *Close the lid and simmer the fish for 10 minutes over low heat. Serve the fish to the containers with tomato sauce.*

Nutrition Calories 113 | Fat 1.2g | Fiber 1.9g | Carbs 7.2g | Protein 18.9g

422) ***Garlic Mussels***

Ingredients

- *1-pound mussels*
- *1 chili pepper, chopped*
- *1 cup chicken stock*
- *½ cup milk*
- *1 teaspoon olive oil*
- *1 teaspoon minced garlic*
- *1 teaspoon ground coriander*
- *½ teaspoon salt*
- *1 cup fresh parsley, chopped*
- *4 tablespoons lemon juice*

DIRECTIONS: Servings: 4Preparation time: 10 minutes

- ✓ *Pour milk into the saucepan.*
- ✓ *Add chili pepper, chicken stock olive oil, minced garlic, ground coriander, salt, and lemon juice.*
- ✓ *Bring the liquid to a boil and add mussels.*
- ✓ *Boil the mussel for 4 minutes or until thee will open shells.*
- ✓ *Then add chopped parsley and mix up the meal well.*
- ✓ *Remove it from the heat.*

Nutrition Calories 136 | Fat 4.7g | Fiber 0.6g | Carbs 7.5g | Protein 15.3g

423) ***Mahi Mahi And Pomegranate Sauce***

Ingredients:

- *1 and ½ cups chicken stock*
- *1 tablespoon olive oil*
- *4 mahi-mahi fillets, boneless*
- *4 tablespoons tahini paste*
- *Juice of 1 lime*
- *Seeds from 1 pomegranate*
- *1 tablespoon parsley, chopped*

Directions: Servings: 4Preparation time: 10 minutes

- ✓ *Heat up a pan with the oil over medium-high heat, add the fish and cook for 3 minutes on each side.*
- ✓ *Add the rest of the ingredients, flip the fish again, cook for 4 minutes more, divide everything between plates and serve.*

NUTRITION Calories 224 | Fat 11.1g | Fiber 5.5g | Carbs 16.7g | Protein 11.4g

424) ***Honey Balsamic Salmon***

Ingredients

- *2 salmon fillets*
- *¼ tsp red pepper flakes*
- *2 tbsp honey*
- *2 tbsp balsamic vinegar*
- *1 cup of water*
- *Pepper and Salt*

DIRECTIONS: Servings: 2Preparation time: 3 minutes

- ✓ *Pour water into the instant pot and place trivet to the pot.*
- ✓ *In a small container, mix together honey, red pepper flakes, and vinegar.*
- ✓ *Brush fish fillets with honey mixture and place on top of the trivet*
- ✓ *Seal pot with lid and cook on high for 3 minutes.*

- ✓ *Once done, release pressure using quick release. Remove lid.*
- ✓ *Serve and enjoy.*

NUTRITION Calories 303 | Fat 11g | Carbs 17.6g | Sugar 17.3g | Protein 34.6g | Cholesterol 78mg

425) Sage Salmon Fillet

Ingredients

- 4 oz salmon fillet
- ½ teaspoon salt
- 1 teaspoon sesame oil
- ½ teaspoon same

Directions: Servings: 1Preparation time: 25 minutes

- ✓ *Rub the fillet with salt and sage.*
- ✓ *Place the fish on the tray and sprinkle it with sesame oil.*
- ✓ *Cook the fish for 25 minutes at 365F.*
- ✓ *Flip the fish carefully onto another side after 12 minutes of cooking.*

NUTRITION Calories 191| Fat 11.6g | Fiber 0.1g |Carbs 0.2g |Protein 22g

426) Seafood Stew Cioppino

Ingredients

- ¼ cup Italian parsley. chopped
- ¼ tsp dried basil
- ¼ tsp dried these
- ½ cup dry white wine like pinot grigio
- ½ lb. King crab legs. cut at each joint
- ½ onion. chopped
- ½ tsp red pepper Blakes (adjust to the desired spiciness)
- 1 28-oz can crushed tomatoes
- 1 lb. Mahi-mahi. cut into ½-inch cubes
- 1 lb. raw shrimp
- 1 tbsp olive oil
- 2 bay leaves
- 2 cups clam juice
- 50 live clams, washed
- 6 cloves garlic, minced
- Pepper and salt to taste

DIRECTIONS: Servings: 6Preparation time: 40 minutes

- ✓ *On medium fire, place a stockpot and heat oil.*
- ✓ *Add onion and for 4 minutes sauté until soft.*
- ✓ *Add bay leaves, thyme, basil, red pepper flakes, and garlic. Cook for a minute while stirring a bit.*
- ✓ *Add clam juice and tomatoes. Once simmering, place fire to medium heat and cook for 20 minutes uncovered.*
- ✓ *Add white vine and clams. Cover and cook for 5 minutes or until clams have slightly opened.*
- ✓ *Stir the pot and add fish pieces, crab legs, and shrimp. Do not stir the soup to maintain the fish's shape. Cook, while covered for 4 minutes or until clams are fully opened: fish and shrimps are opaque and cooked.*
- ✓ *Season with pepper and salt to taste.*
- ✓ *Transfer Cioppino to serving containers and garnish with parsley before serving.*

NUTRITION Cal371|Carbs 15.5g|Protein 62g|Fat 6.8

427) Feta Tom Shrimp Soup

Ingredients

- 4 sea bass fillets
- 1 ½ cups water
- 1 tbsp olive oil
- 1 tsp garlic, minced
- 1 tsp basil, chopped
- 1 tsp parsley, chopped
- ½ cup feta cheese, crumbled
- 1 cup canned tomatoes, diced
- Pepper
- Salt

DIRECTIONS: Servings: 4Preparation time: 8 minutes

- ✓ *Season fish fillets with pepper and salt.*
- ✓ *Pour 2 cups of water into the instant pot, then place a steamer rack to the pot.*
- ✓ *Place fish fillets on the steamer rack to the pot.*
- ✓ *Seal pot with lid and cook on high for 5 minutes.*
- ✓ *Once done, release pressure using quick release. Remove lid.*
- ✓ *Remove fish fillets from the pot and clean the pot.*
- ✓ *Add oil into the inner pot of the instant pot and set the pot on sauté mode.*
- ✓ *Add garlic and sauté for 1 minute.*
- ✓ *Add tomatoes, parsley, and basil and stir well and cook for 1 minute.*
- ✓ *Add fish fillets and top with crumbled cheese and cook for a minute.*
- ✓ *Serve and enjoy*

NUTRITION Calories 219| Fat 10g | Carbs 4g | Sugar 2.8g | Protein 27.1g | Cholesterol 70mg

428) Mussels Containers

Ingredients

- 2 pounds mussels, scrubbed
- 1 tablespoon garlic, minced
- 1 tablespoon basil, chopped
- 1 yellow onion, chopped
- 6 tomatoes, cubed
- 1 cup heavy cream

- *2 tablespoons olive oil*
- *1 tablespoon parsley, chopped*

DIRECTIONS:Servings: 4 Preparation time:20 minutes

- ✓ *Heat up a pan with the oil over medium-high heat, add the garlic and the onion and sauté for 2 minutes.*
- ✓ *Add the mussels and the rest of the ingredients, toss, cook for 7 minutes more, divide into containers and serve.*

NUTRITION Calories 266 | Fat 11.8g | Fiber 5.8g | Carbs 16.5g | Protein 10.5g

429) Tasty Crabby Panini

Ingredients

- *1 tbsp Olive oil*
- *French bread split and sliced diagonally*
- *1 lb. blue crab meat or shrimp or spiny lobster or stone crab*
- *½ cup celery*
- *½ cup green onion chopped*
- *1 tsp Worcestershire sauce*
- *1 tsp lemon juice*
- *1 tbsp Dijon mustard*
- *½ cup light mayonnaise*

DIRECTIONS: Servings:4 Preparation time: 10 minutes

- ✓ *In a medium container, mix the following thoroughly: celery, onion, Worcestershire, lemon juice, mustard, and mayonnaise. Season with pepper and salt. Then gently add to the almonds and crabs.*
- ✓ *Spread olive oil on sliced sides of bread and smear with crab mixture before covering with another bread slice.*
- ✓ *Grill the sandwich in a Panini press until bread is crisped and ridged.*

Nutrition Calories 248 |Carbs 12g | Protein 24.5g |

430) Tasty Crabby Panini

Ingredients

- *1 tbsp Olive oil*
- *French bread split and sliced diagonally*
- *1 lb. blue crab meat or shrimp or spiny lobster or stone crab*
- *½ cup celery*
- *½ cup green onion chopped*
- *1 tsp Worcestershire sauce*
- *1 tsp lemon juice*
- *1 tbsp Dijon mustard*
- *½ cup light mayonnaise*

DIRECTIONS: Servings: 4 Preparation time: 10 minutes

- ✓ *In a medium container, mix the following thoroughly: celery, onion, Worcestershire, lemon juice, mustard, and mayonnaise. Season with pepper and salt. Then gently add to the almonds and crabs.*
- ✓ *Spread olive oil on sliced sides of bread and smear with crab mixture before covering with another bread slice.*
- ✓ *Grill the sandwich in a Panini press until bread is crisped and ridged.*

Nutrition Calories 248 | Carbs 12g | Protein 24.5g | Fat 10.9g

431) Halibut And Quinoa Mix

Ingredients

- *4 halibut fillets, boneless*
- *2 tablespoons olive oil*
- *1 teaspoon rosemary, dried*
- *2 teaspoons cumin, ground*
- *1 tablespoons coriander, ground*
- *2 teaspoons cinnamon powder*
- *2 teaspoons oregano, dried*
- *A pinch of salt and black pepper*
- *2 cups quinoa, cooked*
- *1 cup cherry tomatoes, halved*
- *1 avocado, peeled, pitted, and sliced*
- *1 cucumber, cubed*
- *½ cup black olives pitted and sliced Juice of 1 lemon*

DIRECTIONS: Servings: 4Preparation time: 12 minutes

- ✓ *In a container, combine the fish with rosemary, cumin, coriander, cinnamon, oregano, salt, and pepper, and toss.*
- ✓ *Heat up a pan with the oil over medium heat, add the fish, and sear for 2 minutes on each side.*
- ✓ *Introduce the pan to the oven and bake the fish at 435 degrees F for 7 minutes.*
- ✓ *Meanwhile, mix the quinoa with the resting ingredients, toss and divide between plates in a container.*
- ✓ *Add the fish next to the quinoa mix and Serve right away.*

NUTRITION Calories 364 | Fat 15.4g | Fiber 11.2g |Carbs 56.4g | Protein 24.5g

432) Crab Stew

Ingredients

- *½ lb lump crab meat*
- *2 tbsp heavy cream*
- *1 tbsp olive oil*
- *2 cups fish stock*
- *½ lb shrimp, shelled and chopped*
- *1 celery stalk, chopped*
- *½ tsp garlic, chopped*

- ¼ onion, chopped
- Pepper
- Salt

DIRECTIONS: Servings:2 Preparation time: 13 minutes

- ✓ Add oil into the inner pot of the instant pot and set the pot on sauté mode.
- ✓ Add onion and sauté for 3 minutes.
- ✓ Add garlic and sauté for 30 seconds.
- ✓ Add resting ingredients except for heavy cream and stir well.
- ✓ Seal pot with lid and cook on high for 10 minutes.
- ✓ Once done, release pressure using quick release. Remove lid. Stir in heavy cream and serve.

NUTRITION **Calories 376 | Fat 23.5g | Carbs 5.8g | Sugar 0.7g |Protein 48g | Cholesterol 326mg**

433) Crazy Saganaki Shrimp

Ingredients

- ¼ tsp salt
- ½ cup Chardonnay
- ½ cup crumbled Greek feta cheese
- 1 medium bulb. Fennel, cored and finely chopped
- 1 small Chile pepper, seeded and minced
- 1 tbsp extra Virgin olive oil
- 12 jumbo shrimps, peeled and deveined with tails left on
- 2 tbsp lemon juice, divided
- 5 scallions sliced thinly
- Pepper to taste

DIRECTIONS:Servings: 4 **Preparation time:** 10 minutes

- ✓ In a medium container, mix salt, juice, and shrimp.
- ✓ On medium fire, place a saganaki pan (or large nonstick saucepan) and heat oil.
- ✓ Sauté chile pepper, scallions, and fennel for 4 minutes, or until soft and starting to brown.
- ✓ Add ride and sauté for another minute.
- ✓ Place the shrimp on top of the fennel and cook for 4 minutes, or until they are pink.
- ✓ Remove only the shrimp and place them on a plate.
- ✓ Add pepper, feta, and 1 tbsp lemon juice to the pan and cook for a minute or until cheese begins to melt.
- ✓ To serve, place cheese and fennel mixture on a serving plate and top with shrimps.

NUTRITION **Cal 310 | Protein 49.7g | Fat 6.8g |Carbs 8.4g**

434) Grilled Tuna

Ingredients

- 3 tuna fillets
- 3 tsp teriyaki sauce
- ½ teaspoon minced garlic
- 1 teaspoon olive oil

DIRECTIONS: Servings: 3Preparation time: 6 minutes

- ✓ Whisk together teriyaki sauce, minced garlic, and olive oil.
- ✓ Brush every tuna fillet with teriyaki mixture.
- ✓ Preheat grill to 390F.
- ✓ Grill the fish for 3 minutes from each side.

Nutrition Calories 382 | Fat 32.6g | Fiber 0g | Carbs 1.1g | Protein 21.4g

435) Rosemary Salmon

Ingredients

- 2-pound salmon fillet
- 2 tablespoons avocado oil
- 2 teaspoons fresh rosemary, chopped
- ½ teaspoon minced garlic
- ½ teaspoon dried cilantro
- ½ teaspoon salt
- 1 teaspoon butter
- ½ teaspoon white pepper

DIRECTIONS: Servings: 3Preparation time: 10 minutes

- ✓ Whisk together avocado oil, fresh rosemary, minced garlic, dried cilantro, salt, and white pepper.
- ✓ Rub the salmon fillet with the rosemary mixture generously and leave fish in the fridge for 20 minutes to marinate.
- ✓ After this, put butter into the saucepan or big skillet and melt it.
- ✓ Then put heat on maximum and place a salmon fillet in the hot butter.
- ✓ Roast it for 1 minute from each side.
- ✓ After this, preheat the grill to 385F and grill the fillet for 8 minutes (for minutes from each side).
- ✓ Cut the cooked salmon on the servings.

Nutrition Calories 257 | Fat 12.8g | Fiber 0.5g | Carbs 0.9g | Protein 35.3g

436) Lime Squid And Capers Mix

Ingredients

- 1 pound baby squid, cleaned, body and tentacles chopped
- ½ teaspoon lime zest, grated
- 1 tablespoon lime juice
- ½ teaspoon orange zest. grated
- 3 tablespoons olive oil
- 1 teaspoon red pepper flakes, crushed
- 1 tablespoon parsley, chopped
- 4 garlic cloves, minced

- 1 shallot, chopped
- 2 tablespoons capers, drained
- 1 cup chicken stock
- 2 tablespoons red wine vinegar
- Salt and black pepper to the taste

DIRECTIONS:Servings: 6 **Preparation time: 20 minutes**

✓ Heat up a pan with the oil over medium-high heat, add the lime zest, lime juice, orange zest, and the rest of the ingredients except the squid and the parsley, stir, bring to a simmer cook over medium heat for 10 minutes.

✓ Add the resting ingredients, stir, cook everything for 10 minutes more, divide into containers, and serve.

Nutrition Calories 302 | Fat 8.5g | Fiber 9.8g |Carbs 21.8g | Protein 11.3g

437) Salmon And Pineapple Sauce

Ingredients

- 1 cup pineapple, chopped
- 14 oz salmon fillet
- ½ teaspoon salt
- ¾ teaspoon ground turmeric
- ¼ teaspoon cayenne pepper
- 1 teaspoon butter
- 1 teaspoon olive oil
- 1 tablespoon water
- ¼ teaspoon ground thyme
- ¼ cup of water

DIRECTIONS: Servings:4Preparation time: 15 minutes

✓ Rub the salmon fillet with salt and ground turmeric.

✓ Brush the fish with oil and grill to the drill for 3 minutes from each side at 385F.

✓ Meanwhile, make the pineapple dip: blend the pineapple until smooth and transfer into the skillet.

✓ Add water, butter, ground thyme, and cayenne pepper.

✓ Bring the pineapple dip to a boil and cook it without a lid for 5 minutes over high heat.

✓ Cut the salmon fillet into 4 servings and arrange them to the seeing plates.

✓ Then top every salmon piece with pineapple dip.

Nutrition Calories 172 | Fat 8.4g | Fiber 0.7g | Carbs 5.8g | Protein 19.5g

438) Lime Squid And Capers Mix

Ingredients

- 1 pound baby squid, cleaned, body and tentacles chopped
- ½ teaspoon lime zest, grated
- 1 tablespoon lime juice
- ½ teaspoon orange zest. grated
- 3 tablespoons olive oil
- 1 teaspoon red pepper flakes, crushed
- 1 tablespoon parsley, chopped
- 4 garlic cloves, minced
- 1 shallot, chopped
- 2 tablespoons capers, drained
- 1 cup chicken stock
- 2 tablespoons red wine vinegar
- Salt and black pepper to the taste

Directions: Servings: 6Preparation time: 20 minutes

✓ Heat up a pan with the oil over medium-high heat, add the lime zest, lime juice, orange zest, and the rest of the ingredients except the squid and the parsley, stir, bring to a simmer cook over medium heat for 10 minutes.

✓ Add the resting ingredients, stir, cook everything for 10 minutes more, divide into containers, and serve.

Nutrition Calories 302 | Fat 8.5g | Fiber 9.8g | Carbs 21.8g | Protein 11.3g

439) Salmon And Pineapple Sauce

Ingredients

- 1 cup pineapple, chopped
- 14 oz salmon fillet
- ½ teaspoon salt
- ¾ teaspoon ground turmeric
- ¼ teaspoon cayenne pepper
- 1 teaspoon butter
- 1 teaspoon olive oil
- 1 tablespoon water
- ¼ teaspoon ground thyme
- ¼ cup of water

DIRECTIONS: Servings: 4Preparation time: 15 minutes

✓ Rub the salmon fillet with salt and ground turmeric.

✓ Brush the fish with oil and grill to the drill for 3 minutes from each side at 385F.

✓ Meanwhile, make the pineapple dip: blend the pineapple until smooth and transfer into the skillet.

✓ Add water, butter, ground thyme, and cayenne pepper.

✓ Bring the pineapple dip to a boil and cook it without a lid for 5 minutes over high heat.

✓ Cut the salmon fillet into 4 servings and arrange them to the seeing plates.

✓ Then top every salmon piece with pineapple dip.

Nutrition Cal 172 | Fat 8.4g | Carbs 5.8g | Protein 19.5g

440) Wrapped Scallops

INGREDIENTS:

- *12 medium scallops*
- *12 thin bacon slices*
- *2 teaspoons lemon juice*
- *2 teaspoons olive oil*
- *A pinch of chili powder*
- *A pinch of cloves, ground*
- *Salt and black pepper to the taste*

DIRECTIONS: Servings: 12

Preparation time: 6 minutes

- ✓ *Wrap each scallop in a bacon slice and secure it with toothpicks.*
- ✓ *Heat up a pan with the oil o 2r medium-high heat, add the scallops and the rest of the ingredients, Cook for 3 minutes on each side, divide between plates, and serve.*

Nutrition Calories 297 | Fat 24.3g | Fiber 9.6g | Carbs 22.4g | Protein 17.6g

441) Walnut Salmon Mix

Ingredients

- *12 oz salmon fillet*
- *1/3 cup walnuts*
- *1 tablespoon panko breadcrumbs*
- *1 tablespoon dried oregano*
- *1 tablespoon sunflower oil*
- *½ teaspoon salt*
- *½ teaspoon ground black pepper*
- *1 tablespoon mustard*

DIRECTIONS: Servings: 4Preparation time: 25 minutes

- ✓ *Put the walnuts, panko bread crumbs, dried oregano, sunflower oil, salt, and ground black pepper into the blender.*
- ✓ *Blend the ingredients until you set smooth and sticky mass.*
- ✓ *After this, line the baking tray with baking paper.*
- ✓ *Brush the salmon fillet with mustard from all sides and coat to the blended walnut mixture generously.*
- ✓ *Bake the salmon for 25 minutes at 365F. Flip the salmon fillet on another side after 15 minutes of cooking.*

NUTRITION Calories 233 | Fat 15.9g | Fiber 1.9g | Carbs 4.7g | Protein 20.1g

442) Pan Fried Tuna With Herbs And Nut

Ingredients

- *¼ cup almonds, chopped finely*
- *¼ cup fresh tangerine juice*
- *½ tsp fennel seeds, chopped finely*
- *½ tsp ground pepper, divided*
- *½ tsp sea salt, divided*
- *1 tbsp olive oil*
- *2 tbsp fresh mint, chopped finely*
- *2 tbsp red onion, chopped finely*
- *4 pieces of 6-oz Tuna steak cut in half*

DIRECTIONS: Servings: 4Preparation time: 5 minute

- ✓ *Mix fennel seeds, olive oil, mint, onion, tangerine juice, and almonds in a small container. Season with ¼ each of pepper and salt.*
- ✓ *Season fish with the resting pepper and salt.*
- ✓ *On medium-high fire, place a large nonstick fry pan and grease with Cooking spray.*
- ✓ *Pan fry tuna until the desired doneness is reached or for one minute per side.*
- ✓ *Transfer cooked tuna to a serving plate, drizzle with dressing and serve.*

NUTRITION Cal 272 | Fat: 9.7g | Protein 42g | Carbs 4.2g

443) Cayenne Cod And Tomatoes

Ingredients:

- *1 teaspoon lime juice*
- *Salt and black pepper to the taste*
- *1 teaspoon sweet paprika*
- *1 teaspoon cayenne pepper*
- *2 tablespoons olive oil*
- *1 yellow onion, chopped*
- *2 garlic cloves, minced*
- *4 cod fillets, boneless*
- *A pinch of cloves, ground*
- *½ cup chicken stock*
- *½ pound cherry tomatoes, cubed*

DIRECTIONS: Servings: 4Preparation time: 25 minutes

- ✓ *Heat up a pan with the oil over medium-high heat, add the cod, salt, pepper, and cayenne, Cook for 4 minutes on each side, and divide between plates.*
- ✓ *Heat up the same pan over medium-high heat, add the onion and garlic, and sauté for 5 minutes.*
- ✓ *Add the rest of the ingredients, stir, bring to a simmer and cook for 10 minutes more.*
- ✓ *Divide the mix next to the fish and serve.*

NUTRITION Calories 232 | Fat 16.5g | Fiber 11.1g | Carbs 24.8g | Protein 16.5g

444) . Mediterranean Fish Fillets

Ingredients:

- *4 cod fillets*
- *1 lb grape tomatoes, halved*
- *1 cup olives, pitted and sliced*

- *2 tbsp capers*
- *1 tsp dried thyme*
- *2 tbsp olive oil*
- *1 tsp garlic, minced*
- *Pepper*
- *Salt*

Direction: Preparation Time: 10 minutes Cooking Time: 3 minutes Servings: 4

✓ *Pour 1 cup of water into the instant pot, then place steamer rack to the pot.*

✓ *Spray heat-safe baking dish with cooking spray.*

✓ *Add half grape tomatoes into the dish and season with pepper and salt.*

✓ *Arrange fish fillets on top of cherry tomatoes. Drizzle with oil and season with garlic, thyme, capers, pepper, and salt.*

✓ *Spread olives and resting grape tomatoes on top of fish fillets.*

✓ *Place dish on top of steamer rack to the pot.*

✓ *Seal the pot with a lid and select manual, and cook on high for 3 minutes.*

✓ *Once done, release pressure using quick release. Remove lid.*

✓ *Serve and enjoy.*

Nutrition: Calories 212 Fat 11.9 g Carbohydrates 7.1 g Sugar 3 g Protein 21.4 g Cholesterol 55 mg

445) Flavors Cioppino

Ingredients:

- *1 lb codfish, cut into chunks*
- *1 1/2 lbs shrimp*
- *28 oz canned tomatoes, diced*
- *1 cup dry white wine*
- *1 bay leaf*
- *1 tsp cayenne*
- *1 tsp oregano*
- *1 shallot, chopped*
- *1 tsp garlic, minced*
- *1 tbsp olive oil*
- *1/2 tsp salt*

Direction: Preparation Time: 10 minutes Cooking Time: 5 minutes Servings: 6

✓ *Add oil into the inner pot of the instant pot and set the pot on sauté mode.*

✓ *Add shallot and garlic and sauté for 2 minutes.*

✓ *Add wine, bay leaf, cayenne, oregano, and salt and cook for 3 minutes.*

✓ *Add resting ingredients and stir well.*

✓ *Seal the pot with a lid and select manual, and cook on low for 0 minutes.*

✓ *Once done, release pressure using quick release. Remove lid.*

✓ *Serve and enjoy.*

Nutrition Cal 281 Fat 5 g Carbs 10.5 g Protein 40.7

446) Delicious Shrimp Alfredo

Ingredients:

- *12 shrimp, remove shells*
- *1 tbsp garlic, minced*
- *1/4 cup parmesan cheese*
- *2 cups whole wheat rotini noodles*
- *1 cup fish broth*
- *15 oz alfredo sauce*
- *1 onion, chopped*
- *Salt*

Direction: Preparation Time: 10 minutes Cooking Time: 3 minutes Servings: 4

✓ *In the instant pot, combine all ingredients except the parmesan cheese and stir well.*

✓ *Seal pot with lid and cook on high for 3 minutes.*

✓ *Once done, release pressure using quick release. Remove lid.*

✓ *Stir in cheese and serve.*

Nutrition: Calories 669 Fat 23.1 g Carbohydrates 76 g Sugar 2.4 g Protein 37.8 g Cholesterol 190 mg

447) Tomato Olive Fish Fillets

Ingredients:

- *2 lbs halibut fish fillets*
- *2 oregano sprigs*
- *2 rosemary sprigs*
- *2 tbsp fresh lime juice*
- *1 cup olives, pitted*
- *28 oz can tomatoes, diced*
- *1 tbsp garlic, minced*
- *1 onion, chopped*
- *2 tbsp olive oil*

Direction: Preparation Time: 10 minutes Cooking Time: 8 minutes Servings: 4

✓ *Add oil into the inner pot of the instant pot and set the pot on sauté mode.*

✓ *Add onion and sauté for 3 minutes.*

✓ *Add garlic and sauté for a minute.*

✓ *Add lime juice, olives, herb sprigs, and tomatoes, and stir well.*

✓ *Seal pot with lid and cook on high for 3 minutes.*

✓ *Once done, release pressure using quick release. Remove lid.*

✓ *Add fish fillets and seal pot again with lid and cook on high for 2 minutes.*

✓ *Once done, release pressure using quick release. Remove lid.*

✓ *Serve and enjoy.*

Nutrition: Calories 333 Fat 19.1 g Carbohydrates 31.8 g Sugar 8.4 g Protein 13.4 g Cholesterol 5 mg

448) Shrimp Scampi

Ingredients:

- 1 lb whole wheat penne pasta
- 1 lb frozen shrimp
- 2 tbsp garlic, minced
- 1/4 tsp cayenne
- 1/2 tbsp Italian seasoning
- 1/4 cup olive oil
- 3 1/2 cups fish stock
- Pepper
- Salt

Direction: Preparation Time: 10 minutes Cooking Time: 8 minutes Servings: 6

- ✓ Add all ingredients into the inner pot of the instant pot and stir well.
- ✓ Seal pot with lid and cook on high for 6 minutes.
- ✓ Once done, release pressure using quick release. Remove lid.
- ✓ Stir well and serve.

Nutrition: Calories 435 Fat 12.6 g Carbohydrates 54.9 g Sugar 0.1 g Protein 30.6 g Cholesterol 116 mg

449) Easy Salmon Stew

Ingredients:

- 2 lbs salmon fillet, cubed
- 1 onion, chopped
- 2 cups fish broth
- 1 tbsp olive oil
- Pepper
- salt

Direction: Preparation Time: 10 minutes Cooking Time: 8 minutes Servings: 6

- ✓ Add oil into the inner pot of the instant pot and set the pot on sauté mode.
- ✓ Add onion and sauté for 2 minutes.
- ✓ Add resting ingredients and stir well.
- ✓ Seal pot with lid and cook on high for 6 minutes.
- ✓ Once done, release pressure using quick release. Remove lid.
- ✓ Stir and serve.

Nutrition: Calories 243 Fat 12.6 g Carbohydrates 0.8 g Sugar 0.3 g Protein 31 g Cholesterol 78 mg

450) Italian Tuna Pasta

Ingredients:

- 15 oz whole wheat pasta
- 2 tbsp capers
- 3 oz tuna
- 2 cups can get tomatoes, crushed
- 2 anchovies
- 1 tsp garlic, minced
- 1 tbsp olive oil
- Salt

Direction: Preparation Time: 10 minutes Cooking Time: 5 minutes Servings: 6

- ✓ Add oil into the inner pot of the instant pot and set the pot on sauté mode.
- ✓ Add anchovies and garlic and sauté for 1 minute.
- ✓ Add resting ingredients and stir well. Pour enough water into the pot to cover the pasta.
- ✓ Seal the pot with a lid and select manual, and cook on low for 4 minutes.
- ✓ Once done, release pressure using quick release. Remove lid.
- ✓ Stir and serve.

Nutrition: Calories 339 Fat 6 g Carbohydrates 56.5 g Sugar 5.2 g Protein 15.2 g Cholesterol 10 mg

451) Garlicky Clams

Ingredients:

- 3 lbs clams, clean
- 4 garlic cloves
- 1/4 cup olive oil
- 1/2 cup fresh lemon juice
- 1 cup white wine
- Pepper
- Salt

Direction: Preparation Time: 10 minutes Cooking Time: 5 minutes Servings: 4

- ✓ Add oil into the inner pot of the instant pot and set the pot on sauté mode.
- ✓ Add garlic and sauté for 1 minute.
- ✓ Add wine and cook for 2 minutes.
- ✓ Add resting ingredients and stir well. Seal pot with lid and cook on high for 2 minutes.
- ✓ Once done, allow to release pressure naturally. Remove lid.
- ✓ Serve and enjoy

Nutrition:: Calories 332 Fat 13.5 g Carbohydrates 40.5 g Sugar 12.4 g Protein 2.5 g Cholesterol 0 mg

452) Delicious Fish Tacos

Ingredients:

- 4 tilapia fillets
- 1/4 cup fresh cilantro, chopped
- 1/4 cup fresh lime juice
- 2 tbsp paprika
- 1 tbsp olive oil
- Pepper
- Salt

Direction: Preparation Time: 10 minutes Cooking Time: 8 minutes Servings: 8

- ✓ Pour 2 cups of water into the instant pot, then place steamer rack to the pot.

- ✓ *Place fish fillets on parchment paper.*
- ✓ *Season fish fillets with paprika, pepper, and salt and drizzle with oil and lime juice.*
- ✓ *Fold parchment paper around the fish fillets and place them on a steamer rack to the pot.*
- ✓ *Seal pot with lid and cook on high for 8 minutes.*
- ✓ *Once done, release pressure using quick release. Remove lid.*
- ✓ *Remove fish packet from the pot and open it.*
- ✓ *Shred the fish with a fork and served.*

Nutrition: Calories 67 Fat 2.5 g Carbohydrates 1.1 g Sugar 0.2 g Protein 10.8 g Cholesterol 28 mg

453) ***Pesto Fish Fillet***

Ingredients:

- *4 halibut fillets*
- *1/2 cup water*
- *1 tbsp lemon zest, grated*
- *1 tbsp capers*
- *1/2 cup basil, chopped*
- *1 tbsp garlic, chopped*
- *1 avocado, peeled and chopped*
- *Pepper*
- *Salt*

Direction: Preparation Time: 10 minutes Cooking Time: 8 minutes Servings: 4

- ✓ *Add lemon zest, capers, basil, garlic, avocado, pepper, and salt into the blender blend until smooth.*
- ✓ *Place fish fillets on aluminum foil and spread a blended mixture on fish fillets.*
- ✓ *Fold foil around the fish fillets.*
- ✓ *Pour water into the instant pot and place trivet to the pot.*
- ✓ *Place foil fish packet on the trivet.*
- ✓ *Seal pot with lid and cook on high for 8 minutes.*
- ✓ *Once done, allow to release pressure naturally. Remove lid.*
- ✓ *Serve and enjoy.*

Nutrition: Calories 426 Fat 16.6 g Carbohydrates 5.5 g Sugar 0.4 g Protein 61.8 g Cholesterol 93 mg

454) ***Tuna Risotto***

Ingredients:

- *1 cup of rice*
- *1/3 cup parmesan cheese, grated*
- *1 1/2 cups fish broth*
- *1 lemon juice*
- *1 tbsp garlic, minced*
- *1 onion, chopped*
- *2 tbsp olive oil*
- *2 cups can tuna, cut into chunks*
- *Pepper*
- *Salt*

Direction: Preparation Time: 10 minutes Cooking Time: 23 minutes Servings: 6

- ✓ *Add oil into the inner pot of the instant pot and set the pot on sauté mode.*
- ✓ *Add garlic, onion, and tuna and cook for 3 minutes.*
- ✓ *Add resting ingredients except for parmesan cheese and stir well.*
- ✓ *Seal pot with lid and cook on high for 20 minutes.*
- ✓ *Once done, release pressure using quick release. Remove lid.*
- ✓ *Stir in parmesan cheese and serve.*

Nutrition: Calories 228 Fat 7 g Carbohydrates 27.7 g Sugar 1.2 g Protein 12.6 g Cholesterol 21 mg

455) ***Salsa Fish Fillets***

Ingredients:

- *1 lb tilapia fillets*
- *1/2 cup salsa*
- *1 cup of water*
- *Pepper*
- *Salt*

Direction: Preparation Time: 10 minutes Cooking Time: 2 minutes Servings: 4

- ✓ *Place fish fillets on aluminum foil and top with salsa, and season with pepper and salt.*
- ✓ *Fold foil around the fish fillets.*
- ✓ *Pour water into the instant pot and place trivet to the pot.*
- ✓ *Place foil fish packet on the trivet.*
- ✓ *Seal pot with lid and cook on high for 2 minutes.*
- ✓ *Once done, release pressure using quick release. Remove lid.*
- ✓ *Serve and enjoy.*

Nutrition: Calories 342 Fat 10.5 g Carbohydrates 41.5 g Sugar 1.9 g Protein 18.9 g Cholesterol 31 mg

456) ***Coconut Clam Chowder***

Ingredients:

- *6 oz clams, chopped*
- *1 cup heavy cream*
- *1/4 onion, sliced*
- *1 cup celery, chopped*
- *1 lb cauliflower, chopped*
- *1 cup fish broth*
- *1 bay leaf*
- *2 cups of coconut milk*
- *Salt*

Direction: Preparation Time: 10 minutes Cooking Time: 7 minutes Servings: 6

- ✓ *Add all ingredients except clams and heavy cream and stir well.*

- ✓ Seal pot with lid and cook on high for 5 minutes.
- ✓ Once done, release pressure using quick release. Remove lid.
- ✓ Add heavy cream and clams and stir well and cook on sauté mode for 2 minutes.
- ✓ Stir well and serve.

Nutrition: Calories 301 Fat 27.2 g Carbohydrates 13.6 g Sugar 6 g Protein 4.9 g Cholesterol 33 mg

457) Feta Tomato Sea Bass

Ingredients:

- 4 sea bass fillets
- 1 1/2 cups water
- 1 tbsp olive oil
- 1 tsp garlic, minced
- 1 tsp basil, chopped
- 1 tsp parsley, chopped
- 1/2 cup feta cheese, crumbled
- 1 cup can tomatoes, diced
- Pepper
- Salt

Direction: Preparation Time: 10 minutes Cooking Time: 8 minutes Servings: 4

- ✓ Season fish fillets with pepper and salt.
- ✓ Pour 2 cups of water into the instant pot, then place steamer rack to the pot.
- ✓ Place fish fillets on the steamer rack to the pot.
- ✓ Cook on high for 5 minutes after sealing the pot with the lid.
- ✓ Once done, release pressure using quick release. Remove lid.
- ✓ Remove fish fillets from the pot and clean the pot.
- ✓ Add oil into the inner pot of the instant pot and set the pot on sauté mode.
- ✓ Add garlic and sauté for 1 minute.
- ✓ Add tomatoes, parsley, and basil and stir well and cook for 1 minute.
- ✓ Add fish fillets and top with crumbled cheese and cook for a minute.
- ✓ Serve and enjoy.

Nutrition: Calories 219 Fat 10.1 g Carbohydrates 4 g Sugar 2.8 g Protein 27.1 g Cholesterol 70 mg

458) Stewed Mussels & Scallops

Ingredients:

- 2 cups mussels
- 1 cup scallops
- 2 cups fish stock
- 2 bell peppers, diced
- 2 cups cauliflower rice
- 1 onion, chopped
- 1 tbsp olive oil
- Pepper
- Salt

Direction: Preparation Time: 10 minutes Cooking Time: 11 minutes Servings: 4

- ✓ Add oil into the inner pot of the instant pot and set the pot on sauté mode.
- ✓ Add onion and peppers and sauté for 3 minutes.
- ✓ Add scallops and cook for 2 minutes.
- ✓ Add resting ingredients and stir well.
- ✓ Seal pot with lid and cook on high for 6 minutes.
- ✓ Once done, allow to release pressure naturally. Remove lid.
- ✓ Stir and serve.

Nutrition: Calories 191 Fat 7.4 g Carbohydrates 13.7 g Sugar 6.2 g Protein 18 g Cholesterol 29 mg

459) Healthy Halibut Soup

Ingredients:

- 1 lb halibut, skinless, boneless, & cut into chunks
- 2 tbsp ginger, minced
- 2 celery stalks, chopped
- 1 carrot, sliced
- 1 onion, chopped
- 1 cup of water
- 2 cups fish stock
- 1 tbsp olive oil
- Pepper
- Salt

Direction: Preparation Time: 10 minutes Cooking Time: 13 minutes Servings: 4

- ✓ Add oil into the inner pot of the instant pot and set the pot on sauté mode.
- ✓ Add onion and sauté for 3-4 minutes.
- ✓ Stir in the water, celery, carrots, ginger, and stock.
- ✓ Seal pot with lid and cook on high for 5 minutes.
- ✓ Once done, release pressure using quick release. Remove lid.
- ✓ Add fish and stir well. Seal pot again and cook on high for 4 minutes.
- ✓ Once done, release pressure using quick release. Remove lid.
- ✓ Stir and serve.

Nutrition: Calories 4586 Fat 99.6 g Carbohydrates 6.3 g Sugar 2.1 g Protein 861 g Cholesterol 1319 mg

460) Creamy Fish Stew

Ingredients:

- 1 lb white fish fillets, cut into chunks
- 2 tbsp olive oil
- 1 cup kale, chopped
- 1 cup cauliflower, chopped
- 1 cup broccoli, chopped

- 3 cups fish broth
- 1 cup heavy cream
- 2 celery stalks, diced
- 1 carrot, sliced
- 1 onion, diced
- Pepper
- Salt

Direction: Preparation Time: 10 minutes Cooking Time: 8 minutes Servings: 6

✓ Add oil into the inner pot of the instant pot and set the pot on sauté mode.

✓ Add onion and sauté for 3 minutes.

✓ Add resting ingredients except for heavy cream and stir well.

✓ Seal pot with lid and cook on high for 5 minutes.

✓ Once done, allow to release pressure naturally. Remove lid.

✓ Stir in heavy cream and serve.

Nutrition: Calories 296 Fat 19.3 g Carbohydrates 7.5 g Sugar 2.6 g Protein 22.8 g Cholesterol 103 mg

461) Nutritious Broccoli Salmon

Ingredients:

- 4 salmon fillets
- 10 oz broccoli florets
- 1 1/2 cups water
- 1 tbsp olive oil
- Pepper
- Salt

Direction: Preparation Time: 10 minutes Cooking Time: 4 minutes Servings: 4

✓ Pour water into the instant pot, then place the steamer basket to the pot.

✓ Place salmon in the steamer basket and season with pepper and salt, and drizzle with oil.

✓ Add broccoli on top of salmon to the steamer basket.

✓ Seal pot with lid and cook on high for 4 minutes.

✓ Once done, release pressure using quick release. Remove lid.

✓ Serve and enjoy.

Nutrition: Calories 290 Fat 14.7 g Carbohydrates 4.7 g Sugar 1.2 g Protein 36.5 g Cholesterol 78 mg

462) Shrimp Zoodles

Ingredients:

- 2 zucchini, spiralized
- 1 lb shrimp, peeled and deveined
- 1/2 tsp paprika
- 1 tbsp basil, chopped
- 1/2 lemon juice
- 1 tsp garlic, minced
- 2 tbsp olive oil
- 1 cup vegetable stock
- Pepper
- Salt

Direction: Preparation Time: 10 minutes Cooking Time: 5 minutes Servings: 4

✓ Add oil into the inner pot of the instant pot and set the pot on sauté mode.

✓ Add garlic and sauté for a minute.

✓ Add shrimp and lemon juice and stir well and cook for 1 minute.

✓ Add resting ingredients and stir well.

✓ Seal pot with lid and cook on high for 3 minutes.

✓ Once done, release pressure using quick release. Remove lid.

✓ Serve and enjoy.

Nutrition: Calories 215 Fat 9.2 g Carbohydrates 5.8 g Sugar 2 g Protein 27.3 g Cholesterol 239 mg

463) Healthy Carrot & Shrimp

Ingredients:

- 1 lb shrimp, peeled and deveined
- 1 tbsp chives, chopped
- 1 onion, chopped
- 1 tbsp olive oil
- 1 cup fish stock
- 1 cup carrots, sliced
- Pepper
- Salt

Direction: Preparation Time: 10 minutes Cooking Time: 6 minutes Servings: 4

✓ Add oil into the inner pot of the instant pot and set the pot on sauté mode.

✓ Add onion and sauté for 2 minutes.

✓ Add shrimp and stir well.

✓ Add resting ingredients and stir well.

✓ Seal pot with lid and cook on high for 4 minutes.

✓ Once done, release pressure using quick release. Remove lid.

✓ Serve and enjoy.

Nutrition: Calories 197 Fat 5.9 g Carbohydrates 7 g Sugar 2.5 g Protein 27.7 g Cholesterol 239 mg

464) Salmon with Potatoes

Ingredients:

- 1 1/2 lbs Salmon fillets, boneless and cubed
- 2 tbsp olive oil
- 1 cup fish stock
- 2 tbsp parsley, chopped
- 1 tsp garlic, minced
- 1 lb baby potatoes, halved

- *Pepper*
- *Salt*

Direction: Preparation Time: 10 minutes Cooking Time: 15 minutes Servings: 4

✓ *Add oil into the inner pot of the instant pot and set the pot on sauté mode.*

✓ *Add garlic and sauté for 2 minutes.*

✓ *Add resting ingredients and stir well.*

✓ *Seal pot with lid and cook on high for 13 minutes.*

✓ *Once done, release pressure using quick release. Remove lid.*

✓ *Serve and enjoy.*

Nutrition: Calories 362 Fat 18.1 g Carbohydrates 14.5 g Sugar 0 g Protein 37.3 g Cholesterol 76 mg

465) ***Honey Garlic Shrimp***

Ingredients:

- *1 lb shrimp, peeled and deveined*
- *1/4 cup honey*
- *1 tbsp garlic, minced*
- *1 tbsp ginger, minced*
- *1 tbsp olive oil*
- *1/4 cup fish stock*
- *Pepper*
- *Salt*

Direction: Preparation Time: 10 minutes Cooking Time: 5 minutes Servings: 4

✓ *Add shrimp into the large container. Add resting ingredients over shrimp and toss well.*

✓ *Transfer shrimp into the instant pot and stir well.*

✓ *Seal pot with lid and cook on high for 5 minutes.*

✓ *Once done, release pressure using quick release. Remove lid.*

✓ *Serve and enjoy.*

Nutrition: Cal 240 Fat 5.6 g Carbohydrates 20.9 g Sugar 17.5 g Protein 26.5 g Cholesterol 239 mg

466) ***Simple Lemon Clams***

Ingredients:

- *1 lb clams, clean*
- *1 tbsp fresh lemon juice*
- *1 lemon zest, grated*
- *1 onion, chopped*
- *1/2 cup fish stock*
- *Pepper*
- *Salt*

Direction: Preparation Time: 10 minutes Cooking Time: 10 minutes Servings: 4

✓ *Add all ingredients into the inner pot of the instant pot and stir well.*

✓ *Seal pot with lid and cook on high for 10 minutes.*

✓ *Once done, release pressure using quick release. Remove lid.*

✓ *Serve and enjoy.*

Nutrition: Calories 76 Fat 0.6 g Carbohydrates 16.4 g Sugar 5.4 g Protein 1.8 g Cholesterol 0 mg

467) ***Crab Stew***

Ingredients:

- *1/2 lb lump crab meat*
- *2 tbsp heavy cream*
- *1 tbsp olive oil*
- *2 cups fish stock*
- *1/2 lb shrimp, shelled and chopped*
- *1 celery stalk, chopped*
- *1/2 tsp garlic, chopped*
- *1/4 onion, chopped*
- *Pepper*
- *Salt*

Direction: Preparation Time: 10 minutes Cooking Time: 13 minutes Servings: 2

✓ *Add oil into the inner pot of the instant pot and set the pot on sauté mode.*

✓ *Add onion and sauté for 3 minutes.*

✓ *Add garlic and sauté for 30 seconds.*

✓ *Add resting ingredients except for heavy cream and stir well.*

✓ *Seal pot with lid and cook on high for 10 minutes.*

✓ *Once done, release pressure using quick release. Remove lid.*

✓ *Stir in heavy cream and serve.*

Nutrition: Calories 376 Fat 25.5 g Carbohydrates 5.8 g Sugar 0.7 g Protein 48.1 g Cholesterol 326 mg

468) ***Honey Balsamic Salmon***

Ingredients:

- *2 salmon fillets*
- *1/4 tsp red pepper flakes*
- *2 tbsp honey*
- *2 tbsp balsamic vinegar*
- *1 cup of water*
- *Pepper*
- *Salt*

Direction: Preparation Time: 10 minutes Cooking Time: 3 minutes Servings: 2

✓ *Pour water into the instant pot and place trivet to the pot.*

✓ *In a small container, mix together honey, red pepper flakes, and vinegar.*

✓ *Brush fish fillets with honey mixture and place on top of the trivet.*

✓ *Seal pot with lid and cook on high for 3 minutes.*

✓ *Once done, release pressure using quick release.*

Remove lid.

✓ Serve and enjoy.

Nutrition: Calories 303 Fat 11 g Carbohydrates 17.6 g Sugar 17.3 g Protein 34.6 g Cholesterol 78 mg

469) Spicy Tomato Crab Mix

Ingredients:

- 1 lb crab meat
- 1 tsp paprika
- 1 cup grape tomatoes, cut into half
- 2 tbsp green onion, chopped
- 1 tbsp olive oil
- Pepper
- Salt

Direction: Preparation Time: 10 minutes Cooking Time: 12 minutes Servings: 4

✓ Add oil into the inner pot of the instant pot and set the pot on sauté mode.

✓ Add paprika and onion and sauté for 2 minutes.

✓ Add the rest of the ingredients and stir well.

✓ Seal pot with lid and cook on high for 10 minutes.

✓ Once done, release pressure using quick release. Remove lid.

✓ Serve and enjoy.

Nutrition: Calories 142 Fat 5.7 g Carbohydrates 4.3 g Sugar 1.3 g Protein 14.7 g Cholesterol 61 mg

470) Dijon Fish Fillets

Ingredients:

- 2 white fish fillets
- 1 tbsp Dijon mustard
- 1 cup of water
- Pepper
- Salt

Direction: Preparation Time: 10 minutes Cooking Time: 3 minutes Servings: 2

✓ Pour water into the instant pot and place trivet to the pot.

✓ Brush fish fillets with mustard, season with pepper and salt, and place on the trivet.

✓ Seal pot with lid and cook on high for 3 minutes.

✓ Once done, release pressure using quick release. Remove lid.

✓ Serve and enjoy.

Nutrition: Calories 270 Fat 11.9 g Carbohydrates 0.5 g Sugar 0.1 g Protein 38 g Cholesterol 119 mg

471) Lemoney Prawns

Ingredients:

- 1/2 lb prawns
- 1/2 cup fish stock
- 1 tbsp fresh lemon juice
- 1 tbsp lemon zest, grated
- 1 tbsp olive oil
- 1 tbsp garlic, minced
- Pepper
- Salt

Direction: Preparation Time: 10 minutes Cooking Time: 3 minutes Servings: 2

✓ Add all ingredients into the inner pot of the instant pot and stir well.

✓ Seal pot with lid and cook on high for 3 minutes.

✓ Once done, release pressure using quick release. Remove lid.

✓ Drain prawns and serve

Nutrition: Calories 215 Fat 9.5 g Carbohydrates 3.9 g Sugar 0.4 g Protein 27.6 g Cholesterol 239 mg

472) Lemon Cod Peas

Ingredients:

- 1 lb cod fillets, skinless, boneless, and cut into chunks
- 1 cup fish stock
- 1 tbsp fresh parsley, chopped
- 1/2 tbsp lemon juice
- 1 green chili, chopped
- 3/4 cup fresh peas
- 2 tbsp onion, chopped
- Pepper
- Salt

Direction: Preparation Time: 10 minutes Cooking Time: 10 minutes Servings: 4

✓ Add all ingredients into the inner pot of the instant pot and stir well.

✓ Seal pot with lid and cook on high for 10 minutes.

✓ Once done, release pressure using quick release. Remove lid.

✓ Stir and serve.

Nutrition: Calories 128 Fat 1.6 g Carbohydrates 5 g Sugar 2.1 g Protein 23.2 g Cholesterol 41 mg

473) Quick & Easy Shrimp

Ingredients:

- 1 3/4 lbs shrimp, frozen and deveined
- 1/2 cup fish stock
- 1/2 cup apple cider vinegar
- Pepper
- Salt

Direction: Preparation Time: 10 minutes Cooking Time: 1-minute Servings: 6

✓ Add all ingredients into the inner pot of the instant pot and stir well.

✓ Seal pot with lid and cook on high for 1 minute.

✓ Once done, release pressure using quick release. Remove lid.

✓ Stir and serve.
Nutrition: Calories 165 Fat 2.4 g Carbohydrates 2.2 g Sugar 0.1 g Protein 30.6 g Cholesterol 279 mg

474) Creamy Curry Salmon

Ingredients:

- 2 salmon fillets, boneless and cubed
- 1 Tbsp olive oil
- 1 Tbsp basil, chopped
- Sea salt and black pepper to the taste
- 1 cup Greek yogurt
- 2 Tsps curry powder
- 1 garlic clove, minced
- ½ Tsp mint, chopped

Direction: Preparation time: 10 minutes Cooking time: 20 minutes Servings: 2

✓ Heat up a pan with the oil over medium-high heat, add the salmon and cook for 3 minutes.

✓ Add the rest of the ingredients, toss, cook for 15 minutes more, divide between plates and serve
Nutrition: Calories 284, fat 14.1, fiber 8.5, carbs 26.7, protein 31.4

475) Mahi Mahi and Pomegranate Sauce

Ingredients:

- 1 and ½ cups chicken stock
- 1 Tbsp olive oil
- 4 mahi-mahi fillets, boneless
- 4 Tbsps tahini paste
- Juice of 1 lime
- Seeds from 1 pomegranate
- 1 Tbsp parsley, chopped

Direction: Preparation time: 10 minutes Cooking time: 10 minutes Servings: 4

✓ Heat up a pan with the oil over medium-high heat, add the fish and cook for 3 minutes on each side. Add the rest of the ingredients, flip the fish again, cook for 4 minutes more, divide everything between plates and serve.
Nutrition: Calories 224, fat 11.1, fiber 5.5, carbs 16.7, protein 11.4

476) Smoked Salmon and Veggies Mix

Ingredients:

- 3 red onions, cut into wedges
- ¾ cup green olives pitted and halved
- 3 red bell peppers, roughly chopped
- ½ Tsp smoked paprika
- Salt and black pepper to the taste
- 3 Tbsps olive oil
- 4 salmon fillets, skinless and boneless
- 2 Tbsps chives, chopped

Direction: Preparation time: 10 minutes Cooking time: 20 minutes Servings: 4

✓ In a roasting pan, combine the salmon with the onions and the rest of the ingredients, introduce to the oven and bake at 390 degrees F for 20 minutes.

✓ Divide the mix between plates and serve.
Nutrition: Calories 301, fat 5.9, fiber 11.9, carbs 26.4, protein 22.4

477) Salmon and Mango Mix

Ingredients:

- 2 salmon fillets, skinless and boneless
- Salt and pepper to the taste
- 2 Tbsps olive oil
- 2 garlic cloves, minced
- 2 mangos, peeled and cubed
- 1 red chili, chopped
- 1 small piece ginger, grated
- Juice of 1 lime
- 1 Tbsp cilantro, chopped

Direction: Preparation time: 10 minutes Cooking time: 25 minutes Servings: 2

✓ In a roasting pan, combine the salmon with the oil, garlic, and the rest of the ingredients except the cilantro. Toss, introduce to the oven at 350 degrees F, and bake for 25 minutes.

✓ Divide everything between plates and serve with the cilantro sprinkled on top.
Nutrition: Calories 251, fat 15.9, fiber 5.9, carbs 26.4, protein 12.4

478) Salmon and Creamy Endives

Ingredients:

- 4 salmon fillets, boneless
- 2 endives, shredded
- Juice of 1 lime
- Salt and black pepper to the taste
- ¼ cup chicken stock
- 1 cup Greek yogurt
- ¼ cup green olives pitted and chopped
- ¼ cup fresh chives, chopped
- 3 Tbsps olive oil

Direction: Preparation time: 10 minutes Cooking time: 15 minutes Servings: 4

✓ Heat up a pan with half of the oil over medium heat, add the endives and the rest of the ingredients except the chives and the salmon, toss, cook for 6 minutes, and divide between plates.

✓ Heat up another pan with the rest of the oil, add the salmon, season with salt and pepper, cook for 4 minutes on each side, add next to the creamy endives mix, sprinkle the chives on top, and serve.
Nutrition: Calories 266, fat 13.9, fiber 11.1, carbs 23.8, protein 17.5

479) Trout and Tzatziki Sauce

Ingredients:

- Juice of ½ lime
- Salt and black pepper to the taste
- 1 and ½ Tsp coriander, ground
- 1 Tsp garlic, minced
- 4 trout fillets, boneless
- 1 Tsp sweet paprika
- 2 Tbsps avocado oil

For the sauce:

- 1 cucumber, chopped
- 4 garlic cloves, minced
- 1 Tbsp olive oil
- 1 Tsp white vinegar
- 1 and ½ cups Greek yogurt
- A pinch of salt and white pepper

Direction: Preparation time: 10 minutes Cooking time: 10 minutes Servings: 4

- ✓ Heat up a pan with the avocado oil over medium-high heat, add the fish, salt, pepper, lime juice, 1 Tsp garlic, and the paprika, rub the fish gently and cook for 4 minutes on each side.
- ✓ In a container, combine the cucumber with 4 garlic cloves and the rest of the ingredients for the sauce and whisk well.
- ✓ Divide the fish between plates, drizzle the sauce all over and serve with a side salad.

Nutrition: Calories 393, fat 18.5, fiber 6.5, carbs 18.3, protein 39.6

480) Parsley Trout and Capers

Ingredients:

- 4 trout fillets, boneless
- 3 ounces tomato sauce
- Handful parsley, chopped
- 2 Tbsps olive oil
- Salt and black pepper to the taste

Direction: Preparation time: 10 minutes Cooking time: 10 minutes Servings: 4

- ✓ Heat up a pan with the oil over medium-high heat, add the fish, salt, and pepper and cook for 3 minutes on each side.
- ✓ Add the rest of the ingredients, cook everything for 4 minutes more.
- ✓ Divide everything between plates and serve.

Nutrition: Calories 308, fat 17, fiber 1, carbs 3, protein 16

481) Baked Trout and Fennel

Ingredients:

- 1 fennel bulb, sliced
- 2 Tbsps olive oil
- 1 yellow onion, sliced
- 3 Tsps Italian seasoning
- 4 rainbow trout fillets, boneless
- ¼ cup panko breadcrumbs
- ½ cup kalamata olives pitted and halved
- Juice of 1 lemon

Direction: Preparation time: 10 minutes Cooking time: 22 minutes Servings: 4

- ✓ Spread the fennel, the onion, and the rest of the ingredients except the trout and the breadcrumbs on a baking sheet lined with parchment paper, toss them and cook at 400 degrees F for 10 minutes.
- ✓ Add the fish dredged in breadcrumbs, seasoned with salt and pepper, and cook it at 400 degrees F for 6 minutes on each side.
- ✓ Divide the mix between plates and serve.

Nutrition: Calories 306, fat 8.9, fiber 11.1, carbs 23.8, protein 14.5

482) Lemon Rainbow Trout

Ingredients:

- 2 rainbow trout
- Juice of 1 lemon
- 3 Tbsps olive oil
- 4 garlic cloves, minced
- A pinch of salt and black pepper

Direction: Preparation time: 10 minutes Cooking time: 15 minutes Servings: 2

- ✓ Line a baking sheet with parchment paper, add the fish and the rest of the ingredients and rub.
- ✓ Bake at 400 degrees F for 15 minutes, divide between plates and serve with a side salad.

Nutrition: Calories 521, fat 29, fiber 5, carbs 14, protein 52

483) Trout and Peppers Mix

Ingredients:

- 4 trout fillets, boneless
- 2 Tbsps kalamata olives, pitted and chopped
- 1 Tbsp capers, drained
- 2 Tbsps olive oil
- A pinch of salt and black pepper
- 1 and ½ Tsps chili powder
- 1 yellow bell pepper, chopped
- 1 red bell pepper, chopped
- 1 green bell pepper, chopped

Direction: Preparation time: 10 minutes Cooking time: 20 minutes Servings: 4

- ✓ Heat up a pan with the oil over medium-high heat, add the trout, salt, and pepper and cook for 10 minutes.

✓ *Flip the fish, add the peppers and the rest of the ingredients, cook for 10 minutes more, divide the whole mix between plates and serve.*
Nutrition: Calories 572, fat 17.4, fiber 6, carbs 71, protein 33.7

484) Cod and Cabbage

Ingredients:

- *3 cups green cabbage, shredded*
- *1 sweet onion, sliced*
- *A pinch of salt and black pepper*
- *½ cup feta cheese, crumbled*
- *4 Tsps olive oil*
- *4 cod fillets, boneless*
- *¼ cup green olives, pitted and chopped*

Direction: Preparation time: 10 minutes Cooking time: 15 minutes Servings: 4

✓ *Grease a roasting pan with the oil, add the fish, the cabbage, and the rest of the ingredients, introduce into the pan and cook at 450 degrees F for 15 minutes.*

✓ *Divide the mix between plates and serve.*
Nutrition: Calories 270, fat 10, fiber 3, carbs 12, protein 31

485) Mediterranean Mussels

Ingredients:

- *1 white onion, sliced*
- *3 Tbsps olive oil*
- *2 Tsps fennel seeds*
- *4 garlic cloves, minced*
- *1 Tsp red pepper, crushed*
- *A pinch of salt and black pepper*
- *1 cup chicken stock*
- *1 Tbsp lemon juice*
- *2 and ½ pounds mussels, scrubbed*
- *½ cup parsley, chopped*
- *½ cup tomatoes, cubed*

Direction: Preparation time: 10 minutes Cooking time: 10 minutes Servings: 4

✓ *Heat up a pan with the oil over medium-high heat, add the onion and the garlic and sauté for 2 minutes.*

✓ *Add the rest of the ingredients except the mussels, stir and cook for 3 minutes more.*

✓ *Add the mussels, cook everything for 6 minutes more, divide everything into containers and serve.*
Nutrition: Calories 276, fat 9.8, fiber 4.8, carbs 6.5, protein 20.5

486) Mussels Containers

Ingredients:

- *2 pounds mussels, scrubbed*
- *1 Tbsp garlic, minced*
- *1 Tbsp basil, chopped*
- *1 yellow onion, chopped*
- *6 tomatoes, cubed*
- *1 cup heavy cream*
- *2 Tbsps olive oil*
- *1 Tbsp parsley, chopped*

Direction: Preparation time: 10 minutes Cooking time: 10 minutes Servings: 4

✓ *Heat up a pan with the oil over medium-high heat, add the garlic and the onion and sauté for 2 minutes.*

✓ *Add the mussels and the rest of the ingredients, toss, cook for 7 minutes more, divide into containers and serve.*
Nutrition: Calories 266, fat 11.8, fiber 5.8, carbs 16.5, protein 10.5

487) Calamari and Dill Sauce

Ingredients:

- *1 and ½ pound calamari, sliced into rings*
- *10 garlic cloves, minced*
- *2 Tbsps olive oil*
- *Juice of 1 and ½ lime*
- *2 Tbsps balsamic vinegar*
- *3 Tbsps dill, chopped*
- *A pinch of salt and black pepper*

Direction: Preparation time: 10 minutes Cooking time: 15 minutes Servings: 4

✓ *Heat up a pan with the oil over medium-high heat, add the garlic, lime juice, and the other ingredients except for the calamari and cook for 5 minutes.*

✓ *Add the calamari rings, cook everything for 10 minutes more, divide between plates and serve*
Nutrition: Calories 282, fat 18.6, fiber 4, carbs 9.2, protein 18.5

488) Chili Calamari and Veggie Mix

Ingredients:

- *1 pound calamari rings*
- *2 red chili peppers, chopped*
- *2 Tbsps olive oil*
- *3 garlic cloves, minced*
- *14 ounces canned tomatoes, chopped*
- *2 Tbsps tomato paste*
- *1 Tbsp thyme, chopped*
- *Salt and black pepper to the taste*
- *2 Tbsps capers, drained*
- *12 black olives, pitted and halved*

Direction: Preparation time: 10 minutes Cooking time: 40 minutes Servings: 4

✓ *Heat up a pan with the oil over medium-high heat,*

add the garlic and the chili peppers and sauté for 2 minutes.

✓ *Add the rest of the ingredients except the olives and capers, stir, bring to a simmer and cook for 22 minutes.*

✓ *Add the olives and capers, cook everything for 15 minutes more, divide everything into containers and serve.*

Nutrition: Calories 274, fat 11.6, fiber 2.8, carbs 13.5, protein 15.4

489) Horseradish Cheesy Salmon Mix

Ingredients:

- *2 ounces feta cheese, crumbled*
- *4 ounces cream cheese, soft*
- *3 Tbsps already prepared horseradish*
- *1 pound smoked salmon, skinless, boneless, and flaked*
- *2 Tsps lime zest, grated*
- *1 red onion, chopped*
- *3 Tbsps chives, chopped*

Direction: Preparation time: 1 hour Cooking time: 0 minutes Servings: 8

✓ *In your food processor, mix cream cheese with horseradish, goat cheese, and lime zest and blend very well.*

✓ *In a container, combine the salmon with the rest of the ingredients, toss, and serve cold.*

Nutrition: Calories 281, fat 17.9, fiber 1, carbs 4.2, protein 25.3

490) Greek Trout Spread

Ingredients:

- *4 ounces smoked trout, skinless, boneless, and flaked*
- *1 Tbsp lemon juice*
- *1 cup Greek yogurt*
  Tbsp dill, chopped
- *Salt and black pepper to the taste*
- *A drizzle of olive oil*

Direction: Preparation time: 5 minutes Cooking time: 0 minutes Servings: 8

✓ *Combine the trout with the lemon juice and the rest of the ingredients in a container and whisk really well.*

✓ *Divide the spread into containers and serve.*

Nutrition: Cal 258, fat 4,5, fiber 2, carbs 5.5, protein 7.6

491) Scallions and Salmon Tartar

Ingredients:

- *4 Tbsps scallions, chopped*
- *2 Tsps lemon juice*
- *1 tbsp chives, minced*
- *1 Tbsp olive oil*
- *1 pound salmon, skinless, boneless, and minced*
- *Salt and black pepper to the taste*
- *1 Tbsp parsley, chopped*

Direction: Preparation time: 5 minutes Cooking time: 0 minutes Servings: 4

✓ *In a container, combine the scallions with the salmon and the rest of the ingredients, stir well, divide into small moulds between plates and serve.*

Nutrition: Calories 224, fat 14.5, fiber 5.2, carbs 12.7, protein 5.3

492) Salmon and Green Beans

Ingredients:

- *3 Tbsps balsamic vinegar*
- *2 Tbsps olive oil*
- *1 garlic clove, minced*
- *½ Tsps red pepper flakes, crushed*
- *½ Tsp lime zest, grated*
- *1 and ½ pounds green beans, chopped*
- *Salt and black pepper to the taste*
- *1 red onion, sliced*
- *4 salmon fillets, boneless*

Direction: Preparation time: 10 minutes Cooking time: 15 minutes Servings: 4

✓ *Heat up a pan with half of the oil, add the vinegar, onion, garlic, and the other ingredients except the salmon, toss, cook for 6 minutes, and divide between plates.*

✓ *Heat up the same pan with the rest of the oil over medium-high heat, add the salmon, salt, and pepper, cook for 4 minutes on each side, add next to the green beans and serve.*

Nutrition: Calories 224, fat 15.5, fiber 8.2, carbs 22.7, protein 16.3

493) Cayenne Cod and Tomatoes

Ingredients:

- *1 Tsp lime juice*
- *Salt and black pepper to the taste*
- *1 Tsp sweet paprika*
- *1 Tsp cayenne pepper*
- *2 Tbsps olive oil*
- *1 yellow onion, chopped*
- *2 garlic cloves, minced*
- *4 cod fillets, boneless*
- *A pinch of cloves, ground*
- *½ cup chicken stock*
- *½ pound cherry tomatoes, cubed*

Direction: Preparation time: 10 minutes Cooking time: 25 minutes Servings: 4

✓ *Heat up a pan with the oil over medium-high heat, add the cod, salt, pepper, and cayenne, cook for 4 minutes on each side, and divide between plates.*

✓ Heat up the same pan over medium-high heat, add the onion and garlic, and sauté for 5 minutes.

✓ Add the rest of the ingredients, stir, bring to a simmer and cook for 10 minutes more.

✓ Divide the mix next to the fish and serve.

Nutrition: Calories 232, fat 16.5, fiber 11.1, carbs 24.8, protein 16.5

494) Salmon and Watermelon Gazpacho

Ingredients:

- ¼ cup basil, chopped
- 1 pound tomatoes, cubed
- 1 pound watermelon, cubed
- ¼ cup red wine vinegar
- 1/3 cup avocado oil
- 2 garlic cloves, minced
- 1 cup smoked salmon, skinless, boneless, and cubed
- A pinch of salt and black pepper

Direction: Preparation time: 4 hours Cooking time: 0 minutes Servings: 4

✓ In your blender, combine the basil with the watermelon and the rest of the ingredients except the salmon, pulse well, and divide into containers.

✓ Top each serving with the salmon and serve cold.

Nutrition: Cal 252, fat 16.5, carbs 24.8, protein 15.5

495) Shrimp and Calamari Mix

Ingredients:

- 1 pound shrimp, peeled and deveined
- Salt and black pepper to the taste
- 3 garlic cloves, minced
- 1 Tbsp avocado oil
- ½ pound calamari rings
- ½ Tsp basil, dried
- 1 Tsp rosemary, dried
- 1 red onion, chopped
- 1 cup chicken stock
- Juice of 1 lemon
- 1 Tbsp parsley, chopped

Direction: Preparation time: 10 minutes Cooking time: 12 minutes Servings: 4

✓ Heat up a pan with the oil over medium-high heat, add the onion and the garlic and sauté for 4 minutes.

✓ Add the shrimp, the calamari, and the rest of the ingredients except the parsley, stir, bring to a simmer and cook for 8 minutes.

✓ Add the parsley, divide everything into containers and serve.

Nutrition: Calories 288, fat 12.8, carbs 22.2, protein 6.8

496) Shrimp and Dill Mix

Ingredients:

- 1 pound shrimp, cooked, peeled, and deveined
- ½ cup raisins
- 1 cup spring onion, chopped
- 2 Tbsps olive oil
- 2 Tbsps capers, chopped
- 2 Tbsps dill, chopped
- Salt and black pepper to the taste

Direction: Preparation time: 10 minutes Cooking time: 10 minutes Servings: 4

✓ Heat up a pan with the oil over medium-high heat, add the onions and raisins and sauté for 2-3 minutes.

✓ Add the shrimp and the rest of the ingredients, toss, cook for 6 minutes more, divide between plates and serve with a side salad

Nutrition: Calories 218, fat 12.8, fiber 6.2, carbs 22.2, protein 4.8

497) Minty Sardines Salad

Ingredients:

- 4 ounces canned sardines in olive oil, skinless, boneless, and flaked
- 2 Tsps avocado oil
- 2 Tbsps mint, chopped
- A pinch of salt and black pepper
- 1 avocado, peeled, pitted, and cubed
- 1 cucumber, cubed
- 2 tomatoes, cubed
- 2 spring onions, chopped

Direction: Preparation time: 10 minutes Cooking time: 0 minutes Servings: 4

✓ In a container, combine the sardines with the oil and the rest of the ingredients, toss, divide into small cups and keep in the fridge for 10 minutes before serving.

Nutrition: Calories 261, fat 7.6, fiber 2.2, carbs 22.8, protein 12.5

Vegetable Recipes

498) Potato Salad

Ingredients:

- 5 cups potato, cubed
- 1/4 cup fresh parsley, chopped
- 1/4 tsp red pepper flakes
- 1 tbsp olive oil
- 1/3 cup mayonnaise
- 1/2 tbsp oregano
- 2 tbsp capers
- 3/4 cup feta cheese, crumbled
- 1 cup olives, halved
- 3 cups of water
- 3/4 cup onion, chopped
- Pepper
- Salt

Direction: Preparation Time: 10 minutes Cooking Time: 10 minutes Servings: 8

- ✓ Add potatoes, onion, and salt into the instant pot.
- ✓ Seal pot with lid and cook on high for 3 minutes.
- ✓ Once done, release pressure using quick release. Remove lid.
- ✓ Remove potatoes from the pot and place them in a large mixing container.
- ✓ Add resting ingredients and stir everything well.
- ✓ Serve and enjoy.

Nutrition: Calories 152 Fat 9.9 g Carbohydrates 13.6 g Sugar 2.1 g Protein 3.5 g Cholesterol 15 mg

499) Greek Green Beans

Ingredients:

- 1 lb green beans, remove stems
- 2 potatoes, quartered
- 1 1/2 onion, sliced
- 1 tsp dried oregano
- 1/4 cup dill, chopped
- 1/4 cup fresh parsley, chopped
- 1 zucchini, quartered
- 1/2 cup olive oil
- 1 cup of water
- k14.5 oz can tomatoes, diced
- Pepper
- Salt

Direction: Preparation Time: 10 minutes Cooking Time: 15 minutes Servings: 4

- ✓ Add all ingredients into the inner pot of the instant pot and stir everything well.
- ✓ Seal pot with lid and cook on high for 15 minutes.
- ✓ Once done, release pressure using quick release. Remove lid.
- ✓ Stir well and serve.

Nutrition: Calories 381 Fat 25.8 g Carbohydrates 37.7 g Sugar 9 g Protein 6.6 g Cholesterol 0 mg

500) Healthy Vegetable Medley

Ingredients:

- 3 cups broccoli florets
- 1 sweet potato, chopped
- 1 tsp garlic, minced
- 14 oz coconut milk
- 28 oz can tomatoes, chopped
- 14 oz can chickpeas, drained and rinsed
- 1 onion, chopped
- 1 tbsp olive oil
- 1 tsp Italian seasoning
- Pepper
- Salt

Direction: Preparation Time: 10 minutes Cooking Time: 17 minutes Servings: 6

- ✓ Add oil into the inner pot of the instant pot and set the pot on sauté mode.
- ✓ Add garlic and onion and sauté until onion is softened.
- ✓ Add resting ingredients and stir everything well.
- ✓ Seal pot with lid and cook on high for 12 minutes.
- ✓ Once done, allow to release pressure naturally for 10 minutes, then release resting using quick release. Remove lid.
- ✓ Stir well and serve.

Nutrition: Calories 322 Fat 19.3 g Carbohydrates 34.3 g Sugar 9.6 g Protein 7.9 g Cholesterol 1 mg

501) Spicy Zucchini

Ingredients:

- 4 zucchini, cut into 1/2-inch pieces
- 1 cup of water
- 1/2 tsp Italian seasoning
- 1/2 tsp red pepper flakes
- 1 tsp garlic, minced
- 1 tbsp olive oil
- 1/2 cup can tomato, crushed
- Salt

Direction: Preparation Time: 10 minutes Cooking Time: 5 minutes Servings: 4

- ✓ Add water and zucchini into the instant pot.
- ✓ Seal pot with lid and cook on high for 2 minutes.
- ✓ Once done, release pressure using quick release. Remove lid.
- ✓ Drain zucchini well and clean the instant pot.
- ✓ Add oil into the inner pot of the instant pot and set the pot on sauté mode.
- ✓ Add garlic and sauté for 30 seconds.

✓ Add resting ingredients and stir well and cook for 2-3 minutes.

✓ Serve and enjoy.

Nutrition: Calories 69 Fat 4.1 g Carbohydrates 7.9 g Sugar 3.5 g Protein 2.7 g Cholesterol 0 mg

502) Healthy Garlic Eggplant

Ingredients:

- 1 eggplant, cut into 1-inch pieces
- 1/2 cup water
- 1/4 cup can tomato, crushed
- 1/2 tsp Italian seasoning
- 1 tsp paprika
- 1/2 tsp chili powder
- 1 tsp garlic powder
- 2 tbsp olive oil
- Salt

Direction: Preparation Time: 10 minutes Cooking Time: 10 minutes Servings: 4

✓ Add water and eggplant into the instant pot.

✓ Seal pot with lid and cook on high for 5 minutes.

✓ Once done, release pressure using quick release. Remove lid.

✓ Drain eggplant well and clean the instant pot.

✓ Add oil into the inner pot of the instant pot and set the pot on sauté mode.

✓ Add eggplant along with resting ingredients and stir well and cook for 5 minutes.

✓ Serve and enjoy.

Nutrition: Calories 97 Fat 7.5 g Carbohydrates 8.2 g Sugar 3.7 g Protein 1.5 g Cholesterol 0 mg

503) Carrot Potato Medley

Ingredients:

- 4 lbs baby potatoes, clean and cut in half
- 1 1/2 lbs carrots, cut into chunks
- 1 tsp Italian seasoning
- 1 1/2 cups vegetable broth
- 1 tbsp garlic, chopped
- 1 onion, chopped
- 2 tbsp olive oil
- Pepper
- Salt

Direction: Preparation Time: 10 minutes Cooking Time: 15 minutes Servings: 6

✓ Add oil into the inner pot of the instant pot and set the pot on sauté mode.

✓ Add onion and sauté for 5 minutes.

✓ Add carrots and cook for 5 minutes.

✓ Add resting ingredients and stir well.

✓ Seal pot with lid and cook on high for 5 minutes.

✓ Once done, allow to release pressure naturally for 10 minutes, then release resting using quick release. Remove lid.

✓ Stir and serve.

Nutrition: Calories 283 Fat 5.6 g Carbohydrates 51.3 g Sugar 6.6 g Protein 10.2 g Cholesterol 1 mg

504) Lemon Herb Potatoes

Ingredients:

- 1 1/2 lbs baby potatoes, rinsed and pat dry
- 1/2 fresh lemon juice
- 1 tsp dried oregano
- 1/2 tsp garlic, minced
- 1 tbsp olive oil
- 1 cup vegetable broth
- 1/2 tsp sea salt

Direction: Preparation Time: 10 minutes Cooking Time: 11 minutes Servings: 6

✓ Add broth and potatoes into the instant pot.

✓ Seal pot with lid and cook on high for 8 minutes.

✓ Once done, release pressure using quick release. Remove lid.

✓ Drain potatoes well and clean the instant pot.

✓ Add oil into the inner pot of the instant pot and set the pot on sauté mode.

✓ Add potatoes, garlic, oregano, lemon juice, and salt and cook for 3 minutes.

✓ Serve and enjoy.

Nutrition: Calories 94 Fat 2.7 g Carbohydrates 14.6 g Sugar 0.2 g Protein 3.8 g Cholesterol 0 mg

505) Flavors Basil Lemon Ratatouille

Ingredients:

- 1 small eggplant, cut into cubes
- 1 cup fresh basil
- 2 cups grape tomatoes
- 1 onion, chopped
- 2 summer squash, sliced
- 2 zucchini, sliced
- 2 tbsp vinegar
- 2 tbsp tomato paste
- 1 tbsp garlic, minced
- 1 fresh lemon juice
- 1/4 cup olive oil
- Salt

Direction: Preparation Time: 10 minutes Cooking Time: 10 minutes Servings: 8

✓ Add basil, vinegar, tomato paste, garlic, lemon juice, oil, and salt into the blender and blend until smooth.

✓ Add eggplant, tomatoes, onion, squash, and zucchini into the instant pot.

✓ Pour blended basil mixture over vegetables and stir

well.

- Seal pot with lid and cook on high for 10 minutes.
- Once done, allow to release pressure naturally. Remove lid.
- Stir well and serve.

Nutrition: Calories 103 Fat 6.8 g Carbohydrates 10.6 g Sugar 6.1 g Protein 2.4 g Cholesterol 0 mg

506) Garlic Basil Zucchini

Ingredients:

- 14 oz zucchini, sliced
- 1/4 cup fresh basil, chopped
- 1/2 tsp red pepper flakes
- 14 oz can tomatoes, chopped
- 1 tsp garlic, minced
- 1/2 onion, chopped
- 1/4 cup feta cheese, crumbled
- 1 tbsp olive oil
- Salt

Direction: Preparation Time: 10 minutes Cooking Time: 8 minutes Servings: 4

- Add oil into the inner pot of the instant pot and set the pot on sauté mode.
- Add onion and garlic and sauté for 2 minutes.
- Add resting ingredients except for feta cheese and stir well.
- Seal pot with lid and cook on high for 6 minutes.
- Once done, allow to release pressure naturally. Remove lid.
- Top with feta cheese and serve.

Nutrition: Calories 99 Fat 5.7 g Carbohydrates 10.4 g Sugar 6.1 g Protein 3.7 g Cholesterol 8 mg

507) Feta Green Beans

Ingredients:

- 1 1/2 lbs green beans, trimmed
- 1/4 cup feta cheese, crumbled
- 28 oz can tomatoes, crushed
- 2 tsp oregano
- 1 tsp cumin
- 1/2 cup water
- 1 tbsp olive oil
- 1 tbsp garlic, minced
- 1 onion, chopped
- 1 lb baby potatoes, clean and cut into chunks
- Pepper
- Salt

Direction: Preparation Time: 10 minutes Cooking Time: 15 minutes Servings: 4

- Add oil into the inner pot of the instant pot and set the pot on sauté mode.
- Add onion and garlic and sauté for 3-5 minutes.
- Add resting ingredients except for feta cheese and stir well.
- Seal pot with lid and cook on high for 10 minutes.
- Once done, allow to release pressure naturally for 5 minutes, then release resting using quick release. Remove lid.
- Top with feta cheese and serve.

Nutrition: Calories 234 Fat 6.1 g Carbohydrates 40.7 g Sugar 10.7 g Protein 9.7 g Cholesterol 8 mg

508) Garlic Parmesan Artichokes

Ingredients:

- 4 artichokes, wash, trim, and cut top
- 1/2 cup vegetable broth
- 1/4 cup parmesan cheese, grated
- 1 tbsp olive oil
- 2 tsp garlic, minced

Direction: Preparation Time: 10 minutes Cooking Time: 10 minutes Servings: 4

- Pour broth into the instant pot, then place steamer rack to the pot.
- Place artichoke steam side down on steamer rack into the pot.
- Sprinkle garlic and grated cheese on top of artichokes and season with salt. Drizzle oil over artichokes.
- Seal pot with lid and cook on high for 10 minutes.
- Once done, release pressure using quick release. Remove lid.
- Serve and enjoy.

Nutrition: Calories 132 Fat 5.2 g Carbohydrates 17.8 g Sugar 1.7 g Protein 7.9 g Cholesterol 4 mg

509) Delicious Pepper Zucchini

Ingredients:

- 1 zucchini, sliced
- 2 poblano peppers, sliced
- 1 tbsp sour cream
- 1/2 tsp ground cumin
- 1 yellow squash, sliced
- 1 tbsp garlic, minced
- 1/2 onion, sliced
- 1 tbsp olive oil
- Salt

Direction: Preparation Time: 10 minutes Cooking Time: 10 minutes Servings: 6

- Add oil into the inner pot of the instant pot and set the pot on sauté mode.
- Add poblano peppers and sauté for 5 minutes
- Add onion and garlic and sauté for 3 minutes.
- Add resting ingredients except for sour cream and stir well.
- Seal pot with lid and cook on high for 2 minutes.

✓ Once done, release pressure using quick release. Remove lid.

✓ Add sour cream and stir well and serve.

Nutrition: Calories 42 Fat 2.9 g Carbohydrates 4 g Sugar 1.7 g Protein 1 g Cholesterol 1 mg

510) Celery Carrot Brown Lentils

Ingredients:

- 2 cups dry brown lentils, rinsed and drained
- 2 1/2 cups vegetable stock
- 2 tomatoes, chopped
- 1/2 tsp red pepper flakes
- 1/2 tsp ground cinnamon
- 1 bay leaf
- 1 tbsp tomato paste
- 2 celery stalks, diced
- 2 carrots, grated
- 1 tbsp garlic, minced
- 2 onions, chopped
- 1/4 cup olive oil
- Pepper
- Salt

Direction: Preparation Time: 10 minutes Cooking Time: 25 minutes Servings: 6

✓ Add oil into the inner pot of the instant pot and set the pot on sauté mode.

✓ Add celery, carrot, garlic, onion, pepper, and salt and sauté for 3 minutes.

✓ Add resting ingredients and stir everything well.

✓ Seal pot with lid and cook on high for 22 minutes.

✓ Once done, release pressure using quick release. Remove lid.

✓ Stir well and serve.

Nutrition: Calories 137 Fat 8.8 g Carbohydrates 12.3 g Sugar 4.7 g Protein 3.1 g Cholesterol 0 mg

511) Easy Chili Pepper Zucchinis

Ingredients:

- 4 zucchinis, cut into cubes
- 1/2 tsp red pepper flakes
- 1/2 tsp cayenne
- 1 tbsp chili powder
- 1/4 cup vegetable stock

Direction: Preparation Time: 10 minutes Cooking Time: 10 minutes Servings: 4

✓ Add all ingredients into the inner pot of the instant pot and stir well.

✓ Seal pot with lid and cook on high for 10 minutes.

✓ Once done, allow to release pressure naturally for 10 minutes, then release resting using quick release. Remove lid.

✓ Stir and serve.

Nutrition: Calories 38 Fat 0.7 g Carbohydrates 8.8 g Sugar 3.6 g Protein 2.7 g Cholesterol 0 m

512) Delicious Okra

Ingredients:

- 2 cups okra, chopped
- 2 tbsp fresh dill, chopped
- 1 tbsp paprika
- 1 cup can tomato, crushed
- Pepper
- Salt

Direction: Preparation Time: 10 minutes Cooking Time: 10 minutes Servings: 4

✓ Add all ingredients into the inner pot of the instant pot and stir well.

✓ Seal pot with lid and cook on high for 10 minutes.

✓ Once done, allow to release pressure naturally for 5 minutes, then release resting using quick release. Remove lid.

✓ Stir well and serve.

Nutrition: Calories 37 Fat 0.5 g Carbohydrates 7.4 g Sugar 0.9 g Protein 2 g Cholesterol 0 mg

513) Tomato Dill Cauliflower

Ingredients:

- 1 lb cauliflower florets, chopped
- 1 tbsp fresh dill, chopped
- 1/4 tsp Italian seasoning
- 1 tbsp vinegar
- 1 cup can get tomatoes, crushed
- 1 cup vegetable stock
- 1 tsp garlic, minced
- Pepper
- Salt

Direction: Preparation Time: 10 minutes Cooking Time: 12 minutes Servings: 4

✓ Add all ingredients except dill into the instant pot and stir well.

✓ Seal pot with lid and cook on high for 12 minutes.

✓ Once done, allow to release pressure naturally for 10 minutes, then release resting using quick release. Remove lid.

✓ Garnish with dill and serve.

Nutrition: Calories 47 Fat 0.3 g Carbohydrates 10 g Sugar 5 g Protein 3.1 g Cholesterol 0 mg

514) Parsnips with Eggplant

Ingredients:

- 2 parsnips, sliced
- 1 cup canned tomatoes, crushed
- 1/2 tsp ground cumin
- 1 tbsp paprika

- *1 tsp garlic, minced*
- *1 eggplant, cut into chunks*
- *1/4 tsp dried basil*
- *Pepper*
- *Salt*

Direction: Preparation Time: 10 minutes Cooking Time: 12 minutes Servings: 4

- ✓ *Add all ingredients into the instant pot and stir well.*
- ✓ *Seal pot with lid and cook on high for 12 minutes.*
- ✓ *Once done, release pressure using quick release. Remove lid.*
- ✓ *Stir and serve.*

Nutrition: Calories 98 0.7 g Carbohydrates 23 g Sugar 8.8 g Protein 2.8 g Cholesterol 0 mg

515) Easy Garlic Beans

Ingredients:

- *1 lb green beans, trimmed*
- *1 1/2 cup vegetable stock*
- *1 tsp garlic, minced*
- *1 tbsp olive oil*
- *Pepper*
- *Salt*

Direction: Preparation Time: 10 minutes Cooking Time: 5 minutes Servings: 4

- ✓ *Add all ingredients into the instant pot and stir well.*
- ✓ *Seal pot with lid and cook on high for 5 minutes.*
- ✓ *Once done, release pressure using quick release. Remove lid.*
- ✓ *Stir and serve.*

Nutrition: Calories 69 Fat 3.7 g Carbohydrates 8.7 g Sugar 1.9 g Protein 2.3 g Cholesterol 0 mg

516) Eggplant with Olives

Ingredients:

- *4 cups eggplants, cut into cubes*
- *1/2 cup vegetable stock*
- *1 tsp chili powder*
- *1 cup olives, pitted and sliced*
- *1 onion, chopped*
- *1 tbsp olive oil*
- *1/4 cup grape tomatoes*
- *Pepper*
- *Salt*

Direction: Preparation Time: 10 minutes Cooking Time: 12 minutes Servings: 4

- ✓ *Add oil into the inner pot of the instant pot and set the pot on sauté mode.*
- ✓ *Add onion and sauté for 2 minutes.*
- ✓ *Add resting ingredients and stir everything well.*
- ✓ *Seal pot with lid and cook on high for 12 minutes.*
- ✓ *Once done, allow to release pressure naturally for 10 minutes, then release resting using quick release. Remove lid.*
- ✓ *Stir and serve.*

Nutrition: Calories 105 Fat 7.4 g Carbohydrates 10.4 g Sugar 4.1 g Protein 1.6 g Cholesterol 0 mg

517) Vegan Carrots & Broccoli

Ingredients:

- *4 cups broccoli florets*
- *2 carrots, peeled and sliced*
- *1/4 cup water*
- *1/2 lemon juice*
- *1 tsp garlic, minced*
- *1 tbsp olive oil*
- *1/4 cup vegetable stock*
- *1/4 tsp Italian seasoning*
- *Salt*

Direction: Preparation Time: 10 minutes Cooking Time: 5 minutes Servings: 6

- ✓ *Add oil into the inner pot of the instant pot and set the pot on sauté mode.*
- ✓ *Add garlic and sauté for 30 seconds.*
- ✓ *Add carrots and broccoli and cook for 2 minutes.*
- ✓ *Add resting ingredients and stir everything well.*
- ✓ *Seal pot with lid and cook on high for 3 minutes.*
- ✓ *Once done, release pressure using quick release. Remove lid.*
- ✓ *Stir well and serve.*

Nutrition: Calories 51 Fat 2.6 g Carbohydrates 6.3 g Sugar 2.2 g Protein 2 g Cholesterol 0 mg

518) Zucchini Tomato Potato Ratatouille

Ingredients:

- *1 1/2 lbs potatoes, cut into cubes*
- *1/2 cup fresh basil*
- *28 oz fire-roasted tomatoes, chopped*
- *1 onion, chopped*
- *4 mushrooms, sliced*
- *1 bell pepper, diced*
- *12 oz eggplant, diced*
- *8 oz zucchini, diced*
- *8 oz yellow squash, diced*
- *Pepper*
- *Salt*

Direction: Preparation Time: 10 minutes Cooking Time: 10 minutes Servings: 6

- ✓ *Add all ingredients except basil into the instant pot and stir well.*
- ✓ *Seal pot with lid and cook on high for 10 minutes.*

- ✓ Once done, release pressure using quick release. Remove lid.
- ✓ Add basil and stir well and serve

Nutrition: Calories 175 Fat 1.9 g

519) Creamy Carrot Chowder

Ingredients:

- 8 fresh mint sprigs
- ½ cup 2% Greek Style Plain yogurt
- 1 tsp fresh ginger, peeled and grated
- 2 cups chicken broth
- 1 lb. baby carrots, peeled and cut into 2-inch lengths
- 1/3 cup sliced shallots
- 2 tsp sesame oil

Direction: Cooking Time: 40 minutes Servings: 8

- ✓ On medium fire, place a medium heavy bottom pot and heat oil.
- ✓ Sauté shallots until tender, around 2 minutes.
- ✓ Add carrots and sauté for another 4 minutes.
- ✓ Pour broth, cover, and bring to a boil once the soup is boiling, slow fire to a simmer, and cook carrots until tender, around 22 minutes.
- ✓ Add ginger and continue cooking while covered for another eight minutes.
- ✓ Turn off the fire and let it cool for 10 minutes.
- ✓ Pour mixture into blender and puree. If needed, puree carrots in batches, then return to pot.
- ✓ Heat pureed carrots until heated through around 2 minutes.
- ✓ Turn off fire and evenly pour into 8 serving containers.
- ✓ Serve and enjoy. Or you can store it in the freezer in 8 different lidded containers for a quick soup to the middle of the week.

Nutrition: Cal: 47; Carbs: 6.5g; Protein: 2.2g; Fat: 1.6g

520) Creamy Corn Soup

Ingredients:

- 4 slices crisp-cooked bacon, crumbled
- 2 tbsp cornstarch
- 1/4 cup water
- 2 tsp soy sauce
- 4 cups chicken broth
- 1 (14.75 oz) can cream-style corn
- 2 egg whites
- 1/4 tsp salt
- 1 tbsp sherry
- 1/2 lb. skinless, boneless chicken breast meat, finely chopped

Direction: Cooking Time: 20 minutes Servings: 4

- ✓ Combine chicken with sherry, egg whites, salt in a container. Stir to the cream-style corn. Mix well.
- ✓ Boil the soy sauce and chicken broth in a wok. Then stir to the chicken mixture while it continues boiling. Then simmer for about 3 minutes, frequently stir to avoid burning.
- ✓ Mix corn starch and water until well combined. Mix to the simmering broth while constantly stirring until it slightly thickens. Cook for about 2 minutes more.
- ✓ Serve topped with the crumbled bacon.

Nutrition: Calories: 305; Carbs: 28.0g; Protein: 21.1g; Fat: 13.0g

521) Creamy Kale and Mushrooms

Ingredients:

- 3 Tbsps coconut oil
- 3 cloves of garlic, minced
- 1 onion, chopped
- 1 bunch kale, stems removed, and leaves chopped
- 5 white button mushrooms, chopped
- 1 cup coconut milk
- Salt and pepper to taste

Direction: Cooking Time: 15 minutes Servings: 3,

- ✓ Heat oil in a pot.
- ✓ Sauté the garlic and onion until fragrant for 2 minutes.
- ✓ Stir in mushrooms. Season with pepper and salt. Cook for 8 minutes.
- ✓ Stir in kale and coconut milk. Simmer for 5 minutes.
- ✓ Adjust seasoning to taste.

Nutrition: Cal: 365; Carbs: 17.9g; Protein: 6g; Fat: 33.5g

522) Crunchy Kale Chips

Ingredients:

- 2 tbsp filtered water
- ½ tsp sea salt
- 1 tbsp raw honey
- 2 tbsp nutrition al yeast
- 1 lemon, juiced
- 1 cup sweet potato, grated
- 1 cup fresh cashews, soaked 2 hours
- 2 bunches green curly kale, washed, ribs and stem removed, leaves torn into bite-sized pieces

Direction: Cooking Time: 2 hours Servings: 8

- ✓ Prepare a baking sheet by covering it with unbleached parchment paper. Preheat oven to 1500F.
- ✓ In a large mixing container, place kale.
- ✓ In a food processor, process resting ingredients until smooth. Pour over kale.
- ✓ With your hands, coat kale with marinade.

- ✓ Evenly spread kale onto parchment paper and pop in the oven. Dehydrate for 2 hours and turn leaves after the first hour of baking.
- ✓ Remove from oven; let it cool completely before serving.

Nutrition: Calories: 209; Carbs: 13.0g; Protein: 7.0g; Fat: 15.9g

523) Delicious and Healthy Roasted Eggplant

Ingredients:

- Pinch of sugar
- ¼ tsp salt
- ¼ tsp cayenne pepper or to taste
- 1 tbsp parsley, flat-leaf, and chopped finely
- 2 tbsp fresh basil, chopped
- 1 small chili pepper, seeded and minced, optional
- ½ cup red onion, finely chopped
- ½ cup Greek feta cheese, crumbled
- ¼ cup extra virgin olive oil
- 2 tbsp lemon juice
- 1 medium eggplant, around 1 lb.

Direction: Cooking Time: 30 minutes Servings: 6,

- ✓ Preheat broiler and position rack 6 inches away from heat source.
- ✓ Pierce the eggplant with a knife or fork. Then with a foil, line a baking pan and place the eggplant and broil. Make sure to turn eggplant every five minutes or until the skin is charred and eggplant is soft, which takes around 14 to 18 minutes of broiling. Once done, remove from heat and let cool.
- ✓ In a medium container, add lemon. Then cut eggplant in half, lengthwise, and scrape the flesh, and place to the container with lemon. Add oil and mix until well combined. Then add salt, cayenne, parsley, basil, chili pepper, bell pepper, onion, and feta. Toss until well combined and add sugar to taste if wanted.

Nutrition: Calories: 97; Carbs: 7.4g; Protein: 2.9g; Fat: 6.7g

524) Delicious Stuffed Squash

Ingredients:

- ¼ cup sour cream
- ½ cup shredded cheddar
- 3 tbsp taco sauce
- 1 small tomato, chopped
- ½ small green bell pepper, seeded and chopped
- ½ medium onion, chopped
- 1 tsp cumin
- 1 tsp onion powder
- ¼ tsp cayenne
- 1 ½ tsp chili powder
- 1 can 15-oz black beans, drained and rinsed
- 1 clove garlic, minced
- 1 tbsp olive oil
- 2 medium zucchinis
- 2 medium yellow squash
- Salt and pepper

Direction: Cooking Time: 30minutes Servings: 4 servings

- ✓ Boil until tender in a large pot of water zucchini and yellow squash, then drain. Lengthwise, slice the squash and trim the ends. Take out the center flesh and chop.
- ✓ On medium-high fire, place the skillet with oil and sauté garlic until fragrant. Add onion and tomato and sauté for 8 minutes. Add chopped squash, bell pepper, cumin, onion powder, cayenne, chili powder, and black beans, and continue cooking until veggies are tender.
- ✓ Season with pepper and salt to taste. Remove from fire.
- ✓ Spread 1 tsp of taco sauce on each squash shell, fill with half of the cooked filling, top with cheese, and garnish with sour cream. Repeat procedure on the other half of the squash shell. Serve and enjoy.

Nutrition: Calories: 318; Carbs: 28.0g; Protein: 21.0g; Fat: 16.0g

525) Easy and Healthy Baked Vegetables

Ingredients:

- 2 lbs. Brussels sprouts, trimmed
- 3 lbs. Butternut Squash, peeled, seeded, and cut into the same size as sprouts
- 1 lb Pork breakfast sausage
- 1 tbsp fat from the fried sausage

Direction: Cooking Time: 1 hour and 15 minutes Servings: 6,

- ✓ Grease a 9x13 inch baking pan and preheat the oven to 350oF.
- ✓ On medium-high fire, place a large nonstick saucepan and cook sausage. Break up sausages and cook until browned.
- ✓ In a greased pan, mix browned sausage, squash, sprouts, sea salt, and fat. Toss to mix well. Pop into the oven and cook for an hour.
- ✓ Remove from oven and serve warm.

Nutrition: Cal: 364; Carbs: 41.2g; Protein: 19.0g; Fat: 16.5g

526) Eggplant Bolognese With Zucchini Noodles

Ingredients:

- 6 leaves of fresh basil, chopped
- 1 28-ounce can plum tomatoes
- ½ cup red wine

- *1 Tbsp tomato paste*
- *4 sprigs of thyme, chopped*
- *2 bay leaves*
- *3 cloves garlic, minced*
- *1 large yellow onion, chopped*
- *Salt and pepper to taste*
- *2 Tbsp extra-virgin olive oil*
- *½ pound ground beef*
- *1 ½ pounds eggplant, diced*
- *2 cups zucchini noodles*

Direction: Cooking Time: 20 minutes Servings: 4

- ✓ *Heat the skillet over medium-high heat and add oil. Sauté the onion and beef and sprinkle with salt and pepper. Sauté for 10 minutes until the meat is brown. Add to the eggplants bay leaves, garlic, and thyme. Cook for another 15 minutes.*
- ✓ *Once the eggplant is tender, add the tomato paste and wine. Add the tomatoes and crush using a spoon. Bring to a boil and reduce the heat to low. Simmer for 10 minutes.*
- ✓ *In a skillet, add oil and sauté the zucchini noodles for five minutes. Turn off the heat.*
- ✓ *Pour the tomato sauce over the zucchini noodles and garnish with fresh basil.*

Nutrition: Cal: 320; Carbs: 24.8g; Protein: 19.2g; Fat: 17.0g

527) ***Feta and Roasted Eggplant Dip***

Ingredients:

- *¼ tsp salt*
- *¼ tsp cayenne pepper*
- *1 tbsp finely chopped flat-leaf parsley*
- *2 tbsp chopped fresh basil*
- *1 small Chile pepper*
- *1 small red bell pepper, finely chopped*
- *½ cup finely chopped red onion*
- *½ cup crumbled Greek nonfat feta cheese*
- *¼ cup extra-virgin olive oil*
- *2 tbsp lemon juice*
- *1 medium eggplant, around 1 lb.*

Direction: Cooking Time: 20 minutes Servings: 12,

- ✓ *Preheat the broiler, position the rack on the topmost part of the oven, and line a baking pan with foil.*
- ✓ *With a fork or knife, poke eggplant, place on a prepared baking pan, and broil for 5 minutes per side until skin is charred all around.*
- ✓ *Once eggplant skin is charred, remove from broiler and allow to cool to handle.*
- ✓ *Once the eggplant is cool enough to handle, slice in half lengthwise, scoop out the flesh, and place in a medium container.*
- ✓ *Pour in lemon juice and toss eggplant to coat with lemon juice and prevent it from discoloring.*
- ✓ *Add oil; continue mixing until the eggplant absorbs oil.*
- ✓ *Stir in salt, cayenne pepper, parsley, basil, Chile pepper, bell pepper, onion, and feta.*
- ✓ *Toss to mix well and serve.*

Nutrition: Calories: 58; Carbs: 3.7g; Protein: 1.2g; Fat: 4.6g

528) ***Garlic 'n Sour Cream Zucchini Bake***

Ingredients:

- *1/4 cup grated Parmesan cheese*
- *paprika to taste*
- *1 Tbsp minced garlic*
- *1 large zucchini, cut lengthwise then in half*
- *1 cup sour cream*
- *1 (8 ounces) package cream cheese, softened*

Direction: Cooking Time: 20 minutes Servings: 3

- ✓ *Lightly grease a casserole dish with cooking spray.*
- ✓ *Place zucchini slices in a single layer in the dish.*
- ✓ *In a container, whisk well, resting ingredients except for paprika. Spread on top of zucchini slices. Sprinkle paprika.*
- ✓ *Cover dish with foil.*
- ✓ *For 10 minutes, cook in preheated 390oF oven.*
- ✓ *Remove foil and cook for 10 minutes.*
- ✓ *Serve and enjoy.*

Nutrition: Calories: 385; Carbs: 13.5g; Protein: 11.9g; Fat: 32.4g

529) ***Garlicky Rosemary Potatoes***

Ingredients:

- *1-pound potatoes, peeled and sliced thinly*
- *2 garlic cloves*
- *½ Tsp salt*
- *1 Tbsp olive oil*
- *2 sprigs of rosemary*

Direction: Cooking Time: 2 minutes Servings: 4

- ✓ *Place a trivet or steamer basket to the Instant Pot and pour in a cup of water.*
- ✓ *In a baking dish that can fit inside the Instant Pot, combine all ingredients and toss to coat everything.*
- ✓ *Cover the baking dish with aluminum foil and place it on the steamer basket.*
- ✓ *Close the lid and activate the Steam.*
- ✓ *Adjust the cooking time to 30 minutes*
- ✓ *Do quick pressure release.*
- ✓ *Once cooled, evenly divide into serving size, keep in your preferred container, and refrigerate until ready to eat*

Nutrition: Calories: 119; Carbs: 20.31g; Protein: 2.39g; Fat: 3.48g

530) Ginger and Spice Carrot Soup

Ingredients:

- ¼ cup Greek yogurt
- 2 tsp fresh lime juice
- 5 cups low-salt chicken broth
- 1 ½ tsp finely grated lime peel
- 4 cups of carrots, peeled, thinly sliced into rounds
- 2 cups chopped onions
- 1 tbsp minced and peeled fresh ginger
- ½ tsp curry powder
- 3 tbsp expeller-pressed sunflower oil
- ½ tsp yellow mustard seeds
- 1 tsp coriander seeds

Direction: Cooking Time: 40 minutes Servings: 6,

- ✓ In a food processor, grind mustard seeds and coriander into a powder.
- ✓ On medium-high fire, place a large pot and heat oil.
- ✓ Add curry powder and powdered seeds, and sauté for a minute.
- ✓ Add ginger, cook for a minute.
- ✓ Add lime peel, carrots, and onions. Sauté for 3 minutes or until onions are softened.
- ✓ Season with pepper and salt.
- ✓ Add broth and bring to a boil. Reduce fire to a simmer and simmer uncovered for 30 minutes or until carrots are tender.
- ✓ Cool broth slightly, and puree in batches. Return pureed carrots into the pot.
- ✓ Add lime juice, add more pepper and salt to taste.
- ✓ Transfer to a serving container, drizzle with yogurt, and serve.

Nutrition: Calories: 129; Carbs: 13.6g; Protein: 2.8g; Fat: 7.7g

531) Ginger-Egg Drop Soup with Zoodle

Ingredients:

- ½ Tsps red pepper flakes
- 2 cups thinly sliced scallions, divided
- 2 cups, plus 1 Tbsp water, divided
- 2 Tbsps extra virgin olive oil
- 2 Tbsps minced ginger
- 3 Tbsps corn starch
- 4 large eggs, beaten
- 4 medium to large zucchini, spiralized into noodles
- 5 cups shiitake mushrooms, sliced
- 5 Tbsps low-sodium tamari sauce or soy sauce
- 8 cups vegetable broth, divided
- Salt & pepper to taste

Direction: Cooking Time: 15 minutes Servings: 4,

- ✓ On medium-high, the fire, place a large pot and add oil.
- ✓ Once the oil is hot, stir in ginger and sauté for two minutes.
- ✓ Stir in a Tbsp of water and shiitake mushrooms. Cook for 5 minutes or until mushrooms starts to give off liquid.
- ✓ Stir in 1 ½ cups scallions, tamari sauce, red pepper flakes, resting water, and 7 cups of vegetable broth. Mix well and bring to a boil.
- ✓ Meanwhile, whisk well cornstarch and resting cup of vegetable broth in a small container and set aside.
- ✓ Once the pot is boiling, slowly pour in eggs while stirring the pot continuously. Mix well.
- ✓ Add the cornstarch slurry to the pot and mix well. Continue mixing every now and then until thickened, about 5 minutes.
- ✓ Taste and adjust seasoning with pepper and salt.
- ✓ Stir in zoodles and cook until heated for about 2 minutes.
- ✓ Serve with a sprinkle of resting scallions and enjoy.

Nutrition: Calories: 238; Protein: 10.6g; Carbs: 34.3g; Sugar: 12.8g; Fat: 8.6g

532) Ginger Vegetable Stir Fry

Ingredients:

- 1 Tbsp oil
- 3 cloves of garlic, minced
- 1 onion, chopped
- 1 thumb-size ginger, sliced
- 1 Tbsp water
- 1 large carrot, peeled and julienned
- 1 seeded and julienned large green bell pepper
- 1 large yellow bell pepper, seeded and julienned
- 1 large red bell pepper, seeded and julienned
- 1 zucchini, julienned
- Salt and pepper to taste

Direction: Cooking Time: 5 minutes Servings: 4

- ✓ Heat oil in a skillet over medium flame and sauté the garlic, onion, and ginger until fragrant.
- ✓ Stir to the rest of the ingredients and adjust the flame to high.
- ✓ Keep on stirring for at least 5 minutes until vegetables are half-cooked.
- ✓ Place in individual containers.
- ✓ Put a label and store it in the fridge.
- ✓ Allow thawing at room temperature before heating to the microwave oven.

Nutrition: Calories: 102; Carbs: 13.6g; Protein:0 g; Fat: 2g; Fiber: 7.6g

533) Gobi Masala Soup

Ingredients:

- 1 tsp salt
- 1 tsp ground turmeric
- 1 tsp ground coriander
- 2 tsp cumin seeds
- 3 tsp dark mustard seeds
- 1 cup water
- 3 cups beef broth
- 1 head cauliflower, chopped
- 3 carrots, chopped
- 1 large onion, chopped
- 2 tbsp coconut oil
- Chopped cilantro for topping
- Crushed red pepper to taste
- Black pepper to taste
- 1 tbsp lemon juice

Direction: Cooking Time: 35 minutes Servings: 4

✓ On medium-high fire, place a large, heavy-bottomed pot and heat coconut oil.

✓ Once hot, sauté garlic cloves for a minute. Add carrots and continue sautéing for 4 minutes more.

✓ Add turmeric, coriander, cumin, mustard seeds, and cauliflower. Sauté for 5 minutes.

✓ Add water and beef broth and simmer for 10 to 15 minutes.

✓ Turn off fire and transfer to a blender. Puree until smoot and creamy.

✓ Return to pot, continue simmering for another ten minutes.

✓ Season with crushed red pepper, lemon juice, pepper, and salt.

✓ To serve, garnish with cilantro, and enjoy.

Nutrition: Calories: 148; Carbs: 16.1g; Protein: 3.7g; Fat: 8.8g

534) Greek Styled Veggie-Rice

Ingredients:

- pepper and salt to taste
- ¼ cup extra virgin olive oil
- 3 tbsp chopped fresh mint
- ½ cup grape tomatoes halved
- ½ red bell pepper, diced small
- 1 head cauliflower, cut into large florets
- ¼ cup fresh lemon juice
- ½ yellow onion, minced

Direction: Cooking Time: 20 minutes Servings: 6

✓ In a container, mix lemon juice and onion and leave for 30 minutes. Then drain the onion and reserve the juice and onion bits.

✓ In a blender, shred cauliflower until the size of a grain of rice.

✓ On medium fire, place a medium nonstick skillet, and for 8-10 minutes, cook cauliflower while covered.

✓ Add grape tomatoes and bell pepper and cook for 3 minutes while stirring occasionally.

✓ Add mint and onion bits. Cook for another three minutes.

✓ Meanwhile, whisk pepper, salt, 3 tbsp reserved lemon juice, and olive oil until well blended in a small container.

✓ Remove cooked cauliflower, transfer to a serving container, pour lemon juice mixture, and toss to mix.

✓ Before serving, if needed, season with pepper and salt to taste.

Nutrition: Calories: 120; Carbs: 8.0g; Protein: 2.3g; Fat: 9.5g

535) Green Vegan Soup

Ingredients:

- 1 medium head cauliflower, cut into bite-sized florets
- 1 medium white onion, peeled and diced
- 2 cloves garlic, peeled and diced
- 1 bay leaf crumbled
- 5-oz watercress
- fresh spinach or frozen spinach
- 1-liter vegetable stock or bone broth
- 1 cup cream or coconut milk + 6 tbsp for garnish
- 1/4 cup ghee or coconut oil
- 1 tsp salt or to taste
- freshly ground black pepper
- Optional: fresh herbs such as parsley or chives for garnish

Direction: Cooking Time: 20 minutes Servings: 6

✓ On medium-high, the fire, place a Dutch oven greased with ghee. Once hot, sauté garlic for a minute. Add onions and sauté until soft and translucent, about 5 minutes.

✓ Add cauliflower florets and crumbled bay leaf. Mix well and cook for 5 minutes.

✓ Stir in watercress and spinach. Sauté for 3 minutes.

✓ Add vegetable stock and bring to a boil.

✓ When cauliflower is crisp-tender, stir in coconut milk.

✓ Season with pepper and salt.

✓ With a hand blender, puree soup until smooth and creamy.

✓ Serve and enjoy.

Nutrition: Calories: 392; Protein: 4.9g; Carbs: 9.7g; Sugar: 6.8g; Fat: 37.6g

536) Grilled Eggplant Caprese

Ingredients:

- *1 eggplant aubergine, small/medium*
- *1 tomato large*
- *2 basil leaves or a little more as needed*
- *4-oz mozzarella*
- *good quality olive oil*
- *Pepper and salt to taste*

Direction: Cooking Time: 10 minutes Servings: 4

- ✓ *Cut the ends of the eggplant and then cut it lengthwise into ¼-inch thick slices. Discard the smaller pieces that are mostly skin and short.*
- ✓ *Slice the tomatoes and mozzarella into thin slices just like the eggplant.*
- ✓ *On medium-high, the fire, place a griddle and let it heat up.*
- ✓ *Brush eggplant slices with olive oil and place on grill. Grill for 3 minutes. Turnover and grill for a minute. Add a slice of cheese on one side and tomato on the other side. Continue cooking for another 2 minutes.*
- ✓ *Sprinkle with basil leaves. Season with pepper and salt.*
- ✓ *Fold eggplant in half and skewer with a cocktail stick.*
- ✓ *Serve and enjoy.*

Nutrition: Calories: 59; Protein: 3.0g; Carbs: 4.0g; Sugar: 2.0g; Fat: 3.0g

537) Grilled Zucchini Bread and Cheese Sandwich

Ingredients:

- *1 large egg*
- *1/2 cup freshly grated Parmesan*
- *1/4 cup almond flour*
- *2 cup grated zucchini*
- *2 cup shredded Cheddar*
- *2 green onions thinly sliced*
- *Freshly ground black pepper*
- *kosher salt*
- *Vegetable oil, for cooking*

Direction: Cooking Time: 40 minutes Servings: 2

- ✓ *With a paper towel, squeeze dry the zucchinis and place them in a container. Add almond flour, green onions, Parmesan, and egg. Season with pepper and salt. Whisk well to combine.*
- ✓ *Place a large nonstick pan on medium fire and add oil to cover the pan. Once hot, add ¼ cup of zucchini mixture and shape it into a square-like bread. Add another batch as many as you can put into the pan. If needed, cook in batches. Cook for four minutes per side and place on a paper towel-lined plate.*
- ✓ *Once done cooking zucchinis, wipe off the oil from the pan. Place one zucchini piece on the pan, spread ½ of shredded cheese, and then top with another piece of zucchini. Grill for two minutes per side. Repeat process to make 2 sandwiches.*
- ✓ *Serve and enjoy.*

Nutrition: Calories: 667; Protein: 41.5g; Carbs: 14.4g; Fat: 49.9g

538) Homemade Egg Drop Soup

Ingredients:

- *1 tbsp cornstarch*
- *1 tbsp dried minced onion*
- *1 tsp dried parsley*
- *2 eggs*
- *4 cubes chicken bouillon*
- *4 cups water*
- *1 cup chopped carrots*
- *½ cup thinly shredded cabbage*

Direction: Cooking Time: 15 minutes Servings: 4

- ✓ *Combine water, bouillon, parsley, cabbage, carrots, and onion flakes in a saucepan, and then bring to a boil.*
- ✓ *Beat the eggs lightly and stir into the soup.*
- ✓ *Dissolve cornstarch with a little water. Stir until smooth and stir into the soup. Let it boil until the soup thickens.*

Nutrition: Calories: 98; Carbs: 6.9g; Protein: 5.1g; Fat: 5.3g

539) Hot and Sour Soup

Ingredients:

- *½ tsp sesame oil*
- *1 cup fresh bean sprouts*
- *1 egg, lightly beaten*
- *1 tsp black pepper*
- *1 tsp ground ginger*
- *3 tbsp white vinegar*
- *3 tbsp soy sauce*
- *¼ lb. sliced mushrooms*
- *½ lb. tofu, cubed*
- *2 tbsp corn starch*
- *3 ½ cups chicken broth*

Direction: Cooking Time: 25 minutes Servings: 4

- ✓ *Mix corn starch and ¼ cup chicken broth and put aside.*
- ✓ *Over high heat, place a pot, then combine and boil: pepper, ginger, vinegar, soy sauce, mushrooms, tofu, and chicken broth.*
- ✓ *Once boiling, add the corn starch mixture. Stir constantly and reduce the fire. Once the concoction is thickened, drop the slightly beaten egg while stirring vigorously.*
- ✓ *Add bean sprouts and for one to two minutes, allow simmering.*

✓ Remove from fire and transfer to serving containers and enjoy while hot.

Nutrition: Calories: 141; Carbs: 12.9g; Protein: 10.0g; Fat: 6.6g

540) Indian Bell Peppers and Potato Stir Fry

Ingredients:

- 1 Tbsp oil
- ½ Tsp cumin seeds
- 4 cloves of garlic, minced
- 4 potatoes, scrubbed and halved
- Salt and pepper to taste
- 5 Tbsps water
- 2 bell peppers, seeded and julienned
- Chopped cilantro for garnish

Direction: Cooking Time: 15 minutes Servings: 2,

✓ Heat oil in a skillet over medium flame and toast the cumin seeds until fragrant.

✓ Add the garlic until fragrant.

✓ Stir to the potatoes, salt, pepper, water, and bell peppers.

✓ Close the lid and allow to simmer for at least 10 minutes.

✓ Garnish with cilantro before cooking time ends.

✓ Place in individual containers.

✓ Put a label and store it in the fridge.

✓ Allow thawing at room temperature before heating to the microwave oven.

Nutrition: Calories: 83; Carbs: 7.3g; Protein: 2.8g; Fat: 6.4g; Fiber:1.7 g

541) Indian Style Okra

Ingredients:

- 1 lb. small to medium okra pods, trimmed
- ¼ tsp curry powder
- ½ tsp kosher salt
- 1 tsp finely chopped serrano chili
- 1 tsp ground coriander
- 1 tbsp canola oil
- ¾ tsp brown mustard seeds

Direction: Cooking Time: 12 minutes Servings: 4,

✓ Place a large and heavy skillet on medium-high fire and cook mustard seeds until fragrant, around 30 seconds.

✓ Add canola oil. Add okra, curry powder, salt, chili, and coriander. Sauté for a minute while stirring every once in a while.

✓ Cover and cook low fire for at least 8 minutes. Stir occasionally.

✓ Uncover, increase the fire to medium-high and cook until okra is lightly browned, around 2 minutes more.

✓ Serve and enjoy.

Nutrition: Calories: 78; Carbs: 6.4g; Protein: 2.1g; Fat: 5.7g

542) Instant Pot Artichoke Hearts

Ingredients:

- 4 artichokes, rinsed and trimmed
- Juice from 2 small lemons, freshly squeezed
- 2 cups bone broth
- 1 Tbsp tarragon leaves
- 1 stalk, celery
- ½ cup extra virgin olive oil
- Salt and pepper to taste

Direction: Cooking Time: 30 minutes Servings: 6

✓ Place all ingredients in a pressure cooker.

✓ Give a good stir.

✓ Close the lid and seal the valve.

✓ Pressure cook for 4 minutes.

✓ Allow the pressure cooker to release steam naturally.

✓ Then serve and enjoy.

Nutrition: Cal: 133; Carbs: 14.3g; Protein: 4.4g; Fat: 11.7g

543) Instant Pot Fried Veggies

Ingredients:

- 1 Tbsp olive oil
- 1 onion, chopped
- 4 cloves of garlic, minced
- 2 carrots, peeled and julienned
- 1 zucchini, julienned
- 1 large potato, peeled and julienned
- ½ cup chopped tomatoes
- 1 Tsp rosemary sprig
- Salt and pepper to taste

Direction: Cooking Time: 6 minutes Servings: 3

✓ Press the Sauté button and heat the oil.

✓ Sauté the onion and garlic until fragrant.

✓ Stir to the rest of the ingredients.

✓ Close the lid and make sure that the vents are sealed.

✓ Press the Manual button and adjust the cooking time to 1 minute.

✓ Do a quick pressure release.

✓ Once the lid is open, press the Sauté button and continue stirring until the liquid has reduced.

✓ Once cooled, evenly divide into serving size, keep in your preferred container, and refrigerate until ready to eat.

Nutrition: Calories: 97; Carbs: 10.4g; Protein: 0.5g; Fat: 4.2g

*544) **Instant Pot Sautéed Kale***

Ingredients:

- *3 Tbsps coconut oil*
- *2 cloves of garlic, minced*
- *1 onion, chopped*
- *2 Tsps crushed red pepper flakes*
- *4cups kale, chopped*
- *¼ cup water*
- *Salt and pepper to taste*

Direction: Cooking Time: minutes Servings: 6

- ✓ *Press the "Sauté" button on the Instant Pot.*
- ✓ *Heat the oil and sauté the garlic and onions until fragrant.*
- ✓ *Stir to the rest of the ingredients.*
- ✓ *Close the lid and make sure that the steam release valve is set to "Sealing."*
- ✓ *Press the "Manual" button and adjust the cooking time to 4 minutes.*
- ✓ *Do a quick pressure release.*

Nutrition: Calories: 82; Carbs: 5.1g; Protein: 1.1g; Fat: 7.9g

Soup Recipes

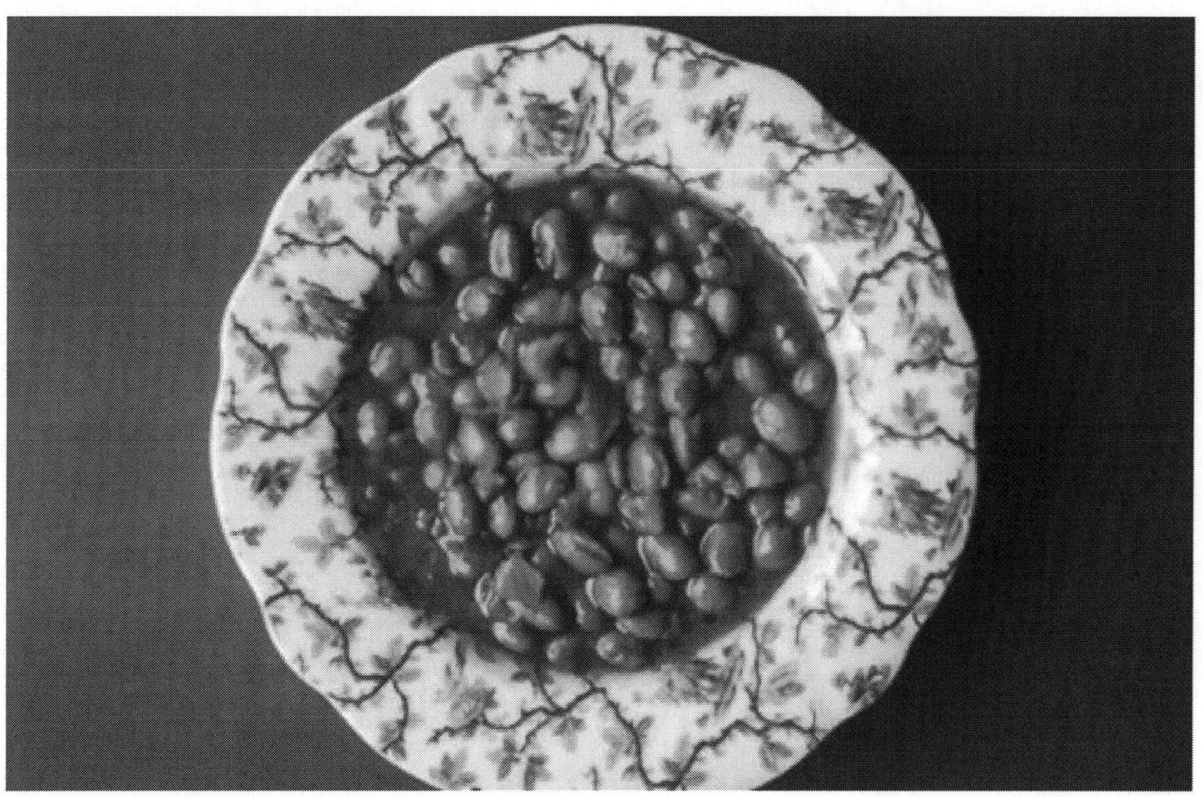

545) Lentil Soup

Ingredients:

- 10 cups water 2 cups brown lentils, picked over and rinsed
- 2 Tsps salt, divided
- ¼ cup long-grain rice, rinsed
- 3 Tbsps extra-virgin olive oil
- 1 large onion, chopped
- 2 medium potatoes, peeled
- 1 Tsp ground cumin
- ½ Tsp freshly ground black pepper

Direction: Prep time: 25 minutes | Cook time: 1 hour 20 minutes | Serves 6 to 8

✓ In a large pot over medium heat, bring the water, lentils, and 1 Tsp of salt to a simmer and continue to cook, occasionally stirring, for 30 minutes.

✓ At the 30-minute mark, add the rice to the lentils. Cover and continue to simmer, occasionally stirring, for another 30 minutes.

✓ Remove the pot from the heat and blend the lentils and rice for 1 to 2 minutes until smooth using a handheld immersion blender.

✓ Return the pot to the stove over low heat.

✓ In a small skillet over medium heat, cook the olive oil and onions for 5 minutes until the onions are golden brown. Add the onions to the soup.

✓ Cut the potatoes into ¼-inch pieces and add them to the soup.

✓ Add resting 1 Tsp of salt, cumin, and black pepper to the soup. Stir and continue to cook for 10 to 15 minutes, or until potatoes are thoroughly cooked. Serve warm.

Nutrition: calories: 348 | fat: 9g | protein: 18g | carbs: 53g | fiber: 20g | sodium: 795mg

546) Lemon Chicken Orzo Soup

Ingredients:

- 1 Tbsp extra-virgin olive oil
- 1 cup chopped onion
- ½ cup chopped carrots
- ½ cup chopped celery
- 3 garlic cloves, minced
- 9 cups low-sodium chicken broth
- 2 cups shredded cooked chicken breast
- ½ cup freshly squeezed lemon juice
- Zest of 1 lemon, grated
- 1 to 2 Tsps dried oregano
- 8 ounces (227 g) cooked orzo pasta

Direction: Prep time: 10 minutes | Cook time: minutes | Serves 8

✓ Heat the oil over medium heat in a large pot and add the onion, carrots, celery, and garlic and cook for about 5 minutes until the onions are translucent. Add the broth and bring to a boil.

✓ Reduce to a simmer, cover, and cook for 10 more minutes until the flavors meld. Then add the shredded chicken, lemon juice and zest, and oregano.

✓ Plate the orzo in serving containers first, then add the chicken soup

Nutrition: calories: 215 | fat: 5g | protein: 16g | carbs: 27g | fiber: 2g | sodium: 114mg

547) Tomato Basil Soup

Ingredients:

- ¼ cup extra-virgin olive oil
- 2 garlic cloves, minced
- 1 (14½-ounce / 411-g) can plum tomatoes, whole or diced
- 1 cup vegetable broth
- ¼ cup chopped fresh basil

Direction: Prep time: 10 minutes | Cook time: 10 minutes | Serves 2

✓ In a medium pot, heat the oil over medium heat, then add the garlic and cook for 2 minutes, until fragrant.

✓ Meanwhile, in a container using an immersion blender or in a blender, purée the tomatoes and their juices.

✓ Add the puréed tomatoes and broth to the pot and mix well. Simmer for 10 to 15 minutes and serve, garnished with basil.

Nutrition: calories: 307 | fat: 27g | protein: 3g | carbs: 11g | fiber: 4g | sodium: 661mg

548) White Bean Soup with Kale

Ingredients:

- 1 to 2 Tbsps extra-virgin olive oil
- 1 large shallot, minced
- 1 large purple carrot, chopped
- 1 celery stalk, chopped
- 1 Tsp garlic powder
- 3 cups low-sodium vegetable broth
- 1 (15-ounce / 425-g) can cannellini beans
- 1 cup chopped baby kale
- 1 Tsp salt (optional)
- ½ Tsp freshly ground black pepper (optional)
- 1 lemon, juiced, and zested
- 1½ Tbsps chopped fresh thyme (optional)
- 3 Tbsps chopped fresh oregano (optional)

Direction: Prep time: 25 minutes | Cook time: 30 minutes | Serves 4

✓ In a large, deep pot, heat the oil. Add the shallot, carrot, celery, and garlic powder and sauté on medium-low heat for 3 to 5 minutes until the vegetables are golden.

✓ Add the vegetable broth and beans and bring to a

simmer. Cook for 15 minutes.

- ✓ *Add to the kale salt (if using) and pepper (if using). Cook for another 5 to 10 minutes until the kale is soft. Before serving, stir to the lemon juice and zest, thyme (if using), and oregano (if using).*

Nutrition: calories: 165 | fat: 4g | protein: 7g | carbs: 26g | fiber: 7g | sodium: 135mg

549) Greek Chicken Artichoke Soup

Ingredients:

- *4 cups chicken stock*
- *2 cups riced cauliflower, divided*
- *2 large egg yolks*
- *¼ cup freshly squeezed lemon juice (about 2 lemons)*
- *¾ cup extra-virgin olive oil, divided*
- *8 ounces (227 g) cooked chicken, coarsely chopped*
- *1 (13¾-ounce / 390-g) can artichoke hearts, drained and quartered*
- *¼ cup chopped fresh dill*

Direction: Prep time: 10 minutes | Cook time: 15 minutes | Serves 4

- ✓ *In a large saucepan, bring the stock to a low boil. Reduce the heat to low and simmer, covered.*
- ✓ *Transfer 1 cup of the hot stock to a blender or food processor. Add ½ cup raw riced cauliflower, egg yolks, and lemon juice, and purée. While the processor or blender is running, stream in ½ cup olive oil and blend until smooth.*
- ✓ *Whisking constantly, pour the purée into the simmering stock until well blended together and smooth. Add the chicken and artichokes and simmer until thickened slightly at 8 to 10 minutes. Stir to the dill and resting 1½ cups riced cauliflower. Serve warm, drizzled with the resting ¼ cup olive oil.*

Nutrition: calories: 566 | fat: 46g | protein: 24g | carbs: 14g | fiber: 7g | sodium: 754mg

550) Tomato Hummus Soup

Ingredients:

- *1 (14½-ounce / 411-g) can crushed tomatoes with basil*
- *1 cup roasted red pepper hummus*
- *2 cups low-sodium chicken stock*
- *Salt, to taste*
- *¼ cup fresh basil leaves, thinly sliced (optional, for garnish)*
- *Garlic croutons (optional, for garnish)*

Direction: Prep time: 10 minutes | Cook time: 10 minutes | Serves 2

- ✓ *Combine the canned tomatoes, hummus, and chicken stock in a blender and blend until smooth. Pour the mixture into a saucepan and bring it to a boil.*
- ✓ *Season with salt and fresh basil if desired. Serve with garlic croutons as a garnish, if desired.*

Nutrition: calories: 148 | fat: 6g | protein: 5g | carbs: 19g | fiber: 4g | sodium: 680mg

551) Chicken Provençal Soup

Ingredients:

- *1 Tbsp extra-virgin olive oil*
- *2 fennel bulbs,*
- *2 Tbsps fronds minced, stalks discarded, bulbs halved, cored, and cut into ½-inch pieces*
- *1 onion, chopped*
- *1¾ Tsps table salt*
- *2 Tbsps tomato paste*
- *4 garlic cloves, minced*
- *1 Tbsp minced fresh thyme or 1 Tsp dried*
- *2 anchovy fillets, minced*
- *7 cups water, divided*
- *1 (14½-ounce / 411-g) can diced tomatoes, drained 2 carrots,*
- *peeled, halved lengthwise, and sliced ½ inch thick*
- *2 (12-ounce / 340-g) bone-in split chicken breasts, trimmed*
- *4 (5-to 7-ounce / 142-to 198-g) bone-in chicken thighs, trimmed*
- *½ cup pitted brine-cured green olives, chopped*
- *1 Tsp grated orange zest*

Direction: Prep time: 20 minutes | Cook time: 30 minutes | Serves 6 to 8

- ✓ *Heat the oil in the Instant Pot on the highest sauté setting until it shimmers. Cook for about 5 minutes until the fennel pieces, onion, and salt have softened. Cook for 30 seconds after adding the tomato paste, garlic, thyme, and anchovies. Stir in 5 cups water, scraping up any browned bits from the bottom of the pan, and then add the tomatoes and carrots. In a large pot, place the chicken breasts and thighs.*
- ✓ *Close the pressure release valve and secure the lid. Cook for 20 minutes using the high-pressure cook function. Quick-release pressure and turn off Instant Pot. Remove the lid with care, allowing steam to escape away from you. Transfer chicken to the cutting board, set aside to cool slightly before shredding with 2 forks into bite-size pieces; discard skin and bones.*
- ✓ *Using a wide, shallow spoon, skim excess fat from the surface of the soup. Stir chicken and any accumulated juices, olives, and resting 2 cups water into the soup and let sit until heated through about 3 minutes. Stir in fennel fronds and orange zest, and season with salt and pepper to taste. Serve.*

Nutrition: 170 | fat: 5g | protein: 19g | carbs: 11g | fiber: 3g | sodium: 870mg

552) Pastina Chicken Soup

Ingredients:

- 1 Tbsp extra-virgin olive oil
- 2 garlic cloves, minced (about 1 Tsp)
- 3 cups packed chopped kale (center ribs removed)
- 1 cup minced carrots (about 2 carrots)
- 8 cups low-sodium or no-salt-added chicken (or vegetable) broth
- ¼ Tsp kosher or sea salt
- ¼ Tsp freshly ground black pepper
- ¾ cup (6 ounces / 170 g) uncooked acini de Pepe or pastina pasta
- 2 cups shredded cooked chicken (about 12 ounces / 340 g)
- 3 Tbsps grated Parmesan cheese

Direction: Prep time: 5 minutes | Cook time: 25 minutes | Serves 6

- ✓ In a large stockpot over medium heat, heat the oil. Add the garlic and cook for 30 seconds, stirring frequently. Add the kale and carrots and cook for 5 minutes, stirring occasionally.
- ✓ Add the broth, salt, and pepper, and turn the heat to high. Bring the broth to a boil, and add the pasta. Lower the heat to medium and cook for 10 minutes, or until the pasta is cooked through, stirring every few minutes, so the pasta doesn't stick to the bottom.
  Add the chicken, and cook for 2 more minutes to warm through.
- ✓ Ladle the soup into six containers, top each with ½ Tbsp of cheese, and serve.

Nutrition: calories: 275 | fat: 19g | protein: 16g | carbs: 11g | fiber: 2g | sodium: 298mg

553) Mushroom Barley Soup

Ingredients:

- 2 Tbsps extra-virgin olive oil
- 1 cup chopped onion (about ½ medium onion)
- 1 cup chopped carrots (about 2 carrots)
- 5½ cups chopped mushrooms (about 12 ounces / 340 g)
- 6 cups low-sodium or no-salt-added vegetable broth
- 1 cup uncooked pearled barley
- ¼ cup red wine
- 2 Tbsps tomato paste
- 4 sprigs fresh thyme or ½ Tsp dried thyme
- 1 dried bay leaf
- 6 Tbsps grated Parmesan cheese

Direction: Prep time: 5 minutes | Cook time: 25 minutes | Serves 6

- ✓ In a large stockpot over medium heat, heat the oil. Add the onion and carrots and cook for 5 minutes, stirring frequently. Turn up the heat to medium-high and add the mushrooms. Cook for 3 minutes, stirring frequently.
- ✓ Add the broth, barley, wine, tomato paste, thyme, and bay leaf. Stir, cover the pot and bring the soup to a boil
- ✓ Once it's boiling, stir a few times, reduce the heat to medium-low, cover, and cook for another 12 to 15 minutes until the barley is cooked through.
- ✓ Remove the bay leaf and serve in soup containers with 1 Tbsp of cheese sprinkled on top of each

Nutrition: calories: 195 | fat: 4g | protein: 7g | carbs: 34g | fiber: 6g | sodium: 173mg

554) Pasta Bean Soup

Ingredients:

- 2 Tbsps extra-virgin olive oil
- ½ cup chopped onion (about ¼ onion)
- 3 garlic cloves, minced (about 1½ Tsps)
- 1 Tbsp minced fresh rosemary or 1 Tsp dried rosemary ¼ Tsp crushed red pepper
- 4 cups low-sodium or no-salt-added vegetable broth
- 2 (15½-ounce / 439-g) cans cannellini, great northern, or light kidney beans, undrained
- 1 (28-ounce / 794-g) can low-sodium or no-salt-added crushed tomatoes
- 2 Tbsps tomato paste
- 8 ounces (227 g) uncooked short pasta, such as ditalini, tubetti, or elbows
- 6 Tbsps grated Parmesan cheese (about 1½ ounces / 43 g)

Direction: Prep time: 5 minutes | Cook time: 25 minutes | Serves 6

- ✓ In a large stockpot over medium heat, heat the oil. Add the onion and cook for 4 minutes, stirring frequently. Add the garlic, rosemary, and crushed red pepper. Cook for 1 minute, stirring frequently. Add the broth, canned beans with their liquid, tomatoes, and tomato paste. Simmer for 5 minutes.
- ✓ To thicken the soup, carefully transfer 2 cups to a blender. Purée, then stir it back into the pot.
- ✓ Bring the soup to a boil over high heat. Mix to the pasta, and lower the heat to a simmer. Cook the pasta for the amount of time recommended on the box, stirring every few minutes to prevent the pasta from sticking to the pot. Taste the pasta to make sure it is cooked through (it could take a few more minutes than the recommended cooking time since it's cooking with other ingredients).
- ✓ Ladle the soup into containers, top each with 1 Tbsp of grated cheese, and serve.

Nutrition: calories: 583 | fat: 6g | protein: 32g | carbs: 103g | fiber: 29g | sodium: 234mg

555) Thyme Carrot Soup with Parmesan

Ingredients:

- 2 pounds (907 g) carrots, unpeeled, cut into ½-inch slices (about 6 cups)
- 2 Tbsps extra-virgin olive oil, divided 1 cup chopped onion (about ½ medium onion)
- 2 cups low-sodium or no-salt-added vegetable (or chicken) broth
- 2½ cups water
- 1 Tsp dried thyme
- ¼ Tsp crushed red pepper
- ¼ Tsp kosher or sea salt
- 4 thin slices of whole-grain bread
- ⅓ cup freshly grated Parmesan cheese (about 1 ounce / 28 g)

Direction: Prep time: 10 minutes | Cook time: 20 minutes | Serves 4

- ✓ Place one oven rack about four inches below the broiler element. Place two large, rimmed baking sheets in the oven on an oven rack. Switch on the oven, preheat it setting its temperature to 450°F (235°C).
- ✓ In a large container, toss the carrots with 1 Tbsp of oil to coat. With oven mitts, carefully remove the baking sheets from the oven and evenly distribute the carrots on both sheets. Bake for 20 minutes, until the carrots are just fork-tender, stirring once halfway through. The carrots will still be somewhat firm. Remove the carrots from the oven, and turn the oven to the high broil setting.
- ✓ While the carrots are roasting, in a large stockpot over medium-high heat, heat 1 Tbsp of oil. Add the onion and cook for 5 minutes, stirring occasionally. Add the broth, water, thyme, crushed red pepper, and salt. Bring to a boil, cover, then remove the pan from the heat until the carrots have finished roasting.
- ✓ Add the roasted carrots to the pot, and blend with an immersion blender (or use a regular blender—carefully pour to the hot soup in batches, then return the soup to the pot). Heat the soup for about 1 minute over medium-high heat until warmed through.
- ✓ Turn the oven to the high broil setting. Place the bread on the baking sheet. Sprinkle the cheese evenly across the slices of bread. Broil the bread 4 inches below the heating element for 1 to 2 minutes, or until the cheese melts, watching carefully to prevent burning.
- ✓ Cut the bread into bite-size croutons. Divide the soup evenly among four containers, top each with the Parmesan croutons, and serve.

Nutrition: calories: 312 | fat: 6g | protein: 6g | carbs: 53g | fiber: 10g | sodium: 650mg

556) Paella Soup

Ingredients:

- 1 cup frozen green peas
- 2 Tbsps extra-virgin olive oil
- 1 cup chopped onion (about ½ medium onion)
- 1½ cups coarsely chopped red bell pepper (about 1 large pepper)
- 1½ cups coarsely chopped green bell pepper (about 1 large pepper)
- 2 garlic cloves, chopped (about 1 Tsp)
- 1 Tsp ground turmeric
- 1 Tsp dried thyme
- 2 Tsps smoked paprika
- 2½ cups uncooked instant brown rice
- 2 cups low-sodium or no-salt-added chicken broth
- 2½ cups water
- 1 (28-ounce / 794-g) can low-sodium or no-salt-added crushed tomatoes
- 1 pound (454 g) fresh raw medium shrimp (or frozen raw shrimp completely thawed), shells and tails removed

Direction: Prep time: 5 minutes | Cook time: 25 minutes | Serves 6

- ✓ Put the frozen peas on the counter to partially thaw as the soup is being prepared.
- ✓ In a large stockpot over medium-high heat, heat the oil. Add the onion, red and green bell peppers, and garlic. Cook for 8 minutes, stirring occasionally. Add the turmeric, thyme, and smoked paprika, and cook for 2 minutes more, stirring often. Stir to the rice, broth, and water. Bring to a boil over high heat. Cover, reduce the heat to medium-low and cook for 10 minutes.
- ✓ Stir the peas, tomatoes, and shrimp into the soup. Cook for 4 to 6 minutes until the shrimp is cooked, turning from gray to pink and white. The soup will be very thick, almost like a stew, when ready to serve.

Nutrition: calories: 275 | fat: 5g | protein: 18g | carbs: 41g | fiber: 6g | sodium: 644m

557) Moroccan Lamb Lentil Soup

Ingredients:

- 1 pound (454 g) lamb shoulder chops (blade or round bone),
- 1 to 1½ inches thick, trimmed, and halved
- ¾ Tsp table salt, divided
- ⅛ Tsp pepper
- 1 Tbsp extra-virgin olive oil
- 1 onion, chopped fine
- ¼ cup harissa, plus extra for serving
- 1 Tbsp all-purpose flour

- *8 cups chicken broth*
- *1 cup French green lentils, picked over and rinsed*
- *1 (15-ounce / 425-g) can chickpeas, rinsed*
- *2 tomatoes, cored and cut into ¼-inch pieces*
- *½ cup chopped fresh cilantro*

Direction: Prep time: 15 minutes | Cook time: 28 minutes | Serves 6 to 8

- ✓ *Pat lamb dry with paper towels and sprinkle with ¼ Tsp salt and pepper. Using the highest sauté function, heat oil in Instant Pot for 5 minutes (or until just smoking). Place lamb in the pot and cook until well browned on the first side, about 4 minutes; transfer to plate.*
- ✓ *Add onion and resting ½ Tsp salt to fat left in pot and cook, using highest sauté function, until softened, about 5 minutes. Stir in harissa and flour and cook until fragrant, about 30 seconds. Slowly whisk in broth, scraping up any browned bits and smoothing out any lumps. Stir in lentils, then nestle lamb into multicooker and add any accumulated juices.*
- ✓ *Lock lid in place and close pressure release valve. Select a high-pressure cook function and cook for 10 minutes. Turn off Instant Pot and quick-release pressure. Carefully remove the lid, allowing steam to escape away from you.*
- ✓ *Transfer lamb to the cutting board, let cool slightly, then shred into bite-size pieces using 2 forks; discard excess fat and bones. Stir lamb and chickpeas into a soup and let sit until heated through about 3 minutes. Season with salt and pepper to taste. Top individual portions with tomatoes and sprinkle with cilantro. Serve, passing extra harissa separately.*

Nutrition: calories: 300 | fat: 13g | protein: 22g | carbs: 24g | fiber: 6g | sodium: 940mg

558) Almond and Cauliflower Gazpacho

Ingredients:

- *1 cup raw almonds*
- *½ Tsp salt*
- *½ cup extra-virgin olive oil, plus 1 Tbsp, divided*
- *1 small white onion, minced*
- *1 small head cauliflower, stalk removed and broken into florets (about 3 cups)*
- *2 garlic cloves, finely minced*
- *2 cups chicken or vegetable stock or broth, plus more if needed*
- *1 Tbsp red wine vinegar*
- *¼ Tsp freshly ground black pepper*

Direction: Prep time: 10 minutes | Cook time: 16 minutes | Serves 4 to 6

- ✓ *Bring a small pot of water to a boil. Add the almonds to the water and boil for 1 minute, being careful not to boil longer, or the almonds will become soggy. Drain in a colander and run under cold water. Pat dry and, using your fingers, squeeze the meat of each almond out of its skin. Discard the skins.*
- ✓ *In a food processor or blender, blend together the almonds and salt. With the processor running, drizzle in ½ cup extra-virgin olive oil, scraping down the sides as needed. Set the almond paste aside.*
- ✓ *In a large stockpot, heat the resting 1 Tbsp olive oil over medium-high heat. Add the onion and sauté until golden, 3 to 4 minutes. Add the cauliflower florets and sauté for another 3 to 4 minutes. Add the garlic and sauté for 1 minute more.*
- ✓ *Add 2 cups stock and bring to a boil. Cover, reduce the heat to medium-low and simmer the vegetables until tender, 8 to 10 minutes. Remove from the heat and allow to cool slightly.*
- ✓ *Add the vinegar and pepper. Using an immersion blender, blend until smooth. Alternatively, you can blend in a stand blender, but you may need to divide the mixture into two or three batches. With the blender running, add the almond paste and blend until smooth, adding extra stock if the soup is too thick.*
- ✓ *Serve warm, or chill in the refrigerator for at least 4 to 6 hours to serve a cold gazpacho.*

Nutrition: calories: 505 | fat: 45g | protein: 10g | carbs: 10g | fiber: 5g | sodium: 484mg

559) Avocado and Tomato Gazpacho

Ingredients:

- *2 cups chopped tomatoes*
- *2 large ripe avocados, halved and pitted*
- *1 large cucumber, peeled and seeded*
- *1 medium bell pepper (red, orange, or yellow), chopped*
- *1 cup plain whole-milk Greek yogurt*
- *¼ cup extra-virgin olive oil*
- *¼ cup chopped fresh cilantro*
- *¼ cup chopped scallions, green part only*
- *2 Tbsps red wine vinegar*
- *Juice of 2 limes or 1 lemon*
- *½ to 1 Tsp salt*
- *¼ Tsp freshly ground black pepper*

Direction: Prep time: 15 minutes | Cook time: 0 minutes | Serves 4

- ✓ *In a blender or in a large container, combine the tomatoes, avocados, cucumber, bell pepper, yogurt, olive oil, cilantro, scallions, vinegar, and if using an immersion blender, lime juice. Blend until smooth. If using a stand blender, you may need to blend in two or three batches.*
- ✓ *Season with salt and pepper and blend to combine the flavors.*

✓ Chill in the fridge for 1 to 2 hours before serving. Serve cold.
Nutrition: calories: 392 | fat: 32g | protein: 6g | carbs: 20g | fiber: 9g | sodium: 335mg

560) Vegetable Gazpacho Soup

Ingredients:

- ½ cup water
- 2 slices white bread, crust removed
- 2 pounds (907 g) ripe tomatoes
- 1 Persian cucumber, peeled and chopped
- 1 clove garlic, finely chopped
- ⅓ cup extra-virgin olive oil, plus more for garnish
- 2 Tbsps red wine vinegar
- 1 Tsp salt
- ½ Tsp freshly ground black pepper

Direction: Prep time: 10 minutes | Cook time: 0 minutes | Serves 6 to 8

✓ Soak the bread to the water for 5 minutes; discard water when done.

✓ Blend the bread, tomatoes, cucumber, garlic, olive oil, vinegar, salt, and black pepper in a food processor or blender until completely smooth.

✓ Pour the soup into a glass container and store it in the fridge until completely chilled.

✓ When you are ready to serve, pour the soup into a container and top with a drizzle of olive oil.
Nutrition: calories: 163 | fat: 13g | protein: 2g | carbs: 12g | fiber: 2g | sodium: 442mg

561) White Bean and Carrot Soup

Ingredients:

- 3 Tbsps extra-virgin olive oil
- 1 large onion, finely chopped
- 3 large garlic cloves, minced
- 2 cups carrots, diced
- 2 cups celery, diced
- 2 (15-ounce / 425-g) cans of white beans, rinsed and drained
- 8 cups vegetable broth
- 1 Tsp salt
- ½ Tsp freshly ground black pepper

Direction: | Serves 6 Prep time: 10 minutes | Cook time: 20 minutes

✓ In a large pot over medium heat, cook the olive oil, onion, and garlic for 2 to 3 minutes.

✓ Add the carrots and celery, and cook for another 3 to 5 minutes, stirring occasionally.

✓ Add the beans, broth, salt, and pepper. Stir and let simmer for 15 to 17 minutes, stirring occasionally. Serve warm.
Nutrition: calories: 244 | fat: 7g | protein: 9g | carbs: 36g | fiber: 10g | sodium: 1160mg

562) Red Lentil and Carrot Soup

Ingredients:

- 1 cup red lentils, picked over and rinsed
- ½ cup long-grain or basmati rice, rinsed
- 10 cups water
- 2 Tsps salt
- 3 Tbsps extra-virgin olive oil
- 1 large onion, finely chopped
- 2 cups carrots, finely diced
- 1 Tsp turmeric
- 1 lemon, cut into wedges

Direction: Serves 6 to 8 Prep time: 10 minutes | Cook time: 20 minutes |

✓ In a large pot over medium heat, heat the lentils, rice, water, and salt. Bring to a simmer for 40 minutes, stirring occasionally.

✓ In a small skillet over medium-low heat, cook the olive oil and onions for 5 minutes until the onions are golden brown.

✓ Add the cooked onions, carrots, and turmeric to the soup and cook for 15 minutes, stirring occasionally.

✓ Serve the soup with a big squeeze of lemon over the top and a lemon wedge on the side.
Nutrition: calories: 230 | fat: 7g | protein: 9g | carbs: 36g | fiber: 9g | sodium: 806mg

563) Beans and Kale Fagioli

Ingredients:

- 1 Tbsp olive oil
- 2 medium carrots, diced
- 2 medium celery stalks, diced
- ½ medium onion, diced
- 1 large garlic clove, minced
- 3 Tbsps tomato paste
- 4 cups low-sodium vegetable broth
- 1 cup packed kale, stemmed and chopped
- 1 (15-ounce / 425-g) can be drained and rinsed red kidney beans,
- 1 (15-ounce / 425-g) can be drained and rinsed cannellini beans,
- ½ cup fresh basil, chopped
- Salt, to taste
- Freshly ground black pepper, to taste

Direction: Prep time: 15 minutes | Cook time: 46 minutes | Serves 2

✓ Heat the olive oil in a stockpot over medium-high heat. Add the carrots, celery, onion, and garlic and sauté for 10 minutes, or until the vegetables start to turn golden.

✓ Stir to the tomato paste and cook for about 30 seconds.

✓ Add the vegetable broth and bring the soup to a

boil. Cover, and reduce the heat to low. Cook the soup for 45 minutes or until the carrots are tender.

- ✓ *Using an immersion blender, purée the soup so that it's partly smooth, but with some chunks of vegetables. If you don't have an immersion blender, scoop out about 1/3 of the soup and blend it in a blender, then add it back to the pot.*
- ✓ *Add the kale, beans, and basil. Season with salt and pepper.*

Nutrition: calories: 215 | fat: 4g | protein: 11g | carbs: 35g | fiber: 11g | sodium: 486mg

564) ***Farro, Pancetta, and Leek Soup***

Ingredients:

- *1 cup whole farro*
- *1 Tbsp extra-virgin olive oil, plus extra for drizzling*
- *3 ounces (85 g) pancetta, chopped fine*
- *1 pound (454 g) leeks, ends trimmed, chopped, and washed thoroughly*
- *2 carrots, peeled and chopped*
- *1 celery rib, chopped*
- *8 cups chicken broth, plus extra as needed*
- *½ cup minced fresh parsley Grated Parmesan cheese*

Direction: Prep time: 10 minutes | Cook time: 16 minutes | Serves 6 to 8

- ✓ *Pulse farro in a blender until about half of grains are broken into smaller pieces, about 6 pulses; set aside.*
- ✓ *Using the highest sauté function, heat oil in Instant Pot until shimmering. Add pancetta and cook until lightly browned for 3 to 5 minutes. Stir in leeks, carrots, and celery and cook until softened, about 5 minutes. Stir in broth, scraping up any browned bits, then stir in farro.*
- ✓ *Lock lid in place and close pressure release valve. Select high-pressure cook function and cook for 8 minutes. Turn off Instant Pot and quick-release pressure. Carefully remove the lid, allowing steam to escape away from you.*
- ✓ *Adjust consistency with extra hot broth as needed. Stir in parsley and season with salt and pepper to taste. Drizzle individual portions with extra oil and top with Parmesan before serving.*

Nutrition: calories: 180 | fat: 6g | protein: 22g | carbs: 24g | fiber: 1g | sodium: 950mg

565) ***Lentil and Chorizo Sausage Soup***

Ingredients:

- *1 Tbsp extra-virgin olive oil, plus extra for drizzling*
- *8 ounces (227 g) Spanish-style chorizo sausage, quartered lengthwise and sliced thin*
- *4 garlic cloves, minced*
- *1½ Tsps smoked paprika*
- *5 cups water*
- *1 pound (454 g) French green lentils, picked over and rinsed*
- *4 cups chicken broth*
- *1 Tbsp sherry vinegar, plus extra for seasoning*
- *2 bay leaves*
- *1 Tsp table salt*
- *1 large onion, peeled*
- *2 carrots, peeled and halved crosswise*
- *½ cup slivered almonds, toasted*
- *½ cup minced fresh parsley*

Direction: Prep time: 15 minutes | Cook time: 18 minutes | Serves 6 to 8

- ✓ *Heat the oil in the Instant Pot on the highest sauté setting until it shimmer . Add chorizo and cook until lightly browned for 3 to 5 minutes. Stir in garlic and paprika and cook until fragrant, about 30 seconds. Stir in water, scraping up any browned bits, then stir in lentils, broth, vinegar, bay leaves, and salt. Nestle onion and carrots into the pot.*
- ✓ *Close the pressure release valve and secure the lid. Select a high-pressure cook function and cook for 14 minutes.*
  Turn off Instant Pot and quick-release pressure. Carefully remove the lid, allowing steam to escape away from you.
- ✓ *Discard bay leaves. Using a slotted spoon, transfer onion and carrots to food processor and process until smooth, about 1 minute, scraping downsides of the container as needed. Stir vegetable mixture into lentils and season with salt, pepper, and extra vinegar to taste. Drizzle individual portions with extra oil, and sprinkle with almonds and parsley before serving.*

Nutrition: calories: 360 | fat: 16g | protein: 21g | carbs: 29g | fiber: 7g | sodium: 950mg

566) ***Cheesy Keto Zucchini Soup***

Ingredients:

- *½ medium onion, peeled and chopped*
- *1 cup bone broth*
- *1 Tbsp coconut oil*
- *1½ zucchinis, cut into chunks*
- *½ Tbsp nutritional yeast*
- *Dash of black pepper*
- *½ Tbsp parsley, chopped, for garnish*
- *½ Tbsp coconut cream, for garnish*

Direction: Servings: 2 Preparation time: 20 mins

- ✓ *Melt the coconut oil in a large pan over medium heat and add onions.*
- ✓ *Sauté for about 3 minutes and add zucchinis and bone broth.*
- ✓ *Reduce the heat to simmer for about 15 minutes and cover the pan.*

- ✓ Add nutritional yeast and transfer to an immersion blender.
- ✓ Blend until smooth and season with black pepper.
- ✓ Top with coconut cream and parsley to serve.

Nutrition: Calories: 154 Carbs: 8.9g Fats: 8.1g Proteins: 13.4g Sodium: 93mg Sugar: 3.9g

567) Spring Soup with Poached Egg

Ingredients:

- 32 oz vegetable broth
- 2 eggs
- 1 head romaine lettuce, chopped
- Salt, to taste

Direction: Servings: 2 Preparation time: 20 mins

- ✓ Bring the vegetable broth to a boil and reduce the heat.
- ✓ Poach the eggs for 5 minutes to the broth and remove them into 2 containers.
- ✓ Stir in romaine lettuce into the broth and cook for 4 minutes.
- ✓ Dish out in a container and serve hot

Nutrition: Calories: 158 Sodium: 1513mg Carbs: 6.9g Fats: 7.3g Proteins: 15.4g Sugar: 3.3g

568) Mint Avocado Chilled Soup

Ingredients:

- 2 romaine lettuce leaves
- 1 Tbsp lime juice
- 1 medium ripe avocado
- 1 cup coconut milk, chilled
- 20 fresh mint leaves
- Salt to taste

Direction: Servings: 2 Preparation time: 15 mins

- ✓ In a blender, combine all of the ingredients and blend until smooth.
- ✓ Refrigerate for 10 minutes before serving chilled.

Nutrition: Calories: 432 Sodium: 33mg Carbs: 16.1g Fats: 42.2g Proteins: 5.2g Sugar: 4.5g

569) Easy Butternut Squash Soup

Ingredients:

- 1 small onion, chopped
- 4 cups chicken broth
- 1 butternut squash
- 3 Tbsps coconut oil
- Salt, to taste
- Nutmeg and pepper, to taste

Direction: Servings: 4 Preparation time: 1 hour 45 mins

- ✓ In a large pot, combine the oil and onions, then add the onions.
- ✓ Add chicken broth and butternut squash after 3 minutes of sautéing.
- ✓ Simmer for 1 hour over medium heat, then blend with an immersion blender.
- ✓ Season with salt, pepper, and nutmeg after pulsing until smooth.
- ✓ Return the pot to the stove and cook for another 30 minutes.
- ✓ Dish out and serve hot.

Nutrition: Calories: 149 Sodium: 765mg Carbs: 6.6g Fats: 11.6g Proteins: 5.4g Sugar: 2.2g

570) Spring Soup Recipe with Poached Egg

Ingredients:

- 2 eggs
- 2 Tbsps butter
- 4 cups chicken broth
- 1 head of romaine lettuce, chopped
- Salt, to taste

Direction: Servings: 2 Preparation time: 20 mins

- ✓ Boil the chicken broth and lower the heat.
- ✓ Poach the eggs into the broth for about 5 minutes and remove the eggs.
- ✓ Place each egg into a container and add chopped romaine lettuce into the broth.
- ✓ Cook for about 10 minutes and ladle the broth with the lettuce into the containers.

Nutrition: Calories: 264 Carbs: 7g Fats: 18.9g Proteins: 16.1g Sodium: 1679mg Sugar: 3.4g

571) Cauliflower, leek & bacon soup

Ingredients:

- 4 cups chicken broth
- ½ cauliflower head, chopped
- 1 leek, chopped
- Salt and black pepper, to taste
- 5 bacon strips

Direction: Servings: 4 Preparation time: 10 mins

- ✓ Put the cauliflower, leek, and chicken broth into the pot and cook for about 1 hour on medium heat.
- ✓ Transfer into an immersion blender and pulse until smooth.
- ✓ Return the soup into the pot and microwave the bacon strips for 1 minute.
- ✓ Cut the bacon into small pieces and put it into the soup.
- ✓ Cook on for about 30 minutes on low heat.
- ✓ Season with salt and pepper and serve.

Nutrition: Calories: 185 Sodium: 1153mg Carbs: 5.8g Fats: 12.7g Proteins: 10.8g Sugar: 2.4g

572) Swiss Chard Egg Drop Soup

Ingredients:

- 3 cups bone broth
- 2 eggs, whisked

- *1 Tsp ground oregano*
- *3 Tbsps butter*
- *2 cups Swiss chard, chopped*
- *2 Tbsps coconut aminos*
- *1 Tsp ginger, grated*
- *Salt and black pepper, to taste*

Direction: Servings: 4 Preparation time: 20 mins

- ✓ *Heat the bone broth in a saucepan and add whisked eggs while stirring slowly.*
- ✓ *Add the swiss chard, butter, coconut aminos, ginger, oregano, and salt, and black pepper.*
- ✓ *Cook for about 10 minutes and serve hot.*

Nutrition: Calories: 185 Carbs: 2.9g Fats: 11g Proteins: 18.3g Sodium: 252mg Sugar: 0.4g

573) Mushroom Spinach Soup

Ingredients:

- *1cupspinach, cleaned and chopped*
- *100gmushrooms, chopped*
- *1onion*
- *6 garlic cloves*
- *½ Tsp red chili powder*
- *Salt and black pepper, to taste*
- *3 Tbsps buttermilk*
- *1 Tsp almond flour*
- *2 cups chicken broth*
- *3 Tbsps butter*
- *¼ cup fresh cream for garnish*

Direction: Servings: 4 Preparation time: 25 mins

- ✓ *Heat butter in a pan and add onions and garlic.*
- ✓ *Sauté for about 3 minutes and add spinach, salt, and red chili powder.*
- ✓ *Sauté for about 4 minutes and add mushrooms.*
- ✓ *Transfer into a blender and blend to make a puree.*
- ✓ *Return to the pan and add buttermilk and almond flour for a creamy texture.*
- ✓ *Mix well and simmer for about 2 minutes.*
- ✓ *Garnish with fresh cream and serve hot.*

Nutrition: Calories: 160 Carbs: 7g Fats: 13.3g Proteins: 4.7g Sodium: 462mg Sugar: 2.7g

574) Delicata Squash Soup

Ingredients:

- *1½ cups beef bone broth*
- *1small onion, peeled and grated.*
- *½ Tsp sea salt*
- *¼ Tsp poultry seasoning*
- *2small Delicata Squash, chopped*
- *2 garlic cloves, minced*
- *2Tbsps olive oil*
- *¼ Tsp black pepper*
- *1 small lemon, juiced*
- *5 Tbsps sour cream*

Direction: Servings: 5 Preparation time:

- ✓ *Put Delicata Squash and water in a medium pan and bring to a boil.*
- ✓ *Reduce the heat and cook for about 20 minutes.*
- ✓ *Drain and set aside.*
- ✓ *Put olive oil, onions, garlic, and poultry seasoning in a small saucepan.*
- ✓ *Cook for about 2 minutes and add broth.*
- ✓ *Allow it to simmer for 5 minutes and remove from heat.*
- ✓ *Whisk to the lemon juice and transfer the mixture to a blender.*
- ✓ *Pulse until smooth and top with sour cream.*

Nutrition: Calories: 109 Carbs: 4.9g Fats: 8.5g Proteins: 3g Sodium: 279mg Sugar: 2.4g

575) Broccoli Soup

Ingredients:

- *3 Tbsps ghee*
- *5 garlic cloves*
- *1 Tsp sage*
- *¼ Tsp ginger*
- *2 cups broccoli*
- *1 small onion*
- *1 Tsp oregano*
- *½ Tsp parsley*
- *Salt and black pepper, to taste*
- *6 cups vegetable broth*
- *4 Tbsps butter*

Direction: Servings: 6 Preparation time: 10 mins

- ✓ *Put ghee, onions, spices, and garlic in a pot and cook for 3 minutes.*
- ✓ *Add broccoli and cook for about 4 minutes.*
- ✓ *Add vegetable broth, cover, and allow it to simmer for about 30 minutes.*
- ✓ *Transfer into a blender and blend until smooth.*
- ✓ *Add the butter to give it a creamy, delicious texture and flavor*

Nutrition: Calories: 183 Carbs: 5.2g Fats: 15.6g Proteins: 6.1g Sodium: 829mg Sugar: 1.8g

576) Apple Pumpkin Soup

Ingredients:

- *1 apple, chopped*
- *1 whole kabocha pumpkin, peeled, seeded, and cubed*
- *1 cup almond flour*
- *¼ cup ghee*
- *1 pinch cardamom powder*

- *2 quarts water*
- *¼ cup coconut cream*
- *1 pinch ground black pepper*

Direction: Servings: 8 Preparation time: 10 mins

- ✓ *Heat ghee to the bottom of a heavy pot and add apples.*
- ✓ *Cook for about 5 minutes on a medium flame and add pumpkin.*
- ✓ *Sauté for about 3 minutes and add the almond flour.*
- ✓ *Sauté for about 1 minute and add water.*
- ✓ *Lower the flame and cook for about 30 minutes.*
- ✓ *Transfer the soup into an immersion blender and blend until smooth.*
- ✓ *Top with coconut cream and serve.*

Nutrition: Calories: 186 Carbs: 10.4g Fats: 14.9g Proteins: 3.7g Sodium: 7mg Sugar: 5.4g

577) ***Keto French Onion Soup***

Ingredients:

- *5 Tbsps butter*
- *500 g brown onion medium*
- *4 drops liquid stevia*
- *4 Tbsps olive oil*
- *3 cups beef stock*

Direction: Servings: 6 Preparation time: 40 mins

- ✓ *Put the butter and olive oil in a large pot over medium-low heat and add onions and salt.*
- ✓ *Cook for about 5 minutes and stir in stevia.*
- ✓ *Cook for another 5 minutes and add beef stock.*
- ✓ *Reduce the heat to low and simmer for about 25 minutes.*
- ✓ *Dish out into soup containers and serve hot.*

Nutrition: Calories: 198 Carbs: 6g Fats: 20.6g Proteins: 2.9g Sodium: 883mg Sugar: 1.7g

578) ***Cauliflower and Thyme Soup***

Ingredients:

- *2Tspsthyme powder*
- *1head cauliflower*
- *3cupsvegetable stock*
- *½ Tsp matcha green tea powder*
- *3Tbspsolive oil*
- *Salt and black pepper, to taste*
- *5garlic cloves, chopped*

Direction: Servings: 6Preparation time: 30 mins

- ✓ *Put the vegetable stock, thyme, and matcha powder to a large pot over medium-high heat and bring to a boil.*
- ✓ *Add cauliflower and cook for about 10 minutes.*
- ✓ *Meanwhile, put the olive oil and garlic in a small saucepan and cook for about 1 minute.*
- ✓ *Add the garlic, salt, and black pepper and cook for about 2 minutes.*
- ✓ *Transfer into an immersion blender and blend until smooth.*
- ✓ *Dish out and serve immediately.*

Nutrition: Calories: 79 Carbs: 3.8g Fats: 7.1g Proteins: 1.3g Sodium: 39mg Sugar: 1.5g

579) ***Homemade Thai Chicken Soup***

Ingredients:

- *1 lemongrass stalk, cut into large chunks*
- *5 thick slices of fresh ginger*
- *1 whole chicken*
- *20 fresh basil leaves*
- *1 lime, juiced*
- *1 Tbsp salt*

Direction: Servings: 12Preparation time: 8 hours 25 mins

- ✓ *Place the chicken, 10 basil leaves, lemongrass, ginger, salt, and water into the slow cooker.*
- ✓ *Cook for about 8 hours on low and dish out into a container.*
- ✓ *Stir in fresh lime juice, and basil leaves to serve.*

Nutrition: Calories: 255 Carbs: 1.2g Fats: 17.6g Proteins: 25.2g Sodium: 582mg Sugar: 0.1g

580) ***Chicken Kale Soup***

Ingredients:

- *2poundschicken breast, skinless*
- *1/3cuponion*
- *1Tbspolive oil*
- *14ounceschicken bone broth*
- *½ cup olive oil*
- *4 cups chicken stock*
- *¼ cup lemon juice*
- *5ouncesbaby kale leaves*
- *Salt, to taste*

Direction: Servings: 6Preparation time: 6 hours 10 mins

- ✓ *Season chicken with salt and black pepper.*
- ✓ *Heat olive oil over medium heat in a large skillet and add seasoned chicken.*
- ✓ *Reduce the temperature and cook for about 15 minutes.*
- ✓ *Shred the chicken and placed it in the crockpot.*
- ✓ *Process the chicken broth and onions in a blender and blend until smooth.*
- ✓ *Pour into a crockpot and stir to the resting ingredients.*
- ✓ *Cook on low for about 6 hours, stirring once while cooking.*

Nutrition: Calories: 261 Carbs: 2g Fats: 21g Proteins: 14.1g Sodium: 264mg Sugar: 0.3g

581) Chicken Veggie Soup

Ingredients:

- 5 chicken thighs
- 12 cups water
- 1 Tbsp adobo seasoning
- 4 celery ribs
- 1 yellow onion
- 1½ Tsps whole black peppercorns
- 6 sprigs of fresh parsley
- 2 Tsps coarse sea salt
- 2 carrots
- 6 mushrooms, sliced
- 2 garlic cloves
- 1 bay leaf
- 3 sprigs fresh thyme

Direction: Servings: 6Preparation time: 20 mins

- ✓ Put water, chicken thighs, carrots, celery ribs, onion, garlic cloves, and herbs in a large pot.
- ✓ Bring to a boil and reduce the heat to low.
- ✓ Cover the pot and simmer for about 30 minutes.
- ✓ Dish out the chicken and shred it, removing the bones.
- ✓ Put the bones back into the pot and simmer for about 20 minutes.
- ✓ Strato, the broth, discarding the chunks and put the liquid back into the pot.
- ✓ Bring it to a boil and simmer for about 30 minutes.
- ✓ Put the mushrooms in the broth and simmer for about 10 minutes.
- ✓ Dish out to serve hot.

Nutrition: Calories: 250 Carbs: 6.4g Fats: 8.9g Proteins: 35.1g Sodium: 852mg Sugar: 2.5g

582) Chicken Mulligatawny Soup

Ingredients:

- 1½ Tbsps curry powder
- 3 cups celery root, diced
- 2 Tbsps Swerve
- 10 cups chicken broth
- 5 cups chicken, chopped and cooked
- ¼ cup apple cider
- ½ cup sour cream
- ¼ cup fresh parsley, chopped
- 2 Tbsps butter
- Salt and black pepper, to taste

Direction: Servings: 10Preparation time: 30 mins

- ✓ Combine the broth, butter, chicken, curry powder, celery root, and apple cider in a large soup pot.
- ✓ Bring to a boil and simmer for about 30 minutes.
- ✓ Stir in Swerve, sour cream, fresh parsley, salt, and black pepper.
- ✓ Dish out and serve hot.

Nutrition: Calories: 215 Carbs: 7.1g Fats: 8.5g Proteins: 26.4g Sodium: 878mg Sugar: 2.2g

583) Buffalo Ranch Chicken Soup

Ingredients:

- 2 Tbsps parsley
- 2 celery stalks, chopped
- 6 Tbsps butter
- 1 cup heavy whipping cream
- 4 cups chicken, cooked and shredded
- 4 Tbsps ranch dressing
- ¼ cup yellow onions, chopped
- 8 oz cream cheese
- 8 cups chicken broth
- 7 hearty bacon slices, crumbled

Direction: Servings: 4 Preparation time: 40 mins

- ✓ Heat butter in a pan and add chicken.
- ✓ Cook for about 5 minutes and add 1½ cups water.
- ✓ Cover and cook for about 10 minutes.
- ✓ Put the chicken and rest of the ingredients into the saucepan except parsley and cook for about 10 minutes.
- ✓ Top with parsley and serve hot.

Nutrition: Calories: 444 Carbs: 4g Fats: 34g Proteins: 28g Sodium: 1572mg Sugar: 2g

584) Traditional Chicken Soup

Ingredients:

- 3 pounds chicken
- 4 quarts water
- 4 stalks celery
- 1/3 large red onion
- 1 large carrot
- 3 garlic cloves
- 2 thyme sprigs
- 2 rosemary sprigs
- Salt and black pepper, to taste

Direction: Servings: 6Preparation time: 1 hour 45 mins

- ✓ Put water and chicken in the stockpot on medium-high heat.
- ✓ Bring to a boil and allow it to simmer for about 10 minutes.
- ✓ Add onion, garlic, celery, salt, and pepper and simmer on medium-low heat for 30 minutes.
- ✓ Add thyme and carrots and simmer on low for another 30 minutes.
- ✓ Dish out the chicken and shred the pieces, removing the bones.
- ✓ Return the chicken pieces to the pot and add

rosemary sprigs.

- ✓ *Simmer for about 20 minutes at low heat and dish out to serve.*

Nutrition: Calories: 357 Carbs: 3.3g Fats: 7g Proteins: 66.2g Sodium: 175mg Sugar: 1.1g

585) Chicken Noodle Soup

Ingredients:

- *1 onion, minced*
- *1 rib celery, sliced*
- *3 cups chicken, shredded*
- *3 eggs, lightly beaten*
- *1 green onion for garnish*
- *2 Tbsps coconut oil*
- *1 carrot, peeled and thinly sliced*
- *2 Tsps dried thyme*
- *2½ quarts homemade bone broth*
- *¼ cup fresh parsley, minced*
- *Salt and black pepper, to taste*

Direction: Servings: 6Preparation time: 30 mins

- ✓ *Heat coconut oil over medium-high heat in a large pot and add onions, carrots, and celery.*
- ✓ *Cook for about 4 minutes and stir to the bone broth, thyme, and chicken.*
- ✓ *Simmer for about 15 minutes and stir in parsley.*
- ✓ *Pour beaten eggs into the soup in a slow, steady stream.*
- ✓ *Remove soup from heat and let it stand for about 2 minutes.*
- ✓ *Season with salt and black pepper and dish out to serve.*

Nutrition: Calories: 226 Carbs: 3.5g Fats: 8.9g Proteins: 31.8g Sodium: 152mg Sugar: 1.6g

586) Chicken Cabbage Soup

Ingredients:

- *2celery stalks*
- *2garlic cloves, minced*
- *4 oz. butter*
- *6 oz. mushrooms, sliced*
- *2 Tbsps onions, dried and minced*
- *1 Tsp salt*
- *8 cups chicken broth*
- *1medium carrot*
- *2 cups green cabbage, sliced into strips*
- *2 Tsps dried parsley*
- *¼ Tsp black pepper*
- *1½ rotisserie chickens, shredded*

Direction: Servings: 8 Preparation time: 35 mins

- ✓ *Melt butter in a large pot and add celery, mushrooms, onions, and garlic into the pot.*
- ✓ *Cook for about 4 minutes and add broth, parsley, carrot, salt, and black pepper.*
- ✓ *Simmer for about 10 minutes and add cooked chicken and cabbage.*
- ✓ *Simmer for an additional 12 minutes until the cabbage is tender.*
- ✓ *Dish out and serve hot.*

Nutrition: Calories: 184 Carbs: 4.2g Fats: 13.1g Proteins: 12.6g Sodium: 1244mg Sugar: 2.1g

587) Green Chicken Enchilada Soup

Ingredients:

- *4 oz. cream cheese softened*
- *½ cup salsa verde*
- *1 cup cheddar cheese, shredded*
- *2 cups cooked chicken, shredded*
- *2 cups chicken stock*

Direction: Servings: 5 Preparation time: 20 mins

- ✓ *Put salsa verde, cheddar cheese, cream cheese, and chicken stock in an immersion blender and blend until smooth.*
- ✓ *Pour this mixture into a medium saucepan and cook for about 5 minutes on medium heat.*
- ✓ *Add the shredded chicken and cook for about 5 minutes.*
- ✓ *Garnish with additional shredded cheddar and serve hot.*

Nutrition: Calories: 265 Carbs: 2.2g Fats: 17.4g Proteins: 24.2g Sodium: 686mg Sugar: 0.8g

588) Keto BBQ Chicken Pizza Soup

Ingredients:

- *6 chicken legs*
- *1 medium red onion, diced*
- *4 garlic cloves*
- *1 large tomato, unsweetened*
- *4 cups green beans*
- *¾ cup BBQ Sauce*
- *1½ cups mozzarella cheese, shredded*
- *¼ cup ghee*
- *2 quarts water*
- *2 quarts chicken stock*
- *Salt and black pepper, to taste*
- *Fresh cilantro for garnishing*

Direction: Servings: 6 Preparation time: 1 hour 30 mins

- ✓ *Put chicken, water, and salt in a large pot and bring to a boil.*
- ✓ *Reduce the heat to medium-low and cook for about 75 minutes.*
- ✓ *Shred the meat off the bones using a fork and keep aside.*
- ✓ *Put ghee, red onions, and garlic in a large soup and*

cook over medium heat.

- ✓ Add chicken stock and bring to a boil over high heat.
- ✓ Add green beans and tomato to the pot and cook for about 15 minutes.
- ✓ Add BBQ Sauce, shredded chicken, salt, and black pepper to the pot.
- ✓ Ladle the soup into serving containers and top with shredded mozzarella cheese and cilantro to serve.

Nutrition: Calories: 449 Carbs: 7.1g Fats: 32.5g Proteins: 30.8g Sodium: 252mg Sugar: 4.7g

589) Salmon Stew Soup

Ingredients:

- 4 cups chicken broth
- 3 salmon fillets, chunked
- 2 Tbsps butter
- 1 cup parsley, chopped
- 3 cups Swiss chard, roughly chopped
- 2 Italian squash, chopped
- 1 garlic clove, crushed
- ½ lemon, juiced
- Salt and black pepper, to taste
- 2 eggs

Direction: Servings: 5 Preparation time: 25 mins

- ✓ Put the chicken broth and garlic into a pot and bring to a boil.
- ✓ Add salmon, lemon juice, and butter to the pot and cook for about 10 minutes on medium heat.
- ✓ Add Swiss chard, Italian squash, salt, and pepper and cook for about 10 minutes.
- ✓ Whisk eggs and add to the pot, stirring continuously.
- ✓ Garnish with parsley and serve.

Nutrition: Calories: 262 Carbs: 7.8g Fats: 14g Proteins: 27.5g Sodium: 1021mg Sugar: 1.2g

590) Spicy Halibut Tomato Soup

Ingredients:

- 2garliccloves, minced
- 1Tbspolive oil
- ¼ cup fresh parsley, chopped
- 10anchoviescanned in oil, minced
- 6cupsvegetable broth
- 1Tspblack pepper
- 1poundhalibut fillets, chopped
- 3tomatoes, peeled and diced
- 1Tspsalt
- 1Tspred chili flakes

Direction: Servings: 8 Preparation time: 1 hour 5mins

- ✓ Heat olive oil in a large stockpot over medium heat and add garlic and half of the parsley.
- ✓ Add anchovies, tomatoes, vegetable broth, red chili flakes, salt, and black pepper, and bring to a boil.
- ✓ Reduce the heat to medium-low and simmer for about 20 minutes.
- ✓ Add halibut fillets and cook for about 10 minutes.
- ✓ Dish out the halibut and shred it into small pieces.
- ✓ Mix back with the soup and garnish with the resting fresh parsley to serve.

Nutrition: Calories: 170 Carbs: 3g Fats: 6.7g Proteins: 23.4g Sodium: 2103mg Sugar: 1.8g

Salad Recipes

591) Lentil Salmon Salad

Ingredients:

- Vegetable stock - 2 cups
- Green lentils - 1, rinsed
- Red onion - 1, chopped
- Parsley - 1 2 cup, chopped
- Smoked salmon - 4 oz., shredded
- Cilantro - 2 tbsp., chopped
- Red pepper - 1, chopped
- Lemon - 1, juiced
- Salt and pepper - to taste

Direction: Servings 4 Preparation and Cooking Time 25 minutes

✓ Cook vegetable stock and lentils in a sauce pan for 15 to 20 minutes, on low heat. Ensure all liquid has been absorbed and then removed from heat.

✓ Pour into a salad container and top with red pepper, parsley, cilantro, and salt and pepper (to suit your taste) and mix.

✓ Mix in lemon juice and shredded salmon.

✓ This salad should be served fresh.

Nutrition: Calories: 330.0 Polyunsaturated Fat: 1.2 g Monounsaturated Fat: 8.8 g Saturated Fat: 1.7 g

592) Peppy Pepper Tomato Salad

Ingredients:

- Yellow bell pepper - 1, cored and diced
- Cucumbers - 4, diced
- Red onion - 1, chopped
- Balsamic vinegar – 1 tbsp.
- Extra virgin olive oil – 2 tbsp.
- Tomatoes - 4, diced
- Red bell peppers - 2, cored and diced
- Chili flakes - 1 pinch
- Salt and pepper - to taste

Direction: Servings 4 Preparation Time 20 minutes

✓ Mix all the Ingredients in a salad container, except salt and pepper.

✓ Season with salt and pepper to suit your taste and mix well.

✓ Eat while fresh.

Nutrition: Calories 335.81 Kcal Calories from fat 324.24 Kcal Total Fat 36.03g Sodium 198.38mg Potassium 125.32mg Total Carbs 3.34g Sugars1.87g Dietary Fiber 0.78g Protein 0.6g

593) Bulgur Salad

Ingredients:

- Vegetable stock - 2 cups
- Bulgur - 2 3 cup
- Garlic clove - 1, minced
- Cherry tomatoes - 1 cup, halved
- Almonds - 2 tbsp., sliced
- Dates - 1 4 cup, pitted and chopped
- Lemon juice - 1 tbsp.
- Baby spinach - 8 oz.
- Cucumber - 1, diced
- Balsamic vinegar - 1 tbsp.
- Salt and pepper - to taste
- Mixed seeds - 2 tbsp.

Direction: Servings 4 Preparation and Cooking Time 30 minutes

✓ Pour the stock into the sauce pan and heat until hot, then stir in bulgur and cook until bulgur has absorbed all stock.

✓ Put in salad container and add resting Ingredients. Stir well.
Add salt and pepper to suit your taste.

✓ Serve and eat immediately.

Nutrition: Calories: 151 · Fat: 0.4g · Sodium: 9mg · Carbohydrates: 33.8g · Fiber: 8.2g · Sugars: 0.2g · Protein: 5.6g

594) Tasty Tuna Salad

Ingredients:

- Green olives - 1 4 cups, sliced
- Tuna in water - 1 can drain
- Pine nuts - 2 tbsp.
- Artichoke hearts – 1 jar, drained and chopped
- Extra virgin olive oil - 2 tbsp.
- Lemon – 1, juiced
- Arugula - 2 leaves
- Dijon mustard - 1 tbsp.
- Salt and pepper - to taste

Direction: Servings 4 Preparation Time 15 minutes

✓ Mix mustard, oil, and lemon juice in a container to make a dressing. Combine the artichoke hearts, tuna, green olives, arugula, and pine nuts in a salad container.

✓ In a separate salad container, mix tuna, arugula, pine nuts, artichoke hearts, and tuna.

✓ Pour dressing mix onto a salad and serve fresh.

Nutrition: Calories: 292.0 Dietary Fiber: 2.2 g Protein: 26.3 g Saturated Fat: 2.5 g

595) Sweet and Sour Spinach Salad

Ingredients:

- Red onions - 2, sliced
- Baby spinach leaves - 4
- Sesame oil - 1 2 tsp.
- Apple cider vinegar - 2 tbsp.
- Honey - 1 tsp.
- Sesame seeds - 2 tbsp.
- Salt and pepper - to taste

Direction: Servings 4 Preparation Time 15 minutes

- ✓ Mix together honey, sesame oil, vinegar, and sesame seeds in a small container to make a dressing. Add in salt and pepper to suit your taste.
- ✓ Add red onions and spinach together in a salad container.
- ✓ Pour dressing over the salad and serve while cool and fresh.

Nutrition: Total Fat 10.03g Cholesterol 94.54mg Sodium 474.92mg Total Carbs 16.98g Sugars 12.52g Dietary Fiber 1.39g Protein12.08g

596) Easy Eggplant Salad

Ingredients:

- Salt and pepper - to taste
- Eggplant - 2, sliced
- Smoked paprika - 1 tsp.
- Extra virgin olive oil - 2 tbsp.
- Garlic cloves - 2, minced
- Mixed greens - 2 cups
- Sherry vinegar - 2 tbsp.

Direction: Servings 4 Preparation Time 30 minutes

- ✓ Mix together garlic, paprika, and oil in a small container.
- ✓ Place eggplant on a plate and sprinkle with salt and pepper to suit your taste. Next, brush the oil mixture onto the eggplant.
- ✓ Cook eggplant on a medium heated grill pan until brown on both sides. Once cooked, put eggplant into a salad container.
- ✓ Top with greens and vinegar, serve and eat.

Nutrition: Calories: 150.5 Total Fat: 10.9 g Dietary Fiber: 4.9 g Monounsaturated Fat: 7.6 g

597) Sweetest Sweet Potato Salad

Ingredients:

- Honey - 2 tbsp.
- Sumac spice - 1 tsp.
- Sweet potato - 2, finely sliced
- Extra virgin olive oil - 3 tbsp
- Dried mint - 1 tsp
- Balsamic vinegar – 1 tbsp.
- Salt and pepper - to taste
- Pomegranate - 1, seeded
- Mixed greens - 3 cups

Direction: Servings 4 Preparation and Cooking Time 30 minutes

- ✓ Place sweet potato slices on a plate and add sumac, mint, salt, and pepper on both sides. Next, drizzle oil and honey over both sides.
- ✓ Add oil to a grill pan and heat. Grill sweet potatoes on medium heat until brown on both sides.
- ✓ Put sweet potatoes in a salad container and top with pomegranate and mixed greens.
- ✓ Stir and eat right away.

Nutrition: Calories 343 Total Fat 17ggrams Saturated Fat 2.7g Cholesterol 9.2mg Sodium 710mg Potassium 1014mg Total Carbohydrates 44g Dietary Fiber 7.3g Sugars 15g Protein 4.7g

598) Delicious Chickpea Salad

Ingredients:

- Chickpeas - 1 can drain
- Cherry tomatoes - 1 cup, quartered
- Parsley - 1 2 cup, chopped
- Red seedless grapes - 1 2 cups, halved
- Feta cheese - 4 oz., cubed
- Salt and pepper - to taste
- Lemon juice - 1 tbsp.
- Greek yogurt - 1 4 cup
- Extra virgin olive oil - 2 tbsp.

Direction: Servings 4 Preparation Time 15 minutes

- ✓ In a salad container, mix together parsley, chickpeas, grapes, feta cheese, and tomatoes.
- ✓ Add in resting ingredients, seasoning with salt and pepper to suit your taste.
- ✓ This fresh salad is best when served right away.

Nutrition: Calories: 285.2 Total Fat: 18.4 g Dietary Fiber: 5.1 g Protein: 10.2 g

599) Couscous Arugula Salad

Ingredients:

- Couscous - 1 2 cup
- Vegetable stock - 1 cup
- Asparagus - 1 bunch, peeled
- Lemon - 1, juiced
- Dried tarragon - 1 tsp.
- Arugula - 2 cups
- Salt and pepper - to taste

Direction: Servings 4 Preparation and Cooking Time 20 minutes

- ✓ Heat vegetable stock in a pot until hot. Remove from heat and add in couscous. Cover until the couscous has absorbed all the stock.
- ✓ Pour in a container and fluff with a fork and then set aside to cool.
- ✓ Peel asparagus with a peeler, making them into ribbons, and put into a container with couscous.
- ✓ Add resting Ingredients and add salt and pepper to suit your taste.
- ✓ Serve the salad immediately.

Nutrition: Calories 468.6 Cholesterol 1.1 mg Sodium 603.9 mg Total Carbohydrate 55.5 g Dietary Fiber 8.2 g Sugars 1.6 g Protein 15.4 g

600) Spinach and Grilled Feta Salad

Ingredients:

- Feta cheese - 8 oz., sliced

- *Black olives - 1 4 cups, sliced*
- *Green olives - 1 4 cups, sliced*
- *Baby spinach - 4 cups*
- *Garlic cloves - 2, minced*
- *Capers - 1 tsp., chopped*
- *Extra virgin olive oil - 2 tbsp.*
- *Red wine vinegar - 1 tbsp.*

Direction: Servings 6 Preparation and Cooking Time 20 minutes

✓ *Grill feta cheese slices over medium to high flame until brown on both sides.*

✓ *In a salad container, mix green olives, black olives, and spinach.*

✓ *In a separate container, mix vinegar, capers, and oil together to make a dressing.*

✓ *Top salad with the dressing and cheese, and it's is ready to serve.*

Nutrition: Calories: 133.9 Protein: 8.0 g Dietary Fiber: 2.1 g Saturated Fat: 2.5 g

601) Creamy Cool Salad

Ingredients:

- *Greek yogurt - 1 2 cup*
- *Dill - 2 tbsp., chopped*
- *Lemon juice - 1 tsp.*
- *Cucumbers - 4, diced*
- *Garlic cloves - 2, minced*
- *Salt and pepper - to taste*

Direction: Servings 4 Preparation Time 15 minutes

✓ *Mix all Ingredients in a salad container.*

✓ *Add salt and pepper to suit your taste and eat.*

Nutrition: Total Fat 11g Cholesterol 10mg Sodium 280mg Total Carbohydrate 2g

602) Grilled Salmon Summer Salad

Ingredients:

- *Salmon fillets - 2*
- *Salt and pepper - to taste*
- *Vegetable stock - 2 cups*
- *Bulgur - 1 2 cup*
- *Cherry tomatoes - 1 cup, halved*
- *Sweet corn - 1 2 cup*
- *Lemon - 1, juiced*
- *Green olives - 1 2 cups, sliced*
- *Cucumber - 1, cubed*
- *Green onion - 1, chopped*
- *Red pepper - 1, chopped*
- *Red bell pepper - 1, cored and diced*

Direction: Servings 4 Preparation and Cooking Time 30 minutes

✓ *Heat a grill pan on medium and then place salmon on, seasoning with salt and pepper. Grill, both sides of salmon until brown and set aside.*

✓ *Heat stock in a sauce pan until hot and then add in bulgur and cook until liquid is completely soaked into bulgur.*

✓ *Mix salmon, bulgur, and all other Ingredients in a salad container and again add salt and pepper, if desired, to suit your taste.*

✓ *Serve the salad as soon as completed*

Nutrition: Calories 210 Trans Fat 0g Cholesterol 55mg Sodium 590mg Total Carbohydrate 8g

603) Broccoli Salad with Caramelized Onions

Ingredients:

- *Extra virgin olive oil - 3 tbsp.*
- *Red onions - 2, sliced*
- *Dried thyme - 1 tsp.*
- *Balsamic vinegar - 2 tbsp. vinegar*
- *Broccoli - 1 lb., cut into florets*
- *Salt and pepper - to taste*

Direction: Servings 4 Preparation and Cooking Time 25 minutes

✓ *Heat olive oil in a pan over high heat and add in sliced onions. Cook for approx. 10 minutes or until the onions are caramelized. Stir in vinegar and thyme and then remove from stove.*

✓ *Mix together the broccoli and onion mixture in a container, adding salt and pepper if desired. Serve and eat salad as soon as possible*

Nutrition: 102 cal; protein 3.4g; carbohydrates 9g; dietary fiber 3.1g; sugars 2.6g; fat 6.9g;

604) Baked Cauliflower Mixed Salad

Ingredients:

- *Cauliflower - 1 lb., cut into florets*
- *Extra virgin olive oil - 2 tbsp.*
- *Dried mint - 1 tsp.*
- *Dried oregano - 1 tsp.*
- *Parsley - 2 tbsp., chopped*
- *Red pepper - 1, chopped*
- *Lemon - 1, juiced*
- *Green onion - 1, chopped*
- *Cilantro - 2 tbsp., chopped*
- *Salt and pepper to taste*

Direction: Servings 4 Preparation and Cooking Time 30 minutes

✓ *Heat oven to 350 degrees.*

✓ *In a deep baking pan, combine olive oil, mint, cauliflower, and oregano and bake for 15 minutes.*

✓ *Once cooked, pour into a salad container and add resting Ingredients, stirring together.*

✓ *Plate the salad and eat fresh and warm.*

Nutrition: 86 calories; protein 4.2g; carbs 5.4 g; dietary fiber 3.6g

605) Quick Arugula Salad

Ingredients:

- Roasted red bell peppers - 6, sliced
- Pine nuts - 2 tbsp.
- Dried raisins - 2 tbsp.
- Red onion - 1, sliced
- Arugula - 3 cups
- Balsamic vinegar - 2 tbsp.
- Feta cheese - 4 oz., crumbled
- Extra virgin olive oil – 2 tbsp.
- Feta cheese - 4 oz., crumbled
- Salt and pepper - to taste

Direction: Servings 4 Preparation Time 15 minutes

✓ Using a salad container, combine vinegar, olive oil, pine nuts, raisins, peppers, and onions.

✓ Add arugula and feta cheese to the mix and serve.

Nutrition: 28 calories. 2.2 g protein. 4.4 g carbohydrate. 2.2 g fiber. 88 milligrams (mg) calcium. 15.9 mg iron. 66 mg magnesium.66 mg phosphorus.

606) Bell Pepper and Tomato Salad

Ingredients:

- Roasted red bell pepper - 8, sliced
- Extra virgin olive oil - 2 tbsp.
- Chili flakes - 1 pinch
- Garlic cloves - 4, minced
- Pine nuts - 2 tbsp.
- Shallot - 1, sliced
- Cherry tomatoes - 1 cup, halved
- Parsley - 2 tbsp., chopped
- Balsamic vinegar - 1 tbsp.
- Salt and pepper - to taste

Direction: Servings 4 Preparation Time 15 minutes

✓ Mix all Ingredients except salt and pepper in a salad container.

✓ Season with salt and pepper if you want, to suit your taste.

✓ Eat once freshly made.

Nutrition: Calories: 102.0 Sodium: 9.9 mg Dietary Fiber: 1.8 g Protein: 1.6 g

607) One Container Spinach Salad

Ingredients:

- Red beets - 2, cooked and diced
- Apple cider vinegar - 1 tbsp.
- Baby spinach - 3 cups
- Greek yogurt - 1 4 cup
- Horseradish - 1 tbsp.
- Salt and pepper - to taste

Direction: Servings 4 Preparation Time 20 minutes

✓ Mix beets and spinach in a salad container.

✓ Add in yogurt, horseradish, and vinegar. You can also add salt and pepper if you wish.

✓ Serve the salad as soon as mixed.

Nutrition: Calories 171.3 Total Fat 1.5 g Saturated Fat 0.1 g Polyunsaturated Fat 1.0 g Monounsaturated Fat 0.1 g Cholesterol 0.0 mg Sodium 29.6 mg Potassium 425.5 mg Total Carbohydrate 35.4 g Dietary Fiber 4.8 g Sugars 26.7 g Protein 6.3 g

608) Olive and Red Bean Salad

Ingredients:

- Red onions - 2, sliced
- Garlic cloves - 2, minced
- Balsamic vinegar - 2 tbsp.
- Green olives - 1 4 cups, sliced
- Salt and pepper - to taste
- Mixed greens - 2 cups
- Red beans - 1 can drain
- Chili flakes - 1 pinch
- Extra virgin olive oil - 2 tbsp.
- Parsley - 2 tbsp., chopped

Direction: Servings 4 Preparation Time 20 minutes

✓ In a salad container, mix all Ingredients

✓ Add salt and pepper, if desired, and serve right away.

Nutrition: 43.2g total carbs, 32.1g net carbs, 15.5g fat, 12.8g protein, and 353 calories.

609) Fresh and Light Cabbage Salad

Ingredients:

- Mint - 1 tbsp., chopped
- Ground coriander - 1 2 tsp.
- Savoy cabbage - 1, shredded
- Greek yogurt - 1 2 cup
- Cumin seeds - 1 4 tsp.
- Extra virgin olive oil - 2 tbsp.
- Carrot - 1, grated
- Red onion – 1, sliced
- Honey - 1 tsp.
- Lemon zest - 1 tsp.
- Lemon juice - 2 tbsp.
- Salt and pepper - to taste

Direction: Servings 4 Preparation Time 25 minutes

✓ In a salad container, mix all Ingredients

✓ You can add salt and pepper to suit your taste and then mix again.

✓ This salad is best when cool and freshly made.

Nutrition: Calories 60.2Total Fat 4.7 gr Saturated Fat 0.6 gr Cholesterol 0.0 mg Sodium 94.5 mg Potassium 130.2 mg Total Carbohydrate 4.5 gr Dietary Fiber 1.3 g Sugars 0.8 g Protein 0.9 g

610) Vegetable Patch Salad

Ingredients:

- *Cauliflower - 1 bunch, cut into florets*
- *Zucchini - 1, sliced*
- *Sweet potato - 1, peeled and cubed*
- *Baby carrots - 1 2 lb.*
- *Salt and pepper - to taste*
- *Dried basil - 1 tsp.*
- *Red onions - 2, sliced*
- *Eggplant - 2, cubed*
- *Endive - 1, sliced*
- *Extra virgin olive oil - 3 tbsp.*
- *Lemon – 1, juiced*
- *Balsamic vinegar - 1 tbsp.*

Direction: Servings 6 Preparation and Cooking Time 30 minutes

- ✓ *Preheat oven to 350 degrees. Mix together all vegetables, basil, salt, pepper, and oil in a baking dish and cook for 25 – 30 minutes.*
- ✓ *After cooked, pour into salad container and stir in vinegar and lemon juice.*
- ✓ *Dish up and serve.*

Nutrition: Calories 11 Polyunsaturated Fat0.036g

Monounsaturated Fat 0.008g Sodium15mg Total Carbohydrate2.32gDietary Fiber0.8g Sugars1.33g Protein 0.55g

611) Cucumber Greek yogurt Salad

Ingredients:

- *4tbsp Greek yogurt*
- *4 large cucumbers peeled, seeded, and sliced*
- *1 tbsp dried dill*
- *1 tbsp apple cider vinegar*
- *1/4 tsp garlic powder*
- *1/4 tsp ground black pepper*
- *1/2 tsp sugar*
- *1/2 tsp salt*

Direction: Serves:6/Preparation time: 5 minutes/Cooking Time: 0 minutes

- ✓ *Place all the Ingredients leaving out the cucumber into a container and whisk this until all is incorporated. Add your cucumber slices and toss until all is well mixed.*
- ✓ *Let the salad chill for 10 minutes in the fridge, and then serve.*

Nutrition: Calories: 49.6 Monounsaturated Fat: 0.2 g Dietary Fiber: 0.7 g Polyunsaturated Fat: 0.0 g

612) Chickpea Salad Recipe

Ingredients:

- *Drained chickpeas: 1 can*
- *Halved cherry tomatoes: 1 cup*
- *Sun-dried chopped tomatoes: 1 2 cups*
- *Arugula: 2 cups*
- *Cubed pita bread: 1*
- *Pitted black olives: 1 2 cups*
- *1 sliced shallot*
- *Cumin seeds: 1 2 Tsp*
- *Coriander seeds: 1 2 Tsp*
- *Chili powder: 1 4 Tsp*
- *Chopped mint: 1 Tsp*
- *Pepper and salt to taste*
- *Crumbled goat cheese: 4 oz.*

Direction: Servings: 4 Duration: 15 minutes

- ✓ *In a salad container, mix the tomatoes, chickpeas, pita bread, arugula, olives, shallot, spices, and mint.*
- ✓ *Stir in pepper and salt as desired to the cheese and stir.*
- ✓ *You can now serve the fresh Salad.*

Nutrition: Calories: 166.6 Total Fat: 7.7 g Protein: 4.4 g Dietary Fiber: 4.3 g

613) Orange salad

Ingredients:

- *4 sliced endives*
- *1 sliced red onion*
- *2 oranges already cut into segments*
- *Extra virgin olive oil: 2 Tbsp*
- *Pepper and salt to taste*

Direction: Servings: 4 Cooking Time: 15 minutes

- ✓ *Mix all the Ingredients in a salad container*
- ✓ *Sprinkle pepper and salt to taste.*
- ✓ *You can now serve the salad fresh.*

Nutrition: Calories from Fat 153. Calories 276.

Total Fat 17g. Saturated Fat 1.3g. Cholesterol 0mg. Sodium 317mg. Potassium 602mg. Total Carbohydrates 30g

614) Yogurt lettuce salad recipe

Ingredients:

- *Shredded Romaine lettuce: 1 head*
- *Sliced cucumbers: 2*
- *2 minced garlic cloves*
- *Greek yogurt: 1 2 cup*
- *Dijon mustard: 1 Tsp*
- *Chili powder: 1 pinch*
- *Extra virgin olive oil: 2 Tbsp*
- *Lemon juice: 1 Tbsp*
- *Chopped dill: 2 Tbsp*
- *4 chopped mint leaves*
- *Pepper and salt to taste*

Direction: Servings: 4 Cooking Time: 20 minutes

- ✓ In a salad container, combine the lettuce with the cucumbers.
- ✓ Add the yogurt, chili, mustard, lemon juice, dill, mint, garlic, and oil in a mortar with pepper and salt as desired.
  Then, mix well into a paste. This is the dressing for the salad.
- ✓ Top the Salad with the dressing, then serve fresh.

Nutrition: Calories: 84.8 Total Fat: 2.1 g Dietary Fiber: 1.6 g Monounsaturated Fat: 0.8 g

615) . Fruit de salad recipe

Ingredients:

- Cubed seedless watermelon: 8 oz.
- Halved red grapes: 4 oz.
- 2 Sliced cucumbers
- Halved strawberries: 1 cup
- Cubed feta cheese: 6 oz.
- Balsamic vinegar: 2 Tbsp
- Arugula: 2 cups

Direction: Servings: 4 Cooking Time: 20 minutes

- ✓ In a salad container, mix the strawberries, grapes, arugula, cucumbers, feta cheese, and watermelon together.
- ✓ Top the salad with vinegar and serve fresh.

Nutrition: 57 calories; protein 1g; carbohydrates 13.9g; dietary fiber 3g; sugars 9.1g; fat 0.4g;

616) Chickpea with a mint salad recipe

Ingredients:

- 1 diced cucumber
- Sliced black olives:1 4 cup
- Chopped mint: 2 Tbsp
- Cooked and drained short pasta: 4 oz.
- Arugula: 2 cups
- Drained chickpeas: 1 can
- 1 sliced shallot
- Chopped Parsley: 1 2 cup

Direction: Servings: 6 Duration: 20 minutes

- ✓ Mix the chickpeas with the other Ingredients in a salad container
- ✓ Top with oil and lemon juice, sprinkle pepper and salt, then mix well.
- ✓ Refrigerate the Salad (can last in a sealed container for about 2 days) or serve fresh.

Nutrition: Cholesterol 0 mg, Carbohydrates 28.5g, Protein 8.1g, Fat 2.3g.

617) Grapy Fennel salad

Ingredients:

- Grape seed oil: 1 Tbsp
- Chopped dill: 1 Tbsp
- 1 finely sliced fennel bulb
- Toasted almond slices: 2 Tbsp
- Chopped mint: 1 Tsp
- 1 grapefruit already cut into segments
- 1 orange already cut into segments
- Pepper and salt as desired

Direction: Servings: 2 Time to prepare: 15 minutes

- ✓ Using a platter, mix the grapefruit and orange segments with the fennel bulb
- ✓ Add the mint, almond slices, and dill, top with the oil, and add pepper and salt as desired.
- ✓ You can now serve the Salad fresh.

Nutrition: 127 calories; protein 1.9g; carbohydrates 21.1g; dietary fiber 2.6g; sugars 16.3g; fat 5g

618) Greenie salad recipe

Ingredients:

- Extra virgin olive oil: 2 Tbsp
- Mixed greens: 12 oz.
- Pitted black olives: 1 2 cup
- Pitted green olives: 1 4 cup
- Sherry vinegar: 2 Tbsp
- Pitted Kalamata olives: 1 2 cup
- Almond slices: 2 Tbsp
- Parmesan shavings: 2 oz.
- Sliced Parma ham: 2 oz.
- Pepper and salt as desired

Direction: Servings: 4 Cooking time: 15 minutes

- ✓ Stir the almonds, olives, and mixed greens together in a salad container
- ✓ Drizzle the oil and vinegar, then sprinkle pepper and salt as you want.
- ✓ Top with the Parma ham and Parmesan shavings before serving.
- ✓ You can now serve fresh.

Nutrition: Dietary Fiber: 4.4 g Protein: 7.6 g Calories: 159.9 Monounsaturated Fat: 2.7 g

619) A Refreshing Detox Salad

Ingredients:

- 1 large apple, diced
- 1 large beet, coarsely grated
- 1 large carrot, coarsely grated
- 1 tbsp chia seeds
- 2 tbsp almonds, chopped
- 2 tbsp lemon juice
- 2 tbsp pumpkin seed oil
- 4 cups mixed greens

Direction: Servings: 4, Cooking Time: 0 minutes

- ✓ In a medium salad container, except for mixed greens, combine all ingredients thoroughly.
- ✓ Into 4 salad plates, divide the mixed greens.

✓ Evenly top mixed greens with the salad container mixture.

✓ Serve and enjoy.

Nutrition: Calories: 136.4; Protein: 1.93g; Carbs: 14.4g; Fat: 7.9g

620) Amazingly Fresh Carrot Salad

Ingredients:

- ¼ tsp chipotle powder
- 1 bunch scallions, sliced
- 1 cup cherry tomatoes, halved
- 1 large avocado, diced
- 1 tbsp chili powder
- 1 tbsp lemon juice
- 2 tbsp olive oil
- 3 tbsp lime juice
- 4 cups carrots, spiralized
- salt to taste

Direction: Servings: 4 Cooking Time: 0 minutes

✓ In a salad container, mix and arrange avocado, cherry tomatoes, scallions, and spiralized carrots. Set aside.

✓ In a small container, whisk salt, chipotle powder, chili powder, olive oil, lemon juice, and lime juice thoroughly.

✓ Pour dressing over noodle salad. Toss to coat well.

✓ Serve and enjoy at room temperature.

Nutrition: Calories: 243.6; Fat: 14.8g; Protein: 3g; Carbs: 24.6g

621) Anchovy and Orange Salad

Ingredients:

- 1 small red onion, sliced into thin rounds
- 1 tbsp fresh lemon juice
- 1/8 tsp pepper or more to taste
- 16 oil cure Kalamata olives
- 2 tsp finely minced fennel fronds for garnish
- 3 tbsp extra virgin olive oil
- 4 small oranges, preferably blood oranges
- 6 anchovy fillets

Direction: Servings: 4, Cooking Time: 0 minutes

✓ With a paring knife, peel oranges, including the membrane that surrounds it.

✓ On a plate, slice oranges into thin circles and allow the plate to catch the orange juices.

✓ On the serving plate, arrange orange slices on a layer.

✓ Sprinkle oranges with onion, followed by olives and then anchovy fillets.

✓ Drizzle with oil, lemon juice, and orange juice.

✓ Sprinkle with pepper.

✓ Allow salad to stand for 30 minutes at room temperature to allow the flavors to develop.

✓ To serve, garnish with fennel fronds and enjoy.

Nutrition: Calories: 133.9; Protein: 3.2 g; Carbs: 14.3g; Fat: 7.1g

622) Arugula with Blueberries 'n Almonds

Ingredients:

- ½ cup slivered almonds
- ½ cup blueberries, fresh
- 1 ripe red pear, sliced
- 1 shallot, minced
- 1 tsp minced garlic
- 1 tsp whole grain mustard
- 2 tbsp fresh lemon juice
- 3 tbsp extra virgin olive oil
- 6 cups arugula

Direction: Servings: 2, Cooking Time: 0 minutes

✓ In a big mixing container, mix garlic, olive oil, lemon juice, and mustard.

✓ Once thoroughly mixed, add resting ingredients.

✓ Toss to coat.

✓ Equally divide into two containers, serve and enjoy.

Nutrition: Calories: 530.4; Protein: 6.1g; Carbs: 39.2g; Fat: 38.8g

623) Asian Peanut Sauce Over Noodle Salad

Ingredients:

- 1 cup shredded green cabbage
- 1 cup shredded red cabbage
- 1/4 cup chopped cilantro
- 1/4 cup chopped peanuts
- 1/4 cup chopped scallions
- 4 cups shirataki noodles (drained and rinsed)
- Asian Peanut Sauce Ingredients
- ¼ cup sugar-free peanut butter
- ¼ Tsp cayenne pepper
- ½ cup filtered water
- ½ Tsp kosher salt
- 1 Tbsp fish sauce (or coconut aminos for vegan)
- 1 Tbsp granulated erythritol sweetener
- 1 Tbsp lime juice
- 1 Tbsp toasted sesame oil
- 1 Tbsp wheat-free soy sauce
- 1 Tsp minced garlic
- 2 Tbsps minced ginger

Direction: Servings: 4, Cooking Time: 0 minutes

✓ In a large salad container, combine all noodle

salad ingredients and toss well to mix.

- ✓ Mix all sauce ingredients In a blender, and pulse until smooth and creamy.
- ✓ Pour sauce over the salad and toss well to coat.
- ✓ Evenly divide into four equal servings and enjoy.
- ✓ Calories: 104; Protein: 7.0g; Carbs: 12.0g; Fat: 16.0g

Nutrition: Calories 173.0 Total Fat 6.6 g, Saturated Fat 1.1 g, Cholesterol 0.0 mg Potassium 187.1 mg Total Carbohydrate 27.0 g Dietary Fiber 4.5 g Sugars 1.6 g Protein 6.5 g

624) Asian Salad with pistachios

Ingredients:

- ¼ cup chopped pistachios
- ¼ cup green onions, sliced
- 1 bunch watercress, trimmed
- 1 cup red bell pepper, diced

Direction: Servings: 6 Cooking Time: 0

- ✓ In a large salad container, mix pistachios, green onions, bell pepper, fennel, watercress, and pears.
- ✓ In a small container, mix vegetable oil and lime juice—season with pepper and salt to taste.
- ✓ Pour dressing into the salad and gently mix before serving.

Nutrition: Calories: 160; Protein: 3g; Fat: 1g; Carbs: 16g

625) Balela Salad from the Middle East

Ingredients:

- 1 jalapeno, finely chopped (optional)
- 1/2 green bell pepper, cored and chopped
- 2 1/2 cups grape tomatoes, slice in halves
- 1/2 cup sun-dried tomatoes
- 1/2 cup freshly chopped parsley leaves
- 1/2 cup freshly chopped mint or basil leaves
- 1/3 cup pitted Kalamata olives
- 1/4 cup pitted green olives
- 3 1/2 cups cooked chickpeas, drained and rinsed
- 3–5 green onions, both white and green parts, chopped

Dressing Ingredients

- 1 garlic clove, minced
- 1 tsp ground sumac
- 1/2 tsp Aleppo pepper
- 1/4 cup Early Harvest Greek extra virgin olive oil
- 1/4 to 1/2 tsp crushed red pepper (optional)
- 2 tbsp lemon juice
- 2 tbsp white wine vinegar
- Salt and black pepper, a pinch to your taste

Direction: Servings: 6, Cooking Time: 0 minutes

- ✓ in a large salad container, mix the salad ingredients together.
- ✓ In a separate smaller container or jar, mix together the dressing ingredients.
- ✓ Drizzle the dressing over the salad and gently toss to coat.
- ✓ Set aside for 35 minutes to allow the flavors to mix.
- ✓ Serve and enjoy.

Nutrition: Calories: 257; Carbs: 30.5g; Protein: 8.4g; Fats: 12.6g

626) Blue Cheese and Portobello Salad

Ingredients:

- ½ cup croutons
- 1 tbsp merlot wine
- 1 tbsp water
- 1 tsp minced garlic
- 1 tsp olive oil
- 2 large Portobello mushrooms, stemmed, wiped clean, and cut into bite-sized pieces
- 2 pieces roasted red peppers (canned), sliced
- 2 tbsp balsamic vinegar
- 2 tbsp crumbled blue cheese
- 4 slices red onion
- 6 asparagus stalks cut into 1-inch sections
- 6 cups Bibb lettuce, chopped
- Ground pepper to taste

Direction: Servings: 2, Cooking Time: 15 minutes

- ✓ On medium fire, place a small pan and heat oil. Once hot, add onions and mushrooms. For 4 to 6 minutes, sauté until tender.
- ✓ Add garlic and for a minute continue sautéing.
- ✓ Pour in the wine and cook for a minute.
- ✓ Bring an inch of water to a boil in a pot with a steamer basket. Once boiling, add asparagus, steam for two to three minutes or until crisp and tender while covered. Once cooked, remove the basket from the pot and set it aside.
- ✓ In a small container, whisk thoroughly black pepper, water, balsamic vinegar, and blue cheese
- ✓ To serve, place 3 cups of lettuce on each plate. Add 1 roasted pepper, ½ of asparagus, ½ of the mushroom mixture, whisk blue cheese dressing before drizzling equally onto plates. Garnish with croutons, serve and enjoy.

Nutrition: Calories: 660.8; Protein: 38.5g; Carbs: 30.4g; Fat: 42.8g

627) Blue Cheese and Arugula Salad

Ingredients:

- ¼ cup crumbled blue cheese
- 1 tsp Dijon mustard
- 1-pint fresh figs, quartered
- 2 bags arugula

- *3 tbsp Balsamic Vinegar*
- *3 tbsp olive oil*
- *Pepper and salt to taste*

Direction: Servings: 4, Cooking Time: 0 minutes

- ✓ *Whisk thoroughly together pepper, salt, olive oil, Dijon mustard, and balsamic vinegar to make the dressing. Set aside to the ref for at least 30 minutes to marinate and allow the spices to combine. On four serving plates, evenly arrange arugula and top with blue cheese and figs.*
- ✓ *Drizzle each plate of salad with 1 ½ tbsp of prepared dressing.*
- ✓ *Serve and enjoy.*

Nutrition: Cal : 202; Protein: 2.5g; Carbs: 25.5g; Fat: 10g

628) Broccoli Salad Moroccan Style

Ingredients:

- *¼ tsp sea salt*
- *¼ tsp ground cinnamon*
- *½ tsp ground turmeric*
- *¾ tsp ground ginger*
- *½ tbsp extra virgin olive oil*
- *½ tbsp apple cider vinegar*
- *2 tbsp chopped green onion*
- *1/3 cup coconut cream*
- *½ cup carrots, shredded*
- *1 small head of broccoli, chopped*

Direction: Servings: 4, Cooking Time: 0 minutes

- ✓ *In a large salad container, mix well salt, cinnamon, turmeric, ginger, olive oil, and vinegar.*
- ✓ *Add resting ingredients, tossing well to coat.*
- ✓ *Pop to the ref for at least 30 to 60 minutes before serving.*

Nutrition: Calories: 90.5; Protein: 1.3g; Carbs: 4g; Fat: 7.7g

629) Charred Tomato and Broccoli Salad

Ingredients:

- *¼ cup lemon juice*
- *½ tsp chili powder*
- *1 ½ lb. boneless chicken breast*
- *1 ½ lb. medium tomato*
- *1 tsp freshly ground pepper*
- *1 tsp salt*
- *4 cups broccoli florets*
- *5 tbsp extra virgin olive oil, divided into 2 and 3 Tbsps*

Direction: Servings: 6, Cooking Time: minutes

- ✓ *Place the chicken in a skillet and add just enough water to cover the chicken. Bring to a simmer over high heat. Reduce the heat once the liquid boils and cook the chicken thoroughly for 12 minutes. Once cooked, shred the chicken into bite-sized pieces.*
- ✓ *On a large pot, bring water to a boil and add the broccoli. Cook for 5 minutes until slightly tender. Drain and rinse the broccoli with cold water. Set aside.*
- ✓ *Core the tomatoes and cut them crosswise. Discard the seeds and set the tomatoes cut side down on paper towels. Pat them dry.*
- ✓ *In a heavy skillet, heat the pan over high heat until very hot. Brush the cut sides of the tomatoes with olive oil and place them on the pan. Cook the tomatoes until the sides are charred. Set aside.*
- ✓ *To the same pan, heat the resting 3 Tbsp olive oil over medium heat. Stir the salt, chili powder, and pepper and stir for 45 seconds. Pour over the lemon juice and remove the pan from the heat.*
- ✓ *Plate the broccoli, shredded chicken, and chili powder mixture dressing.*

Nutrition: Calories: 210.8; Protein: 27.5g; Carbs: 6.3g; Fat: 8.4g

630) Chopped Chicken on Greek Salad

Ingredients:

- *¼ tsp pepper*
- *¼ tsp salt*
- *½ cup crumbled feta cheese*
- *½ cup finely chopped red onion*
- *½ cup sliced ripe black olives*
- *1 medium cucumber, peeled, seeded, and chopped*
- *1 tbsp chopped fresh dill*
- *1 tsp garlic powder*
- *1/3 cup red wine vinegar*
- *2 ½ cups chopped cooked chicken*
- *2 medium tomatoes, chopped*
- *2 tbsp extra virgin olive oil*
- *6 cups chopped romaine lettuce*

Direction: Servings: 4, Cooking Time: 0 minutes

- ✓ *In a large container, whisk well pepper, salt, garlic powder, dill, oil, and vinegar.*
- ✓ *Add feta, olives, onion, cucumber, tomatoes, chicken, and lettuce.*
- ✓ *Toss well to combine.*
- ✓ *Serve and enjoy.*

Nutrition: Calories: 461.9; Protein: 19.4g; Carbs: 10.8g; Fat: 37.9g

631) Classic Greek Salad

Ingredients:

- *¼ cup extra virgin olive oil, plus more for drizzling*
- *¼ cup red wine vinegar*
- *1 4-oz block Greek feta cheese packed in brine*

- *1 cup Kalamata olives, halved and pitted*
- *1 lemon, juiced, and zested*
- *1 small red onion, halved and thinly sliced*
- *1 tsp dried oregano*
- *1 tsp honey*
- *14 small vine-ripened tomatoes, quartered*
- *5 Persian cucumbers*
- *Fresh oregano leaves for topping, optional*
- *Pepper to taste*
- *Salt to taste*

Direction: Servings: 4, Cooking Time: 0 minutes

- ✓ *In a container of ice water, soak red onions with 2 tbsp salt.*
- ✓ *In a large container, whisk well ¼ tsp pepper, ½ tsp salt, dried oregano, honey, lemon zest, lemon juice, and vinegar. Slowly pour olive oil in a steady stream as you briskly whisk the mixture. Continue whisking until emulsified.*
- ✓ *Add olives and tomatoes, toss to coat with dressing.*
- ✓ *Alternatingly peel cucumber leaving strips of skin on. Trim ends slice lengthwise and chop in ½-inch thick cubes. Add into the container of tomatoes.*
- ✓ *Drain onions and add them into the container of tomatoes. Toss well to coat and mix.*
- ✓ *Drain feta and slice into four equal rectangles.*
- ✓ *Divide Greek salad into serving plates, top each with oregano and feta.*
- ✓ *To serve, season with pepper and drizzle with oil and enjoy.*

Nutrition: Calories: 365.5; Protein: 9.6g; Carbs: 26.2g; Fat: 24.7g

632) Cold Zucchini Noodle Container

Ingredients:

- *¼ cup basil leaves, roughly chopped*
- *¼ cup olive oil*
- *¼ tsp sea salt*
- *½ tsp salt1 tsp garlic powder*
- *1 lb. peeled and uncooked shrimp*
- *1 tsp lemon zest*
- *1 tsp lime zest*
- *2 tbsp butter*
- *2 tbsp lemon juice*
- *2 tbsp lime juice*
- *3 clementine, peeled and separated*
- *4 cups zucchini, spirals, or noodles*
- *pinch of black pepper*

Direction: Servings: 4, Cooking Time: 20 minutes

- ✓ *Make zucchini noodles and set them aside.*
- ✓ *On medium fire, place a large nonstick saucepan and heat butter.*
- ✓ *Meanwhile, pat dry shrimps and season with salt and garlic. Add into a hot saucepan and sauté for 6 minutes or until opaque and cooked.*
- ✓ *Remove from pan, transfer to a container and put aside.*
- ✓ *Right away, add zucchini noodles to a still-hot pan and stir fry for a minute. Leave noodles on the pan as you prepare the dressing.*
- ✓ *Blend well salt, olive oil, juice, and zest in a small container*
- ✓ *Then place noodles into salad container, top with shrimp, pour oil mixture, basil and clementine. Toss to mix well.*
- ✓ *Refrigerate for an hour before serving.*

Nutrition:Cal: 353.4; Carbs: 14.8g; Protein: 24.5g; Fat: 21.8g

633) Coleslaw Asian Style

Ingredients:

- *½ cup chopped fresh cilantro*
- *1 ½ tbsp minced garlic*
- *2 carrots, julienned*
- *2 cups shredded napa cabbage*
- *2 cups thinly sliced red cabbage*
- *2 red bell peppers, thinly sliced*
- *2 tbsp minced fresh ginger root*
- *3 tbsp brown sugar*
- *3 tbsp soy sauce*
- *5 cups thinly sliced green cabbage*
- *5 tbsp creamy peanut butter*
- *6 green onions, chopped*
- *6 tbsp rice wine vinegar*
- *6 tbsp vegetable oil*

Direction: Servings: 10 Cooking Time: 0 minutes

- ✓ *Mix the following thoroughly in a medium container: garlic, ginger, brown sugar, soy sauce, peanut butter, oil, and rice vinegar.*
- ✓ *In a separate container, blend well cilantro, green onions, carrots, bell pepper, Napa cabbage, red cabbage, and green cabbage. Pour to the peanut sauce above and toss to mix well.*
- ✓ *Serve and enjoy.*

Nutrition: Calories: 193.8; Protein: 4g; Fat: 12.6g; Carbs: 16.1g

634) Cucumber and Tomato Salad

Ingredients:

- *Ground pepper to taste*
- *Salt to taste*
- *1 tbsp fresh lemon juice*
- *1 onion, chopped*
- *1 cucumber, peeled and diced*

- *2 tomatoes, chopped*
- *4 cups spinach*

Direction: Servings: 4, Cooking Time: 0 minutes

✓ *In a salad container, mix onions, cucumbers, and tomatoes.*

✓ *Season with pepper and salt to taste.*

✓ *Add lemon juice and mix well.*

✓ *Add spinach, toss to coat, serve and enjoy.*

Nutrition: Calories: 70.3; Fat: 0.3g; Protein: 1.3g; Carbohydrates: 7.1g

635) Cucumber Salad Japanese Style

Ingredients:

- *1 ½ tsp minced fresh ginger root*
- *1 tsp salt*
- *1/3 cup rice vinegar*
- *2 large cucumbers, ribbon cut*
- *4 tsp white sugar*

Direction: Servings: 5 servings Cooking Time: 0 minutes

✓ *Mix well ginger, salt, sugar, and vinegar in a small container.*

✓ *Add ribbon-cut cucumbers and mix well.*

✓ *Let stand for at least one hour to the ref before serving*

Nutrition: Calories: 29; Fat: .2g; Protein: .7g; Carbs: 6.1g

636) Easy Garden Salad with Arugula

Ingredients:

- *¼ cup grated parmesan cheese*
- *¼ cup pine nuts*
- *1 cup cherry tomatoes, halved*
- *1 large avocado, sliced into ½ inch cubes*
- *1 tbsp rice vinegar*
- *2 tbsp olive oil or grapeseed oil*
- *4 cups young arugula leaves, rinsed and dried*
- *Black pepper, freshly ground*
- *Salt to taste*

Direction: Servings: 2 Cooking Time: 0

✓ *Get a container with a cover, big enough to hold the salad, and mix together the parmesan cheese, vinegar, oil, pine nuts, cherry tomatoes, and arugula.*

✓ *Season with pepper and salt according to how you like it. Place the lid and jiggle the covered container to combine the salad.*

✓ *Serve the salad topped with sliced avocadoes.*

Nutrition: Calories: 490.8; Fat: 43.6g; Protein: 9.1g; Carbs: 15.5g

637) Easy Quinoa & Pear Salad

Ingredients:

- *¼ cup chopped parsley*
- *¼ cup chopped scallions*
- *¼ cup lime juice*
- *¼ cup red onion, diced*
- *½ cup diced carrots*
- *½ cup diced celery*
- *½ cup diced cucumber*
- *½ cup diced red pepper*
- *½ cup dried wild blueberries*
- *½ cup olive oil*
- *½ cup spicy pecans, chopped*
- *1 tbsp chopped parsley*
- *1 tsp honey*
- *1 tsp sea salt*
- *2 fresh pears, cut into chunks*
- *3 cups cooked quinoa*

Direction: Servings: 6, Cooking Time: 0 minutes

✓ *In a small container, mix well olive oil, salt, lime juice, honey, and parsley. Set aside.*

✓ *In a large salad container, add resting ingredients and toss to mix well.*

✓ *Pour dressing and toss well to coat.*

✓ *Serve and enjoy.*

Nutrition: Calories: 382; Protein: 5.6g; Carbs: 31.4g; Fat: 26g

638) Easy-Peasy Club Salad

Ingredients:

- *½ cup cherry tomatoes halved*
- *½ Tsp garlic powder*
- *½ Tsp onion powder*
- *1 cup diced cucumber*
- *1 Tbsp Dijon mustard*
- *1 Tbsp milk*
- *1 Tsp dried parsley*
- *2 Tbsps mayonnaise*
- *2 Tbsps sour cream*
- *3 cups romaine lettuce, torn into pieces*
- *3 large hard-boiled eggs, sliced*
- *4 ounces cheddar cheese, cubed*

Direction: Servings: 3, Cooking Time: 0 minutes

✓ *Make the dressing by mixing garlic powder, onion powder, dried parsley, mayonnaise, and sour cream in a small container. Add a Tbsp of milk and mix well. If you want the dressing thinner, you can add more milk.*

✓ *In a salad platter, layer salad ingredients with Dijon mustard to the middle.*

✓ Evenly drizzle with dressing and toss well to coat.

✓ Serve and enjoy.

Nutrition: Calories: 335.5; Protein: 16.8g; Carbs: 7.9g; Fat: 26.3g

639) Fennel and Seared Scallops Salad

Ingredients:

- ¼ tsp salt
- ½ large fennel bulb halved, cored, and very thinly sliced
- ½ tsp whole fennel seeds, freshly ground
- 1 large pink grapefruit
- 1 lb. fresh sea scallops, muscle removed, room temperature
- 1 tbsp olive oil, divided
- 1 tsp raw honey
- 12 whole almonds chopped coarsely and lightly toasted
- 4 cups red leaf lettuce, cored and torn into bite-sized pieces
- A pinch of ground pepper

Direction: Servings: 4, Cooking Time: 10 minutes

✓ To catch the juices, work over a container. Peel and segment grapefruit. Strato the juice in a cup.

✓ For the dressing, whisk together in a small container black pepper, 1/8 tsp salt, 1/8 tsp ground fennel, honey, 2 tsp water, 2 tsp oil, and 3 tbsp of pomegranate juice. Set aside 1 tbsp of the dressing.

✓ Pat scallops dry with a paper Sheet and season with resting salt and ½ tsp ground fennel.

✓ On medium fire, place a nonstick skillet and brush with 1 tsp oil. Once heated, add ½ of scallops and cook until lightly browned or for 5 minutes on each side. Transfer to a plate and keep warm as you cook the second batch using the same process.

✓ Mix together dressing, lettuce and fennel in a large salad container. Divide evenly onto 4 salad plates.

✓ Evenly top each salad with scallops, grapefruit segments, and almonds. Drizzle with reserved dressing, serve and enjoy.

Nutrition: Calories: 231.9; Protein: 25.3g; Carbs: 18.5g; Fat: 6.3g

640) Fruity Asparagus-Quinoa Salad

Ingredients:

- ¼ cup chopped pecans, toasted
- ½ cup finely chopped white onion
- ½ jalapeno pepper, diced
- ½ lb. asparagus, sliced to 2-inch lengths, steamed and chilled
- ½ tsp kosher salt
- 1 cup fresh orange sections
- 1 cup uncooked quinoa
- 1 tsp olive oil
- 2 cups water
- 2 tbsp minced red onion
- 5 dates, pitted and chopped
- Dressing ingredients
- ¼ tsp ground black pepper
- ¼ tsp kosher salt
- 1 garlic clove, minced
- 1 tbsp olive oil
- 2 tbsp chopped fresh mint
- 2 tbsp fresh lemon juice
- Mint sprigs – optional

Direction: Servings: 8, Cooking Time: 25 minutes

✓ Wash and rub with your hands the quinoa in a container at least three times, discarding the water each and every time.

✓ On medium-high fire, place a large nonstick fry pan and heat 1 tsp olive oil. For two minutes, sauté onions before adding quinoa and sautéing for another five minutes.

✓ Add ½ tsp salt and 2 cups water and bring to a boil. Lower fire to a simmer, cover, and cook for 15 minutes. Turn off fire and let stand until water is absorbed.

✓ Add pepper, asparagus, dates, pecans, and orange sections into a salad container. Add cooked quinoa, toss to mix well.

✓ In a small container, whisk mint, garlic, black pepper, salt, olive oil, and lemon juice to create the dressing.

✓ Pour dressing over salad, serve and enjoy.

Nutrition: Calories: 173; Fat: 6.3g; Protein: 4.3g; Carbohydrates: 24.7g

641) Garden Salad with Balsamic Vinegar

Ingredients:

- 1 cup baby arugula
- 1 cup spinach
- 1 tbsp raisins
- 1 tbsp almonds, shaved or chopped
- 1 tbsp balsamic vinegar
- ½ tbsp extra virgin olive oil

Direction: Servings: 1, Cooking Time: 0 minutes

✓ On a plate, mix arugula and spinach.

✓ Top with raisins and almonds.

✓ Drizzle olive oil and balsamic vinegar.

✓ Serve and enjoy.

Nutrition: Cal: 206; Fat: 15 g; Protein: 5g;Carbs:14g

642) Garden Salad with Oranges and Olives

Ingredients:

- ½ cup red wine vinegar

- *1 tbsp extra virgin olive oil*
- *1 tbsp finely chopped celery*
- *1 tbsp finely chopped red onion*
- *16 large ripe black olives*
- *2 garlic cloves*
- *2 navel oranges, peeled and segmented*
- *4 boneless, skinless chicken breasts, 4-oz each*
- *4 garlic cloves, minced*
- *8 cups leaf lettuce, washed and dried*
- *Cracked black pepper to taste*

Direction: Servings: 4 Cooking Time: 15 minutes

- ✓ *Prepare the dressing by mixing the pepper, celery, onion, olive oil, garlic, and vinegar in a small container. Whisk well to combine.*
- ✓ *Lightly grease grate and preheat grill to high.*
- ✓ *Rub chicken with the garlic cloves and discard garlic.*
- ✓ *Grill chicken for 5-6 minutes per side or until cooked through.*
- ✓ *With dressing, serve, and enjoy.*
- ✓ *Remove from grill and let it stand for 5 minutes before cutting into ½-inch strips.*
- ✓ *In 4 serving plates, evenly arrange two cups of lettuce, ¼ of the sliced oranges, and 4 olives per plate.*
- ✓ *Top each plate with ¼ serving of grilled chicken, evenly drizzle*

Nutrition: Calories: 259.8; Protein: 48.9g; Carbs: 12.9g; Fat: 1.4g

643) Garden Salad with Grapes

Ingredients:

- *¼ tsp black pepper*
- *¼ tsp salt*
- *½ tsp stone-ground mustard*
- *1 tsp chopped fresh thyme*
- *1 tsp honey*
- *1 tsp maple syrup*
- *2 cups red grapes, halved*
- *2 tbsp toasted sunflower seed kernels*
- *2 tsp grapeseed oil*
- *3 tbsp red wine vinegar*
- *7 cups loosely packed baby arugula*

Direction: Servings: 6, Cooking Time: 0 minutes

- ✓ *In a small container, whisk together mustard, syrup, honey, and vinegar. Whisking continuously, slowly add oil.*
- ✓ *In a large salad container, mix thyme, seeds, grapes, and arugula.*
- ✓ *Drizzle with the oil dressing, season with pepper and salt.*
- ✓ *Gently toss to coat salad with the dressing.*

Nutrition: Calories: 85.7; Protein: 1.6g; Carbs: 12.4g; Fat: 3.3g

644) Ginger Yogurt Dressed Citrus Salad

Ingredients:

- *2/3 cup minced crystallized ginger*
- *1 16-oz Greek yogurt*
- *¼ tsp ground cinnamon*
- *2 tbsp honey*
- *½ cup dried cranberries*
- *3 navel oranges*
- *2 large tangerines, peeled*
- *1 pink grapefruit, peeled*

Direction: Servings: 6, Cooking Time: minutes

- ✓ *Into sections, break tangerines and grapefruit.*
- ✓ *Cut tangerine sections into half.*
- ✓ *Into thirds, slice grapefruit sections.*
- ✓ *Cut orange pith and peel in half and slice oranges into ¼ inch thick rounds, then quartered.*
- ✓ *In a medium container, mix oranges, grapefruit, tangerines, and juices.*
- ✓ *Add cinnamon, honey, and ½ cup of cranberries.*
- ✓ *Cover and place to the ref for an hour.*
- ✓ *In a small container, mix ginger and yogurt.*
- ✓ *To serve, add a dollop of yogurt dressing onto a serving of fruit and sprinkle with cranberries.*

Nutrition: Calories: 190; Protein: 2.9g; Carbs: 16.7g; Fat: 12.4g

645) Goat Cheese and Oregano Dressing Salad

Ingredients:

- *¾ cup crumbled soft, fresh goat cheese*
- *1 ½ cups diced celery*
- *1 ½ large red bell peppers, diced*
- *1 tbsp chopped fresh oregano*
- *1/3 cup chopped red onion*
- *2 tbsp extra virgin olive oil*
- *2 tbsp fresh lemon juice*
- *4 cups baby spinach leaves, coarsely chopped*

Direction: Servings: 4, Cooking Time: 0 minutes

- ✓ *In a large salad container, mix oregano, lemon juice, and oil.*
- ✓ *Add pepper and salt to taste.*
- ✓ *Mix in red onion, goat cheese, celery, bell peppers, and spinach.*
- ✓ *Toss to coat well, serve and enjoy. Ingredients*

Nutrition: Calories: 110.9; Protein: 6.9g; Carbs: 10.7g; Fat: 4.5g

646) Grape and Walnut Garden Salad

Ingredients:

- ½ cup chopped walnuts, toasted
- 1 ripe persimmon
- ½ cup red grapes halved lengthwise
- 1 shallot, minced
- 1 tsp minced garlic
- 1 tsp whole grain mustard
- 2 tbsp fresh lemon juice
- 3 tbsp extra virgin olive oil
- 6 cups baby spinach

Direction: Servings: 2, Cooking Time: 0 minutes

✓ Cut persimmon and red pear into ½-inch cubes. Discard seeds.

✓ In a medium container, whisk garlic, shallot, olive oil, lemon juice, and mustard to make the dressing.

✓ In a medium salad container, toss to mix spinach, pear, and persimmon.

✓ Pour in dressing and toss to coat well.

✓ Garnish with pecans.

✓ Serve and enjoy.

Nutrition: Calories: 440; Protein: 6.1g; Carbs: 39.1g; Fat: 28.8g

647) Greek Antipasto Salad

Ingredients:

- ½ cup artichoke hearts chipped
- ½ cup olives, sliced
- ½ cup sweet peppers, roasted
- 1 large head romaine lettuce, chopped
- 4 ounces cooked prosciutto, cut into thin strips
- 4 ounces cooked salami, cubed
- Italian dressing to taste

Direction: Servings: 4, Cooking Time: 0 minutes

✓ In a large mixing container, add all the ingredients except the Italian dressing. Mix everything until the vegetables are evenly distributed.

✓ Add the Italian dressing and toss to combine.

✓ Serve chilled.

Nutrition: Calories: 425.8; Fat: 38.9 g; Protein: 39.2 g; Carbs: 12.6 g

648) Grilled Halloumi Cheese Salad

Ingredients:

- 0.5 oz chopped walnuts
- 1 handful baby arugula
- 1 Persian cucumber, sliced into circles about ½-inch thick
- 3 oz halloumi cheese
- 5 grape tomatoes, sliced in half
- balsamic vinegar
- olive oil
- salt

Direction: Servings: 1, Cooking Time: 10 minutes

✓ Into 1/3 slices, cut the cheese. For 4 to 5 minutes on each side, grill the kinds of cheese until you can see grill marks.

✓ In a salad container, add arugula, cucumber, and tomatoes. Drizzle with olive oil and balsamic vinegar. Season with salt and toss well coat.

✓ Sprinkle walnuts and add grilled halloumi.

✓ Serve and enjoy.

Nutrition: Cal: 543; Protein: 21.0g; Carbs: 9.0g; Fat: 47.0g

649) Grilled Eggplant Salad

Ingredients:

- 1 avocado, halved, pitted, peeled, and cubed
- 1 Italian eggplant, cut into 1-inch thick slices
- 1 large red onion, cut into rounds
- 1 lemon, zested
- 1 tbsp coarsely chopped oregano leaves
- 1 tbsp red wine vinegar
- 1 tsp Dijon mustard
- Canola oil
- Freshly ground black pepper
- Honey
- Olive oil
- Parsley sprigs for garnish
- Salt

Direction: Servings: 4, Cooking Time: 18 minutes

✓ With canola oil, brush onions and eggplant and place on grill.

✓ Grill on high until onions are slightly charred and eggplants are soft, around 5 minutes for onions and 8 to 12 minutes for eggplant.

✓ Remove from grill and let cool for 5 minutes.

✓ Roughly chop eggplants and onions and place them in a salad container.

✓ Add avocado and toss to mix.

✓ Whisk oregano, mustard, and red wine vinegar in a small container

✓ Whisk in olive oil and honey to taste. Season with pepper and salt to taste.

✓ Pour dressing into eggplant mixture, toss to mix well.

✓ Garnish with parsley sprigs and lemon zest before serving.

Nutrition: Cal: 190; Protein: 2.9g; Carbs: 16.7g; Fat: 12.4g

650) Grilled Vegetable Salad

Ingredients:

- ¼ cup extra virgin olive oil for brushing

- *¼ cup fresh basil leaves*
- *¼ lb. feta cheese*
- *½ bunch asparagus, trimmed and cut into bite-size pieces*
- *1 medium onion, cut into ½ inch rings*
- *1-pint cherry tomatoes*
- *1 red bell pepper, quartered, seeds and ribs removed*
- *1 yellow bell pepper, quartered, seeds and ribs removed*
- *Pepper and salt to taste*

Direction: Servings: 3 Cooking Time: 7 minutes

- ✓ *Toss olive oil and vegetables in a big container—season with salt and pepper.*
- ✓ *Frill vegetables in a preheated griller for 5-7 minutes or until charred and tender.*
- ✓ *Transfer veggies to a platter, add feta and basil.*
- ✓ *In a separate small container, mix olive oil, balsamic vinegar, garlic seasoned with pepper, and salt.*
- ✓ *Drizzle dressing over vegetables and serve.*

Nutrition: Calories: 147.6; Protein: 3.8g; Fat: 19.2g; Carbs: 13.9 g

651) Healthy Detox Salad

Ingredients:

- *4 cups mixed greens*
- *2 tbsp lemon juice*
- *2 tbsp pumpkin seed oil*
- *1 tbsp chia seeds*
- *2 tbsp almonds, chopped*
- *1 large apple, diced*
- *1 large carrot, coarsely grated*
- *1 large beet, coarsely grated*

Direction: Servings: 4, Cooking Time: 0 minutes

- ✓ *In a medium salad container, except for mixed greens, combine all ingredients thoroughly.*
- ✓ *Into 4 salad plates, divide the mixed greens.*
- ✓ *Evenly top mixed greens with the salad container mixture.*
- ✓ *Serve and enjoy.*

Nutrition: Cal: 141; Protein: 2.1g; Carbs: 14.7g; Fat: 8.2g

652) Herbed Calamari Salad

Ingredients:

- *¼ cup finely chopped cilantro leaves*
- *¼ cup finely chopped mint leaves*
- *¼ tsp freshly ground black pepper*
- *½ cup finely chopped flat-leaf parsley leaves*
- *¾ tsp kosher salt*
- *2 ½ lbs. cleaned and trimmed uncooked calamari rings and tentacles, defrosted*
- *3 medium garlic cloves, smashed and minced*
- *3 tbsp extra virgin olive oil*
- *A pinch of crushed red pepper flakes*
- *Juice of 1 large lemon*
- *Peel of 1 lemon, thinly sliced into strips*

Direction: Servings: 6, Cooking Time: 25 minutes

- ✓ *On a nonstick large fry pan, heat 1 ½ tbsp olive oil. Once hot, sauté garlic until fragrant for around a minute.*
- ✓ *Add calamari, making sure that they are in one layer. If the pan is too small, then cook in batches.*
- ✓ *Season with pepper and salt. After 2 to 4 minutes of searing, remove calamari from the pan with a slotted spoon and transfer it to a large container.*
- ✓ *Continue cooking the remainder of calamari.*
- ✓ *Season cooked calamari with herbs, lemon rind, lemon juice, red pepper flakes, pepper, salt, and resting olive oil.*
- ✓ *Toss well to coat, serve and enjoy*

Nutrition: Cal: 551.7; Protein: 7.3g; Carbs: 121.4g; Fat: 4.1g

653) Herbed Chicken Salad Greek Style

Ingredients:

- *¼ cup or 1 oz crumbled feta cheese*
- *½ tsp garlic powder*
- *½ tsp salt*
- *¾ tsp black pepper, divided*
- *1 cup grape tomatoes, halved*
- *1 cup peeled and chopped English cucumbers*
- *1 cup plain fat-free yogurt*
- *1 pound skinless, boneless chicken breast, cut into 1-inch cubes*
- *1 tsp bottled minced garlic*
- *1 tsp ground oregano*
- *2 tsp sesame seed paste or tahini*
- *5 tsp fresh lemon juice, divided*
- *6 pitted kalamata olives, halved*
- *8 cups chopped romaine lettuce*
- *Cooking spray*

Direction: Servings: 6 Cooking Time: 0 minutes

- ✓ *In a container, mix together ¼ tsp salt, ½ tsp pepper, garlic powder, and oregano. Then on medium-high heat, place a skillet and coat with cooking spray and sauté together with the spice mixture and chicken until chicken is cooked. Before transferring to a container, drizzle with juice.*
- ✓ *In a small container, mix the following: garlic, tahini, yogurt, ¼ tsp pepper, ¼ tsp salt, and 2 tsp juice thoroughly.*
- ✓ *In another container, mix together olives,*

tomatoes, cucumber, and lettuce.

- ✓ *To Serve salad, place 2 ½ cups of lettuce mixture on the plate, topped with ½ cup chicken mixture, 3 tbsp yogurt mixture, and 1 tbsp of cheese.*

Nutrition: Calories: 170.1; Fat: 3.7g; Protein: 20.7g; Carbs: 13.5g

654) ***Kale Salad Recipe***

Ingredients:

- *¼ cup Kalamata olives*
- *½ of a lemon*
- *1 ½ tbsp flaxseeds*
- *1 garlic clove, minced*
- *1 small cucumber, sliced thinly*
- *1 tbsp extra virgin olive oil*
- *2 tbsp green onion, chopped*
- *2 tbsp red onion, minced*
- *6 cups dinosaur kale, chopped*
- *a pinch of dried basil*
- *a pinch of salt*

Direction: Servings: 4, Cooking Time: 7 minutes

- ✓ *Bring a medium pot, half filled with water, to a boil.*
- ✓ *Rinse kale and cut it into small strips. Place in a steamer and put on top of boiling water and steam for 5 – 7 minutes.*
- ✓ *Transfer steamed kale to a salad container.*
- ✓ *Season kale with oil, salt, basil, and lemon. Toss to coat well.*
- ✓ *Add resting ingredients into salad container, toss to mix.*
- ✓ *Serve and enjoy.*

Nutrition: Calories: 92.7; Protein: 2.4g; Carbs: 6.6g; Fat: 6.3g

655) ***Cauliflower Tabbouleh Salad***

Ingredients:

- *6 Tbsps extra-virgin olive oil, divided*
- *4 cups riced cauliflower*
- *3 garlic cloves, finely minced*
- *1½ Tbsps salt*
- *½ Tsp freshly ground black pepper*
- *½ large cucumber, peeled, seeded, and chopped*
- *½ cup chopped mint leaves*
- *½ cup chopped Italian parsley*
- *½ cup chopped pitted Kalamata olives*
- *2 Tbsps minced red onion*
- *Juice of 1 lemon (about 2 Tbsps)*
- *2 cups baby arugula or spinach leaves*
- *2 medium avocados, peeled, pitted, and diced*
- *1 cup quartered cherry tomatoes*

Direction: Prep time: 15 minutes | Cook time: 5 minutes | Serves 6

- ✓ *In a large skillet, heat 2 Tbsps of olive oil over medium-high heat. Add the riced cauliflower, garlic, salt, and pepper and sauté until just tender but not mushy, 3 to 4 minutes. Remove from the heat and place in a large container.*
- ✓ *Add the cucumber, mint, parsley, olives, red onion, lemon juice, and resting 4 Tbsps olive oil and toss well. A place to the fridge, uncovered, and refrigerate for at least 30 minutes, or up to 2 hours.*
- ✓ *Before serving, add the arugula, avocado, and tomatoes and toss to combine well—season to taste with salt and pepper and serve cold or at room temperature.*

Nutrition: cal: 235 | fat: 21g | protein: 4g | carbs:12g

656) ***Beet Summer Salad***

Ingredients:

- *6 medium to large fresh red or yellow beets*
- *⅓ cup plus 1 Tbsp extra-virgin olive oil, divided*
- *4 heads of Treviso radicchio*
- *2 shallots, peeled and sliced*
- *¼ cup lemon juice*
- *½ Tsp salt*
- *6 ounces (170 g) feta cheese, crumbled*

Direction: Prep time: 20 minutes | Cook time: 40 minutes | Serves 4 to 6

- ✓ *Switch on the oven, preheat it setting its temperature to 400°F (205°C).*
- ✓ *Cut off the stems and roots of the beets. Wash the beets thoroughly and dry them off with a paper towel.*
- ✓ *Peel the beets using a vegetable peeler. Cut into ½-inch pieces and put them into a large container.*
- ✓ *Add 1 Tbsp of olive oil to the container and toss to coat, then pour the beets out onto a baking sheet. Spread the beets so that they are evenly distributed.*
- ✓ *Bake for 35 to 40 minutes until the beets are tender, turning once or twice with a spatula.*
- ✓ *When the beets are done cooking, set them aside and let them cool for 10 minutes.*
- ✓ *While the beets are cooling, cut the radicchio into 1-inch pieces and place it on a serving dish.*
- ✓ *Once the beets have cooled, spoon them over the radicchio, then evenly distribute the shallots over the beets.*
- ✓ *In a small container, whisk together the resting ⅓ cup of olive oil, lemon juice, and salt. Drizzle the layered salad with dressing. Finish off the salad with feta cheese on top.*

Nutrition: calories: 389 | fat: 31g | protein: 10g | carbs: 22g | fiber: 5g | sodium: 893mg

657) Tomato and Lentil Salad with Feta

Ingredients:

- 3 cups water
- 1 cup brown or green lentils, picked over and rinsed
- 1½ Tsp salt, divided
- 2 large ripe tomatoes
- 2 Persian cucumbers
- ⅓ cup lemon juice
- ½ cup extra-virgin olive oil
- 1 cup crumbled feta cheese

Direction: Prep time: 10 minutes | Cook time: 30 minutes | Serves 4

- ✓ In a large pot over medium heat, bring the water, lentils, and 1 Tsp of salt to a simmer, then reduce heat to low. Cover the pot and continue to cook, occasionally stirring, for 30 minutes. (The lentils should be cooked so that they no longer have a crunch but still hold their form. You should be able to smooth the lentil between your two fingers when pinched.)
- ✓ Once the lentils are done cooking, strato them to remove any excess water and put them into a large container. Let cool.
- ✓ Dice the tomatoes and cucumbers, then add them to the lentils.
- ✓ In a small container, whisk together the lemon juice, olive oil, and resting ½ Tsp salt.
- ✓ Pour the dressing over the lentils and vegetables. Add the feta cheese to the container and gently toss all of the ingredients together.

Nutrition: calories: 521 | fat: 36g | protein: 18g | carbs: 35g | fiber: 15g | sodium: 1304mg

658) Quinoa and Garbanzo Salad

Ingredients:

- 4 cups water
- 2 cups red or yellow quinoa
- 2 Tbsps salt, divided
- 1 cup thinly sliced onions (red or white)
- 1 (16-ounce / 454-g) canned garbanzo beans, rinsed and drained
- ⅓ cup extra-virgin olive oil
- ¼ cup lemon juice
- 1 Tsp freshly ground black pepper

Direction: Prep time: 10 minutes | Cook time: 30 minutes | Serves 8

- ✓ In a 3-quart pot over medium heat, bring the water to a boil.
- ✓ Add the quinoa and 1 Tsp of salt to the pot. Stir, cover, and let cook over low heat for 15 to 20 minutes.
- ✓ Turn off the heat, fluff the quinoa with a fork, cover again, and let stand for 5 to 10 more minutes.
- ✓ Put the cooked quinoa, onions, and garbanzo beans in a large container.
- ✓ In a separate small container, whisk together the olive oil, lemon juice, resting 1 Tsp of salt, and black pepper.
- ✓ Add the dressing to the quinoa mixture and gently toss everything together. Serve warm or cold.

Nutrition: calories: 318 | fat: 6g | protein: 9g | carbs: 43g | fiber: 13g | sodium: 585mg

659) Winter Salad with Red Wine Vinaigrette

Ingredients:

- 1 small green apple, thinly sliced
- 6 stalks kale, stems removed and greens roughly chopped
- ½ cup crumbled feta cheese
- ½ cup dried currants
- ½ cup chopped pitted Kalamata olives
- ½ cup thinly sliced radicchio
- 2 scallions, both green and white parts, thinly sliced
- ¼ cup peeled, julienned carrots
- 2 celery stalks, thinly sliced
- ¼ cup Red Wine Vinaigrette
- Salt and freshly ground black pepper, to taste (optional)

Direction: Prep time: 10 minutes | Cook time: 0 minutes | Serves 4

- ✓ In a large container, combine the apple, kale, feta, currants, olives, radicchio, scallions, carrots, and celery and mix well
- ✓ Drizzle with the vinaigrette. Season with salt and pepper (if using), then serve.

Nutrition: calories: 253 | fat: 15g | protein: 6g | carbs: 29g | fiber: 4g | sodium: 480mg

660) Avocado and Hearts of Palm Salad

Ingredients:

- 2 (14-ounce / 397-g) cans hearts of palm, drained and cut into ½-inch-thick slices
- 1 avocado, cut into ½-inch pieces
- 1 cup halved yellow cherry tomatoes
- ½ small shallot, thinly sliced
- ¼ cup coarsely chopped flat-leaf parsley
- 2 Tbsps low-fat mayonnaise
- 2 Tbsps extra-virgin olive oil
- ¼ Tsp salt
- ⅛ Tsp freshly ground black pepper

Direction: Prep time: 10 minutes | Cook time: 0 minutes | Serves 4

- ✓ *In a large container, toss the hearts of palm, avocado, tomatoes, shallot, and parsley.*
- ✓ *In a small container, whisk the mayonnaise, olive oil, salt, and pepper, then mix into the large container.*

Nutrition: calories: 192 | fat: 15g | protein: 5g | carbs: 14g | fiber: 7g | sodium: 841mg

661) Tuna Salad

Ingredients:

- *4 cups spring mix greens*
- *1 (15-ounce / 425-g) canned cannellini beans, drained*
- *2 (5-ounce / 142-g) cans water-packed, white albacore tuna, drained*
- *⅔ cup crumbled feta cheese*
- *½ cup thinly sliced sun-dried tomatoes*
- *¼ cup sliced pitted Kalamata olives*
- *¼ cup thinly sliced scallions, both green and white parts*
- *3 Tbsps extra-virgin olive oil*
- *½ Tsp dried cilantro*
- *2 or 3 leaves thinly chopped fresh sweet basil*
- *1 lime, zested and juiced*
- *Kosher salt and freshly ground black pepper, to taste*

Direction: Prep time: 10 minutes | Cook time: 0 minutes | Serves 4

- ✓ *In a large container, combine greens, beans, tuna, feta, tomatoes, olives, scallions, olive oil, cilantro, basil, and lime juice, and zest. Season with salt and pepper, mix, and enjoy!*

Nutrition: calories: 355 | fat: 19g | protein: 22g | carbs: 25g | fiber: 8g | sodium: 744mg

662) Kale Salad with Anchovy Dressing

Ingredients:

- *1 large bunch lacinato or dinosaur kale*
- *¼ cup toasted pine nuts*
- *1 cup shaved or coarsely shredded fresh Parmesan cheese*
- *¼ cup extra-virgin olive oil*
- *8 anchovy fillets, roughly chopped*
- *2 to 3 Tbsps freshly squeezed lemon juice (from 1 large lemon)*
- *2 Tbsps red pepper flakes (optional)*

Direction: Prep time: 15 minutes | Cook time: 0 minutes | Serves 4

- ✓ *Remove the rough center stems from the kale leaves and roughly tear each leaf into about 4-by-1-inch strips. Place the torn kale in a large container and add the pine nuts and cheese.*
- ✓ *In a small container, whisk together the olive oil, anchovies, lemon juice, and red pepper flakes (if using). Drizzle over the salad and toss to coat well. Let sit at room temperature 30 minutes before serving, tossing again just prior to serving.*

Nutrition: calories: 337 | fat: 25g | protein: 16g | carbs: 12g | fiber: 2g | sodium: 603mg

663) Authentic Greek Salad

Ingredients:

- *2 large English cucumbers*
- *4 Roma tomatoes, quartered*
- *1 green bell pepper, cut into 1-to 1½-inch chunks*
- *¼ small red onion, thinly sliced*
- *4 ounces (113 g) pitted Kalamata olives*
- *¼ cup extra-virgin olive oil*
- *2 Tbsps freshly squeezed lemon juice*
- *1 Tbsp red wine vinegar*
- *1 Tbsp chopped fresh oregano or 1 Tsp dried oregano*
- *¼ Tsp freshly ground black pepper*
- *4 ounces (113 g) crumbled traditional feta cheese*

Direction: Prep time: 10 minutes | Cook time: 0 minutes | Serves 4

- ✓ *Cut the cucumbers in half lengthwise and then into ½-inch-thick half-moons. Place in a large container.*
- ✓ *Add the quartered tomatoes, bell pepper, red onion, and olives.*
- ✓ *In a small container, whisk together the olive oil, lemon juice, vinegar, oregano, and pepper. Drizzle over the vegetables and toss to coat.*
- ✓ *Divide between salad plates and top each with 1 ounce (28 g) of feta.*

Nutrition: calories: 278 | fat: 22g | protein: 8g | carbs: 12g | fiber: 4g | sodium: 572mg

664) Israeli Salad

Ingredients:

- *¼ cup pine nuts*
- *¼ cup shelled pistachios*
- *¼ cup coarsely chopped walnuts*
- *¼ cup shelled pumpkin seeds*
- *¼ cup shelled sunflower seeds*
- *2 large English cucumbers, unpeeled and finely chopped*
- *1-pint cherry tomatoes, finely chopped*
- *½ small red onion, finely chopped*
- *½ cup finely chopped fresh flat-leaf Italian parsley*
- *¼ cup extra-virgin olive oil*
- *2 to 3 Tbsps freshly squeezed lemon juice (from 1 lemon)*

- *1 Tsp salt*
- *¼ Tsp freshly ground black pepper*
- *4 cups baby arugula*

Direction: Prep time: 15 minutes | Cook time: 6 minutes | Serves 4

- ✓ *In a large dry skillet, toast the pine nuts, pistachios, walnuts, pumpkin seeds, and sunflower seeds over medium-low heat until golden and fragrant, 5 to 6 minutes, being careful not to burn them. Remove from the heat and set aside.*
- ✓ *In a large container, combine the cucumber, tomatoes, red onion, and parsley.*
- ✓ *In a small container, whisk together olive oil, lemon juice, salt, and pepper. Pour over the chopped vegetables and toss to coat.*
- ✓ *Add the toasted nuts and seeds and arugula and toss with the salad to blend well. Serve at room temperature or chilled.*

Nutrition: calories: 414 | fat: 34g | protein: 10g | carbs: 17g | fiber: 6g | sodium: 642mg

665) Tahini Barley Salad

Ingredients:

- *1½ cups pearl barley*
- *5 Tbsps extra-virgin olive oil, divided*
- *1½ Tbsps table salt, for cooking barley*
- *¼ cup tahini*
- *1 Tsp grated lemon zest plus ¼ cup juice (2 lemons)*
- *1 Tbsp sumac, divided*
- *1 garlic clove, minced*
- *¾ Tsp table salt*
- *1 English cucumber, cut into ½-inch pieces*
- *1 carrot, peeled and shredded*
- *1 red bell pepper, stemmed, seeded, and chopped*
- *4 scallions, thinly sliced*
- *2 Tbsps finely chopped jarred hot cherry peppers*
- *¼ cup coarsely chopped fresh mint*

Direction: Prep time: 20 minutes | Cook time: 8 minutes | Serves 4 to 6

- ✓ *Combine 6 cups water, barley, 1 Tbsp oil, and 1½ Tbsps salt in Instant Pot. Lock lid in place and close pressure release valve. Select high-pressure cook function and cook for 8 minutes. Turn off Instant Pot and let the pressure release naturally for 15 minutes. Quick-release any resting pressure, then carefully remove the lid, allowing steam to escape away from you. Drain barley spread onto a rimmed baking sheet, and let cool completely for about 15 minutes.*
- ✓ *Meanwhile, whisk resting ¼ cup oil, tahini, 2 Tbsps water, lemon zest and juice, 1 Tsp sumac, garlic, and ¾ Tsp salt in a large container until combined; let sit for 15 minutes*
- ✓ *Measure out and reserve ½ cup dressing for serving. Add barley, cucumber, carrot, bell pepper, scallions, and cherry peppers to a container with dressing and gently toss to combine. Season with salt and pepper to taste. Transfer salad to serving dish and sprinkle with mint and resting 2 Tbsps sumac. Serve, passing reserved dressing separately.*

Nutrition: calories: 370 | fat: 18g | protein: 8g | carbs: 47g | fiber: 10g | sodium: 510mg

666) Arugula, Watermelon, and Feta Salad

Ingredients:

- *3 cups packed arugula*
- *2½ cups watermelon, cut into bite-size cubes*
- *2 ounces (57 g) feta cheese, crumbled*
- *2 Tbsps balsamic glaze*

Direction: Prep time: 10 minutes | Cook time: 0 minutes | Serves 2

- ✓ *Divide the arugula between two plates.*
- ✓ *Divide the watermelon cubes between the beds of the arugula.*
- ✓ *Sprinkle 1 ounce (28 g) of the feta over each salad.*
- ✓ *Drizzle about 1 Tbsp of the glaze (or more if desired) over each salad.*

Nutrition: calories: 159 | fat: 7g | protein: 6g | carbs: 21g | fiber: 1g | sodium: 327mg

667) Orange Avocado and Almond Salad

Ingredients:

- *2 large Gala apples, chopped*
- *2 oranges, segmented and chopped*
- *⅓ cup sliced almonds*
- *½ cup honey*
- *1 Tbsp extra-virgin olive oil*
- *½ Tsp grated orange zest*
- *1 large avocado, semi-ripened, medium diced*

Direction: Prep time: 10 minutes | Cook time: 0 minutes | Serves 5 to 6

- ✓ *In a large container, combine the apples, oranges, and almonds. Mix gently.*
- ✓ *In a small container, whisk the honey, oil, and orange zest. Set aside.*
- ✓ *Drizzle the orange zest mix over the fruit salad and toss. Add the avocado and toss gently one more time.*

Nutrition: calories: 296 | fat: 12g | protein: 3g | carbs: 50g | fiber: 7g | sodium: 4mg

668) Greek Vegetable Salad

Ingredients:

- *1 head iceberg lettuce*
- *2 cups cherry tomatoes*

- *1 large cucumber*
- *1 medium onion*
- *½ cup extra-virgin olive oil*
- *¼ cup lemon juice*
- *1 Tsp salt*
- *1 clove garlic, minced*
- *1 cup Kalamata olives, pitted*
- *1 (6-ounce / 170-g) package feta cheese, crumbled*

Direction: Prep time: 10 minutes | Cook time: 0 minutes | Serves 4 to 6

- ✓ *Cut the lettuce into 1-inch pieces and put them in a large salad container.*
- ✓ *Cut the tomatoes in half and add them to the salad container.*
- ✓ *Slice the cucumber into bite-size pieces and add them to the salad container.*
- ✓ *Thinly slice the onion and add it to the salad container.*
- ✓ *In another small container, whisk together the olive oil, lemon juice, salt, and garlic. Pour the dressing over the salad and gently toss to evenly coat.*
- ✓ *Top the salad with the Kalamata olives and feta cheese and serve.*

Nutrition: calories: 539 | fat: 50g | protein: 9g | carbs: 17g | fiber: 4g | sodium: 1758mg

669) Balsamic Baby Spinach Salad

Ingredients:

- *1 large ripe tomato*
- *1 medium red onion*
- *½ Tsp fresh lemon zest*
- *3 Tbsps balsamic vinegar*
- *¼ cup extra-virgin olive oil*
- *½ Tsp salt*
- *1 pound (454 g) baby spinach, washed, stems removed*

Direction: Prep time: 10 minutes | Cook time: 0 minutes | Serves 4

- ✓ *Dice the tomato into ¼-inch pieces and slice the onion into long slivers.*
- ✓ *In a small container, whisk together the lemon zest, balsamic vinegar, olive oil, and salt.*
- ✓ *Put the spinach, tomatoes, and onions in a large container. Pour the dressing over the salad and lightly toss to coat.*

Nutrition: calories: 172 | fat: 14g | protein: 4g | carbs: 9g | fiber: 4g | sodium: 389mg

670) Tabouli Salad

Ingredients:

- *1 cup bulgur wheat, grind*
- *4 cups Italian parsley, finely chopped*
- *2 cups ripe tomato, finely diced*
- *1 cup green onion, finely chopped*
- *½ cup lemon juice*
- *½ cup extra-virgin olive oil*
- *1½ Tbsps salt*
- *1 Tsp dried mint*

Direction: Prep time: 10 minutes | Cook time: 0 minutes | Serves 8 to 10

- ✓ *Before you chop the vegetables, put the bulgur in a small container. Rinse with water, drain, and let stand to the container while you prepare the other ingredients.*
- ✓ *Put the parsley, tomatoes, green onion, and bulgur into a large container.*
- ✓ *In a small container, whisk together the lemon juice, olive oil, salt, and mint.*
- ✓ *Pour the dressing over the tomato, onion, and bulgur mixture, tossing everything together. Add additional salt to taste. Serve immediately or store in the fridge for up to 2 days.*

Nutrition: calories: 207 | fat: 14g | protein: 4g | carbs: 19g | fiber: 5g | sodium: 462mg

671) Fig, Prosciutto and Arugula Salad

Ingredients:

- *3 cups arugula*
- *4 fresh, ripe figs (or 4 to 6 dried figs), stemmed and sliced*
- *2 Tbsps olive oil*
- *3 very thin slices of prosciutto, trimmed of any fat and sliced lengthwise into 1-inch strips*
- *¼ cup pecan halves, lightly toasted*
- *2 Tbsps crumbled blue cheese*
- *1 to 2 Tbsps balsamic glaze*

Direction: Prep time: 10 minutes | Cook time: 1 minute | Serves 2

- ✓ *In a large container, toss the arugula and figs with olive oil.*
- ✓ *Place the prosciutto on a microwave-safe plate and heat it on high to the microwave for 60 seconds, or until it just starts to crisp.*
- ✓ *Add the crisped prosciutto, pecans, and blue cheese to the container. Toss the salad lightly.*
- ✓ *Drizzle with the balsamic glaze.*

Nutrition: calories: 519 | fat: 38g | protein: 20g | carbs: 29g | fiber: 6g | sodium: 482mg

672) Panzanella Salad

Ingredients:

- *Cooking spray*
- *1 ear corn on the cob, peeled and shucked*
- *4 slices stale French baguette*
- *½ pint cherry or grape tomatoes halved*
- *1 medium sweet pepper, seeded, and cut into 1-*

inch pieces

- *1 medium avocado, pitted, and cut into cubes*
- *4 very thin slices of sweet onion, cut crosswise into thin rings*
- *½ cup fresh whole basil leaves*
- *2 ounces (57 g) mini Mozzarella balls (ciliegine), halved or quartered*
- *¼ cup honey balsamic dressing*

Direction: Prep time: 10 minutes | Cook time: 11 minutes | Serves 2

✓ *Heat the grill to medium-high heat (about 350°F (180°C)) and lightly spray the cooking grates with cooking spray.*

✓ *Grill the corn for 10 minutes, or until it is lightly charred all around.*

✓ *Grill the bread for 30 to 45 seconds on each side, or until it has grill marks.*

✓ *Let the corn sit until it's cool enough to handle. Cut the kernels off the cob and place them in a large container.*

✓ *Cut the bread into chunks and add it to the container.*

✓ *Add the tomatoes, sweet pepper, avocado, onion, basil, Mozzarella, and dressing to the container, and toss lightly to combine. Let the salad sit for about 15 minutes in the fridge, so the bread can soften, and the flavors can blend.*

✓ *This is best served shortly after it's prepared.*

Nutrition: calories: 525 | fat: 26g | protein: 16g | carbs: 60g | fiber: 10g | sodium: 524mg

673) Citrus Fennel and Pecan Salad

Ingredients:

- *For the Dressing:*
- *2 Tbsps fresh orange juice*
- *3 Tbsps olive oil*
- *1 Tbsp blood orange vinegar, other orange vinegar, or cider vinegar*
- *1 Tbsp honey*
- *Salt, to taste*
- *Freshly ground black pepper, to taste*

For the Salad:

- *2 cups packed baby kale*
- *1 medium navel or blood orange, segmented*
- *½ small fennel bulb, stems and leaves removed, sliced into matchsticks*
- *3 Tbsps toasted pecans, chopped*
- *2 ounces (57 g) goat cheese, crumbled*

Direction: Prep time: 10 minutes | Cook time: 0 minutes | Serves 2

✓ *Make the Dressing*

✓ *Combine the orange juice, olive oil, vinegar, and honey in a small container and whisk to combine. Season with salt and pepper. Set the dressing aside.*

✓ *Make the Salad*

✓ *Divide the baby kale, orange segments, fennel, pecans, and goat cheese evenly between two plates.*

✓ *Drizzle half of the dressing over each salad.*

Nutrition: calories: 502 | fat: 39g | protein: 13g | carbs: 30g | fiber: 6g | sodium: 158mg

674) Pistachio-Parmesan Kale and Arugula Salad

Ingredients:

- *6 cups raw kale, center ribs removed and discarded, leaves coarsely chopped*
- *¼ cup extra-virgin olive oil*
- *2 Tbsps freshly squeezed lemon juice*
- *½ Tsp smoked paprika*
- *2 cups arugula*
- *⅓ cup unsalted shelled pistachios*
- *6 Tbsps grated Parmesan or Pecorino Romano cheese*

Direction: Prep time: 10 minutes | Cook time: minutes | Serves 6

✓ *In a large salad container, combine the kale, oil, lemon juice, and smoked paprika. With your hands, gently massage the leaves for about 15 seconds or so until all are thoroughly coated. Let the kale sit for 10 minutes.*

✓ *When you're ready to serve, gently mix to the arugula and pistachios. Divide the salad among six serving containers, sprinkle 1 Tbsp of grated cheese over each, and serve.*

Nutrition: calories: 105 | fat: 9g | protein: 4g | carbs: 3g | fiber: 2g | sodium: 176mg

675) Italian Celery and Orange Salad

Ingredients:

- *3 celery stalks, including leaves, sliced diagonally into ½-inch slices*
- *2 large oranges, peeled and sliced into rounds*
- *½ cup green olives (or any variety)*
- *¼ cup sliced red onion*
- *1 Tbsp extra-virgin olive oil*
- *1 Tbsp olive brine*
- *1 Tbsp freshly squeezed lemon or orange juice*
- *¼ Tsp kosher or sea salt*
- *¼ Tsp freshly ground black pepper*

Direction: Prep time: 10 minutes | Cook time: 0 minutes | Serves 6

✓ *Place the celery, oranges, olives, and onion on a large serving platter or in a shallow, wide container.*

✓ *In a small container, whisk together the oil, olive brine, and lemon juice. Pour over the salad, sprinkle with salt and pepper, and serve.*

Nutrition: calories: 21 | fat: 1g | protein: 1g | carbs: 1g | fiber: 1g | sodium: 138mg

676) Cantaloupe Caprese Salad

Ingredients:

- 1 cantaloupe, quartered and seeded
- ½ small seedless watermelon
- 1 cup grape tomatoes
- 2 cups fresh Mozzarella balls
- ⅓ cup fresh basil or mint leaves, torn into small pieces
- 2 Tbsps extra-virgin olive oil
- 1 Tbsp balsamic vinegar
- ¼ Tsp freshly ground black pepper
- ¼ Tsp kosher or sea salt

Direction: Prep time: 10 minutes | Cook time: 0 minutes | Serves 6

✓ Using a melon baller or a metal, Tsp-size measuring spoon, scoop balls out of the cantaloupe. You should get about 2½ to 3 cups from one cantaloupe. (If you prefer, cut the melon into bite-size pieces instead of making balls.) Put them in a large colander over a large serving container.

✓ Using the same method, ball or cut the watermelon into bite-size pieces; you should get about 2 cups. Put the watermelon balls to the colander with the cantaloupe.

✓ Let the fruit drain for 10 minutes. Pour the juice from the container into a container to refrigerate and save for drinking or adding to smoothies. Wipe the container dry, and put to the cut fruit.

✓ Add the tomatoes, Mozzarella, basil, oil, vinegar, pepper, and salt to the fruit mixture. Gently mix until everything is incorporated and serve.

Nutrition: calories: 58 | fat: 2g | protein: 1g | carbs: 8g | fiber: 1g | sodium: 156mg

677) Zesty Spanish Potato Salad

Ingredients:

- 4 russet potatoes, peeled and chopped
- 3 large hard-boiled eggs, chopped
- 1 cup frozen mixed vegetables, thawed
- ½ cup plain, unsweetened, full-fat Greek yogurt
- 5 Tbsps pitted Spanish olives
- ½ Tsp freshly ground black pepper
- ½ Tsp dried mustard seed
- ½ Tbsp freshly squeezed lemon juice ½ Tsp dried dill
- Salt, to taste

Direction: Prep time: 10 minutes | Cook time: 5 to 7 minutes | Serves 6 to 8

✓ Place the potatoes in a large pot of water and boil for 5 to 7 minutes, until just fork-tender, checking periodically for doneness. You don't have to overcook them.

✓ Meanwhile, in a large container, mix the eggs, vegetables, yogurt, olives, pepper, mustard, lemon juice, and dill—season with salt to taste. Once the potatoes are cooled somewhat, add them to the large container, then toss well and serve.

Nutrition: calories: 192 | fat: 5g | protein: 9g | carbs: 30g | fiber: 2g | sodium: 59mg

678) Arugula and Walnut Salad

Ingredients:

- 4 Tbsps extra-virgin olive oil
- Zest and juice of 2 clementines or 1 orange (2 to 3 Tbsps)
- 1 Tbsp red wine vinegar
- ½ Tsp salt
  ¼ Tsp freshly ground black pepper
- 8 cups baby arugula
- 1 cup coarsely chopped walnuts
- 1 cup crumbled goat cheese
- ½ cup pomegranate seeds

Direction: calories: 355 | fat: 19g | protein: 22g | carbs: 25g | fiber: 8g | sodium: 744mg

✓ In a small container, whisk together the olive oil, zest and juice, vinegar, salt, and pepper and set aside.

✓ To assemble the salad for serving in a large container, combine the arugula, walnuts, goat cheese, and pomegranate seeds. Drizzle with the dressing and toss to coat.

Nutrition: calories: 444 | fat: 40g | protein: 10g | carbs: 11g | fiber: 3g | sodium: 412mg

679) Tricolor Summer Salad

Ingredients:

- ¼ cup while balsamic vinegar
- 2 Tbsps Dijon mustard
- 1 Tbsp sugar
- ½ Tsp garlic salt
- ½ Tsp freshly ground black pepper
- ¼ cup extra-virgin olive oil
- 1½ cups chopped orange, yellow, and red tomatoes
- ½ cucumber, peeled and diced
- 1 small red onion, thinly sliced
- ¼ cup crumbled feta (optional)

Direction: Prep time: 10 minutes | Cook time: 0 minutes | Serves 3 to 4

✓ In a small container, whisk the vinegar, mustard, sugar, pepper, and garlic salt. Then slowly whisk to the olive oil.

✓ In a large container, add the tomatoes, cucumber, and red onion. Add the dressing. Toss once or twice, and serve with the feta crumbles (if desired) sprinkled on top.

Nutrition: calories: 246 | fat: 18g | protein: 1g | carbs: 19g | fiber: 2g | sodium: 483mg

Sauces, Dips, and Dressings

680) Herbed Olive Oil

Ingredients:

- ½ cup extra-virgin olive oil
- 1 Tsp dried basil
- 1 Tsp dried parsley
- 1 Tsp fresh rosemary leaves 2 Tbsps dried oregano
- ⅛ Tsp salt

Direction: Prep time: 5 minutes | Cook time: 0 minutes | Serves 2

✓ Pour the oil into a small container and stir to the basil, parsley, rosemary, oregano, and salt while whisking the oil with a fork.

Nutrition: calories: 486 | fat: 54g | protein:1 g | carbs: 2g | fiber: 1g | sodium: 78mg

681) Red Wine Vinaigrette

Ingredients:

- ¼ cup plus 2 Tbsps extra-virgin olive oil
- 2 Tbsps red wine vinegar
- 1 and ½ Tbsp apple cider vinegar
- 2 Tbsps honey
- 2 Tbsps Dijon mustard
- ½ Tsp minced garlic
- ⅛ Tsp kosher salt
- ⅛ Tsp freshly ground black pepper

Direction: Prep time: 5 minutes | Cook time: 0 minutes | Serves 2

✓ In a jar, combine the vinegar, lemon juice, and zest. Season with salt and pepper, cover, and shake well.

Nutrition: calories: 386 | fat: 41g | protein: 0g | carbs: 6g | fiber: 0g | sodium: 198mg

682) Apple Cider Dressing

Ingredients:

- 2 Tbsps apple cider vinegar
- ⅓ lemon, juiced
- ⅓ lemon, zested
- Salt and freshly ground black pepper, to taste

Direction: Prep time: 5 minutes | Cook time: 0 minutes | Serves 2

✓ In a jar, combine the vinegar, lemon juice, and zest. Season with salt and pepper, cover, and shake well.

Nutrition: calories: 4 | fat: 0g | protein: 0g | carbs: 1g | fiber: 0g | sodium: 0mg

683) Cucumber Yogurt Dip

Ingredients:

- 1 cup plain, unsweetened, full-fat Greek yogurt
- ½ cup cucumber, peeled, seeded, and diced
- 1 Tbsp freshly squeezed lemon juice
- 1 Tbsp chopped fresh mint
- 1 small garlic clove, minced
- Salt and freshly ground black pepper, to taste

Direction: Prep time: 5 minutes | Cook time: 0 minutes | Serves 2 to 3

✓ In a food processor, combine the cucumber, yogurt, lemon juice, mint, and garlic.

✓ Pulse several times to mix, leaving noticeable cucumber chunks.

✓ Taste and season with salt and pepper.

Nutrition: ca: 128 | fat: 6g | protein: 11g | carbs: 7g | fiber: 0g

684) Oregano Cucumber Dressing

Ingredients:

- 1½ cups plain, unsweetened, full-fat Greek yogurt
- 1 cucumber, seeded and peeled
- ½ lemon, juiced and zested
- 1 Tbsp dried, minced garlic
- ½ Tbsp dried dill
- 2 Tbsps dried oregano
- Salt, to taste

Direction: Prep time: 5 minutes | Cook time: 0 minutes | Serves 2

✓ In a food processor, combine the cucumber, yogurt, lemon juice, garlic, dill, oregano, and a pinch of salt and process until smooth.

✓ Adjust the seasonings as needed and transfer them to a serving container.

Nutrition: calories: 209 | fat: 10g | protein: 18g | carbs: 14g | fiber: 2g | sodium: 69mg

685) Easy Tzatziki Sauce

Ingredients:

- 1 medium cucumber, peeled, seeded, and diced
- ½ Tsp salt, divided, plus more
- ½ cup plain, unsweetened, full-fat Greek yogurt
- ½ lemon, juiced
- 1 chopped fresh parsley
- ½ Tsp dried minced garlic
- ½ Tsp dried dill
- Freshly ground black pepper, to taste

Direction: Prep time: 5 minutes | Cook time: 0 minutes | Serves 2

✓ Put the cucumber in a colander.

✓ Sprinkle with ¼ Tsp of salt and toss. Let the cucumber rest at room temperature in the colander for 30 minutes.

✓ Rinse the cucumber in cool water and place it in a single layer on several layers of paper towels to remove the excess liquid.

✓ In a food processer, pulse the cucumber to chop finely and drain off any extra fluid.

✓ Pour the cucumber into a mixing container and add the yogurt, lemon juice, parsley, garlic, dill, and the *resting ¼ Tsp of salt. Season with salt and pepper to taste and whisk the ingredients together.*

✓ *Refrigerate in an airtight container*

Nutrition: calories: 77 | fat: 3g | protein: 6g | carbs: 6g | fiber: 1g | sodium: 607mg

686) Orange Dijon Dressing

Ingredients:

- *¼ cup extra-virgin olive oil*
- *2 Tbsps freshly squeezed orange juice 1 orange, zested*
- *1 Tsp garlic powder*
- *¾ Tsp za'atar seasoning*
- *½ Tsp salt*
- *¼ Tsp Dijon mustard*
- *Freshly ground black pepper, to taste*

Direction: Prep time: 5 minutes | Cook time: 0 minutes | Serves 2

✓ *In a jar, combine the olive oil, orange juice and zest, garlic powder, za'atar, salt, and mustard. Season with pepper and shake vigorously until completely mixed.*

Nutrition: calories: 283 | fat: 27g | protein: 1g | carbs: 11g | fiber:2 g | sodium: 597mg

687) Creamy Yogurt Dressing

Ingredients:

- *1 cup plain, unsweetened, full-fat Greek yogurt*
- *½ cup extra-virgin olive oil*
- *1 Tbsp apple cider vinegar*
- *½ lemon, juiced*
- *1 Tbsp chopped fresh oregano*
- *½ Tsp dried parsley*
- *½ Tsp kosher salt*
- *¼ Tsp garlic powder*
- *¼ Tsp freshly ground black pepper*

Direction: Prep time: 5 minutes | Cook time: 0 minutes | Serves 3

✓ *In a large container, combine the yogurt, olive oil, vinegar, lemon juice, oregano, parsley, salt, garlic powder, and pepper and whisk well.*

Nutrition: calories: 402 | fat: 40g | protein: 8g | carbs: 4g | fiber: 0g

688) Arugula Walnut Pesto

Ingredients:

- *6 cups packed arugula*
- *1 cup chopped walnuts*
- *½ cup shredded Parmesan cheese*
- *2 garlic cloves, peeled*
- *½ Tsp salt*
- *1 cup extra-virgin olive oil*

Direction: Prep time: 5 minutes | Cook time: 0 minutes | Serves 8 to 10

✓ *In a food processor, combine the arugula, walnuts, cheese, and garlic and process until very finely chopped. Add the salt. With the processor running, stream to the olive oil until well blended.*

✓ *If the mixture seems too thick, add warm water, 1 Tbsp at a time, until smooth and creamy. Store in a sealed container to the fridge.*

Nutrition: calories: 296 | fat: 31g | protein: 4g | carbs: 2g | fiber: 1g | sodium: 206mg

689) Tarragon Grapefruit Dressing

Ingredients:

- *½ cup avocado oil mayonnaise*
- *2 Tbsps Dijon mustard*
- *1 Tsp dried tarragon*
- *juice of ½ grapefruit*
- *½ Tsp salt*
- *¼ Tsp freshly ground black pepper*
- *1 to 2 Tbsps water (optional)*

Direction: Prep time: 5 minutes | Cook time: 0 minutes | Serves 4 to 6

✓ *In a large mason jar or glass measuring cup, combine the mayonnaise, Dijon, tarragon, grapefruit zest and juice, salt, and pepper, and whisk well with a fork until smooth and creamy.*

✓ *If a thinner dressing is preferred, thin out with water.*

Nutrition:calories:86| fat: 7g| protein: 1g |carbs: 6g

690) Bagna Cauda

Ingredients:

- *½ cup extra-virgin olive oil*
- *4 Tbsps (½ stick) butter (optional)*
- *8 anchovy fillets, very finely chopped*
- *4 large garlic cloves, finely minced*
- *½ Tsp salt*
- *½ Tsp freshly ground black pepper*

Direction: Prep time: 5 minutes | Cook time: 20 minutes | Serves 8 to 10

✓ *In a small saucepan, heat the olive oil and butter (if desired) over medium-low heat until the butter is melted.*

✓ *Add the anchovies and garlic and stir to combine. Add the salt and pepper and reduce the heat to low. Cook, occasionally stirring, until the anchovies are very soft and the mixture is very fragrant about 20 minutes.*

✓ *Serve warm, drizzled over steamed vegetables as a dipping sauce for raw veggies or cooked artichokes, or use as a salad dressing—store leftovers in an airtight container in the fridge for up to 2 weeks.*

Nutrition: calories: 181 | fat: 20g | protein: 1g | carbs: 1g | fiber: 0g | sodium: 333mg

691) Tahini Dressing

Ingredients:

- ½ cup tahini
- ¼ cup freshly squeezed lemon juice
- ¼ cup extra-virgin olive oil
- 1 garlic clove, finely minced or ½ Tsp garlic powder
- 2 Tbsps salt

Direction: Prep time: 5 minutes | Cook time: 0 minutes | Serves 8 to 10

✓ In a glass mason jar with a lid, combine the tahini, lemon juice, olive oil, garlic, and salt. Cover and shake well until combined and creamy. Store in the fridge for up to 2 weeks.

Nutrition: calories: 121 | fat: 12g | protein: 2g | carbs: 2g | fiber: 1g | sodium: 479mg

692) Marinara Sauce

Ingredients:

- 1 small onion, diced
- 1 small red bell pepper, stemmed, seeded, and chopped
- 2 Tbsps plus ¼ cup extra-virgin olive oil, divided
- 2 Tbsps butter (optional)
- 4 to 6 garlic cloves, minced
- 2 Tsp salt, divided
- ½ Tsp freshly ground black pepper
- 2 (32-ounce / 907-g) cans crushed tomatoes (with basil, if possible), with their juices
- ½ cup thinly sliced basil leaves, divided
- 2 Tbsps chopped fresh rosemary
- 1 to 2 Tbsps crushed red pepper flakes (optional)

Direction: Prep time: 15 minutes | Cook time: 40 minutes | Makes 8 cups

✓ In a food processor, combine the onion and bell pepper and blend until very finely minced.

✓ In a large skillet, heat 2 Tbsps olive oil and the butter (if desired) over medium heat. Add the minced onion and red pepper and sauté until just starting to get tender, about 5 minutes.

✓ Add the garlic, salt, and pepper and sauté until fragrant, another 1 to 2 minutes.

✓ Reduce the heat to low and add the tomatoes and their juices, resting ¼ cup olive oil, ¼ cup basil, rosemary, and red pepper flakes (if using). Stir to combine, then bring to a simmer and cover.

✓ Cook over low heat for 30 to 60 minutes to allow the flavors to blend.

✓ Add resting ¼ cup chopped fresh basil after removing from heat, stirring to combine.

Nutrition: calories: 256 | fat: 20g | protein: 4g | carbs: 19g | fiber: 5g | sodium: 803mg

693) Romesco Sauce

Ingredients:

- 1 (12-ounce / 340-g) jar roasted red peppers, drained
- 1 (14½-ounce / 411-g) can diced tomatoes, undrained
- ½ cup dry-roasted almonds
- 2 garlic cloves
- 2 Tbsps red wine vinegar
- 1 Tsp smoked paprika or ½ Tsp cayenne pepper
- ¼ Tsp kosher or sea salt
- ¼ Tsp freshly ground black pepper
- ¼ cup extra-virgin olive oil
- ⅔ cup torn, day-old bread or toast Assortment of sliced raw vegetables such as carrots, celery, cucumber, green beans, and bell peppers, for serving

Direction: Prep time: 10 minutes | Cook time: 0 minutes | Serves 10

✓ In a high-powered blender or food processor, combine the roasted peppers, tomatoes and their juices, almonds, garlic, vinegar, smoked paprika, salt, and pepper.

✓ Begin puréeing the ingredients at medium speed and slowly drizzle the oil with the blender running. Continue to purée until the dip is thoroughly mixed.

✓ Add the bread and purée.

✓ Serve with raw vegetables for dipping, or store in a jar with a lid for up to one week to the fridge.

Nutrition: calories: 96 | fat: 7g | protein: 3g | carbs: 8g | fiber: 3g | sodium: 2mg

694) Spanakopita Dip

Ingredients:

- Olive oil cooking spray
- 3 Tbsps olive oil, divided
- 2 Tbsps minced white onion
- 2 garlic cloves, minced
- 4 cups fresh spinach
- 4 ounces (113 g) cream cheese, softened
- 4 ounces (113 g) feta cheese, divided
- Zest of 1 lemon ¼ Tsp ground nutmeg
- 1 Tsp dried dill
- ½ Tsp salt
- Pita chips, carrot sticks, or sliced bread for serving (optional)

Direction: Prep time: 15 minutes | Cook time: 14 minutes | Serves 2

✓ Preheat the deep fryer to 360°F (182°C). Coat the inside of a 6-inch ramekin with olive oil spray.

✓ In a large skillet over medium heat, heat 1 tablespoon olive oil. Add the onion and cook for 1-2 minutes.

- ✓ *Add the garlic and cook, stirring for 1 more minute.*
- ✓ *Reduce the heat to low, stir in the spinach and water. Let cook for 2 to 3 minutes, or until the spinach is wilted. Remove the skillet from the heat.*
- ✓ *In a medium container, combine the cream cheese, 2 ounces of feta, and the remaining 2 tablespoons of olive oil, along with the nutmeg, dill, lemon zest, and salt. Mix until just combined.*
- ✓ *Add the vegetables to the cheese base and stir until combined.*
- ✓ *Pour the mixture into the prepared ramekin and top with the remaining 2 ounces of feta cheese.*
- ✓ *Place the sauce in the fryer basket and bake for 10 minutes, or until heated through and bubbly.*
- ✓ *Serve with pita chips, carrot sticks, or sliced bread.*

Nutrition: calories: 550 | fat: 52g | protein: 14g | carbs: 9g | fiber: 2g | sodium: 113mg

695) **Pearl Onion Dip**

Ingredients:

- *2 cups peeled pearl onions*
- *3 garlic cloves*
- *3 Tbsps olive oil, divided*
- *½ Tsp salt*
- *1 cup nonfat plain Greek yogurt*
  1 Tbsp lemon juice
- *¼ Tsp black pepper*
- *⅛ Tsp red pepper flakes*
- *Pita chips, vegetables, or toasted bread for serving (optional)*

Direction: Prep time: 10 minutes | Cook time: 12 minutes | Serves 4

- ✓ *Preheat the fryer to 360°F (182°C).*
- ✓ *In a large bowl, combine pearl onions and garlic with 2 tablespoons olive oil until onions are well coated.*
- ✓ *Pour the garlic and onion mixture into the fryer basket and roast for 12 minutes.*
- ✓ *Transfer the onions and garlic to a food processor. Pulse the vegetables until the onions are chopped but still have chunks.*
- ✓ *In a large container, combine the garlic and onions and the remaining 1 tablespoon olive oil, along with the salt, yogurt, red pepper flakes, lemon juice and, black pepper.*
- ✓ *Cover and chill for 40- 60 minutes before serving with pita chips, vegetables, or toast.*

Nutrition: calories: 150 | fat: 10g | protein: 7g | carbs: 7g | fiber: 1g | sodium: 3mg

696) **Rosemary Garlic Infused Olive Oil**

Ingredients:

- *1 cup extra-virgin olive oil*
- *4 large garlic cloves, smashed*
- *4 (4-to 5-inch) sprigs rosemary*

Direction: Prep time: 5 minutes | Cook time: 30 minutes | Makes 1 cup

- ✓ *In a medium skillet, heat the olive oil, garlic, and rosemary sprigs over low heat. Cook until fragrant and garlic is very tender, 30 to 45 minutes, stirring occasionally. Don't let the oil get too hot, or the garlic will burn and become bitter.*
- ✓ *Remove from the heat and allow to cool slightly. Remove the garlic and rosemary with a slotted spoon and pour the oil into a glass container.*
- ✓ *Allow cooling completely before covering. Store covered at room temperature for up to 3 months.*

Nutrition: calories: 241 | fat: 26g | protein: 0g | carbs: 1g | fiber: 0g | sodium: 1mg

697) **Fresh Herb Butter**

Ingredients:

- *½ cup almond butter, at room temperature*
- *1 garlic clove, finely minced*
- *2 Tbsps finely chopped fresh rosemary*
- *1 Tsp finely chopped fresh oregano*
- *½ Tsp salt*

Direction: Prep time: 5 minutes | Cook time: 0 minutes | Makes ½ cup

- ✓ *In a food processor, combine the almond butter, garlic, rosemary, oregano, and salt and pulse until the mixture is well combined, smooth, and creamy, scraping down the sides as necessary. Alternatively, you can whip the ingredients together with an electric mixer.*
- ✓ *Using a spatula, scrape the almond butter mixture into a small container or glass container and cover. Store in the fridge for up to 1 month.*

Nutrition: calories: 103 | fat: 12g | protein: 0g | carbs: 0g | fiber: 0g | sodium: 227mg

698) **Harissa Sauce**

Ingredients:

- *1 large red bell pepper, deseeded, cored, and cut into chunks*
- *1 yellow onion, cut into thick rings*
- *4 garlic cloves, peeled*
- *1 cup vegetable broth*
- *2 Tbsps tomato paste*
- *1 Tbsp tamari*
- *1 Tsp ground cumin*
- *1 Tbsp Hungarian paprika*

Direction: Prep time: 10 minutes | Cook time: 20 minutes | Makes 3 to 4 cups

- ✓ *Switch on the oven, preheat it setting its temperature to 450°F (235°C). Line a baking sheet with parchment paper.*
- ✓ *Place the bell pepper on the prepared baking sheet, flesh-side up, and space out the onion and garlic around the pepper.*

✓ *Roast to the preheated oven for 20 minutes. Transfer to a blender.*

✓ *Add the vegetable broth, tomato paste, tamari, cumin, and paprika. Purée until smooth. Served chilled or warm.*

Nutrition: calories: 15 | fat: 1g | protein: 1g | carbs: 3g | fiber: 1g | sodium: 201mg

699) Pineapple Salsa

Ingredients:

- *1 pound (454 g) fresh or thawed frozen pineapple, finely diced, juices reserved*
- *1 white or red onion, finely diced*
- *1 bunch cilantro or mint, leaves only, chopped*
- *1 jalapeño, minced (optional)*
- *Salt, to taste*

Direction: Prep time: 10 minutes | Cook time: 0 minutes | Serves 6 to 8

✓ *Stir together the pineapple with its juice, onion, cilantro, and jalapeño (if desired) in a medium container. Season with salt to taste and serve.*

✓ *The salsa can be refrigerated in an airtight container for up to 2 days.*

Nutrition: cal: 55 | fat: 0g | protein: 1g | carbs: 12g | fiber: 2g

Sides

700) Garlic Broccoli with Artichoke Hearts

Ingredients:

- 2 pounds (907 g) fresh broccoli rabe
- ½ cup extra-virgin olive oil, divided
- 3 garlic cloves, finely minced
- 1 Tsp salt
- 1 Tsp red pepper flakes
- 1 (13¾-ounce / 390-g) can artichoke hearts, drained and quartered
- 1 Tbsp water
- 2 Tbsps red wine vinegar
- Freshly ground black pepper, to taste

Direction: Prep time: 4 to 6 minutes Cook time: 10 minutes | Serves 4

- ✓ Trim away any thick lower stems and yellow leaves from the broccoli rabe and discard. Cut into individual florets with a couple of inches of thin stem attached.
- ✓ In a large skillet, heat ¼ cup olive oil over medium-high heat. Add the trimmed broccoli, garlic, salt, and red pepper flakes and sauté for 5 minutes until the broccoli begins to soften. Add the artichoke hearts and sauté for another 2 minutes.
- ✓ Add the water and reduce the heat to low. Cover and simmer until the broccoli stems are tender, 3 to 5 minutes.
- ✓ In a small container, whisk together resting ¼ cup olive oil and the vinegar. Drizzle over the broccoli and artichokes. Season with ground black pepper, if desired.

Nutrition: calories: 358 | fat: 35g | protein: 11g | carbs: 18g | fiber: 10g | sodium: 918mg

701) Lemon and Thyme Roasted Vegetables

Ingredients:

- 1 head garlic, cloves split apart, unpeeled
- 2 Tbsps olive oil, divided
- 2 medium carrots
- ¼ pound (113 g) asparagus
- 6 Brussels sprouts
- 2 cups cauliflower florets
- ½ pint cherry or grape tomatoes
- ½ fresh lemon, sliced
- Salt and black pepper, to taste
- 3 sprigs fresh thyme or ½ Tsp dried thyme
- Freshly squeezed lemon juice

Direction: Prep time: 20 minutes Cook time: 50 minutes Serves 2

- ✓ Preheat the oven to 375°F (190°C) and place the rack in the center position. Line a baking sheet with baking paper or foil.
- ✓ Place the garlic cloves in a small piece of foil and wrap to enclose them, but do not seal the package. Drizzle with 1 tablespoon of olive oil. Place the foil packet on the baking sheet and roast for 30 minutes while you prepare the rest of the vegetables.
- ✓ While the garlic roasts, clean, peel and chop the vegetables: Cut carrots into strips, ½ inch wide and 3 to 4 inches long; break off hard ends of asparagus; cut off hard ends of Brussels sprouts, cut in half if large; cut cauliflower into 2-inch florets; keep tomatoes whole.
- ✓ Vegetables should be cut into similar-sized pieces for even roasting.
- ✓ Place all vegetables and lemon slices in a large container. Drizzle with the remaining 5 tablespoons olive oil and season generously with salt and pepper.
- ✓ Increase the oven temperature to 400°F (205°C).
- ✓ Put the vegetables on the sheet pan in a single layer, leaving the packet of garlic cloves on the pan. Roast for 20 minutes, occasionally turning, until tender.
- ✓ When the vegetables are tender, remove them from the oven and sprinkle them with thyme leaves. Let the garlic cloves sit until cool enough to handle, and then remove the skins. Leave them whole, or gently mash.
- ✓ Toss garlic with the vegetables and an additional squeeze of fresh lemon juice.

Nutrition: calories: 256 | fat: 15g | protein: 7g | carbs: 31g | fiber: 9g | sodium: 168mg

702) Roasted Parmesan Rosemary Potatoes

Ingredients:

- 12 ounces (340 g) red potatoes (3 to 4 small potatoes)
- 1 Tbsp olive oil
- ½ Tsp garlic powder
- ¼ Tsp salt
- 1 Tbsp grated Parmesan cheese
- 1 Tsp minced fresh rosemary (from 1 sprig)

Direction: Prep time: 10 minutes | Cook time: 55 minutes | Serves 2

- ✓ Switch on the oven, preheat it setting its temperature to 425°F (220°C) and set the rack to the bottom position. Line a baking sheet with parchment paper. (Do not use foil, as the potatoes will stick.)
- ✓ Scrub the potatoes and dry them well. Dice into 1-inch pieces.
- ✓ In a mixing container, combine the potatoes, olive oil, garlic powder, and salt. Toss well to coat.
- ✓ Lay the potatoes on the parchment paper and roast for 10 minutes. Flip the potatoes over and return to

the oven for 10 more minutes.

- ✓ *Check the potatoes to make sure they are golden brown on the top and bottom. Toss them again, turn the heat down to 350°F (180°C), and roast for 30 minutes more.*
- ✓ *When the potatoes are golden, crispy, and cooked through, sprinkle the Parmesan cheese over them and toss again. Return to the oven for 3 minutes more to let the cheese melt a bit.*
- ✓ *Remove from the oven and sprinkle with the fresh rosemary.*

Nutrition: calories: 193 | fat: 8g | protein: 5g | carbs: 28g | fiber: 3g | sodium: 334mg

703) Spicy Wilted Greens

Ingredients:

- *1 Tbsp olive oil*
- *2 garlic cloves, minced*
- *3 cups sliced greens (kale, spinach, chard, beet greens, dandelion greens, or a combination)*
- *Pinch salt*
- *Pinch red pepper flakes*

Direction: Prep time: 10 minutes | Cook time: 5 minutes | Serves 2

- ✓ *Heat the olive oil in a sauté pan over medium-high heat. Add garlic and sauté for 40 seconds, or just until it's fragrant.*
- ✓ *Add the greens, salt, and pepper flakes and stir to combine. Let the greens wilt, but do not overcook. Remove the pan from the heat and serve.*

Nutrition: calories: 91 | fat: 7g | protein: 1g | carbs: 7g | fiber: 3g | sodium: 111mg

704) Romano Broccolini

Ingredients:

- *1 bunch broccolini (about 5 ounces / 142 g)*
- *1 Tbsp olive oil*
- *½ Tsp garlic powder*
- *¼ Tsp salt*
- *2 Tbsps grated Romano cheese*

Direction: Prep time: 5-6 minutes | Cook time: 10 minutes | Serves 2

- ✓ *Switch on the oven, preheat it setting its temperature to 400°F (205°C) and set the oven rack to the middle position. Line a sheet pan with parchment paper or foil.*
- ✓ *Slice the tough ends off the broccolini and place them in a medium container. Add the olive oil, garlic powder, and salt and toss to combine. Arrange broccolini on the lined sheet pan.*
- ✓ *Roast for 7 minutes, flipping pieces over halfway through the roasting time.*
- ✓ *Remove the pan from the oven and sprinkle the cheese over the broccolini. With a pair of tongs, carefully flip the pieces over to coat all sides. Return to the oven for another 2 to 3 minutes, or until the cheese melts and starts to turn golden.*

Nutrition: calories: 114 | fat: 9g | protein: 4g | carbs: 5g | fiber: 2g | sodium: 400mg

705) Balsamic Brussels Sprouts and Delicata Squash

Ingredients:

- *½ pound (227 g) Brussels sprouts, ends trimmed and outer leaves removed*
- *1 medium delicata squash, halved lengthwise, seeded, and cut into 1-inch pieces*
- *1 cup fresh cranberries*
- *2 Tbsps olive oil*
- *Salt and black pepper, to taste*
- *½ cup balsamic vinegar*
- *2 Tbsps roasted pumpkin seeds*
- *2 Tbsps fresh pomegranate arils (seeds)*

Direction: Prep time: 10 minutes | Cook time: 30 minutes | Serves 2

- ✓ *Preheat oven to 400°F (205°C) and set the rack to the middle position. Line a sheet pan with parchment paper.*
- ✓ *Combine squash, Brussels sprouts, and cranberries in a large bowl. Drizzle with olive oil, season liberally with salt and pepper. Mix well to coat and arrange in a single layer on the baking sheet.*
- ✓ *Roast for 30 minutes, turning the vegetables halfway through cooking, or until the Brussels sprouts turn brown and crisp in places and the squash has golden spots.*
- ✓ *While the vegetable roast, prepare the balsamic glaze by boiling the vinegar for 10-12 minutes, or until the mixture has reduced to about ¼ cup and is syrupy inconsistency.*
- ✓ *Remove vegetables from oven, drizzle with balsamic syrup and sprinkle with pumpkin seeds and pomegranate seeds*

Nutrition: calories: 201 | fat: 7g | protein: 6g | carbs: 21g | fiber: 8g | sodium: 34mg

706) Honey Roasted Rainbow Carrots

Ingredients:

- *½ pound (227 g) rainbow carrots (about 4)*
- *2 Tbsps fresh orange juice*
- *1 Tbsp honey*
  ½ Tsp coriander
- *Pinch salt*

Direction: Prep time: 10 minutes | Cook time: 20 minutes | Serves 2

- ✓ *Preheat the oven to 400°F (205°C) and set the oven rack to the middle position.*
- ✓ *Peel the carrots and cut them lengthwise into slices of even thickness. Place them in a large container.*
- ✓ *In a small container, mix together the orange juice, honey, coriander, and salt.*

- *Pour the orange juice mixture over the carrots and toss well to coat.*
- *Spread carrots onto a baking dish in a single layer.*
- *Roast for 15 to 20 minutes, or until fork-tender.*

Nutrition: calories: 85 | fat: 0g | protein: 1g | carbs: 21g | fiber: 3g | sodium: 156mg

707) Garlicky Roasted Grape Tomatoes

Ingredients:

- 1-pint grape tomatoes
- 10 whole garlic cloves, skins removed
- ¼ cup olive oil
- ½ Tsp salt
- 1 fresh rosemary sprig
- 1 fresh thyme sprig

Direction: Prep time: 10 minutes | Cook time: 45 minutes | Serves 2

- *Preheat oven to 350°F (180°C).*
- *Toss tomatoes, garlic cloves, oil, salt, and herb sprigs in a baking dish.*
- *Roast tomatoes until they are soft and begin to caramelize for about 45 minutes.*
- *Remove herbs before serving.*

Nutrition: calories: 271 | fat: 26g | protein: 3g | carbs: 12g | fiber: 3g | sodium: 593mg

708) Roasted Lemon Tahini Cauliflower

Ingredients:

- ½ large head cauliflower stemmed and broken into florets (about 3 cups)
- 1 Tbsp olive oil
- 2 Tbsps tahini
- 2 Tbsps freshly squeezed lemon juice
- 1 Tsp harissa paste
- Pinch salt

Direction: Prep time: 10 minutes | Cook time: 20 minutes | Serves 2

- *Switch on the oven, preheat it setting its temperature to 400°F (205°C) and set the rack to the lowest position. Line a sheet pan with parchment paper or foil.*
- *Toss the cauliflower florets with the olive oil in a large container and transfer them to the sheet pan—Reserve the container to make the tahini sauce.*
- *Roast the cauliflower for 15 minutes, turning it once or twice until it starts to turn golden.*
- *To the same container, combine the tahini, lemon juice, harissa, and salt.*
- *When the cauliflower is tender, remove it from the oven and toss it with tahini sauce. Return to the sheet pan and roast for 5 minutes more.*

Nutrition: calories: 205 | fat: 15g | protein: 7g | carbs: 15g | fiber: 7g | sodium: 161mg

709) Spinach and Zucchini Lasagna

Ingredients:

- ½ cup extra-virgin olive oil, divided
- 4 to 5 medium zucchini squash
- 1 Tsp salt
- 8 ounces (227 g) frozen spinach, thawed and well-drained (about 1 cup)
- 2 cups whole-milk ricotta cheese
- ¼ cup chopped fresh basil or 2 Tbsps dried basil
- 1 Tsp garlic powder
- ½ Tsp freshly ground black pepper
- 2 cups shredded fresh whole-milk Mozzarella cheese
- 1¾ cups shredded Parmesan cheese
- ½ (24-ounce / 680-g) jar low-sugar marinara sauce (less than 5 grams sugar)

Direction: Prep time: 15 minutes | Cook time: 1 hour | Serves 8

- *Switch on the oven, preheat it setting its temperature to 425°F (220°C).*
- *Line two baking sheets with parchment paper or aluminum foil and drizzle each with 2 Tbsps olive oil, spreading evenly.*
- *Slice the zucchini lengthwise into ¼-inch-thick long slices and place them on the prepared baking sheet in a single layer. Sprinkle with ½ Tsp salt per sheet. Bake until softened but not mushy, 15 to 18 minutes. Remove from the oven and let them cool slightly before assembling the lasagna.*
- *Reduce the oven temperature to 375°F (190°C).*
- *While the zucchini cooks, prep the filling. In a large container, combine the spinach, ricotta, basil, garlic powder, and pepper. In a small container, mix together the mozzarella and Parmesan cheeses. In a medium container, combine the marinara sauce and resting ¼ cup olive oil and stir to fully incorporate the oil into the sauce.*
- *To assemble the lasagna, spoon a third of the marinara sauce mixture into the bottom of a 9-by-13-inch glass baking dish and spread evenly. Place 1 layer of softened zucchini slices to fully cover the sauce, then add a third of the ricotta-spinach mixture and spread evenly on top of the zucchini. Sprinkle a third of the Mozzarella-Parmesan mixture on top of the ricotta. Repeat with 2 more cycles of these layers: marinara, zucchini, ricotta-spinach, then cheese blend.*
- *Bake until the cheese is bubbly and melted for 30 to 35 minutes. Turn the broiler to low and broil until the top is golden brown, about 5 minutes. Remove from the oven and allow to cool slightly before slicing.*

Nutrition: calories: 521 | fat: 41g | protein: 25g | carbs: 13g | fiber: 3g | sodium: 712mg

710) Pistachio Citrus Asparagus

Ingredients:

- 5 Tbsps extra-virgin olive oil, divided
- Zest and juice of 2 clementines or 1 orange (about ¼ cup juice and 1 Tbsp zest)
- Zest and juice of 1 lemon
- 1 Tbsp red wine vinegar
- 1 Tsp salt, divided
- ¼ Tsp freshly ground black pepper
- ½ cup shelled pistachios
- 1 pound (454 g) fresh asparagus
- 1 Tbsp water

Direction: Prep time: 10 minutes | Cook time: 15 minutes | Serves 4

- ✓ In a small container, whisk together 4 Tbsps olive oil, the clementine and lemon juices and zests, vinegar, ½ Tsp salt, and pepper. Set aside.
- ✓ In a medium dry skillet, toast the pistachios over medium-high heat until lightly browned, 2 to 3 minutes, being careful not to let them burn. Transfer to a cutting board and coarsely chop. Set aside.
- ✓ Trim the rough ends off the asparagus, usually the last 1 to 2 inches of each spear. In a skillet, heat the resting 1 Tbsp olive oil over medium-high heat. Add the asparagus and sauté for 2 to 3 minutes. Sprinkle with the resting ½ Tsp salt and add the water. Reduce the heat to medium-low, cover, and cook until tender, another 2 to 4 minutes, depending on the thickness of the spears.
- ✓ Transfer the cooked asparagus to a serving dish. Add the pistachios to the dressing and whisk to combine. Pour the dressing over the warm asparagus and toss to coat.

Nutrition: calories: 284 | fat: 24g | protein: 6g | carbs: 11g | fiber: 4g | sodium: 594mg

711) Sautéed Riced Cauliflower

Ingredients:

- 1 small head cauliflower, broken into florets
- ¼ cup extra-virgin olive oil
- 2 garlic cloves, finely minced
- 1½ Tbsps salt
- ½ Tsp freshly ground black pepper

Direction: Prep time: 5 minutes | Cook time: 5 minutes | Serves 6 to 8

- ✓ Place the florets in a food processor and pulse several times until the cauliflower is the consistency of rice or couscous.
- ✓ In a large skillet, heat the olive oil over medium-high heat. Add the cauliflower, garlic, salt, and pepper and sauté for 5 minutes, just to take the crunch out but not enough to let the cauliflower become soggy.
- ✓ Remove the cauliflower from the skillet and place it in a container until ready to use. Toss with chopped herbs and additional olive oil for a simple side, top with sautéed veggies and protein, or use in your favorite recipe.

Nutrition: calories: 92 | fat: 8g | protein: 1g | carbs: 3g | fiber: 0g | sodium: 595mg

Beans

712) Bean Balls with Marinara

Ingredients:

Bean Balls:

- *1 tablespoon of extra virgin olive oil*
- *½ yellow onion, chopped*
- *1 teaspoon fennel seeds*
- *2 tablespoons dried oregano*
- *½ teaspoon crushed red pepper flakes*
- *1 teaspoon garlic powder*
- *1 (15-ounce/425-g) can white beans (cannellini or navy), drained and rinsed*
- *½ cup whole-wheat bread crumbs*
- *Sea salt and ground black pepper, to taste*

Marinara:

- *1 tablespoon extra virgin olive oil*
- *3 garlic cloves, minced Handful of basil leaves*
- *1 (28-ounce/794-g) can chopped tomatoes with juice reserved*
- *Sea salt, to taste Make bean balls*

Direction: Preparation time: 15 minutes | Cooking time: 30 minutes | Serves 2 to 4 people

- ✓ *Turn on the oven, preheat it by setting the temperature to 350°F (180°C).*
- ✓ *Line a baking sheet with baking paper*
- ✓ *Heat the olive oil in a nonstick skillet over medium heat until shimmering*
- ✓ *Add the onion and sauté for 4- 5 minutes or until translucent.*
- ✓ *Sprinkle in the fennel seeds, oregano, red pepper flakes and garlic powder, then cook for 1 minute or until aromatic.*
- ✓ *Pour the stir-fry into a food processor , add the beans and bread crumbs. Sprinkle with salt and black pepper, then pulse to combine well and the mixture will hold together.*
- ✓ *Shape the mixture into balls with a 2 ounce (57 g) cookie scoop, then arrange the balls on the baking sheet.*
- ✓ *In the preheated oven, bake for 30 minutes or until lightly browned. Turn the balls over halfway through the baking time.*
- ✓ *Preparing the marinara*
- ✓ *While cooking the bean balls, heat the oil in a saucepan over medium-high heat until shimmering*
- ✓ *Add the garlic and basil and sauté for 2 minutes or until fragrant.*
- ✓ *Add the tomatoes and juice. Bring to a boil. Reduce heat to low. Put the lid on and simmer for 15 minutes. Sprinkle with salt.*
- ✓ *Transfer the bean patties to a large platter and drizzle with the marinara before serving.*

Nutrition: calories: 351 | fat: 16g | protein: 11g | carbs: 42g | fiber: 10g | sodium: 377mg

713) White Bean Lettuce Wraps

Ingredients:

- *1 Tbsp extra-virgin olive oil*
- *½ cup diced red onion*
- *¾ cup chopped fresh tomatoes*
- *¼ Tsp freshly ground black pepper*
- *1 (15-ounce / 425-g) can cannellini or great northern beans, drained and rinsed*
- *¼ cup finely chopped fresh curly parsley*
- *½ cup lemony garlic hummus or ½ cup prepared hummus*
- *8 romaine lettuce leaves*

Direction: Prep time: 10 minutes | Cook time: 9 minutes | Serves 4

- ✓ *In a large skillet over medium heat, heat the oil. Add the onion and cook for 2- 3 minutes, stirring occasionally. Add the tomatoes and pepper and cook for 3 more minutes, stirring occasionally. Add the beans and cook for 3 more minutes, stirring occasionally. Remove from the heat, and mix to the parsley.*
- ✓ *Spread 1 Tbsp of hummus over each lettuce leaf. Evenly spread the warm bean mixture down the center of each leaf. Fold one side of the lettuce leaf over the filling lengthwise, then fold over the other side to make a wrap and serve.*

Nutrition: calories: 188 | fat: 5g | protein: 10g | carbs: 28g | fiber: 9g | sodium: 115mg

714) Chickpeas with Coriander and Sage

Ingredients:

- *1½ Tbsps table salt, for brining*
- *1 pound (454 g) dried chickpeas, picked over and rinsed*
- *2 Tbsps extra-virgin olive oil, plus extra for drizzling*
- *2 onions, halved and sliced thin*
- *¼ Tsp table salt*
- *1 Tbsp coriander seeds, cracked*
- *¼ to ½ Tsp red pepper flakes*
- *2½ cups chicken broth*
- *¼ cup fresh sage leaves*
- *2 bay leaves*
- *1½ Tsps grated lemon*
- *zest plus 2 Tsps juice*
- *2 Tbsps minced fresh parsley*

Direction: Prep time: 15 minutes | Cook time: 21 minutes | Serves 6 to 8

- ✓ *Dissolve 1½ tablespoons salt in 2 quarts cold water in a large Bowl. Add chickpeas and let soak at room temperature for at least 9 hours or up to 24 hours. Drain and rinse well.*

- ✓ Using the highest setting for sautéing, heat the oil in the Instant Pot until it shimmers. Add the onions and ¼ tsp. salt and cook until the onions are softened and nicely browned, 10 to 12 minutes. Stir in the cilantro and pepper flakes and cook until fragrant, about 30 seconds. Add the stock, scraping up all the browned bits, then stir in the chickpeas, sage and bay leaves.
- ✓ Lock the lid and close the pressure release valve. Select the low pressure cooking function and cook for 10 minutes. Turn off the Instant Pot and allow the pressure to release naturally for 15 minutes. Quickly release the remaining pressure, then carefully remove the lid, allowing the steam to escape away from you.
- ✓ Discard the bay leaves. Stir the lemon zest and juice into the chickpeas and season with salt and pepper to taste. Sprinkle with parsley. Serve, drizzling individual servings with extra oil.

Nutrition: calories: 190 | fat: 6g | protein: 11g | carbs: 40g | fiber: 1g | sodium: 360mg

715) Chili Black Bean with Mangoes

Ingredients:

- 2 Tbsps coconut oil
- 1 onion, chopped
- 2 (15-ounce / 425-g) cans black beans, drained and rinsed
- 1 Tbsp chili powder
- 1 Tsp sea salt
- ¼ Tsp freshly ground black pepper
- 1 cup water
- 2 ripe mangoes, sliced thinly
- ¼ cup chopped fresh cilantro, divided
- ¼ cup sliced scallions, divided

Direction: Prep time: 10 minutes | Cook time: 10 minutes | Serves 4

- ✓ Heat the coconut oil in a pot over high heat until melted.
- ✓ Put the onion to the pot and sauté for 5 minutes or until translucent.
- ✓ Add the black beans to the pot. Sprinkle with chili powder, salt, and ground black pepper. Pour to the water. Stir to mix well.
- ✓ Bring to a boil. Reduce the heat to low, then simmering for 5 minutes or until the beans are tender.
- ✓ Turn off the heat and mix to the mangoes, then garnish with scallions and cilantro before serving.

Nutrition: calories: 277 | fat: 9g | protein: 4g | carbs: 45g | fiber: 7g | sodium: 647mg

716) Garbanzo and Fava Bean Fūl

Ingredients:

- 1 (16-ounce / 454-g) can garbanzo beans, rinsed and drained
- 1 (15-ounce / 425-g) can fava beans, rinsed and drained
- 3 cups water
- ½ cup lemon juice
- 3 cloves garlic, peeled and minced
- 1 Tsp salt
- 3 Tbsps extra-virgin olive oil

Direction: Prep time: 10 minutes | Cook time: 10 minutes | Serves 6

- ✓ In a 3-quart pot over medium heat, cook the garbanzo beans, fava beans, and water for 10 minutes.
- ✓ Reserving 1 cup of the liquid from the cooked beans, drato the beans and put them in a container.
- ✓ Mix the reserved liquid, lemon juice, minced garlic, and salt together and add to the beans to the container. Using a potato masher, mash up about half the beans to the container.
- ✓ After mashing half the beans, give the mixture one more stir to make sure the beans are evenly mixed.
- ✓ Drizzle the olive oil over the top.
- ✓ Serve warm or cold with pita bread.

Nutrition: calories: 199 | fat: 9g | protein: 10g | carbs: 25g | fiber: 9g | sodium: 395mg

717) White Cannellini Bean Stew

Ingredients:

- 3 Tbsps extra-virgin olive oil
- 1 large onion, chopped
- 1 (15-ounce / 425-g) can diced tomatoes
- 2 (15-ounce / 425-g) cans white cannellini beans
- 1 cup carrots, chopped
- 4 cups vegetable broth
- 1 Tsp salt
- 1 (1-pound / 454-g) bag baby spinach, washed

Direction: Prep time: 10 minutes | Cook time: 30 minutes | Serves 4 to 6

- ✓ In a large pot over medium heat, cook the olive oil and onion for 5 minutes.
- ✓ Add the tomatoes, beans, carrots, broth, and salt. Stir and cook for 20 minutes.
- ✓ Add the spinach, a handful at a time, and cook for 5 minutes, until the spinach has wilted.
- ✓ Serve warm

Nutrition: calories: 356 | fat: 12g | protein: 15g | carbs: 47g | fiber: 16g | sodium: 1832mg

718) Green Bean and Halloumi Cheese Salad

Ingredients:

For the Dressing:

- ¼ cup plain kefir or buttermilk
- 1 Tbsp olive oil

- *2 Tsps freshly squeezed lemon juice*
- *¼ Tsp onion powder*
- *¼ Tsp garlic powder*
- *Pinch salt*
- *Pinch freshly ground black pepper*

For the Salad:

- *½ pound (227 g) very fresh green beans, trimmed*
- *2 ounces (57 g) Halloumi cheese, sliced into 2 (½-inch-thick) slices*
- *½ cup cherry or grape tomatoes, halved*
- *¼ cup very thinly sliced sweet onion*
- *2 ounces (57 g) prosciutto, cooked crisp and crumbled*

Direction: Prep time: 15 minutes | Cook time: 6 minutes | Serves 2

- ✓ *Make the Dressing*
- ✓ *Combine the kefir or buttermilk, olive oil, lemon juice, onion powder, garlic powder, salt, and pepper in a small container and whisk well. Set the dressing aside*
- ✓ *Make the Salad*
- ✓ *Fill a medium-size pot with about 1 inch of water and add the green beans. Cover and steam them for about 3 to 4 minutes, or just until beans are tender. Do not overcook. Drain beans, rinse them immediately with cold water, and set them aside to cool.*
- ✓ *Heat a nonstick skillet over medium-high heat and place the slices of Halloumi to the hot pan. After about 2 minutes, check to see if the cheese is golden on the bottom. If it is, flip the slices and cook for another minute or until the second side is golden.*
- ✓ *Remove cheese from the pan and cut each piece into cubes (about 1-inch square)*
- ✓ *Place the green beans, halloumi, tomatoes, and sliced onion in a large container and toss to combine.*
- ✓ *Drizzle dressing over the salad and toss well to combine. Sprinkle prosciutto over the top.*

Nutrition: calories: 273 | fat: 18g | protein: 15g | carbs: 16g | fiber: 5g | sodium: 506mg

719) ***Italian-Style Baked Beans***

Ingredients:

- *2 Tsps extra-virgin olive oil*
- *½ cup minced onion*
- *1 (12-ounce / 340-g) can low-sodium tomato paste*
- *¼ cup red wine vinegar*
- *2 Tbsps honey*
- *¼ Tsp ground cinnamon*
- *½ cup water*
- *2 (15-ounce / 425-g) cans cannellini or great northern beans, undrained*

Direction: Prep time: 10 minutes | Cook time: 15 minutes | Serves 6

- ✓ *In a medium saucepan over medium heat, heat the oil. Add the onion and cook for 5 minutes, stirring often. Add the tomato paste, vinegar, honey, cinnamon and water and stir well. Lower the heat to low.*
- ✓ *Drain and rinse one can of beans in a colander and add to the saucepan. Pour the entire second can of beans (including the liquid) into the casserole. Let cook for 10 minutes, stirring occasionally, and serve.*

Nutrition: calories: 290 | fat: 2g | protein: 15g | carbs: 53g | fiber: 11g | sodium: 647mg

720) ***Turkish-Inspired Pinto Bean Salad***

Ingredients:

- *¼ cup extra-virgin olive oil, divided*
- *3 garlic cloves, lightly crushed and peeled 2 (15-ounce / 425-g) cans pinto beans, rinsed*
- *2 cups plus 1 Tbsp water*
- *Salt and pepper, to taste*
- *¼ cup tahini*
- *3 Tbsps lemon juice*
- *1 Tbsp ground dried Aleppo pepper, plus extra for serving*
- *8 ounces (227 g) cherry tomatoes, halved*
- *¼ red onion, sliced thinly*
- *½ cup fresh parsley leaves*
- *2 hard-cooked large eggs, quartered*
- *1 Tbsp toasted sesame seeds*

Direction: Prep time: 10 minutes | Cook time: 3 minutes | Serves 4 to 6

- ✓ *Add 1 tablespoon olive oil and the garlic to a medium saucepan over medium heat. Cook for about 3 minutes, stirring constantly, or until garlic turns golden brown but not brown.*
- ✓ *Add the beans, 2 cups water and 1 tablespoon salt and bring to a boil. Remove from heat, cover and let stand for 20 minutes. Drain the beans and discard the garlic.*
- ✓ *In a large bowl, whisk together the remaining 3 tablespoons oil, tahini, lemon juice, Aleppo, the remaining 1 tablespoon water and ¼ teaspoon salt. Stir in the beans, tomatoes, onion and parsley.*
- ✓ *Season with salt and pepper to taste.*
- ✓ *Transfer to a serving dish and top with the eggs. Sprinkle with the extra sesame and Aleppo seeds before serving.*

Nutrition: calories: 402 | fat: 18g | protein: 16g | carbs: 44g | fiber: 11g | sodium: 456mg

721) ***Garbanzo and Pita Casserole***

Ingredients:

- *4 cups Greek yogurt 3 cloves garlic, minced*
- *1 Tsp salt*
- *2 (16-ounce / 454-g) cans garbanzo beans, rinsed and drained*
- *2 cups water*
- *4 cups pita chips*
- *5 Tbsps unsalted butter (optional)*

Direction: Prep time: 10 minutes | Cook time: 10 minutes | Serves 4

- ✓ *In a large container, whisk together the yogurt, garlic, and salt. Set aside.*
- ✓ *Put the garbanzo beans and water in a medium pot. Bring to a boil; let beans boil for about 5 minutes.*
- ✓ *Pour the garbanzo beans and the liquid into a large casserole dish.*
- ✓ *Top the beans with pita chips. Pour the yogurt sauce over the pita chip layer.*
- ✓ *In a small saucepan, melt and brown the butter (if desired), about 3 minutes. Pour the brown butter over the yogurt sauce.*

Nutrition: calories: 772 | fat: 36g | protein: 39g | carbs: 73g | fiber: 13g | sodium: 1003mg

722) Turmeric-Spiced Organic Chickpeas

Ingredients:

- *2 (15-ounce / 425-g) cans organic chickpeas, drained and rinsed*
- *3 Tbsps extra-virgin olive oil*
- *2 Tsps Turkish or smoked paprika*
- *2 Tsps turmeric*
- *½ Tsp dried oregano*
- *½ Tsp salt*
- *¼ Tsp ground ginger*
- *⅛ Tsp ground white pepper (optional)*

Direction: Prep time: 10 minutes | Cook time: 30 minutes | Serves

- ✓ *Switch on the oven, preheat it setting its temperature to 400°F (205°C). Line a baking sheet with parchment paper and set aside.*
- ✓ *Completely dry the chickpeas. Lay the chickpeas out on a baking sheet, roll them around with paper towels, and allow them to air-dry.*
- ✓ *let them dry for at least 3 hours, but can also be left to dry overnight.*
- ✓ *In a medium container, combine the olive oil, paprika, turmeric, oregano, salt, ginger, and white pepper (if using).*
- ✓ *Add the dry chickpeas to the container and toss to combine.*
- ✓ *Put the chickpeas on the prepared baking sheet and cook for 30 minutes, or until the chickpeas turn golden brown. At 15 minutes, move the chickpeas around on the baking sheet to avoid burning. Check every 10 minutes in case the chickpeas begin to crisp up before the full cooking time has elapsed.*
- ✓ *Remove from the oven and set them aside to cool.*

Nutrition: (½ cup) calories: 308 | fat: 12g | protein: 11g | carbs: 40g | fiber: 10g | sodium: 292mg

723) Lentil Sloppy Joes

Ingredients:

- *1 Tbsp extra-virgin olive oil*
- *1 cup chopped onion*
- *1 cup chopped bell pepper, any color*
- *2 garlic cloves, minced*
- *1 (15-ounce / 425-g) can lentils, drained and rinsed*
- *1 (14½-ounce / 411-g) can low-sodium or no-salt-added diced tomatoes, undrained*
- *1 Tsp ground cumin*
- *1 Tsp dried thyme*
- *¼ Tsp kosher or sea salt*
- *4 whole-wheat pita breads, split open*
- *1½ cups chopped seedless cucumber*
- *1 cup chopped romaine lettuce*

Direction: Prep time: 15 minutes | Cook time: 15 minutes | Serves 4

- ✓ *In a medium saucepan over medium-high heat, heat the oil. Add the onion and bell pepper and cook for 4 minutes, stirring frequently. Add the garlic and cook for 1 minute, stirring frequently. Add the lentils, tomatoes (with their liquid), cumin, thyme, and salt. Turn the heat to medium and cook, occasionally stirring, for 10 minutes, or until most of the liquid has evaporated.*
- ✓ *Stuff the lentil mixture inside each pita. Lay the cucumbers and lettuce on top of the lentil mixture and serve.*

Nutrition: calories: 241 | fat: 3g | protein: 13g | carbs: 43g | fiber: 12g | sodium: 317mg

724) Garlic and Parsley Chickpeas

Ingredients:

- *¼ cup extra-virgin olive oil , divided*
- *4 garlic cloves, sliced thinly*
- *⅛ Tsp red pepper flakes*
- *1 onion, chopped finely*
- *¼ Tsp salt, plus more to taste*
- *Black pepper , to taste*
- *2 (15-ounce / 425-g) cans chickpeas, rinsed*
- *1 cup vegetable broth*
- *2 Tbsps minced fresh parsley*
- *2 Tsps lemon juice*

Direction: Prep time: 10 minutes | Cook time: 18 to 20 minutes | Serves 4 to 6

- ✓ Add 3 tablespoons olive oil, the garlic and pepper flakes to a skillet over medium heat. Cook for about 3 minutes, stirring constantly, or until garlic turns golden brown but not brown.
- ✓ Stir in the onion and ¼ tsp salt and cook for 5-7 minutes, or until softened and lightly browned.
- ✓ Add the chickpeas and broth to the pan and bring to a boil. Reduce the heat to medium-low, cover and cook for about 7 minutes, or until the chickpeas are cooked through and the flavors blend.
- ✓ Uncover, increase the heat to high and continue to cook for about 3 more minutes, or until almost all the liquid has evaporated.
- ✓ Turn off the heat, stir in the parsley and lemon juice. Season to taste with salt and pepper and drizzle with remaining 1 tablespoon olive oil.
- ✓ Serve warm.

Nutrition: calories: 220 | fat: 11g | protein: 6g | carbs: 24g | fiber: 6g | sodium: 467mg

725) Black-Eyed Peas Salad with Walnuts

Ingredients:

- 3 Tbsps extra-virgin olive oil
- 3 Tbsps dukkah, divided
- 2 Tbsps lemon juice
- 2 Tbsps pomegranate molasses
- ¼ Tsp salt, or more to taste
- ⅛ Tsp pepper, or more to taste
- 2 (15-ounce / 425-g) cans black-eyed peas, rinsed
- ½ cup pomegranate seeds
- ½ cup minced fresh parsley
- ½ cup walnuts, toasted and chopped
- 4 scallions, sliced thinly

Direction: Prep time: 10 minutes | Cook time: 0 minutes | Serves 4 to 6

- ✓ In a large container, whisk together the olive oil, 2 Tbsps of the dukkah, lemon juice, pomegranate molasses, salt and pepper.
- ✓ Stir to the resting ingredients. Season with salt and pepper.
- ✓ Sprinkle with the resting 1 Tbsp of the dukkah before serving.

Nutrition: calories: 155 | fat: 11g | protein: 2g | carbs: 12g | fiber: 2g | sodium: 105mg

726) Mashed Beans with Cumin

Ingredients:

- 1 Tbsp extra-virgin olive oil, plus extra for serving
- 4 garlic cloves, minced
- 1 Tsp ground cumin
- 2 (15-ounce / 425-g) cans fava beans
- 3 Tbsps tahini
- 2 Tbsps lemon juice, plus lemon wedges for serving
- Salt and pepper, to taste 1 tomato, cored and cut into ½-inch pieces
- 1 small onion, chopped finely
- 2 hard-cooked large eggs, chopped
- 2 Tbsps minced fresh parsley

Direction: Prep time: 10 minutes | Cook time: 10 to 12 minutes | Serves 4 to 6

- ✓ Add the olive oil, garlic and cumin to a medium saucepan over medium heat. Cook for about 2 minutes, or until fragrant.
- ✓ Stir to the beans with their liquid and tahini. Bring to a simmer and cook for 8 to 10 minutes, or until the liquid thickens slightly.
- ✓ Turn off the heat, mash the beans to a coarse consistency with a potato masher. Stir to the lemon juice and 1 Tsp pepper. Season with salt and pepper.
- ✓ Transfer the mashed beans to a serving dish. Top with the tomato, onion, eggs and parsley. Drizzle with the extra olive oil.
- ✓ Serve with the lemon wedges.

Nutrition: calories: 125 | fat: 8g | protein: 5g | carbs: 9g | fiber: 3g | sodium: 131mg

Bread and pizza Recipes

727) Garlic-Rosemary Dinner Rolls

Ingredients:

- 2 garlic cloves, minced
- 1 tsp dried crushed rosemary
- ½ tsp apple cider vinegar
- 2 tbsp olive oil
- 2 eggs
- 1 ¼ tsp salt
- 1 ¾ tsp xanthan gum
- ½ cup tapioca starch
- ¾ cup brown rice flour
- 1 cup sorghum flour
- 2 tsp dry active yeast
- 1 tbsp honey
- ¾ cup hot water

Direction: Cooking Time: 20 minutes Servings: 8

- ✓ Mix well water and honey in a small container and add yeast. Leave it for exactly 7 minutes.
- ✓ In a large container, mix garlic, rosemary, salt, xanthan gum, sorghum flour, tapioca starch, and brown rice flour with a paddle mixer.
- ✓ In a medium container, whisk well vinegar, olive oil, and eggs.
- ✓ Into container of dry ingredients pour in vinegar and yeast mixture and mix well.
- ✓ Grease a 12-muffin tin with cooking spray. Transfer dough evenly into 12 muffin tins and leave it 20 minutes to rise.
- ✓ Then preheat oven to 375oF and bake dinner rolls until tops are golden brown, around 17 to 19 minutes.
- ✓ Remove dinner rolls from oven and muffin tins immediately and let it cool.
- ✓ Best served when warm.

Nutrition: Calories: 200; Carbs: 34.3g; Protein: 4.2g; Fat: 5.4g

728) Grilled Burgers with Mushrooms

Ingredients:

- 2 Bibb lettuce, halved
- 4 slices red onion
- 4 slices tomato
- 4 whole wheat buns, toasted
- 2 tbsp olive oil
- ¼ tsp cayenne pepper, optional
- 1 garlic clove, minced
- 1 tbsp sugar
- ½ cup water
- 1/3 cup balsamic vinegar
- 4 large Portobello mushroom caps, around 5-inches in diameter

Direction: Cooking Time: 10 minutes Servings: 4

- ✓ Remove stems from mushrooms and clean with a damp cloth. Transfer into a baking dish with gill-side up.
- ✓ In a container, mix thoroughly olive oil, cayenne pepper, garlic, sugar, water and vinegar. Pour over mushrooms and marinate mushrooms to the ref for at least an hour.
- ✓ Once the one hour is nearly up, preheat grill to medium high fire and grease grill grate.
- ✓ Grill mushrooms for five minutes per side or until tender. Baste mushrooms with marinade so it doesn't dry up.
- ✓ To assemble, place ½ of bread bun on a plate, top with a slice of onion, mushroom, tomato and one lettuce leaf. Cover with the other top half of the bun. Repeat process with resting ingredients, serve and enjoy.

Nutrition: Cal: 244.1; Carbs: 32g; Protein: 8.1g; Fat: 9.3g

729) Grilled Sandwich with Goat Cheese

Ingredients:

- ½ cup soft goat cheese
- 4 Kaiser rolls 2-oz
- ¼ tsp freshly ground black pepper
- ¼ tsp salt
- 1/3 cup chopped basil
- Cooking spray
- 4 big Portobello mushroom caps
- 1 yellow bell pepper, cut in half and seeded
- 1 red bell pepper, cut in half and seeded
- 1 garlic clove, minced
- 1 tbsp olive oil
- ¼ cup balsamic vinegar

Direction: Cooking Time: 8 minutes Servings: 4

- ✓ In a large container, mix garlic, olive oil and balsamic vinegar. Add mushroom and bell peppers. Gently mix to coat. Remove veggies from vinegar and discard vinegar mixture.
- ✓ Coat with cooking spray a grill rack and the grill preheated to medium high fire.
- ✓ Place mushrooms and bell peppers on the grill and grill for 4 minutes per side. Remove from grill and let cool a bit.
- ✓ Into thin strips, cut the bell peppers.
- ✓ In a small container, combine black pepper, salt, basil and sliced bell peppers.
- ✓ Horizontally, cut the Kaiser rolls and evenly spread cheese on the cut side. Arrange 1 Portobello per roll, top with 1/3 bell pepper mixture and cover with the other half of the roll.
- ✓ Grill the rolls as you press down on them to create

a Panini like line on the bread. Grill until bread is toasted.

Nutrition: Calories: 317; Carbs: 41.7g; Protein: 14.0g; Fat: 10.5g

730) Halibut Sandwiches Mediterranean Style

Ingredients:

- *2 packed cups arugula or 2 oz.*
- *Grated zest of 1 large lemon*
- *1 tbsp capers, drained and mashed*
- *2 tbsp fresh flat leaf parsley, chopped*
- *¼ cup fresh basil, chopped*
- *¼ cup sun dried tomatoes, chopped*
- *¼ cup reduced fat mayonnaise*
- *1 garlic clove, halved*
- *1 pc of 14 oz of ciabatta loaf bread with ends trimmed and split in half, horizontally*
- *2 tbsp plus 1 tsp olive oil, divided*
- *Kosher salt and freshly ground pepper*
- *2 pcs or 6 oz halibut fillets, skinned*
- *Cooking spray*

Direction: Cooking Time: 23 minutes Servings: 4

- ✓ *Heat oven to 450oF.*
- ✓ *With cooking spray, coat a baking dish. Season halibut with a pinch of pepper and salt plus rub with a tsp of oil and place on baking dish. Then put in oven and bake until cooked or for ten to fifteen minutes. Remove from oven and let cool.*
- ✓ *Get a slice of bread and coat with olive oil the sliced portions. Put in oven and cook until golden, around six to eight minutes. Remove from heat and rub garlic on the bread.*
- ✓ *Combine the following in a medium container: lemon zest, capers, parsley, basil, sun dried tomatoes and mayonnaise. Then add the halibut, mashing with fork until flaked. Spread the mixture on one side of bread, add arugula and cover with the other bread half and serve.*

Nutrition: Calories: 125; Carbs: 8.0g; Protein: 3.9g; Fat: 9.2g

731) Herbed Panini Fillet O'Fish

Ingredients:

- *4 slices thick sourdough bread*
- *4 slices mozzarella cheese*
- *1 portabella mushroom, sliced*
- *1 small onion, sliced*
- *6 tbsp oil*
- *4 garlic and herb fish fillets*

Direction: Cooking Time: 25 minutes Servings: 4

- ✓ *Prepare your fillets by adding salt, pepper and herbs (rosemary, thyme, parsley whatever you like). Then dredged in flour before deep frying in very hot oil. Once nicely browned, remove from oil and set aside.*
- ✓ *On medium high fire, sauté for five minutes the onions and mushroom in a skillet with 2 tbsp oil.*
- ✓ *Prepare sourdough breads by layering the following over it: cheese, fish fillet, onion mixture and cheese again before covering with another bread slice.*
- ✓ *Grill in your Panini press until cheese is melted and bread is crisped and ridged.*

Nutrition: Calories: 422; Carbs: 13.2g; Protein: 51.2g; Fat: 17.2g

732) Italian Flat Bread Gluten Free

Ingredients:

- *1 tbsp apple cider*
- *2 tbsp water*
- *½ cup yogurt*
- *2 tbsp butter*
- *2 tbsp sugar*
- *2 eggs*
- *1 tsp xanthan gum*
- *½ tsp salt*
- *1 tsp baking soda*
- *1 ½ tsp baking powder*
- *½ cup potato starch, not potato flour*
- *½ cup tapioca flour*
- *¼ cup brown rice flour*
- *1/3 cup sorghum flour*

Direction: Cooking Time: 30 minutes Servings: 8

- ✓ *With parchment paper, line an 8 x 8-inch baking pan and grease parchment paper. Preheat oven to 375oF.*
- ✓ *Mix xanthan gum, salt, baking soda, baking powder, all flours, and starch in a large container.*
- ✓ *Whisk well sugar and eggs in a medium container until creamed. Add vinegar, water, yogurt, and butter. Whisk thoroughly.*
- ✓ *Pour in egg mixture into container of flours and mix well.*
- ✓ *Transfer sticky dough into prepared pan and bake to the oven for 25 to 30 minutes.*
- ✓ *If tops of bread start to brown a lot, cover top with foil and continue baking until done.*
- ✓ *Remove from oven and pan right away and let it cool.*
- ✓ *Best served when warm.*

Nutrition: Calories: 166; Carbs: 27.8g; Protein: 3.4g; Fat: 4.8g

733) Lemon, Buttered Shrimp Panini

Ingredients:

- *3 tbsp butter*
- *1 baguette*
- *1 tsp hot sauce*
- *1 tbsp parsley*
- *2 tbsp lemon juice*
- *4 garlic cloves, minced*
- *1 lb. shrimp peeled*

Direction: Cooking Time: 10 minutes Servings: 4

- ✓ *Make a hollowed portion on your baguette.*
- ✓ *Sauté the following on a skillet with melted butter: parsley, hot sauce, lemon juice and garlic. After a minute or two mix to the shrimps and sautéing for five minutes.*
- ✓ *Scoop shrimps into baguette and grill in a Panini press until baguette is crisped and ridged.*

Nutrition: Calories: 262; Carbs: 14.1g; Protein: 26.1g; Fat: 10.8g

734) Mediterranean Baba Ghanoush

Ingredients:

- *1 bulb garlic*
- *1 red bell pepper, halved and seeded*
- *1 tbsp chopped fresh basil*
- *1 tbsp olive oil*
- *1 tsp black pepper*
- *2 eggplants, sliced lengthwise*
- *2 rounds of flatbread or pita*
- *Juice of 1 lemon*

Direction: Cooking Time: 25 minutes Servings: 4

- ✓ *Grease grill grate with cooking spray and preheat grill to medium high.*
- ✓ *Slice tops of garlic bulb and wrap in foil. Place to the cooler portion of the grill and roast for at least 20 minutes.*
- ✓ *Place bell pepper and eggplant slices on the hottest part of grill.*
- ✓ *Grill for at least two to three minutes each side.*
- ✓ *Once bulbs are done, peel off skins of roasted garlic and place peeled garlic into food processor.*
- ✓ *Add olive oil, pepper, basil, lemon juice, grilled red bell pepper and grilled eggplant.*
- ✓ *Puree until smooth and transfer into a container.*
- ✓ *Grill bread at least 30 seconds per side to warm.*
- ✓ *Serve bread with the pureed dip and enjoy.*

Nutrition: Calories: 213.6; Carbs: 36.3g; Protein: 6.3g; Fat: 4.8g

735) Multi Grain & Gluten Free Dinner Rolls

Ingredients:

- *½ tsp apple cider vinegar*
- *3 tbsp olive oil*
- *2 eggs*
- *1 tsp baking powder*
- *1 tsp salt*
- *2 tsp xanthan gum*
- *½ cup tapioca starch*
- *¼ cup brown teff flour*
- *¼ cup flax meal*
- *¼ cup amaranth flour*
- *¼ cup sorghum flour*
- *¾ cup brown rice flour*

Direction: Cooking Time: 20 minutes Servings: 8

- ✓ *Mix well water and honey in a small container and add yeast. Leave it for exactly 10 minutes.*
- ✓ *In a large container, mix the following with a paddle mixer: baking powder, salt, xanthan gum, flax meal, sorghum flour, teff flour, tapioca starch, amaranth flour, and brown rice flour.*
- ✓ *In a medium container, whisk well vinegar, olive oil, and eggs.*
- ✓ *Into container of dry ingredients pour in vinegar and yeast mixture and mix well.*
- ✓ *Grease a 12-muffin tin with cooking spray. Transfer dough evenly into 12 muffin tins and leave it for an hour to rise.*
- ✓ *Then preheat oven to 375oF and bake dinner rolls until tops are golden brown, around 20 minutes.*
- ✓ *Remove dinner rolls from oven and muffin tins immediately and let it cool.*
- ✓ *Best served when warm.*

Nutrition: Calories: 207; Carbs: 28.4g; Protein: 4.6g; Fat: 8.3g

736) Mushroom and Eggplant Vegan Panini

Ingredients:

- *4 thin slices Asiago Cheese*
- *4 thin slices Swiss cheese*
- *¼ cup fat free ranch dressing*
- *8 slices focaccia bread*
- *2 tsp grated parmesan cheese*
- *1 tsp onion powder*
- *1 tsp garlic powder*
- *4 slices ½-inch thick eggplant, peeled*
- *1 cup fat-free balsamic vinaigrette*
- *4 portobello mushroom caps*
- *2 red bell peppers*

Direction: Cooking Time: 18 minutes Servings: 4

- ✓ *Broil peppers in oven for five minutes or until its skin has blistered and blackened. Remove peppers and place in container while quickly covering with plastic wrap, let cool for twenty minutes before peeling off the skin and refrigerating overnight.*
- ✓ *In a re-sealable bag, place mushrooms and vinaigrette and marinate to the ref for a night.*
- ✓ *Next day, grill mushrooms while discarding*

marinade. While seasoning eggplant with onion and garlic powder then grill along with mushrooms until tender, around four to five minutes.

- ✓ *Remove mushrooms and eggplant from griller and top with parmesan.*
- ✓ *On four slices of focaccia, smear ranch dressing evenly then layer: cheese, mushroom, roasted peppers and eggplant slices and cover with the resting focaccia slices.*
- ✓ *Grill in a Panini press until cheese has melted and bread is crisped and ridged.*

Nutrition: Calories: 574; Carbs: 77.1g; Protein: 29.6g; Fat: 19.9g

737) Open Face Egg and Bacon Sandwich

Ingredients:

- *¼ oz reduced fat cheddar, shredded*
- *½ small jalapeno, thinly sliced*
- *½ whole grain English muffin, split*
- *1 large organic egg*
- *1 thick slice of tomato*
- *1-piece turkey bacon*
- *2 thin slices red onion*
- *4-5 sprigs fresh cilantro*
- *Cooking spray*
- *Pepper to taste*

Direction: Cooking Time: 20 minutes Servings: 1,

- ✓ *On medium fire, place a skillet, cook bacon until crisp tender and set aside.*
- ✓ *In same skillet, drain oils, and place ½ of English muffin and heat for at least a minute per side. Transfer muffin to a serving plate.*
- ✓ *Coat the same skillet with cooking spray and fry egg to desired doneness. Once cooked, place egg on top of muffin.*
- ✓ *Add cilantro, tomato, onion, jalapeno and bacon on top of egg. Serve and enjoy.*

Nutrition: Calories: 245; Carbs: 24.7g; Protein: 11.8g; Fat: 11g

738) Paleo Chocolate Banana Bread

Ingredients:

- *¼ cup dark chocolate, chopped*
- *½ cup almond butter*
- *½ cup coconut flour, sifted*
- *½ Tsp cinnamon powder*
- *1 Tsp baking soda*
  1 Tsp vanilla extract
- *4 bananas, mashed*
- *4 eggs*
- *4 Tbsp coconut oil, melted*
- *A pinch of salt*

Direction: Cooking Time: 50 minutes Servings: 10

- ✓ *Switch on the oven, preheat it setting its temperature to 350oF.*
- ✓ *Grease an 8" x 8" square pan and set aside.*
- ✓ *In a large container, mix together the eggs, banana, vanilla extract, almond butter and coconut oil. Mix well until well combined.*
- ✓ *Add the cinnamon powder, coconut flour, baking powder, baking soda and salt to the wet ingredients. Fold until well combined. Add to the chopped chocolates then fold the batter again.*
- ✓ *Pour the batter into the greased pan. Spread evenly.*
- ✓ *Bake to the oven for about 50 minutes or until a toothpick inserted to the center comes out clean.*
- ✓ *Remove from the hot oven and cool in a wire rack for an hour.*

Nutrition: Calories: 150.3; Carbs: 13.9g; Protein: 3.2g; Fat: 9.1g

739) Panini and Eggplant Caponata

Ingredients:

- *¼ cup packed fresh basil leaves*
- *¼ of a 7oz can of eggplant caponata*
- *4 oz thinly sliced mozzarella*
- *1 tbsp olive oil*
- *1 ciabatta roll 6-7-inch length, horizontally split*

Direction: Cooking Time: 10 minutes Servings: 4

- ✓ *Spread oil evenly on the sliced part of the ciabatta and layer on the following: cheese, caponata, basil leaves and cheese again before covering with another slice of ciabatta.*
- ✓ *Then grill sandwich in a Panini press until cheese melts and bread gets crisped and ridged.*

Nutrition: Calories: 295; Carbs: 44.4g; Protein: 16.4g; Fat: 7.3g

740) Panini with Chicken-Fontina

Ingredients:

- *¼ Cup Arugula*
- *2 oz sliced cooked chicken*
- *3 oz fontina cheese thinly sliced*
- *1 tbsp Dijon mustard*
- *1 ciabatta roll*
- *¼ cup water*
- *1 tbsp + 1 tsp olive oil*
- *1 large onion, diced*

Direction: Cooking Time: 45 minutes Servings: 2

- ✓ *On medium low fire, place a skillet and heat 1 tbsp oil. Sauté onion and cook for 5 minutes. Pour in water while stirring and cooking continuously for 30 minutes until onion is golden brown and tender.*
- ✓ *Slice bread roll lengthwise and spread the*

following on one bread half, on the cut side: mustard, caramelized onion, chicken, arugula and cheese. Cover with the resting bread half.

- ✓ *Place the sandwich in a Panini maker and grill for 5 to 8 minutes or until cheese is melted and bread is ridged and crisped.*

Nutrition: Calories: 216; Carbs: 18.7g; Protein: 22.3g; Fat: 24.5g

741) Quinoa Pizza Muffins

Ingredients:

- *1 cup uncooked quinoa*
- *2 large eggs*
- *½ medium onion, diced*
- *1 cup diced bell pepper*
- *1 cup shredded mozzarella cheese*
- *1 tbsp dried basil*
- *1 tbsp dried oregano*
- *2 tsp garlic powder*
- *1/8 tsp salt*
- *1 tsp crushed red peppers*
- *½ cup roasted red pepper, chopped**
- *Pizza Sauce, about 1-2 cups*

Direction: Servings: 4 Cooking Time: 30 minutes

- ✓ *Preheat oven to 350oF.*
- ✓ *Cook quinoa according to directions.*
- ✓ *Combine all ingredients (except sauce) into container. Mix all ingredients well.*
- ✓ *Scoop quinoa pizza mixture into muffin tin evenly. Makes 12 muffins.*
- ✓ *Bake for 30 minutes until muffins turn golden in color and the edges are getting crispy.*
- ✓ *Top with 1 or 2 tbsp pizza sauce and enjoy!*

Nutrition: Calories: 303; Carbs: 41.3g; Protein: 21.0g; Fat: 6.1g

742) Rosemary-Walnut Loaf Bread

Ingredients:

- *½ cup chopped walnuts*
- *4 tbsp fresh, chopped rosemary*
- *1 1/3 cups lukewarm carbonated water*
- *1 tbsp honey*
- *½ cup extra virgin olive oil*
- *1 tsp apple cider vinegar*
- *3 eggs*
- *5 tsp instant dry yeast granules*
- *1 tsp salt*
- *1 tbsp xanthan gum*
- *¼ cup buttermilk powder*
- *1 cup white rice flour*
- *1 cup tapioca starch*
- *1 cup arrowroot starch*
- *1 ¼ cups all-purpose Bob's Red Mill gluten-free flour mix*

Direction: Cooking Time: 45 minutes Servings: 8,

- ✓ *In a large mixing container, whisk well eggs. Add 1 cup warm water, honey, olive oil, and vinegar.*
- ✓ *While continuously beating, add the rest of the ingredients except the rosemary and walnuts.*
- ✓ *Continue beating. If the dough is too stiff, add a little hot water. The dough should be shaggy and thick. Then add rosemary and walnuts continue kneading until evenly distributed.*
- ✓ *Cover container of dough with a clean towel, place in a warm spot, and let it rise for 30 minutes.*
- ✓ *Fifteen minutes into rising time, preheat oven to 400oF.*
- ✓ *Generously grease with olive oil a 2-quart Dutch oven and preheat inside oven without the lid.*
- ✓ *Once dough is done rising, remove pot from oven, and place dough inside. With a wet spatula, spread top of dough evenly in pot.*
- ✓ *Brush tops of bread with 2 tbsp of olive oil, cover Dutch oven and bake for 35 to 45 minutes.*
- ✓ *Once bread is done, remove from oven. And gently remove bread from pot.*
- ✓ *Allow bread to cool at least ten minutes before slicing.*
- ✓ *Serve and enjoy.*

Nutrition: Calories: 424; Carbs: 56.8g; Protein: 7.0g; Fat: 19.0g

743) Sandwich with Hummus

Ingredients:

- *4 cups alfalfa sprouts*
- *1 cup cucumber sliced 1/8 inch thick*
- *4 red onion sliced ¼-inch thick*
- *8 tomatoes sliced ¼-inch thick*
- *2 cups shredded Bibb lettuce*
- *12 slices 1-oz whole wheat bread*
- *1 can 15.5-oz chickpeas, drained*
- *2 garlic cloves, peeled*
- *¼ tsp salt*
- *½ tsp ground cumin*
- *1 tbsp tahini*
- *1 tbsp lemon juice*
- *2 tbsp water*
- *3 tbsp plain fat free yogurt*

Direction: Cooking Time: 0 minutes Servings: 4

- ✓ *In a food processor, blend chickpeas, garlic, salt, cumin, tahini, lemon juice, water and yogurt until smooth to create hummus.*
- ✓ *On 1 slice of bread, spread 2 tbsp hummus, top with 1 onion slice, 2 tomato slices, ½ cup lettuce, another*

bread slice, 1 cup sprouts, ¼ cup cucumber and cover with another bread slice. Repeat procedure for the rest of the ingredients.

Nutrition: Calories: 407; Carbs: 67.7g; Protein: 18.8 g; Fat: 6.8g

744) ***Sandwich with Spinach and Tuna Salad***

Ingredients:

- *1 cup fresh baby spinach*
- *8 slices 100% whole wheat sandwich bread*
- *¼ tsp freshly ground black pepper*
- *½ tsp salt free seasoning blend*
- *Juice of one lemon*
- *2 tbsp olive oil*
- *½ tsp dill weed*
- *2 ribs celery, diced*

Direction: Cooking Time: 0 minutes Servings: 4

- ✓ *In a medium container, mix well dill weed, celery, onion, cucumber and tuna.*
- ✓ *Add lemon juice and olive oil and mix thoroughly.*
- ✓ *Season with pepper and salt-free seasoning blend.*
- ✓ *To assemble sandwich, you can toast bread slices, on top of one bread slice layer ½ cup tuna salad, top with ¼ cup spinach and cover with another slice of bread.*
- ✓ *Repeat procedure to resting ingredients, serve and enjoy.*

Nutrition: Calories: 272.5; Carbs: 35.9g; Protein: 10.4g; Fat: 9.7g

745) ***Spiced Roast Beef Panini***

Ingredients:

- *Creamy horseradish sauce*
- *Butter*
- *1 roasted red peppers*
- *1 crusty bread, halved lengthwise*
- *2 slices Havarti cheese*
- *4 Slices deli roast beef*

Direction: Cooking Time: 15 minutes Servings: 2

- ✓ *On one bread slice, butter one side, spread over the horseradish sauce, then add evenly the cheese and roast beef and topped with roasted peppers.*
- ✓ *Cover the filling with the other bread half and start grilling in a Panini press for around three to five minutes while pressing down for a ridged effect.*
- ✓ *Serve and enjoy.*

Nutrition: Calories: 311; Carbs: 33.8g; Protein: 17.3g; Fat: 11.7g

746) ***Sun-Dried Tomatoes Panini***

Ingredients:

- *½ cup shredded mozzarella cheese*
- *8 slices country style Italian bread*
- *1/8 tsp freshly ground black pepper*
- *Cooking spray*
- *3/8 tsp salt, divided*
- *1 6oz package fresh baby spinach*
- *8 garlic cloves, thinly sliced*
- *1/8 tsp crushed red pepper*
- *¼ cup chopped drained oil packed sun-dried tomato*
- *4 4oz chicken cutlets*
- *1 tsp chopped rosemary*
- *2 tbsp extra virgin olive oil, divided*

Direction: Cooking Time: 15 minutes Servings: 4

- ✓ *In a re-sealable bag mix chicken, rosemary and 2 tsp olive oil. Allow to marinate for 30 minutes to the ref.*
- ✓ *On medium high fire, place a skillet and heat 4 tsp oil. Sauté for a minute garlic, red pepper and sun-dried tomato. Add 1/8 tsp salt and spinach and cook for a minute and put aside.*
- ✓ *On a grill pan coated with cooking spray, grill chicken for three minutes per side. Season with black pepper and salt.*
- ✓ *To assemble the sandwich, evenly layer the following on one bread slice: cheese, spinach mixture, and chicken cutlet. Cover with another bread slice.*
- ✓ *Place sandwich in a Panini press and grill for around five minutes or until cheese is melted and bread is crisped and ridged.*

Nutrition: Calories: 369; Carbs: 25.7g; Protein: 42.7g; Fat: 10.1g

747) ***Sunflower Gluten Free Bread***

Ingredients:

- *1 tsp apple cider vinegar*
- *3 tbsp olive oil*
- *3 egg whites*
- *Extra seeds for sprinkling on top of loaf*
- *1 ¼ tsp sea salt*
- *2 ¾ tsp xanthan gum*
- *2 tbsp hemp seeds*
- *2 tbsp poppy seeds*
- *¼ cup flax meal*
- *¼ cup buckwheat flour*
- *½ cup brown rice flour*
- *1 cup tapioca starch*
- *1 ½ cups sorghum flour*
- *2 ½ tsp dry active yeast*
- *1 tbsp honey*
- *1 ¼ cup hot water*

Direction: Cooking Time: 30 minutes Servings: 8

- ✓ *Mix honey and water in a small container. Add*

yeast and stir a bit and leave on for 7 minutes.

- ✓ *In a large mixing container, mix well salt, xanthan gum, hemp, poppy, flax meal, buckwheat flour, brown rice four, tapioca starch, and sorghum flour and beat with a paddle mixer.*
- ✓ *In a medium container, beat well vinegar, oil, and eggs.*
- ✓ *In container of dry ingredients, pour in container of egg mixture and yeast mixture and mix well until you have a smooth dough.*
- ✓ *In a greased 10-inch cast iron skillet, transfer dough. Lightly wet hands with warm water and smoothen surface of dough until the surface is even. (A 9-inch cake pan will also do nicely if you don't have a cast iron skillet).*
- ✓ *Sprinkle extra seeds on top of dough and leave dough in a warm corner for 45 to 60 minutes to rise.*
- ✓ *Then pop risen dough in a 3750F preheated oven until tops are golden brown, around 30 minutes.*
- ✓ *Once done cooking, immediately remove dough from pan and let it cool a bit before slicing and serving.*

Nutrition: Calories: 291; Carbs: 49.1g; Protein: 6.0g; Fat: 8.5g

748) Tasty Crabby Panini

Ingredients:

- *1 tbsp Olive oil*
- *French bread split and sliced diagonally*
- *1 lb. blue crab meat or shrimp or spiny lobster or stone crab*
- *½ cup celery*
- *¼ cup green onion chopped*
- *1 tsp Worcestershire sauce*
- *1 tsp lemon juice*
- *1 tbsp Dijon mustard*
- *½ cup light mayonnaise*

Direction: Cooking Time: 10 minutes Servings: 4

- ✓ *In a medium container mix the following thoroughly: celery, onion, Worcestershire, lemon juice, mustard and mayonnaise. Season with pepper and salt. Then gently add to the almonds and crabs.*
- ✓ *Spread olive oil on sliced sides of bread and smear with crab mixture before covering with another bread slice.*
- ✓ *Grill sandwich in a Panini press until bread is crisped and ridged*

Nutrition: Calories: 248; Carbs: 12.0g; Protein: 24.5g; Fat: 10.9g

749) Tuna Melt Panini

Ingredients:

- *2 tbsp softened unsalted butter*
- *16 pcs of 1/8-inch kosher dill pickle*
- *8 pcs of ¼ inch thick cheddar or Swiss cheese*
- *Mayonnaise and Dijon mustard*
- *4 ciabatta rolls, split*
- *Pepper and salt*
- *½ tsp crushed red pepper*
- *1 tbsp minced basil*
- *1 tbsp balsamic vinegar*
- *¼ cup extra virgin olive oil*
- *¼ cup finely diced red onion*
- *2 cans of 6oz albacore tuna*

Direction: Cooking Time: 10 minutes Servings: 4

- ✓ *Combine thoroughly the following in a container: salt pepper, crushed red pepper, basil, vinegar, olive oil, onion and tuna.*
- ✓ *Smear with mayonnaise and mustard the cut sides of the bread rolls then layer on: cheese, tuna salad and pickles. Cover with the resting slice of roll.*
- ✓ *Grill in a Panini press ensuring that cheese is melted and bread is crisped and ridged.*

Nutrition: Calories: 539; Carbs: 27.7g; Protein: 21.6g; Fat: 38.5g

750) Tuscan Bread Dipper

Ingredients:

- *¼ cup balsamic vinegar*
- *¼ cup extra virgin olive oil*
- *¼ Tsp salt*
- *½ tbsp fresh basil, minced*
- *½ Tsp pepper*
- *1 ½ Tsp Italian seasoning*
- *2 cloves garlic minced*
- *8 pieces Food for Life Brown Rice English Muffins*

Direction: Cooking Time: 0 minutes Servings: 8

- ✓ *In a small container mix well all ingredients except for bread. Allow herbs to steep in olive oil-balsamic vinegar mixture for at least 30 minutes.*
- ✓ *To serve, toast bread, cut each muffin in half and serve with balsamic vinegar dip.*

Nutrition: Calories: 168.5; Carbs: 27.7g; Protein: 5.2g; Fat: 4.1g

751) Coconut Flour Pizza

Ingredients:

- *2 Tbsps psyllium husk powder*
- *¾ cup coconut flour*
- *1 Tsp garlic powder*
- *½ Tsp salt*
- *½ Tsp baking soda*

- *1 cup boiling water*
- *1 Tsp apple cider vinegar*
- *3 eggs*
- *Toppings*
- *3 Tbsps tomato sauce*
- *1½ oz. Mozzarella cheese*
- *1 Tbsp basil, freshly chopped*

Direction: Preparation time: 35 mins Servings: 4

✓ *Switch on the oven, preheat it setting its temperature to 350 degrees F and grease a baking sheet.*

✓ *Mix coconut flour, salt, psyllium husk powder, and garlic powder until fully combined.*

✓ *Add eggs, apple cider vinegar, and baking soda and knead with boiling water.*

✓ *Place the dough out on a baking sheet and top with the toppings.*

✓ *Transfer to the oven and bake for about 20 minutes.*

✓ *Dish out and serve warm.*

Nutrition: Calories: 173 Carbs: 16.8g Fats: 7.4g Proteins: 10.4g Sodium: 622mg Sugar: 0.9g

752) Mini Pizza Crusts

Ingredients:

- *1 cup coconut flour, sifted*
- *8 large eggs, 5 whole eggs and 3 egg whites*
- *½ Tsp baking powder*
- *Italian spices, to taste*
- *Salt and black pepper, to taste*

For the pizza sauce

- *2 garlic cloves, crushed*
- *1 Tsp dried basil*
- *½ cup tomato sauce*
- *¼ Tsp sea salt*

Direction: Preparation time: 20 mins Servings: 4

✓ *Switch on the oven, preheat it setting its temperature to 350 degrees F and grease a baking tray.*

✓ *Whisk together eggs and egg whites in a large container and stir to the coconut flour, baking powder, Italian spices, salt, and black pepper.*

✓ *Make small dough balls from this mixture and press on the baking tray.*

✓ *Transfer to the oven and bake for about 20 minutes.*

✓ *Allow pizza bases to cool and keep aside.*

✓ *Combine all ingredients for the pizza sauce together and sit at room temperature for half an hour.*

✓ *Spread this pizza sauce over the pizza crusts and serve.*

Nutrition: Calories: 170 Carbs: 5.7g Fats: 10.5g Proteins: 13.6g Sodium: 461mg Sugar: 2.3g

753) Keto Pepperoni Pizza

Ingredients:

- *Crust*
- *6 oz. mozzarella cheese, shredded*
- *4 eggs*
- *Topping*
- *1 Tsp dried oregano*
- *1½ oz. pepperoni*
- *3 Tbsps tomato paste*
- *5 oz. mozzarella cheese, shredded*
- *Olives*

Direction: Preparation time: 40 mins Servings: 4

✓ *Switch on the oven, preheat it setting its temperature to 400 degrees F and grease a baking sheet.*

✓ *Whisk together eggs and cheese in a container and spread on a baking sheet.*

✓ *Transfer to the oven and bake for about 15 minutes until golden.*

✓ *Remove from the oven and allow it to cool.*

✓ *Increase the oven temperature to 450 degrees F.*

✓ *Spread the tomato paste on the crust and top with oregano, pepperoni, cheese, and olives on top.*

✓ *Bake for 10 minutes more and serve hot.*

Nutrition: Calories: 356 Carbs: 6.1g Fats: 23.8g Proteins: 30.6g Sodium: 790mg Sugar: 1.8g

754) BBQ Chicken Pizza

Ingredients:

- *Dairy Free Pizza Crust*
- *6 Tbsps Parmesan cheese*
- *6 large eggs*
- *3 Tbsps psyllium husk powder*
- *Salt and black pepper, to taste*
- *1½ Tsps Italian seasoning*

Toppings

- *6 oz. rotisserie chicken, shredded*
- *4 oz. cheddar cheese*
- *1 Tbsp mayonnaise*
- *4 Tbsps tomato sauce*
- *4 Tbsps BBQ sauce*

Direction: Preparation time: 30 mins Servings: 4

✓ *Switch on the oven, preheat it setting its temperature to 400 degrees F and grease a baking dish.*

✓ *Place all Pizza Crust ingredients in an immersion blender and blend until smooth.*

✓ *Spread dough mixture onto the baking dish and transfer in the oven.*

✓ *Bake for about 10 minutes and top with favorite toppings.*

✓ *Bake for about 3 minutes and dish out.*

Nutrition: Calories: 356 Carbs: 2.9g Fats: 24.5g Proteins: 24.5g Sodium: 396mg Sugar: 0.6g

755) Buffalo Chicken Crust Pizza

Ingredients:

- *1 cup whole milk mozzarella, shredded*
- *1 Tsp dried oregano*
- *2 Tbsps butter*
- *1 pound chicken thighs, boneless and skinless*
- *1 large egg*
- *¼ Tsp black pepper*
- *¼ Tsp salt*
- *1 stalk celery*
- *3 Tbsps Franks Red Hot Original*
- *1 stalk green onion*
- *1 Tbsp sour cream*
- *1 ounce bleu cheese, crumbled*

Direction: Preparation time: 25 mins Servings: 6

✓ *Switch on the oven, preheat it setting its temperature to 400 degrees F and grease a baking dish.*

✓ *Process chicken thighs in a food processor until smooth.*

✓ *Transfer to a large container and add egg, ½ cup of shredded mozzarella, oregano, black pepper, and salt to form a dough.*

✓ *Spread the chicken dough to the baking dish and transfer to the oven*

✓ *Bake for about 25 minutes and keep aside.*

✓ *Meanwhile, heat butter and add celery, and cook for about 4 minutes.*

✓ *Mix Franks Red Hot Original with the sour cream in a small container.*

✓ *Spread the sauce mixture over the crust, layer with the cooked celery and resting ½ cup of mozzarella and the bleu cheese.*

✓ *Bake 10 minutes more , until the cheese is melted*

Nutrition: Calories: 172 Carbs: 1g Fats: 12.9g Proteins: 13.8g Sodium: 172mg Sugar: 0.2g

756) Fresh Bell Pepper Basil Pizza

Ingredients:

- *Pizza Base*
- *½ cup almond flour*
- *2 Tbsps cream cheese*
- *1 Tsp Italian seasoning*
- *½ Tsp black pepper*
- *6 ounces mozzarella cheese*
- *2 Tbsps psyllium husk*
- *2 Tbsps fresh Parmesan cheese*
- *1 large egg*
- *½ Tsp salt*

Toppings

- *4 ounces cheddar cheese, shredded*
- *¼ cup Marinara sauce*
- *2/3 medium bell pepper*
- *1 medium vine tomato*
- *3 Tbsps basil, fresh chopped*

Direction: Preparation time: 25 mins Servings: 3

✓ *Switch on the oven, preheat it setting its temperature to 400 degrees F and grease a baking dish.*

✓ *Microwave mozzarella cheese for about 30 seconds and top with the resting pizza crust.*

✓ *Add the resting pizza ingredients to the cheese and mix together.*

✓ *Flatten the dough and transfer in the oven.*

✓ *Bake for about 10 minutes and remove pizza from the oven.*

✓ *Top the pizza with the toppings and bake for another 10 minutes.*

✓ *Remove pizza from the oven and allow to cool.*

Nutrition: Calories:411 Carbs: 6.4g Fats: 31.3g Proteins: 22.2g Sodium: 152mg Sugar: 2.8g

757) Keto Thai Chicken Flatbread Pizza

Ingredients:

- *Peanut Sauce*
- *2 Tbsps rice wine vinegar*
- *4 Tbsps reduced sugar ketchup*
- *4 Tbsps soy sauce*
- *4 Tbsps coconut oil*
- *½ lime, juiced*
- *1 Tsp fish sauce*
- *Pizza Base*
- *¾ cup almond flour*
- *3 Tbsps cream cheese*
- *½ Tsp garlic powder*
- *8 oz. mozzarella cheese*
- *1 Tbsp psyllium husk powder*
- *1 large egg*
- *½ Tsp onion powder*
- *½ Tsp ginger*
- *½ Tsp black pepper*
- *½ Tsp salt*
- *Toppings*
- *3 oz. mung bean sprouts*

- *2 medium green onions*
- *2 Tbsps peanuts*
- *2 chicken thighs*
- *6 oz. mozzarella cheese*
- *1½ oz. carrots, shredded*

Direction: Preparation time: 25 mins Servings: 12

- ✓ *Preheat oven to 400 degrees F and grease a baking tray.*
- ✓ *Mix together all peanut sauce ingredients and set aside.*
- ✓ *Microwave cream cheese and mozzarella cheese for the pizza base for 1 minute.*
- ✓ *Add eggs, then mix together with all dry ingredients.*
- ✓ *Arrange dough onto a baking tray and bake for about 15 minutes.*
- ✓ *Flip pizza and top with sauce, chopped chicken, shredded carrots, and mozzarella.*
- ✓ *Bake again for 10 minutes, or until cheese has melted.*
- ✓ *Top with bean sprouts, spring onion, peanuts, and cilantro.*

Nutrition: Calories: 268 Carbs: 3.2g Fats: 21g Proteins: 15g Sodium: 94mg Sugar: 0.2g

Pasta Rice and Grains Recipes

758) Cucumber Olive Rice

Ingredients:

- 2 cups rice, rinsed
- 1/2 cup olives, pitted
- 1 cup cucumber, chopped
- 1 tbsp red wine vinegar
- 1 tsp lemon zest, grated
- 1 tbsp fresh lemon juice
- 2 tbsp olive oil
- 2 cups vegetable broth
- 1/2 tsp dried oregano
- One red bell pepper, chopped
- 1/2 cup onion, chopped
- 1 tbsp olive oil
- Pepper
- Salt

Direction: Preparation Time: 10 minutes Cooking Time: 10 minutes Servings: 8

- ✓ Set the Instant Pot to sauté mode after adding the oil to the inner pot..
- ✓ Sauté for 3 minutes after adding the onion.
- ✓ Add the bell pepper and oregano and sauté for 1 minute.
- ✓ Add the rice and broth and stir well.
- ✓ Close the pot's lid and cook on high heat for 6 minutes.
- ✓ Once it's done, allow the natural release of pressure for 10 minutes, then release by resting using the quick release. Remove the lid.
- ✓ Add the resting ingredients and stir well to combine.
- ✓ Serve immediately and enjoy.

Nutrition: Cal 229 Fat 5.1 g Carbs 40.2 g Sugar 1.6 g Protein 4.9 g Cholesterol 0 mg

759) Flavors Herb Risotto

Ingredients:

- 2 cups of rice
- 2 tbsp parmesan cheese, grated
- 3.5 oz heavy cream
- 1 tbsp fresh oregano, chopped
- 1 tbsp fresh basil, chopped
- 1/2 tbsp sage, chopped
- One onion, chopped
- 2 tbsp olive oil
- 1 tsp garlic, minced
- 4 cups vegetable stock
- Pepper
- Salt

Direction: Preparation Time: 10 minutes Cooking Time: 15 minutes Servings: 4

- ✓ Set the instant pot to sauté mode and pour in the oil.
- ✓ Sauté for 2-3 minutes with the garlic and onion.
- ✓ Combine the remaining ingredients, excluding parmesan cheese and heavy cream and mix well.
- ✓ Close the pot's lid and cook on high heat for 12 minutes.
- ✓ Once done, let release pressure naturally for 10 minutes, then release by resting using the quick release.
- ✓ Remove the lid.
- ✓ Stir in cream and cheese and serve.

Nutrition: Cal 514 Fat 17.6 g Carbs 79.4 g Sugar 2.1 g Protein 8.8 g Cholesterol 36 mg

760) Delicious Pasta Primavera

Ingredients:

- 8 ounces whole-wheat penne pasta
- One tablespoon fresh lemon juice
- Two tablespoons fresh parsley, chopped
- 1/4 cup chopped almonds
- 1/4 cup Parmesan cheese, grated
- 14 ounces canned tomatoes, diced
- 1/3 cup prunes
- 1/3 cup zucchini, chopped
- 1/3 cup asparagus, cut into 1-inch
- 1/3 cup carrots, shredded
- 1/3 cup broccoli, chopped
- 1 3/4 cups vegetable broth
- Pepper
- Salt

Direction: Preparation Time: 10 minutes Cooking Time: 4 minutes Servings: 4

- ✓ Add the broth, pars, tomatoes, plums, zucchini, asparagus, carrots, and broccoli to the Instant Pot and mix well.
- ✓ Close the pot's lid and cook on high heat for 4 minutes.
- ✓ Once done, using the quick release, release the pressure. Remove the lid.
- ✓ Add remaining ingredients, mix well and serve.

Cal per serving: 303 Carbs 63.5 g Sugar 13.4 g Protein 12.8 g Cholesterol 1 mg Fat 2.6 g Carbs 63.5 g Cholesterol 1 mg

761) Roasted Pepper Pasta

Ingredients:

- 1 lb whole wheat penne pasta
- 1 tbsp Italian seasoning
- 4 cups vegetable broth
- 1 tbsp garlic, minced
- 1/2 onion, chopped

- 14 oz jar roasted red peppers
- 1 cup feta cheese, crumbled
- 1 tbsp olive oil
- Pepper and Salt

Direction: Preparation Time: 10 minutes Cooking Time: 13 minutes Servings: 6

- ✓ Add the roasted bell pepper to the blender and blend until smooth.
- ✓ Add the oil to the inner pot of the Instant Pot and set the pot to sauté mode.
- ✓ Sauté for 2-3 minutes with the garlic and onion.
- ✓ Add the blended roasted bell pepper and sauté for 2 minutes.
- ✓ Mix in the remaining ingredients, except the feta cheese, thoroughly..
- ✓ Close the pot's lid and cook on high heat for 8 minutes.
- ✓ Once done, let release pressure naturally for 5 minutes, then release by resting using the quick release. Remove the lid.
- ✓ Add the feta cheese and serve.

Nutrition: Cal 459 Fat 10.6 g Carbs 68.1 g Sugar 2.1 g Protein 21.3 g Cholesterol 24 mg

762) Cheese Basil Tomato Rice

Ingredients:

- 1 1/2 cups brown rice
- 1 cup parmesan cheese, grated
- 1/4 cup fresh basil, chopped
- 2 cups grape tomatoes, halved
- 8 oz can tomato sauce
- 1 3/4 cup vegetable broth
- 1 tbsp garlic, minced
- 1/2 cup onion, diced
- 1 tbsp olive oil
- Pepper
- Salt

Direction: Preparation Time: 10 minutes Cooking Time: 26 minutes Servings: 8

- ✓ Set the instant pot to sauté mode after adding oil to the inner pot.
- ✓ Add garlic and onion and sauté for 4 minutes.
- ✓ Add the rice, tomato sauce, broth, pepper, and salt and mix well.
- ✓ Close the pot's lid and cook on high heat for 22 minutes.
- ✓ Once done, allow pressure to release naturally for 10 minutes, then release by resting using the quick release. Remove the lid.
- ✓ Add resting ingredients and stir well.
- ✓ Serve and enjoy.

Nutrition: Cal 208 Fat 5.6 g Carbs 32.1 g Sugar 2.8 g Protein 8.3 g Cholesterol 8 mg

763) Mac & Cheese

Ingredients:

- 1 lb whole grain pasta
- 1/2 cup parmesan cheese, grated
- 4 cups cheddar cheese, shredded
- 1 cup milk
- 1/4 tsp garlic powder
- 1/2 tsp ground mustard
- 2 tbsp olive oil
- 4 cups of water
- Pepper and Salt

Direction: Preparation Time: 10 minutes Cooking Time: 4 minutes Servings: 8

- ✓ Add the pasta, garlic powder, mustard, oil, water, pepper, and salt to the Instant Pot.
- ✓ Close the pot's lid and cook on high heat for 4 minutes.
- ✓ After that, use the quick release to relieve the pressure. Remove the lid.
- ✓ Add the rest of the ingredients and mix well and serve.

Cal are 509 in this recipe. Cholesterol 66 mg Fat 25.7 g Carbs 43.8 g Sugar 3.8 g Protein 27.3 g

764) Tuna Pasta

Ingredients:

- 10 oz canned tuna, drained
- 15 oz whole wheat rotini pasta
- 4 oz mozzarella cheese, cubed
- 1/2 cup parmesan cheese, grated
- 1 tsp dried basil
- 14 oz canned tomatoes, diced
- 4 cups vegetable broth
- 1 tbsp garlic, minced
- 8 oz mushrooms, sliced
- Two zucchini, sliced
- One onion, chopped
- 2 tbsp olive oil
- Pepper
- Salt

Direction: Preparation Time: 10 minutes Cooking Time: 8 minutes Servings: 6

- ✓ Add the oil to the inner pot of the Instant Pot and set the pot to sauté mode.
- ✓ Add the mushrooms, zucchini, and onion and sauté until the onion is softened.
- ✓ Add the garlic and sauté for one minute.
- ✓ Add the pasta, basil, tuna, tomatoes, and broth and mix well.
- ✓ Close the pot's lid and cook on high heat for 4

minutes.

- ✓ Once done, allow pressure to release naturally for 5 minutes, then release by resting using the quick release. Remove the lid.
- ✓ Add resting ingredients, stir well and serve.

Nutrition: Cal 346 Fat 11.9 g Carbs 31.3 g Sugar 6.3 g Protein 6.3 g

765) Vegan Olive Pasta

Ingredients:

- 4 cups whole grain penne pasta
- 1/2 cup olives, sliced
- 1 tbsp capers
- 1/4 tsp red pepper flakes
- 3 cups of water
- 4 cups pasta sauce, homemade
- 1 tbsp garlic, minced
- Pepper
- Salt

Direction: Preparation Time: 10 minutes Cooking Time: 5 minutes Servings: 4

- ✓ Add all ingredients to the inner pot of the Instant Pot and mix well.
- ✓ Seal the pot with the lid and cook on high heat for 5 minutes. After that, use the quick release to relieve the pressure. Remove the lid.
- ✓ Stir and serve.

Nutrition: Cal 441 Fat 10.1 g Carbs 77.3 g Sugar 24.1 g Protein 11.8 g

766) Italian Mac & Cheese

Ingredients:

- 1 lb whole grain pasta
- 2 tsp Italian seasoning
- 1 1/2 tsp garlic powder
- 1 1/2 tsp onion powder
- 1 cup sour cream
- 4 cups of water
- 4 oz parmesan cheese, shredded
- 12 oz ricotta cheese
- Pepper
- Salt

Direction: Preparation Time: 10 minutes Cooking Time: 6 minutes Servings: 4

- ✓ Add all ingredients except ricotta to the inner pot of the Instant Pot and mix well.
- ✓ Seal the pot with the lid and cook on high for 6 minutes.
- ✓ Once done, let release pressure naturally for 5 minutes, then release rest using the quick release.
- ✓ Remove the lid.
- ✓ Add the ricotta cheese and mix well and serve.

Nutrition: Cal 388 Fat 25.8 g Carbs 18.1 g Sugar 4 g Protein 22.8 g Cholesterol 74 mg

767) Italian Chicken Pasta

Ingredients:

- 1 pound chicken breast, skinless, boneless, and cut into pieces
- 1/2 cup cream cheese
- 1 cup mozzarella cheese, shredded
- 1 1/2 teaspoons Italian seasoning
- One teaspoon minced garlic
- 1 cup mushrooms, diced
- 1/2 onion, diced
- Two tomatoes, diced
- 2 cups water
- 16 ounces whole-wheat penne pasta
- pepper and salt

Direction: Preparation time: 10 minutes Cooking time: 9 minutes Portions: 8

- ✓ Add all ingredients except the cheeses to the inner pot of the Instant Pot and mix well.
- ✓ Seal the pot with the lid and cook on high heat for 9 minutes.
- ✓ Once done, let release pressure naturally for 5 minutes, then release rest using the quick release. Remove the lid.
- ✓ Add cheeses and mix well and serve.

Nutrition: Cal 328 Fat 8.5 g Carbs 42.7 g Sugar 1.4 g Protein 23.7 g Cholesterol 55 mg

768) Delicious Greek Chicken Pasta

Ingredients:

- Two chicken breasts, skinless, boned, and cut into pieces
- 1/2 cup olives, sliced
- 2 cups vegetable broth
- 12 ounces Greek vinaigrette dressing
- 1 pound whole-wheat pasta
- pepper
- salt

Direction: Preparation time: 10 minutes Cooking time: 10 minutes Portions: 6

- ✓ Add all ingredients to the inner pot of the Instant Pot and mix well.
- ✓ Seal the pot with the lid and cook on high heat for 10 minutes.
- ✓ After that, use the quick release to relieve the pressure. Remove the lid.
- ✓ Stir well and serve.

Nutrition: Cal 325 Fat 25.8 g Carbs 10.5 g Sugar 4 g Protein 15.6 g Cholesterol 43 mg

769) Pesto Chicken Pasta

Ingredients:

- *1 pound chicken breast, skinless, boned, and diced*
- *Three tablespoons olive oil*
- *1/2 cup Parmesan cheese, shredded*
- *One teaspoon Italian seasoning*
- *1/4 cup heavy cream*
- *16 ounces whole-wheat pasta*
- *6 ounces basil pesto*
- *3 1/2 cups water*
- *pepper*
- *salt*

Direction: Preparation time: 10 minutes Cooking time: 10 minutes Portions: 6

- ✓ *Season the chicken with Italian seasoning, pepper, and salt.*
- ✓ *Add the oil to the inner pot of the Instant Pot and set the pot to sauté mode.*
- ✓ *Add the chicken to the pot and sauté until brown.*
- ✓ *Add the rest of the ingredients except the parmesan cheese, heavy cream, and pesto, and mix well.*
- ✓ *Close the pot's lid and cook on high pressure for 5 minutes.*
- ✓ *After that, use the quick release to relieve the pressure. Remove the lid.*
- ✓ *Add the parmesan cheese, cream, and pesto and serve.*

Nutrition: Cal 475 Fat 14.7 g Carbs 57 g Sugar 2.8 g Protein 28.7 g Cholesterol 61 mg

770) ***Spinach Pesto Pasta***

Ingredients:

- *8 oz whole-grain pasta*
- *1/3 cup mozzarella cheese, grated*
- *1/2 cup pesto*
- *5 oz fresh spinach*
- *1 3/4 cup water*
- *8 oz mushrooms, chopped*
- *1 tbsp olive oil*
- *Pepper*
- *Salt*

Direction: Preparation Time: 10 minutes Cooking Time: 10 minutes Servings: 4

- ✓ *Set the instant pot to sauté mode after adding oil to the inner pot.*
- ✓ *Add mushrooms and sauté for 4- 5 minutes.*
- ✓ *Add water and pasta and stir well*
- ✓ *Seal pot with lid and cook on high for 5 minutes*
- ✓ *Once done, release pressure using quick release. Remove lid.*
- ✓ *Stir in resting ingredients and serve.*

Nutrition: Cal 213 Fat 17.3 g Carbs 9.5 g Sugar 4.5 g Protein 7.4 g Cholesterol 9 mg

771) ***Fiber Packed Chicken Rice***

Ingredients:

- *1 lb chicken breast, skinless, boneless, and cut into pieces*
- *14.5 oz canned cannellini beans*
- *4 cups chicken broth*
- *2 cups wild rice*
- *1 tbsp Italian seasoning*
- *One small onion, chopped*
- *1 tbsp garlic, chopped*
- *1 tbsp olive oil*
- *Pepper*
- *Salt*

Direction: Preparation Time: 10 minutes Cooking Time: 16 minutes Servings: 6

- ✓ *Set the instant pot to sauté mode after adding oil to the inner pot.*
- ✓ *Sauté for 2-3 minutes with the garlic and onion.*
- ✓ *Add the chicken and cook for 2 minutes.*
- ✓ *Add the rest of the ingredients and mix well*
- ✓ *Seal the pot with the lid and cook on high heat for 11-12 minutes.*
- ✓ *After that, use the quick release to relieve the pressure. Remove the lid. Stir well and serve.*

Nutrition: Cal 399 Fat 6.4 g Carbs 53.4 g Sugar 3 g Protein 31.6 g Cholesterol 50 mg

772) ***Tasty Greek Rice***

Ingredients:

- *1 3/4 cup brown rice, rinsed and drained*
- *3/4 cup roasted red peppers, chopped*
- *1 cup olives, chopped*
- *1 tsp dried oregano*
- *1 tsp Greek seasoning*
- *1 3/4 cup vegetable broth*
- *2 tbsp olive oil*
- *Salt*

Direction: Preparation Time: 10 minutes Cooking Time: 10 minutes Servings: 6

- ✓ *Set the instant pot to sauté mode after adding oil to the inner pot.*
- ✓ *Add rice and cook for 5 minutes.*
- ✓ *Add resting ingredients except for red peppers and olives and stir well*
- ✓ *Seal pot with lid and cook on high for 4- 5 minutes*
- ✓ *Once done, release pressure naturally for 10 minutes, then release resting using quick release. Remove lid.*
- ✓ *Add red peppers and olives and stir well.*
- ✓ *Serve and enjoy. Ingredients*

Nutrition: Cal 285 Fat 9.1 g Carbs 45.7 g Sugar 1.2

g Protein 6 g Cholesterol 0 mg

773) Perfect Herb Rice

Ingredients:

- 1 cup brown rice, rinsed
- 1 tbsp olive oil
- 1 1/2 cups water
- 1/2 cup fresh mix herbs, chopped
- 1 tsp salt

Direction: Preparation Time: 10 minutes Cooking Time: 4 minutes Servings: 4

- ✓ Add all ingredients to the inner pot of the Instant Pot and mix well.
- ✓ Seal the pot with the lid and cook on high heat for 4 minutes.
- ✓ Once done, allow pressure to release naturally for 10 minutes, then release rest using the quick release. Remove the lid.
- ✓ Stir well and serve.

Nutrition: Cal 264 Fat 9.9 g Carbs 36.7 g Sugar 0.4 g Protein 7.3 g Cholesterol 0 mg

774) Herb Polenta

Ingredients:

- 1 cup polenta
- 1/4 tsp nutmeg
- 3 tbsp fresh parsley, chopped
- 1/4 cup milk
- 1/2 cup parmesan cheese, grated
- 4 cups vegetable broth
- 2 tsp thyme, chopped
- 2 tsp rosemary, chopped
- 2 tsp sage, chopped
- One small onion, chopped
- 2 tbsp olive oil
- Salt

Direction: Preparation Time: 10 minutes Cooking Time: 12 minutes Servings: 6

- ✓ Set the instant pot to sauté mode after adding oil to the inner pot.
- ✓ Add onion and herbs and sauté for 4 minutes.
- ✓ Add polenta, broth, and salt and stir well.
- ✓ Seal pot with lid and cook on high for 8 minutes.
- ✓ Once done, allow to release pressure naturally. Remove lid.
- ✓ Stir in resting ingredients and serve.

Nutrition: Cal 196 Fat 7.8 g Carbs 23.5 g Sugar 1.7 g Protein 8.2 g Cholesterol 6 mg

775) Pecorino Pasta with Sausage and Fresh Tomato

Ingredients:

- ¼ cup torn fresh basil leaves
- 1/8 tsp black pepper
- ¼ tsp salt
- 6 tbsp grated fresh pecorino Romano cheese, divided
- One ¼ lbs. tomatoes, chopped
- 2 tsp minced garlic
- 1 cup vertically sliced onions
- 2 tsp olive oil
- 8 oz sweet Italian sausage
- 8 oz uncooked penne, cooked and drained

Direction: Servings: 4, Cooking Time: 20 minutes

- ✓ On medium-high fire, place a nonstick fry pan with oil and cook for five minutes onion and sausage. Stir constantly to break sausage into pieces.
- ✓ Stir in garlic and continue cooking for two minutes more.
- ✓ Add tomatoes and cook for another two minutes.
- ✓ Remove pan from the fire, season with pepper and salt. Mix well.
- ✓ Stir in 2 tbsp cheese and pasta. Toss well.
- ✓ Transfer to a serving dish, garnish with basil, and resting cheese before serving.

Nutrition: Cal : 376; Carbs: 50.8g; Prot: 17.8g; Fat: 11.6g

776) Pesto Pasta and Shrimps

Ingredients:

- ¼ cup pesto, divided
- ¼ cup shaved Parmesan Cheese
- One ¼ lbs. large shrimp, peeled and deveined
- 1 cup halved grape tomatoes
- 4-oz angel hair pasta, cooked, rinsed, and drained

Direction: Servings: 4, Cooking Time: 15 minutes

- ✓ On medium-high fire, place a nonstick large fry pan and grease with cooking spray.
- ✓ Add tomatoes, pesto, and shrimp. Cook for 15 minutes or until shrimps is opaque while covered.
- ✓ Stir in cooked pasta and cook until heated through.
- ✓ Transfer to a serving plate and garnish with Parmesan cheese.

Nutrition: Cal : 319; Carbs: 23.6g; Protein: 31.4g; Fat: 11g

777) . Prosciutto e Faggioli

Ingredients:

- 12 oz pasta, cooked and drained
- Pepper and salt to taste
- 3 tbsp snipped fresh chives
- 3 cups arugula or watercress leaves, loosely packed

- *½ cup chicken broth, warm*
- *1 tbsp Herbed garlic butter*
- *½ cup shredded pecorino Toscano*
- *4 oz prosciutto, cut into bite sizes*
- *2 cups cherry tomatoes, halved*
- *One can of 19oz white kidney beans, rinsed and drained*

Direction: Servings: 4, Cooking Time: 15 minutes

- ✓ *Heat over medium-low fire herbed garlic butter, cheese, prosciutto, tomatoes, and beans in a big saucepan for 2 minutes.*
- ✓ *Once the mixture is simmering, constantly stir to melt cheese while gradually stirring to the broth.*
- ✓ *Once the cheese is fully melted and incorporated, add chives, arugula, pepper, and salt.*
- ✓ *Turn off the fire and toss to the cooked pasta. Serve and enjoy.*

Nutrition: Cal : 452; Carbs: 57.9g; Protein: 30.64g;

778) Puttanesca Style Bucatini

Ingredients:

- *1 tbsp capers, rinsed*
- *1 tsp coarsely chopped fresh oregano*
- *1 tsp finely chopped garlic*
- *1/8 tsp salt*
- *12-oz bucatini pasta*
- *2 cups coarsely chopped canned no-salt-added whole peeled tomatoes with their juice*
- *3 tbsp extra virgin olive oil, divided*
- *Four anchovy fillets, chopped*
- *Eight black Kalamata olives, pitted and sliced into slivers*

Direction: Servings: 4, Cooking Time: 40 minutes

- ✓ *Cook bucatini pasta according to package directions. Drain, keep warm and set aside.*
- ✓ *On medium fire, place a large nonstick saucepan and heat 2 tbsp oil.*
- ✓ *Sauté anchovies until it starts to disintegrate.*
- ✓ *Add garlic and sauté for 15 seconds.*
- ✓ *Add tomatoes, sauté for 15 to 20 minutes or until no longer watery; season with 1/8 tsp salt.*
- ✓ *Add oregano, capers, and olives.*
- ✓ *Add pasta, sautéing until heated through.*
- ✓ *To serve, drizzle pasta with resting olive oil and enjoy.*

Nutrition: Cal : 207.4; Carbs: 31g; Protein: 5.1g;

779) Quinoa & Black Bean Stuffed Sweet Potatoes

Ingredients:

- *Four sweet potatoes*
- *½ onion, diced*
- *One garlic clove, crushed and diced*
- *½ large bell pepper diced (about 2/3 cups)*
- *A handful of diced cilantro*
- *½ cup cooked quinoa*
- *½ cup black beans*
- *1 tbsp olive oil*
- *1 tbsp chili powder*
- *½ tbsp cumin*
- *½ tbsp paprika*
- *½ tbsp oregano*
- *2 tbsp lime juice*
- *2 tbsp honey*
- *Sprinkle salt*
- *1 cup shredded cheddar cheese*
- *Chopped spring onions for garnish (optional)*

Direction: Servings: 8, Cooking Time: 60 minutes

- ✓ *Preheat oven to 400oF.*
- ✓ *Wash and scrub outside of potatoes. Poke with a fork a few times and then place on parchment paper on cookie sheet. Bake for 40-45 minutes or until it is cooked.*
- ✓ *While potatoes are baking, sauté onions, garlic, olive oil, and spices are in a pan on the stove until onions are translucent and soft.*
- ✓ *For the last 10 minutes while the potatoes are cooking, combine the onion mixture with the beans, quinoa, honey, lime juice, cilantro, and ½ cup cheese in a large container. Mix well.*
- ✓ *When potatoes are cooked, remove them from the oven and let cool slightly. When cool to touch, cut in half (hot dog style) and scoop out most of the insides. Leave a thin ring of potato so that it will hold its shape. You can save the sweet potato guts for another recipe, such as my veggie burgers (recipe posted below).*
- ✓ *Fill with bean and quinoa mixture. Top with resting cheddar cheese.*
- ✓ *(If making this a freezer meal, stop here. Individually wrap potato skins in plastic wrap and place them on a flat surface to freeze. Once frozen, place all potatoes in a large zip lock container or Tupperware.)*
- ✓ *Return to oven for an additional 10 minutes or until cheese is melted.*

Nutrition: Cal : 243; Carbs: 37.6g; Protein: 8.5g; Fat: 7.3g

780) Quinoa and Three Beans Recipe

Ingredients:

- *1 cup grape tomatoes, sliced in half*
- *1 cup quinoa*
- *1 cup seedless cucumber, chopped*
- *One red bell pepper, seeds removed and chopped*

- *1 Tbsp balsamic vinegar*
- *One yellow bell pepper, seeds removed and chopped*
- *1/2-pound green beans, trimmed and snapped into 2-inch pieces*
- *1/3 cup pitted kalamata olives, cut in half*
- *1/4 cup chopped fresh basil*
- *1/4 cup diced red onion*
- *1/4 cup feta cheese crumbles*
- *1/4 cup olive oil*
- *1/4 Tsp dried basil*
- *1/4 Tsp dried oregano*
- *15 ounces garbanzo beans, drained and rinsed*
- *15 ounces white beans, drained and rinsed*
- *2 cups water*
- *Two garlic cloves smashed*
- *kosher salt and black pepper to taste*

Direction: Servings: 8, Cooking Time: 35 minutes

✓ *Bring water and quinoa to a boil in a medium saucepan. Cover, reduce heat to low and cook until quinoa is tender, around 15 minutes.*

✓ *Remove from heat and let stand for 5 minutes, covered.*

✓ *Remove lid and fluff with a fork. Transfer to a large salad container.*

✓ *Meanwhile, bring a large pot of salted water to a boil and blanch the green beans for two minutes. Drain and place in a container of ice water. Drain well.*

✓ *Add the fresh basil, olives, feta cheese, red onion, tomatoes, cucumbers, peppers, white beans, garbanzo beans, and green beans in a container of quinoa.*

✓ *Whisk together the pepper, salt, oregano, dried basil, balsamic, and olive oil in a small container. Pour dressing over the salad and toss salad until coated with dressing.*

✓ *Season with more salt and pepper if needed.*

✓ *Serve and enjoy.*

Nutrition: Cal : 249; Carbs: 31.0g; Protein: 8.0g; Fat: 10.0g

781) ***Quinoa Buffalo Bites***

Ingredients:

- *2 cups cooked quinoa*
- *1 cup shredded mozzarella*
- *1/2 cup buffalo sauce*
- *1/4 cup +1 Tbsp flour*
- *One egg*
- *1/4 cup chopped cilantro*
- *One small onion, diced*

Direction: Servings: 4, Cooking Time: 15 minutes

✓ *Preheat oven to 350oF.*

✓ *Mix all ingredients in a large container.*

✓ *Press mixture into greased mini muffin tins.*

✓ *Bake for approximately 15 minutes or until bites is golden.*

✓ *Enjoy on its own or with blue cheese or ranch dip.*

Nutrition: Cal : 212; Carbs: 30.6g; Protein: 15.9g; Fat: 3.0g

782) ***Raisins, Nuts, and Beef on Hashweh Rice***

Ingredients:

- *½ cup dark raisins, soaked in 2 cups water for an hour*
- *1/3 cup slivered almonds, toasted and soaked in 2 cups water overnight*
- *1/3 cup pine nuts, toasted and soaked in 2 cups water overnight*
- *½ cup fresh parsley leaves, roughly chopped*
- *Pepper and salt to taste*
- *¾ tsp ground cinnamon, divided*
- *¾ tsp cloves, divided*
- *1 tsp garlic powder*
- *One ¾ tsp allspice, divided*
- *One lb. lean ground beef*
- *One small red onion, finely chopped*
- *Olive oil*
- *1 ½ cups medium-grain rice*

Direction: Servings: 8, Cooking Time: 50 minutes

✓ *For 15 to 20 minutes, soak rice in cold water. You will know that soaking is enough when you can snap a grain of rice easily between your thumb and index finger. Once soaking is done, drain the rice well.*

✓ *Meanwhile, drain pine nuts, almonds, and raisins for at least a minute and transfer them to one container. Set aside.*

✓ *On a heavy cooking pot on medium-high fire, heat 1 tbsp olive oil*

✓ *Once the oil is hot, add red onions. Sauté for a minute before adding ground meat and sauté for another minute.*

✓ *Season ground meat with pepper, salt, ½ tsp ground cinnamon, ½ tsp ground cloves, 1 tsp garlic powder, and one ¼ tsp allspice.*

✓ *Sauté ground meat for 10 minutes or until browned and cooked fully. Drain fat.*

✓ *In the same pot with cooked ground meat, add rice on top of the meat.*

✓ *Season with pepper and salt. Add resting cinnamon, ground cloves, and allspice. Do not mix.*

✓ *Add 1 tbsp olive oil and 2 ½ cups of water. Bring to a boil, and once boiling, lower the fire to a simmer. Cook while covered until liquid is fully absorbed,* around 20 to 25 minutes.

- ✓ Turn of fire.
- ✓ To serve, place a large serving platter that fully covers the mouth of the pot. Place platter upside down on the mouth of the pot, and invert pot. The inside of the pot should now rest on the platter with the rice on the bottom of the plate and ground meat on top of it.
- ✓ Garnish the top of the meat with raisins, almonds, pine nuts, and parsley.
- ✓ Serve and enjoy.

Nutrition: 357; Carbs: 39.0g; Protein: 16.7g; Fat: 15.9g

783) . Raw Tomato Sauce & Brie on Linguine

Ingredients:

- ¼ cup grated low-fat Parmesan cheese
- ½ cup loosely packed fresh basil leaves, torn
- 12 oz whole wheat linguine
- 2 cups loosely packed baby arugula
- Two green onions, green parts only, sliced thinly
- 2 tbsp balsamic vinegar
- 2 tbsp extra virgin olive oil
- Three large vine-ripened tomatoes
- 3 oz low-fat Brie cheese, cubed, rind removed, and discarded
- 3 tbsp toasted pine nuts
- Pepper and salt to taste

Direction: Servings: 4, Cooking Time: 12 minutes

- ✓ Toss together pepper, salt, vinegar, oil, onions, Parmesan, basil, arugula, Brie, and tomatoes in a large container and set aside.
- ✓ Cook linguine following package instructions. Reserve 1 cup of pasta cooking water after linguine is cooked. Drain and discard the rest of the pasta. Do not run under cold water. Instead, immediately add into a container of salad. Let it stand for a minute without mixing.
- ✓ Add ¼ cup of reserved pasta water into the container to make a creamy sauce. Add more pasta water if desired. Toss to mix well.
- ✓ Serve and enjoy.

Nutrition: Cal : 274.7; Carbs: 30.9g; Protein: 14.6g; Fat: 10.3g

784) Red Quinoa Peach Porridge

Ingredients:

- ¼ cup old fashioned rolled oats
- ¼ cup red quinoa
- ½ cup milk
- 1 ½ cups water
- Two peaches, peeled and sliced

Direction: Servings: 1, Cooking Time: 30 minutes

- ✓ On a small saucepan, place the peaches and quinoa. Add water and cook for 30 minutes.
- ✓ Add the oatmeal and milk last and cook until the oats become tender.
- ✓ Stir occasionally to avoid the porridge from sticking on the bottom of the pan.

Nutrition: Cal : 456.6; Carbs: 77.3g; Protein: 16.6g; Fat: 9g

785) Red Wine Risotto

Ingredients:

- Pepper to taste
- 1 cup finely shredded Parmigiano-Reggiano cheese, divided
- 2 tsp tomato paste
- One ¾ cups dry red wine
- ¼ tsp salt
- broth
- 1 ½ cups Italian 'risotto' rice
- Two cloves garlic, minced
- One medium onion, freshly chopped
- 2 tbsp extra-virgin olive oil
- 4 ½ cups reduced-sodium beef

Direction: Servings: 8, Cooking Time: 25 minutes

- ✓ On medium-high fire, bring to a simmering broth in a medium fry pan. Lower fire, so the broth is steaming but not simmering.
- ✓ On medium-low heat, place a Dutch oven and heat oil.
- ✓ Sauté onions for 5 minutes. Add garlic and cook for 2 minutes.
- ✓ Add rice, mix well, and season with salt.
- ✓ Into rice, add a generous splash of wine and ½ cup of broth.
- ✓ Lower fire to a gentle simmer, cook until liquid is fully absorbed while stirring the rice every once in a while.
- ✓ Add another splash of wine and ½ cup of broth. Stirring once in a while.
- ✓ Add tomato paste and stir to mix well.
- ✓ Continue cooking and adding wine and broth until broth is used up.
- ✓ Once done cooking, turn off the fire and stir in pepper and ¾ cup cheese.
- ✓ To serve, sprinkle with resting cheese and enjoy.

Nutrition: Cal : 231; Carbs: 33.9g; Protein: 7.9g; Fat: 5.7g

786) Rice & Currant Salad Mediterranean Style

Ingredients:

- 1 cup basmati rice
- salt

- *2 1/2 Tbsps lemon juice*
- *1 Tsp grated orange zest*
- *2 Tbsps fresh orange juice*
- *1/4 cup olive oil*
- *1/2 Tsp cinnamon*
- *Salt and pepper to taste*
- *Four chopped green onions*
- *1/2 cup dried currants*
- *3/4 cup shelled pistachios or almonds*
- *1/4 cup chopped fresh parsley*

Direction: Servings: 4, Cooking Time: 50 minutes

- ✓ *Place a nonstick pot on medium-high fire and add rice. Toast rice until opaque and starts to smell, around 10 minutes.*
- ✓ *Add 4 quarts of boiling water to the pot and 2 tsp salt. Boil until tender, around 8 minutes uncovered.*
- ✓ *Drato the rice and spread it out on a lined cookie sheet to cool completely.*
- ✓ *In a large salad container, whisk well the oil, juices, and spices. Add salt and pepper to taste.*
- ✓ *Add half of the green onions, half of parsley, currants, and nuts.*
- ✓ *Toss with the cooled rice and let stand for at least 20 minutes.*
- ✓ *If needed, adjust seasoning with pepper and salt.*
- ✓ *Garnish with resting parsley and green onions.*

Nutrition: Cal : 450; Carbs: 50.0g; Protein: 9.0g;

787) ***Ricotta and Spinach Ravioli***

Ingredients:

- *1 cup chicken stock*
- *1 cup frozen spinach, thawed*
- *One batch pasta dough*

Filling

- *3 tbsp heavy cream*
- *1 cup ricotta*
- *One ¾ cups baby spinach*
- *One small onion, finely chopped*
- *2 tbsp butter*

Direction: Servings: 2, Cooking Time: 15 minutes

- ✓ *Create the filling: In a frying pan, sauté onion and butter for around five minutes. Add the baby spinach leaves and continue simmering for another four minutes. Remove from fire, drain liquid and mince the onion and leaves. Then combine with 2 tbsp cream and the ricotta, ensuring that it is well combined. Add pepper and salt to taste.*
- ✓ *With your pasta dough, divide it into four balls. Roll out one ball to ¼ inch thick rectangular spread. Cut 1 ½ inch by 3-inch rectangles. Place filling on the middle of the rectangles, around 1 Tbspful, and brush is filling with cold water. Fold the rectangles in half, ensure no air is trapped within, and seal using a cookie cutter. Use up all the filling.*
- ✓ *Create Pasta Sauce: Until smooth, puree chicken stock and spinach. Pour into a heated fry pan and for two minutes cook it. Add 1 tbsp cream and season with pepper and salt. Continue cooking for a minute and turn of the fire.*
- ✓ *Cook the ravioli by submerging them in a boiling pot of water with salt. Cook until al dente, then drain. Then quickly transfer the cooked ravioli into the frying pan of pasta sauce, toss to mix, and serve.*

Nutrition: Cal : 443; Carbs: 12.3g; Protein: 18.8g; Fat: 36.8g

788) ***. Roasted Red Peppers and Shrimp Pasta***

Ingredients:

- *12 oz pasta, cooked and drained*
- *1 cup finely shredded Parmesan Cheese*
- *¼ cup snipped fresh basil*
- *½ cup whipping cream*
- *½ cup dry white wine*
- *1 12oz jar roasted red sweet peppers, drained and chopped*
- *¼ tsp crushed red pepper*
- *Six cloves garlic, minced*
- *1/3 cup finely chopped onion*
- *2 tbsp olive oil*
- *¼ cup butter*
- *1 ½ lbs. fresh, peeled, deveined, rinsed, and drained medium shrimps*

Direction: Servings: 6, Cooking Time: 10 minutes

- ✓ *On medium-high fire, heat butter in a big fry pan and add garlic and onions. Stir fry until onions are soft, around two minutes. Add crushed red pepper and shrimps, sauté for another two minutes before adding wine and roasted peppers.*
- ✓ *Allow mixture to a boil before lowering the heat to low fire and for two minutes, let the mixture simmer uncovered. Stirring occasionally, add cream once shrimps are cooked, and simmer for a minute.*
- ✓ *Add basil and remove from fire. Toss to the pasta and mix gently—transfer to serving plates and top with cheese.*

Nutrition: Cal : 418; Carbs: 26.9g; Protein: 37.1g; Fat: 18.8g

789) ***Seafood and Veggie Pasta***

Ingredients:

- *¼ tsp pepper*
- *¼ tsp salt*
- *1 lb raw shelled shrimp*
- *One lemon, cut into wedges*

- *1 tbsp butter*
- *1 tbsp olive oil*
- *Two 5-oz cans chopped clams, drained (reserve 2 tbsp clam juice)*
- *2 tbsp dry white wine*
- *Four cloves garlic, minced*
- *4 cups zucchini, spiraled (use a veggie spiralizer)*
- *4 tbsp Parmesan Cheese*
- *Chopped fresh parsley to garnish*

Direction: Servings: 4, Cooking Time: 20 minutes

✓ *Ready the zucchini and spiralize with a veggie spiralizer. Arrange 1 cup of zucchini noodles per container—a total of 4 containers.*

✓ *On medium fire, place a large nonstick saucepan and heat oil and butter.*

✓ *For a minute, sauté garlic. Add shrimp and cook for 3 minutes until opaque or cooked.*

✓ *Add white wine, reserved clam juice, and clams. Bring to a simmer and continue simmering for 2 minutes or until half of the liquid has evaporated. Stir constantly.*

✓ *Season with pepper and salt. And if needed, add more to taste.*

✓ *Remove from fire and evenly distribute seafood sauce to 4 containers.*

✓ *Top with a Tbsp of Parmesan cheese per container, serve, and enjoy.*

Nutrition: Cal : 324.9; Carbs: 12g; Protein: 43.8g; Fat: 11.3g

790) Seafood Paella with Couscous

Ingredients:

- *½ cup whole wheat couscous*
- *4 oz small shrimp, peeled and deveined*
- *4 oz bay scallops, tough muscle removed*
- *¼ cup vegetable broth*
- *1 cup freshly diced tomatoes and juice*
- *Pinch of crumbled saffron threads*
- *¼ tsp freshly ground pepper*
- *¼ tsp salt*
- *½ tsp fennel seed*
- *½ tsp dried thyme*
- *One clove garlic, minced*
- *One medium onion, chopped*
- *2 tsp extra virgin olive oil*

Direction: Servings: 4, Cooking Time: 15 minutes

✓ *Put it on medium fire in a large saucepan and add oil. Stir to the onion and sauté for three minutes before adding: saffron, pepper, salt, fennel seed, thyme, and garlic. Continue to sauté for another minute.*

✓ *Then add the broth and tomatoes and let boil. Once boiling, reduce the fire, cover, and continue to cook for another 2 minutes.*

✓ *Add the scallops and increase the fire to medium and stir occasionally, and cook for two minutes. Add the shrimp and wait for two minutes more before adding the couscous. Then remove from fire, cover, and set aside for five minutes before carefully mixing.*

Nutrition: Cal : 117; Carbs: 11.7g; Protein: 11.5g; Fat: 3.1g

791) Shrimp Paella Made with Quinoa

Ingredients:

- *1 pound large shrimp, shelled, peeled, and thawed*
- *One teaspoon seafood seasoning*
- *1 cup frozen green peas*
- *One red bell pepper, stripped of core, seeds, and membrane, cut into ½-inch strips*
- *- ½ cup sliced sun-dried tomatoes, packed in olive oil Salt to taste*
- *½ tsp black pepper*
- *½ tsp Spanish paprika*
- *½ tsp saffron threads (optional turmeric)*
- *One bay leaf*
- *¼ tsp crushed red pepper flakes*
- *3 cups chicken broth, fat-free, low sodium*
- *1 ½ cups dry quinoa, rinse well*
- *1 tbsp olive oil*
- *Two cloves garlic, minced*
- *One yellow onion, diced*

Direction: Servings: 7, Cooking Time: 40 minutes

✓ *Season shrimps with seafood seasoning and a pinch of salt. Toss to mix well and refrigerate until ready to use.*

✓ *Prepare and wash quinoa. Set aside.*

✓ *On medium-low fire, place a large nonstick skillet and heat oil. Add onions and for 5 minutes sauté until soft and tender.*

✓ *Add paprika, saffron (or turmeric), bay leaves, red pepper flakes, chicken broth, and quinoa. Season with salt and pepper*

✓ *Cover skillet and bring to a boil. Once boiling, lower the fire to a simmer and cook until all liquid is absorbed, around ten minutes.*

✓ *Add shrimp, peas, and sun-dried tomatoes. For 5 minutes, cover and cook.*

✓ *Once done, turn off the fire, and for ten minutes, allow the paella to set while still covered.*

✓ *To serve, remove bay leaf and enjoy with a squeeze of lemon if desired.*

Nutrition: Cal : 324.4; Protein: 22g; Carbs: 33g; Fat: 11.6g

792) Shrimp, Lemon, and Basil Pasta

Ingredients:

- *2 cups baby spinach*
- *½ tsp salt*
- *2 tbsp fresh lemon juice*
- *2 tbsp extra virgin olive oil*
- *3 tbsp drained capers*
- *¼ cup chopped fresh basil*
- *One lb. peeled and deveined large shrimp*
- *8 oz uncooked spaghetti*
- *3 quarts water*

Direction: Servings: 4, Cooking Time: 25 minutes

- ✓ *In a pot, bring to a boil 3 quarts of water. Add the pasta and allow it to a boil for another eight minutes before adding the shrimp and boiling for another three minutes or until pasta is cooked.*
- ✓ *Drato the pasta and transfer it to a container. Add salt, lemon juice, olive oil, capers, and basil while mixing well.*
- ✓ *To serve, place baby spinach on a plate around ½ cup and topped with ½ cup of pasta.*

Nutrition: Cal : 151; Carbs: 18.9g; Protein: 4.3g; Fat: 7.49

793) Simple Penne Anti-Pasto

Ingredients:

- *¼ cup pine nuts, toasted*
- *½ cup grated Parmigiano-Reggiano cheese, divided*
- *8oz penne pasta, cooked and drained*
- *1 6oz jar drained, sliced, marinated, and quartered artichoke hearts*
- *1 7 oz jar drained and chopped sun-dried tomato halves packed in oil*
- *3 oz chopped prosciutto*
- *1/3 cup pesto*
- *½ cup pitted and chopped Kalamata olives*
- *One medium red bell pepper*

Direction: Servings: 4, Cooking Time: 15 minutes

- ✓ *Slice bell pepper, discard membranes, seeds, and stem. Place bell pepper halves on a foiled lined baking sheet, press down by hand, and broil in the oven for eight minutes. Remove from oven, put in a sealed bag for 5 minutes before peeling and chopping.*
- ✓ *Place chopped bell pepper in a container and mix artichokes, tomatoes, prosciutto, pesto, and olives.*
- ✓ *Toss in ¼ cup cheese and pasta. Transfer to a serving dish and garnish with ¼ cup cheese and pine nuts. Serve and enjoy!*

Nutrition: Cal : 606; Carbs: 70.3g; Prot: 27.2g; Fat: 27.6g

794) Spaghetti in Lemon Avocado White Sauce

Ingredients:

- *Freshly ground black pepper*
- *Zest and juice of 1 lemon*
- *One avocado pitted and peeled*
- *1-pound spaghetti*
- *Salt*
- *1 tbsp Olive oil*
- *8 oz small shrimp, shelled and deveined*
- *¼ cup dry white wine*
- *One large onion, finely sliced*

Direction: Servings: 6, Cooking Time: 30 minutes

- ✓ *Let a big pot of water boil. Once boiling, add the spaghetti or pasta and cook following the manufacturer's instructions until al dente. Drain and set aside.*
- ✓ *In a large fry pan, sauté wine and onions over medium fire for ten minutes or until onions are translucent and soft.*
- ✓ *Add the shrimps into the frying pan and increase the fire to high while constantly sautéing until shrimps are cooked for around five minutes. Turn the fire off. Season with salt and add the oil right away. Then quickly toss to the cooked pasta, mix well.*
- ✓ *In a blender, until smooth, puree the lemon juice and avocado. Pour into the frying pan of pasta, combine well. Garnish with pepper and lemon zest, then serve.*

Nutrition:Cal : 206; Carbs: 26.3g; Protein: 10.2g;Fat:8.0g

795) Spanish Rice Casserole with Cheesy Beef

Ingredients:

- *2 Tbsps chopped green bell pepper*
- *1/4 Tsp Worcestershire sauce*
- *1/4 Tsp ground cumin*
- *1/4 cup shredded Cheddar cheese*
- *1/4 cup finely chopped onion*
- *1/4 cup chile sauce*
- *1/3 cup uncooked long-grain rice*
- *1/2-pound lean ground beef*
- *1/2 Tsp salt*
- *1/2 Tsp brown sugar*
- *1/2 pinch ground black pepper*
- *1/2 cup water*
- *1/2 (14.5 ounces) can canned tomatoes*
- *1 Tbsp chopped fresh cilantro*

Direction: Servings: 2, Cooking Time: 32 minutes

- ✓ *Place a nonstick saucepan on medium fire and brown beef for 10 minutes while crumbling beef. Discard fat.*

- ✓ Stir in pepper, Worcestershire sauce, cumin, brown sugar, salt, chile sauce, rice, water, tomatoes, green bell pepper, and onion. Mix well and cook for 10 minutes until blended and a bit tender.
- ✓ Transfer to an ovenproof casserole and press down firmly. Sprinkle cheese on top and cook for 7 minutes at 4000F preheated oven. Broil for 3 minutes until the top is lightly browned.
- ✓ Serve and enjoy with chopped cilantro.

Nutrition: Cal : 460; Carbs : 35.8g; Protein: 37.8g; Fat: 17.9g

796) Squash and Eggplant Casserole

Ingredients:

- ½ cup dry white wine
- One eggplant halved and cut into 1-inch slices
- One large onion, cut into wedges
- One red bell pepper, seeded and cut to julienned strips
- One small butternut squash, cut into 1-inch slices
- 1 tbsp olive oil
- 12 baby corn
- 2 cups low sodium vegetable broth
- Salt and pepper to taste
- Polenta Ingredients
- ¼ cup parmesan cheese, grated
- 1 cup instant polenta
- 2 tbsp fresh oregano, chopped
- Topping Ingredients
- One garlic clove, chopped
- 2 tbsp slivered almonds
- 5 tbsp parsley, chopped
- Grated zest of 1 lemon

Direction: Servings: 2, Cooking Time: 45 minutes

- ✓ Switch on the oven, preheat it setting its temperature to 350 degrees Fahrenheit.
- ✓ In a casserole, heat the oil and add the onion wedges and baby corn. Sauté over medium-high heat for five minutes. Stir occasionally to prevent the onions and baby corn from sticking at the bottom of the pan.
- ✓ Add the butternut squash to the casserole and toss the vegetables. Add the eggplants and the red pepper.
- ✓ Cover the vegetables and cook over low to medium heat.
- ✓ Cook for about ten minutes before adding the wine. Let the wine sizzle before stirring to the broth. Bring to a boil and cook in the oven for 30 minutes.
- ✓ While the casserole is cooking inside the oven, make the topping by spreading the slivered almonds on a baking tray and toasting under the grill until they are lightly browned.
- ✓ Place the toasted almonds in a small container and mix the resting ingredients for the toppings.
- ✓ Prepare the polenta. In a large saucepan, bring 3 cups of water to a boil over high heat.
- ✓ Add the polenta and continue whisking until it absorbs all the water.
- ✓ Reduce the heat to medium until the polenta is thick. Add the parmesan cheese and oregano.
- ✓ Serve the polenta on plates and add the casserole on top. Sprinkle the toppings on top.

Nutrition: Cal : 579.3; Carbs: 79.2g; Protein: 22.2g; Fat: 19.3g

797) Stuffed Tomatoes with Green Chili

Ingredients:

- 4 oz Colby-Jack shredded cheese
- ¼ cup water
- 1 cup uncooked quinoa
- Six large ripe tomatoes
- ¼ tsp freshly ground black pepper
- ¾ tsp ground cumin
- 1 tsp salt, divided
- 1 tbsp fresh lime juice
- 1 tbsp olive oil
- 1 tbsp chopped fresh oregano
- 1 cup chopped onion
- 2 cups fresh corn kernels
- Two poblano chilies

Direction: Servings: 6, Cooking Time: 55 minutes

- ✓ Preheat broiler to high.
- ✓ Slice lengthwise the chilies and press on a baking sheet lined with foil. Broil for 8 minutes. Remove from oven and let cool for 10 minutes. Peel the chilies and chop them coarsely and place them in a medium-sized container.
- ✓ Place onion and corn on a baking sheet and broil for ten minutes. Stir two times while broiling. Remove from oven and mix in with chopped chilies.
- ✓ Add black pepper, cumin, ¼ tsp salt, lime juice, oil, and oregano. Mix well.
- ✓ Cut off the tops of tomatoes and set them aside. Leave the tomato shell intact as you scoop out the tomato pulp.
- ✓ Drain tomato pulp as you press down with a spoon. Reserve 1 ¼ cups of tomato pulp liquid and discard the rest. Invert the tomato shells on a wire rack for 30 mins and then wipe the insides dry with a paper towel.
  Season with ½ tsp salt the tomato pulp.
- ✓ On a sieve over a container, place quinoa. Add water until it covers quinoa. Rub quinoa grains for 30 seconds together with hands; rinse and drain. Repeat this procedure two times and drain well at the end.

- ✓ *In a medium saucepan, bring resting salt, ¼ cup water, quinoa, and tomato liquid to a boil.*
- ✓ *Once boiling, reduce heat and simmer for 15 minutes or until liquid is fully absorbed. Remove from heat and fluff quinoa with a fork. Transfer and mix the quinoa well with the corn mixture.*
- ✓ *Spoon ¾ cup of the quinoa-corn mixture into the tomato shells, top with cheese, and cover with the tomato top. Bake in a preheated 350oF oven for 15 minutes and then broil high for another 1.5 minutes.*

Nutrition: Cal : 276; Carbs: 46.3g; Protein: 13.4g; Fat: 4.1g

798) Tasty Lasagna Rolls

Ingredients:

- *¼ tsp crushed red pepper*
- *¼ tsp salt*
- *½ cup shredded mozzarella cheese*
- *½ cups parmesan cheese, shredded*
- *One 14-oz package tofu, cubed*
- *One 25-oz canned of low-sodium marinara sauce*
- *1 tbsp extra virgin olive oil*
- *12 whole wheat lasagna noodles*
- *2 tbsp Kalamata olives, chopped*
- *Three cloves minced garlic*
- *3 cups spinach, chopped*

Direction: Servings: 6, Cooking Time: 20 minutes

- ✓ *Put enough water on a large pot and cook the lasagna noodles according to package instructions. Drain, rinse and set aside until ready to use.*
- ✓ *In a large skillet, sauté garlic over medium heat for 20 seconds. Add the tofu and spinach and cook until the spinach wilts. Transfer this mixture to a container and add parmesan olives, salt, red pepper, and 2/3 cup of marinara sauce.*
- ✓ *In a pot, spread a cup of marinara sauce on the bottom. To make the rolls, place noodles on a surface and spread ¼ cup of the tofu filling. Roll up and place it on the pan with the marinara sauce. Do this procedure until all lasagna noodles are rolled.*
- ✓ *Place the pot over high heat and bring to a simmer. Reduce the heat to medium and let it cook for three more minutes. Sprinkle mozzarella cheese and let the cheese melt for two minutes. Serve hot.*

Nutrition: Cal : 304; Carbs: 39.2g; Protein: 23g; Fat: 19.2g

799) Tasty Mushroom Bolognese

Ingredients:

- *¼ cup chopped fresh parsley*
- *oz Parmigiano-Reggiano cheese, grated*
- *1 tbsp kosher salt*
- *10-oz whole wheat spaghetti, cooked and drained*
- *¼ cup milk*
- *1 14-oz can whole peeled tomatoes*
- *½ cup white wine*
- *2 tbsp tomato paste*
- *1 tbsp minced garlic*
- *8 cups finely chopped cremini mushrooms*
- *½ lb. ground pork*
- *½ tsp freshly ground black pepper, divided*
- *¾ tsp kosher salt, divided*
- *2 ½ cups chopped onion*
- *1 tbsp olive oil*
- *1 cup boiling water*
- *½-oz dried porcini mushrooms*

Direction: Servings: 6, Cooking Time: 65 minutes

- ✓ *Let porcini stand in a boiling water container for twenty minutes, drain (reserve liquid), rinse, and chop. Set aside.*
- ✓ *Place a Dutch oven with olive oil on medium-high fire and cook for ten minutes; cook pork, ¼ tsp pepper, ¼ tsp salt, and onions. Constantly mix to break ground pork pieces.*
- ✓ *Stir in ¼ tsp pepper, ¼ tsp salt, garlic, and cremini mushrooms. Continue cooking until liquid has evaporated, around fifteen minutes.*
- ✓ *Stirring constantly, add porcini and sauté for a minute.*
- ✓ *Stir in wine, porcini liquid, tomatoes, and tomato paste. Let it simmer for forty minutes. Stir occasionally. Pour milk and cook for another two minutes before removing it from the fire.*
- ✓ *Stir in pasta and transfer to a serving dish. Garnish with parsley and cheese before serving.*

Nutrition: Cal : 358; Carbs: 32.8g; Protein: 21.1g; Fat: 15.4g

800) Tortellini Salad with Broccoli

Ingredients:

- *One red onion, chopped finely*
- *1 cup sunflower seeds*
- *1 cup raisins*
- *Three heads fresh broccoli, cut into florets*
- *2 tsp cider vinegar*
- *½ cup white sugar*
- *½ cup mayonnaise*
- *20-oz fresh cheese-filled tortellini*

Direction: Servings: 12, Cooking Time: 20 minutes

- ✓ *In a large pot of boiling water, cook tortellini according to the manufacturer's instructions. Drain and rinse with cold water and set aside.*
- ✓ *Whisk vinegar, sugar, and mayonnaise to create your salad dressing.*

- ✓ Mix in a large container red onion, sunflower seeds, raisins, tortellini, and broccoli. Pour dressing and toss to coat.
- ✓ Serve and enjoy.

Nutrition: Cal : 272; Carbs: 38.7g; Protein: 5.0g; Fat: 8.1g

801) Turkey and Quinoa Stuffed Peppers

Ingredients:

- Three large red bell peppers
- 2 tsp chopped fresh rosemary
- 2 tbsp chopped fresh parsley
- 3 tbsp chopped pecans, toasted
- ¼ cup extra virgin olive oil
- ½ cup chicken stock
- ½ lb. fully cooked smoked turkey sausage, diced
- ½ tsp salt
- 2 cups water
- 1 cup uncooked quinoa

Direction: Servings: 6, Cooking Time: 55 minutes

- ✓ On high fire, place a large saucepan and add salt, water, and quinoa. Bring to a boil.
- ✓ Once boiling, reduce fire to a simmer, cover, and cook until all water is absorbed, around 15 minutes.
- ✓ Uncover quinoa, turn off the fire and let it stand for another 5 minutes.
- ✓ Add rosemary, parsley, pecans, olive oil, chicken stock, and turkey sausage into a pan of quinoa. Mix well.
- ✓ Slice peppers lengthwise in half and discards membranes and seeds. In another boiling pot of water, add peppers, boil for 5 minutes, drain and discard water.
- ✓ Grease a 13 x 9 baking dish and preheat the oven to 3500F.
- ✓ Place boiled bell pepper onto a prepared baking dish, evenly fill with the quinoa mixture, and pop into the oven.
- ✓ Bake for 15 minutes.

Nutrition: Cal : 255.6; Carbs: 21.6g; Protein: 14.4g; Fat: 12.4g

802) Veggie Pasta with Shrimp, Basil, and Lemon

Ingredients:

- 2 cups baby spinach
- ½ tsp salt
- 2 tbsp fresh lemon juice
- 2 tbsp extra virgin olive oil
- 3 tbsp drained capers
- ¼ cup chopped fresh basil
- One lb. peeled and deveined large shrimp
- 4 cups zucchini, spirals

Direction: Servings: 4, Cooking Time: 5 minutes

- ✓ divide into four serving plates, top with ¼ cup of spinach, serve and enjoy.

Nutrition: Cal : 51; Carbs: 4.4g; Protein: 1.8g; Fat: 3.4g

803) Veggies and Sun-Dried Tomato Alfredo

Ingredients:

- 2 tsp finely shredded lemon peel
- ½ cup finely shredded Parmesan cheese
- One ¼ cups milk
- 2 tbsp all-purpose flour
- Eight fresh mushrooms, sliced
- 1 ½ cups fresh broccoli florets
- 4 oz fresh trimmed and quartered Brussels sprouts
- 4 oz trimmed fresh asparagus spears
- 1 tbsp olive oil
- 4 tbsp butter
- ½ cup chopped dried tomatoes
- 8 oz dried fettuccine

Direction: Servings: 4, Cooking Time: 30 minutes

- ✓ In a boiling pot of water, add fettuccine and cook following the manufacturer's instructions. Two minutes before the pasta is cooked, add the dried tomatoes. Drain pasta and tomatoes and return to pot to keep warm. Set aside.
- ✓ In a big fry pan with 1 tbsp butter, fry mushrooms, broccoli, Brussels sprouts, and asparagus on medium-high fire, cook for eight minutes while covered, transfer to a plate and put aside.
- ✓ Using the same frypan, add resting butter and flour. Stirring vigorously, cook for a minute or until thickened. Add Parmesan cheese, milk and mix until cheese is melted around five minutes.
- ✓ Toss to the pasta and mix; transfer to a serving dish. Garnish with Parmesan cheese and lemon peel before serving.

Nutrition: Cal : 439; Carbs: 52.0g; Protein: 16.3g; Fat: 19.5g

804) Yangchow Chinese Style Fried Rice

Ingredients:

- 4 cups cold cooked rice
- 1/2 cup peas
- One medium yellow onion, diced
- 5 tbsp olive oil
- 4 oz frozen medium shrimp, thawed, shelled, deveined, and chopped finely
- 6 oz roast pork

- *Three large eggs*
- *Salt and freshly ground black pepper*
- *1/2 tsp cornstarch*

Direction: Servings: 4, Cooking Time: 20 minutes

- ✓ *Combine the salt and ground black pepper and 1/2 tsp cornstarch, coat the shrimp with it. Chop the roasted pork. Beat the eggs and set them aside.*
- ✓ *Stir-fry the shrimp in a wok on high fire with 1 tbsp heated oil until pink, around 3 minutes. Set the shrimp aside and stir fry the roasted pork briefly. Remove both from the pan.*
- ✓ *To the same pan, stir-fry the onion until soft; stir the peas and cook until bright green. Remove both from the pan.*
- ✓ *Add 2 tbsp oil to the same pan, add the cooked rice. Stir and separate the individual grains. Add the beaten eggs, toss the rice. Add the roasted pork, shrimp, vegetables, and onion. Toss everything together, season with salt and pepper to taste.*

Nutrition: Cal : 556; Carbs: 60.2g; Protein: 20.2g; Fat: 25.2g

805) Dinner Meaty Baked Penne

Ingredients:

- *1 pound (454 g) penne pasta*
- *1 pound (454 g) ground beef*
- *1 Tsp salt*
- *1 (25-ounce / 709-g) jar marinara sauce*
- *1 (1-pound / 454-g) bag baby spinach, washed*
- *3 cups shredded Mozzarella cheese, divided*

Direction: Prep time: 5 minutes | Cook time: 50 minutes | Serves 8

- ✓ *Bring a large pot of salted water to a boil, add penne and cook for 7 minutes. Reserve 2 cups of the pasta water and drate the pasta.*
- ✓ *Turn on the oven, preheat it by setting the temperature to 350°F (180°C).*
- ✓ *In a large saucepan over medium heat, cook ground beef and season with salt; brown the ground beef for 5 minutes.*
- ✓ *Add the marinara sauce and 2 cups of pasta water. Allow simmering for 5 minutes.*
- ✓ *Add a handful of spinach at a time into the sauce and cook for another 3 minutes.*
- ✓ *To assemble, in a 9-by-13-inch baking dish, add the pasta and pour the pasta sauce over it. Add 1 1/2 cups of mozzarella cheese. Cover the dish with aluminum foil and bake for 20 minutes.*
- ✓ *After 20 minutes, remove the foil, cover with the rest of the mozzarella and bake for another 10 minutes. Serve warm.*

Nutrition: Cal : 497 | fat: 17g | protein: 31g | carbs: 54g | fiber: 4g | sodium: 619mg

806) Whole-Wheat Fusilli with Chickpea Sauce

Ingredients:

- *¼ cup extra-virgin olive oil*
- *½ large shallot, chopped*
- *Five garlic cloves, thinly sliced*
- *1 (15-ounce / 425-g) canned chickpeas, drained and rinsed, reserving*
- *½ cup canning liquid Pinch red pepper flakes*
- *1 cup whole-grain fusilli pasta*
- *¼ Tsp salt*
- *⅛ Tsp freshly ground black pepper*
- *¼ cup shaved fresh Parmesan cheese*
- *¼ cup chopped fresh basil*
- *2 Tsp dried parsley*
- *1 Tsp dried oregano*
- *Red pepper flakes*

Direction: Prep time: 15 minutes | Cook time: 15 minutes | Serves 4

- ✓ *In a medium skillet, heat the oil over medium heat and sauté the shallots and garlic for 3-5 minutes until the garlic is golden brown. Add ¾ of the chickpeas plus two tablespoons of the liquid from the can and bring to a boil.*
- ✓ *Remove from heat, transfer to a standard blender and blend until smooth. At this point, add the remaining chickpeas. Add more of the reserved chickpea liquid if it becomes thick.*
- ✓ *Bring a large pot of salted water to a boil and cook the pasta until al dente, about 8 minutes.*
- ✓ *Reserve ½ cup of the pasta water, dehydrate the pasta, and return it to the pot.*
- ✓ *Add the chickpea sauce to the hot pasta and add up to ¼ cup of the pasta water. You may need to add more water to reach the desired consistency.*
- ✓ *Place the pasta pot over medium heat and occasionally mix until the sauce thickens; season with salt and pepper.*
- ✓ *Serve garnished with parmesan, basil, parsley, oregano, and red pepper flakes.*

Nutrition: Cal : 310 | fat: 16g | protein: 10g | carbs: 33g | fiber: 6g | sodium: 243mg

807) Bow Ties with Zucchini

Ingredients:

- *3 Tbsps extra-virgin olive oil*
- *Two garlic cloves, minced*
- *Three large or four medium zucchini, diced*
- *½ Tsp freshly ground black pepper*
- *¼ Tsp kosher or sea salt*
- *½ cup 2% milk*
- *¼ Tsp ground nutmeg*
- *8 ounces (227 g) uncooked farfalle (bow ties) or other small pasta shapes*
- *½ cup grated Parmesan or Romano cheese*

- 1 Tbsp freshly squeezed lemon juice

Direction: Prep time: 10 minutes | Cook time: 32 minutes | Serves 4

- ✓ In a large skillet over medium heat, heat the oil. Add the garlic and cook for 1 minute, stirring frequently. Add the zucchini, pepper, and salt. Stir well, cover, and cook for 15 minutes, stirring once or twice.
- ✓ In a small, microwave-safe container, warm the milk to the microwave on high for 30 seconds. Stir the milk and nutmeg into the skillet and cook uncovered for another 5 minutes, stirring occasionally.
- ✓ While the zucchini is cooking, cook the pasta according to the package directions in a large stockpot.
- ✓ Drato, the pasta in a colander, saving about 2 Tbsps of pasta water. Add the pasta and pasta water into the skillet. Mix everything and remove from the heat. Stir to the cheese and lemon juice and serve.

Nutrition: Cal : 190 | fat: 9g | protein: 7g | carbs: 20g | fiber: 2g | sodium: 475mg

808) Linguine with Artichokes and Peas

Ingredients:

- 1 pound (454 g) linguine
- 5 cups water, plus extra as needed
- 1 Tbsp extra-virgin olive oil
- 1 Tsp table salt
- 1 cup whole artichokes in a jar packed in water, quartered
- 1 cup frozen peas, thawed
- 4 ounces (113 g) finely grated Pecorino Romano, plus extra for serving
- ½ Tsp pepper
- 2 Tsp grated lemon zest
- 2 Tbsps chopped fresh tarragon

Direction: Prep time: 10 minutes | Cook time: 5 minutes | Serves 4 to 6

- ✓ Loosely wrap half of the pasta in a dish towel, then press bundle against the corner of the counter to break noodles into 6-inch lengths; repeat with resting pasta.
- ✓ Add the pasta, water, oil, and salt to the Instant Pot, ensuring the pasta is completely submerged. Lock the lid and close the pressure release valve. Select the high-pressure cooking function and cook for 4 minutes. Turn off the Instant Pot and quickly release the pressure. Carefully remove the lid, allowing steam to escape away from you.
- ✓ Stir artichokes and peas into paste, cover, and let stand until heated through about 3 minutes. Gently stir in pecorino and pepper until cheese is melted and fully combined for 1 to 2 minutes. Adjust consistency with additional hot water, if necessary. Add the lemon zest and tarragon, and season with salt and pepper to taste. Serve, passing the extra pecorino separately.

Nutrition: Cal : 390 | fat: 7g | protein: 17g | carbs: 59g | fiber: 3g | sodium: 680mg

809) Rigatoni with Pancetta and Veggie

Ingredients:

- 4 ounces (113 g) pancetta, chopped fine one onion, chopped fine
- ¼ teaspoon cooking salt
- Three garlic cloves, minced
- Two anchovy fillets, rinsed, dried, and chopped
- Two tablespoons fennel seeds, slightly crushed
- ¼ teaspoon red pepper flakes
- 1 (28-ounce/794-g) can diced tomatoes
- 2 cups chicken broth
- 1½ cups water
- 1 pound (454 g) of rigatoni pasta
- ¼ cup grated Pecorino Romano cheese, plus extra for serving
- Two tablespoons fresh chopped parsley

Direction: Preparation time: 15 minutes | Cooking time: 22 minutes | Serves 4-6 people

- ✓ Using the highest sauté function, cook bacon in Instant Pot, frequently stirring, until golden brown and fat are well-rendered, 6 to 10 minutes. Using a slotted spoon, transfer bacon to a paper towel-lined plate; set aside to serve.
- ✓ Add the onion and salt to the remaining fat in the pot and cook, using the highest sauté function, until the onion is softened, about 5 minutes. Add the garlic, anchovies, fennel seeds, and pepper flakes and cook until fragrant, about 1 minute. Add the tomatoes and their juice, broth, and water, scraping up all the browned bits, then stir in the pasta.
- ✓ Lock the lid and close the pressure release valve. Select the high-pressure cooking function and cook for 5 minutes. Turn off Instant Pot and quickly release the pressure. Carefully remove the lid, allowing steam to escape away from you.
- ✓ Stir in Pecorino cheese and season with salt and pepper to taste. Transfer to serving dish and let stand until sauce thickens slightly, about 5 minutes. Sprinkle with parsley and reserved bacon. Serve, passing extra Pecorino separately.

Nutrition: Cal : 400 | fat: 7g | protein: 17g | carbs: 64g | fiber: 5g | sodium: 1020mg

810) Orecchiette with Italian Sausage and Broccoli

Ingredients:

- 2 Tbsps extra-virgin olive oil, divided
- 1 pound (454 g) broccoli rabe, trimmed and cut

into 1½-inch pieces

- ¼ Tsp table salt
- 8 ounces (227 g) hot or sweet Italian sausage, casings removed
- Six garlic cloves, minced
- ¼ Tsp red pepper flakes
- ¼ cup dry white wine
- 4½ cups chicken broth
- 1 pound (454 g) orecchiette
- 2 ounces (57 g) parmesan cheese, grated, plus extra for serving

Direction: Preparation time: 10 minutes | Cooking time: 13 minutes | For 4 or 6 people

- ✓ Using the highest sauté setting, heat one tablespoon of oil in the Instant Pot until shimmering.
- ✓ Add broccoli rabe and salt, cover partially and cook, occasionally stirring, until broccoli rabe is softened, 3 to 5 minutes.
- ✓ Using a slotted spoon, transfer broccoli rabe to container; set aside.
- ✓ Add sauté and remaining one tablespoon oil to now-empty pot. Using the highest sauté setting, cook sausage, breaking up meat with a wooden spoon until lightly browned, about 5 minutes. Stir in garlic and pepper flakes and cook until fragrant, about 30 seconds. Add wine, scraping up browned bits, then stir in broth and pasta.
- ✓ Lock the lid and close the pressure release valve. Select the high-pressure cooking function and cook for 4 minutes. Turn off Instant Pot and quickly release the pressure.
- ✓ Carefully remove the lid, allowing steam to escape away from you.
- ✓ Stir broccoli rabe and any accumulated juices and parmesan into pasta.
- ✓ Season with salt and pepper to taste. Serve, passing extra parmesan separately.

Nutrition: Cal : 440 | fat: 12g | protein: 22g | carbs: 59g | fiber: 1g | sodium: 930mg

811) Orzo with Shrimp and Feta Cheese

Ingredients:

- 1 pound (454 g) large shrimp, peeled and deveined
- 1 Tbsp grated lemon zest plus 1 Tbsp juice
- ¼ Tsp table salt
- ¼ Tsp pepper
- 2 Tbsps extra-virgin olive oil, plus extra for serving
- One onion, chopped fine
- Two garlic cloves, minced
- 2 cups orzo
- 2 cups chicken stock, plus extra as needed
- 1¼ cups water
- ½ cup pitted kalamata olives, chopped coarsely
- 1 ounce (28 g) feta cheese, crumbled, plus extra for serving
- 1 Tbsp chopped fresh dill

Direction: Prep time: 15 minutes | Cook time: 13 minutes | Serves 4 to 6

- ✓ Toss shrimp with lemon zest, salt, and pepper in the container; refrigerate until ready to use.
- ✓ Using the highest sauté function, heat the oil in the Instant Pot until it shimmers. Add onion and cook until softened, about 5 minutes. Stir in garlic and cook until fragrant, about 30 seconds. Add orzo and cook, often stirring, until orzo is coated in oil and lightly browned, about 5 minutes. Add broth and water, scraping up any browned bits.
- ✓ Lock the lid and close the pressure release valve. Select the high-pressure cooking function and cook for 2 minutes. Turn off Instant Pot and quickly release the pressure. Carefully remove the lid, allowing steam to escape away from you.
- ✓ Stir shrimp, olives, and feta into barley. Cover and let stand until shrimp are opaque throughout, 5 to 7 minutes.
- ✓ Adjust consistency with more hot broth if needed. Stir in dill and lemon juice, and season with salt and pepper to taste.
- ✓ Sprinkle individual portions with extra feta and drizzle with extra oil before serving.

Nutrition: alories: 320 | fat: 7g | protein: 18g | carbs: 46g | fiber: 2g | sodium: 670mg

812) Triple-Green Pasta with Parmesan

Ingredients:

- 8 ounces (227 g) uncooked penne
- 1 Tbsp extra-virgin olive oil
- Two garlic cloves, minced
- ¼ Tsp crushed red pepper
- 2 cups chopped fresh flat-leaf (Italian) parsley, including stems 5 cups loosely packed baby spinach)
- ¼ Tsp ground nutmeg
- ¼ Tsp freshly ground black pepper
- ¼ Tsp kosher or sea salt
- ⅓ cup Castelvetrano olives, pitted and sliced
- ⅓ cup grated Pecorino Romano or Parmesan cheese

Direction: Prep time: 10 minutes | Cook time: 14 minutes | Serves 4

- ✓ Cook pasta according to package directions in a large pot, but boil 1 minute less than directed. Drain the pasta, and reserve ¼ cup of the cooking water.
- ✓ While the pasta is cooking, in a large skillet over

medium heat, heat the oil.

- ✓ Add the garlic and crushed red pepper and cook for 30 seconds, stirring constantly. Add the parsley and cook for 1 minute, stirring constantly.
- ✓ Add the spinach, nutmeg, pepper, and salt and cook for 3 minutes, occasionally stirring, until the spinach is wilted.
- ✓ Add the pasta and reserve ¼ cup of the pasta water in the skillet. Stir in the olives, and cook for about 2 minutes until most of the pasta water has been absorbed.
- ✓ Remove from heat, stir in cheese, and serve.

Nutrition: Cal : 262 | fat: 3g | protein: 15g | carbs: 51g | fiber: 12g | sodium: 1180mg

813) Asparagus and Grape Tomato Pasta

Ingredients:

- 8 ounces (227 g) uncooked small pasta, like orecchiette (little ears) or farfalle (bow ties)
- 1½ pounds (680 g) fresh asparagus, ends trimmed, and stalks chopped into 1-inch pieces
- 1½ cups grape tomatoes halved
- 2 Tbsps extra-virgin olive oil
- ¼ Tsp freshly ground black pepper
- ¼ Tsp kosher or sea salt
- 2 cups fresh mozzarella, drained and cut into bite-size pieces
- ⅓ cup torn fresh basil leaves
- 2 Tbsps balsamic vinegar

Direction: Prep time: 10 minutes | Cook time: 25 minutes | Serves 6

- ✓ Switch on the oven, preheat it setting its temperature to 400°F (205°C).
- ✓ Cook pasta according to package directions in a large pot, but boil 1 minute less than directed. Drain pasta and reserve ¼ cup of the cooking water.
- ✓ While the pasta is cooking, in a large skillet over medium heat, heat the oil. Add the garlic and crushed red pepper and cook for 30 seconds, stirring constantly. Add the parsley and cook for 1 minute, stirring constantly.
- ✓ Add the spinach, nutmeg, pepper, and salt and cook for 3 minutes, occasionally stirring, until the spinach is wilted.
- ✓ Add the pasta and reserve ¼ cup of the pasta water in the skillet. Add the olives and cook for about 2 minutes, until most of the pasta water has been absorbed.
- ✓ Remove from heat, stir in cheese and serve. Gently mix the Mozzarella and basil.
- ✓ Drizzle with balsamic vinegar. Serve from the baking sheet or pour the pasta into a large container.
- ✓ If you want to make this dish ahead of time or serve it cold, follow the recipe up to step 4, then refrigerate the pasta and vegetables. When you are ready to serve, follow step 5 either with the cold pasta or with warm pasta that's been gently reheated in a pot on the stove.

Nutrition: Cal : 147 | fat: 2g | protein: 16g | carbs: 17g | fiber: 4g | sodium: 420mg

814) Garlic Shrimp Fettuccine

Ingredients:

- 8 ounces (227 g) fettuccine pasta
- ¼ cup extra-virgin olive oil
- 3 Tbsps garlic, minced
- 1 pound (454 g) large shrimp, peeled and deveined
- ⅓ cup lemon juice
- 1 Tbsp lemon zest
- ½ Tsp salt
- ½ Tsp freshly ground black pepper

Direction: Prep time: 10 minutes | Cook time: 15 minutes | Serves 4 to 6

- ✓ Bring a large pot of salted water to a boil. Add the fettuccine and cook for 8 minutes. Reserve ½ cup of the cooking liquid and drate the pasta.
- ✓ In a large saucepan over medium heat, heat the olive oil. Add the garlic and sauté for 1 minute.
- ✓ Add the shrimp to the casserole and cook each side for 3 minutes. Remove the shrimp from the pan and set it aside.
- ✓ Add the rest of the ingredients to the casserole and stir until cooked through. Add the pasta and toss it together to evenly coat the pasta.
- ✓ Transfer the pasta to a serving dish and serve topped with the cooked shrimp.

Nutrition: Cal : 485 | fat: 17g | protein: 33g | carbs: 50g | fiber: 4g | sodium: 407mg

815) Simple Pesto Pasta

Ingredients:

- 1 pound (454 g) spaghetti
- 4 cups fresh basil leaves, stems removed
- Three cloves garlic
- 1 Tsp salt
- ½ Tsp freshly ground black pepper
- ½ cup toasted pine nuts
- ¼ cup lemon juice
- ½ cup grated Parmesan cheese
- 1 cup extra-virgin olive oil

Direction: Prep time: 10 minutes | Cook time: 8 minutes | Serves 4 to 6

- ✓ Bring a large pot of salted water to a boil. Add the spaghetti to the pot and cook for 8 minutes.
- ✓ In a food processor, place the resting ingredients, except for the olive oil and pulse.

- ✓ While the processor is running, slowly drizzle the olive oil through the top opening. Process until all the olive oil has been added.
- ✓ Reserve ½ cup of the cooking liquid. Drato the pasta and put it into a large container. Add the pesto and cooking liquid to the container of pasta and toss everything together.
- ✓ Serve immediately.

Nutrition: 1067 | fat: 72g | protein: 23g | carbs: 91g | fiber: 6g | sodium: 817mg

816) Spaghetti with Pine Nuts and Cheese

Ingredients:

- 8 ounces (227 g) spaghetti
- 4 Tbsps almond butter
- 1 Tsp freshly ground black pepper
- ½ cup pine nuts
- 1 cup fresh grated Parmesan cheese, divided

Direction: Prep time: 10 minutes | Cook time: 11 minutes | Serves 4 to 6

- ✓ Bring a large pot of salted water to a boil. Add the pasta and cook for 8 minutes.
- ✓ In a large saucepan over medium heat, combine the butter, black pepper, and pine nuts.
- ✓ Cook for 2 to 3 minutes, or until the pine nuts are lightly toasted.
- ✓ Reserve ½ cup of the pasta water. Dredge the pasta and place it in the skillet with the pine nuts.
- ✓ Add ¾ cup of the Parmesan cheese and the pasta water reserved for the pasta and toss to coat the pasta evenly.
- ✓ Transfer the pasta to a serving dish and top with the remaining ¼ cup of Parmesan cheese. Serve immediately.

Nutrition: Cal : 542 | fat: 32g | protein: 20g | carbs: 46g | fiber: 2g | sodium: 552mg

817) Creamy Garlic Parmesan Chicken Pasta

Ingredients:

- 3 Tbsps extra-virgin olive oil
- Two boneless, skinless chicken breasts, cut into thin strips
- One large onion, thinly sliced
- 3 Tbsps garlic, minced
- 1½ Tsps salt
- 1 pound (454 g) fettuccine pasta
- 1 cup heavy whipping cream
- ¾ cup freshly grated Parmesan cheese, divided
- ½ Tsp freshly ground black pepper

Direction: Prep time: 5 minutes | Cook time: 15 minutes | Serves 4

- ✓ In a large skillet over medium heat, heat the olive oil. Add the chicken and cook for 3 minutes.
- ✓ Add the onion, garlic, and salt to the skillet. Cook for 7 minutes, stirring occasionally.
- ✓ Meanwhile, bring a large pot of salted water to a boil, add the pasta, and then cook for 7 minutes.
- ✓ While the pasta is cooking, add the heavy cream, ½ cup Parmesan cheese, and black pepper to the chicken. Simmer for 3 minutes.
- ✓ Reserve ½ cup of the pasta water. Drato the pasta and add it to the chicken cream sauce.
- ✓ Add the reserved pasta water to the pasta and toss it together. Simmer for 2 minutes. Top with the resting ¼ cup of the Parmesan cheese and serve warm.

Nutrition: Cal : 879 | fat: 42g | protein: 35g | carbs: 90g | fiber: 5g | sodium: 1283mg

818) Couscous Confetti Salad

Ingredients:

- 3 Tbsps extra-virgin olive oil
- One large onion, chopped
- Two carrots, chopped
- 1 cup fresh peas
- ½ cup golden raisins
- 1 Tsp salt
- 2 cups vegetable broth
- 2 cups couscous

Direction: Prep time: 5 minutes | Cook time: 20 minutes | Serves 4 to 6

- ✓ In a medium saucepan over medium heat, gently sauté the olive oil, onions, carrots, peas, and raisins and cook for 5 minutes.
- ✓ Add the salt and broth and stir to combine. Bring to a boil and let the ingredients simmer for 5 minutes.
- ✓ Add the couscous. Stir, lower the heat, cover and let cook for 10 minutes. Stir with a fork and serve.

Nutrition: Cal : 511 | fat: 12g | protein: 14g | carbs: 92g | fiber: 7g | sodium: 504mg

819) Rustic Lentil-Rice Pilaf

Ingredients:

- ¼ cup extra-virgin olive oil
- One large onion, chopped 6 cups water
- 1 Tsp ground cumin
- 1 Tsp salt
- 2 cups brown lentils, picked over and rinsed
- 1 cup basmati rice

Direction: Prep time: 5 minutes | Cook time: 50 minutes | Serves 6

- ✓ In a medium saucepan over medium heat, cook the olive oil and onions for 7-10 minutes until the edges are golden brown.
- ✓ Turn the heat to high, add the water, cumin, and salt, and bring this mixture to a boil, simmering for

about 3 minutes.

- ✓ *Add the lentils and bring the heat to medium-low. Cover the pot and cook for 20 minutes, stirring occasionally.*
- ✓ *Stir in rice and cover; cook for another 20 minutes.*
- ✓ *Stir the rice with a fork and serve hot.*

Nutrition: Cal : 397 | fat: 11g | protein: 18g | carbs: 60g | fiber: 18g | sodium: 396mg

820) Bulgur Pilaf with Garbanzos

Ingredients:

- *Three tablespoons of extra virgin olive oil*
- *One large onion, chopped*
- *1 (16-ounce / 454-g) canned chickpeas, rinsed and drained*
- *2 cups bulgur wheat, rinsed and drained*
- *1½ teaspoons salt*
- *½ teaspoon cinnamon*
- *4 cups water*

Direction: Preparation time: 5 minutes | Cooking time: 20 minutes | Servings 4 to 6

- ✓ *In a large pot over medium heat, cook the olive oil and onion for 5 minutes.*
- ✓ *Add the chickpeas and cook for another 5 minutes.*
- ✓ *Add the bulgur, salt, cinnamon, and water and stir to combine. Cover the pot, lower the heat and cook for 10 minutes.*
- ✓ *When the cooking is done, fluff the pilaf with a fork. Cover and let stand for another 5 minutes.*

Nutrition: Cal : 462 | fat: 13g | protein: 15g | carbs: 76g | fiber: 19g | sodium: 890mg

821) Lentil Bulgur Pilaf

Ingredients:

- *½ cup extra virgin olive oil*
- *Four large onions, chopped*
- *Two teaspoons salt, divided*
- *6 cups water 2 cups brown lentils, picked and rinsed*
- *One teaspoon freshly ground black pepper*
- *1 cup bulgur wheat*

Direction: Preparation time: 10 minutes | Cooking time: 50 minutes | Serves six people

- ✓ *In a large pot over medium heat, cook and stir olive oil, onions, and one teaspoon salt for 12-15 minutes, until onions are a medium brown/gold.*
- ✓ *Place half of the cooked onions in a container.*
- ✓ *Add the water, remaining one tablespoon salt, and lentils to the resting onions. Stir, cover, and cook for 30 minutes.*
- ✓ *Stir in black pepper and bulgur, cover, and cook for 5 minutes. Stir with a fork, cover, and let stand for another 5 minutes.*
- ✓ *Pour the lentils and bulgur onto a serving platter and top with the reserved onions. Serve warm.*

Nutrition: Cal : 479 | fat: 20g | protein: 20g | carbs: 60g | fiber: 24g | sodium: 789mg

822) Simple Spanish Rice

Ingredients:

- *2 Tbsps extra-virgin olive oil*
- *One medium onion, finely chopped*
- *One large tomato, finely diced*
- *2 Tbsps tomato paste*
- *1 Tsp smoked paprika*
- *1 Tsp salt*
- *1½ cups basmati rice*
- *3 cups water*

Direction: Prep time: 10 minutes | Cook time: 20 minutes | Serves 4

- ✓ *In a medium saucepan over medium heat, cook olive oil, onion, and tomato for 3 minutes.*
- ✓ *Stir in the tomato paste, paprika, salt, and rice, cook for 1 minute.*
- ✓ *Add water, cover pot, and lower heat to low; cook for 12 minutes.*
- ✓ *Gently toss in rice, cover, and cook for three more minutes.*

Nutrition: Cal : 328 | fat: 7g | protein: 6g | carbs: 60g | fiber: 2g | sodium: 651mg

823) Creamy Parmesan Garlic Polenta

Ingredients:

- *4 Tbsps (½ stick) unsalted butter, divided (optional)*
- *1 Tbsp garlic, finely chopped*
- *4 cups water*
- *1 Tsp salt*
- *1 cup polenta*
- *¾ cup Parmesan cheese, divided*

Direction: Prep time: 5 minutes | Cook time: 30 minutes | Serves 4

- ✓ *In a large saucepan over medium heat, cook three tablespoons of butter (if desired) and garlic for 2 minutes.*
- ✓ *Add the water and salt and bring to a boil. Add the polenta and immediately whisk until it begins to thicken about 3 minutes. Lower the heat, cover, and cook for 25 minutes, whisking every 5 minutes.*
- ✓ *Using a wooden spoon, stir in ½ cup Parmesan cheese.*
- ✓ *To serve, pour the polenta into a large serving bowl. Sprinkle top with remaining one tablespoon butter (if desired) and remaining ¼ cup Parmesan cheese. Serve warm.*

Nutrition: Cal : 297 | fat: 16g | protein: 9g | carbs: 28g | fiber: 2g | sodium: 838mg

824) Mushroom Parmesan Risotto

Ingredients:

- 6 cups vegetable broth
- Three tablespoons extra-virgin olive oil, divided
- 1 pound (454 g) cremini mushrooms, cleaned and sliced
- One medium onion, finely chopped
- Two cloves of garlic, minced ½ cup Arborio rice
- One teaspoon salt
- ½ cup freshly grated Parmesan cheese
- ½ teaspoon freshly ground black pepper

Direction: Preparation time: 10 minutes | Cooking time: 30 minutes | Serves 4

- ✓ In a saucepan over medium heat, bring the broth to a simmer.
- ✓ In a large skillet over medium heat, cook one tablespoon olive oil and sliced mushrooms for 5-7 minutes. Set the cooked mushrooms aside.
- ✓ In the same skillet over medium heat, add the remaining two tablespoons of olive oil, onion, and garlic, cook for 3 minutes.
- ✓ Add the rice, salt, and 1 cup of broth to the skillet. Stir ingredients together and cook over low heat until most of the liquid is absorbed. Continue adding ½ cup of broth at a time, stirring until absorbed. Repeat until all the broth is used up.
- ✓ With the last addition of broth, add the cooked mushrooms, Parmesan cheese, and black pepper.
- ✓ Cook for an additional 2 minutes. Serve immediately.

Nutrition: Cal : 410 | fat: 12g | protein: 11g | carbs: 65g | fiber: 3g | sodium: 2086mg

825) Brown Rice Containers with Roasted Vegetables

Ingredients:

- Nonstick cooking spray
- 2 cups broccoli florets
- 2 cups cauliflow1 (15-ounce / 425-g) can chickpeas, drained and rinsed
- 1 cup carrots sliced
- 1 inch thick
- 2 or 3 tablespoons of extra virgin olive oil, divided
- Salt and freshly ground black pepper, to taste
- 2 to 3 tablespoons sesame seeds

for garnish

- 2 cups cooked brown rice florets Condiment:
- 3 to 4 tablespoons tahini
- Two tablespoons honey
- One lemon, squeezed
- One garlic clove, minced
- Salt and freshly ground black pepper, to taste

Direction: Preparation time: 15 minutes | Cooking time: 20 minutes | Serves four people

- ✓ Turn on the oven, preheat it by setting the temperature to 400°F (205°C). Spray two baking sheets with cooking spray.
- ✓ Cover the first baking sheet with broccoli and cauliflower and the second with chickpeas and carrots. Coat each baking sheet with half the oil and season with salt and pepper before placing it in the oven.
- ✓ Cook the carrots and chickpeas for 10 minutes, leaving the carrots still just crisp, and the broccoli and cauliflower for 20 minutes, until tender.
- ✓ Stir each halfway through cooking.
- ✓ To make the dressing, mix the tahini, honey, lemon juice, and garlic in a small container. Season with salt and pepper and set aside.
- ✓ Divide the rice into individual containers, then layer with vegetables and drizzle dressing over the dish.

Nutrition: Cal : 454 | fat: 18g | protein: 12g | carbs: 62g | fiber: 11g | sodium: 61mg

826) Spanish Chicken and Rice

Ingredients:

- 2 Tsp smoked paprika
- 2 Tsp ground cumin
- 1½ Tsp garlic salt
- ¾ Tsp chili powder
- ¼ Tsp dried oregano
- One lemon
- Two boneless, skinless chicken breasts
- 3 Tbsps extra-virgin olive oil, divided
- Two large shallots, diced
- 1 cup uncooked white rice
- 2 cups vegetable stock
- 1 cup broccoli florets
- ⅓ cup chopped parsley

Direction: Prep time: 15 minutes | Cook time: 30 minutes | Serves 2

- ✓ Whisk together the paprika, cumin, garlic salt, chili powder, and oregano in a small container. Divide in half and set aside. Into another small container, juice the lemon and set aside.
- ✓ Put the chicken in a medium container. Coat the chicken with 2 Tbsps of olive oil and rub with half of the seasoning mix.
- ✓ In a large pan, heat the resting 1 Tbsp of olive oil and cook the chicken for 2 to 3 minutes on each side, until just browned but not cooked through.
- ✓ Add the scallions to the same skillet and cook until translucent, then add the rice and cook for one more minute to toast.

- ✓ Add the vegetable broth, lemon juice, and resting seasoning mix and stir to combine. Return the chicken to the pan on top of the rice; cover and cook for 15 minutes.
- ✓ Uncover and add the broccoli florets. Cover and cook another 5 minutes until the liquid is absorbed, the rice is tender, and the chicken is cooked.
- ✓ Add the chopped fresh parsley and serve immediately.

Nutrition: Cal : 750 | fat: 25g | protein: 36g | carbs: 101g | fiber: 7g | sodium: 1823mg

827) Toasted Barley and Almond Pilaf

Ingredients:

- One tablespoon olive oil
- One garlic clove, minced
- Three shallots, chopped
- 2 ounces (57 g) mushrooms, sliced ¼ cup almonds, sliced
- ½ cup uncooked pearl barley
- 1½ cups low-sodium chicken broth
- ½ teaspoon dried thyme
- One tablespoon chopped fresh parsley
- Salt, to taste

Direction: Preparation time: 10 minutes | Cooking time: 5 minutes | Serves two people

- ✓ Heat the oil in a saucepan over medium-high heat. Add the garlic, scallions, mushrooms, and almonds, and sauté for 3 minutes.
- ✓ Add the barley and cook, stirring, for 1 minute to toast it.
- ✓ Add the chicken broth and thyme and bring the mixture to a boil.
- ✓ Cover and reduce the heat to low. Simmer the barley for 30 minutes or until the liquid is absorbed and the barley is tender.
- ✓ Sprinkle with fresh parsley and salt before serving.

Nutrition: Cal : 333 | fat: 13g | protein: 10g | carbs: 46g | fiber: 9g | sodium: 141mg

828) Mediterranean Lentils and Brown Rice

Ingredients:

- 2¼ cups low-sodium vegetable broth or no added salt
- ½ cup uncooked brown or green lentils
- ½ cup uncooked instant brown rice
- ½ cup diced carrots
- ½ cup diced celery
- 1 (2¼-ounce/64-g) can sliced olives, drained
- ¼ cup diced red onion
- ¼ cup fresh curly-leaf parsley, chopped
- 1½ tablespoons extra-virgin olive oil
- 1 tablespoon freshly squeezed lemon juice
- 1 clove garlic, minced
- ¼ tablespoon kosher salt or sea salt
- ¼ tablespoon freshly ground black pepper

Direction: Preparation time: 15 minutes | Cooking time: 23 minutes | Serves four people

- ✓ In a medium saucepan over high heat, bring the broth and lentils to a boil, cover and lower the heat to medium-low, cook for 8 minutes.
- ✓ Raise the heat to medium, and stir in the rice. Cover the pot and cook the mixture for 15 minutes or until the liquid is absorbed. Remove pot from heat and let stand, covered, for 1 minute, then stir.
- ✓ While the lentils and rice are cooking, stir the carrots, celery, olives, onion, and parsley in a large bowl.
- ✓ Whisk together the oil, lemon juice, garlic, salt, and pepper in a small container. Set aside.
- ✓ When the lentils and rice are cooked, add them to the serving container. Pour the dressing over them and toss to combine.
- ✓ Serve hot or cold, or store in a sealed container in the refrigerator for up to 7 days.

Nutrition: Cal : 170 | fat: 5g | protein: 5g | carbs: 25g | fiber: 2g | sodium: 566mg

829) Wild Mushroom Farrotto with Parmesan

Ingredients:

- 1½ cups whole spelt
- 3 tablespoons extra-virgin olive oil, divided, plus extra for drizzle
- 12 ounces (340 g) cremini or white mushrooms, cut and thinly sliced
- ½ onion, finely chopped
- ½ teaspoon table salt
- ¼ teaspoon pepper
- 1 clove of garlic, minced
- ¼ ounce (7 g) dried porcini mushrooms, rinsed and finely chopped
- 2 teaspoons chopped fresh thyme or ½ teaspoon dried thyme
- ¼ cup dry white wine
- 2½ cups chicken or vegetable stock, plus more if necessary
- 2 ounces (57 g) Parmesan cheese, grated, plus extra to serve
- 2 tablespoons lemon juice
- ½ cup chopped fresh parsley

Direction: Preparation time: 15 minutes | Cooking time: 7 minutes | Serves four people

- ✓ Pulse the farro in the blender until about half of the grains have broken down into smaller pieces, about six pulses.
- ✓ Using the highest sauté function, heat two

tablespoons of oil in the Instant Pot until shimmering. Add cremini mushrooms, onion, salt, and pepper, cover partially and cook until mushrooms are softened and have released their liquid, about 5 minutes.

- ✓ *Stir in farro, garlic, porcini mushrooms, and thyme and cook until fragrant, about 1 minute. Add wine and cook until almost evaporated about 30 seconds. Add the broth.*
- ✓ *Lock the lid and close the pressure release valve. Select the high-pressure cooking function and cook for 12 minutes. Turn off Instant Pot and quickly release the pressure. Carefully remove the lid, allowing steam to escape away from you.*
- ✓ *If necessary, adjust the consistency with extra hot broth, or continue cooking the farrotto, using the highest sauté function, often stirring, until the correct consistency is reached.*
- ✓ *(The farrotto should be slightly thickened, and the spoon dragged along the bottom of the multicooker should leave a quickly filling trail.)*
- ✓ *Add the Parmesan cheese and remaining one tablespoon oil and mix vigorously until the farrotto becomes creamy.*
- ✓ *Add the lemon juice and season with salt and pepper to taste. Sprinkle individual servings with parsley and extra Parmesan cheese, and drizzle with extra oil before serving.*

Nutrition: Cal : 280 | fat: 9g | protein: 13g | carbs: 35g | fiber: 3g | sodium: 630mg

830) Bulgur with Za'Atar, Chickpeas, and Spinach

Ingredients:

- *3 Tbsps extra-virgin olive oil, divided*
- *1 onion, chopped fine*
- *½ Tsp table salt*
- *3 garlic cloves, minced*
- *2 Tbsps za'atar, divided*
- *1 cup medium-grind bulgur, rinsed*
- *1 (15-ounce / 425-g) can chickpeas, rinsed*
- *1½ cups water*
- *5 ounces (142 g) baby spinach, chopped*
- *1 tablespoon lemon juice, plus lemon wedges to serve*

Direction: Preparation time: 10 minutes | Cooking time: 7 minutes | Serves 4-6 people

- ✓ *Using the highest sauté setting, heat two tablespoons of oil in the Instant Pot until shimmering.*
- ✓ *Add onion and salt and cook until onion is softened about 5 minutes. Stir in garlic and one tablespoon za'atar and cook until fragrant, about 30 seconds. Add the bulgur, chickpeas, and water.*
- ✓ *Lock the lid and close the pressure release valve. Select the high-pressure cooking function and cook for 1 minute.*
- ✓ *Turn off Instant Pot and quickly release the pressure. Carefully remove the lid, allowing steam to escape away from you.*
- ✓ *Gently fluff the bulgur with a fork. Lay a clean dish towel over the pot, replace the lid and let stand for 5 minutes.*
- ✓ *Add the spinach, lemon juice, one tablespoon za'atar, and one tablespoon oil and toss gently, season with salt and pepper to taste.*
- ✓ *Serve with lemon wedges.*

Nutrition: Cal : 200 | fat: 8g | protein: 6g | carbs: 28g | fiber: 6g | sodium: 320mg

831) Pearl Barley Risotto with Parmesan Cheese

Ingredients:

- *4 cups of low-sodium or no-salt vegetable stock*
- *1 tablespoon extra virgin olive oil*
- *1 cup chopped yellow onion*
- *2 cups uncooked pearl barley*
- *½ cup dry white wine*
- *1 cup freshly grated Parmesan cheese, divided*
- *¼ tablespoon kosher salt or sea salt*
- *¼ teaspoon freshly ground black pepper*
- *Chopped fresh chives and lemon wedges for serving (optional)*

Direction: Preparation time: 5 minutes | Cooking time: 20 minutes | Serves six people

- ✓ *Pour the broth into a medium saucepan and bring to a boil.*
- ✓ *Heat the olive oil in a large saucepan over medium-high heat. Add the onion and cook for about 4 minutes, stirring occasionally.*
- ✓ *Add the barley and cook for 2 minutes, stirring, or until the barley is toasted. Pour in the wine and cook for about 1 minute, or until most of the liquid evaporates. Add 1 cup of the hot broth to the pot and cook, stirring, for about 2 minutes, or until most of the liquid is absorbed.*
- ✓ *Add the remaining broth, 1 cup at a time, cooking until each cup is absorbed (about 2 minutes each time) before adding the next.*
- ✓ *The last addition of broth will take a little longer to be absorbed, about 4 minutes.*
- ✓ *Remove the pot from the heat and stir in ½ cup cheese, salt, and pepper.*
- ✓ *Serve with the remaining ½ cup of cheese on the side, along with the chives and lemon wedges. (if desired).*

Nutrition: Cal : 421 | fat: 11g | protein: 15g | carbs: 67g | fiber: 11g | sodium: 641mg

832) Israeli Couscous with Asparagus

Ingredients:

- *1½ pounds (680 g) asparagus spears, ends cut off, and stalks cut into 1-inch pieces*
- *1 clove of garlic, minced*
- *1 tablespoon extra-virgin olive oil*
- *¼ tablespoon freshly ground black pepper*
- *1¾ cup water*
- *1 (8-ounce / 227-g) uncooked box of whole wheat or regular Israeli couscous (about 1⅓ cups)*
- *¼ Tsp kosher salt*
- *1 cup garlic-herb goat cheese, room temperature*

Directions: Preparation time: 5 minutes | Cooking time: 25 minutes | Serves six people

- ✓ *Turn on the oven, preheat it by setting the temperature to 425°F (220°C).*
- ✓ *In a large bowl, mix the asparagus, garlic, oil, and pepper.*
- ✓ *Spread the asparagus on a large rimmed baking sheet and roast for 10 minutes, stirring a few times. Remove the baking sheet from the oven and pour the asparagus into a large serving container.*
- ✓ *Set aside.*
- ✓ *While the asparagus roasts, bring the water to a boil in a medium saucepan, add the couscous and salt, stirring well.*
- ✓ *Reduce the heat to medium-low, cover, and cook for 12 minutes until the water is absorbed.*
- ✓ *Pour the hot couscous into the container with the asparagus. Add the goat cheese and stir thoroughly until completely melted.*
- ✓ *Serve immediately*

Nutrition: Cal : 103 | fat: 2g | protein: 6g | carbs: 18g | fiber: 5g | sodium: 343mg

833) Freekeh Pilaf with Dates and Pistachios

Ingredients:

- *2 Tbsps extra-virgin olive oil, plus extra for drizzling*
- *1 shallot, minced*
- *1½ Tsp grated fresh ginger*
- *¼ Tsp ground coriander*
- *¼ Tsp ground cumin*
- *Salt and pepper, to taste*
- *1¾ cups water*
- *1½ cups cracked freekeh, rinsed*
- *3 ounces (85 g) pitted dates, chopped*
- *¼ cup shelled pistachios, toasted and coarsely chopped*
- *1½ Tbsp lemon juice*
- *¼ cup chopped fresh mint*

Direction: Prep time: 10 minutes | Cook time: 10 minutes | Serves 4 to 6

- ✓ *Set the Instant Pot in Sauté mode and heat the olive oil until it shimmers.*
- ✓ *Add the shallots, ginger, cilantro, cumin, salt, and pepper to the pot and cook for about 2 minutes until the shallots are softened. Stir in the water and freekeh.*
- ✓ *Secure the lid. Select manual mode and set the cooking time for 4 minutes on high pressure. Once cooking is complete, do a quick release of pressure. Gently open the lid.*
- ✓ *Add the dates, pistachios, and lemon juice and gently stir in the freekeh with a fork; season to taste with salt and pepper.*
- ✓ *Transfer to a serving dish and sprinkle with the mint. Serve drizzled with extra olive oil.*

Nutrition: Cal : 280 | fat: 8g | protein: 8g | carbs: 46g | fiber: 9g | sodium: 200mg

834) Quinoa with Baby Potatoes and Broccoli

Ingredients:

- *2 tablespoons olive oil*
- *1 cup new potatoes, cut in half*
- *1 cup broccoli florets*
- *2 cups cooked quinoa*
- *Peel of 1 lemon*
- *Sea salt and freshly ground pepper, to taste*

Direction: Preparation time: 5 minutes | Cooking time: 10 minutes | Serves 4

- ✓ *Heat olive oil in a large skillet over medium heat until shimmering.*
- ✓ *Add the potatoes and cook for about 6 to 7 minutes, or until softened and golden brown. Add the broccoli and cook for about 3 minutes, or until tender.*
- ✓ *Remove from heat and add the quinoa and lemon zest. Season with salt and pepper to taste, then serve.*

Nutrition: Cal : 205 | fat: 8g | protein: 5g | carbs: 27g | fiber: 3g | sodium: 158m

Air Frier Recipes

835) Air Fryer Crusted Salmon

Ingredients:

- 10 oz. salmon filets
- 8 fresh mint leaves, chopped
- 1/2 cup salad cream
- Seasoning
- Lemon juice

Direction: Total time: 12 minutes Servings: 4

- ✓ Preheat air fryer to 200C.
- ✓ Spray lightly with cooking spray and fry for 6 minutes or until cooked properly.
- ✓ Season salmon with seasoning to taste.
- ✓ Mix the cream with mint and lemon juice in a bowl and apply a medium amount over each salmon.

Nutrition values: Calories 136.2 Total Fat 0.1 g Saturated Fat 0.0 g Polyunsaturated Fat 0.0 g Monounsaturated Fat 0.0 g Cholesterol 0.0 mg

836) Avocado Toast with Poached Eggs

Ingredients:

- Olive oil cooking spray
- 4 large eggs
- Salt and black pepper, to taste
- 4 pieces whole grain bread
- 1 avocado Red pepper flakes (optional)

Direction: Prep time: 5 minutes | Cook time: 7 minutes | Serves 4

- ✓ Preheat the air fryer to 320°F (160°C).
- ✓ Coat the inside of four oven-safe ramekins with oil cooking spray.
- ✓ Season each ramekin with salt and black pepper after cracking one egg.
- ✓ Place the ramekins into the air fryer. Set the timer to 7 minutes and Close
- ✓ Toast the bread while the eggs are cooking,
- ✓ Cut the avocado in half lengthwise, remove the pit, and scoop out the flesh into a container; season to taste with salt and pepper.
- ✓ Using a fork, smash the avocado lightly.
- ✓ Spread a quarter of the smashed avocado on each slice of toast.
- ✓ Remove the eggs from the air fryer, spoon one onto each slice of avocado toast before serving.

Nutrition: calories: 232 | fat: 14g | protein: 11g | carbs: 18g | fiber: 6g | sodium: 175mg

837) Air Fryer Loaded Potatoes

Ingredients:

- 8 baby Yukon gold potatoes
- 1 tsp olive oil
- 1 1/2 tbsp chopped chives
- 1/8 tsp kosher salt
- 2 bacon slices,
- 2 tbsp reduced-fat cream/ cheddar.

Direction: Total time: 25 minutes Servings: 2

- ✓ Coat potatoes with oil and place in air fryer basket to cook for 25 minutes at 350 F, until fork tender.
- ✓ Stir occasionally.
- ✓ Still, at the same time, cook bacon in a pan over medium heat for 7 minutes until crispy.
- ✓ Remove and crumble with your hand.
- ✓ Place potatoes on a flat plate and crush lightly till it splits open.
- ✓ Top with crumbled bacon, drippings, chives, sour cream, cheese, and salt.
- ✓ Serve.

Nutrition values: Calories: 142kcal | Carbohydrates: 31g | Protein: 4g | Fat: 1g | Saturated Fat: 1g | Sodium: 299mg | Potassium: 721mg | Fiber: 2g | Sugar: 1g | Vitamin C: 10mg | Calcium: 22mg

838) Shoestring Carrots

Ingredients:

- 10-oz. of julienned carrots
- 1 tbsp olive oil
- salt and pepper
- apple cider vinegar in a spray bottle
- 1 tsp orange zest

Direction: Total Time: 18 minutes Serving: 3

- ✓ In a medium bowl, blend the carrots in with the olive oil, covering them softly.
- ✓ Move them to a serving bowl, mix with orange zest, splash a little apple juice vinegar and salt and pepper.
- ✓ Season with salt and pepper.
- ✓ Put the carrots florets in an air fryer set at 390 F. Cook for 13 minutes, shaking at regular intervals.
- ✓ Serve immediately.

Nutrition values: Calories 34.9 Total Fat 0g Carbohydrates 8g Net carbs 6g Sugar 5g Fiber 2g Protein 1g Calcium 20.4mg Iron 0.4mg

839) Feta and Pepper Frittata

Ingredients:

- Olive oil cooking spray
- 8 large eggs
- 1 medium red bell pepper, diced
- ½ Tsp salt
- ½ Tsp black pepper
- 1 garlic clove, minced
- ½ cup feta, divided

Direction: Prep time: 10 minutes | Cook time: 20 minutes | Serves 4

- Preheat the air fryer to 360°F (182°C). Coat the inside of a 6-inch round cake pan with oil cooking spray.
- In a large container, beat the eggs until well combined.
- Add the bell pepper, black pepper, salt, and garlic to the eggs, and mix together until the bell pepper is distributed throughout.
- Fold in ¼ cup of feta cheese.
- Pour the mixture into the prepared cake pan, and sprinkle the resting ¼ cup of feta over the top.
- Place into the air fryer, bake for 18 to 20 minutes
- Remove from the air fryer and allow to cool for 5 minutes serve.

Nutrition: calories: 204 |fat: 14g |protein: 16g |carbs: 4g

840) Veggie Stuffed Hash Browns

Ingredients:

- Olive oil cooking spray
- 1 Tbsp plus 2 Tsps olive oil, divided
- 4 ounces (113 g) baby Bella mushrooms, diced
- 1 garlic clove, minced
- 2 cups shredded potatoes
- ½ Tsp salt
- ¼ Tsp black pepper
- 1 scallion, white and green parts, diced
- 1 Roma tomato, diced
- ½ cup shredded Mozzarella

Direction: Serves 4 | Prep time: 10 minutes | Cook time: 20 minutes

- Preheat the air fryer to 380 degrees Fahrenheit. Using oil cooking spray, lightly coat the inside of a 6-inch cake pan.
- Heat 2 Tsps olive oil in a small skillet over medium heat. Add the mushrooms, scallion, and garlic, cook until they have softened, and begin to show some color. Remove from heat.
- Meanwhile, combine the potatoes, salt, pepper, and the resting Tbsp olive oil in a large container. Toss until all potatoes are well coated.
- Pour half of the potatoes into the cake pan. Add the mushroom mixture, tomato, and Mozzarella to the top. Spread the resting potatoes over the top.
- Bake to the air fryer until the top is golden brown.
- Remove and allow to cool for 7-8 minutes before slicing and serving.

Nutrition: calories: 164 | fat: 9g | protein: 6g | carbs: 16g | fiber: 3g | sodium: 403mg

841) Hearty Honey-Apricot Granola

Ingredients:

- 1 cup rolled oats
- 1/3 cup dried apricots, diced
- 1/3 cup almond slivers
- 1/3 cup walnuts, chopped
- 1/3 cup hemp hearts
- ¼ to ⅓ cup raw honey, plus more for drizzling
- 1 Tbsp olive oil
- 1 Tsp ground cinnamon
- 1/3 Tsp ground nutmeg
- ¼ Tsp salt
- 2 Tbsps sugar-free dark chocolate chips (optional)
- 3 cups nonfat plain Greek yogurt

Direction: Prep time: 15 minutes | Cook time: 30 minutes | Serves 6

- Preheat the air fryer to 260°F (127°C). Cover the air fryer basket using parchment paper.
- In a large container, combine the oats, apricots, almonds, walnuts, honey, hemp hearts, nutmeg, olive oil, cinnamon, and salt, mixing so that the oil, honey, and spices are well distributed.
- Put the mixture onto the paper, spread it into an even layer.
- Bake for 10-11 mins, then stir and spread back out into an even layer.
- Baking for 11 minutes more, then repeat the process of stirring the mixture—Bake for an additional 9 minutes before removing from the air fryer.
- Leave the granola to cool before stirring to the chocolate chips (if using) and pouring into an airtight container for storage.
- For each serving, top ½ cup Plain Greek yogurt with ⅓ cup granola and a drizzle of honey, if needed.

Nutrition: calories: 342 | fat: 16g | protein: 20g | carbs: 31g | fiber: 4g | sodium: 162mg

842) Simple and Quick Steak

Ingredients:

- ½ lb steak, quality-cut
- Salt and freshly cracked black pepper

Direction: Preparation time: 15 minutes Cooking time: 10 minutes Servings: 2

- Switch on the air fryer, set the frying basket in it, set its temperature to 385°F, and let it preheat.
- Meanwhile, prepare the steaks, and for this, season steaks with salt and freshly cracked black pepper on both sides.
- When the air fryer has preheated, add prepared steaks to the fryer basket, shut it with a lid and cook for 15 minutes.
- When done, transfer steaks to a dish and then serve immediately.
- For meal prepping, evenly divide the steaks between two heatproof containers, close them with a lid and refrigerate for up to 4 days until ready to serve.

✓ When ready to eat, reheat steaks into the microwave until hot and then serve.

Nutrition: Calories 301, Total Fat 25.1, Total Carbs 0, Protein 19.1g, Sugar 0g, Sodium 65mg

843) Quinoa-Feta Stuffed Mushrooms

Ingredients:

- 2 Tbsps finely diced red bell pepper
- 1 garlic clove, minced
- ¼ cup cooked quinoa
- ⅛ Tsp salt
- ¼ Tsp dried oregano
- 24 button mushrooms, stemmed
- 2 ounces (57 g) crumbled feta
- 3 Tbsps whole wheat bread crumbs Olive oil
- cooking spray

Direction: Prep time: 5 minutes | Cook time: 8 minutes | Serves 6

✓ Preheat the air fryer to 360°F (182°C).

✓ In a small container, combine the bell pepper, garlic, quinoa, salt, and oregano.

✓ Fill the mushroom caps halfway with quinoa before spooning it out.

✓ Add a piece of feta to the top of the mushroom.

✓ Sprinkle a pinch of bread crumbs over the feta on each mushroom.

✓ Spray the air fryer's basket using olive oil spray, then coat the mushrooms into the basket, making sure that they don't touch each other.

✓ Coat the basket into the air fryer and bake for 8 minutes.

✓ Remove from the air fryer and serve.

Nutrition: calories: 97 | fat: 4g | protein: 7g | carbs: 11g | fiber: 2g | sodium: 167mg

844) Falafel Balls with Garlic-Yogurt Sauce

Ingredients:

- Falafel:
- 1 (15-ounce / 425-g) can chickpeas, drained and rinsed
- ½ cup fresh parsley
- 2 garlic cloves, minced
- ½ Tbsp ground cumin
- 1 Tbsp whole wheat flour
- Salt, to taste

Garlic-Yogurt Sauce:

- 1 cup nonfat plain Greek yogurt
- 1 garlic clove, minced
- 1 Tbsp chopped fresh dill
- 2 Tbsps lemon juice

Direction: Prep time: 5 minutes | Cook time: 15 minutes | Serves 4

✓ Make the Falafel

✓ Preheat the air fryer to 360°F (182°C).

✓ Put the chickpeas into a food processor. Pulse until mostly chopped, add the garlic, parsley, and cumin, and pulse until the ingredients are combined and turned into a dough.

✓ Add the flour, Pulse until combined. Although the dough will have texture, the chickpeas should be pulsed into small chunks.

✓ Using hands, roll the dough into 8 balls of equal size, pat the balls down a bit, so they are about ½-thick disks.

✓ Spray the basket with olive oil spray, place the falafel patties in the basket in a single layer, then making sure they don't touch each other.

✓ Fry to the for 15 minutes.

✓ Make the Garlic-Yogurt Sauce

✓ In a small container, combine the yogurt, garlic, dill, and lemon juice.

✓ Once the falafel is cooked and nicely browned on all sides, remove them from the air fryer and season with salt.

✓ Serve hot with dipping sauce.

Nutrition: calories: 151 | fat: 2g | protein: 12g | carbs: 22g | fiber: 5g | sodium: 141mg

845) Fried Green Beans

Ingredients:

- Green Beans:
- 1 egg
- 2 Tbsps water
- 1 Tbsp whole wheat flour
- ¼ Tsp paprika
- ½ Tsp garlic powder
- ½ Tsp salt
- ¼ cup whole wheat bread crumbs
- ½ pound (227 g) whole green beans

Lemon-Yogurt Sauce

- ½ cup nonfat plain Greek yogurt
- 1 Tbsp lemon juice
- ¼ Tsp salt
- ⅛ Tsp cayenne pepper

Direction: Prep time: 5 minutes | Cook time: 5 minutes | Serves 4

✓ Make the Green Beans

✓ Preheat the air fryer to 380°F (193°C).

✓ In a medium shallow container, beat together the egg and water until frothy.

✓ In a separate medium shallow container, whisk the flour, paprika, garlic powder, and salt, then mix the bread crumbs.

✓ Spray the basket's bottom with olive oil spray.

- ✓ *Dip green bean into the egg mixture, then into the bread crumb mixture, coating the outside with the crumbs. Coat the green beans in a single layer to the bottom of the air fryer basket.*
- ✓ *Air fryer until the breading is golden brown.*
- ✓ *Make the Lemon-Yogurt Sauce*
- ✓ *In a small container, combine the yogurt, lemon juice, salt, and cayenne.*
- ✓ *Serve alongside the lemon-yogurt sauce.*

Nutrition: ***calories: 88 | fat: 2g | protein: 7g | carbs: 12g | fiber: 2g | sodium: 502mg***

846) ***Whole Wheat Pita Chips***

Ingredients:

- *2 whole-wheat pitas*
- *1 Tbsp olive oil*
- *½ Tsp kosher salt*

Direction: Prep time: 2 minutes | Cook time: 8 minutes | Serves 2

- ✓ *Preheat the air fryer to 360°F (182°C).*
- ✓ *Cut each pita into 8 wedges.*
- ✓ *In a medium container, toss the pita wedges, olive oil, and salt until the wedges are coated, and the olive oil and salt are evenly distributed.*
- ✓ *Place the pita wedges into the basket in an even layer and fry for 7 to 8 minutes. (The cooking time will vary depending upon how thick the pita is and how browned you prefer a chip.)*
- ✓ *Season with additional salt, if desired. Serve alone or with a favorite dip.*

Nutrition: calories: 230 | fat: 8g | protein: 6g | carbs: 35g |

847) ***Greek-Style Potato Skins***

Ingredients:

- *2 russet potatoes*
- *3 Tbsps olive oil, divided, plus more for drizzling (optional)*
- *1 Tsp kosher salt, divided*
- *¼ Tsp black pepper*
- *2 Tbsps fresh cilantro, chopped, plus more for serving*
- *¼ cup Kalamata olives, diced*
- *¼ cup crumbled feta*
- *Chopped fresh parsley for garnish (optional)*

Direction: Prep time: 5 minutes | Cook time: 45 minutes | Serves 4

- ✓ *Preheat the air fryer to 380°F (193°C).*
- ✓ *Using a fork, poke 2 to 3 holes in the potatoes, then arrange each with about ½ Tbsp olive oil and ½ Tsp salt.*
- ✓ *Put the potatoes into the air fryer and bake for 30 minutes.*
- ✓ *Cut the potatoes in half after removing them from the air fryer. Scoop out the flesh of the potatoes with a spoon, leaving a 12-inch layer of potato inside the skins, and set aside.*
- ✓ *In a medium container, combine the scooped potato middles with the resting 2 Tbsps of olive oil, ½ Tsp of salt, black pepper, and cilantro. Mix until well combined.*
- ✓ *Fill the now-empty potato skins with the potato filling, spreading it evenly. Top potato with a Tbsp each of the olives and feta.*
- ✓ *Return the loaded potato skins to the air fryer and bake for an additional 15 minutes.*
- ✓ *Serve with additional chopped cilantro or parsley*

Nutrition: calories: 270 | fat: 13g | protein: 5g | carbs: 34g | fiber: 3g | sodium: 748mg

848) ***Crunchy Chili Chickpeas***

Ingredients:

- *1 (15-ounce / 425-g) can cooked chickpeas, drained and rinsed*
- *1 Tbsp olive oil*
- *¼ Tsp salt*
- *⅛ Tsp chili powder*
- *⅛ Tsp garlic powder*
- *⅛ Tsp paprika*

Direction: Prep time: 5 minutes | Cook time: 15 minutes | Serves 4

- ✓ *Preheat the air fryer to 380°F (193°C).*
- ✓ *In a medium container, toss all of the ingredients together until the chickpeas are well coated.*
- ✓ *Pour the chickpeas into the air fryer basket and spread them out in a single layer.*
- ✓ *Roast for 15 minutes, stirring once halfway through the cooking time.*

Nutrition: calories: 109 | fat: 5g | protein: 4g | carbs: 13g | fiber: 4g | sodium: 283mg

849) ***Mediterranean White Beans with Basil***

Ingredients:

- *1 (15-ounce / 425-g) can cooked white beans*
- *2 Tbsps olive oil 1 Tsp fresh sage, chopped*
- *¼ Tsp garlic powder*
- *¼ Tsp salt, divided*
- *1 Tsp chopped fresh basil*

Direction: Prep time: 2 minutes | Cook time: 19 minutes | Serves 2

- ✓ *Preheat the air fryer to 380°F (193°C).*
- ✓ *Mix together the beans, olive oil, sage, garlic, ⅛ Tsp salt, and basil in a medium container.*
- ✓ *Pour the white beans into the air fryer and spread them out in a single layer.*
- ✓ *Bake for 10 minutes. Stir and continue cooking until they reach your preferred level of crispiness.*

✓ Toss with the resting ⅛ Tsp salt before serving.
Nutrition: calories: 308 | fat: 14g | protein: 13g | carbs: 34g | fiber: 9g | sodium: 294mg

850) Beet Chips

Ingredients:

- 4 medium beets, rinse and thinly sliced
- 1 Tsp sea salt
- 2 Tbsps olive oil
- Hummus, for serving

Direction: Prep time: 10 minutes | Cook time: 30 minutes | Serves 6

✓ Preheat the air fryer to 380°F (193°C).

✓ In a large container, toss the beets with sea salt and olive oil until well coated.

✓ Put the beet slices into the air fryer and spread them out in a single layer.

✓ Air Fry for 10 minutes. Stir, and fry for an additional 10 minutes. Stir again, then fry until the chips reach the desired crispiness.

✓ Serve with a favorite hummus.
Nutrition: calories: 63 | fat: 5g | protein: 1g | carbs: 5g | fiber: 2g | sodium: 430mg

851) Healthy Deviled Eggs with Greek Yogurt

Ingredients:

- 4 eggs
- ¼ cup nonfat plain Greek yogurt
- 1 Tsp chopped fresh dill
- ⅛ Tsp salt
- ⅛ Tsp paprika
- ⅛ Tsp garlic powder
- Chopped fresh parsley for garnish

Direction: Prep time: 15 minutes | Cook time: 15 minutes | Serves 4

✓ Preheat the air fryer to 270°F (132°C).

✓ Put the eggs in a single layer to the air fryer basket and cook for 15 minutes.

✓ Quickly remove the eggs from the air fryer, place them into a cold water bath. Let the eggs cool to the water for 10 minutes before removing and peeling them.

✓ After peeling the eggs, cut them in half.

✓ Spoon the yolk into a small container. Add the yogurt, salt, dill, paprika, and garlic powder and mix until smooth.

✓ Pipe the yolk mixture into the halved egg whites. Serve with a sprinkle of fresh parsley on top.
Nutrition: calories: 80 | fat: 5g | protein: 8g | carbs: 1g | fiber: 0g | sodium: 149mg

852) Spiced Cashews

Ingredients:

- 2 cups raw cashews
- 2 Tbsps olive oil
- ¼ Tsp salt
- ¼ Tsp chili powder
- ⅛ Tsp garlic powder
- ⅛ Tsp smoked paprika

Direction: Prep time: 7 minutes | Cook time: 10 minutes | Serves 4

✓ Preheat the air fryer to 360°F (182°C).

✓ In a large container, toss all of the ingredients together.

✓ Put the cashews into the air fryer and roast them for 5 minutes. Shake the basket, cook for 5 minutes more.

✓ Serve immediately.
Nutrition: calories: 476 | fat: 40g | protein: 14g | carbs: 23g | fiber: 3g | sodium: 151mg

853) Sweet Potato Chips

Ingredients:

- 1 large sweet potato, thinly sliced
- ⅛ Tsp salt
- 2 Tbsps olive oil

Direction: Prep time: 5 minutes | Cook time: 15 minutes | Serves 2

✓ Preheat the air fryer to 380°F (193°C).

✓ Toss the sweet potatoes, salt, and olive oil together in a small container until the potatoes are well coated.

✓ Pour the sweet potato slices into the air fryer and spread them out in a single layer.

✓ Fry for 10 minutes. Stir and air fry until the chips reach the preferred level of crispiness.
Nutrition: calories: 175 | fat: 14g | protein: 1g | carbs: 13g | fiber: 2g | sodium: 191mg

854) Cranberry Chocolate Granola Bars

Ingredients:

- 2 cups certified gluten-free quick oats
- 2 Tbsps sugar-free dark chocolate chunks
- 2 Tbsps unsweetened dried cranberries
- 3 Tbsps unsweetened shredded coconut
- ½ cup raw honey
- 1 Tsp ground cinnamon
- ⅛ Tsp salt
- 2 Tbsps olive oil

Direction: Prep time: 5 minutes | Cook time: 15 minutes | Serves 6

✓ Preheat the air fryer to 360°F (182°C). Line an 8-by-8-inch baking dish with parchment paper.

✓ In a large container, mix together all of the ingredients until well combined.

- ✓ Press the oat mixture into the pan in an even layer.
- ✓ Put the pan into the air fryer and bake for 15 minutes.
- ✓ Remove the pan from the air fryer, lift the granola cake out of the pan with the edges of the parchment paper.
- ✓ Allow cooling for 10 minutes before slicing into 6 equal bars.
- ✓ Serve immediately,

Nutrition: calories: 272 | fat: 10g | protein: 6g | carbs: 55g | fiber: 5g | sodium: 74mg

855) Carrot Cake Cupcakes with Walnuts

Ingredients:

- Cooking spray with olive oil
- 1 cup grated carrots
- ¼ cup raw honey
- ¼ cup olive oil
- ½ Tsp vanilla extract
- 1 egg
- ¼ cup unsweetened applesauce
- 1 ⅓ flour made from whole wheat
- ¾ Tsp baking powder
- ½ Tsp baking soda
- ½ Tsp ground cinnamon
- ¼ Tsp ground nutmeg
- ⅛ Tsp ground ginger
- ⅛ Tsp salt
- ¼ cup chopped walnuts
- 2 Tbsps chopped golden raisins

Direction: Prep time: 10 minutes | Cook time: 12 minutes | Serves 6

- ✓ Preheat the air fryer to 380°F (193°C). Coat the inside of six silicone muffin cups or a six-cup muffin tin with olive oil spray.
- ✓ Mix together the carrots, honey, olive oil, vanilla extract, egg, and unsweetened applesauce in a medium container.
- ✓ Whisk together the flour, baking powder, baking soda, cinnamon, nutmeg, ginger, and salt in a separate medium container.
- ✓ Combine the wet ingredients to the dry ingredients, mixing until just combined.
- ✓ Gently fold to the walnuts and raisins. Fill the muffin cups or tin three-quarters full with the batter, and place them in the air fryer basket.
- ✓ Bake until a toothpick inserted into the center of a cupcake comes out clean.
- ✓ Serve immediately

Nutrition: calories: 277 | fat: 14g | protein: 6g | carbs: 36g | fiber: 4g | sodium: 182mg

856) Roasted Figs with Goat Cheese

Ingredients:

- 8 fresh figs
- 2 ounces (57 g) goat cheese
- ¼ Tsp ground cinnamon
- 1 Tbsp honey, plus more for serving
- 1 Tbsp olive oil

Direction: Prep time: 8 minutes | Cook time: 10 minutes | Serves 4

- ✓ Preheat the air fryer to 360°F (182°C).
- ✓ Cut the stem off of each fig.
- ✓ Cut an X into the top of each fig, cutting halfway down the fig. Leave the base intact.
- ✓ In a small container, mix together the goat cheese, cinnamon, and honey.
- ✓ Spoon the goat cheese mixture into the cavity of each fig.
- ✓ Arrange the figs in a single layer to the air fryer. Drizzle the oil over the top of the figs and roast for 10 minutes.
- ✓ Serve with an additional drizzle of honey.

Nutrition: calories: 158 | fat: 7g | protein: 3g | carbs: 24g | fiber: 3g | sodium: 61mg

857) Air-Fried Popcorn with Garlic Salt

Ingredients:

- 1 Tsp garlic
- salt

Direction: Prep time: 5 minutes | Cook time: 8 minutes | Serves 2

- ✓ Preheat the air fryer to 380°F (193°C).
- ✓ Tear a square of aluminum foil the size of the bottom of the air fryer and coat it into the air fryer basket.
- ✓ Drizzle olive oil over the top of the foil, and then pour to the popcorn kernels.
- ✓ Roast until the popcorn stops popping.
- ✓ Transfer the popcorn to a large container and sprinkle with garlic salt before serving.

Nutrition: calories: 245 | fat: 14g | protein: 4g | carbs: 25g | fiber: 5g | sodium: 885mg

858) Chicken Skewers with Veggies

Ingredients:

- ¼ cup olive oil
- 1 Tsp garlic powder
- 1 Tsp onion powder
- 1 Tsp ground cumin
- ½ Tsp dried oregano
- ½ Tsp dried basil
- ¼ cup lemon juice
- 1 Tbsp apple cider vinegar Olive oil cooking spray

- *1 pound (454 g) boneless skinless chicken thighs, cut into 1-inch pieces*
- *1 red bell pepper, cut into 1-inch pieces*
- *1 red onion, cut into 1-inch pieces*
- *1 zucchini, cut into 1-inch pieces*
- *12 cherry tomatoes*

Direction: Prep time: 30 minutes | Cook time: 25 minutes | Serves 4

- ✓ *Mix together the olive oil, garlic powder, onion powder, cumin, oregano, basil, lemon juice, and apple cider vinegar in a large container.*
- ✓ *Spray six skewers with olive oil cooking spray.*
- ✓ *On each skewer, slide on a piece of chicken, then a piece of bell pepper, onion, zucchini, and finally a tomato, and then repeat. Each skewer should have at least two pieces of each item.*
- ✓ *Once all of the skewers are prepared, place them in a 9-by-13-inch baking dish and pour the olive oil marinade over the top of the skewers. Turn each skewer so that all sides of the chicken and vegetables are coated.*
- ✓ *Cover the dish with plastic wrap and place it in the refrigerator for 30 minutes.*
- ✓ *After 30 minutes, preheat the air fryer to 380°F (193°C). (If using a grill attachment, make sure it is inside the air fryer during preheating.)*
- ✓ *Remove the skewers from the marinade and lay them in a single layer to the air fryer basket. If the air fryer has a grill attachment, you can also lay them on this instead.*
- ✓ *Cook for 10 minutes. Rotate the kebabs, then cook them for 15 minutes more.*
- ✓ *Remove the skewers from the air fryer and let them rest for 5 minutes before serving.*

Nutrition: calories: 304 | fat: 17g | protein: 27g | carbs: 10g | fiber: 3g | sodium: 62mg

859) Shrimp Pesto Rice Containers

Ingredients:

- *1 pound (454 g) medium shrimp, peeled and deveined*
- *¼ cup pesto sauce*
- *1 lemon, sliced*
- *2 cups cooked wild rice pilaf*

Direction: Prep time: 5 minutes | Cook time: 5 minutes | Serves 4

- ✓ *Preheat the air fryer to 360°F (182°C).*
- ✓ *In a medium container, toss the shrimp with the pesto sauce until well coated.*
- ✓ *Place the shrimp in a single layer to the air fryer basket.*
- ✓ *Put the lemon slices over the shrimp and roast for 5 minutes*
- ✓ *Remove the lemons and discard them. Serve a quarter of the shrimp over ½ cup wild rice with some favorite steamed vegetables.*

Nutrition: calories: 249 | fat: 10g | protein: 20g | carbs: 20g | fiber: 2g | sodium: 277mg

860) Salmon with Tomatoes and Olives

Ingredients:

- *2 Tbsps olive oil*
- *4 (1½-inch-thick) salmon fillets*
- *½ Tsp salt*
- *¼ Tsp cayenne*
- *1 Tsp chopped fresh dill*
- *2 Roma tomatoes, diced*
- *¼ cup sliced Kalamata olives*
- *4 lemon slices*

Direction: Prep time: 5 minutes | Cook time: 8 minutes | Serves 4

- ✓ *Preheat the air fryer to 380°F (193°C).*
- ✓ *Brush the olive oil on both sides of the salmon fillets, and then season them lightly with salt, cayenne, and dill.*
- ✓ *Place the fillets in a single layer to the air fryer's basket, then layer the tomatoes and olives over the top. Top each fillet with a lemon slice.*
- ✓ *Bake for 8 minutes or until the salmon has reached an internal temperature of 145°F (63°C).*

Nutrition: calories: 241 | fat: 15g | protein: 23g | carbs: 3g | fiber: 1g | sodium: 595mg

861) Baked Trout with Lemon

Ingredients:

- *4 trout fillets*
- *2 Tbsps olive oil*
- *½ Tsp salt*
- *1 Tsp black pepper*
- *2 garlic cloves, sliced*
- *1 lemon, sliced, plus additional wedges for serving*

Direction: Prep time: 5 minutes | Cook time: 15 minutes | Serves 4

- ✓ *Preheat the air fryer to 380°F (193°C).*
- ✓ *Brush each fillet with olive oil on both sides and season with salt and pepper. Place the fillets in an even layer to the air fryer basket.*
- ✓ *Place the sliced garlic over the tops of the trout fillets, then top the garlic with lemon slices and cook for 12 to 15 minutes, or until it has reached an internal temperature of 145°F (63°C).*
- ✓ *Serve with fresh lemon wedges.*

Nutrition: calories: 231 | fat: 12g | protein: 29g | carbs: 1g | fiber: 0g | sodium: 341mg

862) Shrimp and Veggie Pita

Ingredients:

- *1 pound (454 g) medium shrimp, peeled and deveined*

- 2 Tbsps olive oil
- 1 Tsp dried oregano
- ½ Tsp dried thyme
- ½ Tsp garlic powder
- ¼ Tsp onion powder
- ½ Tsp salt
- ¼ Tsp black pepper
- 4 whole-wheat pitas
- 4 ounces (113 g) feta cheese, crumbled
- 1 cup shredded lettuce
- 1 tomato, diced
- ¼ cup black olives, sliced
- 1 lemon

Direction: Prep time: 15 minutes | Cook time: 6 minutes | Serves 4

- ✓ Switch on the oven, preheat it setting its temperature to 380°F (193°C).
- ✓ Combine the shrimp with olive oil, oregano, thyme, garlic powder, onion powder, salt, and black pepper in a medium container.
- ✓ Pour shrimp in a single layer into the air fryer basket and cook for 6 to 8 minutes, or until cooked through.
- ✓ Remove from the air fryer and divide into warmed pitas with feta, lettuce, tomato, olives, and a squeeze of lemon.

Nutrition: calories: 395 | fat: 15g | protein: 26g | carbs: 40g | fiber: 4g | sodium: 728mg

863) Sea Bass with Roasted Root Veggie

Ingredients:

- 1 carrot, diced small
- 1 parsnip, diced small
- 1 rutabaga, diced small
- ¼ cup olive oil
- 2 Tsps salt, divided
- 4 sea bass fillets
- ½ Tsp onion powder
- 2 garlic cloves, minced
- 1 lemon, sliced, plus additional wedges for serving

Direction: Prep time: 10 minutes | Cook time: 15 minutes | Serves 15

- ✓ Preheat the air fryer to 380°F (193°C).
- ✓ Toss the carrot, parsnip, and rutabaga with olive oil and 1 Tsp salt in a small container.
- ✓ Lightly season the sea bass with the resting 1 Tsp of salt and the onion powder, then place it into the air fryer basket in a single layer.
- ✓ Spread the garlic over the top of each fillet, then cover with lemon slices.
- ✓ Pour the prepared vegetables into the basket around and on top of the fish. Roast for 15 minutes.
- ✓ Serve with additional lemon wedges if desired.

Nutrition: calories: 299 | fat: 15g | protein: 25g | carbs: 13g | fiber: 2g | sodium: 1232mg

864) Cod Fillet with Swiss Chard

Ingredients:

- 1 Tsp salt
- ½ Tsp dried oregano
- ½ Tsp dried thyme
- ½ Tsp garlic powder
- 4 cod fillets
- ½ white onion, thinly sliced
- 2 cups Swiss chard, washed, stemmed, and torn into pieces
- ¼ cup olive oil
- 1 lemon, quartered

Direction: Prep time: 10 minutes | Cook time: 12 minutes | Serves 4

- ✓ Preheat the air fryer to 380°F (193°C).
- ✓ In a small container, whisk together the salt, oregano, thyme, and garlic powder.
- ✓ Tear off four pieces of aluminum foil, with each sheet being large enough to envelop one cod fillet and a quarter of the vegetables.
- ✓ Place a cod fillet in the middle of each sheet of foil, then sprinkle on all sides with the spice mixture.
- ✓ In each foil packet, place a quarter of the onion slices and ½ cup Swiss chard, then drizzle 1 Tbsp olive oil and squeeze ¼ lemon over the contents of each foil packet.
- ✓ Fold and seal the sides of the foil packets and then place them into the air fryer basket. Steam for 12 minutes.
- ✓ Remove from the basket, and carefully open each packet to avoid a steam burn.

Nutrition: calories: 252 | fat: 13g | protein: 26g | carbs: 4g | fiber: 1g | sodium: 641mg

865) Pollock and Vegetable Pitas

Ingredients:

- 1 pound (454 g) pollock, cut into 1-inch pieces
- ¼ cup olive oil
- 1 Tsp salt
- ½ Tsp dried oregano
- ½ Tsp dried thyme
- ½ Tsp garlic powder
- ¼ Tsp cayenne
- 4 whole-wheat pitas
- 1 cup shredded lettuce
- 2 Roma tomatoes, diced
- Nonfat plain Greek yogurt

- *Lemon, quartered*

Direction: Prep time: 10 minutes | Cook time: 15 minutes | Serves 4

✓ *Preheat the air fryer to 380°F (193°C).*

✓ *Combine the pollock with olive oil, salt, oregano, thyme, garlic powder, and cayenne in a medium container.*

✓ *Put the pollock into the air fryer basket and cook for 15 minutes.*

✓ *Serve inside pitas with lettuce, tomato, and Greek yogurt with a lemon wedge on the side.*

Nutrition: calories: 368 | fat: 1g | protein: 21g | carbs: 38g | fiber: 5g | sodium: 514mg

866) Dill and Garlic Stuffed Red Snapper

Ingredients:

- *1 Tsp salt*
- *½ Tsp black pepper*
- *½ Tsp ground cumin*
- *¼ Tsp cayenne*
- *1 (1-to 1½-pound / 454-to 680-g) whole red snapper, cleaned and patted dry*
- *2 Tbsps olive oil*
- *2 garlic cloves, minced*
- *¼ cup fresh dill Lemon wedges, for serving*

Direction: Prep time: 10 minutes | Cook time: 35 minutes | Serves 4

✓ *Preheat the air fryer to 360°F (182°C)*

✓ *In a small container, mix together the salt, pepper, cumin, and cayenne.*

✓ *Coat the outside of the fish with olive oil, then sprinkle the seasoning blend over the outside of the fish. Stuff the minced garlic and dill inside the cavity of the fish.*

✓ *Place the snapper into the basket of the air fryer and roast for 20 minutes. Flip the snapper over, and roast for 15 minutes more, or until the snapper reaches an internal temperature of 145°F (63°C).*

Nutrition: calories: 125 | fat: 1g | protein: 23g | carbs: 2g | fiber: 0g | sodium: 562mg

867) Easy Tuna Steaks

Ingredients:

- *1 Tsp garlic powder*
- *½ Tsp salt*
- *¼ Tsp dried thyme*
- *¼ Tsp dried oregano*
- *4 tuna steaks*
- *2 Tbsps olive oil*
- *1 lemon, quartered*

Direction: Prep time: 10 minutes | Cook time: 8 minutes | Serves 4

✓ *Preheat the air fryer to 380°F (193°C).*

✓ *In a small container, whisk together the garlic powder, salt, thyme, and oregano.*

Coat the tuna steaks with olive oil. Season both sides of each steak with the seasoning blend. Place the steaks in a single layer to the air fryer basket.

✓ *Cook for 5 minutes, then flip and cook for an additional 3 to 4 minutes.*

Nutrition: calories: 269 | fat: 13g | protein: 33g | carbs: 1g | fiber: 0g | sodium: 231mg

868) Honey-Garlic Glazed Salmon

Ingredients:

- *¼ cup raw honey*
- *4 garlic cloves, minced*
- *1 Tbsp olive oil*
- *½ Tsp salt*
- *Olive oil cooking spray*
- *4 (1½-inch-thick) salmon fillets*

Direction: Serves 4 | Prep time: 5 minutes | Cook time: 10 minutes

✓ *Preheat the air fryer to 380°F (193°C).*

✓ *In a small container, mix together the honey, garlic, olive oil, and salt.*

✓ *Spray the bottom of the air fryer basket with olive oil cooking spray, and place the salmon in a single layer on the bottom of the air fryer basket.*

✓ *Brush the top of each fillet with the honey-garlic mixture, and roast for 10 to 12 minutes, or until the internal temperature reaches 145°F (63°C).*

Nutrition: calories: 260 | fat: 10g | protein: 23g | carbs: 18g | fiber: 0g | sodium: 342mg

869) Balsamic Shrimp on Tomato and Olive

Ingredients:

- *½ cup olive oil*
- *4 garlic cloves, minced*
- *1 Tbsp balsamic vinegar*
- *¼ Tsp cayenne pepper*
- *¼ Tsp salt*
- *1 Roma tomato, diced*
- *¼ cup Kalamata olives*
- *1 pound (454 g) medium shrimp, cleaned and deveined*

Direction: Prep time: 10 minutes | Cook time: 6 minutes | Serves 4

✓ *Preheat the air fryer to 380°F (193°C).*

✓ *In a small container, combine the olive oil, garlic, balsamic, cayenne, and salt.*

✓ *Divide the tomatoes and olives among four small ramekins. Then divide shrimp among the ramekins, and pour a quarter of the oil mixture over the shrimp.*

- ✓ Cook for 6 to 8 minutes, or until the shrimp are cooked through.

Nutrition: calories: 160 | fat: 8g | protein: 16g | carbs: 4g | fiber: 1g | sodium: 213mg

870) Grouper Fillet with Tomato and Olive

Ingredients:

- 4 grouper fillets
- ½ Tsp salt
- 3 garlic cloves, minced 1 tomato, sliced
- ¼ cup sliced Kalamata olives
- ¼ cup fresh dill, roughly chopped
- Juice of 1 lemon
- ¼ cup olive oil

Direction: Prep time: 10 minutes | Cook time: 10 minutes | Serves 4

- ✓ Preheat the air fryer to 380°F (193°C).
- ✓ Season the grouper fillets on all sides with salt, then place them into the air fryer basket and top with the minced garlic, tomato slices, olives, and fresh dill.
- ✓ Drizzle the lemon juice and olive oil over the top of the grouper, then bake for 10 to 12 minutes, or until the internal temperature reaches 145°F (63°C),

Nutrition: calories: 271 | fat: 15g | protein: 28g | carbs: 3g | fiber: 1g | sodium: 324mg

871) Shrimp, Mushrooms, Basil Cheese Pasta

Ingredients:

- 1 pound (454 g) small shrimp, peeled and deveined
- ¼ cup plus 1 Tbsp olive oil, divided
- ¼ Tsp garlic powder
- ¼ Tsp cayenne
- 1 pound (454 g) whole-grain pasta 5 garlic cloves, minced
- 8 ounces (227 g) baby Bella mushrooms, sliced
- ½ cup Parmesan, plus more for serving (optional)
- 1 Tsp salt
- ½ Tsp black pepper
- ½ cup fresh basil

Direction: Prep time: 10 minutes | Cook time: 10 minutes | Serves 6

- ✓ Preheat the air fryer to 380°F (193°C).
- ✓ Combine the shrimp, 1 Tbsp olive oil, garlic powder, and cayenne in a small container. Toss to coat the shrimp.
- ✓ Place the shrimp into the air fryer basket and roast for 5 minutes. Remove the shrimp and set it aside.
- ✓ Cook the pasta according to package directions. Once done cooking, reserve ½ cup pasta water, then drain.
- ✓ Meanwhile, in a large skillet, heat ¼ cup of olive oil over medium heat. Add the garlic and mushrooms and cook down for 5 minutes.
- ✓ Pour the pasta, reserved pasta water, Parmesan, salt, pepper, and basil into the skillet with the vegetable-and-oil mixture, and stir to coat the pasta.
- ✓ Toss to the shrimp and remove from heat, then let the mixture sit for 5 minutes before serving with additional Parmesan if desired.

Nutrition: calories: 457 | fat: 14g | protein: 25g | carbs: 60g | fiber: 6g | sodium: 411mg

872) Rosemary Roasted Red Potatoes

Ingredients:

- 1 pound (454 g) red potatoes, quartered
- ¼ cup olive oil
- ½ Tsp kosher salt
- ¼ Tsp black pepper
- 1 garlic clove, minced
- 4 rosemary sprigs

Direction: Serves 6| Prep time: 5 minutes | Cook time: 20 minutes

- ✓ Preheat the air fryer to 360°F (182°C).
- ✓ Tossing the potatoes with olive oil, salt, pepper, and garlic in a large container until well coated.
- ✓ Pour the potatoes into the air fryer basket and top with the sprigs of rosemary.
- ✓ Roast for 10 minutes, then stir or toss the potatoes and roast for 10 minutes more.
- ✓ Remove the rosemary sprigs and serve the potatoes. Season with additional salt and pepper, if needed.

Nutrition: calories: 133 | fat: 9g | protein: 1g | carbs: 12g | fiber: 1g | sodium: 199mg

873) Easy Roasted Radishes

Ingredients:

- 1 pound (454 g) radishes, ends trimmed if needed
- 2 Tbsps olive oil
  ½ Tsp sea salt

Direction: Prep time: 5 minutes | Cook time: 18 minutes | Serves 4

Preheat the air fryer to 360°F (182°C).

- ✓ In a large container, combine the radishes with olive oil and sea salt.
- ✓ Pour the radishes into the air fryer and cook for 10 minutes. Stir or turn the radishes over and cook for 8 minutes more, then serve.

Nutrition: calories: 78 | fat: 9g | protein: 1g | carbs: 4g | fiber: 2g | sodium: 335mg

874) Zucchini with Garlic and Red Pepper

Ingredients:

- 2 medium zucchini, cubed
- 1 red bell pepper, diced
- 2 garlic cloves, sliced
- 2 Tbsps olive oil
- ½ Tsp salt

Direction: Prep time: 5 minutes | Cook time: 15 minutes | Serves 6

✓ Preheat the air fryer to 380°F (193°C).

✓ Mix together the zucchini, bell pepper, and garlic with olive oil and salt in a large container.

✓ Pour the mixture into the air fryer basket, and roast for 7 minutes. Shake or stir, then roast for 7 to 8 minutes more.

Nutrition: calories: 60 | fat: 5g | protein: 1g | carbs: 4g | fiber: 1g | sodium: 195mg

875) Savory Sweet Potatoes with Parmesan

Ingredients:

- 2 large sweet potatoes, peeled and cubed
- ¼ cup olive oil
- 1 Tsp dried rosemary
- ½ Tsp salt
- 2 Tbsps shredded Parmesan

Direction: Prep time: 10 minutes | Cook time: 18 minutes | Serves 4

✓ Preheat the air fryer to 360°F (182°C).

✓ In a large container, toss the sweet potatoes with olive oil, rosemary, and salt.

✓ Pour the potatoes into the air fryer basket, roast for 10 minutes, then stir the potatoes and sprinkle the Parmesan over the top. Continue roasting for 8 minutes more.

✓ Serve hot and enjoy.

Nutrition: calories: 186 | fat: 14g | protein: 2g | carbs: 13g | fiber: 2g | sodium: 369mg

876) Orange Roasted Brussels Sprouts

Ingredients:

- 1 pound (454 g) Brussels sprouts, quartered
- 2 garlic cloves, minced
- 2 Tbsps olive oil
- ½ Tsp salt
- 1 orange, cut into rings

Direction: Prep time: 5 minutes | Cook time: 10 minutes | Serves 4

✓ Preheat the air fryer to 360°F (182°C).

✓ Tossing the quartered Brussels sprouts with garlic, olive oil, and salt in a large container until well coated.

✓ Pour the Brussels sprouts into the air fryer, lay the orange slices on top of them, and roast for 10 minutes.

✓ Remove from the air fryer and set the orange slices aside. Toss the Brussels sprouts before serving.

Nutrition: calories: 111 | fat: 7g | protein: 4g | carbs: 11g | fiber: 4g | sodium: 319mg

877) Crispy Artichoke s with Lemon

Ingredients:

- 1 (15-ounce / 425-g) can artichoke hearts in water, drained
- 1 egg
- 1 Tbsp water
- ¼ cup whole wheat bread crumbs
- ¼ Tsp salt
- ¼ Tsp paprika
- ½ lemon

Direction: Prep time: 10 minutes | Cook time: 15 minutes | Serves 2

✓ Preheat the air fryer to 380°F (193°C).

✓ In a medium shallow container, beat together the egg and water until frothy.

✓ In a separate medium shallow container, mix together the bread crumbs, salt, and paprika.

✓ Dip each artichoke heart into the egg mixture, then into the bread crumb mixture, coating the outside with the crumbs. Place the artichoke's hearts in a single layer of the air fryer basket.

✓ Fry the artichoke hearts for 15 minutes.

✓ Remove the artichokes from the air fryer, and squeeze fresh lemon juice over the top before serving.

Nutrition: calories: 91 | fat: 2g | protein: 5g | carbs: 16g | fiber: 8g | sodium: 505mg

878) Lemon Green Beans with Red Onion

Ingredients:

- 1 pound (454 g) fresh green beans, trimmed
- ½ red onion, sliced
- 2 Tbsps olive oil
- ½ Tsp salt
- ¼ Tsp black pepper
- 1 Tbsp lemon juice
- Lemon wedges, for serving

Direction: Prep time: 5 minutes | Cook time: 10 minutes | Serves 6

✓ Preheat the air fryer to 360°F (182°C). In a large container, toss the green beans, onion, olive oil, salt, pepper, and lemon juice until combined.

✓ Pour the mixture into the air fryer and roast for 5 minutes. Stir well and roast for 5 minutes more.

✓ Serve with lemon wedges.

Nutrition: calories: 67 | fat: 5g | protein: 1g | carbs: 6g | fiber: 2g | sodium: 199mg

879) Walnut Carrots with Honey Glaze

Ingredients:

- 1 pound (454 g) baby carrots
- 2 Tbsps olive oil
- ¼ cup raw honey
- ¼ Tsp ground cinnamon
- ¼ cup black walnuts, chopped

Direction: Prep time: 5 minutes | Cook time: 12 minutes | Serves 6

✓ Preheat the air fryer to 360°F (182°C).

✓ Tossing the baby carrots with olive oil, honey, and cinnamon in a large container until well coated.

✓ Pour into the air fryer and roast for 6 minutes. Shake the basket, sprinkle the walnuts on top, and roast for 6 minutes more.

✓ Remove the carrots from the air fryer and serve.

Nutrition: cal: 146 | fat: 8g | protein: 1g | carbs: 20g

880) Roasted Asparagus and Tomatoes

Ingredients:

- 2 cups grape tomatoes
- 1 bunch asparagus, trimmed
- 2 Tbsps olive oil
- 3 garlic cloves, minced
- ½ Tsp kosher salt

Direction: Prep time: 5 minutes | Cook time: 12 minutes | Serves 6

✓ Preheat the air fryer to 380°F (193°C).

✓ In a large container, combine all of the ingredients, tossing until the vegetables are well coated with oil.

✓ Pour the vegetable mixture into the air fryer basket and spread into a single layer, then roast for 12 minutes.

Nutrition: calories: 57 | fat: 5g | protein: 1g | carbs: 4g | fiber: 1g | sodium: 197mg

881) Ricotta Stuffed Bell Peppers

Ingredients:

- 2 red bell peppers
- 1 cup cooked brown rice
- 2 Roma tomatoes, diced
- 1 garlic clove, minced
- ¼ Tsp salt
- ¼ Tsp black pepper
- 4 ounces (113 g) ricotta
- 3 Tbsps fresh basil, chopped
- 3 Tbsps fresh oregano, chopped
- ¼ cup shredded Parmesan, for topping

Direction: Prep time: 10 minutes | Cook time: 20 minutes | Serves 4

✓ Preheat the air fryer to 360°F (182°C).

✓ Cut the bell peppers in half and remove the seeds and stem.

✓ In a medium container, combine the brown rice, tomatoes, garlic, salt, and pepper.

✓ Distribute the rice filling evenly among the four bell pepper halves.

✓ In a small container, combine the ricotta, basil, and oregano. Put the herbed cheese over the top of the rice mixture in each bell pepper.

✓ Place the bell peppers into the air fryer and roast for 20 minutes.

✓ Remove and serve with shredded Parmesan on top.

Nutrition: calories: 156 | fat: 6g | protein: 8g | carbs: 19g | fiber: 3g |

882) Ratatouille

Ingredients:

- 2 russet potatoes, cubed
- ½ cup Roma tomatoes, cubed
- 1 eggplant, cubed
- 1 zucchini, cubed
- 1 red onion, chopped
- 1 red bell pepper, chopped
- 2 garlic cloves, minced
- 1 Tsp dried mint
- 1 Tsp dried parsley
- 1 Tsp dried oregano
- ½ Tsp salt
- ½ Tsp black pepper
- ¼ Tsp red pepper flakes ⅓ cup olive oil
- 1 (8-ounce / 227-g) can tomato paste
- ¼ cup vegetable broth
- ¼ cup water

Direction: Prep time: 15 minutes | Cook time: 40 minutes | Serves 6

✓ Preheat the air fryer to 320°F (160°C).

✓ Combine the potatoes, tomatoes, eggplant, zucchini, onion, bell pepper, garlic, mint, parsley, oregano, salt, black pepper, and red pepper flakes in a large container.

✓ In a small container, mix together the olive oil, tomato paste, broth, and water.

✓ Pour the oil-and-tomato-paste mixture over the vegetables and toss until everything is coated.

✓ Pour the coated vegetables into the air fryer basket in an even layer and roast for 20 minutes. After 20 minutes, stir well and spread out again. Roast for an additional 10 minutes, then repeat the process and cook for another 10 minutes.

Nutrition: calories: 280 | fat: 13g | protein: 6g | carbs: 40g | fiber: 7g | sodium: 264mg

883) Parmesan Butternut Squash

Ingredients:

- 2½ cups butternut squash, cubed into 1-inch pieces (approximately 1 medium)
- 2 Tbsps olive oil
- ¼ Tsp salt
- ¼ Tsp garlic powder
- ¼ Tsp black pepper
- 1 Tbsp fresh thyme
- ¼ cup grated Parmesan

Direction: Prep time: 15 minutes | Cook time: 20 minutes | Serves 4

- ✓ Preheat the air fryer to 360°F (182°C).
- ✓ In a large container, combine the cubed squash with the olive oil, salt, garlic powder, pepper, and thyme until the squash is well coated.
- ✓ Pour this mixture into the air fryer basket, and roast for 10 minutes. Stir and roast another 8 to 10 minutes more.
- ✓ Remove the squash from the air fryer and toss with freshly grated Parmesan before serving.

Nutrition: calories: 127 | fat: 9g | protein: 3g | carbs: 11g | fiber: 2g | sodium: 262mg

884) Garlic Eggplant Slices

Ingredients:

- 1 egg
- 1 Tbsp water
- ½ cup whole wheat bread crumbs
- 1 Tsp garlic powder
- ½ Tsp dried oregano
- ½ Tsp salt
- ½ Tsp paprika
- 1 medium eggplant, sliced into ¼-inch-thick rounds
- 1 Tbsp olive oil

Direction: Prep time: 5 minutes | Cook time: 25 minutes | Serves 4

- ✓ Preheat the air fryer to 360°F (182°C).
- ✓ In a medium shallow container, beat together the egg and water until frothy.
- ✓ Mix together bread crumbs, garlic powder, oregano, salt, and paprika in a separate medium shallow container.
- ✓ Dip each eggplant slice into the egg mixture, then into the bread crumb mixture, coating the outside with crumbs. Place the slices in a single layer to the bottom of the air fryer basket.
- ✓ Drizzle the tops of the eggplant slices with the olive oil, then fry for 15 minutes. Turn each slice and cook for an additional 10 minutes.

Nutrition: calories: 137 | fat: 5g | protein: 5g | carbs: 19g | fiber: 5g | sodium: 409mg

885) Dill Beets

Ingredients:

- 4 beets, cleaned, peeled, and sliced
- 1 garlic clove, minced
- 2 Tbsps chopped fresh dill
- ¼ Tsp salt
- ¼ Tsp black pepper
- 3 Tbsps olive oil

Direction: Prep time: 10 minutes | Cook time: 30 minutes | Serves 4

- ✓ Preheat the air fryer to 380°F (193°C).
- ✓ In a large container, mix together all of the ingredients, so the beets are well coated with the oil.
- ✓ Pour the beet mixture into the air fryer basket, and roast for 15 minutes before stirring, then continue roasting for 15 minutes more.

Nutrition: calories: 126 | fat: 10g | protein: 1g | carbs: 8g | fiber: 2g | sodium: 210mg

886) Orange-Honey Roasted Broccoli

Ingredients:

- 4 cups broccoli florets (approximately 1 large head)
- 2 Tbsps olive oil
- ½ Tsp salt
- ½ cup orange juice
- 1 Tbsp raw honey
- Orange wedges, for serving (optional)

Direction: Prep time: 5 minutes | Cook time: 12 minutes | Serves 6

- ✓ Preheat the air fryer to 360°F (182°C).
- ✓ Combine the broccoli, olive oil, salt, orange juice, and honey in a large container. Toss the broccoli into the liquid until well coated.
- ✓ Pour the broccoli mixture into the air fryer basket and cook for 6 minutes. Stir and cook for 6 minutes more.
- ✓ Serve alone or with orange wedges for additional citrus flavor, if desired.

Nutrition: calories: 80 | fat: 5g | protein: 2g | carbs: 9g | fiber: 2g | sodium: 203mg

887) Baked Sweet Potato Black Bean Burgers

Ingredients:

- 1 (15-ounce / 425-g) can black beans, drained and rinsed
- 1 cup mashed sweet potato
- ½ Tsp dried oregano
- ¼ Tsp dried thyme
- ¼ Tsp dried marjoram
- 1 garlic clove, minced
- ¼ Tsp salt
- ¼ Tsp black pepper

- *1 Tbsp lemon juice*
- *1 cup cooked brown rice*
- *¼ to ½ cup whole wheat bread crumbs*
- *1 Tbsp olive oil*

For Serving:

- *Whole wheat buns or whole wheat pitas Plain Greek yogurt*
- *Avocado*
- *Lettuce*
- *Tomato*
- *Red onion*

Direction: Prep time: 10 minutes | Cook time: 10 minutes | Serves 4

✓ *Preheat the air fryer to 380°F (193°C).*

✓ *In a large container, use the back of a fork to mash the black beans until there are no large pieces left.*

✓ *Add the mashed sweet potato, oregano, thyme, marjoram, garlic, salt, pepper, and lemon juice, and mix until well combined.*

✓ *Stir to the cooked rice.*

✓ *Add in ¼ cup of the whole wheat bread crumbs and stir. Check to see if the mixture is dry enough to form patties. If it seems too wet and loose, add an additional ¼ cup bread crumbs and stir.*

✓ *Form the dough into 4 patties. Place them into the air fryer basket in a single layer, ensuring they don't touch each other.*

✓ *Brush half of the oil onto the patties and bake for 5 minutes.*

✓ *Flip the patties over, brush the other side with the resting oil, and bake for an additional 4 to 5 minutes.*

✓ *Serve on toasted whole wheat buns or whole wheat pitas with a spoonful of yogurt and lettuce, avocado, tomato, and red onion as desired.*

Nutrition: calories: 263 | fat: 5g | protein: 9g | carbs: 47g | fiber: 8g | sodium: 247mg

888) Herb Lentil-Rice Balls

Ingredients:

- *½ cup cooked green lentils*
- *2 garlic cloves, minced*
- *¼ white onion, minced*
- *¼ cup parsley leaves*
- *5 basil leaves*
  1 cup cooked brown rice
- *1 Tbsp lemon juice*
- *1 Tbsp olive oil*
- *½ Tsp salt*

Direction: Prep time: 5 minutes | Cook time: 11 minutes | Serves 6

✓ *Preheat the air fryer to 380°F (193°C).*

✓ *In a food processor, pulse the cooked lentils with the garlic, onion, parsley, and basil until mostly smooth. (You will want some bits of lentils to the mixture.)*

✓ *Pour the lentil mixture into a large container, and stir in brown rice, lemon juice, olive oil, and salt. Stir until well combined.*

✓ *Form the rice mixture into 1-inch balls. Place the rice balls in a single layer to the air fryer basket, ensuring they don't touch each other.*

✓ *Fry for 6 minutes. Turn the rice balls and then fry for an additional 4 to 5 minutes, or until browned on all sides.*

Nutrition: calories: 80 | fat: 3g | protein: 2g | carbs: 12g | fiber: 2g | sodium: 198mg

889) Lentil Stuffed Tomatoes

Ingredients:

- *4 tomatoes*
- *½ cup cooked red lentils*
- *1 garlic clove, minced*
- *1 Tbsp minced red onion*
- *4 basil leaves, minced*
- *¼ Tsp salt*
- *¼ Tsp black pepper*
- *4 ounces (113 g) goat cheese*
- *2 Tbsps shredded Parmesan cheese*

Direction: Prep time: 10 minutes | Cook time: 15 minutes | Serves 4

✓ *Preheat the air fryer to 380°F (193°C).*

✓ *Slice the top off of each tomato.*

✓ *Using a knife and spoon, cut and scoop out half of the flesh inside of the tomato. Place it into a medium container.*

✓ *To the container with the tomato, add the cooked lentils, garlic, onion, basil, salt, pepper, and goat cheese. Stir until well combined.*

✓ *Spoon the filling into the scooped-out cavity of each of the tomatoes, then top each one with ½ Tbsp of shredded Parmesan cheese.*

✓ *Place the tomatoes in a single layer to the air fryer basket and bake for 15 minutes.*

Nutrition: calories: 138 | fat: 7g | protein: 9g | carbs: 11g | fiber: 4g | sodium: 317mg

890) Oregano Lentil and Carrot Patties

Ingredients:

- *1 cup cooked brown lentils*
- *¼ cup fresh parsley leaves*
- *½ cup shredded carrots*
- *¼ red onion, minced*
- *¼ red bell pepper, minced*
- *1 jalapeño, seeded and minced*
- *2 garlic cloves, minced*

- *1 egg*
- *2 Tbsps lemon juice*
- *2 Tbsps olive oil, divided*
- *½ Tsp onion powder*
- *½ Tsp smoked paprika*
- *½ Tsp dried oregano*
- *¼ Tsp salt*
- *¼ Tsp black pepper*
- *½ cup whole wheat bread crumbs*
- *For Serving:*
- *Whole wheat buns or whole wheat pitas*
- *Plain Greek yogurt*
- *Tomato*
- *Lettuce*
- *Red Onion*

Direction: Prep time: 16 minutes | Cook time: 9-10 minutes | Serves 4

- ✓ *Preheat the air fryer to 380°F (193°C).*
- ✓ *In a food processor, pulse the lentils and parsley mostly smooth. (You will want some bits of lentils to the mixture.)*
- ✓ *Pour the lentils into a large container, and combine with the carrots, onion, bell pepper, jalapeño, garlic, egg, lemon juice, and 1 Tbsp olive oil.*
- ✓ *Add the onion powder, paprika, oregano, salt, pepper, and bread crumbs. Stir everything together until the seasonings and bread crumbs are well distributed.*
- ✓ *Form the dough into 4 patties. Place them into the air fryer basket in a single layer, ensuring they don't touch each other. Brush the resting 1 Tbsp of olive oil over the patties.*
- ✓ *Bake for 5 minutes. Flip the patties over and bake for an additional 5 minutes.*
- ✓ *Serve on toasted whole wheat buns or whole wheat pitas with a spoonful of yogurt and lettuce, tomato, and red onion as desired.*

Nutrition: calories: 206 | fat: 9g | protein: 8g | carbs: 25g | fiber: 6g | sodium: 384mg

891) **Roasted White Beans with Herb**

Ingredients:

- *Olive oil cooking spray*
- *2 (15-ounce / 425-g) cans of white beans, or cannellini beans, drained and rinsed*
- *1 red bell pepper, diced*
- *½ red onion, diced*
- *3 garlic cloves, minced*
- *1 Tbsp olive oil*
- *¼ to ½ Tsp salt*
- *½ Tsp black pepper*
- *1 rosemary sprig*
- *1 bay leaf*

Direction: Prep time: 10 minutes | Cook time: 15 minutes | Serves 4

- ✓ *Preheat the air fryer to 360 degrees Fahrenheit (182 degrees Celsius). Using olive oil cooking spray, lightly coat the inside of a 5-cup casserole dish. (The casserole dish's shape will be determined by the size of the air fryer, but it must hold at least 5 cups.)*
- ✓ *Combine the beans, bell pepper, onion, garlic, olive oil, salt, and pepper in a large container.*
- ✓ *Pour the bean mixture into the prepared casserole dish, place the rosemary and bay leaf on top, and then place the casserole dish into the air fryer.*
- ✓ *Roast for 15 minutes.*
- ✓ *Remove the rosemary and bay leaves, then stir well before serving.*

Nutrition: calories: 196 | fat: 5g | protein: 10g | carbs: 30g | fiber: 1g | sodium: 150mg

892) **Greek Baked Two Beans**

Ingredients:

- *Olive oil cooking spray*
- *1 (15-ounce / 425-g) can cannellini beans, drained and rinsed*
- *1 (15-ounce / 425-g) can great northern beans, drained and rinsed ½ yellow onion, diced*
- *1 (8-ounce) can tomato sauce*
- *1½ Tbsps raw honey*
- *¼ cup olive oil 2 garlic cloves, minced*
- *2 Tbsps chopped fresh dill*
- *½ Tsp salt*
- *½ Tsp black pepper 1 bay leaf*
- *1 Tbsp balsamic vinegar*
- *2 ounces (57 g) feta cheese, crumbled, for serving*

Direction: Prep time: 15 minutes | Cook time: 30 minutes | Serves 4

- ✓ *Preheat the air fryer to 360 degrees Fahrenheit (182 degrees Celsius). Using olive oil cooking spray, lightly coat the inside of a 5-cup casserole dish. (The casserole dish's shape will be determined by the size of the air fryer, but it must hold at least 5 cups.)*
- ✓ *In a large container, combine all ingredients except the feta cheese and stir until well combined.*
- ✓ *Pour the bean mixture into the prepared casserole dish.*
- ✓ *Bake to the air fryer for 30 minutes.*
- ✓ *Remove the bay leaf from the air fryer and discard it. Before serving, top with crumbled feta cheese.*

Nutrition: calories: 397 | fat: 18g | protein: 14g | carbs: 48g | fiber: 16g | sodium: 886mg

893) **Butter Beans Casserole with Parsley**

Ingredients:

- Olive oil cooking spray
- 1 (15-ounce / 425-g) can cooked butter beans, drained and rinsed
- 1 cup diced fresh tomatoes
- ½ Tbsp tomato paste
- 2 garlic cloves, minced
- ½ yellow onion, diced
- ½ Tsp salt
- ¼ cup olive oil
- ¼ cup fresh parsley, chopped

Direction: Prep time: 10 minutes | Cook time: 30 minutes | Serves 4

- ✓ Preheat the air fryer to 380°F (193°C). Lightly coat the inside of a 5-cup capacity casserole dish with olive oil cooking spray. (The shape of the casserole dish will depend upon the size of the air fryer, but it needs to be able to hold at least 5 cups.)
- ✓ In a large container, combine the butter beans, tomatoes, tomato paste, garlic, onion, salt, and olive oil, mixing until all ingredients are combined.
- ✓ Pour the mixture into the prepared casserole dish and top with the chopped parsley.
- ✓ Bake to the air fryer for 15 minutes. Stir well, then return to the air fryer and bake for 15 minutes more.

Nutrition: calories: 212 | fat: 14g | protein: 5g | carbs: 17g | fiber: 1g | sodium: 298mg

894) Mediterranean Green Peas with Parmesan

Ingredients:

- 1 cup cauliflower florets, fresh or frozen
- ½ white onion, roughly chopped
- 2 Tbsps olive oil
- ½ cup unsweetened almond milk
- 3 cups green peas, fresh or frozen
- 3 garlic cloves, minced
- 2 Tbsps fresh thyme leaves, chopped
- 1 Tsp fresh rosemary leaves, chopped
- ½ Tsp salt
- ½ Tsp black pepper
- Shredded Parmesan cheese (garnish)
- Fresh parsley (garnish)

Direction: Prep time: 15 minutes | Cook time: 25 minutes | Serves 8

- ✓ Preheat the air fryer to 380°F
- ✓ Combine the cauliflower florets and onion with the olive oil in a large container and toss well to coat.
- ✓ Put the cauliflower-and-onion mixture into the air fryer basket in an even layer and bake for 15 minutes.
- ✓ Transfer the cauliflower and onion to a food processor. Add the almond milk and pulse until smooth.
- ✓ In a medium saucepan, combine the cauliflower purée, peas, garlic, thyme, rosemary, salt, and pepper and mix well. Cook over medium heat for 10 minutes more, stirring regularly.
- ✓ Serve with a sprinkle of Parmesan cheese and chopped fresh parsley.

Nutrition: calories: 87 | fat: 4g | protein: 4g | carbs: 10g | fiber: 3g | sodium: 163mg

895) Tropical Almond Pancakes

Ingredients:

- 2 cups creamy milk
- 3½ cups almond flour
- 1 Tsp baking soda
- ½ Tsp salt
- 1 Tsp allspice
- 2 Tbsps vanilla
- 1 Tsp cinnamon
- 1 Tsp baking powder
- ½ cup club soda

Direction: Preparation time: 15 mins Servings: 8

- ✓ Preheat the Air fryer at 290 degrees F and grease the cooking basket of the air fryer.
- ✓ Whisk together salt, almond flour, baking soda, allspice, and cinnamon in a large container.
- ✓ Mix together the vanilla, baking powder, and club soda and add to the flour mixture.
- ✓ Stir the mixture thoroughly and pour the mixture into the cooking basket.
- ✓ Cook for about 10 minutes and dish it out on a serving platter.

Nutrition: Calories: 324 Carbs: 12.8g Fats: 24.5g Proteins: 11.4g Sodium: 342mg Sugar: 1.6g

896) Bacon & Hot Dogs Omelet

Ingredients:

- 4 hot dogs, chopped
- 8 eggs
- 2 bacon slices, chopped
- 4 small onions, chopped

Direction: Preparation time: 15 mins Servings: 4

- ✓ Preheat the Airfryer to 325 degrees F.
- ✓ Crack the eggs in an Air fryer baking pan and beat well.
- ✓ Stir to the resting ingredients and cook for about 10 minutes until completely done.

Nutrition: Calories: 298 Carbs: 9g Fats: 21.8g Proteins: 16.9g Sodium: 628mg Sugar: 5.1g

897) Simple Cheese Sandwiches

Ingredients:

- 8 American cheese slices

- *8 bread slices*
- *8 Tsps butter*

Direction: Preparation time: 10 mins Servings: 4

- ✓ *Preheat the Air fryer to 365 degrees F and arrange cheese slices between bread slices.*
- ✓ *Spread butter over the outer sides of the sandwich and repeat with the resting butter, slices, and cheese.*
- ✓ *Arrange the sandwiches in an Air fryer basket and cook for about 8 minutes, flipping once to the middle way.*

Nutrition: Calories: 254 Carbs: 12.4g Fats: 18.8g Proteins: 9.2g Sodium: 708mg Sugar:3.9g

898) Ham, Spinach & Egg in a Cup

Ingredients:

- *2 Tbsps olive oil*
- *2 Tbsps unsalted butter, melted*
- *2 pounds fresh baby spinach*
- *8 eggs*
- *8 Tsps milk*
- *14ounce ham, sliced*
- *Salt and black pepper, to taste*

Direction: Preparation time: 35 mins Servings: 8

- ✓ *Preheat the Airfryer to 360 degrees F and grease 8 ramekins with butter.*
- ✓ *Heat oil in a skillet on medium heat and add spinach.*
- ✓ *Cook for about 3 minutes and drato the liquid completely from the spinach.*
- ✓ *Divide the spinach into prepared ramekins and layer with ham slices.*
- ✓ *Crack 1 egg over ham slices into each ramekin and drizzle evenly with milk.*
- ✓ *Sprinkle with salt and black pepper and bake for about 20 minutes.*

Nutrition: Calories: 228 Carbs: 6.6g Fats: 15.6g Proteins: 17.2g Sodium: 821mg Sugar: 1.1g

899) Eggs with Sausage & Bacon

Ingredients:

- *4 chicken sausages*
- *4 bacon slices*
- *2 eggs*
- *Salt and freshly ground black pepper, to taste*

Direction: Preparation time: 25 mins Servings: 2

- ✓ *Preheat the Airfryer to 330 degrees F and place sausages and bacon slices in an Airfryer basket.*
- ✓ *Cook for about 10 minutes and lightly grease 2 ramekins.*
- ✓ *Crack 1 egg in each prepared ramekin and season with salt and black pepper.*
- ✓ *Cook for about 10 minutes and divide sausages and bacon slices on serving plates.*

Nutrition: Calories: 245 Carbs: 5.7g Fats: 15.8g Proteins: 17.8g Sodium: 480mg Sugar: 0.7g

900) Toasted Bagels

Ingredients:

- *6 Tsps butter*
- *3 bagels, halved*

Direction: Preparation time: 10 mins Servings: 6

- ✓ *Preheat the Airfryer to 375 degrees F and arrange the bagels into an Airfryer basket.*
- ✓ *Cook for about 3 minutes and remove the bagels from Airfryer.*
- ✓ *Spread butter evenly over bagels and cook for about 3 more minutes.*

Nutrition: Calories: 169 Carbs: 26.5g Fats: 4.7g Proteins: 5.3g Sodium: 262mg Sugar: 2.7g

901) Eggless Spinach & Bacon Quiche

Ingredients:

- *1 cup fresh spinach, chopped*
- *4 slices of bacon, cooked and chopped*
- *½ cup mozzarella cheese, shredded*
- *4 Tbsps milk*
- *4 dashes of Tabasco sauce*
- *1 cup Parmesan cheese, shredded*
- *Salt and freshly ground black pepper, to taste*

Direction: Preparation time: 20 mins Servings: 8

- ✓ *Preheat the Airfryer to 325 degrees F and grease a baking dish.*
- ✓ *Put all the ingredients in a container and mix well.*
- ✓ *Transfer the mixture into a prepared baking dish and cook for about 8 minutes.*
- ✓ *Dish out and serve.*

Nutrition: Calories: 72 Carbs: 0.9g Fats: 5.2g Proteins: 5.5g Sodium: 271mg Sugar: 0.4g

902) Ham Casserole

Ingredients:

- *4-ounce ham, sliced thinly*
- *4 Tsps unsalted butter, softened*
- *8 large eggs, divided*
- *4 Tbsps heavy cream*
- *¼ Tsp smoked paprika*
- *4 Tsps fresh chives, minced*
- *Salt and freshly ground black pepper, to taste*
- *6 Tbsps Parmesan cheese, grated finely*

Direction: Preparation time: 25 mins Servings: 4

- ✓ *Preheat the Airfryer to 325 degrees F and spread butter to the pie pan.*
- ✓ *Place ham slices to the bottom of the pie pan.*
- ✓ *Whisk together 2 eggs, cream, salt, and black pepper until smooth.*

- ✓ Place the egg mixture evenly over the ham slices and crack the resting eggs on top.
- ✓ Season with paprika, salt, and black pepper.
- ✓ Top evenly with chives and cheese and place the pie pan in an Airfryer.
- ✓ Cook for about 12 minutes and serve with toasted bread slices.

Nutrition: Calories: 410 Carbs: 3.9g Fats: 30.8g Proteins: 31.2g Sodium: 933mg Sugar: 0.8g

903) Sausage & Bacon with Beans

Ingredients:

- 12 medium sausages
- 12 bacon slices
- 8 eggs
- 2 cans baked beans
- 12 bread slices, toasted

Direction: Preparation time: 30 mins Servings: 12

- ✓ Preheat the Airfryer at 325 degrees F and place sausages and bacon in a fryer basket.
- ✓ Cook for about 10 minutes and place the baked beans in a ramekin.
- ✓ Place eggs in another ramekin and the Airfryer to 395 degrees F.
- ✓ Cook for about 10 more minutes and divide the sausage mixture, beans, and eggs on serving plates
- ✓ Serve with bread slices.

Nutrition: Calories: 276 Carbs: 14.1g Fats: 17g Proteins: 16.3g Sodium: 817mg Sugar: 0.6g

904) French Toasts

Ingredients:

- ½ cup evaporated milk
- 4 eggs
- 6 Tbsps sugar
- ¼ Tsp vanilla extract
- 8 bread slices
- 4 Tsps olive oil

Direction: Preparation time: 15 mins Servings: 4

- ✓ Preheat the Airfryer to 395 degrees F and grease a pan.
- ✓ Put all the ingredients in a large shallow dish except the bread slices.
- ✓ Beat till well combined and dip each bread slice in egg mixture from both sides.
- ✓ Arrange the bread slices to the prepared pan and cook for about 3 minutes per side.

Nutrition: Calories: 261 Carbs: 30.6g Fats: 12g Proteins: 9.1g Sodium: 218mg Sugar: 22.3g

905) Veggie Hash

Ingredients:

- 2 medium onions, chopped
- 2 Tsps dried thyme, crushed
- 4 Tsps butter
- 1 green bell pepper, seeded and chopped
- 3 pounds russet potatoes, peeled and cubed
- Salt and freshly ground black pepper, to taste
- 10 eggs

Direction: Preparation time: 55 mins Servings: 8

- ✓ Preheat the Airfryer to 395 degrees F and grease the Airfryer pan with butter.
- ✓ Add bell peppers and onions and cook for about 5 minutes.
- ✓ Add the herbs, potatoes, salt, and black pepper and cook for about 30 minutes.
- ✓ Heat a greased skillet on medium heat and add beaten eggs.
- ✓ Cook for about 1 minute on each side and remove from the skillet.
- ✓ Cut it into small pieces and add egg pieces into the Airfryer pan.
- ✓ Cook for about 5 more minutes and dish out.

Nutrition: Calories: 229 Carbs: 31g Fats: 7.6g Proteins: 10.3g Sodium: 102mg Sugar: 4.3g

906) Parmesan Garlic Rolls

Ingredients:

- 1 cup Parmesan cheese, grated
- 4 dinner rolls
- 4 Tbsps unsalted butter, melted
- 1 Tbsp garlic bread seasoning mix

Direction: Preparation time: 15 mins Servings: 4

- ✓ Preheat the Airfryer at 360 degrees F and cut the dinner rolls into cross style.
- ✓ Stuff the slits evenly with the cheese and coat the tops of each roll with butter.
- ✓ Sprinkle with the seasoning mix and cook for about 5 minutes until cheese is fully melted.

Nutrition: Calories: 391 Carbs: 45g Fats: 18.6g Proteins: 11.7g Sodium: 608mg Sugar: 4.8g

907) Pickled Toasts

Ingredients:

- 4 Tbsps unsalted butter, softened
- 8 bread slices, toasted
- 4 Tbsps Branston pickle
- ½ cup Parmesan cheese, grated

Direction: Preparation time: 25 mins Servings: 4

- ✓ Preheat the Airfryer to 385 degrees F and place the bread slice in a fryer basket.
- ✓ Cook for about 5 minutes and spread butter evenly over bread slices.
- ✓ Layer with Branston pickle and top evenly with cheese.
- ✓ Cook for about 5 minutes until cheese is fully

melted.

Nutrition: Calories: 186 Carbs: 16.3g Fats: 12.9g Proteins: 2.6g Sodium: 397mg Sugar: 6.8g

908) Potato Rosti

Ingredients:

- *½ pound russet potatoes, peeled and grated roughly*
- *Salt and freshly ground black pepper, to taste*
- *3.5 ounces smoked salmon, cut into slices*
- *1 Tsp olive oil*
- *1 Tbsp chives, chopped finely*
- *2 Tbsps sour cream*

Direction: Preparation time: 15 mins Servings: 4

- ✓ *Preheat the Airfryer to 360 degrees F and grease a pizza pan with olive oil.*
- ✓ *Add chives, potatoes, salt, and black pepper in a large container and mix until well combined.*
- ✓ *Place the potato mixture into the prepared pizza pan and transfer the pizza pan to an Airfryer basket.*
- ✓ *Cook for about 15 minutes and cut the potato rosti into wedges.*
- ✓ *Top with the smoked salmon slices and sour cream and serve.*

Nutrition: Calories: 91 Carbs: 9.2g Fats: 3.6g Proteins: 5.7g Sodium: 503mg Sugar: 0.7g

909) Pumpkin Pancakes

Ingredients:

- *2 squares puff pastry*
- *6 Tbsps pumpkin filling*
- *2 small eggs, beaten*
- *¼ Tsp cinnamon*

Direction: Preparation time: 20 mins Servings: 8

- ✓ *Preheat the Airfryer to 360 degrees F and roll out a square of puff pastry.*
- ✓ *Layer it with pumpkin pie filling, leaving about ¼-inch space around the edges.*
- ✓ *Cut it up into equal-sized square pieces and cover the gaps with beaten egg.*
- ✓ *Arrange the squares into a baking dish and cook for about 12 minutes.*
- ✓ *Sprinkle some cinnamon and serve.*

Nutrition: Calories: 51 Carbs: 5g Fats: 2.5g Proteins: 2.4g Sodium: 48mg Sugar: 0.5g

910) Moroccan-Style Brown Rice and Chickpea

Ingredients:

- *Olive oil cooking spray*
- *1 cup long-grain brown rice*
- *2¼ cups chicken broth*
- *1 (15½-ounce / 439-g) can chickpeas, drained and rinsed*
- *½ cup diced carrots*
- *½ cup green peas*
- *1 teaspoon ground cumin*
- *½ teaspoon ground turmeric*
- *½ teaspoon ground ginger*
- *½ teaspoon onion powder*
- *½ teaspoon salt*
- *¼ teaspoon ground cinnamon*
- *¼ teaspoon garlic powder*
- *¼ teaspoon black pepper*
- *Fresh parsley, for garnish*

Direction: Preparation time: 15 minutes | Cooking time: 45 minutes | Serves 6

- ✓ *Preheat the fryer to 380°F (193°C). Lightly coat the inside of a 5-cup casserole dish with olive oil spray.*
- ✓ *(The shape of the casserole dish will depend on the size of the air fryer, but it should be able to hold at least 5 cups).*
- ✓ *Combine the rice, broth, chickpeas, carrot, peas, cumin, turmeric, ginger, onion powder, salt, cinnamon, garlic powder, and black pepper in the casserole dish. Mix well to combine.*
- ✓ *Loosely cover with aluminum foil.*
- ✓ *Place the covered casserole dish in the air fryer and cook for 20 minutes. Remove from the fryer and stir well.*
- ✓ *Return the casserole to the fryer, uncovered, and cook for another 25 minutes.*
- ✓ *Stir with a spoon and sprinkle with chopped fresh parsley before serving.*

Nutrition: calories: 204 | fat: 1g | protein: 7g | carbs: 40g | fiber: 4g | sodium: 623mg

911) Buckwheat Groats with Root Vegetables

Ingredients:

- *Olive oil cooking spray*
- *2 large potatoes, cubed*
- *2 carrots, sliced*
- *1 small rutabaga, cubed*
- *2 celery stalks, chopped*
- *½ Tsp smoked paprika*
- *¼ cup plus*
- *1 Tbsp olive oil, divided*
- *2 rosemary sprigs*
- *1 cup buckwheat groats*
- *2 cups vegetable broth*
- *2 garlic cloves, minced*
- *½ yellow onion, chopped*
- *1 Tsp salt*

Direction: Prep time: 15 minutes | Cook time: 40 minutes | Serves 6

- ✓ *Preheat the deep fryer to 380°F (193°C). Lightly coat the inside of a 5-cup casserole dish with olive oil spray. (The shape of the casserole depends on the size of the fryer, but it should be able to hold at least 5 cups.)*
- ✓ *In a large pot, sauté the potatoes, carrots, rutabaga, and celery with paprika and ¼ cup olive oil.*
- ✓ *Pour the vegetable mixture into the prepared casserole dish and cover with the rosemary sprigs. Place the casserole dish in the air fryer and cook for 15 minutes.*
- ✓ *While the vegetables are cooking, rinse and dehydrate the buckwheat groats.*
- ✓ *In a medium saucepan over medium-high heat, combine the semolina, vegetable broth, garlic, onion, and salt with the remaining 1 tablespoon olive oil. Bring the mixture to a boil, then reduce the heat to low, cover, and cook for 10-12 minutes.*
- ✓ *Remove the casserole from the fryer. Remove the rosemary sprigs and discard them. Pour the cooked buckwheat into the casserole with the vegetables and stir to combine. Cover with aluminum foil and bake for an additional 15 minutes.*
- ✓ *Stir before serving.*

Nutrition: calories: 344 | fat: 12g | protein: 8g | carbs: 50g | fiber: 7g | sodium: 876mg

912) __Farro Risotto with Fresh Sage__

Ingredients:

- *Olive oil cooking spray*
- *1½ cups uncooked farro*
- *2 ½ cups chicken broth*
- *1 cup tomato sauce*
- *1 yellow onion, diced*
- *3 garlic cloves, minced*
- *1 Tbsp fresh sage, chopped*
- *½ Tsp salt*
- *2 Tbsps olive oil*
- *1 cup Parmesan cheese, grated, divided*

Direction: Prep time: 10 minutes | Cook time: 35 minutes | Serves 6

- ✓ *Preheat the air fryer to 380°F (193°C). Lightly coat the inside of a 5-cup casserole dish with olive oil spray. (The shape of the casserole depends on the size of the fryer, but it should be able to hold at least 5 cups.)*
- ✓ *Combine the farro, broth, tomato sauce, onion, garlic, sage, salt, olive oil, and ½ cup Parmesan cheese in a large container.*
- ✓ *Pour the farro mixture into the prepared casserole dish and cover with aluminum foil.*
- ✓ *Bake for 20 minutes, then uncover and stir. Sprinkle the remaining ½ cup Parmesan cheese over the top and bake for another 15 minutes.*
- ✓ *Stir well before serving.*

Nutrition: calories: 284 | fat: 9g | protein: 12g | carbs: 40g | fiber: 3g | sodium: 564mg

913) __Olive Oil Almond Cake__

Ingredients:

- *Olive oil cooking spray*
- *1½ cups whole wheat flour, plus more for dusting*
- *3 eggs*
- *⅓ cup honey*
- *½ cup olive oil*
- *½ cup unsweetened almond milk*
- *½ Tsp vanilla extract*
- *½ Tsp almond extract*
- *1 Tsp baking powder*
- *½ Tsp salt*

Direction: Prep time: 10 minutes | Cook time: 12 minutes | Serves 4

- ✓ *Preheat the air fryer to 380°F (193°C). Lightly coat the interior of an 8-by-8-inch baking dish with olive oil cooking spray and a dusting of whole wheat flour. Knock out any excess flour.*
- ✓ *In a large container, beat the eggs and honey until smooth.*
- ✓ *Slowly mix the olive oil, then the almond milk, and finally the vanilla and almond extracts until combined.*
- ✓ *In a separate container, whisk together the flour, baking powder, and salt.*
- ✓ *Slowly incorporate the dry ingredients into the wet ingredients with a rubber spatula until combined, making sure to scrape down the sides of the container as you mix.*
- ✓ *Pour the batter into the prepared pan and place it in the air fryer. Bake for 12 to 15 minutes, or until a toothpick inserted into the center comes out clean.*

Nutrition: calories: 546 | fat: 31g | protein: 12g | carbs: 58g | fiber: 3g | sodium: 361mg

914) __Tropical Almond Pancakes__

ingredients

- *2 cups creamy milk*
- *3 ½ cups almond flour*
- *1 tsp baking soda*
- *½ tsp salt*
- *1 tsp allspice*
- *2 tbsp vanilla*
- *1 tsp cinnamon*
- *1 tsp baking powder*
- *½ cup club soda*

Directions: Servings: 8| Preparation Time: 15

Minutes

- ✓ Preheat the Airfryer at 290F and grease the cooking basket of the air fryer.
- ✓ Whisk together salt, almond flour, baking soda, allspice, and cinnamon in a large container.
- ✓ Mix together the vanilla, baking powder, and club soda and add to the flour mixture.
- ✓ Stir the mixture thoroughly, pour the mixture into the cooking basket.
- ✓ Cook for about 10 minutes and dish out on a serving platter.

Nutrition Calories 324 | Fat 24.5g | Carbs 12.8g | Protein 11.5g | Sugar 1.6g | Sodium 342mg

915) Mushroom Barley Pilaf

Ingredients:

- Olive oil cooking spray
- 2 Tbsps olive oil
- 8 ounces (227 g) button mushrooms, diced
- ½ yellow onion, diced
- 2 garlic cloves, minced
- 1 cup pearl barley
  2 cups vegetable broth
- 1 Tbsp fresh thyme, chopped ½ Tsp salt
- ¼ Tsp smoked paprika
- Fresh parsley, for garnish

Direction: Prep time: 5 minutes | Cook time: 37 minutes | Serves 4

- ✓ Preheat the deep fryer to 380°F (193°C). Lightly coat the inside of a 5-cup casserole dish with olive oil spray. (The shape of the casserole dish will depend on the size of the air fryer, but it should be able to hold at least 5 cups).
- ✓ In a large skillet, heat the olive oil over medium heat. Add the mushrooms and onion and cook, occasionally stirring, for 5 minutes, or until the mushrooms begin to brown.
- ✓ Add the garlic and cook for an additional 2 minutes. Transfer the vegetables to a large container.
- ✓ Add the barley, broth, thyme, salt, and paprika.
- ✓ Pour the barley and vegetable mixture into the prepared casserole dish and place it in the fryer. Cook for 15 minutes.
- ✓ Stir in the barley mixture. Reduce the heat to 360°F (182°C), then return the barley to the fryer and cook for another 15 minutes.
- ✓ Remove from fryer and let rest for 5 minutes before smashing with a fork and garnishing with fresh parsley.

Nutrition: calories: 263 | fat: 8g | protein: 7g | carbs: 44g | fiber: 9g | sodium: 576mg

916) Pumpkin Pancakes

Ingredients

- 2 squares puff pastry
- 6 tbsp pumpkin filling
- 2 small eggs, beaten
- ¼ tsp cinnamon

Directions: Servings: 8Preparation Time: 20 Minutes

- ✓ Preheat the Airfryer to 360 F and roll out a square of puff pastry.
- ✓ Layer it with pumpkin pie filling, leaving about 1/4 -inch space around the edges.
- ✓ Cut it up into equal-sized square pieces and cover the gaps with beaten egg.
- ✓ Arrange the squares into a baking dish and cook for about 12 minutes.
- ✓ Sprinkle some cinnamon and serve

NUTRITION Calories 51| Carbs 5g |Fat 2.5g | Protein 2.4g | Sugar 0.5g

917) Eggless Spinach & Bacon Quiche

Ingredients

- 1 cup fresh spinach, chopped
- 4 slices of bacon, cooked and chopped
- ½ cup mozzarella cheese. shredded
- 4 tablespoons milk
- 4 dashes of Tabasco sauce
- 1 cup Parmesan cheese, shredded
- Salt and freshly ground black pepper. to taste

DIRECTIONS: Servings: 8 Preparation time:20 minutes

- ✓ Preheat the Airfryer to 325 degrees F and grease a baking dish.
- ✓ Put all the ingredients in a bowl and mix well.
- ✓ Transfer the mixture into a prepared baking dish and cook for about 8 minutes.
- ✓ Dish out and serve.

Nutrition: Calories 72, Carbs 0.9g, Fat 5,2g, Protein 5.5g, Sodium 271mg, Sugar: 0.4g

918) Sausage & Bacon with Beans

Ingredients

- 12 medium sausages
- 12 bacon slices
- 8 eggs
- 2 cans baked beans
- 12 bread slices, toasted

DIRECTIONS: Servings: 12 Preparation time: 30 Minute

- ✓ Preheat the Airfryer at 325 degrees F and place sausages and bacon in a fryer basket.
- ✓ Cook for about 10 minutes and place the baked beans in a ramekin.
- ✓ Place eggs in another ramekin and the Airfryer to 395 degrees F.

- ✓ Cook for about 10 more minutes and divide the sausage mixture. beans and eggs in serving plates
- ✓ Serve with bread slices.

Nutrition: Calories 276, Carbs 14.1g, Fat 17g, Protein 16.3g, Sodium 817mg, Sugar: 0.6g

919) Classic French Fries

Ingredients:

- (2 Servings)
- 2 russet potatoes, peeled and cut into strips
- 1 tbsp olive oil
- Salt and black pepper to taste
- ½ cup garlic aioli (or garlic mayo)

Direction: (Prep + Cook Time: 30 minutes)

- ✓ Preheat the air fryer to 400 F.
- ✓ Spray the frying basket with cooking spray.
- ✓ Place the potato strips in a tub, and toss with the olive oil, salt, and pepper.
- ✓ Arrange on the frying basket. Air fry for 20-22 minutes, turning once halfway through, until crispy.
- ✓ Serve with garlic aioli.

Nutritional Value: For every 100 grams Calories: 93 g Fat: 0.12 g Protein: 2.5 g Carbs: 21.2 g Fiber: 2.2 g Vitamin C: 28% Vitamin B6: 27% Potassium: 26% Manganese: 19% Magnesium: 12% Phosphorus: 12% Niacin: 12% Folate: 12%

920) Curly Fries with Paprika

Ingredients:

- (2 Servings)
- 2 Yukon gold potatoes, spiralized
- 1 tbsp olive oil
- 1 tsp all-purpose seasoning blend
- 1 tsp paprika

Direction::(Prep + Cook Time: 30 minutes)

- ✓ Coat the potatoes with olive oil.
- ✓ Place them in the frying basket and air fry for 20-22 minutes at 390 F, tossing them at the 10-minute mark.
- ✓ Sprinkle with the blend and paprika and serve immediately.

Nutritional Value: For every 10grams; Calories: 30Protein: less than 1 gFat: less than 1 gCarbs: 6.3 gFiber: 3.2 g

921) Simple Baked Potatoes

Ingredients:

- 4 Servings)
- 4 Yukon gold potatoes, clean and dried
- 2 tbsp olive oil
- 2 tbsp butter Salt and black pepper to taste.

Direction:Prep + Cook Time: 45 minutes)

- ✓ Preheat the air fryer to 400 F.
- ✓ Brush the potatoes with olive oil and season with salt and black pepper.
- ✓ Arrange them on the frying basket and air fry for 30 minutes at 400 F until fork-tender, flipping once.
- ✓ Let cool slightly, then cut slit down the center of each baked potato.
- ✓ Use a fork to fluff the insides of the potatoes. Top with butter, sprinkle with salt and black pepper.
- ✓ Serve immediately and enjoy!

Nutritional Value: For every 100 grams Calories: 93 g Fat: 0.12 g Protein: 2.5 g Carbs: 21.2 g Fiber: 2.2 g Vitamin C: 28% Vitamin B6: 27%Potassium: 26% Manganese: 19% Magnesium: 12% Phosphorus: 12%

922) Avocado Egg Rolls

Ingredients:

- (4 Servings)
- 2 ripe avocados, roughly chopped
- 8 egg roll wrappers
- 1 tomato, peeled and chopped
- salt and black pepper to taste.

Direction:(Prep + Cook Time: 15 minutes)

- ✓ Place the avocados, tomato, salt, and black pepper in a bowl.
- ✓ Mash with a fork until somewhat smooth.
- ✓ Divide the mixture between the egg wrappers.
- ✓ Fold the edges in and over the filling, roll up tightly, and seal the wrappers with a bit of water.
- ✓ Arrange them on the greased frying basket.
- ✓ Spray the rolls with cooking spray and Bake for 10 minutes at 350 F, turning halfway through until crispy and golden.

Nutrition : A 50g portion of an avocado contains:Calories: 95KcalProtein: 3.1g Fat: 3.8g Carbohydrates: 3.1g Fibre: 3.8g Potassium: 225mg Vit E: 35mg

923) Balsamic Brussels Sprouts

Ingredients:

- (2 Servings)
- ½ lb Brussels sprouts, trimmed and halved
- 1 tbsp butter, melted
- salt and black pepper to taste
- 1 tbsp balsamic vinegar

Direction:(Prep + Cook Time: 20 minutes

- ✓ Preheat the air fryer to 380 F.
- ✓ In a bowl, mix Brussels sprouts with butter, salt, and black pepper.
- ✓ Place the sprouts in the greased frying basket and air fry for 5-7 minutes.
- ✓ Shake and cook until the sprouts are caramelized but tender on the inside, 5-7 more minutes.

- ✓ Drizzle with balsamic vinegar to serve.

Nutrition: For every 1 cup serving,

Calories: 56Fat: 0 gCarbohydrates: 11 gFiber: 4 gProtein: 4 g Vitamin C: 18% Vitamin K: 12%F

924) Zucchini-Parmesan Chips

Ingredients:

- 4 Servings)
- 2 medium zucchinis, sliced
- 1 cup breadcrumbs
- 2 eggs, beaten
- 1 cup Parmesan cheese, grated
- salt and black pepper to taste
- 1 tsp smoked paprika

Direction:Prep + Cook Time: 20 minutes

- ✓ Preheat the air fryer to 390 F.
- ✓ In a bowl, mix breadcrumbs, Salt, pepper, Parmesan, and paprika.
- ✓ Dip zucchini slices in the eggs and then in the cheese mix; press to coat well.
- ✓ Spray the coated slices with cooking spray and place them in the frying basket.
- ✓ Airfry for 12-14 minutes, flipping once. Serve hot.

Nutrition: Every 1 cup serving of Zucchini's

Calories: 62 Protein: 2 g Fat: Less than 1 g Carbs: 14 g Fiber: 8 gSugar: 7 gLutein: 29%Zeaxanthin: 18%

925) Onion Rings

Ingredients:

- (2 Servings)
- 1 onion, sliced into 1-inch rings
- 1 egg, beaten
- ¼ cup milk
- Salt and garlic powder to taste
- ½ cup all-purpose flour
- ¼ cup panko breadcrumbs

Direction:Prep + Cook Time: 20 minutes

- ✓ Preheat the air fryer to 350 F.
- ✓ Dust the onion rings with some flour and set them aside. In a bowl, mix the remaining flour, garlic powder, and salt.
- ✓ Stir in the egg and milk.
- ✓ Dip onion rings into the flour mixture, then coat them in the crumbs.
- ✓ Lay the rings into the frying basket and spray with cooking spray.
- ✓ Airfry for 8-11 minutes until golden and crispy, shaking once.
- ✓ Serve with honey-mustard dipping sauce.

Nutrition : One cup of chopped onion provides

64 caloriesCarbs: 14.9 grams (g) Fat: 0.16 g Cholesterol: 0 g Fiber: 2.72 g Sugar: 6.78 g Protein: 1.76 g Vitamin C: 38%

Vitamin B-6: 54Manganese: 29%Calcium: 5%Iron: 12%Folate: 9%Magnesium: 17%Phosphorus: 8%Potassium: 7%Antioxidants quercetin and sulfur: 32%

926) Breaded Mushrooms

Ingredients:

- (4 Servings)
- 1 lb white button mushrooms, cleaned
- 1 cup breadcrumbs
- 2 eggs, beaten
- salt and black pepper to taste
- 1 cup Parmesan cheese, grated.

Direction:(Prep + Cook Time: 20 minutes

- ✓ Preheat the air fryer to 360 F.
- ✓ Pour breadcrumbs into a bowl and add in the Parmesan cheese, salt, and pepper; mix well.
- ✓ Dip each mushroom into the eggs, then coat in the cheese mixture.
- ✓ Spray with cooking spray and Bake in the fryer for 10-12 minutes, shaking once halfway through.
- ✓ Serve warm.

Nutrition: From every 1 cup of mushrooms, you get

Calories: 15 Protein: 2.2 g Fat: 0.2 g Carbs: 2.3 g Fiber: 0.7 g Sugar: 1.4 gSelenium: 4%Copper: 6%Thiamin: 13%Magnesium: 9%Phosphorous: 17%

927) Herb & Cheese Stuffed Mushrooms

Ingredients:

- 4 Servings)
- 1 lb brown mushrooms, stems removed
- 1 cup Grana Padano cheese, grated
- ½ tsp dried thyme
- ½ tsp dried rosemary
- salt and black pepper to taste
- 1 tbsp olive oil

Direction:(Prep + Cook Time: 20 minutes

- ✓ Preheat the air fryer to 360 F.
- ✓ In a bowl, mix Grana Padano cheese, herbs, salt, and black pepper.
- ✓ Spoon the mixture into the mushrooms and press down so that it sticks. Drizzle with olive oil and place in the air fryer.
- ✓ Bake for 8-10 minutes or until the cheese has melted.
- ✓ Serve warm.

Nutrition : 104 calories Protein: 5 g Fat: 9 g of (5 g saturated)Carb: 1 g Fibre: 0 g Sugar: 0.6 g Calcium: 293 mg 468 mg sodium Protein: 34%

928) Hot Air Fried Green Tomatoes

Ingredients:

- *(4 Servings)*
- *8 green tomato slices*
- *2 egg whites*
- *½ cup flour*
- *1 cup breadcrumbs*
- *1 tsp cayenne pepper*
- *½ tsp mustard powder*
- *Salt and black pepper to taste.*

Direction:(Prep + Cook Time: 15 minutes

- ✓ *Preheat the air fryer to 390 F.*
- ✓ *In a bowl, beat the egg whites with a pinch of salt.*
- ✓ *Mix the flour, mustard powder, cayenne pepper, salt, and black pepper in a separate bowl.*
- ✓ *Add the breadcrumbs to a third bowl Dredge the tomato slices in the flour mixture, then in the egg whites, and finally in the crumbs.*
- ✓ *Spray with oil and arrange in the greased frying basket.*
- ✓ *Airfry for 8 minutes, turning once. Serve warm.*

Nutrition : Calories: 18Water: 95%Protein: 0.9gCarbs: 3.9gSugar: 2.6gFiber: 1.2gFat: 0.2gLycopene36%Vitamin C:23%Potassium: 19%Folate: 17%Vitamin K: 20%

*929) **Classic Zucchini Fries***

Ingredients:

- *(2 Servings)*
- *1 zucchini, cut lengthways into strips*
- *½ cup panko breadcrumbs*
- *½ cup all-purpose flour*
- *1 egg*
- *Salt and garlic powder to taste*
- *½ cup garlic*
- *mayonnaise*

Direction:: (Prep + Cook Time: 20 minutes

- ✓ *Preheat the air fryer to 400 F.*
- ✓ *Sift the flour into a bowl with a pinch of salt.*
- ✓ *Whisk the egg in another bowl with some salt.*
- ✓ *Pour the breadcrumbs into a third one and mix with garlic powder.*
- ✓ *Coat the zucchini strips in the flour, then in the beaten egg, and finally in the crumbs.*
- ✓ *Lightly spray the strips with cooking spray and AirFry until crispy, 10-12 minutes, flipping once halfway through.*
- ✓ *Serve with garlic mayo.*

Nutrition Every 1 cup serving of Zuchinis Calories: 62 Protein: 2 g Fat: Less than 1 g Carbs: 14 g Fiber: 8 gSugar: 7 gLutein: 29%Zeaxanthin: 18%

*930) **Corn on the Cob***

Ingredients:

- *(2 Servings)*
- *2 ears fresh corn, cut into halves*
- *2 tbsp fresh parsley, chopped*
- *2 tbsp butter, softened*
- *Garlic salt to taste.*

Direction:Prep + Cook Time: 20 minutes

- ✓ *Preheat the air fryer to 390 F.*
- ✓ *Spritz the corn with cooking spray and Bake for 12-14 minutes, turning a few times until slightly charred.*
- ✓ *Brush the corn with the butter.*
- ✓ *Sprinkle with garlic salt and parsley*

Nutrition : Calories: 90 Protein: 3g Fat: 1g Carbs: 19g Fiber: 1g Sugars: 5g Vitamin C: 3.6 mg

*931) **Perfect Air Fryer Eggs***

Ingredients:

- *6 Servings)*
- *6 large eggs*
- *Salt and black pepper to taste.*

Direction:(Prep + Cook Time: 20 minutes

- ✓ *Preheat the air fryer to 270 F.*
- ✓ *Lay the eggs in the basket (or in a muffin tray) and cook for 10 minutes for runny or 15 minutes for hard.*
- ✓ *Using tongs, place the eggs in a bowl with cold water to cool for 5 minutes. When cooled, remove the shells, cut them in half, and sprinkle with salt and pepper.*
- ✓ *Serve.*

Nutrition : Calories: 77 Protein: 6g Healthy fats: 5g

*932) **Air Fried Mac & Cheese***

Ingredients:

- *2 Servings)*
- *8 oz elbow macaroni*
- *, cooked 1 cup cheddar cheese, grated*
- *1 cup warm milk*
- *1 tbsp Parmesan cheese, grated*
- *salt and black pepper to taste*

Direction:Prep + Cook Time: 20 minutes

- ✓ *Preheat the air fryer to 350 F.*
- ✓ *Add the macaroni to a baking dish and stir in cheddar, milk, salt, and pepper.*
- ✓ *Place the dish in the fryer and Bake for 16 minutes.*
- ✓ *Serve sprinkled with Parmesan cheese*

Nutrition : Calories: 100 Carbs: 1g Fat: 9g Protein: 5g Calcium: 150mg Sodium: 170mg Vitamin A: 17%Vitamin B-12: 32%Vitamin K: 23%Zinc: 8%

*933) **Morning Frittata***

Ingredients:

- *(4 Servings)*
- *8 eggs*
- *½ cup heavy cream*
- *Salt and black pepper to taste*
- *1 cup spinach, finely chopped*
- *½ red onion chopped*
- *½ cup tomatoes, diced*
- *1 cup mozzarella cheese, shredded*
- *2 tsp fresh parsley for garnishing*

Direction: : (Prep + Cook Time: 30 minutes

- ✓ *Preheat the air fryer to 330 F.*
- ✓ *Grease a baking dish that fits in your air fryer with cooking spray.*
- ✓ *In a bowl, whisk the eggs and heavy cream until pale.*
- ✓ *Add in spinach,*
- ✓ *red onion, tomatoes, mozzarella, salt, and pepper.*
- ✓ *Mix to combine.*
- ✓ *Pour the mixture into the baking dish and Bake in the air fryer for 20-23 minutes, or until the eggs are set in the center.*
- ✓ *Sprinkle with parsley and cut into wedges to serve.*

Nutrition : One large egg contains:Calories: 77Protein: 6gHealthy fats: 5gVitamin A: 65%Vitamin B5: 32%Vitamin B12: 21%Vitamin D: 16%Vitamin E: 10%Vitamin K: 10%Vitamin B6: 7%Folate: 17%Phosphorus: 8%Selenium: 11%Calcium: 6%Zinc: 6%

934) ***. Mediterranean Bruschetta***

Ingredients:

- *(4 Servings)*
- *12 oz mozzarella cheese sticks*
- *½ cup flour*
- *1 cup breadcrumbs*
- *2 eggs,*
- *¼ cup Parmesan cheese, grated*
- *1 cup marinara sauce (optional).*

Direction:(Prep + Cook Time: 15 minutes

- ✓ *Brush the bread with olive oil and rub with garlic.*
- ✓ *Scatter mozzarella cheese on top. Arrange the slices in the frying basket and Bake for 8-10 minutes at 360 F.*
- ✓ *Top with cherry tomatoes and basil to serve.*

Nutrition : Here are the nutrients in 100g raw tomatoesCalories: 18Water: 95%Protein: 0.9gCarbs: 3.9gSugar: 2.6gFiber: 1.2gFat: 0.2g

935) ***Mozzarella Cheese Sticks***

Ingredients:

- *(4 Servings)*
- *12 oz mozzarella cheese sticks*
- *½ cup flour*
- *1 cup breadcrumbs*
- *2 eggs,*
- *¼ cup Parmesan cheese, grated*
- *1 cup marinara sauce (optional).*

Direction:(Prep + Cook Time: 15 minutes)

- ✓ *Preheat the air fryer to 380 F.*
- ✓ *Pour the breadcrumbs into a bowl.*
- ✓ *Beat the eggs in another bowl.*
- ✓ *In a third bowl, mix Parmesan cheese and flour.*
- ✓ *Dip each cheese stick in the flour, then in the eggs, and finally in breadcrumbs.*
- ✓ *Place them in the greased frying basket and AirFry until golden brown, about 6-8 minutes, shaking the basket once or twice.*
- ✓ *Serve with marinara sauce.*

Nutrition : From everv 1 ounce of cheese consumed, vhere is Calories: 100 Carbs: 1g Fat: 9g Protein: 5g Calcium: 150mg Sodium: 170mg Vitamin A: 17%Vitamin B-12: 32%Vitamin K: 23%Zinc: 8% Calcium: 19% Vitamin D: 11%

936) ***"Bikini" Ham & Cheese Sandwich***

Ingredients:

- *(1 Serving)*
- *2 tbsp butter*
- *2 slices bread*
- *2 slices cheddar cheese*
- *1 slice ham*

Direction:(Prep + Cook Time: 15 minutes

- ✓ *Preheat the air fryer to 370 F.*
- ✓ *Spread 1 tsp of butter on the outside of each of the bread slices.*
- ✓ *Place the cheese on the inside of one bread slice.*
- ✓ *Top with ham and the other cheese slice. Close with the second bread slice.*
- ✓ *Airfry for 8 minutes, flipping once halfway through.*
- ✓ *Cut diagonally and serve.*

Nutrition : Calories: 100 Carbs: 1g Fat: 9g Protein: 5g Calcium: 150mg Sodium: 170mg Vitamin A: 17%Vitamin B-12: 32%Vitamin K: 23%Zinc: 8% Calcium: 19%

937) ***Homemade Arancini (Rice Balls***

Ingredients:

- *4 Servings)*
- *2 cups cooked rice*
- *½ cup flour*
- *1 green onion, chopped*
- *2 garlic cloves, minced*

- *2 eggs, lightly beaten*
- *½ cup Parmesan cheese, grated*
- *salt and black pepper to taste*
- *1 cup breadcrumbs*
- *1 tsp dried mixed herbs*
- *1 cup arrabbiata sauce*

Direction:Prep + Cook Time: 25 minutes + chilling time)

- ✓ *Place the flour, beaten eggs, and breadcrumbs into 3 separate bowls.*
- ✓ *Combine the cooked rice, onion, garlic, Parmesan cheese, herbs, salt, and pepper in a bowl.*
- ✓ *Shape into 10 balls.*
- ✓ *Roll them in the flour, shake off any excess, then dip in the eggs, and finally coat in the breadcrumbs.*
- ✓ *Let chill for 20 minutes.*
- ✓ *Preheat the air fryer to 390 F.*
- ✓ *Spray the arancini with cooking spray and AirFry them for 12-14 minutes, turning once halfway through cooking, until golden and crispy.*
- ✓ *Serve with arrabbiata sauce.*

Nutrition : Calories: 250 Fat: 16g Carbs: 19g Protein: 6g Sodium: 295mg Dietary fiber: 1g Sugars: 1g

938) Cheddar Hash Browns

Ingredients:

- *4 Servings)*
- *4 russet potatoes, peeled and grated*
- *1 brown onion, chopped*
- *2 garlic cloves, minced*
- *½ cup cheddar cheese, grated*
- *1 egg, lightly beaten*
- *salt and black pepper to taste*
- *1 tbsp fresh thyme, chopped*

Direction:Prep + Cook Time: 30 minutes

- ✓ *Mix the potatoes, onion, garlic, cheddar cheese, egg, salt, black pepper, and thyme in a bowl.*
- ✓ *Spread the mixture in the greased frying basket and AirFry in the preheated air fryer for 20-22 minutes at 400 F.*
- ✓ *Shake once halfway through cooking, until golden and crispy.*
- ✓ *Serve hot with ketchup (optional).*

Nutrition : Calories: 93 g Fat: 0.12 g Protein: 2.5 gCarbs: 21.2 gFiber: 2.2 g Vitamin C: 28%

939) Bacon-Wrapped Chicken Breasts

Ingredients:

- *(4 Servings)*
- *2 chicken breasts*
- *8 oz cream cheese*
- *1 tbsp butter*
- *6 turkey*
- *bacon slices*
- *salt to taste*
- *1 tbsp fresh parsley, chopped.*

Direction:(Prep + Cook Time: 25 minutes

- ✓ *Preheat the air fryer to 390 F.*
- ✓ *Stretch out the bacon and lay the slices in 2 sets; 3 bacon strips together on each side.*
- ✓ *Place the chicken on each bacon set. Use a knife to smear the cream cheese on both.*
- ✓ *Spread the butter on top and sprinkle with salt.*
- ✓ *Wrap the turkey bacon around the chicken and secure the ends into the wrap.*
- ✓ *Place the wrapped chicken in the greased frying basket and air fry for 16-18 minutes, turning halfway through.*
- ✓ *Top with fresh parsley and serve with steamed greens (optional).*

Nutrition : Calories: 120 Protein: 26 g Fat: 2 g Carbs: 0 g

940) Air-Fried Chicken Popcorn

Ingredients:

- *4 Servings)*
- *2 chicken breasts,*
- *cut into small cubes*
- *2 cups panko breadcrumbs*
- *Salt and black pepper to taste*
- *1 tsp garlic powder*

Direction: Prep + Cook Time: 30 minutes)

- ✓ *Preheat the air fryer to 360 F.*
- ✓ *Rub the chicken cubes with salt, garlic powder, and black pepper.*
- ✓ *Coat in the panko breadcrumbs and place them in the greased frying basket.*
- ✓ *Spray with cooking spray and AirFry for 16-18 minutes, flipping once until nice and crispy.*
- ✓ *Serve with tzatziki sauce if desired*

Nutrition : Calories: 120 Protein: 26 g Fat: 2 g Carbs: 0 g Fiber: 0 gSugar: 0 gVitamin B12: 8%Tryptophan: 9%

941) Sweet Garlicky Chicken Wings

Ingredients:

- *(4 Servings)*
- *16 chicken wings*
- *¼ cup butter*
- *1 tsp honey*
- *½ tbsp salt*

- *4 garlic cloves, minced*
- *¾ cup potato starch*

Direction:(Prep + Cook Time: 20 minutes

- ✓ *Preheat the air fryer to 370 F.*
- ✓ *Coat the chicken with potato starch and place it in the greased frying basket.*
- ✓ *Bake for 5 minutes.*
- ✓ *Whisk the rest of the ingredients in a bowl.*
- ✓ *Remove the wings from the fryer, pour the sauce over them, and bake until crispy for another 10 minutes.*
- ✓ *Serve immediately.*

Nutrition : For everv 100g of chicken wings served, Carbs: 20gProteins: 30gFats: 20gVitamin B1: 16% Vitamin B9: 21%Vitamin B12: 19%Vitamin B6: 32%Vitamin B2: 13%Vitamin A: 5%Vitamin E: 22%Vitamin D: 15% Vitamin K: 22%Phosphorus: 19%Potassium: 14%Iron: 13%Magnesium: 30%Calcium: 33%Zinc: 10%Selenium: 14%Iodine: 22%Copper: 2%Sulphur: 3%

942) Spicy Buffalo Chicken Wings

Ingredients:

- *(4 Servings)*
- *2 lb chicken wings*
- *½ cup cayenne pepper*
- *sauce 2 tbsp*
- *coconut oil 2 tbsp Worcestershire sauce*
- *Salt to taste*
- *½ cup sour cream*
- *¼ cup mayonnaise*
- *1 tbsp scallions, chopped*
- *1 tbsp fresh parsley, chopped 1*
- *garlic clove minced*

Direction:Prep + Cook Time: 25 minutes + marinating time)

- ✓ *In a mixing bowl, combine cayenne pepper sauce, coconut oil, Worcestershire sauce, and salt.*
- ✓ *Add in the chicken wings and toss to coat.*
- ✓ *Cover with a lid and marinate for 1 hour in the fridge.*
- ✓ *Preheat the air fryer to 400 F.*
- ✓ *Place the chicken in a greased frying basket and air fry for 15-18 minutes or until the marinade becomes sticky and the wings are cooked through.*
- ✓ *Meanwhile, mix together sour cream, mayonnaise, garlic, parsley, and salt in a small bowl.*
- ✓ *Top the wings with scallions and serve with the prepared sauce on the side. Enjoy*

Nutrition: Scallions are high in vitamin C and B-complex vitamins like thiamine, riboflavin, and B3 (niacin). Scallions are high in carotenoids, calcium, potassium, and antioxidants, among other vitamins and minerals.

943) Hot Chicken Wingettes

Ingredients:

- *(4 Servings)*
- *1 lb chicken wingettes*
- *salt and black pepper to taste*
- *⅓ cup hot sauce*
- *½ tbsp white wine vinegar.*

Direction:Prep + Cook Time: 25 minutes

- ✓ *Preheat the air fryer to 360 F.*
- ✓ *Season the wingettes with black pepper and salt and spray them with oil.*
- ✓ *AirFry them for 15-18 minutes, until golden, tossing every 5 minutes.*
- ✓ *In a bowl, mix vinegar with hot sauce.*
- ✓ *When the wingettes are ready, transfer them to a plate and pour the sauce over.*
- ✓ *Serve warm.*

Nutritional Value: Calories 50 Calories from Fat 29.7 (59.4%) Total Fat 3.3g Saturated fat 0.9g Cholesterol 21mg Sodium 340mg Carbohydrates 1.3g Net carbs 1g Sugar 0.3g Fiber 0.3g Protein 4.3g

944) Turkey Scotch Eggs

Ingredients:

- *(4 Servings)*
- *4 hard-boiled eggs, peeled*
- *1 cup panko breadcrumbs*
- *1 egg, beaten in a bowl*
- *1 lb ground turkey*
- *½ tsp dried rosemary*
- *Salt and black pepper to taste*

Direction:(Prep + Cook Time: 20 minutes

- ✓ *Preheat the air fryer to 400 F.*
- ✓ *In a bowl, mix panko breadcrumbs with rosemary.*
- ✓ *In another bowl, pour the ground turkey and mix it with salt and pepper*
- ✓ *Shape into 4 balls. Wrap the balls around the boiled eggs to form a large ball with the egg in the center.*
- ✓ *Dip in the beaten egg and coat with breadcrumbs.*
- ✓ *Place in the greased frying basket and Bake for 12-14 minutes, shaking once. Serve and enjoy!*

Nutrition: Fat 14.6g Saturates 4.3g Carbohydrate 14.9g Sugars 0.7g Fibre 2.2g Protein 9.8g Salt 0.8g

945) Air Fried Pork Popcorn Bites

Ingredients:

- *4 boneless pork chops, cut into 1-inch cubes,*

- salt and black pepper to taste,
- 1 cup flour, ¼ tsp garlic powder ¼ tsp onion powder,
- 1 tsp paprika
- 2 eggs
- 1 cup ranch sauce.

Direction:(Prep + Cook Time): 20 minutes: (4 Servings)

- ✓ Preheat the Air fryer to 390 F.
- ✓ Spray the basket with cooking spray.
- ✓ Combine the flour, garlic and onion powders, paprika, salt, and black pepper in a bowl and mix well.
- ✓ In another bowl, whisk the eggs with a bit of salt.
- ✓ Dip the pork in the flour first, then in the eggs, and back again in the flour; coat well.
- ✓ Spray with cooking spray and place in the frying basket.
- ✓ Airfry for 15 minutes, shaking once halfway through.
- ✓ Remove to a serving plate and serve with ranch sauce.

Nutritional Value: calories: 590kcal, carbohydrates: 1g, protein: 11g, fat: 60g, saturated fat: 22g, cholesterol: 82mg, sodium: 342mg, potassium: 222mg, sugar: 1g

946) Sesame Pork Skewers

Ingredients:

- (4 Servings)
- 1 lb pork tenderloin, cut into 1-inch chunks
- 1 red pepper, cut into 1-inch chunks
- 2 tbsp sesame oil
- 1 garlic clove, minced
- 2 tbsp soy sauce
- Salt and black pepper to taste
- 1 tbsp honey
- 1 tsp sesame seeds

Direction:(Prep + Cook Time: 20 minutes + marinating time)

- ✓ Mix the honey, sesame oil, soy sauce, salt, and black pepper in a bowl.
- ✓ Coat the pork in the mixture.
- ✓ Cover with a lid and let sit for 30 minutes.
- ✓ Preheat the air fryer to 400 F.
- ✓ Thread the pork onto skewers, alternating the cubes of meat with chunks of red pepper. Place them in the greased frying basket.
- ✓ Spritz them with cooking spray and AirFry the skewers for 8-10 minutes.
- ✓ Flip them over and cook further for 5-7 minutes until golden brown.
- ✓ Top with sesame seeds and serve

nutritional value: calories 176 energy 737 kg fat 2g saturates 1g protein 34g sodium 1158mg carbs 2g sugar 1g

947) Teriyaki Pork Ribs

Ingredients:

- 4 Servings)
- 1 lb pork ribs
- 2 tbsp olive oil
- Salt and black pepper to taste
- 1 tsp sugar
- 1 tsp ginger paste
- 1 tsp five-spice powder
- 1 tbsp teriyaki sauce
- 1 tbsp light soy sauce
- 1 garlic clove, minced
- ½ tsp honey
- 2 tbsp water
- 1 tbsp tomato sauce.

Direction:(Prep + Cook Time: 20 minutes + marinating time)

- ✓ Mix teriyaki sauce, sugar, five-spice powder, ginger paste, salt, and black pepper in a bowl.
- ✓ Add in the pork ribs and stir to coat.
- ✓ Cover with foil and marinate for 2 hours in the fridge.
- ✓ Preheat the air fryer to 350 F. Add the ribs to the greased frying basket and Bake for 18-20 minutes, flipping once until crispy.
- ✓ Heat the olive oil in a skillet over medium heat and stir in the soy sauce, garlic, honey, water, and tomato sauce.
- ✓ Cook the sauce for 1-2 minutes until it thickens slightly.
- ✓ Pour it over the ribs and serve

nutritional value: Total Fat 28g. Saturated Fat 9.9g. Trans Fat 0.2g. Cholesterol 177mg. Sodium 1748mg. Potassium 783mg. Total Carbohydrates 6.6g. Dietary Fiber 0g.

948) Gorgonzola Cheese Burgers

Ingredients:

- (4 Servings)
- 1 lb ground beef
- ½ cup Gorgonzola cheese, crumbled
- 1 tbsp olive oil
- 1 tsp Worcestershire, sauce
- ½ tsp hot sauce
- ½ garlic clove, Minced
- 4 bread buns
- 4 yellow cheese slices

- *2 tbsp mayonnaise*
- *1 tsp ketchup*
- *1 dill pickle,*
- *sliced salt and black pepper to taste*

Direction:Prep + Cook Time: 35 minutes

- ✓ *Preheat the air fryer to 360 F.*
- ✓ *In a mixing bowl, place the ground beef, Worcestershire sauce, hot sauce, gorgonzola cheese, garlic, salt, and pepper*
- ✓ *Mix well. Shape the mixture into 4 burgers.*
- ✓ *Grease the frying basket with a thin layer of olive oil.*
- ✓ *Add the burgers and AirFry for 20 minutes, flipping once ha On bread buns, spread the mayonnaise, and add the dill pickles.*
- ✓ *Place the burgers over the top and lay the yellow cheese.*
- ✓ *Top with ketchup and serve.*

nutritional value: Total Fat 39g Saturated Fat 14g Trans Fat 2g Sodium 1040mg Cholesterol 125mg Total Carbohydrates 4g Dietary Fiber 1g Total Sugars 1g Includes 1g Added Sugars Protein 29g

949) Beef Steak Fingers

Ingredients:

- *4 Servings)*
- *1 lb beef steak, cut into strips*
- *1 tbsp olive oil*
- *½ cup flour*
- *½ cup panko breadcrumbs*
- *¼ tsp cayenne pepper*
- *2 eggs, beaten*
- *½ cup milk*
- *Salt and black pepper to taste*
- *1 lb tomatoes, chopped*
- *1 tbsp tomato paste*
- *1 tsp honey*
- *1 tbsp white wine vinegar*

Direction:(Prep + Cook Time: 30 minutes

- ✓ *Place the tomatoes, tomato paste, honey, and vinegar in a deep skillet over medium heat.*
- ✓ *Cook for 6-8 minutes, occasionally stirring until the sauce thickens; set aside to cool.*
- ✓ *Grease the basket with oil.*
- ✓ *Preheat the air fryer to 390 F.*
- ✓ *In a bowl, combine flour, salt, black pepper, and cayenne pepper.*
- ✓ *In a second bowl, whisk the eggs with the milk.*
- ✓ *Dredge the steak strips in the flour mixture, then coat with the egg mixture, and finally in the breadcrumbs until completely coated.*
- ✓ *AirFry the dredged steak strips for 8 minutes. Turn them over and spray with a little bit of olive oil.*
- ✓ *Continue to cook for another 5-7 minutes until golden and crispy.*
- ✓ *Spoon into paper cones and serve with the tomato sauce.*

nutritional: Total Fat 18g Saturated Fat 5g Cholesterol 20mg Sodium 540mg Total Carbs 14g Dietary Fiber 1g Sugars 1g Protein 8g

950) Easy Salmon Fillets

Ingredients:

- *(2 Servings)*
- *2 salmon fillets*
- *1 tbsp olive oil*
- *Salt to taste*
- *1 lemon, cut into wedges.*

Direction:Prep + Cook Time: 15 minutes

- ✓ *Preheat the air fryer to 380 F.*
- ✓ *Brush the salmon with olive oil and season with salt Place the fillets in the greased frying basket and Bake for 8 minutes until tender, turning once.*
- ✓ *Serve with lemon wedges.*

nutritional value: Calories259.5 Total Fat 14.4 g Saturated Fat4.1 g Polyunsaturated Fat 0.0 g Monounsaturated Fat0.0 g Cholesterol 60.0 mg Sodium 200.5 mg Potassium 30.0 mg Total Carbohydrate 7.2 g Dietary Fiber 1.1 g Sugars 0.7 g Protein 24.6 g

951) Classic Fish & Chips

Ingredients:

- *(4 Servings)*
- *2 tbsp olive oil*
- *4 potatoes, cut into thin slices*
- *salt and black pepper to taste,*
- *4 white fish fillets*
- *1 cup flour*
- *2 eggs, beaten*
- *1 cup breadcrumbs*
- *Salt and black pepper to taste*

Direction:Prep + Cook Time: 30 minutes)

- ✓ *Preheat the air fryer to 400 F.*
- ✓ *Drizzle the potatoes with olive oil and season with salt and black pepper; toss to coat.*
- ✓ *Place them in the greased frying basket and air fry for 10 minutes.*
- ✓ *Season the fillets with salt and black pepper*
- ✓ *Coat them with flour, then dip in the eggs, and finally into the crumbs.*
- ✓ *Shake the potatoes and add in the fish; cook until the fish is crispy, 8-10 minutes.*
- ✓ *Serve.*

nutritional value: Calories 1590 Total Fat 104g

Saturated Fat 11g Trans Fat 1g Cholesterol 60mg Sodium 3430mg Total Carbohydrates 134g Dietary Fiber 11g Sugars 7g Protein 28g

952) Chipotle-Lime Prawn Bowls

Ingredients:

- *(4 Servings)*
- *1 lb prawns, deveined, peeled*
- *2 tsp olive oil*
- *2 tsp lime juice*
- *1 tsp honey*
- *1 garlic clove, minced*
- *1 tsp chipotle powder*
- *2 cups cooked brown rice*
- *1 (15-oz) can black beans, warmed*
- *1 large avocado, chopped*
- *1 cup sliced cherry tomatoes*

Direction:(Prep + Cook Time: 25 minutes + marinating time)

- ✓ *Toss the lime juice, olive oil, honey, garlic, and chipotle powder in a bowl.*
- ✓ *Mix well to make a marinade. Add the prawns and toss to coat.*
- ✓ *Transfer them to the fridge for at least 30 minutes*
- ✓ *Preheat the air fryer to 390 F. Remove the prawns to the fryer and AirFry them for 10-15 minutes, tossing once, until golden and cooked through.*
- ✓ *Divide the rice, beans, avocado, and tomatoes between 4 bowls and top with the prawns.*
- ✓ *Serve.*

nutritional value: kcal564 fat18g saturates5g carbs70g sugars18g fibre14g protein23g salt1.7g Dietary Fiber 0g Sugars 0g Protein 22g Calcium 1.2% Iron 1.9%

953) Simple Calamari Rings

Ingredients:

- *(4 Servings)*
- *1 lb calamari rings*
- *½ cup cornstarch*
- *2 large eggs, beaten 2 garlic cloves, minced*
- *1 cup breadcrumbs*
- *1 lemon, sliced*

Direction:(Prep + Cook Time: 30 minutes

- ✓ *In a bowl, coat the calamari with cornstarch.*
- ✓ *In another bowl, mix the eggs with garlic.*
- ✓ *Dip the calamari in the egg and roll them up in the crumbs.*
- ✓ *Transfer to the fridge for 10 minutes.*
- ✓ *Remove calamari from the fridge and arrange them on the greased frying basket.*
- ✓ *Air fry for 12 minutes at 390 F, shaking once halfway through cooking.*
- ✓ *Serve with lemon slices.*

nutritional value: Calories 79.5 Total Fat 0.5g Sodium 200.5mg Carbohydrates 0g Net carbs 0g Sugar 0g Fiber 0g Protein 17g Calcium 0mg Iron 1.4mg

954) Gambas al Ajillo (Garlic Shrimp)

Ingredients:

- *(4 Servings)*
- *1 lb shrimp, peeled and deveined*
- *½ tsp Cajun seasoning*
- *10 lettuce leaves*
- *1 tbsp olive oil*
- *¼ tsp garlic powder*
- *2 tbsp lemon juice,*

Direction:(Prep + Cook Time: 25 minutes)

- ✓ *Mix the garlic powder, half of the lemon juice, olive oil, and Cajun seasoning in a bowl to make a marinade.*
- ✓ *Toss the shrimp to coat thoroughly.*
- ✓ *Cover with plastic wrap and refrigerate for 30 minutes.*
- ✓ *Preheat the air fryer to 400 F. Place the shrimp in the greased frying basket and air fry for 5 minutes.*
- ✓ *Shake the basket and cook for 7-8 more minutes, until cooked through.*
- ✓ *Arrange the lettuce leaves on a plate and top with the shrimp.*
- ✓ *Drizzle with the remaining lemon juice and serve.*

nutritional value: Carbs5 g Dietary Fiber1 g Sugar1 g Fat25 g Saturated3 gPolyunsaturated3 g Monounsaturated17 g Protein16 g Sodium310 mg Potassium285 mg Cholesterol115 mg

955) Crispy Fish Finger Sticks

Ingredients:

- *(4 Servings)*
- *2 fresh white fish fillets, cut into 4 fingers each*
- *1 egg*
- *½ cup buttermilk*
- *1 cup panko breadcrumbs*
- *Salt and black pepper to taste*
- *1 cup aioli (or garlic mayo*

Direction:Prep + Cook Time: 20 minutes

- ✓ *Preheat the air fryer to 380 F.*
- ✓ *In a bowl, beat the egg and buttermilk. On a plate, combine breadcrumbs, salt, and pepper.*
- ✓ *Dip each finger into the egg mixture, roll it up in the crumbs, and spritz it with cooking spray.*

- ✓ *Arrange on the greased frying basket and air fry for 10 minutes, turning once.*
- ✓ *Serve with aioli.*

nutritional value: Calories 200 Total Fat 4 g Saturated Fat 2 g Trans Fat 0.1 g Cholesterol 20 mg Sodium 400 mg Potassium 300 mg Total Carbohydrate 28 g Dietary Fiber 2 g Sugars 3 g Protein 13 g Calcium 20 mg

956) Raspberry & Vanilla Pancakes

Ingredients:

- (4 Servings)
- 1 ½ cups all-purpose flour
- 1 cup milk
- 3 eggs, beaten
- 1 tsp baking powder
- 2 tbsp brown sugar
- 1 tsp vanilla extract
- ½ cup frozen raspberries, thawed
- 2 tbsp maple syrup

Direction:Prep + Cook Time: 15 minutes

- ✓ *Preheat the air fryer to 370 F.*
- ✓ *Mix the flour, baking powder, milk, eggs, vanilla, and brown sugar in a bowl.*
- ✓ *Gently stir in the raspberries to avoid coloring the batter*
- ✓ *Working in batches, drop the batter into a greased baking pan using a spoon.*
- ✓ *Bake for 6-8 minutes, flipping once.*
- ✓ *Repeat the process with the remaining batter.*
- ✓ *Serve the pancakes with maple syrup.*

nutritional value: Calories: 241 calories Fat: 5 g Carbohydrates: 11 g Fiber: 13 g Protein: 20 g

957) Cinnamon French Toast ticks

Ingredients:

- (2 Servings)
- 4 white bread slices, cut them into strips
- 2 eggs
- 1 ½ tbsp butter
- ¼ tsp cinnamon powder + some for dusting
- ¼ nutmeg powder
- ¼ clove powder
- 2 tbsp brown sugar
- 1 tbsp icing sugar

Direction:Prep + Cook Time: 15 minutes

- ✓ *Preheat the air fryer to 350 F. Add the eggs, brown sugar, clove powder, nutmeg powder, and cinnamon powder to a bowl.*
- ✓ *Beat the mixture using a whisk until well combined.*
- ✓ *Dip the strips into the egg mixture*
- ✓ *Arrange them on the greased frying basket and spritz with cooking spray.*
- ✓ *Bake for 2 minutes. Flip the toasts and cook for 3 more minutes.*
- ✓ *Dust the toasts with cinnamon and icing sugar to serve*

nutritional: Calories330 Total Fat 15g Saturated Fat 2g Trans Fat 0g Cholesterol 20mg Sodium 340mg Total Carbs 44g Dietary Fiber 2g Sugars 17g

958) Air Fried Cinnamon Apples

Ingredients:

- (2 Servings)
- 2 apples, cored, bottom intact
- 2 tbsp butter, cold
- 3 tbsp sugar
- 3 tbsp crushed walnuts
- 2 tbsp raisins
- 1 tsp cinnamon.

Direction:Prep + Cook Time: 25 minutes)

- ✓ *Preheat the air fryer to 350 F.*
- ✓ *In a bowl, add butter, sugar, walnuts, raisins, and cinnamon*
- ✓ *Mix well until you obtain a crumble.*
- ✓ *Stuff the apples with the filling mixture.*
- ✓ *Bake in the air fryer for 20 minutes.*

nutritional value: Calories: 120kcal Carbohydrates: 31g Protein: 1g Fat: 1g Saturated Fat: 1g Polyunsaturated Fat: 1g Monounsaturated Fat: 1g

959) Easy Breakfast Potatoes

Ingredients:

- (6 Servings)
- 4 large potatoes,
- cubed 2 bell peppers, cut into 1-inch chunks
- ½ onion, diced
- 2 tsp olive oil
- 1 garlic clove Minced
- ½ tsp dried thyme
- ½ tsp cayenne pepper Salt to taste.

Direction:Prep + Cook Time: 35 minutes

- ✓ *Preheat the air fryer to 390 F. Place the potato cubes in a bowl and sprinkle with garlic, cayenne pepper, and salt.*
- ✓ *Drizzle with some olive oil and toss to coat.*
- ✓ *Arrange the potatoes in an even layer in the greased frying basket.*
- ✓ *AirFry for 10 minutes, shaking once halfway through cooking.*
- ✓ *In the meantime, add the remaining olive oil, garlic, thyme, and salt to a mixing bowl. Add in the bell peppers and onion and mix well.*
- ✓ *Pour the veggies over the potatoes and continue cooking for 10 more minutes.*

- ✓ *At the 5-minute mark, shake the basket and cook for 5 minutes.*
- ✓ *Serve warm.*

nutritional value: Calories: 128 Fat: 0.2 g Saturated Fat: 0.1 g Percent Calories from Fat: 1.7% Cholesterol: 0 mg Protein: 3.1 g Carbohydrate: 29.9 g Sugar: 2.7 g Fiber: 4.1 g Sodium: 309 mg Calcium: 39 mg Iron: 2.7 mg Beta-Carotene: 89 mcg

960) Morning Potato Skins

Ingredients:

- *(4 Servings)*
- *4 eggs*
- *2 large russet potatoes, scrubbed*
- *1 tbsp olive oil*
- *2 tbsp cooked bacon, chopped*
- *1 cup cheddar cheese, shredded*
- *1 tbsp chopped chives*
- *¼ tsp red pepper flakes*
- *Salt and black pepper to taste*

Direction:Prep + Cook Time: 35 minutes

- ✓ *Preheat the air fryer to 360 F.*
- ✓ *Using a fork, poke holes all over the potatoes, then cook them in the microwave on high for 5 minutes.*
- ✓ *Flip them and cook in the microwave for another 3-5 minutes.*
- ✓ *Test with a fork to make sure they are tender.*
- ✓ *Halve the potatoes lengthwise and scoop out most of the 'meat,' leaving enough potato so 'boat' sides don't collapse.*
- ✓ *Coat the skin side of the potatoes with olive oil, salt, and black pepper for taste.*
- ✓ *Arrange the potatoes, skin down, in the lightly greased frying basket.*
- ✓ *Crack an egg and put it in the scooped potato, one egg for each half.*
- ✓ *Divide the bacon and cheddar cheese between the potatoes and sprinkle with salt and pepper.*
- ✓ *For a runny yolk, AirFry for 5-6 minutes, and for a solid yolk, AirFry for 7-10 minutes.*
- ✓ *Sprinkle with red pepper flakes and chives to serve.*

nutritional value: Calories 340 Total Fat 24g Saturated fat 9.9g Cholesterol 30mg Sodium 320mg Carbohydrates 20g Net carbs 15g Fiber 5g Glucose 1.1g Protein 11g Calcium 60mg

961) Chili Potato Latkes (Hash Browns)

Ingredients:

- *(4 Servings)*
- *1 lb potatoes, peeled and shredded*
- *salt and black pepper to taste*
- *1 tsp garlic powder*
- *1 tsp chili flakes*
- *1 tsp onion powder*
- *1 egg, beaten*
- *1 tbsp olive oil*

Direction:(Prep + Cook Time: 25 minutes + cooling time)

- ✓ *Heat olive oil in a skillet over medium heat and sauté potatoes for 10 minutes; transfer to a bowl to cool.*
- ✓ *When cooled, add in the egg, black pepper, salt, chili flakes, onion powder, and garlic powder; mix well.*
- ✓ *On a flat plate, spread the mixture and pat it firmly with your fingers.*
- ✓ *Refrigerate for 20 minutes.*
- ✓ *Preheat the air fryer to 350 F.*
- ✓ *Shape the cooled mixture into patties.*
- ✓ *Arrange them on the greased frying basket and AirFry for 12 minutes, flipping once halfway through.*
- ✓ *Serve warm.*

nutritional value: Calories150 Total Fat 8g Saturated Fat2g Trans Fat0g Polyunsaturated Fat2.0g Monounsaturated Fat4.0g Cholesterol 0.0mg Sodium 270mg Total Carbohydrate 18g Dietary Fiber2g Sugars<1.0g Protein 2g Potassium300mg Calcium0%

962) Kaiserschmarrn (German Torn Pancake

Ingredients:

- *(4 Servings)*
- *3 eggs*
- *, whites and yolks separated*
- *1 tbsp sugar*
- *2 tbsp butter, melted*
- *1 cup flour*
- *2 tbsp sugar, powdered*
- *½ cup milk*
- *2 tbsp raisins, soaked in rum*
- *1 cup plum sauce.*

Direction:Prep + Cook Time: 30 minutes

- ✓ *Preheat the air fryer to 350 F.*
- ✓ *Mix flour, milk, and egg yolks in a bowl until fully incorporated; stir in the drained raisins.*
- ✓ *Beat the egg whites with sugar until stiff.*
- ✓ *Gently fold the whites into the yolk mixture.*
- ✓ *Grease a baking pan with butter and pour in the batter.*
- ✓ *Place the pan inside the frying basket.*
- ✓ *Bake for 6-8 minutes until the pancake is fluffy and golden brown.*

- ✓ Break the pancake into pieces using two forks and dust with powdered sugar.
- ✓ Serve with plum sauce and enjoy!

nutritional value: Cals 526 Fat 23.8g Saturated Fat 10.1g Cholesterol 199 mg Potassium 552 mg Carbs 65.9g Fiber 3.2g Sugar 25.5g Protein 15.4g

963) Three Meat Cheesy Omelet

Ingredients:

- (2 Servings)
- 1 beef sausage, chopped
- 4 slices prosciutto, chopped
- 3 oz salami, chopped
- 1 cup mozzarella cheese, grated
- 4 eggs
- 1 green onion, chopped
- 1 tbsp ketchup
- 1 tsp fresh parsley, chopped

Direction:(Prep + Cook Time: 20 minutes

- ✓ Preheat the air fryer to 350 F. Whisk the eggs with ketchup in a bowl.
- ✓ Stir in the green onion, mozzarella, salami, and prosciutto.
- ✓ AirFry the sausage in a greased baking pan inside the fryer for 2 minutes.
- ✓ Slide-out and pour the egg mixture over.
- ✓ Bake for 8-10 more minutes until golden.
- ✓ Serve topped with parsley.

nutritional value: Calories 1210 Total Fat 94g Saturated Fat 34g Trans Fat 0.5g Cholesterol 740mg Sodium 3400mg Total Carbohydrates 21g Dietary Fiber 3g Sugars 9g Protein 70g

964) Masala Omelet The Indian Way

Ingredients:

- (1 Serving)
- 1 garlic clove, crushed
- 1 green onion
- ½ chili powder
- ½ tsp garam masala 2 eggs
- 1 tbsp olive oil
- 1 tbsp fresh cilantro, chopped
- salt and black pepper to taste

Direction:Prep + Cook Time: 15 minutes

- ✓ Preheat the air fryer to 360 F.
- ✓ In a bowl, whisk the eggs with salt and black pepper.
- ✓ Add in the green onion, garlic, chili powder, and garam masala; stir well.
- ✓ Transfer to a greased baking pan.
- ✓ Bake in the fryer for 8 minutes until the top is golden and the eggs are set. Scatter with fresh cilantro and serve

nutrition: Calories230.8 Total Fat15.2 g Cholesterol425.0 mg Potassium404.1 mg Total Carbohydrate10.2 g Dietary Fiber2.2 g Sugars0.5 g

965) Japanese-Style Omelet

Ingredients:

- (1 Serving)
- ½ cup cubed tofu
- 3 whole
- eggs
- Salt and black pepper to taste
- ¼ tsp ground coriander
- ¼ tsp cumin
- 1 tsp soy sauce
- 1 tbsp green onions, chopped
- ¼ onion, chopped

Direction:Prep + Cook Time: 20 minutes

- ✓ Mix eggs, onion, soy sauce, ground coriander, cumin, black pepper, and salt in a bowl.
- ✓ Add in the tofu and pour the mixture into a greased baking pan.
- ✓ Place in the preheated air fryer and Bake for 8 minutes at 360 F.
- ✓ Remove, and let cool for 2 minutes.
- ✓ Sprinkle with green onions and serve.

nutrition: Calories 60 Protein 4.32g Fat 3.64g Carbohydrate 2.56g

966) Baked Kale Omelet

Ingredients:

- (2 Servings)
- 5 eggs
- 3 tbsp cottage cheese, crumbled
- 1 cup kale, chopped
- ½ tbsp fresh basil, chopped
- ½ tbsp fresh parsley, chopped
- salt and black pepper to taste

Direction:(Prep + Cook Time: 15 minutes

- ✓ Beat the eggs, salt, and black pepper in a bowl.
- ✓ Stir in the rest of the ingredients
- ✓ Pour the mixture into a greased baking pan and fit in the air fryer.
- ✓ Bake for 10 minutes at 330 F until slightly golden and set.

nutrition: 1 piece- 107 g, 76 cal, 33% protein. Contains 134% of your DV of Vitamin A, 94% of

967) Ham & Cheddar Omelet

Ingredients:

- 2 Servings)
- 4 eggs

- *3 tbsp cheddar cheese, grated*
- *1 tsp soy sauce*
- *½ cup ham, chopped.*

Direction:(Prep + Cook Time: 20 minutes

- ✓ *Preheat the air fryer to 350 F.*
- ✓ *In a bowl, whisk the eggs with soy sauce.*
- ✓ *Fold in the chopped ham and mix well to combine. Spoon the egg mixture into a greased baking pan and pour into the frying basket.*
- ✓ *Bake for 6-8 minutes until golden on top.*
- ✓ *Sprinkle with the cheddar cheese and serve warm.*

nutrition: Calories 512 Total Fat 37g Saturated Fat 16g Trans Fat 0.3g Polyunsaturated Fat 4.3g Monounsaturated Fat 12g Cholesterol 712mg Potassium 454mg Total Carbohydrates 2.9g Dietary Fiber 0.1g Sugars 1.4g Protein 40g

968) Omelet Bread Cups

Ingredients:

- *4 Servings)*
- *4 crusty rolls*
- *5 eggs, beaten*
- *½ tsp thyme, dried*
- *3 strips cooked bacon, chopped*
- *2 tbsp heavy cream*
- *4 Gouda cheese thin slices*

Direction:Prep + Cook Time: 25 minutes

- ✓ *Preheat the air fryer to 330 F.*
- ✓ *Cut the tops off the rolls and remove the inside with your fingers.*
- ✓ *Line the rolls with a slice of cheese and press down so the cheese conforms to the inside of the roll.*
- ✓ *In a bowl, mix the eggs, heavy cream, bacon, and thyme.*
- ✓ *Stuff the rolls with the egg mixture. Lay them in the greased frying basket and Bake for 6-8 minutes or until the eggs become puffy and the roll shows a golden brown texture.*
- ✓ *Remove and let them cool for a few minutes before serving.*

nutrition: Calories 356 Total Fat 16g Saturated Fat 3.9g Trans Fat 0.2g Cholesterol 372mg Sodium 608mg Potassium 364mg Total Carbohydrates 33g Dietary Fiber 2.9g Sugars 5.7g Protein 18g Calcium 15%

969) Greek-Style Frittata

Ingredients:

- *4 Servings)*
- *5 eggs*
- *1 cup baby spinach*
- *½ cup grape tomatoes halved*
- *½ cup feta cheese, crumbled*
- *10 Kalamata olives, sliced*
- *salt and black pepper to taste*
- *2 tbsp fresh parsley, chopped*

Direction:(Prep + Cook Time: 30 minutes)

- ✓ *Preheat the air fryer to 360 F.*
- ✓ *Beat the eggs, salt, and black pepper in a bowl, until well combined.*
- ✓ *Add in the spinach and stir until well mixed.*
- ✓ *Pour half the mixture into a greased baking pan. On top of the mixture, add half of the tomatoes, olives, and feta cheese.*
- ✓ *Cover the pan with foil, making sure to close it tightly around the edges, then place it inside the air fryer and Bake for 12 minutes.*
- ✓ *Remove the foil and cook for an additional 5-7 minutes until the eggs are fully cooked.*
- ✓ *Place the finished frittata on a serving plate and repeat the above instructions for the remaining ingredients.*
- ✓ *Decorate with fresh parsley and cut into wedges.*
- ✓ *Serve hot or at room temperature. S*

nutritional value: Calories 1465 Carbs 33g Fat 116g Protein 76g Fiber 8g Net carbs 24g Sodium 7238mg Cholesterol 1243mg

970) panish Chorizo Frittata

Ingredients:

- *(2 Servings)*
- *4 eggs*
- *1 large potato, boiled and cubed*
- *¼ cup Manchego cheese, grated*
- *1 tbsp parsley, chopped*
- *1 Spanish chorizo, chopped*
- *½ small red onion, chopped*
- *¼ tsp paprika*
- *Salt and black pepper to taste*

Direction:Prep + Cook Time: 20 minutes)

- ✓ *Preheat the air fryer to 330 F.*
- ✓ *In a bowl, beat the eggs with paprika, salt, and pepper.*
- ✓ *Stir in all of the remaining ingredients, except for the parsley Spread the egg batter on the greased baking pan and insert it into the air fryer.*
- ✓ *Bake for 8-10 minutes until the top is golden.*
- ✓ *Garnish with parsley to serve.*

nutritional value: Calories 481cal Kilojoules 2010kJ Protein 27g Total fat 27g Saturated fat 7g Carbohydrates 30g Sugars 12g Dietary fiber 7g Sodium 620mg Calcium 210mg Iron 4mg

971) Vienna Sausage & Cherry Tomato Frittata

Ingredients:

- *(2 Servings)*
- *2 Vienna sausages, sliced*
- *salt and black pepper to taste*
- *1 tbsp fresh parsley, chopped*
- *½ cup milk 4 eggs*
- *½ tsp red pepper flakes, crushed*
- *4 cherry tomatoes, halved*
- *2 tbsp Parmesan cheese, shredded*

Direction:(Prep + Cook Time: 15 minutes)

- ✓ *Preheat the air fryer to 360 F. In a bowl, whisk the eggs and milk.*
- ✓ *Stir in the Parmesan cheese, red pepper flakes, salt, parsley, and black pepper.*
- ✓ *Add the mixture to a lightly greased baking pan and top with sausage slices and cherry tomatoes.*
- ✓ *Bake in the fryer for 8 minutes until the eggs are set.*
- ✓ *Serve hot.*

nutritional value: Calories Per Serving: 155 Total Fat 7.7g Sodium 270.3mg Dietary Fiber 0.5g Protein 17.6g Saturated Fat 2.3g Total Carbohydrate 3.2g Sugars 2.4g

972) Air Fried Shirred Eggs

Ingredients:

- *(2 Servings)*
- *2 tsp butter, melted*
- *4 eggs*
- *2 tbsp heavy cream*
- *4 smoked ham slices*
- *3 tbsp Parmesan cheese, grated*
- *¼ tsp paprika*
- *Salt and black pepper to taste*
- *2 tsp fresh chives, chopped*

Direction:Prep + Cook Time: 20 minutes)

- ✓ *Preheat the air fryer to 320 F. Lightly grease 4 ramekins with butter.*
- ✓ *Line the bottom of each ramekin with a piece of smoked ham.*
- ✓ *Crack the eggs on top of the ham and season with salt and pepper*
- ✓ *Drizzle with heavy cream and sprinkle with Parmesan cheese.*
- ✓ *AirFry for 10-12 minutes until the eggs are completely set.*
- ✓ *Garnish with paprika and fresh chives to serve.*

nutritional value: Calories 177 Fat 10g Saturated Fat 4g Polyunsaturated Fat 1g Monounsaturated Fat 1g Cholesterol 171mg Sodium 255mg Potassium 617mg Carbohydrates 11g Fiber 3g Sugar 3g Protein 12g Calcium 162mg Iron 3mg

973) Prosciutto, Mozzarella & Eggs in a Cup

Ingredients:

- *2 Servings)*
- *4 prosciutto slices*
- *2 eggs*
- *4 tomato slices*
- *¼ tsp balsamic vinegar*
- *2 tbsp mozzarella cheese, grated*
- *¼ tsp maple syrup*
- *2 tbsp mayonnaise*
- *Salt and black pepper to taste*

Direction:(Prep + Cook Time: 20 minutes

- ✓ *Preheat the air fryer to 350 F.*
- ✓ *Grease 2 cups with cooking spray.*
- ✓ *Line the bottom and sides of each cup with prosciutto, patching up any holes using little pieces if necessary.*
- ✓ *Place the tomato slices on top and divide the mozzarella cheese between the cups.*
- ✓ *Crack the eggs over the mozzarella cheese and drizzle with maple syrup and balsamic vinegar.*
- ✓ *Season with salt and pepper.*
- ✓ *Bake in the fryer until the egg whites are just set, about 10-12 minutes.*
- ✓ *Top with mayonnaise and serve.*

nutritional value: Calories 229.2 Total Fat 18.2 g Saturated Fat 8.6 g Polyunsaturated Fat 1.0 g Monounsaturated Fat 4.3 g Cholesterol 261.7 mg Sodium 857.2 mg Potassium 79.9 mg Total Carbohydrate 2.2 g Dietary Fiber 0.0 g Sugars 0.1 g Protein 14.3 g

974) Buttered Eggs in Hole

Ingredients:

- *2 Servings)*
- *2 bread slices*
- *2 eggs*
- *Salt and black pepper to taste*
- *1 tbsp butter, softened*

Direction:Prep + Cook Time: 15 minutes

- ✓ *Preheat the air fryer to 360 F.*
- ✓ *Place a heatproof pan in the frying basket and brush with butter.*
- ✓ *Make a hole in the middle of the bread slices with a bread knife and place in the heatproof pan in 2 batches.*
- ✓ *Crack an egg into the center of each hole; adjust the seasoning.*
- ✓ *Bake in the air fryer for 4 minutes.*
- ✓ *Turn the bread with a spatula and cook for another 4 minutes.*
- ✓ *Serve warm*

nutritional value: Calories 130 Total Fat 11g Saturated fat 5g Cholesterol 195mg Sodium 95mg Carbohydrates 0g Net carbs 0g Sugar 0g Fiber 0g Protein 6g

975) Breakfast Shrimp & Egg Muffins

Ingredients:

- 4 Servings)
- 4 eggs, beaten
- 2 tbsp olive oil
- ½ small red bell pepper, finely diced
- 1 garlic clove, minced
- 4 oz shrimp, cooked, chopped
- 4 tsp ricotta cheese, crumbled
- 1 tsp dry dill
- Salt and black pepper to taste

Direction:Prep + Cook Time: 35 minutes

- ✓ Preheat the air fryer to 360 F.
- ✓ Warm the olive oil in a skillet over medium heat.
- ✓ Sauté the bell pepper and garlic until the pepper is soft, then add the shrimp.
- ✓ Season with dill, salt, and pepper and cook for about 5 minutes.
- ✓ Remove from the heat and mix in the eggs.
- ✓ Grease 4 ramekins with cooking spray.
- ✓ Divide the mixture between the ramekins.
- ✓ Place them in the air fryer and Bake for 6 minutes.
- ✓ Remove and stir the mixture.
- ✓ Sprinkle with ricotta and return to the fryer.
- ✓ Bake for 5 more minutes until the eggs are set and the top is lightly browned.
- ✓ Let sit for 2 minutes, invert on a plate while warm, and serve.

nutritional value: Calories 73 Fat 1g Potassium 159mg Carbohydrates 5g Fiber 1g Sugar 1g Protein 9g

976) Cheese & Ham Breakfast Egg Cups

Ingredients:

- 6 Servings)
- 4 eggs, beaten
- 1 tbsp olive oil
- ½ cup Colby cheese, shredded
- 2 ¼ cups frozen hash browns, thawed
- 1 cup smoked ham, chopped
- ½ tsp Cajun seasoning

Direction:Prep + Cook Time: 20 minutes)

- ✓ Preheat the air fryer to 360 F.
- ✓ Gather 12 silicone muffin cups and coat them with olive oil.
- ✓ Whisk the eggs, hash browns, smoked ham, Colby cheese, and Cajun seasoning in a large bowl and add a heaping spoonful into each muffin cup.
- ✓ Put the muffin cups in the frying basket and AirFry 8-10 minutes until golden brown and the center is set.
- ✓ Transfer to a wire rack to cool completely.
- ✓ Serve.

nutritional value: Calories 82.1 Total Fat 5.2 g Saturated Fat 1.6 g Polyunsaturated Fat0.1 g Monounsaturated Fat 0.8 g Cholesterol 111.4 mg Sodium 416.5 mg Potassium 31.5 mg Total Carbohydrate 2.0 g Dietary Fiber 0.3 Sugars 0.8 Protein 7.1

977) Turkey & Mushroom Sandwich

Ingredients:

- 1 Serving)
- ⅓ cup leftover turkey, shredded
- ⅓ cup sliced mushrooms, sauteed
- ½ tbsp butter softened
- 2 tomato slices
- ½ tsp red pepper flakes
- Salt and black pepper to taste
- 1 hamburger bun, halved

Direction:(Prep + Cook Time: 10 minutes)

- ✓ Preheat the air fryer to 350 F.
- ✓ Brush the bun bottom with butter and top with shredded turkey.
- ✓ Arrange the mushroom slices on top of the turkey.
- ✓ Cover with tomato slices and sprinkle with salt, black pepper, and red flakes.
- ✓ Top with the bun top and AirFry for 5-8 minutes until crispy.
- ✓ Serve and enjoy!

nutritional value: Calories 156.2Total Fat8.2 g Saturated Fat 4.3 g Polyunsaturated Fat 1.3 g Monounsaturated Fat 2.2 g Cholesterol 17.8 mg Sodium 316.3 mg Potassium 579.8 mg Total Carbohydrate 13.6 g Dietary Fiber 2.6 g Sugars 2.8 g Protein 9.5 g Calcium 13.4 %

978) Air Fried Sourdough Sandwiches

Ingredients:

- (2 Servings)
- 4 slices sourdough bread
- 2 tbsp mayonnaise
- 2 slices ham
- 2 lettuce leaves
- 1 tomato, sliced
- 2 slices mozzarella cheese

Direction:Prep + Cook Time: 20 minutes

- ✓ *Preheat the air fryer to 350 F.*
- ✓ *On a clean working board, lay the bread slices and spread them with mayonnaise.*
- ✓ *Top 2 of the slices with ham, lettuce leaves, tomato slices, and mozzarella.*
- ✓ *Cover with the remaining bread slices to form two sandwiches.*
- ✓ *AirFry for 12 minutes, flipping once.*
- ✓ *Serve hot.*

nutritional value: Calories: 210kcal Carbohydrates: 25g Protein: 9g Fat: 8g Saturated Fat: 4g Trans Fat: 1g Cholesterol: 20mg Sodium: 367mg Potassium: 94mg Fiber: 1g Sugar: 3g Calcium: 270mg Iron: 2mg

979) Loaded Egg Pepper Rings

Ingredients:

- *(4 Servings)*
- *4 eggs*
- *1 bell pepper, cut into four*
- *¾-inch rings*
- *5 cherry tomatoes, halved*
- *salt and black pepper to taste*

Direction:Prep + Cook Time: 15 minutes

- ✓ *Preheat the air fryer to 360 F.*
- ✓ *Add the bell pepper rings to a greased baking pan and crack an egg into each one.*
- ✓ *Season with salt and black pepper Top with the halved cherry tomatoes.*
- ✓ *Put the pan into the air fryer and AirFry for 6-9 minutes, or until the eggs are halve set.*
- ✓ *Serve and enjoy*

nutritional value:
Calories: 102 kcal · Carbohydrates: 4 g · Protein: 7 g · Fat: 6 g · Saturated Fat: 3 g · Polyunsaturated Fat: 1 g · Monounsaturated Fat: 2 g · Trans Fat: 1 g · Cholesterol: 171 mg · Sodium: 165 mg Fiber : 1 g · Sugar: 3 g 47 mg

980) Sausage & Egg Casserole

Ingredients:

- *6 Servings)*
- *2 tbsp olive oil*
- *1 lb Italian sausages*
- *6 eggs*
- *1 red pepper, diced*
- *1 green pepper, diced*
- *1 yellow pepper, diced*
- *1 sweet onion, diced*
- *1 cup cheddar cheese, shredded*
- *salt and black pepper to taste*
- *2 tbsp fresh parsley, chopped.*

Direction:Prep + Cook Time: 20 minutes)

- ✓ *Warm the olive oil in a skillet over medium heat.*
- ✓ *Add the sausages and brown them slightly, occasionally turning, for about 5 minutes. Once done, drain any excess fat derived from cooking and set aside.*
- ✓ *Arrange the sausages on the bottom of a greased casserole dish that fits in your air fryer.*
- ✓ *Top with onion, red pepper, green pepper, and yellow pepper.*
- ✓ *Sprinkle with cheddar cheese on top.*
- ✓ *In a bowl, beat the eggs with salt and pepper.*
- ✓ *Pour the mixture over the cheese.*
- ✓ *Place the casserole dish in the frying basket and Bake at 360 F for 15 minutes.*
- ✓ *Serve warm garnished with fresh parsley.*

nutritional value: Calories 312.9 Total Fat 22.5 g Saturated Fat 8.2 g Polyunsaturated Fat 2.4 g Monounsaturated Fat 9.0 g Cholesterol 152.1 mg Sodium 846.3 mg Potassium 209.8 mg Total Carbohydrate 12.4 g Dietary Fiber 0.6 g Sugars 3.0 g Protein 15.7 g Calcium 24.9 %

981) Grilled Tofu Sandwich with Cabbage

Ingredients:

- *(1 Serving)*
- *2 slices of bread*
- *1 tofu slice, 1-inch thick*
- *¼ cup red cabbage, shredded*
- *2 tsp olive oil*
- *¼ tsp vinegar Salt to taste*

Direction:(Prep + Cook Time: 20 minutes

- ✓ *Preheat the air fryer to 350 F.*
- ✓ *Add the bread slices to the frying basket and AirFry for 3 minutes; set aside.*
- ✓ *Brush the tofu with some olive oil and place it in the air fryer.*
- ✓ *AirFry for 5 minutes on each side.*
- ✓ *Mix the cabbage, remaining olive oil, and vinegar.*
- ✓ *Season with salt.*
- ✓ *Place the tofu on top of one bread slice, place the cabbage over, and top with the other bread slice.*
- ✓ *Serve with cream cheese-mustard dip.*

nutritional value: 271 calories; protein 12.5g; carbohydrates 33.1g; dietary fiber 5.1g; sugars 10.9g; fat 11.1g; saturated fat 1.7g; cholesterol 1.9mg;

982) French Toast with Vanilla Filling

Ingredients:

- *(3 Servings)*
- *6 white bread slices*
- *2 eggs*
- *¼ cup milk*

- *3 tbsp caramel sauce*
- *⅓ cup cream cheese softened*
- *1 tsp vanilla extract*
- *⅓ cup sugar mixed with*
- *1 tsp ground cinnamon*

Direction:Prep + Cook Time: 15 minutes

- ✓ *In a bowl, mix the cream cheese, caramel sauce, and vanilla.*
- ✓ *Spread three of the bread slices with the cheese mixture around the center.*
- ✓ *Place the remaining three slices on top to form three sandwiches.*
- ✓ *Whisk the eggs and milk in a bowl.*
- ✓ *Dip the sandwiches into the egg mixture.*
- ✓ *Arrange them in the greased frying basket and AirFry for 10 minutes at 340 F, turning once.*
- ✓ *Dust with the cinnamon mi*

nutritional value: Calories 566 Total Fat 15g Saturated fat 9g Cholesterol 84mg Sodium 659mg Net carbs 52g Fiber 3g Glucose 24g Protein 11g

983) Brioche Toast with Nutella

Ingredients:

- *(2 Servings)*
- *4 slices of brioche*
- *3 eggs*
- *4 tbsp butter*
- *6 oz Nutella spread*
- *½ cup heavy cream*
- *1 tsp vanilla extract*
- *1 tbsp icing sugar*
- *½ cup fresh strawberries, sliced.*

Direction:Prep + Cook Time: 15 minutes

- ✓ *Preheat the air fryer to 350 F.*
- ✓ *Beat the eggs along with heavy cream and vanilla in a small bowl.*
- ✓ *Dip the brioche slices in the egg mixture and AirFry in the greased frying basket for 7-8 minutes in total, shaking once or twice.*
- ✓ *Spread two pieces of the toast with a thin layer of Nutella and cover with the remaining toast pieces.*
- ✓ *Dust with icing sugar and top with strawberries.*
- ✓ *Serve and enjoy!*

nutritional value: Calories 596.1 Total Fat 30.0 g Saturated Fat 12.2 g Polyunsaturated Fat 0.5 g Monounsaturated Fat 3.1 g Cholesterol 30.5 mg Sodium 494.4 mg Potassium 237.1 mg Total Carbohydrate 68.0 g Dietary Fiber 3.0 g Sugars 34.4 g Protein 15.1 g Calcium 8.7 %

984) Bacon & Egg Sandwich

Ingredients:

- *(1 Serving)*
- *1 egg, fried*
- *1 slice English bacon*
- *Salt and black pepper to taste,*
- *2 bread slices*
- *½ tbsp butter softened.*

Direction:Prep + Cook Time: 10 minutes

- ✓ *Preheat the air fryer to 400 F.*
- ✓ *Spread butter on one side of the bread slices.*
- ✓ *Add the fried egg on top and season with salt and black pepper*
- ✓ *Top with the bacon and cover with the other slice of the bread.*
- ✓ *Place in the frying basket and AirFry for 4-6 minutes.*
- ✓ *Serve warm.*

nutritional value: Calories 433 Total Fat 27g Saturated Fat 12g Saturated Fat 12g Cholesterol 238mg Sodium 838mg Potassium 263mg Total Carbohydrates 27g Dietary Fiber 1.5g Sugars 0.2g Protein 19g Calcium 13%

985) Mediterranean Avocado Toast

Ingredients:

- *2 Serving)*
- *2 slices thick whole grain bread*
- *4 thin tomato slices*
- *1 ripe avocado, pitted, peeled, and sliced*
- *1 tbsp olive oil*
- *pinch of salt*
- *½ tsp chili flakes*

Direction:Prep + Cook Time: 7 minutes

- ✓ *Preheat the air fryer to 370 F.*
- ✓ *Arrange the bread slices in the frying basket and toast them for 3 minutes.*
- ✓ *Add the avocado to a bowl and mash it up with a fork until smooth.*
- ✓ *Season with salt*
- ✓ *When the toasted bread is ready, remove it to a plate.*
- ✓ *Spread the avocado and cover with thin tomato slices.*
- ✓ *Drizzle with olive oil, sprinkle the toasts with chili flakes and serve.*

nutritional value: Calorie 300 Carbs37 g Fat 13g Sodium 705 Dietary Fiber7 g Sugar1 g Fat13 g Saturated3 g Protein8 g Sodium705 mg Cholesterol0 mg

986) Very Berry Breakfast Puffs

Ingredients:

- *4 Servings)*

- *1 puff pastry sheet*
- *1 tbsp strawberries, mashed*
- *1 tbsp raspberries; mashed,*
- *¼ tsp vanilla extract*
- *1 cup cream cheese*
- *1 tbsp honey*

Direction:Prep + Cook Time: 30 minutes

- ✓ *Preheat the air fryer to 375 F.*
- ✓ *Roll the puff pastry out on a lightly floured surface into a 1-inch thick rectangle.*
- ✓ *Cut into 4 squares. Spread the cream cheese evenly on top of them.*
- ✓ *In a bowl, combine the berries, honey, and vanilla.*
- ✓ *Spoon the mixture onto the pastry squares.*
- ✓ *Fold in the sides over the filling.*
- ✓ *Pinch the ends to form a puff.*
- ✓ *Place the puffs in the greased frying basket.*
- ✓ *Bake in the air fryer for 15 minutes until the pastry is puffed and golden all over.*
- ✓ *Let it cool for 10 mins before serving.*

nutritional value: Calories 170 Total Fat 1.5g Saturated Fat 0g Trans Fat 0 Cholesterol 0mg Sodium 180mg Total Carbohydrates 37g Dietary Fiber 2g Total Sugars 11g Added Sugars 11g Protein 2g Iron 2% Calcium 4%

987) Romanian Polenta Fries

Ingredients:

- *(4 Servings)*
- *2 cups milk*
- *1 cup instant polenta*
- *Salt and black pepper to taste*
- *2 tbsp fresh thyme, chopped*

Direction:(Prep + Cook Time: 30 minutes + cooling time)

- ✓ *Line a baking dish with parchment paper.*
- ✓ *Pour 2 cups of milk and 2 cups of water into a saucepan and let simmer.*
- ✓ *Keep whisking as you pour in the polenta.*
- ✓ *Continue to whisk until the polenta thickens and bubbles; season to taste.*
- ✓ *Add polenta into the lined dish and spread out.*
- ✓ *Refrigerate for 45 minutes.*
- ✓ *Preheat the air fryer to 380 F.*
- ✓ *Slice the polenta into batons.*
- ✓ *Arrange the chips in the greased frying basket and sprinkle with thyme.*
- ✓ *AirFry for 14-16 minutes, turning once until the fries are crispy.*

nutritional value: Calories 500 Total Fat 40g Saturated fat 6g Cholesterol 15mg Sodium 750mg Carbohydrates 32g Net carbs 30g Sugar 1g Fiber 2g Protein 3g

988) Soppressata Pizza

Ingredients:

- *2 Servings)*
- *1 pizza crust*
- *½ tsp dried oregano*
- *½ cup passata*
- *½ cup mozzarella cheese, shredded*
- *4 oz soppressata, chopped*
- *4 basil leaves.*

Direction:Prep + Cook Time: 15 minutes

- ✓ *Preheat the air fryer to 370 F.*
- ✓ *Spread the passata over the pizza crust, sprinkle with oregano, mozzarella, and finish with soppressata.*
- ✓ *Bake in the fryer for 10 minutes.*
- ✓ *Top with basil leaves and serve.*

nutrition: Calorie 460 Fat 16g Sodium 1,440g Cholesterol 40mg Carbs 54 g Dietary Fiber 2g Sugar 6g Saturated 7g Protein 20g Calcium 40% Iron 8%

989) Air Fried Italian Calzone

Ingredients:

- *(4 Servings)*
- *1 pizza dough*
- *4 oz cheddar cheese, grated*
- *1 oz mozzarella cheese, grated*
- *1 oz bacon, diced*
- *2 cups cooked turkey, shredded*
- *1 egg, beaten*
- *4 tbsp tomato paste*
- *½ tsp dried basil*
- *½ tsp dried oregano*
- *Salt and black pepper to taste.*

Direction:Prep + Cook Time: 20 minutes

- ✓ *Preheat the air fryer to 350 F.*
- ✓ *Divide the pizza dough into 4 equal pieces, so you have the dough for 4 pizza crusts.*
- ✓ *Combine the tomato paste, basil, and oregano in a small bowl.*
- ✓ *Brush the mixture onto the crusts; make sure not to go all the way to avoid brushing near the edges of each crust.*
- ✓ *Scatter half of the turkey on top and season with salt and black pepper.*
- ✓ *Top with bacon, mozzarella, and cheddar cheeses.*
- ✓ *Brush the edges with the beaten egg.*
- ✓ *Fold the crusts and seal with a fork.*
- ✓ *Bake for 10-12 minutes until puffed and golden,*

turning it over halfway through cooking.

- ✓ *Serve warm*

nutritional value: Calories 348 Fat 12g Sat fat 3g Unsatfat 7g Protein 21g Carbohydrate 44g Fiber 5g Sugars 3g Added sugars 0g Sodium 710mg Calcium 21% DV Potassium 3% DV

990) Breakfast Banana Bread

Ingredients:

- (2 Servings)
- 1 cup flour
- ¼ tsp baking soda 1 tsp baking powder
- ⅓ cup sugar
- 2 bananas, mashed
- ¼ cup vegetable oil
- 1 egg, beaten
- 1 tsp vanilla extract
- ¾ cup walnuts, chopped
- ¼ tsp salt
- 2 tbsp peanut butter, softened
- 2 tbsp sour cream.

Direction:Prep + Cook Time: 35 minutes

- ✓ Preheat the air fryer to 350 F.
- ✓ Sift the flour into a large bowl and add salt, baking powder, and baking soda; stir to combine.
- ✓ In another bowl, combine bananas, vegetable oil, egg, peanut butter, vanilla, sugar, and sour cream; stir well.
- ✓ Mix both mixtures and fold in the walnuts.
- ✓ Pour the batter into a greased baking dish and place it in the fryer.
- ✓ Bake for 20-25 minutes until nice and golden.
- ✓ Serve chilled

nutrition: Calories 135 Total Fat 2.4g Saturated Fat 0.9g Unsaturated Fat 0.9g Cholesterol 1.7mg Sodium 166.9mg Total Carbohydrate 25.5g Dietary Fiber 3.4g Sugars 7.9g Protein 4.6 g

991) Prosciutto & Mozzarella Bruschetta

Ingredients:

- (2 Servings)
- ½ cup tomatoes, finely chopped
- 3 oz mozzarella cheese, grated
- 3 prosciutto slices, chopped
- 1 tbsp olive oil
- 1 tsp dried basil
- 6 small French bread slices

Direction:Prep + Cook Time: 7 minutes

- ✓ Preheat the air fryer to 350 F.
- ✓ Add in the bread slices and fry for 3 minutes to toast them.
- ✓ Remove and top the slices with tomatoes, prosciutto, and mozzarella cheese
- ✓ Sprinkle basil all over and drizzle with olive oil.
- ✓ Return to the fryer and AirFry for 1 more minute, just to heat through.
- ✓ Serve warm.

nutrition: Calories 150 Total Fat 10g Saturated fat 4.5g Cholesterol 25mg Carbohydrates 12g Sodium 400mg Net carbs 11g Sugar 6g Fiber 1g Protein 4g

992) Quick Feta Triangles

Ingredients:

- (3 Servings)
- 1 cup feta cheese
- 1 onion, chopped
- ½ tsp parsley dried 1 egg yolk
- 2 tbsp olive oil
- 3 sheets filo pastry.

Direction:Prep + Cook Time: 30 minutes

- ✓ Cut each of the filo sheets into 3 equal-sized strips.
- ✓ Brush the strips with some olive oil.
- ✓ In a bowl, mix onion, feta cheese, egg yolk, and parsley.
- ✓ Divide the mixture between the strips and fold each diagonally to make triangles.
- ✓ Arrange them in the greased frying basket and brush the tops with the remaining olive oil.
- ✓ Place in the fryer and Bake for 8 minutes at 360 F.
- ✓ Serve warm.

nutritional value: Cals 89 Fat3.60g Saturated Fat1.700g Carbohydrates11.70g Sugar0.30g Sodium116mg

993) Toasted Herb & Garlic Bagel

Ingredients:

- (1 Serving)
- 1 tbsp butter, softened
- ¼ tsp dried basil
- ¼ tsp dried parsley
- ¼ tsp garlic powder
- 1 tbsp Parmesan cheese, grated
- salt and black pepper to taste
- 1 bagel, halved.

Direction:(Prep + Cook Time: 10 minutes

- ✓ Preheat the air fryer to 370 degrees.
- ✓ Place the bagel halves in the frying basket and AirFry for 3 minutes. Mix butter, Parmesan

cheese, garlic, basil, and parsley in a bowl.

- ✓ *Season with salt and pepper.*
- ✓ *Spread the mixture onto the toasted bagel and return to the fryer to AirFry for 3 more minutes.*

nutritional value: Calories 130 Total Fat 4.5g Carbs 19g Fiber 0.5g Total Sugars 1g Protein 4g

994) Pumpkin & Sultanas' Bread

Ingredients:

- *(6 Servings)*
- *1 cup pumpkin, peeled and shredded*
- *1 cup flour*
- *1 tsp ground nutmeg*
- *½ tsp salt*
- *¼ tsp baking powder*
- *2 eggs*
- *½ cup sugar*
- *¼ cup milk*
- *2 tbsp butter, melted*
- *½ tsp vanilla extract*
- *2 tbsp sultanas, soaked*
- *1 tbsp honey*
- *1 tbsp canola oil.*

Direction:Prep + Cook Time: 30 minutes + cooling time

- ✓ *Preheat the air fryer to 350 F.*
- ✓ *Beat the eggs and add pumpkin, sugar, milk, canola oil, sultanas, and vanilla in a bowl.*
- ✓ *In a separate bowl, sift the flour and mix in nutmeg, salt, butter, and baking powder.*
- ✓ *Combine the 2 mixtures and stir until a thick cake mixture forms*
- ✓ *Spoon the batter into a greased baking dish and place it in the air fryer.*
- ✓ *Bake for 25 minutes until a toothpick inserted in the center comes out clean and dry.*
- ✓ *Remove to a wire rack to cool completely.*
- ✓ *Drizzle with honey and serve.*

nutritional value: Calories 86 Total Fat 2g Cholesterol 11mg Sodium 120mg Carbohydrates 15g Net carbs 14g Fiber 1g Protein 2g

995) Grilled Apple & Brie Sandwich

Ingredients:

- *(1 Serving)*
- *2 bread slices*
- *½ apple, thinly sliced*
- *2 tsp butter*
- *2 oz brie cheese, thinly sliced*

Direction:Prep + Cook Time: 10 minutes

- ✓ *Spread butter on the outside of the bread slices and top with apple slices.*
- ✓ *Place the brie slices on top of the apple and cover with the other slice of bread.*
- ✓ *Bake in the air fryer for 5 minutes at 350 F.*
- ✓ *When ready, remove and cut diagonally to serve.*

nutritional value: Calories 67 Total Fat 0g Sodium 133mg Carbohydrates 10g Net carbs 10g Sugar 0g Fiber 0g Protein 5g Calcium 2400mg Iron 0mg

996) Blueberry & Maple Toast

Ingredients:

- *(2 Servings)*
- *2 eggs, beaten*
- *4 bread slices*
- *1 tbsp maple syrup*
- *1 ½ cups corn flakes*
- *⅓ cup milk*
- *¼ tsp ground nutmeg*
- *1 cup fresh blueberries*

Direction:(Prep + Cook Time: 15 minutes

- ✓ *Preheat the air fryer to 390 F.*
- ✓ *In a bowl, mix the eggs, nutmeg, and milk.*
- ✓ *Dip the bread slices in the egg mixture, then thoroughly coat them in corn flakes*
- ✓ *AirFry them in the greased frying basket for 8 minutes, turning once halfway through cooking.*
- ✓ *Drizzle with maple syrup and top blueberries.*
- ✓ *Serve.*

nutritional value: Calories 200 Calories From Fat 20 Total Fat 2g Saturated Fat 0.5g Trans Fat 0g Cholesterol 0mg Sodium 250mg Total Carbohydrates 40g Dietary Fiber 2g Sugars 12g Protein 6g

997) Spicy Egg & Bacon Tortilla raps

Ingredients:

- *(3 Servings)*
- *3 flour tortillas*
- *2 eggs, scrambled*
- *3 slices bacon, cut into strips*
- *3 tbsp salsa*
- *3 tbsp cream cheese*
- *1 cup Pepper Jack cheese, grated.*

Direction:Prep + Cook Time: 15 minutes

- ✓ *Preheat the air fryer to 390 F.*
- ✓ *Spread cream cheese on the tortillas.*
- ✓ *Add the eggs and bacon and top with salsa.*
- ✓ *Scatter with grated Pepper Jack cheese and roll up tightly.*
- ✓ *Place in the frying basket and AirFry for 10 minutes or until golden.*
- ✓ *Cut in half and serve warm*

nutritional value: 195 calories; protein 11g; carbohydrates 18g; dietary fiber 1.3g; sugars 2g; fat 8.7g; saturated fat 2.9g; cholesterol 10.6mg; vitamin a iu 962.5IU; vitamin c 17mg; folate 7.6mcg; calcium 56.6mg; iron 2.3mg; magnesium 14.2mg; potassium 246mg; sodium 462mg.

998) Paprika Rarebit

Ingredients:

- *(2 Servings)*
- *4 toasted bread slices*
- *1 tsp smoked paprika*
- *2 eggs, beaten*
- *1 tsp Dijon mustard*
- *4 ½ oz cheddar cheese, grated*
- *salt and black pepper to taste.*

Direction:Prep + Cook Time: 15 minutes

- ✓ *Preheat the fryer to 360 F.*
- ✓ *In a bowl, combine the eggs, mustard, cheddar, and paprika.*
- ✓ *Season with salt and pepper.*
- ✓ *Spread the mixture on the bread slices and AirFry them for 10 minutes or until golden.*

nutritional value: Calories 19 Total Fat 0.9g Saturated Fat 0.1g Trans Fat 0g Cholesterol 0mg Total Carbs 3.7g Dietary Fiber 2.4g Total Sugars 0.7g Protein 1g

999) Mango Bread

Ingredients:

- *(6 Servings)*
- *½ cup butter, melted*
- *1 egg, lightly beaten*
- *½ cup brown sugar*
- *1 tsp vanilla extract*
- *3 ripe mangoes, mashed*
- *1 ½ cups flour*
- *1 tsp baking powder*
- *½ tsp grated nutmeg*
- *½ tsp ground cinnamon*

Direction:Prep + Cook Time: 30 minutes

- ✓ *Line a loaf tin with baking paper.*
- ✓ *In a bowl, whisk melted butter, egg, sugar, vanilla, and mangoes.*
- ✓ *Sift in flour, baking powder, nutmeg, and ground cinnamon and stir without overmixing.*
- ✓ *Pour the batter into the tin and place it in the frying basket.*
- ✓ *Bake for 18-20 minutes at 330 F.*
- ✓ *Let cool before slicing.*
- ✓ *Serve.*

nutritional value: Calories 273 Total Fat 13g Cholesterol 47mg Sodium 336mg Carbohydrates 37g Net carbs 35.6g Fiber 1.4g Glucose 23.1g Protein 3g Calcium 20mg Iron 0.2mg

1000) Crustless Mediterranean Feta Quiche

Ingredients:

- *(2 Servings)*
- *4 eggs*
- *½ cup tomatoes, chopped*
- *1 cup feta cheese, crumbled*
- *½ tbsp fresh basil, chopped*
- *½ tbsp fresh oregano, chopped*
- *¼ cup Kalamata olives, sliced*
- *¼ cup onions, chopped*
- *½ cup milk*
- *Salt and black pepper to taste.*

Direction:(Prep + Cook Time: 40 minutes

- ✓ *Preheat the air fryer to 340 F.*
- ✓ *Beat the eggs with milk, salt, and pepper in a bowl.*
- ✓ *Stir in all the remaining ingredients.*
- ✓ *Pour the egg mixture into a greased baking pan that fits in your air fryer and Bake for 30 minutes or until lightly golden.*
- ✓ *Serve warm with a green salad if desired.*

nutritional value: Calories 224 Total Fat13.03g Saturated Fat6.318g Trans Fat0g Polyunsaturated Fat0.692g Monounsaturated Fat1.908g Cholesterol241mg Sodium934mg Total Carbohydrate9g Dietary Fiber3.4g Sugars3.14g Protein16.5g Calcium39mg Iron1.21mg

1001) Crustless Broccoli & Mushroom Pie

Ingredients:

- *(4 Servings)*
- *4 eggs, beaten*
- *1 cup mushrooms, sliced*
- *1 cup broccoli florets, steamed*
- *½ cup cheddar cheese, shredded*
- *½ cup mozzarella cheese, shredded*
- *2 tbsp olive oil*
- *¼ tsp ground allspice*
- *Salt and black pepper to taste.*

Direction:Prep + Cook Time: 25 minutes

- ✓ *Preheat the air fryer to 360 F.*
- ✓ *Warm the olive oil in a pan over medium heat.*
- ✓ *Sauté the mushrooms for 3-4 minutes or until soft.*
- ✓ *Stir the broccoli for 1 minute; set aside.*
- ✓ *Place the eggs, cheddar cheese, mozzarella cheese, allspice, salt, and pepper in a medium*

bowl and whisk well. Pour the mushrooms' mixture into the egg mixture and gently fold it in.

- ✓ *Transfer the batter to a greased baking pan and into the fryer.*
- ✓ *AirFry for 5 minutes, then stir the mixture and cook until the eggs are done about 3-5 more minutes.*
- ✓ *Cut into wedges and serve.*

Nutritional value: Calories 158.4 Total Fat 8.4 g Saturated Fat 2.5 g Polyunsaturated Fat 1.1 g Monounsaturated Fat 3.4 g Cholesterol 105.2 mg Sodium 442.5 mg Potassium 248.3 mg Total Carbohydrate 14.6 g Dietary Fiber 2.0 g Sugars 3.3 g Protein 7.0 g Calcium 7.2 %

1002) Flaxseed Porridge

Ingredients:

- (4 Servings)
- 1 cup steel-cut oats
- 1 tbsp flax seeds
- 1 tbsp peanut butter
- 1 tbsp butter
- 1 cup milk
- 2 tbsp honey.

Direction:Prep + Cook Time: 15 minutes

- ✓ *Preheat the air fryer to 350 F.*
- ✓ *Combine all ingredients in an ovenproof bowl.*
- ✓ *Place the bowl in the air fryer and Bake for 10 minutes.*
- ✓ *Let cool for a few minutes before serving. Enjoy!*

nutritional value: Calories 229.6 Total Fat 14.1 g Saturated Fat 0.0 g Polyunsaturated Fat 10.9 g Monounsaturated Fat 2.7 g Cholesterol 0.0 mg Sodium133.4 mg Potassium 24.7 mg Total Carbohydrate 11.1 g Dietary Fiber 11.0 g Sugars0.0 g Protein16.3 g

1003) Zucchini Muffins

Ingredients:

- (4 Servings)
- 1 ½ cups flour
- 1 tsp cinnamon
- 3 eggs
- 2 tsp baking powder
- ½ tsp sugar 1 cup milk
- 2 tbsp butter, melted
- 1 tbsp yogurt
- 1 zucchini, shredded
- A pinch of salt
- 2 tbsp cream cheese

Direction:(Prep + Cook Time: 25 minutes

- ✓ *Preheat the air fryer to 350 F.*
- ✓ *Whisk the eggs with sugar, salt, cinnamon, cream cheese, flour, and baking powder in a bowl.*
- ✓ *In another bowl, combine the remaining ingredients, except for the zucchini.*
- ✓ *Gently combine the dry and liquid mixtures. Stir in the zucchini.*
- ✓ *Grease 4 muffin tins with oil and pour the batter inside them.*
- ✓ *Place them in the air fryer and Bake for 18-20 minutes until golden.*
- ✓ *Serve.*

nutritional value: Calories 188 Total Fat 7.8g Saturated Fat 3.2g Trans Fat 0.2g Cholesterol 25mg Sodium 154mg Potassium 167mg Total Carbohydrates 28g Dietary Fiber 1.3g Sugars 15ggrams Protein 3.1g

1004) Banana & Hazelnut Muffins

Ingredients:

- (6 Servings)
- ¼ cup butter, melted
- ¼ cup honey
- 1 egg, lightly beaten
- 2 ripe bananas, mashed
- ½ tsp vanilla extract 1 cup flour
- ½ tsp baking powder
- ½ tsp ground cinnamon
- ¼ cup hazelnuts, chopped
- ¼ cup dark chocolate chips.

Direction:Prep + Cook Time: 30 minutes

- ✓ *Spray a muffin tin that fits in your air fryer with cooking spray.*
- ✓ *In a bowl, whisk butter, honey, egg, bananas, and vanilla until well combined.*
- ✓ *Sift in flour, baking powder, and cinnamon without overmixing.*
- ✓ *Stir in the hazelnuts and chocolate chips.*
- ✓ *Pour the batter into the muffin holes and place it in the air fryer.*
- ✓ *Bake for 20 minutes at 350 F, checking them around the 15-minute mark.*
- ✓ *Serve chilled.*

nutritional value: Calories 589 Total Fat 29g Saturated Fat 12g Trans Fat 0.7g Cholesterol 91mg Sodium 480mg Potassium 328mg Total Carbohydrates 79g Dietary Fiber 3.9g Sugars 45g Protein 7.2g

1005) Italian Sausage Patties

Ingredients:

- (4 Servings)
- 1 lb ground Italian sausage
- ¼ cup breadcrumbs

- 1 tsp red pepper flakes
- salt and black pepper to taste
- ¼ tsp garlic powder
- 1 egg, beaten

Direction:Prep + Cook Time: 20 minutes

- ✓ Preheat the air fryer to 350 F.
- ✓ Mix all the ingredients thoroughly in a big tub.
- ✓ Make balls out of the mixture using your hands.
- ✓ Flatten the balls to make the patties. Arrange them on the greased frying basket.
- ✓ Place them in the fryer and AirFry for 15 minutes, flipping once halfway through.
- ✓ Serve.

nutritional value: Calories 210 Total Fat 15g Saturated fat 7g Cholesterol 55mg Sodium 650mg Carbohydrates 1g Net carbs 1g Fiber 0g Glucose 1g Protein 15g Calcium 0mg

1006) Kiwi Muffins with Pecans

Ingredients:

- (4 Servings)
- 1 cup flour
- 1 kiwi, mashed
- ¼ cup powdered sugar
- 1 tbsp milk
- 1 tbsp pecans, chopped
- ½ tsp baking powder
- ¼ cup oats
- ¼ cup butter, room temperature

Direction:Prep + Cook Time: 25 minutes

- ✓ Preheat the air fryer to 350 F.
- ✓ Place the sugar, pecans, kiwi, and butter in a bowl and mix well.
- ✓ In another bowl, mix the flour, baking powder, and oats and stir well
- ✓ Combine the two mixtures and stir in the milk.
- ✓ Pour the batter into a greased muffin tin that fits in the fryer and Bake for 15 minutes.
- ✓ Remove to a wire rack and leave to cool for a few minutes before removing the muffin from the tin.
- ✓ Enjoy!

nutritional value: Calories 348.46 Kcal Calories from fat 137.26 Kcal Total Fat 15.25g Cholesterol 21.07mg Sodium 1075.09mg Potassium 380.53mg Total Carbs 47.72g Sugars 8.17g Dietary Fiber 4.82g Protein 6.57g Iron 2.6mg Calcium 239.3mg

1007) Orange Creamy Cupcakes

Ingredients:

- (4 Servings)
- Lemon Frosting:
- 1 cup plain yogurt
- 2 tbsp sugar
- 1 orange, juiced
- 1 tbsp orange zest
- 7 oz cream cheese Cake.
- 1 tsp dark rum
- 2/3 cup flour
- ¼ tsp salt
- ½ cup sugar
- 1 tsp vanilla extract
- 2 eggs
- ½ cup butter softened.

Direction:(Prep + Cook Time: 25 minutes

- ✓ In a bowl, add yogurt and cream cheese and mix until smooth.
- ✓ Add in orange juice and zest and whisk well.
- ✓ Gradually add the sugar and stir until smooth.
- ✓ Make sure the frosting is not runny.
- ✓ Set aside.
- ✓ Preheat the air fryer to 360 F. In a bowl, put the flour, rum, softened butter, eggs, vanilla extract, sugar, and salt for the cake.
- ✓ Beat with a whisk until smooth.
- ✓ Spoon the batter into 4 cupcake cases, ¾ way up. Place them in the air fryer and Bake for 12 minutes or until an inserted toothpick comes out clean.
- ✓ Once ready, remove and let cool.
- ✓ Design the cupcakes with the frosting and serve.

nutritional value: Calories 215 Total Fat 8g Saturated Fat 2g Trans Fat 2g Cholesterol 27mg Sodium 172mg Total Carbohydrates 35g Dietary Fiber 0g Sugars 21g Protein 2g

1008) Coconut & Oat Cookies

Ingredients:

- (4 Servings)
- ¾ cup flour
- 4 tbsp sugar
- ½ cup oats
- 1 egg
- ¼ cup coconut flakes Filling.
- 1 tbsp white chocolate, melted
- 4 tbsp butter
- ½ cup powdered sugar
- 1 tsp vanilla extract

Direction:(Prep + Cook Time: 30 minutes

- ✓ Beat egg, sugar, oats, and coconut flakes in a bowl with an electric hand mixer.
- ✓ Fold in the flour.

- ✓ *Drop spoonfuls of the batter into a greased baking sheet and Bake in the air fryer at 350 F for 18 minutes.*
- ✓ *Let cool to firm up and to resemble cookies.*
- ✓ *Cook in batches if needed*
- ✓ *Meanwhile, prepare the filling by beating all filling ingredients together.*
- ✓ *Spread the filling on half of the cookies.*
- ✓ *Top with the other halves to make cookie sandwiches like oreo.*
- ✓ *Serve and enjoy!*

nutritional value: Cals 45 Fat1.70g Saturated Fat0.700g Carbohydrates6.00g Sugar1.20g Fibre0.9g Protein0.90g

1009) Cherry & Almond Scones

Ingredients:

- *(4 Servings)*
- *2 cups flour + some more*
- *⅓ cup sugar*
- *2 tsp baking powder*
- *½ cup sliced almonds*
- *¾ cup dried cherries, chopped*
- *¼ cup cold butter, cut into cubes*
- *½ cup milk 1 egg.*

Direction:(Prep + Cook Time: 25 minutes

- ✓ *Preheat the air fryer to 390 F.*
- ✓ *Line the frying basket with baking paper.*
- ✓ *Mix together flour, sugar, baking powder, sliced almonds, and dried cherries in a bowl.*
- ✓ *Rub the butter with hands into the dry ingredients to form a sandy, crumbly texture.*
- ✓ *Whisk together egg and milk.*
- ✓ *Pour into the dry ingredients and stir to combine*
- ✓ *Sprinkle a working board with flour, lay the dough onto the board, and give it a few kneads.*
- ✓ *Shape into a rectangle and cut into 9 squares.*
- ✓ *Arrange the squares in the frying basket and AirFry for 12-14 minutes at 390 F.*
- ✓ *Work in batches if needed.*
- ✓ *Serve.*

nutritional value: Calories 460.2 Total Fat 26.5 g Saturated Fat 15.5 g Polyunsaturated Fat 0.8 g Monounsaturated Fat 5.6 g Cholesterol 66.7 mg Sodium 320.4 mg mg Total Carbs 50.2 g Dietary Fiber 2.5 g Sugars 25.8 g Protein 4.8 g

1010) Blueberry Oat Bars

Ingredients:

- *(12 bars)*
- *2 cups rolled oats*
- *¼ cup ground almonds*
- *¼ cup sugar*
- *1 tsp baking powder*
- *½ tsp ground cinnamon*
- *2 eggs, lightly beaten*
- *½ cup canola oil*
- *½ cup milk*
- *1 tsp vanilla extract*
- *2 cups blueberries*

Direction:Prep + Cook Time: 20 minutes

- ✓ *Spray a baking pan that fits in your air fryer with oil.*
- ✓ *Add oats, almonds, sugar, baking powder, and cinnamon; stir well.*
- ✓ *In another bowl, whisk eggs, canola oil, milk, and vanilla.*
- ✓ *Stir the wet ingredients into the oat mixture. Fold in the blueberries. Pour the mixture into the pan and place it inside the fryer. Bake for 10 minutes.*
- ✓ *Remove to a wire rack to cool and then cut into 12 bars.*

nutritional value: Calories 370 Total Fat 14g Saturated fat 7g Cholesterol 30mg Carbohydrates 47g Net carbs 42g Sugar 19g Fiber 5g Protein 6g

1011) Sweet Bread Pudding with Raisins

Ingredients:

- *(4 Servings)*
- *8 bread slices, cubed*
- *½ cup buttermilk*
- *¼ cup honey*
- *1 cup milk*
- *2 eggs*
- *½ tsp vanilla extract*
- *2 tbsp butter, softened*
- *¼ cup sugar*
- *4 tbsp raisins*
- *2 tbsp chopped hazelnuts*
- *Ground cinnamon for garnish*

Direction:Prep + Cook Time: 45 minutes

- ✓ *Preheat the air fryer to 350 F.*
- ✓ *Beat the eggs and buttermilk, honey, milk, vanilla, sugar, and butter in a bowl.*
- ✓ *Stir in raisins and hazelnuts, then add in the bread to soak, about 10 minutes. Transfer to a greased tin and bake the pudding in the air fryer for 25 minutes.*
- ✓ *Dust with cinnamon.*
- ✓ *Serve.*

nutritional value: Calories 360 Total Fat 12g

Saturated fat 9g Cholesterol 150mg Sodium 140mg Carbs 52g Net carbs 51g Fiber 1g Protein 26g

1012) Simple Crispy Bacon

Ingredients:

- *4 Servings)*
- *8 oz bacon, sliced*

Direction:(Prep + Cook Time: 15 minutes

- ✓ *Preheat the fryer to 390 F.*
- ✓ *Place the bacon slices in the frying basket*
- ✓ *AirFry for 10 minutes, flipping once.*

Nutritional value: 120 calories, 9 grams fat, 3.8 grams saturated fat, 30 mg cholesterol, 7.5 grams protein, and 435 mg sodium.

1013) Crispy Croutons

Ingredients:

- *(4 Servings)*
- *2 cups bread cubes*
- *2 tbsp butter, melted*
- *1 tsp dried parsley Garlic*
- *salt and black pepper to taste*

Direction:Prep + Cook Time: 20 minutes

- ✓ *Mix the cubed bread with butter, parsley, garlic salt, and black pepper until well coated.*
- ✓ *Place them in the frying basket and AirFry for 6-8 minutes at 380 F, shaking once until golden brown.*

nutritional value: Calories 32.3 Total Fat 2.5 g Saturated Fat 1.3 g Polyunsaturated Fat 0.1 g Monounsaturated Fat 0.6 g Cholesterol 5.8 mg Sodium 52.9 mg Potassium 3.9 mg Total Carbohydrate 2.3 g Dietary Fiber 1.0 g Sugars 0.2 g Protein 1.2 g

1014) Avocado Tempura

Ingredients:

- *(4 Servings)*
- *½ cup breadcrumbs*
- *½ tsp salt*
- *1 avocado, pitted, peeled, and sliced*
- *½ cup soda water (club soda)*

Direction:(Prep + Cook Time: 15 minutes

- ✓ *Preheat the air fryer to 360 F.*
- ✓ *In a bowl, add the breadcrumbs and salt and mix well.*
- ✓ *Sprinkle the avocado with soda water and then coat in the breadcrumbs.*
- ✓ *Arrange the slices in the grease frying basket in one layer and AirFry for 8-10 minutes, shaking once or twice.*
- ✓ *Serve warm.*

nutritional value: Calories540 Total Fat 43g Saturated Fat 6g Trans Fat 0g Cholesterol 45mg Sodium 25mg Total Carbohydrates 33g Dietary Fiber 8g Total Sugars < 1g includes 0g Added Sugars Protein 7g Iron 1mg Potassium 540mg

1015) Baked Avocado with Eggs & Cilantro

Ingredients:

- *(1 Serving)*
- *1 ripe avocado, pitted and halved*
- *2 eggs*
- *Salt and black pepper, to taste*
- *1 tsp fresh cilantro, chopped*

Direction:(Prep + Cook Time: 20 minutes

- ✓ *Preheat the air fryer to 400 F.*
- ✓ *Crack one egg into each avocado half and place it in the air fryer.*
- ✓ *Bake for 8-12 minutes until the eggs are cooked through.*
- ✓ *Let cool slightly and season to taste.*
- ✓ *Top with freshly chopped cilantro and serve warm.*

nutritional value: Calories270 Total Fat 21g Saturated Fat 4.5g Trans Fat 0g Cholesterol 190mg Sodium 190mg Total Carbohydrates 12g Dietary Fiber 9g Total Sugars 4g Includes 0g Added Sugars Calcium 44mg

1016) Roasted Asparagus with Serrano Ham

Ingredients:

- *4 Servings)*
- *12 spears asparagus, trimmed*
- *12 Serrano ham slices*
- *¼ cup Parmesan cheese, grated*
- *Salt and black pepper to taste*

Direction:Prep + Cook Time: 20 minutes

- ✓ *Preheat the air fryer to 350 F.*
- ✓ *Season asparagus with salt and black pepper.*
- ✓ *Wrap each ham slice around each asparagus spear from one end to the other end to cover completely.*
- ✓ *Arrange them on the greased frying basket and AirFry for 10 minutes, shaking once or twice throughout cooking.*
- ✓ *When ready, scatter with Parmesan cheese and serve immediately.*

nutritional value: Calories: 225 Total Fat: 16g Saturated Fat: 2g Polyunsaturated Fat: 2g Monounsaturated Fat: 11g Trans Fat: 0g Cholesterol: 8mg Sodium: 403mg Total Carbohydrates: 17g Dietary Fiber: 3g Sugar: 11g Protein: 7g Calcium: 58mg Iron: 2mg Potassium: 418mg

1017) Hearty Banana Pastry

Ingredients:

- 2 Servings)
- 3 bananas, sliced
- 3 tbsp honey
- 2 puff pastry sheets, cut into thin strips
- 1 cup fresh berries to serve

Direction:Prep + Cook Time: 20 minutes

- ✓ Preheat the air fryer to 340 F.
- ✓ Place banana slices into a greased baking dish.
- ✓ Cover with pastry strips and drizzle with honey
- ✓ Bake inside the air fryer for 12 minutes until golden.
- ✓ Serve with berries.

nutritional value:Calories 83.7 Total Fat 0.6 g Saturated Fat 0.2 g Polyunsaturated Fat 0.1 g Monounsaturated Fat 0.2 g Cholesterol 0.1 mg Sodium 109.6 mg Potassium 109.8 mg Total Carbohydrate 21.5 g Dietary Fiber 0.7 g Sugars9.2 g Protein 0.5 g Calcium 2.6 % Copper 1.8 % Folate 1.0 % Iron 1.0 % Magnesium 2.0 % Manganese 2.6 % Niacin 0.6 %

1018) Air-Fried Hot Wings

Ingredients:

- (4 Servings)
- ¼ tsp celery salt
- ¼ tsp bay leaf powder
- Black pepper to taste
- ½ tsp cayenne pepper
- ¼ tsp allspice
- 1 tbsp thyme leaves
- 1 lb chicken wings

Direction:(Prep + Cook Time: 25 minutes

- ✓ Preheat the air fryer to 360 F.
- ✓ Mix celery salt, bay leaf powder, black pepper, paprika, thyme, cayenne pepper, and allspice in a bowl.
- ✓ Coat the wings in the mixture.
- ✓ Arrange the wings on the greased frying basket and AirFry for 10 minutes.
- ✓ Flip and cook for 6-8 more minutes until crispy on the outside.

nutritional value: Calories 226.7 Total Fat 10.7 g Saturated Fat 3.7 g Polyunsaturated Fat 0.4 g Monounsaturated Fat 0.6 g Cholesterol 153.7 mg Sodium 268.2 mg Potassium 76.8 mg Total Carbohydrate 14.2 g Dietary Fiber 0.6 g Sugars 4.6 g Protein 19.2 g Calcium 1.4 %

1019) Crispy Alfredo Chicken Wings

Ingredients:

- (4 Servings)
- 1 ½ lb chicken wings, pat-dried
- Salt to taste
- ½ cup Alfredo sauce

Direction: (Prep + Cook Time: 25 minutes

- ✓ Preheat the air fryer to 370 F.
- ✓ Season the wings with salt.
- ✓ Arrange them in the greased frying basket, without overlapping, and AirFry for 12 minutes until no longer pink in the center
- ✓ Flip them, increase the heat to 390 F, and cook for 5 more minutes.
- ✓ Work in batches if needed.
- ✓ Plate the wings and drizzle with Alfredo sauce to serve.

nutritional value: Calories: 225 Net Carbs: 1g Carbs: 1g Fat: 17g Protein: 16g Fiber: 0g

1020) Crunchy Ranch Chicken Wings

Ingredients:

- (4 Servings)
- 2 lb chicken wings
- 2 tbsp olive oil
- 1 tbsp ranch
- seasoning mix
- Salt to taste

Direction:(Prep + Cook Time: 25 minutes

- ✓ Preheat the air fryer to 390 F.
- ✓ Put the ranch seasoning, olive oil, and salt in a large, resealable bag and mix well.
- ✓ Add the wings, seal the bag, and toss until the wings are thoroughly coated.
- ✓ Put the wings in the greased frying basket in one layer, spritz them with a nonstick cooking spray, and AirFry for 7 minutes.
- ✓ Turn them over and fry for 5-8 more minutes until the wings are light brown and crispy.
- ✓ Test for doneness with a meat thermometer.
- ✓ Serve with your favorite dipping sauce and enjoy!

nutritional value: Calories 774.37 Kcal Calories from fat 513.56 Kcal Total Fat 57.06g Cholesterol 245.06mg Sodium 2125.29mg Potassium 401.21mg Total Carbs 23.87g Sugars 5.7g Dietary Fiber 3.34g Protein 40.89g Iron 4.8mg Calcium 221.7mg

1021) Korean Chili Chicken Wings

Ingredients:

- (4 Servings)
- 8 chicken wings
- Salt to taste
- 1 tsp sesame oil
- Juice from half lemon
- ¼ cup sriracha chili sauce

- *1-inch piece ginger, grated*
- *1 tsp garlic powder*
- *1 tsp sesame seeds*

Direction:(Prep + Cook Time: 20 minutes

- ✓ *Preheat the air fryer to 370 F.*
- ✓ *Grease the air frying basket with cooking spray. Mix salt, ginger, garlic, lemon juice, sesame oil, and chili sauce in a bowl.*
- ✓ *Coat the wings in the mixture.*
- ✓ *Transfer the wings to the basket and AirFry for 15 minutes, flipping once.*
- ✓ *Sprinkle with sesame seeds and serve.*

nutritional value: Cal 143 Total Fat 8.3g Saturated Fat 1.1g Cholesterol 38mg Potassium 144mg Total Carbohydrates 8.8g Dietary Fiber 0.4g Protein 7.7g

1022) Teriyaki Chicken Wings

Ingredients:

- *(4 Servings)*
- *1 lb chicken wings*
- *1 cup soy sauce.*
- *½ cup brown sugar*
- *½ cup apple cider vinegar*
- *2 tbsp fresh ginger,*
- *minced*
- *1 garlic clove,*
- *minced*
- *Black pepper to taste*
- *2 tbsp cornstarch*
- *2 tbsp cold water*
- *1 tsp sesame seeds*

Direction:Prep + Cook Time: 20 minutes+ marinating time)

- ✓ *In a bowl, add the chicken wings and cover with half a cup of soy sauce.*
- ✓ *Refrigerate for 20 minutes.*
- ✓ *Drain and pat dry.*
- ✓ *Arrange them on the greased frying basket and AirFry for 14 minutes at 380 F, turning once halfway through cooking.*
- ✓ *In a skillet over medium heat, stir the sugar, remaining soy sauce, vinegar, ginger, garlic, and black pepper, for 4 minutes.*
- ✓ *Dissolve 2 tbsp of cornstarch in cold water and stir in the sauce until it thickens, about 2 minutes.*
- ✓ *Pour the sauce over the wings and sprinkle with sesame seeds.*
- ✓ *Serve hot.*

Nutritional value: Calories 699 Total Fat 53.4g Sat. Fat 10.5g Trans Fat 0g Cholesterol 150.1mg Sodium 1701mg Tot. Carb. 14.8g Dietary Fiber 0g Sugars 6.7g Protein 44.1g

1023) Chicken Wings with Gorgonzola Dip

Ingredients:

- *(4 Servings)*
- *8 chicken wings*
- *1 tsp cayenne pepper*
- *Salt to taste*
- *2 tbsp olive oil*
- *1 tsp red chili flakes*
- *1 cup heavy cream*
- *3 oz gorgonzola cheese, crumbled*
- *½ lemon, juiced*
- *½ tsp garlic powder*

Direction:(Prep + Cook Time: 30 minutes

- ✓ *Preheat the air fryer to 380 F.*
- ✓ *Coat the wings with cayenne pepper, salt, and olive oil.*
- ✓ *Place in the fryer and AirFry for 16 minutes until crispy and golden brown, flipping once.*
- ✓ *Mix heavy cream, gorgonzola cheese, chili flakes, lemon juice, and garlic powder in a bowl.*
- ✓ *Serve the wings with the cheese dip.*

nutritional value: Calories 78 Total Fat 6.7g Saturated Fat 1.4g Trans Fat 0g Cholesterol 17mg Sodium 43mg Total Carbs 0g Dietary Fiber 0g Total Sugars 0g Protein 4g Calcium 10mg Iron 0.2mg

1024) Piri Piri Chicken Wings

Ingredients:

- *2 Servings)*
- *8 chicken wings*
- *Salt and black pepper to taste*
- *1 tsp smoked paprika*
- *1 tbsp lemon juice*
- *½ tsp ground ginger*
- *½ tsp red chili powder*
- *1 tsp ground cumin*
- *1 cup mayonnaise mixed with*

Direction:Prep + Cook Time: 25 minutes

- ✓ *Preheat the air fryer to 380 F.*
- ✓ *In a bowl, mix paprika, ginger, chili powder, cumin, salt, and pepper.*
- ✓ *Add the chicken wings and toss to coat.*
- ✓ *Place in the greased frying basket and AirFry for 16-18 minutes, flipping once halfway through.*
- ✓ *Let cool for a few minutes. Serve with lemon mayonnaise.*

nutritional value: Calories 598 Total Fat 35.4g Saturated fat 10.4g Sodium 0mg Carbohydrates 0g Net carbs 0g Fiber 0g Protein 69.8g Calcium 0mg Iron 0mg

1025) Air-Fried Chicken Thighs

Ingredients:

- 4 Servings)
- 1 ½ lb chicken thighs
- 2 eggs, lightly beaten
- 1 cup seasoned breadcrumbs
- ½ tsp oregano
- Salt and black pepper to taste

Direction:(Prep + Cook Time: 20 minutes

- ✓ Preheat the air fryer to 390 F.
- ✓ Season the thighs with oregano, salt, and black pepper.
- ✓ In a bowl, add the beaten eggs.
- ✓ In a separate bowl, add the breadcrumbs
- ✓ Dip the thighs in the egg wash. Then roll them in the breadcrumbs and press firmly so the breadcrumbs stick well.
- ✓ Spray the thighs with cooking spray and arrange them in the frying basket in a single layer, skin-side up.
- ✓ AirFry for 12 minutes, turn the thighs over and cook for 6-8 more minutes until crispy.
- ✓ Serve and enjoy!

nutritional value: Calories 243 Total Fat 16g Saturated Fat5g Trans Fat0.0g Polyunsaturated Fat3.7 gb Monounsaturated Fat7.2g Cholesterol 145mg Sodium 396mg Total Carbohydrate 0.2g Dietary Fiber0g Sugars0.0g Protein 27g Calcium1% Iron7%

1026) Mustard-Honey Chicken Thighs

Ingredients:

- 4 Servings)
- 1 lb chicken thighs
- Salt and garlic powder to taste
- 2 tbsp olive oil
- 1 tsp yellow mustard
- 1 tsp honey
- ¼ cup mayo mixed with
- 2 tbsp hot sauce

Direction:Prep + Cook Time: 30 minutes + marinating time)

- ✓ Preheat the air fryer to 360 F.
- ✓ In a bowl, whisk the olive oil, honey, mustard, salt, and garlic powder.
- ✓ Add the thighs and stir to coat.
- ✓ Marinate for 10 minutes.
- ✓ Transfer the thighs to the greased frying basket, skin side down, and insert in the air fryer.
- ✓ AirFry for 18-20 minutes, flipping once until golden and crispy.
- ✓ Serve immediately with the hot mayo sauce. Enjoy!

nutritional value: Calories 163 Total Fat 2.6g Saturated Fat 0.6g Trans Fat 0g Cholesterol 49mg Sodium 334mg Potassium 187mg Total Carbohydrates 17g Dietary Fiber 0.7g Sugars 16g Protein 19g Calcium 2% Iron 5%

1027) Crispy Chicken Nuggets

Ingredients:

- (4 Servings)
- 1 lb chicken breasts, cut into large cubes
- Salt and black pepper to taste
- 2 tbsp olive oil
- 5 tbsp plain breadcrumbs
- 2 tbsp panko breadcrumbs
- 2 tbsp grated Parmesan cheese

Direction:Prep + Cook Time: 25 minutes)

- ✓ Preheat the air fryer to 380 F.
- ✓ Season the chicken with black pepper and salt.
- ✓ In a bowl, mix the breadcrumbs and Parmesan cheese.
- ✓ Coat the chicken pieces with olive oil. Then dip into the breadcrumb mixture, shake off the excess, and place in the greased frying basket.
- ✓ Lightly spray the nuggets with cooking spray and AirFry for 13-15 minutes, flipping once.
- ✓ Serve warm

nutritional value: Calories 187.5 Total Fat 2.6 g Saturated Fat 0.6 g Polyunsaturated Fat 1.0 g Monounsaturated Fat 0.7 g Cholesterol 66.0 mg Sodium 321.8 mg Potassium 307.0 mg Total Carbohydrate 12.6 g Dietary Fiber 0.4 g Sugars 1.6 g Protein 27.3 g Calcium 1.4 %

1028) Paprika Chicken Fingers

Ingredients:

- 4 Servings)
- 2 chicken breasts, cut into chunks
- 1 tsp paprika
- 2 tbsp milk
- 2 eggs
- 1 tsp garlic powder
- Salt and black pepper to taste
- 1 cup flour
- 2 cups breadcrumbs

Direction:Prep + Cook Time: 20 minutes + cooling time

- ✓ Preheat the air fryer to 370 F.
- ✓ In a bowl, mix paprika, garlic powder, salt, pepper, flour, and breadcrumbs.
- ✓ In another bowl, beat eggs with milk.
- ✓ Dip the chicken in the egg mixture, then roll in the crumbs.
- ✓ Place in the frying basket and spray with cooking spray.

✓ AirFry for 14-16 minutes, flipping once. Yummy!
nutritional value: Calories 650 Total Fat 49g Saturated Fat 10g Trans Fat 0g Cholesterol 125mg Sodium 1350mg Total Carbohydrate 14g Total Carbohydrate 14g Dietary Fiber 5g Total Sugars 5g Includes 0g Added Sugars Protein 40g Calcium 201mg Iron 2mg Potassium 609mg

1029) Corn-Crusted Chicken Tenders

Ingredients:

- 4 Servings)
- 2 chicken breasts, cut into strips
- Salt and black pepper to taste
- 2 eggs
- 1 cup ground cornmeal

Direction:Prep + Cook Time: 25 minutes

✓ Preheat the air fryer to 390 F.
✓ In a bowl, mix cornmeal, salt, and black pepper.
✓ In another bowl, beat the eggs; season with salt and pepper.
✓ Dip the chicken in the eggs and then coat in the cornmeal.
✓ Spray the strips with cooking spray and place them in the frying basket in a single layer.
✓ AirFry for 6 minutes, slide the basket out and flip the sticks.
✓ Cook for 6-8 more minutes until golden brown.
✓ Serve hot.

nutritional value: Calories 368 Total Fat 15g Saturated Fat 5.9g Trans Fat 0.2g Cholesterol 99mg Sodium 441mg Potassium 268mg Total Carbohydrates 34g Dietary Fiber 1.3g Sugars 2.4g Protein 24g Calcium 6% Iron 49%

1030) Chicken & Oat Croquettes

Ingredients:

- (4 Servings)
- 1 lb ground chicken
- 2 eggs
- Salt and black pepper to taste
- 1 cup oats, crumbled
- ½ tsp garlic powder
- 1 tsp dried parsley

Direction:Prep + Cook Time: 20 minutes

✓ Preheat the air fryer to 360 F.
✓ Mix the chicken with garlic, parsley, salt, and pepper.
✓ In a bowl, beat the eggs with a pinch of salt.
✓ In a third bowl, add the oats.
✓ Form croquettes out of the chicken mixture.
✓ Dip in the eggs and coat in the oats.
✓ AirFry them in the greased frying basket for 10 minutes, shaking once.
✓

nutritional value: Calories 173.6 Total Fat 4.4 g Saturated Fat 1.7 g Polyunsaturated Fat 0.5 g Monounsaturated Fat 0.6 g Cholesterol 89.1 mg Sodium 193.4 mg Potassium 300.8 mg Total Carbohydrate 9.2 g Dietary Fiber 0.6 g Sugars 1.7 g Protein 23.8 g

1031) Crunchy Chicken Egg Rolls

Ingredients:

- (4 Servings)
- 2 tsp olive oil
- 2 garlic cloves, minced
- ¼ cup soy sauce
- 1 tsp grated fresh ginger
- 1 lb ground chicken
- 2 cups white cabbage, shredded
- 1 onion, chopped
- 1 egg, beaten
- 8 egg roll wrappers

Direction:Prep + Cook Time: 30 minutes

✓ Heat olive oil in a pan over medium heat and add garlic, onion, ginger, and ground chicken.
✓ Sauté for 5 minutes until the chicken is no longer pink.
✓ Pour in the soy sauce and shredded cabbage and stir-fry for another 5-6 minutes until the cabbage is tender.
✓ Remove from the heat and let cool slightly.
✓ Fill each egg wrapper with the mixture, arranging it just below the center of the wrappers
✓ Fold in both sides and roll up tightly.
✓ Use the beaten egg to seal the edges.
✓ Brush the tops with the remaining beaten egg.
✓ Place the rolls in the greased frying basket, spray them with cooking spray, and AirFry for 12-14 minutes at 370 F until golden, turning once halfway through.
✓ Let cool slightly and serve.

nutritional value: Calories 160.1 Total Fat 4g Saturated fat 1g Sodium 489.8mg Potassium 180.1mg Carbohydrates 24g Net carbs 22g Sugar 7g Fiber 2g Protein 6g Calcium 40mg Iron 1.1mg

1032) Asian Veggie Spring Rolls

Ingredients:

- (4 Servings)
- 4 spring roll wrappers
- ½ cup cooked vermicelli noodles
- 1 garlic clove, minced
- 1 tbsp fresh ginger, minced
- 1 tbsp soy sauce
- 2 tsp sesame oil

- *½ red bell pepper, seeds removed, chopped*
- *½ cup mushrooms, finely chopped*
- *½ cup carrots, finely chopped*
- *¼ cup scallions, finely chopped*

Direction:(Prep + Cook Time: 30 minutes

- ✓ *Warm sesame oil in a saucepan over medium heat and add garlic, ginger, soy sauce, bell pepper, mushrooms, carrots, and scallions and stir-fry for 5 minutes.*
- ✓ *Stir in vermicelli noodles and set aside.*
- ✓ *Place the wrappers onto a working board.*
- ✓ *Spoon the veggie-noodle mixture at the center of the roll wrappers.*
- ✓ *Roll and tuck in the corners and edges to create neat and secure rolls.*
- ✓ *Spray with oil and place them in the frying basket.*
- ✓ *AirFry for 12-14 minutes at 340 F, turning once or twice until golden.*

nutritional value: Calories 210 Total Fat 7g Saturated fat 2.5g Sodium 550mg Carbohydrates 33g Net carbs 31g Fiber 2g Glucose 4g Protein 4g Calcium 0mg Iron 0mg

1033) Herby Meatballs

Ingredients:

- *4 Servings)*
- *1 lb ground beef*
- *1 onion, finely chopped*
- *2 garlic cloves, finely chopped*
- *1 egg*
- *1 cup breadcrumbs*
- *½ cup Mediterranean herbs*
- *Salt and black pepper to taste*
- *1 tbsp olive oil.*

Direction:(Prep + Cook Time: 30 minutes

- ✓ *Add the ground beef, onion, garlic, egg, breadcrumbs, herbs, salt, and pepper in a bowl and mix with your hands to combine.*
- ✓ *Shape into balls and brush them with olive oil.*
- ✓ *Arrange the meatballs in the frying basket and AirFry for 15-16 minutes at 380 F, turning once halfway through.*
- ✓ *Serve immediately.*

nutritional value: Cals 185 Fat11.20g Saturated Fat4.900g Carbohydrates1.30g Sugar0.20g Fibre0.1g Protein19.60g Salt1.50g

1034) Chili Cheese Balls

Ingredients:

- *(4 Servings)*
- *2 cups cottage cheese, crumbled*
- *2 cups Parmesan cheese, grated*
- *2 red potatoes, boiled and mashed*
- *1 medium onion, finely chopped*
- *1 ½ tsp red chili flakes*
- *1 green chili, finely chopped*
- *Salt to taste*
- *2 tbsp fresh cilantro, chopped*
- *1 cup flour*
- *1 cup breadcrumbs*

Direction:Prep + Cook Time: 25 minutes

- ✓ *Combine the cottage and Parmesan cheeses, onion, chili flakes, green chili, salt, cilantro, flour, and mashed potatoes in a bowl.*
- ✓ *Mold balls out of the mixture and roll them in breadcrumbs.*
- ✓ *Place them in the greased frying basket and AirFry for 14-16 minutes at 350 F, shaking once or twice.*
- ✓ *Serve warm.*

nutritional value: Calories 372.25 Kcal Total Fat 29.76g Cholesterol 91.85mg Sodium 721.66mg Potassium 146.14mg Total Carbs 3.39g Sugars 1.66g Dietary Fiber 1.1g Protein 23.04g Iron 0.7mg Calcium 649.3mg

1035) Cheesy Sticks with Sweet Thai Sauce

Ingredients:

- *(4 Servings)*
- *12 sticks mozzarella cheese*
- *2 cups breadcrumbs*
- *3 eggs*
- *1 cup sweet Thai sauce*
- *4 tbsp skimmed milk.*

Direction:Prep + Cook Time: 25 minutes + freezing time)

- ✓ *Pour the breadcrumbs into a bowl.*
- ✓ *Beat the eggs with milk in another bowl.*
- ✓ *After the other, dip the sticks in the egg mixture, in the crumbs, then in the egg mixture again, and lastly in the crumbs again.*
- ✓ *Freeze for 1 hour.*
- ✓ *Preheat the air fryer to 380 F.*
- ✓ *Arrange the sticks in the greased frying basket and AirFry for 10-12 minutes, flipping halfway through. Work in batches.*
- ✓ *Serve with sweet Thai sauce.*

nutritional: Calories 311 Total Fat 18.3g Saturated Fat 4g Trans Fat 0g Cholesterol 53.3mg Sodium 482.5mg Potassium 0mg Total Carbohydrate 17g Dietary Fiber 0.4g Sugars 0g Protein 19.3g Calcium 20% Iron 4%

1036) Potato Chips with Chives

Ingredients:

- *(4 Servings)*
- *1 lb potatoes, cut into thin slices*
- *¼ cup olive oil*
- *1 tbsp garlic paste*
- *2 tbsp chives, chopped A*
- *pinch of salt*

Direction:Prep + Cook Time: 40 minutes + marinating time)

- ✓ *Preheat the air fryer to 390 F.*
- ✓ *Add olive oil, garlic paste, and salt in a bowl and mix to obtain a marinade.*
- ✓ *Add the potatoes and let them sit for 30 minutes. Lay the potato slices into the frying basket and AirFry for 20 minutes.*
- ✓ *At the 10-minute mark, give the chips a turn and sprinkle with freshly chopped chives.*

nutritional value: Calories 218 Total Fat 14g Saturated Fat 1.3g Sodium 222mg Total Carbohydrates 21g Sugars 1g Protein 2.8g

1037) Quick Pickle Chips

Ingredients:

- *(4 Servings)*
- *36 sweet pickle chips, drained 1 cup flour*
- *¼ cup cornmeal*

Direction:Prep + Cook Time: 15 minutes

- ✓ *Preheat the air fryer to 400 F.*
- ✓ *In a bowl, mix flour, cayenne pepper, and cornmeal*
- ✓ *Dip the pickles in the flour mixture and spritz with cooking spray.*
- ✓ *AirFry for 10 minutes until golden brown, turning once.*

nutritional value: Calories 20.0 Total Fat 0.1 g Saturated Fat 0.0 g Polyunsaturated Fat 0.0 g Monounsaturated Fat 0.0 g Cholesterol 0.0 mg Sodium 293.0 mg Potassium 139.1 mg Total Carbohydrate 5.8 g Dietary Fiber 0.5 g Sugars 3.7 g Protein 0.5 g Calcium 1.7 % Copper 2.1 % Folate 1.8 % Iron 3.1 % Magnesium 4.4 % Manganese 9.0 % Niacin 0.7 % Pantothenic Acid 1.1 % Phosphorus 1.8 % Riboflavin 0.9 % Selenium 0.3 % Thiamin 1.1 % Zinc 0.9 %

1038) Garlicky Potato Chips with Herbs

Ingredients:

- *(2 Servings)*
- *2 potatoes, thinly sliced*
- *1 tbsp olive oil*
- *1 garlic cloves, crushed*
- *1 tsp each of fresh rosemary, thyme, oregano, chopped*
- *Salt and black pepper to taste*

Direction:Prep + Cook Time: 40 minutes

- ✓ *In a bowl, mix olive oil, garlic, herbs, salt, and pepper.*
- ✓ *Coat the potatoes thoroughly in the mixture.*
- ✓ *Arrange them in the frying basket and AirFry for 18-20 minutes at 360 F, shaking every 4-5 minutes*

nutritional value: Calories140 Total Fat 8g Saturated Fat 1g Trans Fat 0g Cholesterol 0mg Total Carbohydrates 17g Dietary Fiber 2g Sugars 4g Includes 0ggrams Added Sugars Protein 1g

1039) Hot Carrot Crisps

Ingredients:

- *(2 Servings)*
- *2 large carrots, cut into strips*
- *½ tsp oregano*
- *½ tsp hot paprika*
- *½ tsp garlic powder*
- *1 tbsp olive oil*
- *Salt to taste*

Direction:Prep + Cook Time: 25 minutes

- ✓ *Put the carrots in a bowl and stir in the remaining ingredients; toss to coat*
- ✓ *Arrange the carrots in the greased frying basket and AirFry for 13-15 minutes at 390 F, shaking once.*
- ✓ *Serve warm.*

nutritional value: 71 Calories, 1 g Fat, 0 g Saturated Fat, 0 mg Cholesterol, 213 mg Sodium, 16 g Carbohydrate, 5 g fiber, 7 g Sugar, 2 g Protein

1040) Root Vegetable Chips

Ingredients:

- *4 Servings)*
- *1 carrot, sliced*
- *1 parsnip, sliced*
- *1 potato, sliced*
- *1 daikon, sliced*
- *2 tbsp olive oil*
- *1 tbsp soy sauce*

Direction:(Prep + Cook Time: 25 minutes

- ✓ *Preheat the air fryer to 400 F.*
- ✓ *In a bowl, mix olive oil and soy sauce.*
- ✓ *Add in the veggies and toss to coat; marinate for 5 minutes.*
- ✓ *Transfer them to the fryer and AirFry for 15 minutes, tossing once*

nutritional value: Calories 150 Total Fat 8g Saturated Fat 1g Trans Fat 0g Cholesterol 0mg Sodium 90mg Total Carbohydrates 17g Dietary Fiber 2g Sugars 5g Protein 1g Calcium 2% Iron 2%

1041) Mexican-Style Air Fryer Nachos

Ingredients:

- *(4 Servings)*

- *8 corn tortillas, cut into wedges*
- *1 tbsp olive oil*
- *½ tsp ground cumin*
- *½ tsp chili powder*
- *½ tsp paprika*
- *½ tsp cayenne pepper*
- *½ tsp salt*
- *½ tsp ground coriander*

Direction:(Prep + Cook Time: 20 minutes

- ✓ *Preheat the air fryer to 370 F.*
- ✓ *Brush the tortilla wedges with olive oil and arrange them in the frying basket in an even layer.*
- ✓ *Mix the spices thoroughly in a small bowl.*
- ✓ *Sprinkle the tortilla wedges with the spice mixture. AirFry for 2-3 minutes, shake the basket, and fry for another 2-3 minutes until crunchy and nicely browned.*
- ✓ *Serve the nachos immediately.*

nutritional:Calories: 352kcal | Carbohydrates: 41.7 g | Protein: 119g | Fat: 16.5g | Saturated Fat: 4.7g | Cholesterol: 12mg | Sodium: 508mg | Pot assium: 450mg | Fiber: 6.1g | Sugar: 1.6g | Calcium: 65mg | Iron: 2mg

1042) Air Fried Asparagus with Romesco Sauce

Ingredients:

- *(4 Servings)*
- *1 cup panko breadcrumbs*
- *Salt and black pepper to taste*
- *½ cup almond flour*
- *1 lb asparagus spears, trimmed and washed*
- *2 eggs*
- *2 tomatoes, chopped*
- *Romesco Sauce*
- *2 roasted peppers, chopped*
- *½ cup almond flour*
- *½ tsp garlic powder*
- *1 tbsp vinegar*
- *2 slices toasted bread, torn into pieces*
- *½ tsp paprika*
- *1 tsp crushed red chili flakes*
- *1 tbsp tomato purée*
- *½ cup extra-virgin olive oil*

Direction:Prep + Cook Time: 25 minutes)

- ✓ *Preheat the air fryer to 390 F.*
- ✓ *On a plate, combine panko breadcrumbs, salt, and black pepper.*
- ✓ *On another shallow plate, whisk the eggs with salt and black pepper.*
- ✓ *On a third plate, pour the almond flour Dip asparagus in the almond flour, followed by a dip in the eggs, and finally, coat with breadcrumbs.*
- ✓ *Place in the greased frying basket and AirFry for 10 minutes, turning once halfway.*
- ✓ *Pulse all romesco sauce ingredients in a food processor until smooth.*
- ✓ *Serve asparagus with romesco sauce.*

nutritional value: Calories 90 Total Fat 5g Saturated Fat 0.6g Trans Fat 0g Polyunsaturated Fat 0.7g Fat Cholesterol 0mg Sodium 595mg Total Carbs 10g Dietary Fiber 5g Sugars 4g Protein 5g

1043) Parmesan Artichoke Hearts

Ingredients:

- *(4 Servings)*
- *1 can (14-oz) artichoke hearts, drained*
- *2 eggs*
- *¼ cup flour*
- *¼ Parmesan cheese, grated*
- *⅓ cup panko breadcrumbs*
- *1 tsp garlic powder*
- *Salt and black pepper to taste*

Direction:(Prep + Cook Time: 25 minutes

- ✓ *Preheat the air fryer to 390 F.*
- ✓ *Pat dry the artichokes with a paper towel and cut them into wedges.*
- ✓ *In a bowl, whisk the eggs with a pinch of salt.*
- ✓ *In another bowl, combine Parmesan cheese, breadcrumbs, and garlic powder*
- ✓ *In a third bowl, pour the flour mixed with salt and black pepper.*
- ✓ *Dip the artichokes in the flour, then dip the eggs, and finally coat with breadcrumbs.*
- ✓ *Place them in the frying basket and AirFry for 10 minutes, flipping once.*
- ✓ *Serve with mayo sauce if desired.*

nutritional value: Calories 134.5 Total Fat 0.5 g Saturated Fat 0.3 g Cholesterol 1.3 mg Sodium 721.4 mg Potassium 57.8 mg Total Carbohydrate 20.9 g Dietary Fiber 3.0 g Sugars 4.0 g Protein 9.7 g

1044) Air Fried Cheesy Brussels Sprouts

Ingredients:

- *4 Servings)*
- *1 lb Brussels sprouts, halved*
- *2 tbsp canola oil*
- *1 cup breadcrumbs*
- *1 tbsp paprika*
- *2 tbsp Grana Padano cheese, grated*
- *1 tbsp sage, chopped*

Direction:: (Prep + Cook Time: 30 minutes)

- ✓ *Preheat the air fryer to 400 F. Line the frying basket with parchment paper.*

- ✓ In a bowl, mix breadcrumbs and paprika with Grana Padano cheese.
- ✓ Drizzle the Brussels sprouts with canola oil and add them to the crumbs/cheese mixture; toss to coat.
- ✓ Place in the frying basket and AirFry for 15 minutes, shaking every 4-5 minutes.
- ✓ Serve sprinkled with chopped sage.

nutritional value: Calories 103 Fat 6.7g Carbohydrates 7.4g Fiber 3g Protein 4.4g

1045) Crispy Kale Chips

Ingredients:

- (4 Servings)
- 4 cups kale leaves, stems removed, chopped
- 2 tbsp olive oil
- 1 tsp garlic powder
- Salt and black pepper to taste
- ¼ tsp onion powder

Direction:(Prep + Cook Time: 20 minutes + cooling time

- ✓ In a bowl, mix kale and olive oil.
- ✓ Add in garlic and onion powders, salt, and black pepper; toss to coat.
- ✓ Arrange the kale in the frying basket and AirFry for 8 minutes at 350 F, shaking once.
- ✓ Serve cool.

nutritional value: Calories: 140 Fat: 10g Sodium: 380mg Carbohydrates: 7g Fiber: 3g Sugars: 1g Protein: 7g

1046) Crispy Cauliflower in Buffalo Sauce

Ingredients:

- 4 Servings)
- 3 tbsp butter, melted
- 3 tbsp buffalo hot sauce
- 1 egg white
- 1 cup panko breadcrumbs
- Salt and black pepper to taste
- ½ head cauliflower, cut into florets

Direction:Prep + Cook Time: 35 minutes

- ✓ In a bowl, whisk butter, buffalo sauce, and egg white.
- ✓ In a separate bowl, mix breadcrumbs with salt and black pepper.
- ✓ Toss the florets in the buffalo mixture and roll them in the breadcrumbs to coat.
- ✓ Spritz with cooking spray and AirFry them for 14-16 minutes at 340 F, shaking twice.
- ✓ Serve hot.

nutritional: Cal 289.9 Total Fat 0.7 g Saturated Fat 0.1 g Monounsaturated Fat 0.1 g Cholesterol 0.0 mg Sodium 5,717.5 mg Potassium 940.2 mg Total Carbohydrate 36.9 g Dietary Fiber 7.2 g Sugars 4.0 g Protein 6.2 g

1047) Crunchy Cauliflower Bites

Ingredients:

- (4 Servings)
- 1 tbsp Italian seasoning
- 1 cup flour
- 1 cup milk
- 1 egg, beaten
- 1 head cauliflower, cut into florets

Direction:Prep + Cook Time: 25 minutes

- ✓ Preheat the air fryer to 390 F.
- ✓ Grease the frying basket with cooking spray.
- ✓ In a bowl, mix flour, milk, egg, and Italian seasoning.
- ✓ Coat the cauliflower in the mixture and drain the excess liquid.
- ✓ Place the florets in the frying basket, spray with cooking spray, and AirFry for 7 minutes.
- ✓ Shake and continue cooking for another 5 minutes.
- ✓ Allow cooling before serving.

nutritional value: Calories 710 Total Fat 34g Saturated Fat 6g Trans Fat 0g Cholesterol 35mg Sodium 1210mg Total Carbohydrates 85g Dietary Fiber 3g Sugars 44g Protein 19g

1048) Crispy Yellow Squash Chips

Ingredients:

- (4 Servings)
- 2 yellow squash, sliced into rounds
- ½ cup flour
- Salt and black pepper to taste
- ¼ cup Parmesan cheese, grated
- Greek yogurt dressing, for serving
- 2 eggs
- 1 tbsp soy sauce
- ¾ cup panko breadcrumbs
- ¼ tsp dried dill

Direction:(Prep + Cook Time: 25 minutes

- ✓ Preheat the air fryer to 380 F.
- ✓ Spray the frying basket with cooking spray.
- ✓ In a bowl, mix the flour, dill, salt, and black pepper.
- ✓ In another bowl, beat the eggs with soy sauce.
- ✓ In a third, pour the breadcrumbs and Parmesan cheese, mix well.
- ✓ Dip the squash rounds in the flour, then in the eggs, and then coat with breadcrumbs.
- ✓ Place in the frying basket and AirFry for 10 minutes, flipping once halfway through.

✓ *Serve with Greek yogurt dressing.*

nutritional value: **Calories 196 Fat 12g Saturated Fat 4g Cholesterol 14mg Sodium 331mg Potassium 388mg Carbohydrates 12g Fiber 2g Sugar 3g Protein 9g**

1049) Air Fryer Avocado Wedges

Ingredients:

- *4 Servings)*
- *2 avocados, peeled, stoned, cut into wedges*
- *1 cup panko breadcrumbs*
- *2 egg, beaten*
- *½ cup Greek yogurt*
- *1 tbsp fresh cilantro, chopped*
- *½ tsp sriracha sauce*
- *Salt and garlic powder to taste*

Direction:(Prep + Cook Time: 25 minutes

✓ *Preheat the air fryer to 390 F.*

✓ *Add the yogurt, sriracha sauce, salt, garlic powder, and cilantro to a small bowl.*

✓ *Mix together until well incorporated.*

✓ *Place in the fridge to chill for 15 minutes.*

✓ *In a bowl, whisk the eggs with a pinch of salt until frothy.*

✓ *In another bowl, mix the breadcrumbs with garlic powder and salt.*

✓ *Dip the avocado wedges into the eggs and then dredge in the breadcrumbs.*

✓ *Arrange the wedges in the greased frying basket.*

✓ *Spritz with cooking spray, AirFry for 4 minutes, flip and cook for 3-4 more minutes until crispy.*

✓ *Serve the avocado wedges with yogurt sauce.*

nutritional value: **CALORIES 87 Total Fat 7g Saturated Fat 1g Cholesterol 15mg Sodium 127mg Total Carbohydrate 6g Dietary Fiber 2g Total Sugars 1g Protein 2g Calcium 27mg**

1050) Fried Pimiento-Stuffed Green Olives

Ingredients:

- *(4 Servings)*
- *½ (13-oz) jar pimiento-stuffed green olives*
- *¼ cup flour*
- *¼ cup Parmesan cheese, grated*
- *Salt and black pepper to taste*
- *½ cup panko breadcrumbs*
- *1 egg, beaten*
- *1 tsp cayenne pepper*

Direction:(Prep + Cook Time: 30 minutes)

✓ *Preheat the air fryer to 390 F.*

✓ *In a bowl, combine flour, cayenne pepper, salt, and black pepper.*

✓ *In another bowl, add the beaten egg.*

✓ *Mix the breadcrumbs with Parmesan cheese in a third bowl.*

✓ *Drain and pat dry the olives with a paper towel.*

✓ *Dredge the olives in flour, then in the egg, and finally in the breadcrumbs.*

✓ *Place in the frying basket, spray them with cooking spray and AirFry for 8-10 minutes.*

✓ *Shake and cook for 3 more minutes.*

✓ *Let cool before serving.*

nutritional value: **Calories 25 Total Fat 2.5g Saturated Fat 0g Trans Fat 0g Cholesterol 0mg Sodium 210mg Total Carbohydrates 0g Protein 0g**

1051) Mini Spinach & Mushroom Empanadas

Ingredients:

- *(4 Servings)*
- *2 tbsp olive oil*
- *10 oz spinach, chopped*
- *1 onion, chopped*
- *2 garlic cloves, minced*
- *¼ cup mushrooms, chopped*
- *1 cup ricotta cheese, crumbled*
- *1 (13-oz) pizza crust 1 tbsp Italian seasoning Salt and black pepper to taste 1 ½ cups marinara sauce*

Direction:Prep + Cook Time: 30 minutes

✓ *Heat olive oil in a pan over medium heat and sauté garlic, onion, and mushrooms for 4 minutes or until tender.*

✓ *Stir in spinach for 2-3 minutes.*

✓ *Season with Italian seasoning, salt, and pepper.*

✓ *Pour in marinara sauce and cook until the sauce thickens about 5 minutes.*

✓ *Turn off and mix in ricotta cheese.*

✓ *On a floured work surface, roll the pizza crust out.*

✓ *Slice into 4 rectangles.*

✓ *Divide the mixture between the rectangles and close them by folding them in half.*

✓ *Seal the edges and lightly flatten.*

✓ *Spritz with cooking spray and transfer to the frying basket.*

✓ *Bake for 14-16 minutes, turning once halfway through.*

✓ *Serve.*

nutritional value: **Calories 550 Total Fat34g Saturated Fat15g Trans Fat0g Cholesterol45mg Sodium710mg Potassium290mg Total Carbohydrate48g Dietary Fiber2g Sugars1g Protein12g Calcium25% Iron20%**

1052) Kielbasa & Mushroom Pierogi

Ingredients:

- *(4 Servings)*
- *½ package puff pastry dough, at room temperature*
- *½ lb Kielbasa smoked sausage, chopped*
- *½ onion, chopped*
- *½ lb mushrooms, chopped*
- *½ tsp ground cumin*
- *¼ tsp paprika*
- *Salt and black pepper to taste*
- *1 egg, beaten*

Direction:(Prep + Cook Time: 25 minutes

- ✓ *Preheat the air fryer to 360 F.*
- ✓ *Mix Kielbasa sausage, onion, mushrooms, cumin, paprika, salt, and pepper in a bowl.*
- ✓ *Place the pastry on a lightly floured surface.*
- ✓ *Using a glass, cut out 8 circles of the pastry.*
- ✓ *Place 1 tbsp of the sausage mixture on each pastry circle, brush the edges with the beaten egg, and fold over.*
- ✓ *Seal the edges with a fork.*
- ✓ *Brush the empanadas with the remaining egg and spray with cooking spray.*
- ✓ *Place in the greased frying basket and Bake for 12-14 minutes until golden brown.*

nutritional value: 339 calories; fat 18g; cholesterol 81mg; saturated fat 7g; carbohydrates 29g; mono fat 3g; poly fat 1g; insoluble fiber 2g; sugars 4g; Protein 18g; vitamin a 1700.7IU; vitamin c 6.5mg;

1053) ***Low-Carb Radish Chips***

Ingredients:

- *4 Servings)*
- *10-15 radishes, thinly sliced*
- *Salt to season.*

Direction:Prep + Cook Time: 15 minutes

- ✓ *Preheat the air fryer to 400 F.*
- ✓ *Grease the frying basket with cooking spray.*
- ✓ *Add in the sliced radishes and AirFry for 8 minutes, flipping once halfway through.*
- ✓ *Season with salt and consume immediately.*

nutritional value: Calories: 35, Total fat: 3g, Saturated fat: 50g, Cholesterol: 0mg, Sodium: 180mg, Total carbs: 3g, Fiber: 1g, Sugar: 1g, Protein: 1g.NET CARBS: 2g.

1054) ***Green Bean Crisps***

Ingredients:

- *(4 Servings)*
- *lb green beans, trimmed*
- *2 tbsp olive oil*
- *½ tsp garlic powder*
- *½ tsp onion powder*
- *½ tsp paprika*
- *Salt and black pepper to taste*

Direction:Prep + Cook Time: 15 minutes)

- ✓ *Preheat the air fryer to 390 F.*
- ✓ *Mix olive oil, garlic and onion powders, paprika, salt, and black pepper in a bowl.*
- ✓ *Coat the green beans in the mixture and place them in the greased frying basket.*
- ✓ *AirFry for 10-12 minutes, shaking once halfway through cooking.*
- ✓ *Serve warm*

nutritional value: Calories 130 kCal Total Carbs 20 g Net Carbs 16 g Fiber 4 g Sugar 2 g Protein 1 g Fat 4.5 g Calcium 40 mg Iron 0.8 mg Potassium 400 mg Sodium 45 mg

1055) ***Smoked Fish Balls***

Ingredients:

- *(4 Servings)*
- *1 cup smoked mackerel, flaked*
- *2 cups cooked rice*
- *2 eggs, lightly beaten*
- *1 cup Grana Padano cheese, grated*
- *¼ cup fresh thyme, chopped*
- *Salt and black pepper to taste*
- *1 cup panko breadcrumbs Cooking spray*

Direction:(Prep + Cook Time: 25 minutes

- ✓ *Add fish, rice, eggs, Grana Padano cheese, thyme, salt, and black pepper; stir to combine.*
- ✓ *Shape the mixture into 12 even-sized balls.*
- ✓ *Add fish, rice, eggs, Grana Padano cheese, thyme, salt, and black pepper; stir to combine.*
- ✓ *Shape the mixture into 12 even-sized balls.*

nutritional value: Calorie 290 Carbs 25g Dietary Fiber 2g Sugar 0g Fat 14g Saturated 3g Polyunsaturated 3g Trans0 g Protein15 g Sodium560 mg Potassium0 mg Cholesterol30 mg

1056) ***Salmon Mini Tarts***

Ingredients:

- *(4-6 Servings)*
- *15 mini tart shells*
- *4 eggs, lightly beaten*
- *2 tbsp fresh dill, chopped*
- *½ cup heavy cream*
- *3 oz smoked salmon*
- *6 oz cream cheese, divided into 15 pieces*

Direction:Prep + Cook Time: 20 minutes

- ✓ *Mix together the eggs and heavy cream in a bowl.*
- ✓ *Arrange the tarts on a greased air fryer muffin tray.*
- ✓ *Pour the mixture into the tarts, about halfway*

up the side, and top with a piece of salmon and cheese.

- ✓ *Bake in the fryer for 10 minutes at 340 F, regularly checking them to avoid overcooking.*
- ✓ *When ready, remove them from the tray and let them cool.*
- ✓ *Sprinkle with freshly chopped dill and enjoy*

***nutritional value:** Calories 333.8 Total Fat 23.8 g Saturated Fat 9.2 g Polyunsaturated Fat 3.2 g Monounsaturated Fat 9.7 g Cholesterol 223.0 mg Sodium 295.0 mg Potassium 372.2 mg Total Carbohydrate 0.7 g Dietary Fiber 0.1 g Sugars 0.0 g Protein 28.4 g Calcium 40.6 %*

1057) Easy Coconut Shrimp

Ingredients:

- *(4 Servings)*
- *1 lb jumbo shrimp, peeled and deveined*
- *¾ cup coconut, shredded*
- *1 tsp maple syrup*
- *½ cup breadcrumbs*
- *⅓ cup cornstarch*
- *½ cup milk*

Direction:Prep + Cook Time: 30 minutes

- ✓ *Pour the cornstarch and shrimp in a zipper bag and shake vigorously to coat.*
- ✓ *Mix maple syrup and milk in a bowl and set aside.*
- ✓ *In a separate bowl, mix the breadcrumbs and shredded coconut.*
- ✓ *Remove the shrimp from the bag while shaking off excess starch.*
- ✓ *Dip each piece in the milk mixture and then in the crumbs mixture.*
- ✓ *Lay the shrimp in the frying basket and AirFry for 12-14 minutes at 350 F, flipping once halfway through.*
- ✓ *Serve with a coconut-based dip or sautéed green beans if desired.*

***nutritional value:** CALORIES220 CALORIES FROM Fat 110 TOTAL FAT 12g SATURATED FAT 4.5g TRANS FAT 0g CHOLESTEROL 45mg SODIUM 440mg POTASSIUM 140mg TOTAL CARBOHYDRATE 20g DIETARY FIBER 2g SUGARS 6g PROTEIN 8g CALCIUM 2% IRON10%*

1058) Salmon Croquettes

Ingredients:

- *(4 Servings)*
- *1 (15 oz) tinned salmon, flaked*
- *1 cup onions, grated*
- *1 cup carrots, grated*
- *3 large eggs*
- *1 ½ tbsp fresh chives, chopped*
- *4 tbsp mayonnaise*
- *4 tbsp breadcrumbs 2*
- *½ tsp Italian seasoning*
- *Salt and black pepper to taste*
- *2 ½ tsp lemon juice*

Direction:Prep + Cook Time: 20 minutes + refrigerating time)

- ✓ *Mix well the salmon, onions, carrots, eggs, chives, mayonnaise, crumbs, Italian seasoning, salt, black pepper, and lemon juice in a bowl.*
- ✓ *Form croquettes out of the mixture and refrigerate for 45 minutes.*
- ✓ *Preheat the air fryer to 400 F.*
- ✓ *Grease the basket with cooking spray.*
- ✓ *Arrange the croquettes in a single layer and spray with cooking spray.*
- ✓ *AirFry for 10-12 minutes until golden, flipping once.*

***nutritional value:** Calories 422 Total Fat 23g Saturated Fat 4.3g Polyunsaturated Fat 6.7g Monounsaturated Fat 11g Cholesterol 548mg Total Carbohydrates 20g Dietary Fiber 1.7g Sugars 1.9g Protein 31g*

1059) Rich Cod Fingers

Ingredients:

- *(4 Servings)*
- *2 cups flour*
- *Salt and black pepper to taste*
- *1 tsp seafood seasoning*
- *1 cup cornmeal*
- *1 lb cod fillets, cut into fingers*
- *2 tbsp milk*
- *2 eggs, beaten*
- *1 cup breadcrumbs*

Direction:Prep + Cook Time: 20 minutes

- ✓ *Preheat the air fryer to 400 F.*
- ✓ *In a bowl, mix the eggs with milk, salt, and black pepper.*
- ✓ *In a separate bowl, mix the flour, cornmeal, and seafood seasoning.*
- ✓ *In a third bowl, pour the breadcrumbs Preheat the air fryer to 400 F.*
- ✓ *In a bowl, mix the eggs with milk, salt, and black pepper.*
- ✓ *In a separate bowl, mix the flour, cornmeal, and seafood seasoning.*
- ✓ *In a third bowl, pour the breadcrumbs*

***nutritional value:** Calories 216 Kcal Calories from fat 99 Kcal Total Fat 11g Saturated Fat 1g Sodium 250mg Total Carbs 17g Sugars 1g Dietary Fiber 1g Protein 13g*

1060) Parsley & Lemon Fried Shrimp

Ingredients:

- *4 Servings)*
- *1 ½ lb shrimp, peeled and deveined*
- *½ cup fresh parsley, chopped*
- *Juice of 1 lemon*
- *1 egg, beaten*
- *½ cup flour*
- *¾ cup seasoned breadcrumbs*
- *2 tbsp chili garlic sauce*

Direction:Prep + Cook Time: 20 minutes + marinating time

- ✓ *Add the shrimp, parsley, and lemon juice to a resealable bag and massage until well-coated.*
- ✓ *Place in the fridge to marinate for 20 minutes.*
- ✓ *Preheat the air fryer to 400 F.*
- ✓ *Put beaten egg, flour, and breadcrumbs each in a bowl.*
- ✓ *Dredge shrimp in the flour, then in the egg, and finally in the crumbs.*
- ✓ *Add to the frying basket and spray with cooking spray.*
- ✓ *AirFry for 10-12 minutes, shaking once.*
- ✓ *Remove to a serving plate and drizzle with chili garlic sauce to serve.*

nutritional value: Kcal 73 fat 4g saturates 1g carbs 0g sugars 0g fiber 0g protein 9g salt 0.3g

1061) Prawn & Cabbage Egg Rolls

Ingredients:

- *4 Servings)*
- *2 tbsp olive oil*
- *1-inch piece fresh ginger, grated*
- *1 tbsp garlic paste*
- *1 carrot, cut into strips*
- *¼ cup chicken broth*
- *2 tbsp soy sauce*
- *1 tbsp sugar*
- *1 cup Napa cabbage, shredded 1*
- *tbsp sesame oil*
- *8 cooked prawns, chopped*
- *1 egg*
- *8 egg roll wrappers*

Direction:Prep + Cook Time: 30 minutes + cooling time)

- ✓ *Warm olive oil in a skillet over medium heat.*
- ✓ *Sauté ginger, carrot, and garlic paste for 2 minutes.*
- ✓ *Pour in the broth, soy sauce, and sugar and bring to a boil.*
- ✓ *Add the cabbage, lower the heat, and let simmer until softened, about 4 minutes.*
- ✓ *Remove from the heat and stir in sesame oil; let cool for 15 minutes.*
- ✓ *Strain the cabbage mixture and add in the chopped prawns.*
- ✓ *Whisk an egg in a small bowl.*
- ✓ *Divide the prawn mixture between the wrappers.*
- ✓ *Fold the bottom part over the filling and tuck under.*
- ✓ *Fold in both sides and tightly roll up.*
- ✓ *Use the whisked egg to seal the wrappers.*
- ✓ *Place the rolls into the greased frying basket, spray them with oil and AirFry for 12 minutes at 370 F, turning once halfway through.*

nutritional value: Calories 22.3 Total Fat 0.2 g Saturated Fat 0.0 g Polyunsaturated Fat 0.1 g Monounsaturated Fat 0.0 g Cholesterol 0.0 mg Sodium 16.0 mg Total Carbohydrate 4.8 g Dietary Fiber 2.0 g Sugars 0.0 g Protein 1.3 g Calcium 4.2 %

1062) Mouth-Watering Beef Sticks

Ingredients:

- *4 Servings)*
- *1 lb ground beef*
- *1 tbsp thyme*
- *½ tsp garlic powder*
- *½ tsp chili powder*
- *Salt to taste 1 tsp liquid smoke*

Direction:(Prep + Cook Time: 30 minutes

- ✓ *Place the ground beef, thyme, garlic powder, chili powder, salt, and liquid smoke in a bowl; mix well.*
- ✓ *Mold out 4 sticks with your hands and place them on a plate to stand for 10 minutes.*
- ✓ *After, place them in the frying basket and AirFry for 14-16 minutes at 350 F, flipping once halfway through.*
- ✓ *Serve warm.*

nutritional value: Calories 110 Total Fat 8g Saturated Fat 3.5g Trans Fat 0.5g Cholesterol 20mg Sodium 390mg Total Carbohydrate 2g Dietary Fiber 0g Sugars 2g Protein 13g

1063) Cheesy Bacon Fries

Ingredients:

- *(4 Servings)*
- *2 russet potatoes, boiled and chopped*
- *5 slices bacon*
- *2 tbsp olive oil*
- *2 cups cheddar cheese, shredded 3*
- *oz softened cream cheese*
- *Salt and black pepper to taste*
- *¼ cup scallions, chopped*

Direction:(Prep + Cook Time: 35 minutes)

- ✓ Preheat the air fryer to 400 F.
- ✓ Place the bacon in the frying basket and AirFry for 5 minutes, turning once; set aside to cool.
- ✓ To the air fryer, add the potatoes and drizzle them with olive oil. AirFry for 20-22 minutes, shaking once.
- ✓ Remove and season with salt and black pepper In a bowl, mix cheddar and cream cheeses.
- ✓ Pour over the potatoes and cook for 5 more minutes.
- ✓ Chop the fried bacon and scatter over the potatoes.
- ✓ Sprinkle with scallions and serve immediately

nutritional value: Calories 388 Total Fat 22g Saturated Fat 6.8g Trans Fat 0.3g Cholesterol 27mg Sodium 417mg Potassium 565mg Total Carbohydrates 38g Dietary Fiber 3.5g Sugars 0.5g Protein 9.9g Calcium 17% Iron 5%

1064) Crispy Bacon with Butter Bean Dip

Ingredients:

- (2 Servings)
- 1 (14-oz) can butter beans
- 1 tbsp scallions, chopped
- ½ cup feta cheese, crumbled
- Black pepper to taste
- 3 tbsp olive oil
- 2 oz bacon, sliced

Direction:Prep + Cook Time: 15 minutes

- ✓ Preheat the air fryer to 390 F.
- ✓ Arrange the bacon slices in the frying basket and AirFry for 5 minutes.
- ✓ Flip and cook for 5 more minutes or until crispy.
- ✓ Remove to a paper towel-lined plate to drain
- ✓ Meanwhile, blend butter beans, olive oil, and black pepper in a blender.
- ✓ Add in the feta cheese and stir well.
- ✓ Serve the crispy bacon with the feta-bean dip and scatter fresh scallions on top.

nutritional value: Calories 456 Fat 30g Saturated Fat 11g Cholesterol 79mg Sodium 542mg Potassium 423mg Carbohydrates 27g Fiber 1g Sugar 23g Protein 18g Calcium 42mg Iron 2mg

1065) Bacon-Wrapped Avocados

Ingredients:

- (4 Servings)
- 12 thick strips of bacon
- 3 large avocados, sliced
- ⅓ tsp chili powder
- ⅓ tsp c⅓ tsp salt cumin

Direction:Prep + Cook Time: 40 minutes

- ✓ Stretch the bacon strips to elongate and cut in half to make 24 pieces.
- ✓ Wrap each bacon piece around a slice of avocado.
- ✓ Tuck the end of bacon into the wrap, and season with salt, chili powder, and cumin.
- ✓ Arrange the wrapped pieces in the frying basket and AirFry for 8-10 minutes at 350 F, flipping halfway through to cook evenly.
- ✓ Remove to a wire rack and repeat the process for the remaining avocados.

nutritional value: Calories 458 Total Fat 20g Saturated fat 5g Sodium 865mg Carbohydrates 55g Net carbs 48g Sugar 6g Fiber 7g Protein 16g Calcium 360mg Iron 3.4mg

1066) Bacon & Chicken Wrapped Jalapeños

Ingredients:

- (4 Servings)
- 8 jalapeño peppers, halved lengthwise and seeded
- 4 chicken breasts, halved and butterflied
- 6 oz cream cheese, softened
- 16 slices bacon
- 1 cup breadcrumbs
- Salt and black pepper to taste
- 6 oz cheddar cheese, grated
- 2 eggs

Direction:(Prep + Cook Time: 40 minutes

- ✓ Season the chicken with black pepper and salt on both sides.
- ✓ In a bowl, add cream and cheddar cheeses, black pepper, and salt; mix well.
- ✓ Fill the jalapeños with the cheese mixture.
- ✓ On a working board, flatten each piece of chicken and lay 2 bacon slices onto each one.
- ✓ Place a stuffed jalapeño on each laid out chicken and bacon set and wrap around the jalapeños
- ✓ Preheat the air fryer to 350 F.
- ✓ Add the eggs to a bowl and pour the breadcrumbs into another bowl.
- ✓ Dip the wrappers into the eggs first and then in the breadcrumbs.
- ✓ Arrange them on the greased frying basket and AirFry for 7-8 minutes, turn and cook further for 4-5 minutes.
- ✓ Serve warm.

nutritional value: Calories 320 Total Fat 18g Saturated Fat 8g Trans Fat 0g Cholesterol 115mg Sodium 640mg Total Carbohydrates 1g Dietary Fiber 0g Sugars 0g Protein 31g Calcium 8% Iron 2%

1067) Black Bean & Corn Flatbreads+

Ingredients:

- *4 Servings)*
- *4 flatbreads, warm*
- *2 oz cream cheese, softened*
- *¼ cup cheddar cheese, shredded*
- *½ (15-oz) can corn, drained and rinsed*
- *½ (15-oz) can black beans, drained and rinsed*
- *¼ cup chunky salsa*
- *½ tsp ground cumin*
- *½ tsp paprika*
- *Salt and black pepper to taste*
- *2 tbsp fresh cilantro, chopped*

Direction:(Prep + Cook Time: 20 minutes)

- ✓ *Preheat the air fryer to 320 F.*
- ✓ *Add the black beans, corn, chunky salsa, cream cheese, cheddar cheese, cumin, paprika, salt, and pepper in a bowl.*
- ✓ *Mix well.*
- ✓ *Spread the mixture out on a baking dish and insert it in the air fryer. AirFry for 9-11 minutes until heated through.*
- ✓ *Divide the mixture among the flatbreads.*
- ✓ *Top with cilantro and serve warm.*

nutritional value: Energy: 114 kilocalories Protein: 7.62 g Fat: 0.46 g Carbohydrate: 20.39 g Fiber: 7.5 g Sugars: 0.28 g Calcium: 23 milligrams (mg) Iron: 1.81 mg Magnesium: 60 mg Phosphorus: 120 mg Potassium: 305 mg Sodium: 1 mg Zinc: 0.96 mg Thiamin: 0.21 mg Niacin: 0.434 mg Folate: 128 msg

1068) BBQ Chicken Naan Pizza

Ingredients:

- *1 Serving) 1 piece naan bread*
- *¼ cup barbeque sauce*
- *¼ cup mozzarella cheese, shredded*
- *¼ cup Monterrey Jack*
- *cheese, shredded*
- *2 tbsp red onions, thinly sliced*
- *½ chicken sausage, sliced*
- *½ tbsp fresh cilantro, chopped*

Direction:Prep + Cook Time: 20 minutes

- ✓ *Spray naan's bread with cooking spray and place it on the greased frying basket.*
- ✓ *Brush with barbeque sauce, sprinkle with mozzarella and Monterrey Jack cheeses, and red onions.*
- ✓ *Top with the chicken sausage.*
- ✓ *Bake in the preheated fryer for 8-10 minutes at 400 F.*
- ✓ *Sprinkle with cilantro to serve.*

nutritional value: Calories 411.2 Total Fat 11.0 g Saturated Fat 4.9 g Polyunsaturated Fat 0.4 g Monounsaturated Fat 0.4 g Cholesterol 93.4 mg Sodium 1,026.9 mg Potassium 410.4 mg Total Carbohydrate 42.2 g Dietary Fiber 3.2 g Sugars 13.0 g Protein 39.4 g

1069) Italian Pork Sausage Pizza

Ingredients:

- *2 Servings)*
- *1 piece pizza crust dough*
- *½ tsp dried oregano*
- *¼ cup tomato sauce*
- *¼ cup mozzarella cheese, shredded*
- *1 shallot, thinly sliced*
- *1 Italian pork sausage, sliced*
- *4 fresh basil leaves*
- *4 black olives*

Direction:(Prep + Cook Time: 20 minutes

- ✓ *Preheat the air fryer to 390 F.*
- ✓ *Spread tomato sauce over the pizza dough and sprinkle with oregano.*
- ✓ *Top with mozzarella cheese, shallot, and pork sausage slices.*
- ✓ *Place the pizza dough on the greased frying basket.*
- ✓ *Bake for 10 minutes until the crust is golden and the cheese is melted.*
- ✓ *Scatter over basil leaves and olives to serve.*

nutritional value: Calorie 170cl Carbs2 g Dietary Fibero g Sugaro g Fat15 g Saturated5 g Polyunsaturatedo g Monounsaturatedo g Transo g Protein7 g Sodium560 mg

1070) Chorizo Pita Pizzas

Ingredients:

- *(4 Servings) 4 pita bread pieces*
- *4 tbsp marinara sauce*
- *12 chorizo rounds*
- *8 button mushrooms, sliced*
- *8 fresh basil leaves*
- *2 cups cheddar cheese, grated*
- *1 tsp chili flakes Cooking oil*

Direction:(Prep + Cook Time: 25 minutes

- ✓ *Spray the pitas with oil and scatter marinara sauce over.*
- ✓ *Top with chorizo rounds, mushrooms, basil, cheddar cheese, and chili flakes.*
- ✓ *Bake in the fryer for 12-14 minutes at 360 F, regularly checking to ensure an even baking.*
- ✓ *Work in batches if needed. Serve warm with garlic mayo or yogurt dip.*

nutritional value: CALORIES 641 ENERGY 2684 KJ FAT 44g SATURATES 12g FIBRE 8g PROTEIN 20g SODIUM 1605mg CARBS 38g SUGAR 4g

1071) Crispy Pepperoni Pizza

Ingredients:

- *2 Servings)*

- *8 oz fresh pizza dough*
- *⅓ cup mozzarella cheese, shredded*
- *8 pepperonis, sliced*
- *1 tsp oregano, dried Flour to dust*
- *⅓ cup tomato sauce*

Direction:(Prep + Cook Time: 25 minutes

- ✓ *On a floured surface, place pizza dough and dust with flour.*
- ✓ *Stretch with hands into the greased frying basket. Spray the dish with cooking spray and place the pizza dough inside.*
- ✓ *Spread the tomato sauce, leaving some space at the border.*
- ✓ *Scatter with mozzarella cheese and oregano and top with pepperoni slices.*
- ✓ *Bake for 14-16 minutes or until crispy at 340 F.*
- ✓ *Serve sliced*

nutritional value: Calories 319 Total Fat 20g Saturated Fat 9g Cholesterol 45mg Sodium 870mg Total Carbohydrate 23g Dietary Fiber 2.1g Sugar 3g Protein 14g Calcium 199.65mg Iron 1.08mg Potassium mg

1072) Bacon-Wrapped Dates

Ingredients:

- *4 Servings)*
- *2 tbsp maple syrup*
- *16 dates, pits removed*
- *⅓ cup blue cheese softened*
- *8 bacon slices, cut in half*
- *crosswise*

Direction:Prep + Cook Time: 25 minutes)

- ✓ *Preheat the air fryer to 370 F.*
- ✓ *Grease the frying basket with cooking oil.*
- ✓ *Using a sharp knife, make a deep cut into each date to create a pocket.*
- ✓ *Stuff the dates with blue cheese and pinch to lock up.*
- ✓ *Lay the bacon slices on the chopping board.*
- ✓ *Put a date on one side of each slice and roll-up.*
- ✓ *Secure with toothpicks.*
- ✓ *Brush the wrapped dates with maple syrup and AirFry for 10-12 minutes, turning halfway through cooking until the bacon is crispy.*
- ✓ *Let cool for 5 minutes and serve.*

nutritional value: Calories 49.6 Total Fat 2.3 g Saturated Fat 0.8 g Polyunsaturated Fat 0.3 g Monounsaturated Fat 1.1 g Cholesterol 3.9 mg Sodium 72.6 mg Potassium 76.6 mg Total Carbohydrate 6.3 g Dietary Fiber 0.7 g Sugars 5.3 g Protein 1.6 g Calcium 0.4 % Copper 1.2 % Folate 0.5 % Iron 0.9 % Magnesium 1.2 % Manganese 1.2 % Niacin 2.2 % Pantothenic Acid 1.0 % Phosphorus 2.0 % Riboflavin 1.1 % Selenium 2.0 % Thiamin 2.4 % Zinc 1.1 %

1073) Delicious Chicken Tortillas

Ingredients:

- *(4 Servings)*
- *1 cup cooked chicken, shredded*
- *1 cup mozzarella cheese, shredded*
- *¼ cup salsa ¼ cup Greek yogurt*
- *Salt and black pepper to taste*
- *8 flour tortillas*

Direction:Prep + Cook Time: 20 minutes

- ✓ *Mix the chicken, mozzarella, salsa, Greek yogurt, salt, and black pepper in a bowl.*
- ✓ *Lay 2 tbsp of the mixture at the center of the tortillas.*
- ✓ *Roll tightly around the mixture.*
- ✓ *Spray the taquitos with cooking spray and arrange them in the frying basket.*
- ✓ *AirFry for 12-14 minutes at 380 F, turning once.*
- ✓ *Serve.*

nutritional value: Calories 335.3 Total Fat 7.3 g Saturated Fat 2.4 g Polyunsaturated Fat 1.0 g Monounsaturated Fat 3.3 g Cholesterol 17.5 mg Sodium 696.1 mg Potassium 502.0 mg Total Carbohydrate 53.8 g Dietary Fiber 4.9 g Sugars 1.1 g Protein 14.2 g

1074) Chicken Burgers with Horseradish Sauce

Ingredients:

- *(4 Servings)*
- *1 lb ground chicken*
- *½ cup seasoned breadcrumbs*
- *¼ cup Parmesan cheese, grated*
- *1 egg, beaten*
- *1 tbsp minced garlic*
- *1 tbsp olive oil*
- *1 tsp horseradish sauce*
- *4 tbsp Greek yogurt*
- *4 buns, halved*
- *4 tomato slices*

Direction:(Prep + Cook Time: 25 minutes

- ✓ *Preheat the air fryer to 380 F.*
- ✓ *In a bowl, combine ground chicken, breadcrumbs, Parmesan, egg, and garlic.*
- ✓ *Mix well. Form balls and flatten them to make patties.*
- ✓ *Brush them with olive oil and place them in the greased frying basket.*
- ✓ *AirFry for 16-18 minutes, flipping once until nice and golden.*
- ✓ *Mix the yogurt with horseradish sauce.*
- ✓ *Assemble the burgers by spreading the yogurt mixture on the bun bottoms, adding the patties*

and fresh tomato slices.

- ✓ *Cover with the bun tops and serve.*
- ✓ *Mix the yogurt with horseradish sauce.*
- ✓ *Assemble the burgers by spreading the yogurt mixture on the bun bottoms, adding the patties and fresh tomato slices.*
- ✓ *Cover with the bun tops and serve.*

***nutritional value:* Calories 535 Total Fat 20g Saturated Fat 4.1g Trans Fat 0g Polyunsaturated Fat 9.1g Monounsaturated Fat 5.6g Cholesterol 57mg Sodium 1056mg Potassium 382mg Total Carbohydrates 57g Dietary Fiber 4.2g Sugars 6.5g Protein 29g Calcium 17%**

1075) Classic Beef Meatballs

Ingredients:

- *4 Servings)*
- *1 lb ground beef*
- *1 tsp grated ginger*
- *1 tbsp hot sauce*
- *½ tbsp white wine vinegar*
- *½ tsp lemon juice*
- *½ cup tomato ketchup*
- *¼ tsp dry mustard*
- *Salt and black pepper to taste*

Direction:(Prep + Cook Time: 25 minutes)

- ✓ *Mix well ground beef, ginger, hot sauce, vinegar, lemon juice, ketchup, mustard, black pepper, and salt in a bowl.*
- ✓ *With greased hands, shape the mixture into 2-inch sized balls.*

***nutritional value:* Cals 57 Protein 3.47g Fat 3.69g Saturated Fat 1.394g Cholesterol 21mg Carbohydrates 2.12g Sugar 0.42g Fibre 0.1g**

1076) Paprika Beef Fajitas

Ingredients:

- *(4 Servings)*
- *1 lb beef sirloin steak, cut into strips*
- *2 garlic cloves, minced*
- *1 tsp paprika*
- *½ red bell pepper, sliced*
- *½ orange bell pepper, sliced*
- *2 shallots, sliced*
- *2 tbsp Cajun seasoning*
- *2 tbsp olive oil*
- *8 tortilla wraps*
- *½ cup cheddar cheese, shredded*
- *Salt and black pepper to taste.*

Direction:(Prep + Cook Time: 35 minutes)

- ✓ *Preheat the air fryer to 360 F.*
- ✓ *In a bowl, combine the beef, shallots, bell peppers, and garlic.*
- ✓ *Season with Cajun seasoning, paprika, salt, and black pepper; toss to combine*
- ✓ *Transfer the mixture to a greased frying basket and place it inside the frying basket.*
- ✓ *Bake for 10 minutes, shaking once or twice throughout cooking.*
- ✓ *Serve on the tortilla wraps, topped with cheddar cheese.*

***nutritional value:* Calories 392.7 Total Fat 12.0 g Saturated Fat 2.8 g Polyunsaturated Fat 0.7 g Monounsaturated Fat 3.0 g Cholesterol 75.7 mg Sodium 808.5 mg Potassium 749.3 mg Total Carbohydrate 38.4 g Dietary Fiber 6.5 g Sugars 2.0 g Protein 33.9 g**

1077) South Asian Pork Momos

Ingredients:

- *4 Servings)*
- *1 lb ground pork*
- *2 tbsp olive oil*
- *1 carrot, shredded*
- *1 onion, chopped*
- *1 tsp soy sauce*
- *16 wonton wrappers*
- *Salt and black pepper to taste*

Direction:Prep + Cook Time: 25 minutes

- ✓ *Preheat the air fryer to 320 F.*
- ✓ *Warm olive oil in a pan over medium heat and stir-fry ground pork, onion, carrot, soy sauce, salt, and black pepper for 8-10 minutes or until the meat is browned.*
- ✓ *Divide the filling between the wrappers.*
- ✓ *Tuck them around the mixture to form momo shapes and seal the edges.*
- ✓ *Spritz the momos with cooking spray and AirFry them for 9-11 minutes, flipping once.*

***nutritional value:* Calories – 348 kcal Total Fat – 22.14 g Saturated Fat – 5.62 g Polyunsaturated Fat – 5.268 g Cholesterol – 23 g Health Benefits of Sodium – 424 mg Total Carbohydrates – 24.61 g Dietary Fibre – 0.9 sugar – 0.13 g Protein – 12.16 g**

1078) Spanish Chorizo with Brussels Sprouts

Ingredients:

- *(4 Servings)*
- *4 Spanish chorizo sausages, halved*
- *1 lb Brussels sprouts, trimmed and halved*
- *2 tbsp olive oil Salt and black pepper to taste*
- *1 tsp garlic puree*
- *1 thyme sprig, chopped*

Direction:(Prep + Cook Time: 20 minutes

- ✓ *Preheat the air fryer to 390 F. In a bowl, mix olive oil, garlic puree, salt, and black pepper.*

- ✓ *Add the Brussels sprouts and toss to coat*
- ✓ *Arrange chorizo and Brussels sprouts on the greased frying basket and AirFry for 11-14 minutes, tossing once halfway through cooking.*
- ✓ *Top with thyme to serve.*

nutritional value: 127 calories; fat 7.6g; saturated fat 1.7g; mono fat 4.6g; poly fat 0.9g; sodium 245mg

1079) Cheesy Sausage Balls

Ingredients:

- *(4 Servings)*
- *1 lb ground pork sausage meat*
- *1 ¼ cups cheddar cheese, shredded*
- *1 cup flour, sifted*
- *¾ tsp baking soda*
- *2 eggs*
- *½ cup sour cream*
- *½ tsp dried oregano*
- *½ tsp smoked paprika*
- *½ tsp garlic powder*
- *2 tbsp coconut oil*

Direction:Prep + Cook Time: 25 minutes + chilling time

- ✓ *Heat coconut oil in a pan over medium heat and brown the sausage meat for 3-4 minutes.*
- ✓ *Mix flour with baking soda in a bowl.*
- ✓ *Whisk eggs, sour cream, oregano, paprika, and garlic in another bowl.*
- ✓ *Combine egg and flour mixtures using a spatula.*
- ✓ *Mix in the cheese and sausage meat; let cool slightly.*
- ✓ *Mold out balls out of the batter and refrigerate for 15 minutes.*
- ✓ *Remove from the fridge and brush them with the sausage fat.*
- ✓ *Place the balls in the basket and AirFry for 12-14 minutes at 400 F, shaking once.*

nutritional value: Total Fat 10.3g Cholesterol 35.1mg Sodium 209mg Total Carbohydrate 7.7g Dietary Fiber 0.3g Sugars 0.7g Protein 9.6g Vitamin A 49.6µg Vitamin C 0.6mg Calcium 122.9mg Iron 0.6mg

1080) Baked Potatoes with Bacon

Ingredients:

- *4 Servings)*
- *4 potatoes, scrubbed, halved, cut lengthwise*
- *1 tbsp olive oil*
- *Salt and black pepper to taste*
- *4 oz bacon, chopped*

Direction:Prep + Cook Time: 35 minutes

- ✓ *Preheat the air fryer to 390 F.*
- ✓ *Brush the potatoes with olive oil and season with salt and black pepper.*
- ✓ *Arrange them in the greased frying basket, cut-side down.*
- ✓ *Bake for 15 minutes, flip them, top with bacon and bake for 12-15 minutes or until the potatoes are golden and the bacon is crispy.*
- ✓ *Serve.*

Nutritional value: Calories 480 kCal Total Carbs 66 g Net Carbs 59 g Fiber 7 g Sugar 6 g Protein 17 g Fat 17 g Monounsat. Fat 6 g Polyunsat. Fat 2.5 g Saturated Fat 8 g Cholesterol 40 mg Calcium 200 mg Iron 3.6 mg

1081) Chive Roasted Red Potatoes

Ingredients:

- *(4 Servings)*
- *4 red potatoes, cut into wedges*
- *1 tbsp garlic powder.*
- *Salt and black pepper to taste*
- *2 tbsp chives, chopped*
- *3 tbsp butter, melted*

Direction:(Prep + Cook Time: 30 minutes

- ✓ *Preheat the air fryer to 380 F.*
- ✓ *In a bowl, mix butter, garlic powder, salt, and pepper.*
- ✓ *Add the potatoes and shake to coat.*
- ✓ *Place them in the frying basket and Bake for 12 minutes; remove the basket, shake and continue to cook for another 8-10 minutes until golden brown.*
- ✓ *Serve warm topped with chives.*

nutritional value: Calories 110.0 Total Fat 1.5g Saturated Fat 0g Trans Fat 0g Cholesterol 5mg Sodium 300mg Total Carbohydrate 21g Dietary Fiber 3g Sugars 2g Protein 2g

1082) Crispy Hasselback Potatoes

Ingredients:

- *4 Servings)*
- *2 tbsp lard, melted*
- *1 lb russet potatoes*
- *1 tbsp olive oil*
- *Salt and black pepper to taste*
- *1 garlic clove, crushed*
- *1 tbsp fresh dill, chopped*

Direction:(Prep + Cook Time: 25 minutes

- ✓ *Preheat the air fryer to 400 F.*
- ✓ *On the potatoes, make thin vertical slits around 1/5 inch apart.*
- ✓ *Make sure to cut the potatoes 3/4-the way down so that they can hold together.*
- ✓ *Mix together the lard, olive oil, and garlic in a*

bowl

- ✓ Brush the potatoes with some of the mixtures.
- ✓ Season with salt and pepper and place them in the greased frying basket.
- ✓ AirFry for 25-30 minutes, brushing once halfway through so they don't dry during cooking until golden and crispy around the edges.
- ✓ Sprinkle with dill. Serve and enjoy!

nutritional value: Calories 218 Fat 9g Carbohydrates 28g Fiber 4g Sugar 1g Protein 3g

1083) Sweet Potato Boats

Ingredients:

- (4 Servings)
- 4 sweet potatoes, boiled and halved lengthwise
- 2 tbsp olive oil
- 1 shallot, chopped
- 1 cup canned mixed beans
- ¼ cup mozzarella cheese, grated
- Salt and black pepper to taste

Direction:(Prep + Cook Time: 25 minutes)

- ✓ Preheat the air fryer to 400 F.
- ✓ Grease the frying basket with olive oil.
- ✓ Scoop out the flesh from the potatoes, so shells are formed.
- ✓ Chop the potato flesh and put it in a bowl.
- ✓ Add in shallot, mixed beans, salt, and pepper; mix to combine.
- ✓ Fill the potato shells with the mixture and top with the cheese.
- ✓ Arrange on the basket and place inside the fryer.
- ✓ Bake for 10-12 minutes.

nutritional value: Calories: 173 Protein: 3 g Carbohydrate: 40 g Sugar: 8 g Total Fat: 0.2 g Calories from Fat: 1%Fiber: 6 g Sodium: 370 m

1084) Thyme & Garlic Sweet Potato Wedges

Ingredients:

- 2 Servings)
- ½ lb sweet potatoes, cut into wedges
- 1 tbsp coconut oil
- ¼ tsp chili powder
- ¼ tsp salt
- ¼ tsp garlic powder
- ¼ tsp smoked paprika
- ¼ tsp dried thyme
- ¼ tsp cayenne pepper

Direction:(Prep + Cook Time: 30 minutes)

- ✓ Mix coconut oil, salt, chili and garlic powders, paprika, thyme, and cayenne pepper in a bowl.
- ✓ Toss in the potato wedges. Arrange the wedges on the frying basket and AirFry for 23-25 minutes at 380 F, shaking a few times through cooking until golden.
- ✓ Serve and enjoy!

nutritional value: Calories 194 Fat 7g Saturated Fat 1g Sodium 471mg Potassium 528mg Carbohydrates 31g Fiber 4g Sugar 6g Protein 2g Calcium 50mg Iron 1.3mg

1085) Prosciutto & Cheese Stromboli

Ingredients:

- (4 Servings)
- 1 (13-oz) pizza crust
- 4 (1-oz) fontina cheese slices
- 8 slices prosciutto
- 12 cherry tomatoes, halved
- 4 fresh basil leaves, chopped
- ½ tsp dried oregano
- Salt and black pepper to taste

Direction:Prep + Cook Time: 30 minutes

- ✓ Roll out the pizza crust on a lightly floured work surface; slice into 4 squares.
- ✓ Top each one with a slice of fontina cheese, 2 slices of prosciutto, 3 halved cherry tomatoes, oregano, and basil.
- ✓ Season with salt and black pepper
- ✓ Close the rectangles by folding in half, press, and seal the edges with a fork.
- ✓ Spritz with cooking spray and transfer to the greased frying basket.
- ✓ Bake for 15 minutes, turning once.

nutritional value: Calories 1030 Total Fat 50g Saturated Fat 21g Trans Fat 0.5g Cholesterol 170mg Sodium 2985mg Potassium 619mg Total Carbohydrates 91g Dietary Fiber 5g Sugars 7g Protein 52g Calcium 65% Iron 45%

1086) Fava Bean Falafel Bites

Ingredients:

- 4 Servings)
- 1 tbsp olive oil
- 1 can (15.5-oz) fava beans, drained
- 1 red onion, chopped
- 2 tsp chopped fresh cilantro
- 1 tsp ground cumin
- Salt to taste
- 1 garlic clove, minced
- 3 tbsp flour
- 4 lemon wedges to serve

Direction:Prep + Cook Time: 20 minutes

- ✓ Preheat the air fryer to 380 F.
- ✓ In a food processor, pulse all the ingredients until a thick paste is formed.

- ✓ *Shape the mixture into ping pong-sized balls.*
- ✓ *Brush with olive oil and insert in the greased frying basket. AirFry for 12 minutes, turning once halfway through.*
- ✓ *Plate and serve with lemon wedges.*

nutritional value: Calorie 298clCarbs 20 g Dietary Fiber 10 g Sugar 8 g Fat 16 g Saturated 5 g Protein 13 g

1087) Plum & Pancetta Bombs

Ingredients:

- *(4-6 Servings)*
- *1 ¼ cups soft goat cheese, crumbled*
- *1 tbsp fresh rosemary, finely chopped*
- *1 cup almonds, chopped*
- *Salt and black pepper to taste*
- *15 dried plums, soaked and chopped*
- *15 pancetta slices*

Direction:(Prep + Cook Time: 20 minutes

- ✓ *Line the frying basket with baking paper.*
- ✓ *Add goat cheese, rosemary, almonds, salt, black pepper, and plums; stir well.*
- ✓ *Roll into balls and wrap with a pancetta slice*
- ✓ *Place them into the fryer and AirFry for 10 minutes at 400 F, shaking once.*
- ✓ *Let cool for a few minutes.*
- ✓ *Serve with toothpicks*

nutritional value: Calorie 246cl Carbs0 g Fat19 g Saturated0 g Polyunsaturated0 g Monounsaturated0 g Trans0 g Protein17 g Sodium25 mg Potassium50 mg Cholesterol0 mg

1088) Fried Sausage Ravioli

Ingredients:

- *(6 Servings)*
- *2 (18-oz) packages of fresh ravioli*
- *1 cup flour*
- *1 cup marinara sauce*
- *4 eggs, beaten in a bowl*
- *2 cups breadcrumbs*
- *2 tbsp Parmesan cheese, grated*

Direction:Prep + Cook Time: 15 minutes

- ✓ *Preheat the air fryer to 400 F.*
- ✓ *In a bowl, mix breadcrumbs with Parmesan cheese.*
- ✓ *Dip pasta into the flour, then into the eggs, and finally in the breadcrumb mixture.*
- ✓ *Arrange the coated ravioli on the greased frying basket in an even layer and spritz them with cooking spray.*
- ✓ *AirFry for 10-12 minutes, turning once halfway through cooking until nice and golden.*
- ✓ *Serve hot with marinara sauce.*

nutritional value: Calories 98 Total Fat 4.6g Saturated Fat 1g Trans Fat 0.1g Polyunsaturated Fat 2.1g Monounsaturated Fat 1.1g Cholesterol 16mg Sodium 250mg Potassium 88mg Total Carbohydrates 11g Dietary Fiber 0.8g Sugars 1.4g Protein 3.2g Calcium 3% Iron 3.3%

1089) Roasted Hot Chickpeas

Ingredients:

- *(4 Servings)*
- *1 (19-oz) can chickpeas, drained and rinsed*
- *2 tbsp olive oil*
- *½ tsp ground cumin*
- *¼ tsp mustard powder*
- *¼ tsp onion powder*
- *½ tsp chili powder*
- *¼ tsp cayenne pepper*
- *¼ tsp salt*

Direction:(Prep + Cook Time: 25 minutes

- ✓ *Preheat the air fryer to 385 F.*
- ✓ *In a mixing bowl, thoroughly combine the olive oil, cumin, mustard powder, onion powder, chili powder, cayenne pepper, and salt.*
- ✓ *Add in the chickpeas.*
- ✓ *Toss them until evenly coated.*
- ✓ *Transfer the Chickpeas to the frying basket and Air Fry, shaking the basket every 2-3 minutes.*
- ✓ *Cook until they're as crunchy as you like them, about 15-20 minutes.*
- ✓ *Serve.*

nutritional value: Calories 119 Total Fat 3.9g Saturated Fat 0.5g Polyunsaturated Fat 1g Monounsaturated Fat 2.1g Cholesterol 0mg Sodium 6.3mg Potassium 187mg Total Carbohydrates 16g Dietary Fiber 3.2g Sugars 2.8g Protein 5.3g

1090) Paprika Baked Parsnips

Ingredients:

- *(4 Servings)*
- *½ tbsp paprika*
- *1 lb parsnips, peeled and halved*
- *4 tbsp avocado oil*
- *2 tbsp fresh cilantro, chopped*
- *2 tbsp Parmesan cheese, grated*
- *1 tsp garlic powder*
- *Salt and black pepper to taste*

Direction:(Prep + Cook Time: 20 minutes)

- ✓ *Preheat the air fryer to 390 F.*
- ✓ *In a bowl, mix paprika, avocado oil, garlic, salt, and black pepper.*
- ✓ *Toss in the parsnips to coat.*
- ✓ *Arrange them on the greased frying basket and Bake for 14-16 minutes, turning once halfway through cooking, until golden and crunchy.*

- ✓ *Remove and sprinkle with Parmesan cheese and cilantro.*
- ✓ *Serve.*

nutritional value:** **Calories: 237; Total Fat: 8g; Saturated Fat: 1g; Monounsaturated Fat: 5g; Cholesterol: 0mg; Sodium: 314mg; Carbohydrate: 42g; Dietary Fiber: 12g; Sugar: 11g; Protein: 3g

1091) Air-Fried Cheesy Broccoli with Garlic

Ingredients:

- *(2 Servings)*
- *2 tbsp butter, melted*
- *1 egg white*
- *1 garlic clove, grated*
- *Salt and black pepper to taste*
- *½ lb broccoli florets*
- *⅓ cup grated Parmesan cheese*

Direction:Prep + Cook Time: 20 minutes)

- ✓ *`In a bowl, whisk together butter, egg white, garlic, salt, and black pepper.*
- ✓ *Toss in the broccoli to coat.*
- ✓ *Arrange them in a single layer in the greased frying basket and AirFry for 10 minutes at 360 F, shaking once.*
- ✓ *Remove to a plate and sprinkle with Parmesan cheese.*
- ✓ *Serve immediately.*

nutritional value:
Calories: 43kcal | Carbohydrates: 8g | Protein: 3g | Fat: 1g | Saturated
Fat: 1g | Sodium: 37mg | Potassium: 358mg | Fiber: 3g | Sugar: 2g | Vitamin
A: 706IU | Calcium: 53mg | Iron: 1mg

1092) Roasted Coconut Carrots

Ingredients:

- *4 Servings)*
- *1 tbsp coconut oil, melted*
- *1 lb horse carrots, sliced*
- *Salt and black pepper to taste*
- *½ tsp chili powder*

Direction:Prep + Cook Time: 15 minutes)

- ✓ *Preheat the air fryer to 400 F.*
- ✓ *Mix the carrots with coconut oil, chili powder, salt, and black pepper in a bowl.*
- ✓ *Place them in the fryer and AirFry for 7 minutes.*
- ✓ *Shake the basket and cook for another 5 minutes until golden brown.*
- ✓ *Serve.*

Nutrition:Calories: 111.3kcal Carbs: 19g Protein: 2 g Fat: 3.7g Saturated Fat: 2.9g Monounsaturated Fat: 0.2g Sodium: 176.5mg Potassium: 639.4mg Fib er: 5.6g Sugar: 9.5g

1093) Pumpkin Wedges

Ingredients:

- *(4 Servings)*
- *1 lb pumpkin, washed and cut into wedges*
- *1 tbsp paprika*
- *2 tbsp olive oil*
- *1 lime, juiced*
- *1 tbsp balsamic vinegar*
- *Salt and black pepper to taste*
- *1 tsp turmeric*

Direction:Prep + Cook Time: 20 minutes

- ✓ *Preheat the air fryer to 400 F.*
- ✓ *Add the pumpkin wedges to the greased frying basket and AirFry for 10-12 minutes, flipping once.*
- ✓ *Mix olive oil, lime juice, balsamic vinegar, turmeric, salt, black pepper, and paprika in a bowl.*
- ✓ *Drizzle the dressing over the pumpkin and fry for 5 more minutes.*
- ✓ *Serve warm.*

nutritional value: Calories 82.9 Total Fat 1.2 g Cholesterol 0.0 mg Sodium 30.6 mg Potassium 50.0 mg Total Carbohydrate 16.7 g Dietary Fiber 2.4 g Sugars 3.6 g Protein 2.8 g Calcium 0.4 %

1094) Baked Butternut Squash

Ingredients:

- *(4 Servings)*
- *2 cups butternut squash, cubed*
- *2 tbsp olive oil*
- *Salt and black pepper to taste*
- *¼ tsp dried thyme*
- *1 tbsp fresh parsley, finely chopped*

Direction:(Prep + Cook Time: 25 minutes

- ✓ *Add squash, olive oil, salt, black pepper, and thyme; toss to coat.*
- ✓ *Place the squash in the air fryer and AirFry for 12-14 minutes at 360 F, shaking once or twice.*
- ✓ *Serve sprinkled with fresh parsley.*

nutritional value: 26 Kcal/110KJ0.7g protein 0.1g fat 5.9g carbohydrate1.5g fibre 224mg potassium 12mg

1095) Cheesy Mushrooms

Ingredients:

- *2 Servings)*
- *2 tbsp olive oil Salt and black pepper to taste*
- *10 button mushroom caps*
- *2 tbsp mozzarella cheese, grated*
- *2 tbsp cheddar cheese, grated*
- *1 tsp Italian seasoning*

Direction:(Prep + Cook Time: 20 minutes

- ✓ *Preheat the air fryer to 390 F.*

- ✓ In a bowl, mix olive oil, salt, black pepper, and Italian seasoning.
- ✓ Toss in the mushrooms to coat.
- ✓ Mix the cheeses in a separate bowl.
- ✓ Stuff the mushrooms with the cheese mixture and place them in the frying basket.
- ✓ Bake for 10-12 minutes until golden on top.
- ✓ Serve warm.

nutritional value: Calories 53 Total Fat 4.1g Saturated Fat 0.8g Trans Fat 0g Cholesterol 2mg Sodium 114mg Potassium 69mg Total Carbohydrates 3.1g Dietary Fiber 0.5g Sugars 0.5g Protein 1.4g

1096) Walnut & Cheese Filled Mushrooms

Ingredients:

- (4 Servings)
- 4 large portobello mushroom caps
- ⅓ cup walnuts, finely chopped
- 1 tbsp canola oil
- ½ cup mozzarella cheese, shredded
- 2 tbsp fresh parsley, chopped

Direction:Prep + Cook Time: 20 minutes

- ✓ Preheat the air fryer to 350 F.
- ✓ Grease the frying basket with cooking spray.
- ✓ Rub the mushrooms with canola oil and fill them with mozzarella cheese.
- ✓ Top with walnuts and arrange them in the greased frying basket.
- ✓ Bake for 10-12 minutes or until golden on top.
- ✓ Remove and let cool for a few minutes.
- ✓ Sprinkle with freshly chopped parsley and serve

nutritional value: Calories 55.2 Total Fat 3.3 g Saturated Fat 1.0 g Polyunsaturated Fat 1.5 g Cholesterol 4.1 mg Sodium 157.1 mg Potassium 112.4 mg Total Carbohydrate 2.3 g Dietary Fiber 0.4 g Sugars 0.5 g Protein 4.6 g

1097) Paprika Serrano Peppers

Ingredients:

- (4 Servings)
- 4 serrano peppers, halved and seeds removed
- 3 oz ricotta cheese, crumbled
- 1 cup breadcrumbs
- 1 tsp paprika
- 1 tbsp chives, chopped
- 1 tbsp olive oil

Direction:Prep + Cook Time: 20 minutes)

- ✓ Preheat the air fryer to 380 F.
- ✓ Grease the frying basket with cooking spray.
- ✓ In a bowl, combine ricotta cheese, paprika, and chives. Spoon the mixture into the pepper halves and top with breadcrumbs.
- ✓ Drizzle with olive oil.
- ✓ Place in the basket and Bake for 10-12 minutes.
- ✓ Serve warm.

nutritional value: Calories: 34Fat: 0.5g Sodium: 11mg Carbohydrates: 7g Fiber: 3.9g Sugars: 4g Protein: 1.8g

1098) Chili Edamame

Ingredients:

- 4 Servings)
- 1 (16-oz) bag frozen edamame in pods
- 1 red chili, finely chopped
- 1 tbsp olive oil
- ½ tsp garlic salt
- ½ tsp red pepper flakes
- Black pepper to taste

Direction:Prep + Cook Time: 20 minutes)

- ✓ Preheat the air fryer to 380 F.
- ✓ Combine olive oil, garlic salt, red pepper flakes, and black pepper in a mixing bowl and mix well.
- ✓ Add in the edamame and toss to coat.
- ✓ Transfer to the frying basket in a single layer and AirFry for 10 minutes, shaking once.
- ✓ Cook until lightly browned and just crispy.
- ✓ Work in batches if needed.
- ✓ Serve topped with the red chili.

nutritional value: Calories 370 Total Fat 12g Saturated Fat 0g Trans Fat 0g Cholesterol 0mg Sodium 25mg Total Carbohydrates 27g Dietary Fiber 15g Sugars 6ggrams Protein 32g

1099) Brie Cheese Croutons with Herbs

Ingredients:

- 2 Servings)
- 2 tbsp olive oil
- 1 tbsp french herbs
- 6 oz brie cheese, chopped
- 2 slices bread, halved

Direction:Prep + Cook Time: 15 minutes + cooling time

- ✓ Preheat the air fryer to 340 F.
- ✓ Brush the bread slices with olive oil and sprinkle with herbs.
- ✓ Top with brie cheese Place in the greased frying basket and Bake for 10-12 minutes.
- ✓ Let cool, then cut into cubes.

nutritional value: Calories 100 Total Fat 9g Saturated fat 4g Sodium 120.1mg Carbohydrates 0g Net carbs 0g Sugar 0g Fiber 0g Protein 4g Calcium 100mg Iron 1.1mg

1100) Super Cabbage Canapes

Ingredients:

- (2 Servings)

- *1 whole cabbage, cut into rounds*
- *½ cup mozzarella cheese, shredded*
- *½ carrot, cubed*
- *¼ onion, cubed*
- *¼ bell pepper, cubed*
- *1 tbsp fresh basil, chopped*

Direction:Prep + Cook Time: 20 minutes

- ✓ *Preheat the air fryer to 360 F.*
- ✓ *In a bowl, mix onion, carrot, bell pepper, and mozzarella cheese.*
- ✓ *Toss to coat evenly.*
- ✓ *Add the cabbage rounds to the greased frying basket, top with the cheese mixture, and Bake for 5-8 minutes.*
- ✓ *Garnish with basil and serve*

nutritional value: Calories: 22 Fat: 0.1g Sodium: 16mg Carbohydrates: 5.2g Fiber: 2.2g Sugars: 2.9g Protein: 1.1g Potassium: 151 mg Folate: 38.3 mcg Vitamin K: 67.6mc

1101) ***Broccoli Cheese Quiche***

Ingredients:

- *3 Servings)*
- *1 head broccoli, cut into florets*
- *½ cup Parmesan cheese, grated*
- *¼ cup heavy cream*
- *Salt and black pepper to taste 5 eggs*

Direction:Prep + Cook Time: 30 minutes)

- ✓ *Preheat the air fryer to 340 F.*
- ✓ *Beat the eggs with heavy cream.*
- ✓ *Season with salt and black pepper.*
- ✓ *In a greased baking dish, lay the florets and cover them with the egg mixture.*
- ✓ *Spread Parmesan cheese on top and place inside the frying basket. Bake for 10-12 minutes until golden brown on top.*
- ✓ *Serve warm.*

nutritional value: Calories 411 Total Fat 30g Saturated Fat 15g Trans Fat 0.7g Polyunsaturated Fat 2.4g Monounsaturated Fat 9.6g Cholesterol 210mg Sodium 385mg Potassium 330mg Total Carbohydrates 20g Dietary Fiber 2.6g Sugars 4.4g Protein 16g

1102) ***Easy Parmesan Sandwich***

Ingredients:

- *(1 Serving)*
- *4 tbsp Parmesan cheese, shredded*
- *2 scallions*
- *1 tbsp butter, softened*
- *2 bread slices*

Direction:(Prep + Cook Time: 20 minutes

- ✓ *Preheat the air fryer to 360 F.*
- ✓ *Spread only one side of the bread slices with butter.*
- ✓ *Cover one of the buttered slices with Parmesan and scallions and top with the buttered side of the other slice to form a sandwich.*
- ✓ *Place in the frying basket and Bake for 10-12 minutes.*
- ✓ *Cut into 4 triangles and serve.*

nutritional value: Calories 437.3 Total Fat 13.4 g Saturated Fat 6.9 g Polyunsaturated Fat 1.0 g Monounsaturated Fat 2.5 g Cholesterol 90.1 mg Sodium 947.0 mg Potassium 323.5 mg Total Carbohydrate 34.2 g Dietary Fiber 4.5 g Sugars 8.5 g Protein 44.2 g

1103) ***Salty Carrot Cookies***

Ingredients:

- *(4 Servings)*
- *6 carrots, boiled and mashed*
- *Salt and black pepper to taste*
- *½ tsp parsley*
- *1 ¼ oz oats*
- *1 whole egg, beaten*
- *½ tsp thyme*

Direction:Prep + Cook Time: 25 minutes)

- ✓ *Preheat the air fryer to 360 F.*
- ✓ *Combine carrots, salt, black pepper, egg, oats, thyme, and parsley; mix well to form a batter.*
- ✓ *Shape into cookie shapes.*
- ✓ *Place the cookies in the greased frying basket and Bake for 14-16 minutes, flipping once halfway through.*
- ✓ *Serve.*

nutritional value: Calories 110.9 Total Fat 5.6 g Saturated Fat 0.6 g Polyunsaturated Fat 3.1 g Monounsaturated Fat 1.6 g Cholesterol 0.0 mg Sodium 164.7 mg Potassium 41.8 mg Total Carbohydrate 14.1 g Dietary Fiber 0.5 g Sugars 0.4 Protein 1.4 g

1104) ***Mini Cheese Scones***

Ingredients:

- *(4 Servings)*
- *1 cup flour*
- *A pinch of salt*
- *1 tsp baking powder*
- *2 oz butter, cubed*
- *1 tsp fresh chives, chopped*
- *1 egg*
- *¼ cup milk*
- *½ cup cheddar cheese, shredded*

Direction:Prep + Cook Time: 30 minutes

- ✓ *Preheat the air fryer to 360 F.*
- ✓ *Sith the flour in a bowl and mix in butter, baking powder, and salt until a breadcrumb mixture is formed.*

- ✓ *Add cheese, chives, milk, and egg, and mix to get a sticky dough.*
- ✓ *Roll the dough into small balls.*
- ✓ *Place the balls in the greased frying basket and AirFry for 18-20 minutes, shaking once or twice. Serve warm*

nutritional value: Calories 154 Total Fat 9.5g Saturated Fat 5.6g Trans Fat 0.3g Cholesterol 51mg Sodium 263mg Total Carbohydrates 13g Dietary Fiber 0.4g Sugars 0.3g Protein 4.4g

1105) Cheddar Cheese Biscuits

Ingredients:

- *4 Servings)*
- *½ cup butter softened*
- *1 tbsp melted butter.*
- *1 tsp salt*
- *2 cups flour*
- *½ cup buttermilk*
- *½ cup cheddar cheese, grated*
- *1 egg, beaten*

Direction:Prep + Cook Time: 30 minutes)

- ✓ *Preheat the air fryer to 360 F.*
- ✓ *Mix salt, flour, butter, cheese, and buttermilk to form a batter in a bowl.*
- ✓ *Shape into balls and flatten them into biscuits.*
- ✓ *Arrange them on a greased frying basket and brush with the beaten egg.*
- ✓ *Drizzle with melted butter and Bake in the fryer for 18-20 minutes, flipping once.*

nutritional value: Calories160 kCal Total Carbs 15 g Net Carbs 14 g Fiber 1 g Sugar 1 g Protein v4 g Fat 10 g Saturated Fat 4 g Cholesterol 10 mg Calcium 40 mg Iron 1.1 mg Sodium 240 mg

1106) Cauliflower & Tofu Croquettes

Ingredients:

- *4 Servings)*
- *1 lb cauliflower florets*
- *2 eggs*
- *½ cup tofu, crumbled*
- *½ cup mozzarella cheese*
- *⅓ cup breadcrumbs*
- *1 tsp dried thyme*
- *¼ tsp ground cumin*
- *½ tsp onion powder*
- *Salt and black pepper to taste*
- *1 cup chipotle aioli*

Direction:Prep + Cook Time: 30 minutes

- ✓ *Place the cauliflower florets in your food processor and pulse until it resembles rice.*
- ✓ *Microwave the resulting "rice" in a heatproof dish for 4-6 minutes until it has softened completely.*
- ✓ *Let cool.*
- ✓ *Preheat the air fryer to 390 F.*
- ✓ *Add the eggs, tofu, mozzarella cheese, breadcrumbs, thyme, cumin, onion powder, salt, and pepper to the cauliflower rice and mix to combine.*
- ✓ *Form the mixture into croquettes and arrange them on the greased frying basket.*
- ✓ *Spritz with cooking spray.*
- ✓ *AirFry for 14-16 minutes, turning once, until golden brown.*
- ✓ *Serve warm with the chipotle aioli.*

nutritional value: Kcal 155 Fat 9g Saturates 3g Carbs 12g Sugars 2g Fibre 1g Protein 5g Salt 0.23g

1107) Cheesy Mushroom & Cauliflower Balls

Ingredients:

- *(4 Servings)*
- *½lb mushrooms, diced*
- *3 tbsp olive oil + some more for brushing*
- *1 small red onion, chopped*
- *3 garlic cloves, minced*
- *3 cups cauliflower, chopped*
- *1 cup breadcrumbs*
- *1 cup Grana Padano cheese, grated*
- *2 sprigs fresh thyme, chopped*
- *Salt and black pepper to taste*

Direction:(Prep + Cook Time: 25 minutes + cooling time

- ✓ *Heat 3 tbsp olive oil in a skillet over medium heat and sauté garlic and onion for 3 minutes.*
- ✓ *Add in mushrooms and cauliflower and stir-fry for 5 minutes.*
- ✓ *Add in Grana Padano cheese, black pepper, thyme, and salt.*
- ✓ *Turn off and let cool.*
- ✓ *Make small balls out of the mixture and refrigerate for 30 minutes.*
- ✓ *Preheat the air fryer to 350 F.*
- ✓ *Remove the balls from the refrigerator and roll in the breadcrumbs.*
- ✓ *Brush with olive oil and place in the frying basket without overcrowding. Bake for 14-16 minutes, tossing every 4-5 minutes.*
- ✓ *Serve with sautéed zoodles and tomato sauce, if desired.*

nutritional value: Calories 395.6 Total Fat 33.3g Saturated fat 12.8g Monounsaturated fat 14.6g Polyunsaturated fat 2.2g Trans-fat 0.7g Cholesterol 57.6mg Sodium 375.2mg Potassium 459mg Carbohydrates 10.3gNet carbs 6.7g Sugar 4g Fiber 3.6g Glucose 3.1g Fructose 0.7g Lactose 0.1g Galactose 0.1g

Protein 16.4g

1108) Spicy Cheese Lings

Ingredients:

- (4 Servings)
- ½ cup grated cheddar cheese + extra for rolling
- 1 cup flour + extra for kneading
- ¼ tsp chili powder
- ½ tsp baking powder
- 3 tsp butter, melted
- A pinch of salt

Direction:Prep + Cook Time: 20 minutes)

- ✓ Mix the cheese, flour, baking powder, chili powder, butter, and salt in a bowl.
- ✓ Add some water and mix well to get a dough.
- ✓ Remove the dough onto a flat, floured surface.
- ✓ Using a rolling pin, roll out into a thin sheet and
- ✓ cut into lings' shape.
- ✓ Add the cheese lings to the greased frying basket and AirFry for 10-12 minutes at 350 F, flipping once halfway through.
- ✓ Serve with ketchup if desired

nutritional value: Calories 20 Total Fat 1.5g Sodium 150mg Carbohydrates 2g Net carbs 2g Fiber 0g Protein 0g

1109) Cocktail Meatballs

Ingredients:

- 4 Servings)
- ½ lb ground beef
- ½ lb ground pork
- 2 oz bacon, chopped
- 1 cup jalapeño tomato ketchup
- 1 egg
- Salt and black pepper to taste
- ¼ tsp cayenne pepper
- 2 oz cheddar cheese, shredded

Direction:Prep + Cook Time: 30 MINUTES

- ✓ Preheat the air fryer to 400 F.
- ✓ In a bowl, thoroughly mix all ingredients.
- ✓ Form the mixture into 1-inch balls using an ice cream scoop.
- ✓ Place them into the greased frying basket and spray with cooking oil.
- ✓ AirFry for 8-10 minutes, turning once.
- ✓ Serve with toothpicks and jalapeño tomato ketchup on the side.

nutritional value: Calories 56c Total Fat 2.4g Saturated Fat 0.7g Trans Fat 0.1g Polyunsaturated Fat 0.3g Monounsaturated Fat 1.1g Cholesterol 8.7mg Sodium 136mg Potassium 74mg Total Carbohydrates 5.3g Dietary Fiber 0.2g Sugars 1.7g Protein 3.2g Calcium 0.9%

1110) French Beans with Toasted Almonds

Ingredients:

- (4 Servings)
- 1 lb French beans, trimmed
- Salt and black pepper to taste
- ½ tbsp onion powder
- 2 tbsp olive oil
- ½ cup toasted almonds, chopped

Direction:Prep + Cook Time: 15 minutes

- ✓ Preheat air fryer to 400 F.
- ✓ In a bowl, drizzle the beans with olive oil.
- ✓ Add onion powder, salt, and pepper and toss to coat.
- ✓ AirFry for 10-12 minutes, shaking once.
- ✓ Sprinkle with almonds and serve.

nutritional value: 68 calories; protein 2.2g; carbohydrates 5g; dietary fiber 2.5g; sugars 1g; fat 5.1g; saturated fat 0.5g; vitamin a iu 379.8IU; vitamin c 9mg; folate 21.9mcg; calcium 33.8mg; iron 0.8mg; magnesium 28.6mg; potassium 154.4mg; sodium 60.1mg.

1111) Cheddar Black Bean Burritos

Ingredients:

- (4 Servings)
- 4 tortillas
- 1 cup cheddar cheese, grated
- 1 can (8 oz) black beans, drained
- 1 tsp taco seasoning

Direction:Prep + Cook Time: 10 minutes)

- ✓ Preheat the air fryer to 350 F.
- ✓ Mix the beans with the taco seasoning.
- ✓ Divide the bean mixture between the tortillas and top with cheddar cheese.
- ✓ Roll the burritos and arrange them on the greased frying basket.
- ✓ Place in the air fryer and Bake for 4-5 minutes, flip, and cook for 3 more minutes.
- ✓ Serve warm.

nutritional value: Calories 377.6 Total Fat 14.6 g Saturated Fat 7.2 g Polyunsaturated Fat 0.5 g Monounsaturated Fat 3.2 g Cholesterol 35.5 mg Sodium 581.4 mg Potassium 352.3 mg Total Carbohydrate 45.4 g Dietary Fiber 11.5 g Sugars 1.0 g Protein 19.1 g

1112) Smoky Hazelnuts

Ingredients:

- 4-6 Servings)
- 2 cups almonds
- 2 tbsp liquid smoke
- Salt to taste

- 1 tbsp molasses

Direction:Prep + Cook Time: 20 minutes

- ✓ Preheat the air fryer to 360 F.
- ✓ In a bowl, add salt, liquid smoke, molasses, and almonds; toss to coat.
- ✓ Place the hazelnuts in the greased frying basket and Bake for 5-8 minutes, shaking once.
- ✓ Serve warm.

nutritional value: Calories: 176 Total fat: 17 grams Protein: 4.2 grams Carbs: 4.7 grams Fiber: 2.7 grams Vitamin E: 21% of the RDI Thiamin: 12% Magnesium: 12% Copper: 24%

1113) Spiced Almonds

Ingredients:

- (4 Servings)
- ½ tsp ground cinnamon
- ½ tsp smoked paprika
- 1 cup almonds
- 1 egg white
- Sea salt to taste

Direction:Prep + Cook Time: 15 minutes

- ✓ Preheat the air fryer to 310 F.
- ✓ Grease the frying basket with cooking spray.
- ✓ In a bowl, whisk the egg white with cinnamon and paprika and stir in the almonds.
- ✓ Spread the almonds in the frying basket and AirFry for 12-14 minutes, shaking once or twice.
- ✓ Remove and sprinkle with sea salt to serve.

nutritional value: Calories 7.7 Total Fat 0.7g Saturated Fat 0.1g Trans Fat 0gPolyunsaturated Fat 0.2ggrams Monounsaturated Fat 0.4g Cholesterol 0mg Sodium 6.4mg Potassium 9.2mg Total Carbohydrates 0.3g Dietary Fiber 0.1gSugars 0.1g Protein 0.3g

1114) Roasted Pumpkin Seeds with Cardamom

Ingredients:

- (4 Servings)
- 1 cup pumpkin seeds, pulp removed, rinsed
- 1 tbsp butter, melted
- 1 tbsp brown sugar
- 1 tsp orange zest
- ½ tsp cardamom
- ½ tsp salt

Direction:(Prep + Cook Time: 25 minutes

- ✓ Preheat air fryer to 320 F.
- ✓ Place the pumpkin seeds in a greased baking dish and place the dish in the fryer.
- ✓ AirFry for 4-5 minutes to avoid moisture.
- ✓ In a bowl, whisk butter, sugar, zest, cardamom, and salt.
- ✓ Add the seeds to the bowl and toss to coat well.
- ✓ Transfer the seeds to the baking dish inside the fryer and Bake for 13-15 minutes, shaking the basket every 5 minutes, until lightly browned.
- ✓ Serve warm.

nutritional value: Calories 169 Total Fat 14g Saturated Fat 2.5g Trans Fat 0g Polyunsaturated Fat 5.9g Monounsaturated Fat 4.6g Cholesterol 0mg Sodium 76mg Potassium 232mg Total Carbohydrates 4.3g Dietary Fiber 1.9g Sugars 0.4g Protein 8.8g

1115) Masala Cashew Nuts

Ingredients:

- (2 Servings)
- 1 cup cashew nuts
- Salt and black pepper to taste
- ½ tsp ground coriander
- 1 tsp garam masala

Direction:Prep + Cook Time: 10 minutes

- ✓ Preheat the air fryer to 360 F.
- ✓ In a bowl, mix coriander, garam masala, salt, and pepper. Add cashews and toss to coat.
- ✓ Place in a greased baking dish and AirFry in the fryer for 5-8 minutes, shaking once.

nutritional value: 157 calories 8.56 g carbohydrate1.68 g sugar 0.9 g fiber 5.17 g protein 12.43 g total fat

1116) Sweet Mixed Nuts

Ingredients:

- (5 Servings)
- ½ cup pecans
- ½ cup walnuts
- ½ cup almonds
- A pinch of cayenne pepper
- 1 tbsp sugar
- 2 tbsp egg whites
- 2 tsp ground cinnamon
- Cooking spray

Direction:Prep + Cook Time: 15 minutes

- ✓ Add cayenne pepper, sugar, and cinnamon to a bowl and mix well; set aside.
- ✓ In another bowl, mix pecans, walnuts, almonds, and egg whites.
- ✓ Add in the spice mixture and stir.
- ✓ Grease a baking dish with cooking spray.
- ✓ Pour in the nuts and place the dish in the fryer.
- ✓ Bake for 5-7 minutes.
- ✓ Stir the nuts using a wooden spoon and cook for 4-5 more minutes.
- ✓ Pour the nuts into the bowl and let cool slightly.

nutritional value: Calories 150 Total Fat 11g Saturated Fat 1.5g Trans Fat 0g Cholesterol 0mg Sodium 135mg Total Carbohydrates 11g Dietary Fiber 2g Sugars 7g Protein 4g

1117) Pork, Beef & Lamb Honey & Bbq Spare Ribs

Ingredients:

- (4 Servings)
- 1 rack pork spareribs, fat trimmed
- ½ tsp ginger powder
- Salt and black pepper to taste
- 2 garlic cloves, minced
- 1 tsp olive oil
- 1 tbsp honey + for brushing
- 4 tbsp barbecue sauce
- 1 tsp soy sauce

Direction:(Prep + Cook Time: 30 minutes + marinating time)

- ✓ Chop the ribs into individual bones. I
- ✓ n a large bowl, whisk all the remaining ingredients, reserving some of the honey.
- ✓ Add in the meat and mix to coat.
- ✓ Cover with a lid and place in the fridge for 1 hour
- ✓ Preheat the air fryer to 350 F. Place the ribs in the frying basket and AirFry for 8 minutes.
- ✓ Slide the basket out and brush the ribs with the reserved honey.
- ✓ AirFry for 12-14 minutes until golden and crispy.

nutritional value: Calories 693.4 Total Fat44.8 g Saturated Fat 16.6 g Monounsaturated Fat 20.4 g Cholesterol 178.6 mg Sodium 804.2 mg Potassium 500.3 mg Total Carbohydrate 35.5 g Dietary Fiber 0.2 g Sugars 34.1 g Protein 37.0 g

1118) Char Siew Pork Ribs

Ingredients:

- (4 Servings)
- 2 lb pork ribs
- 2 tbsp char siew sauce
- 2 tbsp minced ginger
- 1 tbsp soy sauce
- 2 tbsp hoisin sauce
- 2 tbsp sesame oil
- 1 tsp honey
- 4 garlic cloves, minced

Direction:Prep + Cook Time: 35 minutes + marinating time)

- ✓ Whisk together all the ingredients, except for the ribs, in a large bowl.
- ✓ Add in the ribs and toss to coat.
- ✓ Cover with a lid. Place the bowl in the fridge to marinate for 2 hours.
- ✓ Preheat the air fryer to 390 F. Put the ribs in the greased frying basket and place them in the fryer; do not throw away the liquid from the bowl.
- ✓ Bake for 15 minutes. Pour in the marinade and cook for 10-12 more minutes. Serve hot.

nutritional value: Calories 449 Total Fat 27g Saturated Fat 12g Sodium 777mg Total Carbs 16g Total Sugars 16gProtein 36g

1119) Memphis-Style Pork Ribs

Ingredients:

- 4 Servings)
- 1 ½ lb St. Louis–style pork spareribs
- Salt and black pepper to taste
- ½ tsp sweet paprika
- ½ tsp dry mustard
- 1 tbsp brown sugar
- 1 tbsp cayenne pepper
- 1 tsp poultry seasoning
- 1 tsp shallot powder
- 1 tsp garlic powder
- ½ cup hot sauce

Direction:Prep + Cook Time: 40 minutes)

- ✓ Preheat the air fryer to 370 F.
- ✓ Cut the ribs individually. In a bowl, mix all the remaining ingredients, except for the hot sauce.
- ✓ Add the ribs to the bowl and rub the seasoning onto the meat.
- ✓ Place the ribs in the greased frying basket and Bake for 20 minutes, turn them over, and cook for 10 more minutes or until the ribs are tender inside and golden brown and crisp on the outside.
- ✓ Serve with hot sauce.

Nutritional value: Calories 430 kCal Total Carbs 7 g Net Carbs 5 g Fiber 2 g Sugar 5 g Protein 32 g Fat 31 g Monounsat. Fat 13 g Polyunsat. Fat 6 g Saturated Fat 11 gCholesterol120 mg Calcium 60 mg Iron 2.7 mg Potassium 430 mg Sodium 200 mg

1120) Roasted Pork Rack with Macadamia Nuts

Ingredients:

- (2 Servings)
- 1 lb pork rack
- 2 tbsp olive oil
- 1 clove garlic, minced
- 1 tbsp rosemary, chopped
- Salt and black pepper to taste
- 1 cup macadamia nuts, finely chopped
- 1 tbsp breadcrumbs
- 1 egg, beaten in a bowl

Direction:(Prep + Cook Time: 65 minutes)

- ✓ Mix the olive oil and garlic vigorously in a bowl to make garlic oil.

- ✓ Place the rack of pork on a chopping board and brush with the garlic oil.
- ✓ Sprinkle with salt and pepper.
- ✓ Preheat the fryer to 370 F.
- ✓ In a bowl, add breadcrumbs, macadamia nuts, and rosemary.
- ✓ Brush the meat with the beaten egg on all sides and generously sprinkle with the nut mixture.
- ✓ Place the coated pork in the frying basket and Bake for 30 minutes.
- ✓ Flip over and cook further for 5-8 minutes.
- ✓ Remove the meat onto a chopping board and let it rest for 10 minutes before slicing.
- ✓ Serve with a salad or steamed rice.

nutritional value: CALORIES 1201ENERGY 5027 KJ FAT 71g SATURATES 22g FIBRE 7g PROTEIN 101g SODIUM 3707gm carbs 36g SUGAR 16g

1121) Chinese Sticky Ribs

Ingredients:

- (4 Servings)
- 1 tbsp sesame oil
- 1 ½ lb pork ribs
- ½ tsp red chili flakes
- 2 tbsp light brown sugar
- 1-inch piece ginger, grated
- 2 scallions, chopped 2 garlic cloves, minced
- 1 tbsp balsamic vinegar
- ½ tsp onion powder
- ½ tsp Chinese Five-spice powder
- 1 tbsp sweet chili sauce
- Salt and black pepper to taste

Direction:(Prep + Cook Time: 45 minutes + marinating time)

- ✓ Mix the red chili flakes, brown sugar, ginger, garlic, vinegar, onion powder, Five-spice powder, chili sauce, salt, and black pepper in a bowl.
- ✓ Add in the ribs and toss to coat.
- ✓ Chill for at least 1 hour.
- ✓ Preheat the air fryer to 370 F.
- ✓ Remove the ribs from the fridge and place them in the greased frying basket.
- ✓ Brush with sesame oil and Bake for 25-30 minutes, flipping once.
- ✓ Serve topped with scallions.

nutritional value: Calories 423 Total Fat 28g Saturated Fat 8.5g Trans Fat 0.2g Cholesterol 95mg Sodium 1277mg Potassium 654mg Total Carbohydrates 21g Dietary Fiber 2.8g Sugars 6.2g Protein 22g

1122) Pork Sausage with Butter Bean Ratatouille

Ingredients:

- (4 Servings)
- 4 pork sausages For Ratatouille
- 1 red bell pepper, chopped
- 2 zucchinis, chopped
- 1 eggplant, chopped
- 1 medium red onion, chopped
- 2 tbsp olive oil
- 1 cup canned butter beans, drained
- 15 oz canned tomatoes, chopped
- 1 tbsp balsamic vinegar
- 2 garlic cloves, minced
- 1 red chili, minced

Direction:Prep + Cook Time: 45 minutes)

- ✓ Preheat the air fryer to 390 F.
- ✓ Add the sausages to the greased frying basket and AirFry for 12-15 minutes, turning once halfway through.
- ✓ Cover with foil to keep warm.
- ✓ Mix all ratatouille ingredients in the frying basket and Bake for 15-18 minutes, shaking once.
- ✓ Serve the sausages with ratatouille.

nutritional value: Calories 540 Total Fa t24g Saturated Fat 8g Trans Fat 0g Cholesterol 60 mg Sodium 1220 mg Potassium 1070mg Total Carbohydrate 54g Dietary Fiber 9g Sugars 7g Protein 27g

1123) Maple Mustard Pork Balls

Ingredients:

- (4 Servings)
- 1 lb ground pork
- 1 large onion, chopped
- ½ tsp maple syrup
- 1 tsp yellow mustard
- ½ cup basil leaves, chopped
- Salt and black pepper to taste
- 2 tbsp cheddar cheese, grated
- 1 cup marinara sauce

Direction:Prep + Cook Time: 25 minutes

- ✓ Add the ground pork, onion, maple syrup, mustard, basil leaves, salt, pepper, and cheddar cheese; mix well and form small balls.
- ✓ Place in the greased air fryer and AirFry for 12 minutes at 400 F.
- ✓ Slide the basket out and shake the meatballs. Cook further for 5 minutes.
- ✓ Serve with marinara sauce.

nutritional value: Calories: 188.4 Protein: 12.1g Carbohydrates: 12.3g Dietary Fiber: 0.6g Sugars: 8.1g Fat: 9.9g Saturated Fat: 4.1g Cholesterol: 68.2mgCalories From Fat: 89.4

1124) Pork Meatball Noodle Bowl

Ingredients:

- *(4 Servings) 2 lb ground pork*
- *2 eggs, beaten*
- *1 tbsp cooking oil for greasing*
- *1cup panko breadcrumbs*
- *1 shallot, chopped*
- *2 tsp soy sauce*
- *2 garlic cloves, minced*
- *½ tsp ground ginger*
- *2 cups rice noodles, cooked*
- *1 gem lettuce, torn*
- *1 carrot, shredded*
- *1 cucumber, peeled, thinly sliced*
- *1 cup Asian sesame dressing*
- *1 lime, cut into wedges*

Direction:Prep + Cook Time: 30 minutes

- ✓ *Preheat the air fryer to 390 F.*
- ✓ *Mix the ground pork, eggs, breadcrumbs, shallot, soy sauce, garlic, and ginger in a mixing bowl.*
- ✓ *Divide the mixture into 24 balls.*
- ✓ *Place them into the greased frying basket.*
- ✓ *AirFry for 12-15 minutes, shaking the basket every 5 minutes to ensure even cooking.*
- ✓ *Cook until the meatballs are golden brown.*
- ✓ *Divide the rice noodles, lettuce, carrot, and cucumber between 4 bowls.*
- ✓ *Top with meatballs and drizzle with the sesame dressing.*
- ✓ *Serve with lime wedges and enjoy.*

nutritional value: Carbs 52 g Dietary Fiber 3 g Sugar 4 g Fat31 g Saturated19 g Protein 27 g

1125) ***Traditional Swedish Meatballs***

Ingredients:

- *(4 Servings)*
- *1 lb ground pork*
- *1 tbsp fresh dill, chopped*
- *½ tsp nutmeg*
- *⅓ cup seasoned breadcrumbs*
- *1 egg, beaten*
- *Salt and white pepper to taste 2*
- *tbsp butter*
- *⅓ cup sour cream*
- *2 tbsp flour*

Direction:Prep + Cook Time: 25 minutes

- ✓ *Preheat the air fryer to 360 F. In a bowl, combine the ground pork, dill, nutmeg, breadcrumbs, egg, salt, and pepper and mix well.*
- ✓ *Shape the mixture into small balls.*
- ✓ *AirFry them in the greased frying basket for 12-14 minutes, flipping once.*
- ✓ *Meanwhile, melt butter in a saucepan over medium heat and stir in the flour until lightly browned for about 2 minutes.*
- ✓ *Gradually pour 1 cup of water and whisk until the sauce thickens.*
- ✓ *Stir in sour cream and cook for 1 minute. Pour the sauce over the meatballs to serve.*

nutritional value: Calories: 370 Total Fat: 17 g Saturated Fat: 6 g Trans Fat: 0 g Cholesterol: 90 mg Sodium: 1120 mg Potassium: 260 mg Total Carbohydrates: 39 g Dietary Fiber: 4 g Sugars: 1 g Protein: 16 g Calcium: 6%

1126) ***Best Ever Pork Burgers***

Ingredients:

- *(2 Servings)*
- *½ lb ground pork*
- *½ medium onion, chopped*
- *½ tsp herbs de Provence*
- *½ tsp garlic powder*
- *½ tsp dried basil*
- *4 slices cheddar cheese*
- *½ tsp mustard*
- *Salt and black pepper to taste*
- *2 bread buns, halved.*
- *½ red onion, sliced in 2-inch rings*
- *1 large tomato, sliced in 2-inch rings*
- *½ lettuce leaves, torn*

Direction:Prep + Cook Time: 30 minutes

- ✓ *Combine the ground pork, onion, herbs de Provence, garlic powder, basil, mustard, salt, and pepper in a bowl and mix evenly.*
- ✓ *Form 2 patties out of the mixture and place them on a flat plate. Preheat the air fryer to 370 F.*
- ✓ *Place the pork patties in the greased frying basket and Bake for 10-12 minutes.*
- ✓ *Slid the basket out and turned the patties. Continue cooking for 5 more minutes.*
- ✓ *Lay lettuce on bun bottoms, add the patties, then slice onion, tomato, and cheddar cheese, and cover with the bun tops.*
- ✓ *Serve with ketchup and french fries if desired.*

nutritional value: Calories 301 Total Fat 21g Saturated Fat 7.8g Trans Fat 0g Cholesterol 95mg Sodium 467mg Potassium 369mg Total Carbohydrates 0.1g Dietary Fiber 0.1g Sugars 0g Protein 26g

1127) ***Pork & Pear Blue Cheese Patties***

Ingredients:

- *(2 Servings)*
- *½ lb ground pork*

- *1 pear, peeled and grated*
- *1 cup breadcrumbs*
- *2 oz blue cheese, crumbled*
- *½ tsp ground cumin*
- *Salt and black pepper to taste.*

Direction:Prep + Cook Time: 20 minutes

- ✓ *In a bowl, add the ground pork, pear, breadcrumbs, cumin, blue cheese, salt, and black pepper, and mix with your hands.*
- ✓ *Shape into 2 even-sized burger patties.*
- ✓ *Arrange the patties on the greased frying basket and AirFry for 12-14 minutes at 380 F, turning once halfway through.*
- ✓ *Serve warm.*

nutritional value: Energy (kJ)3410 kJ Energy (kcal)815 kcal Fat31.0g saturates10.0 g Carbohydrate96 g sugars 14.0 g Protein 42 g

1128) Serbian Pork Skewers with Yogurt Sauce

Ingredients:

- *(4 Servings)*
- *1 lb pork sausage meat*
- *Salt and black pepper to taste*
- *1 onion, chopped*
- *½ tsp garlic puree*
- *1 tsp ground cumin*
- *1 cup Greek yogurt*
- *2 tbsp walnuts, finely chopped*
- *1 tbsp fresh dill, chopped*

Direction:(Prep + Cook Time: 25 minutes

- ✓ *Preheat the air fryer to 340 F.*
- ✓ *Mix the sausage meat, onion, garlic puree, ground cumin, salt, and pepper in a bowl.*
- ✓ *Knead until everything is well incorporated.*
- ✓ *Form patties out the mixture, about ½ inch thick, and thread them onto flat skewers.*
- ✓ *Lay them on the greased frying basket.*
- ✓ *AirFry for 14-16 minutes, turning them over once or twice until golden.*
- ✓ *Whisk the yogurt, walnuts, garlic, dill, and salt in a small bowl to obtain a sauce.*
- ✓ *Serve the skewers with the yogurt sauce.*

nutritional value: Calories: 314 Total Fat: 14g Saturated Fat: 4g Trans Fat: 0g Unsaturated Fat: 8g Cholesterol: 94mg Sodium: 222mg Carbohydrates: 10g Fiber: 1gSugar: 5g Protein: 37g

1129) Italian Fennel & Pork Balls

Ingredients:

- *(4 Servings)*
- *1 lb pork sausage meat*
- *1 whole egg, beaten*
- *1 onion, chopped*
- *2 tbsp fresh sage, chopped*
- *2 tbsp ground almonds*
- *¼ head fennel bulb, chopped*
- *1 cup passata di Pomodoro (tomato sauce)*
- *Salt and black pepper to taste*

Direction:(Prep + Cook Time: 30 minutes

- ✓ *Preheat the air fryer to 350 F.*
- ✓ *Place the sausage meat, onion, almonds, fennel, egg, salt, and pepper in a bowl.*
- ✓ *Mix with hands until well combined.*
- ✓ *Shape the mixture into balls.*
- ✓ *Add them to the greased frying basket and Bake for 14-16 minutes, shaking once.*
- ✓ *Top with sage and serve with passata sauce.*

nutritional value: Calories 429.4 Total Fat 16.1 g Saturated Fat 7.1 g Polyunsaturated Fat 0.0 g Monounsaturated Fat 0.1 g Cholesterol 0.0 mg Sodium 728.5 mg Potassium 666.5 mg Total Carbohydrate 29.4 g Dietary Fiber 1.1 g Sugars 6.8 g Protein 38.1 g

1130) Mediterranean Pork Kabobs

Ingredients:

- *(4 Servings)*
- *Salt and black pepper to taste*
- *1 green bell pepper, cut into chunks*
- *1 lb pork tenderloin, cubed*
- *8 pearl onions, halved*
- *½ tsp Italian seasoning mix*
- *½ tsp smoked paprika*
- *1 zucchini, cut into chunks*

Direction:Prep + Cook Time: 30 minutes

- ✓ *Preheat the air fryer to 350 F.*
- ✓ *In a bowl, mix the pork, paprika, salt, and pepper.*
- ✓ *Thread alternating the vegetables and the pork cubes onto bamboo skewers.*
- ✓ *Spray with cooking spray and transfer to the frying basket.*
- ✓ *Bake for 15-18 minutes, flipping once halfway through.*
- ✓ *Serve sprinkled with Italian mix.*

nutritional value: Calories 260 Total Fat 7g Saturated Fat 1.5g Cholesterol 60mg Sodium 350mg Total Carbohydrate 21g Dietary Fiber 3g Protein 28g

1131) Sausage Sticks Rolled in Bacon

Ingredients:

- *(4 Servings)*
- *Sausage: 8 bacon strips*
- *8 pork sausages Relish:*

- *8 large tomatoes, chopped*
- *1 clove garlic, peeled*
- *1 small onion, peeled*
- *3 tbsp fresh parsley, chopped*
- *Salt and black pepper to taste*
- *2 tbsp sugar*
- *1 tsp smoked paprika*
- *1 tbsp white wine vinegar*

Direction:Prep + Cook Time: 40 minutes + chilling time

- ✓ *Pulse the tomatoes, garlic, and onion in a food processor until the mixture is pulpy.*
- ✓ *Transfer to a saucepan over medium heat and add vinegar, salt, and pepper; simmer for 10 minutes. Stir in the smoked paprika, parsley, and sugar*
- ✓ *Let cool for 1 hour. Neatly wrap each sausage in a bacon strip and stick it in a bamboo skewer at the end of the sausage to secure the bacon ends.*
- ✓ *Place in a greased frying basket and AirFry for 12-14 minutes at 350 F, turning once halfway through.*
- ✓ *Serve the sausages with the cooled relish.*

nutritional value: Cals 438 Fat19.00g Saturated Fat6.600g Carbohydrates43.00g Sugar1.10g Protein22.00g Salt6.75g

1132) Veggies & Pork Pinchos

Ingredients:

- *4 Servings)*
- *1 lb pork tenderloin, cubed*
- *2 tbsp olive oil*
- *1 lime, juiced, and zested*
- *2 cloves garlic, minced*
- *1 tsp chili powder*
- *1 tsp ground fennel seeds*
- *½ tsp ground cumin*
- *Salt and white pepper to taste*
- *1 red pepper, cut into chunks*
- *½ cup mushrooms, quartered*

Direction:Prep + Cook Time: 25 minutes+ marinating time)

- ✓ *Mix half of the olive oil, lime zest, and juice, garlic, chili, ground fennel, cumin, salt, and white pepper in a bowl.*
- ✓ *Add in the pork and stir to coat.*
- ✓ *Cover with cling film and place in the fridge for 1 hour. Preheat the air fryer to 380 F.*
- ✓ *Season the mushrooms and red pepper with salt and black pepper and drizzle with the remaining olive oil.*
- ✓ *Thread alternating the pork, mushroom, and red pepper pieces onto short skewers.*
- ✓ *Place in the greased frying basket and AirFry for 15 minutes, turning once.*
- ✓ *Serve hot.*

nutritional value: Calorie 150cal Fat 5 g Saturated0 g Polyunsaturated0 g Monounsaturated0 g Trans 0 g Protein21 g

1133) Spice-Rubbed Jerk Chicken Wings

Ingredients:

- *4 Servings)*
- *2 lb chicken wings*
- *2 tbsp olive oil*
- *3 garlic cloves, minced*
- *1 tbsp chili powder*
- *½ tbsp cinnamon powder*
- *½ tsp allspice*
- *1 habanero pepper, seeded*
- *1 tbsp soy sauce*
- *½ tbsp lemon pepper*
- *¼ cup red wine vinegar*
- *3 tbsp lime juice*
- *½ tbsp ginger, grated*
- *½ tbsp fresh thyme, chopped*
- *⅓ tbsp sugar*

Direction:(Prep + Cook Time: 30 minutes + marinating time)

- ✓ *In a bowl, add olive oil, garlic, chili powder, cinnamon powder, allspice, habanero pepper, soy sauce, lemon pepper, red wine vinegar, lime juice, ginger, thyme, and sugar; mix well.*
- ✓ *Add the chicken wings to the mixture and toss to coat.*
- ✓ *Cover and refrigerate for 1 hour.*
- ✓ *Preheat the air fryer to 380 F.*
- ✓ *Remove the chicken from the fridge, drain all the liquid, and pat dry with paper towels.*
- ✓ *Working in batches, cook the wings in the greased frying basket for 16 minutes in total.*
- ✓ *Shake once halfway through.*
- ✓ *Remove to a serving platter and serve with a blue cheese dip if desired*

Nutrition values: Calories 5 Total Fat 0g Sodium 95mgCarbohydrates 1g Net carbs 1g Protein 0g

1134) Sticky Chicken Wings with Coleslaw

Ingredients:

- *2 Servings)*
- *10 chicken wings*
- *2 tbsp hot chili sauce*
- *½ tbsp balsamic vinegar*
- *1 tbsp pomegranate molasses*

- *1 tsp brown sugar*
- *1 tsp tomato paste*
- *Salt and black pepper to taste*
- *4 tbsp mayonnaise*
- *½ cup yogurt*
- *1 tbsp lemon juice*
- *½ white cabbage, shredded*
- *1 carrot, grated*
- *1 green onion, sliced*
- *2 tbsp fresh parsley, chopped*

Direction:Prep + Cook Time: 30 minutes + marinating time)

- ✓ *Mix hot chili sauce, balsamic vinegar, pomegranate molasses, brown sugar, tomato paste, salt, and pepper in a bowl.*
- ✓ *Coat the chicken wings with the mixture, cover, and refrigerate for 30 minutes.*
- ✓ *In a salad bowl, combine the cabbage, carrot, green onion, and parsley; mix well.*
- ✓ *In another bowl, whisk the mayonnaise, yogurt, lemon juice, salt, and black pepper.*
- ✓ *Pour over the coleslaw and mix to combine.*
- ✓ *Keep in the fridge until ready to use.*
- ✓ *Preheat the air fryer to 350 F.*
- ✓ *Put the chicken wings in the greased frying basket and AirFry for 14-16 minutes, turning once halfway through.*
- ✓ *Serve with the chilled coleslaw and enjoy!*

Nutrition values: Calories 119.5 Total Fat 7.2 g Saturated Fat 1.0 g Polyunsaturated Fat 0.7 g Monounsaturated Fat 5.0 g Cholesterol 7.2 mg Sodium 457.7 mg Potassium 85.5 mg Total Carbohydrate 11.1 g Dietary Fiber 0.2 g Sugars 10.1 g Protein 3.5 g Calcium 0.7 %

1135) ***Sweet Chili & Ginger Chicken Wings***

Ingredients:

- *(4 Servings)*
- *1 lb chicken wings*
- *1 tsp ginger root powder*
- *1 tbsp tamarind powder*
- *¼ cup sweet chili sauce*

Direction:Prep + Cook Time: 20 minutes)

- ✓ *Preheat the air fryer to 390 F.*
- ✓ *Rub the chicken wings with tamarind and ginger root powders.*
- ✓ *Spray with cooking spray and place in the fryer.*
- ✓ *AirFry for 6 minutes.*
- ✓ *Slide the basket out and cover the wings with sweet chili sauce; cook for 6-8 more minutes until nice and crispy.*
- ✓ *Serve warm.*

Nutrition values: Calories 205.4 Total Fat 4.2 g Saturated Fat 1.1 g Monounsaturated Fat 1.0 g Cholesterol 66.4 mg Total Carbohydrate 14.3 g Dietary Fiber 0.3 g Sugars 12.3 g Protein 27.1 g

1136) ***Crispy Chicken Wings with Buffalo Sauce***

Ingredients:

- *(4 Servings)*
- *1 lb chicken wings*
- *Salt and white pepper to taste*
- *1 tsp garlic powder*
- *½ tsp chili powder*
- *½ tsp ground nutmeg*
- *2 tbsp butter, melted*
- *½ cup red hot sauce*
- *1 tbsp sugar*

Direction:Prep + Cook Time: 30 minutes)

- ✓ *Preheat the air fryer to 390 F.*
- ✓ *Add the garlic powder, chili powder, nutmeg, salt, and white pepper to a bowl.*
- ✓ *Rub the chicken wings with the mixture and transfer them to the greased frying basket*
- ✓ *Brush with some butter and AirFry for 20-22 minutes, flipping once, or until crispy and golden brown.*
- ✓ *In a bowl, whisk the remaining butter, hot sauce, and sugar.*
- ✓ *Serve the wings with the sauce.*

Nutrition values: Calories 220 Total Fat 17g Saturated fat 4g Cholesterol 70mg Sodium 710mg Carbohydrates 9g Net carbs 9g Fiber 0 Protein 13g

1137) ***Italian Parmesan Wings with Herbs***

Ingredients:

- *4 Servings)*
- *1 lb chicken wings*
- *¼ cup butter*
- *¼ cup Parmesan cheese, grated*
- *2 cloves garlic, minced*
- *½ tsp dried oregano*
- *½ tsp dried rosemary*
- *Salt and black pepper to taste*
- *¼ tsp paprika*

Direction:Prep + Cook Time: 30 minutes)

- ✓ *Preheat the air fryer to 370 F.*
- ✓ *Season the wings with salt and pepper and place them in the greased frying basket.*
- ✓ *AirFry for 12-14 minutes, flipping once.*
- ✓ *Remove to a greased frying basket.*
- ✓ *Melt the butter in a skillet over medium heat and*

cook the garlic for 1 minute.

- ✓ Stir in paprika, oregano, and rosemary for another minute.
- ✓ Spread the mixture over the chicken wings, sprinkle with Parmesan cheese, and Bake in the air fryer for 5 minutes or until the cheese is bubbling.
- ✓ Serve immediately.

Nutrition values: Calories130 Total Fat 13g Saturated Fat 2.5g Trans Fat 0g Cholesterol 10mg Sodium 630mg Total Carbohydrates 3g Dietary Fiber 0g Sugars 1g Includes 1g Added Sugars Protein 1g Calcium 26mg Iron 0mg Potassium 0mg

1138) Greek-Style Chicken Wings

Ingredients:

- (4 Servings)
- 1 lb chicken wings
- 1 tbsp fresh parsley, chopped
- Salt and black pepper to taste
- 1 tbsp cashew butter
- 1 garlic clove, minced
- 1 tbsp yogurt
- 1 tsp honey
- ½ tbsp vinegar
- ½ tbsp garlic chili sauce

Direction:Prep + Cook Time: 25 minutes

- ✓ Preheat the air fryer to 360 F.
- ✓ Season the wings with salt and pepper and spritz with cooking spray.
- ✓ AirFry for 14-16 minutes, shaking once.
- ✓ In a bowl, mix the remaining ingredients.
- ✓ Transfer the wings to the greased frying basket, top with the sauce, and cook in the air fryer for 5 more minutes. Serve.

Nutrition values: Calories 190 Total Fat 12g Saturated Fat 3.5g Trans Fat 0.2g Cholesterol 55mg Sodium 660mg Total Carbohydrates 3g Dietary Fiber 0g Sugars 0g Protein 16g

1139) Hot Chili Chicken Wings

Ingredients:

- (2 Servings)
- 8 chicken wings
- 1 cup cornflour
- ½ cup white wine
- 1 tsp chili paste
- 1-inch fresh ginger, grated
- 1 tbsp olive oil.

Direction:Prep + Cook Time: 25 minutes + marinating time)

- ✓ In a bowl, mix wine, chili paste, and ginger.
- ✓ Add in the chicken wings and marinate for 30 minutes. Preheat the air fryer to 360 F.
- ✓ Remove the chicken, drain, and coat in cornflour.
- ✓ Brush with olive oil and place in the frying basket.
- ✓ AirFry for 14-16 minutes, shaking once until crispy.
- ✓ Serve and enjoy!

Nutrition values: Calories 220 Total Fat 15g Saturated fat 3.5g Monounsaturated fat 6g Polyunsaturated fat 3.5g Cholesterol 110mg Sodium 560mg Carbohydrates 1g Net carbs 1g Fiber 0g Protein 20g Calcium 0mg

1140) One-Tray Parmesan Chicken Wings

Ingredients:

- (4 Servings)
- 8 chicken wings
- 1 tsp Dijon mustard
- Salt and black pepper to taste
- 2 tbsp olive oil
- 4 tbsp Parmesan cheese, grated
- 2 tsp fresh parsley, chopped

Direction:(Prep + Cook Time: 25 minutes)

- ✓ Preheat the air fryer to 380 F.
- ✓ Season the wings with salt and pepper.
- ✓ Brush them with mustard.
- ✓ Coat the chicken wings with 2 tbsp of Parmesan cheese, drizzle with olive oil, and place in the greased frying basket.
- ✓ AirFry for 14-16 minutes, turning once. When cooked, sprinkle with the remaining Parmesan cheese and top freshly chopped parsley.

Nutrition: Calories 99 Total Fat 8.4g Saturated Fat 2.7g Trans Fat 0.2g Polyunsaturated Fat 2.6g Monounsaturated Fat 2.7g Cholesterol 34mg Sodium 146mg Potassium 47mg Total Carbohydrates 0.4g Dietary Fiber 0g Sugars 0g Protein 5.2g Calcium1.7%

1141) Korean-Style Chicken Wings

Ingredients:

- (4 Servings)
- 8 chicken wings
- 2 tbsp sesame oil
- 1 tbsp honey
- 3 tbsp light soy sauce
- 2 crushed garlic clove
- 1 small knob fresh ginger, grated
- 2 tbsp black sesame seeds, toasted
- 1green onion, sliced.

Direction:Prep + Cook Time: 30 minutes + marinating time)

- ✓ Add all ingredients to a Ziploc bag, except for the

sesame seeds.

- ✓ Seal up and massage the ingredients until the wings are well coated.
- ✓ Let them marinate for 30 minutes in the fridge. Preheat the air fryer to 400 F.
- ✓ Place the wings in the frying basket and AirFry for 10 minutes, flip, and cook for 8-10 more minutes until golden. S
- ✓ sprinkle with sesame seeds and green onion and serve.

Nutrition values: Calories 146 Total Fat 8.1g Saturated Fat 1.4g Trans Fat 0.1g Cholesterol 27mg Sodium 277mg Potassium 139mg Total Carbohydrates 13g Dietary Fiber 0.5g Sugars 6g Protein 5.4g

1142) Thai Tom Yum Wings

Ingredients:

- 2 Servings)
- 8 chicken wings
- 2 tbsp tom yum paste
- 1 tbsp water
- ½ cup flour
- 2 tbsp cornstarch
- ½ tbsp baking powder.

Direction:Prep + Cook Time: 30 minutes + marinating time)

- ✓ Whisk the tom yum paste and water in a small bowl.
- ✓ Place the wings in a large bowl, pour the tom yum mixture over, and brush to coat well.
- ✓ Cover the bowl with foil and refrigerate for 2 hours.
- ✓ Preheat the air fryer to 370 F.
- ✓ In a shallow bowl, mix the flour, baking powder, and cornstarch.
- ✓ Dredge the chicken wings in the flour mixture, shaking them off, and place them in the greased frying basket.
- ✓ Spritz with cooking spray and AirFry them for 7-8 minutes.
- ✓ Flip and cook for another 5-6 minutes until crispy.

Nutrition: Calories 17 Total Fat 0.6g Saturated Fat 0.1g Trans Fat 0g Polyunsaturated Fat 0g Cholesterol 0mg Sodium 588mg Total Carbs 2g Dietary Fiber 0g Total Sugars 2g Sugar Protein 0g

Dessert and fruit recipes

1143) Fig Crostini with Mascarpone

Ingredients:

- 1 long French baguette
- 4 Tbsps (½ stick) salted butter, melted (optional)
- 1 (8-ounce / 227-g) tub mascarpone cheese
- 1 (12-ounce / 340-g) jar fig jam or preserves

Direction: Prep time: 10 minutes | Cook time: 10 minutes | Serves 6 to 8

- ✓ Switch on the oven, preheat it setting its temperature to 350°F (180°C).
- ✓ Slice the bread into ¼-inch-thick slices.
- ✓ Arrange the sliced bread on a baking sheet and brush each slice with the melted butter (if desired).
- ✓ Put the baking sheet in the oven and toast the bread for 5 to 7 minutes, just until golden brown.
- ✓ Let the bread cool slightly. Spread about a Tsp or so of the mascarpone cheese on each piece of bread.
- ✓ Top with a Tsp or so of the jam. Serve immediately.

Nutrition: calories: 445 | fat: 24g | protein: 3g | carbs: 48g | fiber: 5g | sodium: 314mg

1144) Cranberry Orange Loaf

Ingredients:

- Dough:
- 3 cups all-purpose flour
- 1 (¼-ounce / 7-g) package quick-rise yeast
- ½ Tsp salt
- ⅛ Tsp ground cinnamon
- ⅛ Tsp ground cardamom
- ½ cup water
- ½ cup almond milk
- ⅓ cup butter, cubed (optional) Cranberry

Filling:

- 1 (12-ounce / 340-g) can cranberry sauce
- ½ cup chopped walnuts
- 2 Tbsps grated orange zest
- 2 Tbsps orange juice

Direction: Prep time: 20 minutes | Cook time: 45 minutes | Makes 1 loaf

- ✓ In a large container, combine the flour, yeast, salt, cinnamon, and cardamom.
- ✓ Heat the water, almond milk, and butter (if desired) over medium-high heat in a small pot. Once it boils, it reduces the heat to medium-low. Simmer for 10 to 15 minutes until the liquid thickens.
- ✓ Pour the liquid ingredients into the dry ingredients and, using a wooden spoon or spatula, mix the dough until it forms a ball to the container.
- ✓ Put the dough in a greased container, cover it tightly with a kitchen towel, and set aside for 1 hour.
- ✓ To make the cranberry filling: In a medium container, mix the cranberry sauce with walnuts, orange zest, and orange juice in a large container.
- ✓ Assemble the Bread
- ✓ Roll out the dough to about a 1-inch-thick and 10-by-7-inch-wide rectangle.
- ✓ Spread the cranberry filling evenly on the surface of the rolled-out dough, leaving a 1-inch border around the edges. Starting with the long side, tuck the dough under with your fingertips and roll up the dough tightly. Place the rolled-up dough in an "S" shape in a bread pan.
- ✓ Allow the bread to rise again, about 30 to 40 minutes.
- ✓ Switch on the oven, preheat it setting its temperature to 350°F (180°C).
- ✓ Bake in a preheated oven, 45 minutes.

Nutrition: calories: 483 | fat: 15g | protein: 8g | carbs: 79g | fiber: 4g | sodium: 232mg

1145) Strawberry Shortbread Cookies

Ingredients:

- 2 cups cornstarch
- 1½ cups all-purpose flour
- 2 Tsps baking powder
- 1 Tsp baking soda
- 1 cup (2 sticks) cold butter, cut into 1-inch cubes (optional)
- ⅔ cup sugar
- 4 large egg yolks
- 2 Tbsps brandy
- 1 Tsp vanilla extract
- ½ Tsp salt
- 2 cups strawberry preserves
- Confectioners' sugar, for sprinkling

Direction: Prep time: 20 minutes | Cook time: 10 minutes | Makes 3 dozen cookies

- ✓ Combine the cornstarch, flour, baking powder, and baking soda in a container and mix together. Using your hands or 2 forks, mix the butter (if desired) and sugar just until combined, with small pieces of butter resting.
- ✓ Add the egg yolks, brandy, vanilla, and salt, stirring slowly until all ingredients are blended together. If you have a stand mixer, you can mix these ingredients together with the paddle attachment and then finish mixing by hand, but it is not required.
- ✓ Wrap the dough in plastic wrap and place in a resealable plastic bag for at least 1 hour.
- ✓ Switch on the oven, preheat it setting its temperature to 350°F (180°C).
- ✓ Roll the dough to ¼-inch thickness and cut, placing 12 cookies on a sheet. Bake the sheets one at a time on the top rack of the oven for 12 to 14 minutes.

✓ *Let the cookies cool completely and top with about 1 Tbsp of strawberry preserves.*

✓ *Sprinkle with confectioners' sugar.*

Nutrition: calories: 157 | fat: 6g | protein: 1g | carbs: 26g | fiber: 0g | sodium: 132mg

1146) Pound Cake with Citrus Glaze

Ingredients:

- *Cake:*
- *Nonstick cooking spray*
- *1 cup sugar*
- *⅓ cup extra-virgin olive oil*
- *1 cup unsweetened almond milk*
- *1 lemon, zested and juiced*
- *2 cups all-purpose flour*
- *1 Tsp baking soda*
- *1 Tsp salt*

Glaze:

- *1 cup powdered sugar*
- *1 to 2 Tbsps freshly squeezed lemon juice*
- *½ Tsp vanilla extract*

Direction: Prep time: 10 minutes | Cook time: 45 minutes | Serves 8

✓ *Make the Cake*

✓ *Switch on the oven, preheat it setting its temperature to 350°F (180°C). Line a 9-inch loaf pan with parchment paper and coat the paper with nonstick cooking spray.*

✓ *In a large container, whisk together the sugar and olive oil until creamy. Whisk to the milk and lemon juice and zest. Let it stand for 5 to 7 minutes.*

✓ *In a medium container, combine the flour, baking soda, and salt. Fold the dry ingredients into the milk mixture and stir just until incorporated.*

✓ *Pour the batter into the prepared pan and smooth the top. Bake until a toothpick or skewer inserted into the middle comes out clean with a few crumbs attached, about 45 minutes.*

✓ *Remove the cake from the oven and cool for at least 10 minutes into the pan. Transfer to a cooling rack placed over a baking sheet and cooled completely.*

✓ *Make the Glaze*

✓ *In a small container, whisk together the powdered sugar, lemon juice, and vanilla until smooth. Pour the glaze over the cooled cake, allowing the excess to drip off the cake onto the baking sheet beneath.*

Nutrition: calories: 347 | fat: 9g | protein: 4g | carbs: 64g | fiber: 1g | sodium: 481mg

1147) Apple Pie Pockets

Ingredients:

- *1 organic puff pastry, rolled out, at room temperature*
- *1 Gala apple, peeled and sliced*
- *¼ cup brown sugar*
- *⅛ Tsp ground cinnamon*
- *⅛ Tsp ground cardamom*
- *Nonstick cooking spray*
- *Honey, for topping*

Direction: Prep time: 5 minutes | Cook time: 15 minutes | Serves 6

✓ *Switch on the oven, preheat it setting its temperature to 350°F (180°C).*

✓ *Cut the pastry dough into 4 even discs. Peel and slice the apple. In a small container, toss the slices with brown sugar, cinnamon, and cardamom.*

✓ *Spray a muffin tin very well with nonstick cooking spray. Be sure to spray only the muffin holders you plan to use.*

✓ *Once sprayed, line the bottom of the muffin tin with the dough and place 1 or 2 broken apple slices on top. Fold the resting dough over the apple and drizzle with honey.*

✓ *Bake for 15 minutes or until brown and bubbly.*

Nutrition: calories: 250 | fat: 15g | protein: 3g | carbs: 30g | fiber: 1g | sodium: 98mg

1148) Baked Pears with Mascarpone Cheese

Ingredients:

- *2 ripe pears, peeled*
- *1 Tbsp plus 2 Tsps honey, divided*
- *1 Tsp vanilla, divided*
- *¼ Tsp ginger*
- *¼ Tsp ground coriander*
- *¼ cup minced walnuts*
- *¼ cup mascarpone cheese*
- *Pinch salt*

Direction: Prep time: 10 minutes | Cook time: 20 minutes | Serves 2

✓ *Switch on the oven, preheat it setting its temperature to 350°F (180°C) and set the rack to the middle position. Grease a small baking dish.*

✓ *Cut the pears in half lengthwise. Using a spoon, scoop out the core from each piece. Place the pears with the cut side up to the baking dish.*

✓ *In a small container, combine 1 Tbsp of honey, ½ Tsp of vanilla, ginger, and coriander. Pour this mixture evenly over the pear halves.*

✓ *Sprinkle walnuts over the pear halves.*

✓ *Bake for 20 minutes, or until the pears are golden and you're able to pierce them easily with a knife.*

✓ *While the pears are baking, mix the mascarpone cheese with the resting 2 Tsps honey, ½ Tsp of vanilla, and a pinch of salt. Stir well to combine.*

✓ *Divide the mascarpone among the warm pear halves and serve.*

Nutrition: calories: 307 | fat: 16g | protein: 4g | carbs: 43g | fiber: 6g | sodium: 89mg

1149) Orange Mug Cake

Ingredients:

- 6 Tbsps flour
- 2 Tbsps sugar
- ½ Tsp baking powder
- Pinch salt
- 1 Tsp orange zest
- 1 egg
- 2 Tbsps olive oil
- 2 Tbsps freshly squeezed orange juice
- 2 Tbsps unsweetened almond milk
- ½ Tsp orange extract
- ½ Tsp vanilla extract

Direction: Prep time: 10 minutes | Cook time: 2 minutes | Serves 2

- ✓ Combine the flour, sugar, baking powder, salt, and orange zest in a small container.
- ✓ Whisk together the egg, olive oil, orange juice, milk, orange extract, and vanilla extract in a separate container.
- ✓ Pour the dry ingredients into the wet ingredients and stir to combine. The batter will be thick.
- ✓ Divide the mixture into two small mugs that hold at least 6 ounces 170 g each, or 1 (12-ounce 340-g) mug.
- ✓ Microwave each mug separately. The small ones should take about 60 seconds, and one large mug should take about 90 seconds, but microwaves can vary. The cake will be made when it pulls away from the sides of the mug.

Nutrition: calories: 302 | fat: 17g | protein: 6g | carbs: 33g | fiber: 1g | sodium: 117mg

1150) Fruit and Nut Dark Chocolate Bark

Ingredients:

- 2 Tbsps chopped nuts (almonds, pecans, walnuts, hazelnuts, pistachios, or any combination of those)
- 3 ounces (85 g) good-quality dark chocolate chips (about ⅔ cup)
- ¼ cup chopped dried fruit (apricots, blueberries, figs, prunes, or any combination of those)

Direction: Prep time: 15 minutes | Cook time: 5 minutes | Serves 2

- ✓ Line a sheet pan with parchment paper.
- ✓ Place the nuts in a skillet over medium-high heat and toast them for 60 seconds, or just until they're fragrant.
- ✓ Place the chocolate in a microwave-safe glass container or measuring cup and microwave on high for 1 minute. Stir the chocolate and allow any unmelted chips to warm and melt. If necessary, heat for another 20 to 30 seconds, but keep a close eye on it to ensure it doesn't burn.
- ✓ Pour the chocolate onto the sheet pan. Sprinkle the dried fruit and nuts over the chocolate evenly and gently pat them in, so they stick.
- ✓ Transfer the sheet pan to the refrigerator for at least 1 hour to let the chocolate harden.
- ✓ When solid, break into pieces. Store any leftover chocolate in the fridge or freezer.

Nutrition: calories: 284 | fat: 16g | protein: 4g | carbs: 39g | fiber: 2g | sodium: 2mg

1151) Grilled Fruit Skewers

Ingredients:

- ⅔ cup prepared labneh, or, if making your own,
- ⅔ cup full-fat plain Greek yogurt
- 2 Tbsps honey
- 1 Tsp vanilla extract
- Pinch salt
- 3 cups fresh fruit cut into 2-inch chunks (pineapple, cantaloupe, nectarines, strawberries, plums, or mango)

Direction: Prep time: 15 minutes | Cook time: 10 minutes | Serves 2

- ✓ If making your own labneh, place a colander over a container and line it with cheesecloth. Place the Greek yogurt on the cheesecloth and wrap it up. Put the container in the fridge and let sit for at least 12 to 24 hours, until it's thick like soft cheese.
- ✓ Mix honey, vanilla, and salt into the labneh. Stir well to combine and set it aside.
- ✓ Heat the grill to medium (about 300°F / 150°C) and oil the grill grate. Alternatively, you can cook these on the stovetop in a heavy grill pan (cast iron works well).
- ✓ Thread the fruit onto skewers and grill for 4 minutes on each side, or until the fruit is softened and has grill marks on each side.
- ✓ Serve the fruit with labneh to dip.

Nutrition: cal: 292 | fat: 6g | protein: 5g | carbs: 60g

1152) Pomegranate Blueberry Granita

Ingredients:

- 1 cup frozen wild blueberries
- 1 cup pomegranate or pomegranate blueberry juice
- ¼ cup sugar
- ¼ cup water

Direction: Prep time: 5 minutes | Cook time: 10 minutes | Serves 2

- ✓ Combine the frozen blueberries and pomegranate juice in a saucepan and bring to a boil. Reduce the heat and simmer for 5 minutes, or until the blueberries start to break down.
- ✓ While the juice and berries are cooking, combine the sugar and water in a small microwave-safe

container. Microwave for 60 seconds or until it comes to a rolling boil. Stir to make sure all of the sugar is dissolved, and set the syrup aside.

- ✓ *Combine the blueberry mixture and the sugar syrup in a blender and blend for 1 minute, or until the fruit is completely puréed.*
- ✓ *Pour the mixture into an 8-by-8-inch baking pan or a similar-sized container. The liquid should come about ½ inch up the sides. Let the mixture cool for 30 minutes, and then put it into the freezer.*
- ✓ *Every 30 minutes for the next 2 hours, scrape the granita with a fork to keep it from freezing solid.*
- ✓ *Serve it after 2 hours, or store it in a covered container in the freezer.*

Nutrition: calories: 214 | fat: 0g | protein: 1g | carbs: 54g | fiber: 2g | sodium: 15mg

1153) Chocolate Dessert Hummus

Ingredients:

- *Caramel:*
- *2 Tbsps coconut oil*
- *1 Tbsp maple syrup*
- *1 Tbsp almond butter*
- *Pinch salt*

Hummus:

- *½ cup chickpeas drained and rinsed*
- *2 Tbsps unsweetened cocoa powder*
- *1 Tbsp maple syrup, plus more to taste*
- *2 Tbsps almond milk, or more as needed, to thin*
- *Pinch salt*
- *2 Tbsps pecans*

Direction: Prep time: 15 minutes | Cook time: 0 minutes | Serves 2

- ✓ *Make the Caramel*
- ✓ *To make the caramel, put the coconut oil in a small microwave-safe container. If it's solid, microwave it for about 15 seconds to melt it.*
- ✓ *Stir to the maple syrup, almond butter, and salt.*
- ✓ *Place the caramel in the fridge for 5 to 10 minutes to thicken.*
- ✓ *Make the Hummus*
- ✓ *In a food processor, combine the chickpeas, cocoa powder, maple syrup, almond milk, and a pinch of salt, and process until smooth. Scrape down the sides to make sure everything is incorporated.*
- ✓ *If the hummus seems too thick, add another Tbsp of almond milk.*
- ✓ *Add the pecans and pulse 6 times to roughly chop them.*
- ✓ *Transfer the hummus to a serving container and when the caramel is thickened, swirl it into the hummus. Gently fold it in, but don't mix it in completely.*
- ✓ *Serve with fresh fruit or pretzels.*

Nutrition: 321 | fat: 22g | protein: 7g | carbs: 30g | fiber: 6g | sodium: 100mg

1154) Blackberry Lemon Panna Cotta

Ingredients:

- *¾ cup half-and-half, divided*
- *1 Tsp unflavored powdered gelatin*
- *½ cup heavy cream*
- *3 Tbsps sugar*
- *1 Tsp lemon zest*
- *1 Tbsp freshly squeezed lemon juice*
- *1 Tsp lemon extract*
- *½ cup fresh blackberries*
- *Lemon peels to garnish (optional)*

Direction: Prep time: 20 minutes | Cook time: 10 minutes | Serves 2

- ✓ *Place ¼ cup of half-and-half in a small container.*
- ✓ *Sprinkle the gelatin powder evenly over the half-and-half and set it aside for 10 minutes to hydrate.*
- ✓ *In a saucepan, combine the resting ½ cup of half-and-half, the heavy cream, sugar, lemon zest, lemon juice, and lemon extract. Heat the mixture over medium heat for 4 minutes, or until it's barely simmering—don't let it come to a full boil. Remove from the heat.*
- ✓ *When the gelatin is hydrated (it will look like applesauce), add it into the warm cream mixture, whisking as the gelatin melts.*
- ✓ *If there are any resting clumps of gelatin, strato the liquid or remove the lumps with a spoon.*
- ✓ *Pour the mixture into 2 dessert glasses or stemless wine glasses and refrigerate for at least 6 hours, or up to overnight.*
- ✓ *Serve with the fresh berries and garnish with some strips of fresh lemon peel, if desired.*

Nutrition: calories: 422 | fat: 33g | protein: 6g | carbs: 28g | fiber: 2g | sodium: 64mg

1155) Berry and Honey Compote

Ingredients:

- *½ cup honey*
- *¼ cup fresh berries*
- *2 Tbsps grated orange zest*

Direction: Prep time: 5 minutes | Cook time: 2 to 5 minutes | Serves 2 to 3

- ✓ *In a small saucepan, heat the honey, berries, and orange zest over medium-low heat for 2 to 5 minutes, until the sauce thickens, or heat for 15 seconds to the microwave.*
  Serve the compote drizzled over pancakes, muffins, or French toast.

Nutrition: calories: 272 | fat: 0g | protein: 1g | carbs: 74g

1156) Pomegranate and Quinoa Dark Chocolate Bark

Ingredients:

- Nonstick cooking spray
- ½ cup uncooked tricolor or regular quinoa
- ½ Tsp kosher or sea salt
- 8 ounces (227 g) dark chocolate or 1 cup dark chocolate chips
- ½ cup fresh pomegranate seeds

Direction: Prep time: 5 minutes | Cook time: 13 minutes | Serves 6

✓ In a medium saucepan coated with nonstick cooking spray over medium heat, toast the uncooked quinoa for 2 to 3 minutes, stirring frequently. Do not let the quinoa burn. Remove the pan from the stove, and mix with the salt. Set aside 2 Tbsps of the toasted quinoa to use for the topping.

✓ Break the chocolate into large pieces, and put it in a gallon-size zip-top plastic bag. Using a metal ladle or a meat pounder, pound the chocolate until broken into smaller pieces. (If using chocolate chips, you can skip this step.) Dump the chocolate out of the bag into a medium, microwave-safe container and heat for 1 minute on high to the microwave. Stir until the chocolate is completely melted. Mix the toasted quinoa (except the topping you set aside) into the melted chocolate.

✓ Line a large, rimmed baking sheet with parchment paper. Pour the chocolate mixture onto the sheet and spread it evenly until the entire pan is covered. Sprinkle the resting 2 Tbsps of quinoa and the pomegranate seeds on top. Using a spatula or the back of a spoon, press the quinoa and the pomegranate seeds into the chocolate.

✓ Freeze the mixture for 10 to 15 minutes or until set. Remove the bark from the freezer, and break it into about 2-inch jagged pieces. Store in a sealed container or zip-top plastic bag in the fridge until ready to serve.

Nutrition: 268 | fat: 11g | protein: 4g | carbs: 37g | fiber: 2g | sodium: 360mg

1157) Pecan and Carrot Coconut Cake

Ingredients:

- ½ cup coconut oil, at room temperature, plus more

for greasing the baking dish

- 2 Tsps pure vanilla extract
- ¼ cup pure maple syrup
- 6 eggs
- ½ cup coconut flour
- 1 Tsp baking powder
- 1 Tsp baking soda
- ½ Tsp ground nutmeg
- 1 Tsp ground cinnamon
- ⅛ Tsp sea salt
- ½ cup chopped pecans
- 3 cups finely grated carrots

Direction: Prep time: 10 minutes | Cook time: 45 minutes | Serves 12

✓ Switch on the oven, preheat it setting its temperature to 350°F (180°C). Grease a 13-by-9-inch baking dish with coconut oil.

✓ Combine the vanilla extract, maple syrup, and ½ cup of coconut oil in a large container. Stir to mix well.

✓ Break the eggs into the container and whisk to combine well. Set aside.

✓ Combine the coconut flour, baking powder, baking soda, nutmeg, cinnamon, and salt in a separate container. Stir to mix well.

✓ Make a well to the center of the flour mixture, then pour the egg mixture into the well. Stir to combine well.

✓ Add the pecans and carrots to the container and toss to mix well. Pour the mixture into the single layer on the baking dish.

✓ Bake to the preheated oven for 45 minutes or until puffed, and the cake spring back when lightly pressed with your fingers.

✓ Remove the cake from the oven. Allow to cool for at least 15 minutes, then serve.

Nutrition: calories: 255 | fat: 21g | protein: 5g | carbs: 12g | fiber: 2g | sodium: 202mg

1158) Lemon Fool with Honey Drizzled

Ingredients:

- 1 cup 2% plain Greek yogurt
- 1 medium lemon
- ¼ cup cold water
- 1½ Tsps cornstarch
- 3½ Tbsps honey, divided
- ⅔ cup heavy (whipping) cream
- Fresh fruit and mint leaves, for serving (optional)

Direction: Prep time: 10 minutes | Cook time: 2 minutes | Serves 4

✓ Place a large glass container and the metal beaters from your electric mixer in the fridge to chill. Add the yogurt to a medium glass container, and place that container in the fridge to chill as well.

✓ Using a Microplane or citrus zester, zest the lemon into a medium, microwave-safe container. Halve the lemon, and squeeze 1 Tbsp of lemon juice into the container. Add the water and cornstarch, and stir well. Whisk in 3 Tbsps of honey. Microwave the lemon mixture on high for 1 minute; stir and microwave for an additional 10 to 30 seconds until the mixture is thick and bubbling.

✓ Remove the container of yogurt from the refrigerator, and whisk it into the warm lemon *mixture. Place the yogurt back in the fridge.*

- ✓ *Remove the large chilled container and the beaters from the refrigerator. Assemble your electric mixer with the chilled beaters. Pour the cream into the chilled container, and beat until soft peaks form, 1 to 3 minutes, depending on the freshness of your cream.*
- ✓ *Take the chilled yogurt mixture out of the refrigerator. Gently fold it into the whipped cream using a rubber scraper; lift and turn the mixture to prevent the cream from deflating. Chill until serving, at least 15 minutes but no longer than 1 hour.*
- ✓ *To serve, spoon the lemon fool into four glasses or dessert dishes and drizzle with the resting ½ Tbsp of honey. Top with fresh fruit and mint, if desired.*

Nutrition: 171 | fat: 9g | protein: 3g | carbs: 20g | fiber: 0g | sodium: 37mg

1159) Avocados Chocolate Pudding

Ingredients:

- *2 ripe avocados, halved and pitted*
- *¼ cup unsweetened cocoa powder*
- *¼ cup heavy whipping cream, plus more if needed*
- *2 Tsps vanilla extract*
- *1 to 2 Tsps liquid stevia or monk fruit extract (optional)*
- *½ Tsp ground cinnamon (optional)*
- *¼ Tsp salt*
- *Whipped cream, for serving (optional)*

Direction: Prep time: 10 minutes | Cook time: 0 minutes | Serves 4

- ✓ *Using a spoon, scoop out the ripe avocado into a blender or large container if using an immersion blender. Mash well with a fork.*
- ✓ *Add the cocoa powder, heavy whipping cream, vanilla, sweetener (if using), cinnamon (if using), and salt. Blend well until smooth and creamy, adding additional cream, 1 Tbsp at a time, if the mixture is too thick.*
- ✓ *Cover and refrigerate for at least 1 hour before serving. Serve chilled with additional whipped cream, if desired.*

Nutrition: calories: 230 | fat: 21g | protein: 3g | carbs: 10g | fiber: 5g | sodium: 163mg

1160) Nut Butter Cup

Ingredients:

- *½ cup crunchy almond butter (no sugar added)*
- *½ cup light fruity extra-virgin olive oil*
- *¼ cup ground flaxseed*
- *2 Tbsps unsweetened cocoa powder*
- *1 Tsp vanilla extract*
- *1 Tsp ground cinnamon (optional)*
- *1 to 2 Tsps sugar-free sweetener of choice (optional)*

Direction: Prep time: 10 minutes | Cook time: 0 minutes | Serves 8

- ✓ *In a mixing container, combine the almond butter, olive oil, flaxseed, cocoa powder, vanilla, cinnamon (if using), and sweetener (if using) and stir well with a spatula to combine. The mixture will be a thick liquid.*
- ✓ *Pour into 8 mini muffin liners and freeze until solid, at least 12 hours. Store in the freezer to maintain the ir shape.*

Nutrition: calories: 240 | fat: 23g | protein: 3g | carbs: 5g | fiber: 2g | sodium: 3mg

1161) Dark Chocolate and Avocado Mousse

Ingredients:

- *8 ounces (227 g) dark chocolate (60% cocoa or higher), chopped*
- *¼ cup unsweetened coconut milk*
- *2 Tbsps coconut oil*
- *2 ripe avocados, deseeded*
- *¼ cup raw honey*
- *Sea salt, to taste*

Direction: Prep time: 5 minutes | Cook time: 5 minutes | Serves 4 to 6

- ✓ *Put the chocolate in a saucepan. Pour to the coconut milk and add the coconut oil.*
- ✓ *Cook for 3 minutes or until the chocolate and coconut oil melt. Stir constantly.*
- ✓ *Put the avocado in a food processor, then drizzle with honey and melted chocolate. Pulse to combine until smooth.*
- ✓ *Pour the mixture into a serving container, then sprinkle with salt. Refrigerate to chill for 30 minutes and serve.*

Nutrition: calories: 654 | fat: 46g | protein: 7g | carbs: 55g | fiber: 9g | sodium: 112mg

1162) Quick Marzipan Fat Bomb

Ingredients:

- *1½ cup finely ground almond flour*
- *½ to 1 cup powdered sugar-free sweetener of choice*
- *2 Tsps almond extract*
- *½ cup light fruity extra-virgin olive oil or avocado oil*

Direction: calories: 654 | fat: 46g | protein: 7g | carbs: 55g | fiber: 9g | sodium: 112mg

- ✓ *Add the almond flour and sweetener to a food processor and run until the mixture is very finely ground.*
- ✓ *Add the almond extract and pulse until combined. With the processor running, stream in olive oil until the mixture starts to form a large ball. Turn off the food processor.*

- *Using your hands, form the marzipan into eight (1-inch) diameter balls, pressing to hold the mixture together. Store in an airtight container in the fridge for up to 2 weeks.*

Nutrition: calories: 157 | fat: 16g | protein: 2g | carbs: 0g | fiber: 0g | sodium: 0mg

1163) Summer Strawberry Panna Cotta

Ingredients:

- *2 Tbsps warm water*
- *2 Tsps gelatin powder*
- *2 cups heavy cream1 cup sliced strawberries, plus more for garnish*
- *1 to 2 Tbsps sugar-free sweetener of choice (optional)*
- *1½ Tsps pure vanilla extract*
- *4 to 6 fresh mint leaves for garnish (optional)*

Direction: Prep time: 10 minutes | Cook time: 5 minutes | Serves 4

- *Pour the warm water into a small container. Sprinkle the gelatin over the water and stir well to dissolve. Allow the mixture to sit for 10 minutes.*
- *In a blender or a large container, combine the cream, strawberries, sweetener (if using), and vanilla if using an immersion blender. Blend until the mixture is smooth and the strawberries are well puréed.*
- *Or mint leaves (if using).*
- *Transfer the mixture to a saucepan and heat over medium-low heat until just below a simmer. Remove from the heat and cool for 5 minutes.*
- *Whisking constantly, add to the gelatin mixture until smooth. Divide the custard between ramekins or small glass containers, cover, and refrigerate until set, 4 to 6 hours.*
- *Serve chilled, garnishing with additional sliced strawberries*

Nutrition: calories: 431 | fat: 43g | protein: 4g | carbs: 7g | fiber: 1g | sodium: 49mg

1164) Chocolate Chia Seeds Pudding

Ingredients:

- *2 cups heavy cream*
- *¼ cup unsweetened cocoa powder*
- *1 Tsp almond extract or vanilla extract*
- *½ or 1 Tsp ground cinnamon*
- *¼ Tsp salt*
- *½ cup chia seeds*

Direction: Prep time: 5 minutes | Cook time: 5 minutes | Serves 4

- *In a saucepan, heat the heavy cream over medium-low heat to just below a simmer. Remove from the heat and allow to cool slightly.*
- *In a blender or large container, if using an immersion blender, combine the warmed heavy cream, cocoa powder, almond extract, cinnamon, and salt and blend until the cocoa is well incorporated.*
- *Stir to the chia seeds and let sit for 15 minutes.*
- *Divide the mixture evenly between ramekins or small glass containers and refrigerate for at least 6 hours, or until set. Serve chilled.*

Nutrition: calories: 561 | fat: 52g | protein: 8g | carbs: 19g | fiber: 12g | sodium: 187mg

1165) Orange Almond Cupcakes

Ingredients:

- *1 large egg*
- *2 Tbsps powdered sugar-free sweetener (such as stevia or monk fruit extract)*
- *½ cup extra-virgin olive oil*
- *1 Tsp almond extract*
- *Zest of 1 orange*
- *1 cup almond flour*
- *¾ Tsp baking powder*
- *⅛ Tsp salt*
- *1 Tbsp freshly squeezed orange juice*

Direction: Prep time: 10 minutes | Cook time: 15 minutes | Makes 6 cupcakes

- *Switch on the oven, preheat it setting its temperature to 350°F (180°C). Place muffin liners into 6 cups of a muffin tin.*
- *In a large container, whisk together the egg and powdered sweetener. Add the olive oil, almond extract, and orange zest and whisk to combine well.*
- *In a small container, whisk together the almond flour, baking powder, and salt. Add to wet ingredients along with the orange juice and stir until just combined.*
- *Divide the batter evenly into 6 muffin cups and bake until a toothpick inserted to the center of the cupcake comes out clean, 15 to 18 minutes.*
- *Remove from the oven and cool for 5 minutes to the tin before transferring to a wire rack to cool completely.*

Nutrition: calories: 211 | fat: 21g | protein: 3g | carbs: 2g | fiber: 0g | sodium: 105mg

1166) Ricotta Pumpkin Cheesecake

Ingredients:

- *1 cup almond flour*
- *½ cup butter, melted (optional)*
- *1 (14½-ounce / 411-g) can pumpkin purée 8 ounces (227 g) cream cheese, at room temperature*
- *½ cup whole-milk Ricotta cheese*
- *½ to ¾ cup sugar-free sweetener*
- *4 large eggs*
- *2 Tsps vanilla extract*
- *2 Tsps pumpkin pie spice*

- *Whipped cream for garnish (optional)*

Direction: Prep time: 10 minutes | Cook time: 40 minutes | Serves 10 to 12

✓ *Switch on the oven, preheat it setting its temperature to 350°F (180°C). Line the bottom of a 9-inch springform pan with parchment paper.*

✓ *In a small container, combine the almond flour and melted butter (if desired) with a fork until well combined. Using your fingers, press the mixture into the bottom of the prepared pan.*

✓ *In a large container, beat together the pumpkin purée, cream cheese, ricotta, and sweetener using an electric mixer on medium.*

✓ *Add the eggs, one at a time, beating after each addition. Stir to the vanilla and pumpkin pie spice until just combined.*

✓ *Pour the mixture over the crust and bake until set, 40 to 45 minutes.*

✓ *Allow cooling to room temperature. Refrigerate for at least 6 hours before serving.*

✓ *Serve chilled, garnishing with whipped cream, if desired.*

Nutrition: calories: 242 | fat: 22g | protein: 7g | carbs: 5g | fiber: 1g | sodium: 178mg

1167) Blueberry, Pecan, and Oat Crisp

Ingredients:

- *2 Tbsps coconut oil, melted, plus more for greasing*
- *4 cups fresh blueberries*
- *Juice of ½ lemon*
- *2 Tsps lemon zest*
- *¼ cup maple syrup*
- *1 cup gluten-free rolled oats*
- *½ cup chopped pecans*
- *½ Tsp ground cinnamon Sea salt, to taste*

Direction: Prep time: 10 minutes | Cook time: 20 minutes | Serves 4

✓ *Switch on the oven, preheat it setting its temperature to 350°F (180°C). Grease a baking sheet with coconut oil.*

✓ *Combine the blueberries, lemon juice and zest, and maple syrup in a container. Stir to mix well, then spread the mixture on the baking sheet.*

✓ *Combine the resting ingredients in a small container. Stir to mix well. Pour the mixture over the blueberries mixture.*

✓ *Bake to the preheated oven for 20 minutes or until the oats are golden brown.*

✓ *Serve immediately with spoons.*

Nutrition: calories: 496 | fat: 33g | protein: 5g | carbs: 51g | fiber: 7g | sodium: 41mg

1168) Baklava with Syrup

Ingredients:

- *1½ cups finely chopped walnuts*
- *1 Tsp ground cinnamon*
- *¼ Tsp ground cardamom (optional)*
- *1 cup water*
- *½ cup sugar*
- *½ cup honey*
- *2 Tbsps freshly squeezed lemon juice*
- *1 cup salted butter, melted (optional)*
- *20 large sheets phyllo pastry dough, at room temperature*

Direction: Prep time: 10 minutes | Cook time: 30 minutes | Serves 12

✓ *Switch on the oven, preheat it setting its temperature to 350°F (180°C).*

✓ *In a small container, gently mix the walnuts, cinnamon, and cardamom (if using) and set aside.*

✓ *In a small pot, bring the water, sugar, honey, and lemon juice just to a boil. Remove from the heat.*

✓ *Put the butter in a small container. Onto an ungreased 9-by-13-inch baking sheet, put 1 layer of phyllo dough, and slowly brush with butter. Be careful not to tear the phyllo sheets as you butter them. Carefully layer 1 or 2 more phyllo sheets, brushing each with butter to the baking pan, and then layer ⅛ of the nut mix; layer 2 sheets and add another ⅛ of the nut mix; repeat with 2 sheets and nuts until you run out of nuts and dough, topping with the resting phyllo dough sheets.*

✓ *Slice 4 lines into the baklava lengthwise and make another 4 or 5 slices diagonally across the pan.*

✓ *Put to the oven and cook for 30 to 40 minutes, or until golden brown.*

✓ *Remove the baklava from the oven and immediately cover it with the syrup.*

Nutrition: calories: 443 | fat: 26g | protein: 6g | carbs: 47g | fiber: 3g | sodium: 344mg

1169) Baked Lemon Cookies

Ingredients:

- *Nonstick cooking spray*
- *¾ cup granulated sugar*
- *½ cup butter (optional)*
- *1½ Tsps vinegar*
- *1 large egg*
- *1 Tsp grated lemon zest*
- *1¾ cups flour*
- *1 Tsp baking powder*
- *¼ Tsp baking soda*
- *¾ cup confectioners' sugar*
- *¼ cup freshly squeezed lemon juice*
- *1 Tsp finely grated lemon zest*

Direction: Prep time: 10 minutes | Cook time: 10 minutes | Makes 12 cookies

✓ *Switch on the oven, preheat it setting its*

temperature to 350°F (180°C). Spray a baking sheet with cooking spray and set aside.

- ✓ In a medium container, cream the sugar and butter (if desired). Next, stir to the vinegar, and then add the egg and lemon zest, and mix well. Sift the flour, baking powder, and baking soda into the container and mix until combined.
- ✓ Spoon the mixture onto a prepared baking sheet in 12 equal heaps. Bake for 10 to 12 minutes. Be sure not to burn the bottoms.
- ✓ While the cookies are baking, make the lemon glaze in a small container by mixing the sugar, lemon juice, and lemon zest together.
- ✓ Remove the cookies from the oven and brush with lemon glaze.

Nutrition: calories: 233 | fat: 8g | protein: 2g | carbs: 39g | fiber: 1g | sodium:132 mg

1170) Mixed-Berries, Pecans and Oat Crumbles

Ingredients:

- 1½ cups frozen mixed berries, thawed
- 1 Tbsp butter, softened (optional)
- 1 Tbsp sugar
- ¼ cup pecans
- ¼ cup oats

Direction: Prep time: 5 minutes | Cook time: 30 minutes | Serves 2

- ✓ Switch on the oven, preheat it setting its temperature to 350°F (180°C) and set the rack to the middle position.
- ✓ Divide the berries between 2 (8-ounce) ramekins
- ✓ In a food processor, combine the butter (if desired), sugar, pecans, and oats, and pulse a few times until the mixture resembles damp sand.
- ✓ Divide the crumble topping over the berries.
- ✓ Place the ramekins on a sheet pan and bake for 30 minutes, or until the top is golden and the berries are bubbling.

Nutrition: calories: 267 | fat: 16g | protein: 4g | carbs: 27g | fiber: 6g | sodium: 43mg

1171) Chilled Fruit Kebabs with Dark Chocolate

Ingredients:

- 12 strawberries, hulled
- 12 cherries, pitted
- 24 seedless red or green grapes
- 24 blueberries
- 8 ounces (227 g) dark chocolate

Direction: Prep time: 5 minutes | Cook time: 1 minute | Serves 6

- ✓ Line a large, rimmed baking sheet with parchment paper. On your work surface, lay out six 12-inch wooden skewers.
- ✓ Thread the fruit onto the skewers, following this pattern: 1 strawberry, 1 cherry, 2 grapes, 2 blueberries, 1 strawberry, 1 cherry, 2 grapes, and 2 blueberries (or vary according to taste!). Place the kebabs on the prepared baking sheet.
- ✓ In a medium, microwave-safe container, heat the chocolate to the microwave for 1 minute on high. Stir until the chocolate is completely melted.
- ✓ Spoon the melted chocolate into a small plastic sandwich bag. Twist the bag closed right above the chocolate and snip the corner of the bag off with scissors. Squeeze the bag to drizzle lines of chocolate over the kebabs.
- ✓ Place the sheet in the freezer and chill for 20 minutes before serving.

Nutrition: calories: 297 | fat: 16g | protein: 4g | carbs: 35g | fiber: 5g | sodium: 12m

1172) Flourless Brownies with Balsamic Raspberry Sauce

Ingredients:

- For the Raspberry Sauce:
- ¼ cup good-quality balsamic vinegar
- 1 cup frozen raspberries
- For the Brownie:
- ½ cup black beans with no added salt, rinsed
- 1 large egg
- 1 Tbsp olive oil
- ½ Tsp vanilla extract
- 4 Tbsps unsweetened cocoa powder
- ¼ cup sugar
- ¼ Tsp baking powder
- Pinch salt
- ¼ cup dark chocolate chips
- Make the Raspberry Sauce

Direction: Prep time: 10 minutes | Cook time: 30 minutes | Serves 2

- ✓ Combine the balsamic vinegar and raspberries in a saucepan and bring the mixture to a boil. Reduce the heat to medium and let the sauce simmer for 15 minutes, or until reduced to ½ cup. If desired, strato the seeds and set the sauce aside until the brownie is ready.
- ✓ Make the Brownie
- ✓ Switch on the oven, preheat it setting its temperature to 350°F (180°C) and set the rack to the middle position. Grease two 8-ounce ramekins and place them on a baking sheet.
- ✓ In a food processor, combine the black beans, egg, olive oil, and vanilla. Purée the mixture for 1 to 2 minutes, or until it's smooth and the beans are completely broken down. Scrape down the sides of the container a few times to make sure everything is well incorporated.
- ✓ Undercooked. If you prefer a firmer brownie, leave

it in the oven for another 5 minutes or until a toothpick inserted into the middle comes out clean.

- ✓ *Add the cocoa powder, sugar, baking powder, and salt, and purée again to combine the dry ingredients, scraping down the sides of the container as needed.*
- ✓ *Stir the chocolate chips into the batter by hand. Reserve a few if you like to sprinkle over the top of the brownies when they come out of the oven.*
- ✓ *Pour the brownies into the prepared ramekins and bake for 15 minutes, or until firm. The center will look slightly. Remove the brownies from the oven. If desired, sprinkle any resting chocolate chips over the top and let them melt into the warm brownies.*
- ✓ *Let the brownies cool for a few minutes and top with warm raspberry sauce to serve.*

Nutrition: calories: 447 | fat: 15g | protein: 10g | carbs: 68g | fiber: 13g | sodium: 124mg

1173) Vanilla Apple Compote

Ingredients:

- *3 cups apples, cored and cubed*
- *1 tsp vanilla*
- *3/4 cup coconut sugar*
- *1 cup of water*
- *2 tbsp fresh lime juice*

Direction: Preparation Time: 10 minutes Cooking Time: 15 minutes Servings: 6

- ✓ *Add all ingredients into the inner pot of the instant pot and stir well.*
- ✓ *Seal pot with lid and cook on high for 15 minutes.*
- ✓ *Once done, allow to release pressure naturally for 10 minutes, then release resting using quick release. Remove lid.*
- ✓ *Stir and serve.*

Nutrition: Calories 76 Fat 0.2 g Carbohydrates 19.1 g Sugar 11.9 g Protein 0.5 g Cholesterol 0 mg

1174) Apple Dates Mix

Ingredients:

- *4 apples, cored and cut into chunks*
- *1 tsp vanilla*
- *1 tsp cinnamon*
- *1/2 cup dates, pitted*
- *1 1/2 cups apple juice*

Direction: Preparation Time: 10 minutes Cooking Time: 15 minutes Servings: 4

- ✓ *Add all ingredients into the inner pot of the instant pot and stir well.*
- ✓ *Seal pot with lid and cook on high for 15 minutes.*
- ✓ *Once done, allow to release pressure naturally for 10 minutes, then release resting using quick release. Remove lid.*
- ✓ *Stir and serve.*

Nutrition: Calories 226 Fat 0.6 g Carbohydrates 58.6 g Sugar 46.4 g Protein 1.3 g Cholesterol 0 mg

1175) Choco Rice Pudding

Ingredients:

- *1 1/4 cup rice*
- *1/4 cup dark chocolate, chopped*
- *1 tsp vanilla*
- *1/3 cup coconut butter*
- *1 tsp liquid stevia*
- *2 1/2 cups almond milk*

Direction: Preparation Time: 10 minutes Cooking Time: 20 minutes Servings: 4

- ✓ *Add all ingredients into the inner pot of the instant pot and stir well.*
- ✓ *Seal pot with lid and cook on high for 20 minutes.*
- ✓ *Once done, allow to release pressure naturally. Remove lid.*
- ✓ *Stir well and serve.*

Nutrition: Calories 632 Fat 39.9 g Carbohydrates 63.5 g Sugar 12.5 g Protein 8.6 g Cholesterol 2 mg

1176) Grapes Stew

Ingredients:

- *1 cup grapes, halved*
- *1 tsp vanilla*
- *1 tbsp fresh lemon juice*
- *1 tbsp honey*
- *2 cups rhubarb, chopped*
- *2 cups of water*

Direction: Preparation Time: 10 minutes Cooking Time: 15 minutes Servings: 4

- ✓ *Add all ingredients into the inner pot of the instant pot and stir well.*
- ✓ *Seal pot with lid and cook on high for 15 minutes.*
- ✓ *Once done, allow to release pressure naturally for 10 minutes, then release resting using quick release. Remove lid.*
- ✓ *Stir and serve.*

Nutrition: Calories 48 Fat 0.2 g Carbohydrates 11.3 g Sugar 8.9 g Protein 0.7 g Cholesterol 0 mg

1177) Chocolate Rice

Ingredients:

- *1 cup of rice*
- *1 tbsp cocoa powder*
- *2 tbsp maple syrup*
- *2 cups almond milk*

Direction: Preparation Time: 10 minutes Cooking Time: 20 minutes Servings: 4

- ✓ *Add all ingredients into the inner pot of the instant pot and stir well.*
- ✓ *Seal pot with lid and cook on high for 20 minutes.*
- ✓ *Once done, allow to release pressure naturally for*

10 minutes, then release resting using quick release. Remove lid.

- *Stir and serve.*

Nutrition: Calories 474 Fat 29.1 g Carbohydrates 51.1 g Sugar 10 g Protein 6.3 g Cholesterol 0 mg

1178) Raisins Cinnamon Peaches

Ingredients:

- *4 peaches, cored and cut into chunks*
- *1 tsp vanilla*
- *1 tsp cinnamon*
- *1/2 cup raisins*
- *1 cup of water*

Direction: Preparation Time: 10 minutes Cooking Time: 15 minutes Servings: 4

- *Add all ingredients into the inner pot of the instant pot and stir well.*
- *Seal pot with lid and cook on high for 15 minutes.*
- *Once done, allow to release pressure naturally for 10 minutes, then release resting using quick release. Remove lid.*
- *Stir and serve.*

Nutrition: Calories 118 Fat 0.5 g Carbohydrates 29 g Sugar 24.9 g Protein 2 g Cholesterol 0 mg

1179) Lemon Pear Compote

Ingredients:

- *3 cups pears, cored and cut into chunks*
- *1 tsp vanilla*
- *1 tsp liquid stevia*
- *1 tbsp lemon zest, grated*
- *2 tbsp lemon juice*

Direction: Preparation Time: 10 minutes Cooking Time: 15 minutes Servings: 6

- *Add all ingredients into the inner pot of the instant pot and stir well.*
- *Seal pot with lid and cook on high for 15 minutes.*
- *Once done, allow to release pressure naturally for 10 minutes, then release resting using quick release. Remove lid.*
- *Stir and serve.*

Nutrition: Calories 50 Fat 0.2 g Carbohydrates 12.7 g Sugar 8.1 g Protein 0.4 g Cholesterol 0 mg

1180) Strawberry Stew

Ingredients:

- *12 oz fresh strawberries, sliced*
- *1 tsp vanilla*
- *1 1/2 cups water*
- *1 tsp liquid stevia*
- *2 tbsp lime juice*

Direction: Preparation Time: 10 minutes Cooking Time: 15 minutes Servings: 4

- *Add all ingredients into the inner pot of the instant pot and stir well.*
- *Seal pot with lid and cook on high for 15 minutes.*
- *Once done, allow to release pressure naturally for 10 minutes, then release resting using quick release. Remove lid.*
- *Stir and serve.*

Nutrition: Calories 36 Fat 0.3 g Carbohydrates 8.5 g Sugar 4.7 g Protein 0.7 g Cholesterol 0 mg

1181) Walnut Apple Pear Mix

Ingredients:

- *2 apples, cored and cut into wedges*
- *1/2 tsp vanilla*
- *1 cup apple juice*
- *2 tbsp walnuts, chopped*
- *2 apples, cored and cut into wedges*

Direction: Preparation Time: 10 minutes Cooking Time: 10 minutes Servings: 4

- *Add all ingredients into the inner pot of the instant pot and stir well.*
- *Seal pot with lid and cook on high for 10 minutes.*
- *Once done, allow to release pressure naturally for 10 minutes, then release resting using quick release. Remove lid.*
- *Serve and enjoy.*

Nutrition: Calories 132 Fat 2.6 g Carbohydrates 28.3 g Sugar 21.9 g Protein 1.3 g Cholesterol 0 mg

1182) Cinnamon Pear Jam

Ingredients:

- *8 pears, cored and cut into quarters*
- *1 tsp cinnamon*
- *1/4 cup apple juice*
- *2 apples, peeled, cored, and diced*

Direction: Preparation Time: 10 minutes Cooking Time: 4 minutes Servings: 12

- *Add all ingredients into the inner pot of the instant pot and stir well.*
- *Seal pot with lid and cook on high for 4 minutes.*
- *Once done, allow to release pressure naturally. Remove lid.*
- *Blend pear apple mixture using an immersion blender until smooth.*
- *Serve and enjoy.*

Nutrition: Calories 103 Fat 0.3 g Carbohydrates 27.1 g Sugar 18 g Protein 0.6 g Cholesterol 0 mg

1183) Delicious Apple Pear Cobbler

Ingredients:

- *3 apples, cored and cut into chunks*
- *1 cup steel-cut oats*
- *2 pears, cored and cut into chunks*
- *1/4 cup maple syrup*
- *1 1/2 cups water*

- *1 tsp cinnamon*

Direction: Preparation Time: 10 minutes Cooking Time: 12 minutes Servings: 4

- ✓ *Spray instant pot from inside with cooking spray.*
- ✓ *Add all ingredients into the inner pot of the instant pot and stir well.*
- ✓ *Seal pot with lid and cook on high for 12 minutes.*
- ✓ *Once done, release pressure using quick release. Remove lid.*
- ✓ *Sere and enjoy.*

Nutrition: Calories 278 Fat 1.8 g Carbohydrates 66.5 g Sugar 39.5 g Protein 3.5 g Cholesterol 0 mg

1184) Coconut Rice Pudding

Ingredients:

- *1/2 cup rice*
- *1/4 cup shredded coconut*
- *3 tbsp swerve*
- *1 1/2 cups water*
- *14 oz can coconut milk*
- *Pinch of salt*

Direction: Preparation Time: 10 minutes Cooking Time: 3 minutes Servings: 4

- ✓ *Spray instant pot from inside with cooking spray.*
- ✓ *Add all ingredients into the inner pot of the instant pot and stir well.*
- ✓ *Seal pot with lid and cook on high for 3 minutes.*
- ✓ *Once done, allow to release pressure naturally for 10 minutes, then release resting using quick release. Remove lid.*
- ✓ *Serve and enjoy.*

Nutrition: Calories 298 Fat 23 g Carbohydrates 33.3 sugar 11.6 g Protein 3.8 g Cholesterol 0 mg

1185) Pear Sauce

Ingredients:

- *10 pears, sliced*
- *1 cup apple juice*
- *1 1/2 tsp cinnamon*
- *1/4 tsp nutmeg*

Direction: Preparation Time: 10 minutes Cooking Time: 15 minutes Servings: 6

- ✓ *Add all ingredients into the instant pot and stir well.*
- ✓ *Seal pot with lid and cook on high for 15 minutes.*
- ✓ *Once done, allow to release pressure naturally for 10 minutes, then release resting using quick release. Remove lid.*
- ✓ *Blend the pear mixture using an immersion blender until smooth.*
- ✓ *Serve and enjoy.*

Nutrition: Calories 222 Fat 0.6 g Carbohydrates 58.2 g Sugar 38 g Protein 1.3 g Cholesterol 0 mg

1186) Sweet Peach Jam

Ingredients:

- *1 1/2 lb fresh peaches, pitted and chopped*
- *1/2 tbsp vanilla*
- *1/4 cup maple syrup*

Direction: Preparation Time: 10 minutes Cooking Time: 16 minutes Servings: 20

- ✓ *Add all ingredients into the instant pot and stir well.*
- ✓ *Seal pot with lid and cook on high for 1 minute.*
- ✓ *Once done, allow to release pressure naturally. Remove lid.*
- ✓ *Set pot on sauté mode and cook for 15 minutes or until jam thickened.*
- ✓ *Pour it into the container and store it in the fridge.*

Nutrition: Calories 16 Fat 0 g Carbohydrates 3.7 g Sugar 3.4 g Protein 0.1 g Cholesterol 0 mg

1187) Warm Peach Compote

Ingredients:

- *4 peaches, peeled and chopped*
- *1 tbsp water*
- *1/2 tbsp cornstarch*
- *1 tsp vanilla*

Direction: Preparation Time: 10 minutes Cooking Time: 1-minute Servings: 4

- ✓ *Add water, vanilla, and peaches into the instant pot.*
- ✓ *Seal pot with lid and cook on high for 1 minute.*
- ✓ *Once done, allow to release pressure naturally. Remove lid.*
- ✓ *In a small container, whisk together 1 Tbsp of water and cornstarch and pour into the pot and stir well.*
- ✓ *Serve and enjoy.*

Nutrition: Calories 66 Fat 0.4 g Carbohydrates 15 g Sugar 14.1 g Protein 1.4 g Cholesterol 0 mg

1188) Spiced Pear Sauce

Ingredients:

- *8 pears, cored and diced*
- *1/2 tsp ground cinnamon*
- *1/4 tsp ground nutmeg*
- *1/4 tsp ground cardamom*
- *1 cup of water*

Direction: Preparation Time: 10 minutes Cooking Time: 6 hours Servings: 12

- ✓ *Add all ingredients into the instant pot and stir well.*
- ✓ *Seal the pot with a lid and select slow cook mode and cook on low for 6 hours.*
- ✓ *Mash the sauce using a potato masher.*
- ✓ *Pour it into the container and store it in the fridge.*

Nutrition: Calories 81 Fat 0.2 g Carbohydrates 21.4 g Sugar 13.6 g Protein 0.5 g Cholesterol 0 mg

1189) Honey Fruit Compote

Ingredients:

- *1/3 cup honey*
- *1 1/2 cups blueberries*
- *1 1/2 cups raspberries*

Direction: Preparation Time: 10 minutes Cooking Time: 3 minutes Servings: 4

- ✓ *Add all ingredients into the instant pot and stir well.*
- ✓ *Seal pot with lid and cook on high for 3 minutes.*
- ✓ *Once done, allow to release pressure naturally. Remove lid.*
- ✓ *Serve and enjoy.*

Nutrition: Calories 141 Fat 0.5 g Carbohydrates 36.7 g Sugar 30.6 g Protein 1 g Cholesterol 0 mg

1190) Creamy Brown Rice Pudding

Ingredients:

- *1 cup of rice*
- *1 cup of brown rice*
- *1 cup of water*
- *1 cup half and half*
- *1/2 cup pecans, chopped*
- *2 tsp vanilla*
- *1 tbsp coconut butter*
- *1/2 cup heavy cream*
- *Pinch of salt*

Direction: Preparation Time: 10 minutes Cooking Time: 20 minutes Servings: 8

- ✓ *Add coconut butter into the instant pot and set the pot on sauté mode.*
- ✓ *Add pecans into the pot and stir until toasted.*
- ✓ *Add resting ingredients except for heavy cream and vanilla. Stir well.*
- ✓ *Seal pot with lid and cook on high for 20 minutes.*
- ✓ *Once done, allow to release pressure naturally for 10 minutes, then release resting using quick release. Remove lid.*
- ✓ *Add vanilla and heavy cream. Stir well and serve.*

Nutrition: Calories 276 Fat 10.9 g Carbohydrates 39.2 g Sugar 0.5 g Protein 5 g Cholesterol 21 mg

1191) Lemon Cranberry Sauce

Ingredients:

- *10 oz fresh cranberries*
- *3/4 cup Swerve*
- *1/4 cup water*
- *1 tsp lemon zest*
- *1 tsp vanilla extract*

Direction: Preparation Time: 10 minutes Cooking Time: 14 minutes Servings: 8

- ✓ *Add cranberries and water into the instant pot.*
- ✓ *Seal pot with lid and cook on high for 1 minute.*
- ✓ *Once done, allow to release pressure naturally for 10 minutes, then release resting using quick release. Remove lid. Set pot on sauté mode.*
- ✓ *Add resting ingredients and cook for 2-3 minutes.*
- ✓ *Pour in a container and store in the fridge.*

Nutrition: Calories 21 Fat 0 g Carbohydrates 25.8 g Sugar 23.9 g Protein 0 g Cholesterol 0 mg

1192) Blackberry Jam

Ingredients:

- *3 cups fresh blackberries*
- *1/4 cup chia seeds*
- *4 tbsp Swerve*
- *1/4 cup fresh lemon juice*
- *1/4 cup coconut butter*

Direction: Preparation Time: 10 minutes Cooking Time: 6 hours Servings: 6

- ✓ *Add all ingredients into the instant pot and stir well.*
- ✓ *Seal the pot with a lid and select slow cook mode and cook on low for 6 hours.*
- ✓ *Pour in a container and store in the fridge.*

Nutrition: Calories 101 Fat 6.8 g Carbohydrates 20 g Sugar 14.4 g Protein 2 g Cholesterol 0 mg

1193) Chunky Apple Sauce

Ingredients:

- *4 apples, peeled, cored, and diced*
- *1 tsp vanilla*
- *4 pears, diced*
- *2 tbsp cinnamon*
- *1/4 cup maple syrup*
- *3/4 cup water*

Direction: Preparation Time: 10 minutes Cooking Time: 12 minutes Servings: 16

- ✓ *Add all ingredients into the instant pot and stir well.*
- ✓ *Seal pot with lid and cook on high for 12 minutes.*
- ✓ *Once done, allow to release pressure naturally for 10 minutes, then release resting using quick release. Remove lid.*
- ✓ *Serve and enjoy.*

Nutrition: Calories 75 Fat 0.2 g Carbohydrates 19.7 g Sugar 13.9 g Protein 0.4 g Cholesterol 0 mg

1194) Maple Syrup Cranberry Sauce

Ingredients:

- *12 oz fresh cranberries, rinsed*

- 1 apple, peeled, cored, and chopped
- 1/2 cup maple syrup
- 1/2 cup apple cider
- 1 tsp orange zest, grated
- 1 orange juice

Direction: Preparation Time: 10 minutes Cooking Time: 5 minutes Servings: 8

✓ Add all ingredients into the instant pot and stir well.

✓ Seal pot with lid and cook on high for 5 minutes.

✓ Once done, allow to release pressure naturally for 10 minutes, then release resting using quick release. Remove lid.

✓ Pour in a container and store in the fridge.

Nutrition: Calories 101 Fat 0.1 g Carbohydrates 23.9 g Sugar 18.8 g Protein 0.2 g Cholesterol 0 mg

1195) Raisin Pecan Baked Apples

Ingredients:

- 6 apples, cored and cut into wedges
- 1 cup red wine
- 1/4 cup pecans, chopped
- 1/4 cup raisins
- 1/4 tsp nutmeg
- 1 tsp cinnamon
- 1/3 cup honey

Direction: Preparation Time: 10 minutes Cooking Time: 4 minutes Servings: 6

✓ Add all ingredients into the instant pot and stir well.

✓ Seal pot with lid and cook on high for 4 minutes.

✓ Once done, allow to release pressure naturally for 10 minutes, then release resting using quick release. Remove lid.

✓ Stir well and serve.

Nutrition: Calories 229 Fat 0.9 g Carbohydrates 52.6 g Sugar 42.6 g Protein 1 g Cholesterol 0 mg

1196) Healthy Zucchini Pudding

Ingredients:

- 2 cups zucchini, shredded
- 1/4 tsp cardamom powder
- 5 oz half and half
- 5 oz almond milk
- 1/4 cup Swerve

Direction: Preparation Time: 10 minutes Cooking Time: 10 minutes Servings: 4

✓ Add all ingredients except cardamom into the instant pot and stir well.

✓ Seal pot with lid and cook on high for 10 minutes.

✓ Once done, allow to release pressure naturally for 10 minutes, then release resting using quick release. Remove lid.

✓ Stir in cardamom and serve.

Nutrition: Calories 137 Fat 12.6 g Carbohydrates 20.5 g Sugar 17.2 g Protein 2.6 g Cholesterol 13 mg

1197) Cinnamon Apple Rice Pudding

Ingredients:

- 1 cup of rice
- 1 tsp vanilla
- 1/4 apple, peeled and chopped
- 1/2 cup water
- 1 1/2 cup almond milk
- 1 tsp cinnamon
- 1 cinnamon stick

Direction: Preparation Time: 10 minutes Cooking Time: 15 minutes Servings: 8

✓ Add all ingredients into the instant pot and stir well.

✓ Seal pot with lid and cook on high for 15 minutes.

✓ Once done, release pressure using quick release. Remove lid.

✓ Stir and serve.

Nutrition: Calories 206 Fat 11.5 g Carbohydrates 23.7 g Sugar 2.7 g Protein 3 g Cholesterol 0 mg

1198) Coconut Risotto Pudding

Ingredients:

- 3/4 cup rice
- 1/2 cup shredded coconut
- 1 tsp lemon juice
- 1/2 tsp vanilla
- 1/4 cup maple syrup
- 1 1/2 cups water

Direction: Preparation Time: 10 minutes Cooking Time: 20 minutes Servings: 6

✓ Add all ingredients into the instant pot and stir well.

✓ Seal pot with lid and cook on high for 20 minutes.

✓ Once done, allow to release pressure naturally for 10 minutes, then release resting using quick release. Remove lid.

✓ Blend pudding mixture using an immersion blender until smooth.

✓ Serve and enjoy.

Nutrition: Calories 205 Fat 8.6 g Carbohydrates 29.1 g Sugar 9 g Protein 2.6 g Cholesterol 0 mg

1199) Mediterranean Baked Apples

Ingredients:

- 1.5 pounds apples, peeled and sliced
- Juice from ½ lemon
- A dash of cinnamon

Direction: Cooking Time: 25 minutes Servings: 4

✓ Switch on the oven, preheat it setting its

temperature to 250oF.

- ✓ *Line a baking sheet with parchment paper, then set aside.*
- ✓ *In a medium container, apples with lemon juice and cinnamon.*
- ✓ *Place the apples on the parchment paper-lined baking sheet.*
- ✓ *Bake for 25 minutes until crisp.*

***Nutrition:** Cal: 90; Carbs: 23.9g; Protein: 0.5g; Fat: 0.3g*

1200) Mediterranean Diet Cookie Recipe

Ingredients:

- *1 tsp vanilla extract*
- *½ tsp salt*
- *4 large egg whites*
- *1 ¼ cups sugar*
- *2 cups toasted and skinned hazelnuts*

Direction: Cooking Time: 40 minutes Servings: 12

- ✓ *Preheat oven to 325oF and position oven rack to the center. Then line with baking paper your baking pan.*
- ✓ *In a food processor, finely grind the hazelnuts and then transfer them into a medium-sized container.*
- ✓ *In a large mixing container, at high speed, beat salt and egg whites until stiff and there are peaks. Then gently fold to the ground nut and vanilla until thoroughly mixed.*
- ✓ *Drop a spoonful of the mixture onto the prepared pan and bake the cookies for twenty minutes or until lightly browned per batch. Bake 6 cookies per cookie sheet.*
- ✓ *Let it cool on the pan for five minutes before removing it.*

***Nutrition:** Calorie s: 173; Carbs: 23.0g; Protein: 3.1g; Fats: 7.6g*

1201) Mediterranean Style Fruit Medley

Ingredients:

- *4 Fuyu persimmons, sliced into wedges*
- *1 ½ cups grapes, halved*
- *8 mint leaves, chopped*
- *1 Tbsp lemon juice*
- *1 Tbsp honey*
- *½ cups almond, toasted and chopped*

Direction: Cooking Time: 5 minutes Servings: 7

- ✓ *Combine all Ingredients in a container.*
- ✓ *Toss, then chill before serving.*

***Nutrition:** Cal : 159; Carbs: 32g; Protein: 3g; Fat: 4g*

1202) Mediterranean Watermelon Salad

Ingredients:

- *6 cups mixed salad greens, torn*
- *3 cups watermelon, seeded and cubed*
- *½ cup onion, sliced*
- *1 Tbsp extra-virgin olive oil*
- *1/3 cup feta cheese, crumbled*
- *Cracked black pepper*

Direction: Cooking Time: 2 minutes Servings: 6

- ✓ *In a large container, mix all ingredients. Toss to combine everything.*
- ✓ *Allow chilling before serving.*

***Nutrition:** Cal: 91; Carbs: 15.2g; Protein: 1.9g; Fat: 2.8g*

1203) Melon Cucumber Smoothie

Ingredients:

- *½ cucumber*
- *2 slices of melon*
- *2 Tbsps lemon juice*
- *1 pear, peeled and sliced*
- *3 fresh mint leaves*
- *½ cup almond milk*

Direction: Cooking Time: 5 minutes Servings: 2

- ✓ *Place all Ingredients in a blender.*
- ✓ *Blend until smooth.*
- ✓ *Pour in a glass container and allow to chill to the fridge for at least 30 minutes.*

***Nutrition:** Calories: 253; Carbs: 59.3g; Protein: 5.7g; Fat: 2.1g*

1204) Peanut Banana Yogurt Container

Ingredients:

- *4 cups Greek yogurt*
- *2 medium bananas, sliced*
- *¼ cup creamy natural peanut butter*
- *¼ cup flax seed meal*
- *1 Tsp nutmeg*

Direction: Cooking Time: 15 minutes Servings: 4

- ✓ *Divide the yogurt between four containers and top with banana, peanut butter, and flax seed meal.*
- ✓ *Garnish with nutmeg.*
- ✓ *Chill before serving.*

***Nutrition:** Calories: 370; Carbs: 47.7g; Protein: 22.7g; Fat: 10.6g*

1205) Pomegranate and Lychee Sorbet

Ingredients:

- *¾ cup dragon fruit cubes*
- *8 lychees, peeled and pitted*
- *Juice from 1 lemon*
- *3 Tbsps stevia sugar*
- *2 Tbsps pomegranate seeds*

Direction: Cooking Time: 5 minutes Servings: 6

- ✓ *In a blender, combine the dragon fruit, lychees, lemon, and stevia sugar.*
- ✓ *Pulse until smooth.*
- ✓ *Pour the mixture into a container with a lid and place it inside the fridge.*
- ✓ *Allow sorbet to harden for at least 8 hours.*
- ✓ *Sprinkle with pomegranate seeds before serving.*

Nutrition: Cal : 214; Carbs: 30.4g; Protein: 1.9g; Fat: 1.2g

1206) Pomegranate Granita with Lychee

Ingredients:

- *500 millimeters pomegranate juice, organic and sugar-free*
- *1 cup water*
- *½ cup lychee syrup*
- *2 Tbsps lemon juice*
- *4 mint leaves*
- *1 cup fresh lychees, pitted and sliced*

Direction: Cooking Time: 5 minutes Servings: 7

- ✓ *Place all Ingredients in a large pitcher.*
- ✓ *Place inside the fridge to cool before serving.*

Nutrition: Cal:96; Carbs: 23.8g; Protein: 0.4g; Fat: 0.4g

1207) Roasted Berry and Honey Yogurt Pops

Ingredients:

- *12 ounces mixed berries*
- *A dash of sea salt*
- *2 Tbsps honey*
- *2 cups whole Greek yogurt*
- *½ small lemon, juice*

Direction: Servings: 8, Cooking Time: 15 minutes

- ✓ *Switch on the oven, preheat it setting its temperature to 3500F.*
- ✓ *Line a baking sheet with parchment paper, then set aside.*
- ✓ *In a medium container, toss the berries with sea salt and honey.*
- ✓ *Pour the berries on the prepared baking sheet.*
- ✓ *Roast for 30 minutes while stirring halfway.*
- ✓ *While the fruit is roasting, blend the Greek yogurt and lemon juice. Add honey to taste if desired.*
- ✓ *Once the berries are done, cool for at least ten minutes.*
- ✓ *Fold the berries into the yogurt mixture.*
- ✓ *Pour into popsicle molds and allow to freeze for at least 8 hours.*
- ✓ *Serve chilled.*

Nutrition: Cal: 177; Carbs: 24.8g; Protein: 3.2g; Fat: 7.9g

1208) Scrumptious Cake with Cinnamon

Ingredients:

- *1 lemon*
- *4 eggs*
- *1 tsp cinnamon*
- *¼ lb. sugar*
- *½ lb. ground almonds*

Direction: Cooking Time: 40 minutes Servings: 8

- ✓ *Preheat oven to 3500F. Then grease a cake pan and set it aside.*
- ✓ *At high speed, beat for three minutes the sugar and eggs or until the volume is doubled.*
- ✓ *Then with a spatula, gently fold to the lemon zest, cinnamon, and almond flour until well mixed.*
- ✓ *Then pour batter on prepared pan and bake for forty minutes or until golden brown.*
- ✓ *Let cool before serving.*

Nutrition: Cal: 253; Carbs: 21.1g; Protein:8.8g; Fats:16.3g

1209) Smoothie Container with Dragon Fruit

Ingredients:

- *¼ of dragon fruit, peeled and sliced*
- *1 cup frozen berries*
- *2 cups baby greens (mixed)*
- *½ cup coconut meat*

Direction: Cooking Time: 5 minutes Servings: 4,

- ✓ *Place all Ingredients in a blender and pulse until smooth.*
- ✓ *Place on a container and allow to cool to the fridge for at least 20 minutes.*
- ✓ *Garnish with whatever fruits or nuts are available in your fridge.*

Nutrition: Calories: 190; Carbs: 19g; Protein: 5g; Fat: 13g

1210) Soothing Red Smoothie

Ingredients:

- *4 plums, pitted*
- *¼ cup raspberry*
- *¼ cup blueberry*
- *1 Tbsp lemon juice*
- *1 Tbsp linseed oil*

Direction: Cooking Time: 3 minutes Servings: 2

- ✓ *Place all Ingredients in a blender.*
- ✓ *Blend until smooth.*
- ✓ *Pour in a glass container and allow to chill to the fridge for at least 30 minutes.*

Nutrition: Cal: 201; Carbs: 36.4g; Protein: 0.8g; Fat: 7.1g

1211) Strawberry and Avocado Medley

Ingredients:

- *2 cups strawberry, halved*
- *1 avocado, pitted and sliced*
- *2 Tbsps slivered almonds*

Direction: Cooking Time: 5 minutes Servings: 4

- ✓ *Place all Ingredients in a mixing container.*
- ✓ *Toss to combine.*
- ✓ *Allow chilling to the fridge before serving.*

Nutrition: Cal: 107; Carbs: 9.9g; Protein: 1.6g; Fat: 7.8g

1212) Strawberry Banana Greek Yogurt Parfaits

Ingredients:

- *1 cup plain Greek yogurt, chilled*
- *1 cup pepitas*
- *½ cup chopped strawberries*
- *½ banana, sliced*

Direction: Servings: 4, Cooking Time: 5 minutes

- ✓ *In a parfait glass, add the yogurt at the bottom of the glass.*
- ✓ *Add a layer of pepitas, strawberries, and bananas.*
- ✓ *Continue to layer the Ingredients until the entire glass is filled.*

Nutrition: Calories : 387; Carbs: 69.6g; Protein: 18.1g; Fat: 1g

1213) Summertime Fruit Salad

Ingredients:

- *1-pound strawberries, hulled and sliced thinly*
- *3 medium peaches, sliced thinly*
- *6 ounces blueberries*
- *1 Tbsp fresh mint, chopped*
- *2 Tbsps lemon juice*
- *1 Tbsp honey*
- *2 Tsps balsamic vinegar*

Direction: Cooking Time: 5 minutes Servings: 6

- ✓ *In a salad container, combine all ingredients.*
- ✓ *Gently toss to coat all ingredients.*
- ✓ *Chill for at least 30 minutes before serving.*

Nutrition: Cal: 146; Carbs: 22.8g; Protein: 8.1g; Fat: 3.4g

1214) Sweet Tropical Medley Smoothie

Ingredients:

- *1 banana, peeled*
- *1 sliced mango*
- *1 cup fresh pineapple*
- *½ cup coconut water*

Direction: Preparation Time: 10 minutes Cooking time: 5 minutes Servings: 4

- ✓ *Place all Ingredients in a blender.*
- ✓ *Blend until smooth.*
- ✓ *Pour in a glass container and allow to chill to the fridge for at least 30 minutes.*

Nutrition: Calories : 73; Carbs: 18.6g; Protein: 0.8g; Fat: 0.5g.

1215) Greek Yogurt Muesli Parfaits

Ingredients

- *4 cups Greek yogurt*
- *1 cup whole wheat muesli*
- *2 cups fresh berries of your choice*

DIRECTIONS:Servings: 4 Preparation time:10 minutes

- ✓ *Layer the four classes with Greek yogurt at the bottom, muesli on top, and berries.*
- ✓ *Repeat the layers until the glass is filled.*
- ✓ *Place in the fridge for at least hours to chill.*

Nutrition Calories 280, Fat 36g, Protein 23g, Carbs 4g

1216) Lemon Cream

Ingredients

- *2 eggs, whisked*
- *1 and ¼ cup stevia*
- *10 tablespoons avocado oil*
- *1 cup heavy cream*
- *Juice of 2 lemons*
- *Zest of 2 lemons, grated*

DIRECTIONS: Servings: 6 Preparation time: 10 minutes

- ✓ *In a pan, combine the cream with the lemon juice and the other ingredients, whisk well, cook for 10 minutes, divide into cups and keep to the fridge for 1 hour before serving.*

Nutrition Calories 200, Fat 8.5g, Protein 4.5g, Carbs 8.6g, Fiber 4.5g

1217) Mediterranean Fruit Tart

Ingredients

- *¼ cups all-purpose flour*
- *½ tsp salt*
- *2 TB. sugar*
- *1 cup cold butter*
- *½ cup shortening*
- *5 TB. ice water*
- *2 cups Ashta Custard*
- *10 strawberries, sliced*
- *2 kiwi, peeled and sliced*

- *1 cup blueberries*
- *1 cup peach or apricot jam*
- *3 TB. water*

DIRECTIONS: Servings: 1/8 of tart Preparation time: 15 minutes

- ✓ *In a food processor fitted with a chopping blade, pulse 2 cups of all-purpose flour, salt, and sugar 5 times.*
- ✓ *Add butter and shortening, and blend for 1 minute or until mixture crumbles. Transfer mixture to a medium container.*
- ✓ *Add ice enter to the batter, and mix just until combined.*
- ✓ *Place dough on a piece of plastic wrap, form into a flat disc, and refrigerate for 20 minutes.*
- ✓ *Switch on the oven, preheat it setting its temperature to 450F.*
- ✓ *Dust your workspace with flour, and using a rolling pin, roll out dough to 1/8 inch thickness. Place rolled-out dough into a 9-inch tart pan, press to mold into the pan, and cut off excess dough. Bake for 13 minutes.*
- ✓ *Let the tart cool for 10 minutes.*
- ✓ *Place tart shell on a serving dish and fill with Ashta Custard. Arrange strawberry slices, kick slices, and blueberries on top of the tart.*
- ✓ *In a small saucepan over medium heat, heat peach jam and enter, stirring for 2 minutes.*
- ✓ *Using a pastry brush, brush the top of the fruit and tart with warmed jam.*
- ✓ *Serve chilled and store in the fridge.*

Nutrition Calories 644, Fat 39g, Carbs 70g, Fiber 2g, Protein 6g

1218) Green Tea And Vanilla Cream

Ingredients

- *14 ounces almond milk, hot*
- *2 tablespoons green tea powder*
- *14 ounces heavy cream*
- *3 tablespoons stevia*
- *1 teaspoon vanilla extract*
- *1 teaspoon gelatin powder*

DIRECTIONS: Servings: 4 Preparation time: 0 minutes

- ✓ *In a container, combine the almond milk with the green tea powder and the rest of the ingredients, whisk well, cool down, divide into cups and keep to the fridge for 2 hours before serving.*

Nutrition Calories 120, Fat 3g, Protein 4g, Carbs 7g, Fiber 3g

1219) Honey Walnut Bars

Ingredients

- *5 oz puff pastry*
- *½ cup of water*
- *3 tablespoons of liquid honey*
- *1 teaspoon Erythritol*
- *1/'3 cup butter softened*
- *½ cup walnuts, chopped*
- *1 teaspoon olive oil*

DIRECTIONS: Servings: 8 Preparation time: 30 minutes

- ✓ *Roll up the puff paste and cut it on 6 sheets.*
- ✓ *Then brush the tray with olive oil and arrange the first puff pastry sheet inside.*
- ✓ *Grease it with butter gently and sprinkle it with walnuts.*
- ✓ *Repeat the same steps with 4 puff pastry sheets.*
- ✓ *Then sprinkle the last layer with walnuts and Erythritol and cove with the sixth puff past sheet.*
- ✓ *Cut the baklava on the servings. Bake the baklava for 30 minutes.*
- ✓ *Meanwhile, bring to a boil liquid honey and water*
- ✓ *When the baklava is cooked, remove it from the oven.*
- ✓ *Pour hot honey liquid over baklava and let it cool till room temperature.*

Nutrition Calories 243, Fat 19.6g, Protein 3.3g, Carbs 15.9g

1220) Lime Vanilla Fudge

Ingredients

- *1/3 cup cashew butter*
- *5 tablespoons lime juice*
- *½ teaspoon lime zest, grated*
- *1 tablespoons stevia*

DIRECTIONS: Servings: 6 Preparation time: 0 minutes

- ✓ *In a container, mix the cashew butter with the other ingredients and whisk well.*
- ✓ *Line a muffin tray with parchment paper, scoop 1 tablespoon of lime fudge, mix in each of the muffin tins and keep in the freezer for 3 hours before serving.*

Nutrition Calories 200, Fat 4.5g, Protein 5g, Carbs 13.5g, Fiber 3.4g

1221) Honey Cream

Ingredients

- *½ cup cream*
- *¼ cup milk*
- *2 teaspoons honey*
- *1 teaspoon vanilla extract*
- *1 tablespoons gelatin*
- *2 tablespoons orange juice*

Directions: Servings: 2 Preparation time: 5 minutes

- ✓ *Mix up together milk and gelatin and leave it for 5*

minutes.

- ✓ *Meanwhile, pour cream into the saucepan and bring it to a boil.*
- ✓ *Add honey and vanilla extract.*
- ✓ *Remove the cream from the heat and stir well until honey is dissolved.*
- ✓ *After this, add gelatin mixture (milk+ gelatin) and mix it up until gelatin is dissolved.*
- ✓ *After this, place 1 tablespoon of orange juice in every serving glass.*
- ✓ *Add the cream mixture over the orange juice.*
- ✓ *Refrigerate the pannacotta for 30-50 minutes to the fridge or until it is solid.*

Nutrition Calories 100, Fat 4g, Protein 4.6g, Carbs 11g

1222) Dragon Fruit, Pear, And Spinach Salad

Ingredients

- *5 ounces spinach leaves, torn*
- *1 dragon fruit, peeled and cubed*
- *2 pears, peeled and cubed*
- *10 ounces organic goat cheese*
- *1 cup pecan, halves*
- *6 ounces blackberries*
- *6 ounces raspberries*
- *8 tablespoons olive oil*
- *8 tablespoons red wine vinegar*
- *1 tablespoon poppy seeds*

Directions: Servings: 4 Preparation time: 3 minutes

- ✓ *In a mixing container, combine all ingredients: except for the poppy seeds.*
- ✓ *Place inside the fridge and allow to chill before seizing.*
- ✓ *Sprinkle with poppy seeds on top before serving.*

Nutrition Calories 321, Fat 3g, Protein 3.3g, Carbs 27.2g

1223) Kataifi

Ingredients

- *1 kg almonds, blanched and then chopped*
- *1 tsp cinnamon*
- *¼ kg kataifi phyllo*
- *2 eggs*
- *4 tablespoons sugar*
- *400g butter*
- *1 ½ kilograms sugar*
- *1 lemon rind*
- *1 teaspoon lemon juice*
- *5 cups water*

Directions: Servings: 8-10 Preparation time: 30 minutes

- ✓ *Switch on the oven, preheat it setting its temperature to 340F.*
- ✓ *Put the sugar, eggs, cinnamon, and almonds in a container.*
- ✓ *With your fingers, open the kataifi past gently. Lay it on a piece of marble and wood. Put 1 tablespoon of the almond mixture in one end and then roll the pasts into a log or a cylinder. Make sure you fold the pasts a little tight so that way the filling is enclosed securely. Repeat the process with the resting past and almond mixture.*
- ✓ *Melt the butter and put it into a baking dish.*
- ✓ *Brush the kataifi rolls with melted butter, covering all the sides.*
- ✓ *Place into baking sheets and bake for about 30 minutes.*
- ✓ *Meanwhile, prepare the syrup.*
- ✓ *Except for the lemon juice, cook the rest of the syrup ingredients for about 5-10 minutes. Add the lemon juice and let cook for a few minutes until the syrup is slightly thick.*
- ✓ *After baking the kataifi, pour the syrup over the still warm rolls.*
- ✓ *Cover the pastry with a clean towel. Let cool as the kataifi absorbs the syrup.*

Nutrition Calories 1085, Fat 83.3g, Protein 22.6g, Carbs 76.6g, Sugar 59g, Chol 119mg, Sodium 248, Pot 759mg

1224) Walnuts Kataifi

Ingredients

- *7 oz kataifi dough*
- *1/3 cup walnuts, chopped*
- *½ teaspoon ground cinnamon*
- *¾ teaspoon vanilla extract*
- *4 tablespoons butter, melted*
- *¼ teaspoon ground clove*
- *1/3 cup water*
- *3 tablespoons honey*

Directions: Servings: 2 Preparation time: 50 minutes

- ✓ *For the filling: mix up together walnuts, ground cinnamon, and vanilla extract. Add ground clove and blend the mixture until smooth.*
- ✓ *Make the kataifi dough: grease the casserole mold with butter and place ½ part of the kataifi dough.*
- ✓ *Then sprinkle the filling over the kataifi dough.*
- ✓ *After this, sprinkle the filling with 1 tablespoon of melted butter.*
- ✓ *Sprinkle the filling with the resting kataifi dough.*
- ✓ *Make the roll from ½ part of kataifi dough and cut it. Gently arrange the kataifi roll to the tray.*
- ✓ *Repeat the same steps with the resting dough. To the end, you should get 2 kataifi rolls.*

- ✓ *Switch on the oven, preheat it setting its temperature to 355F and place the tray with kataifi rolls inside.*
- ✓ *Bake the dessert for 50 minutes or until it, is crispy.*
- ✓ *Meanwhile, make the syrup: bring the water to a boil.*
- ✓ *Add honey and heat it up until the honey is dissolved.*
- ✓ *When the kataifi rolls are cooked, pour the hot syrup over the hot kataifi rolls.*
- ✓ *Cut every kataifi roll into 2 pieces.*
- ✓ *Serve the dessert with the resting syrup.*

Nutrition Calories 120, Fat 1.5g, Protein 3g, Carbs 22g

1225) Mediterranean Biscotti

Ingredients

- *2 eggs*
- *1 cup whole-wheat flour*
- *1 cup all-purpose flour*
- *¾ cup parmesan cheese, grated*
- *2 teaspoons baking powder*
- *2 tablespoons sugar*
- *¼ cup sun-dried tomato, finely chopped*
- *¼ cup kalamata olive, finely chopped*
- *1/3 cup olive oil*
- *½ teaspoon salt*
- *½ teaspoon black pepper, cracked*
- *1 teaspoon dried oregano (preferably Greek)*
- *1 teaspoon dried basil*

Directions: Servings: 3 Preparation time: 1 Hour

- ✓ *Into a large-sized container, beat the eggs and the sugar together. Pour to the olive, beat until smooth.*
- ✓ *In another container, combine the flours, baking powder, pepper. Salt, oregano, and basil. Stir the flour mix into the egg mixture, stirring until blended.*
- ✓ *Stir to the cheese, tomatoes, and olives, stirring until thoroughly combined.*
- ✓ *Divide the dough into 2 portions; shape each into 10-inch long logs. Place the logs into a parchment-lined cookie sheet, flatten the low tops slightly.*
- ✓ *Bake for about 30 minutes in a preheated 375F oven or until the loss are pale golden and not quite firm to the touch.*
- ✓ *Remove from the oven; let cool on the baking sheet for 3 minutes, transfer the logs into a cutting board, slice each log into 1/2-inch diagonal slices using a serrated knife.*
- ✓ *Place the biscotti slices on the baking sheet, return them into the 325F oven and bake for about 20 to 25 minutes until dry and firm. Flip the slices halfway through baking. Remove from the oven, transfer on a ride rack and let cool.*

Nutrition Calories 731, Fat 36.5g, Protein 23.3g, Carbs 77.8g, Sugar 10.7, Fiber 3.5g, Chol 146mg, Sodium 1238.4mg

1226) Semolina Pie

Ingredients

- *½ cup milk*
- *3 tablespoons semolina*
- *½ cup butter softened*
- *8 Phyllo sheets*
- *2 eggs, beaten*
- *3 tablespoons Erythritol*
- *1 teaspoon lemon rind*
- *1 tablespoon lemon juice*
- *1 teaspoon vanilla extract*
- *2 tablespoons liquid honey*
- *1 teaspoon ground cinnamon*
- *¼ cup of water*

Directions: Servings: 6 Preparation time: 1 Hour

- ✓ *Melt ½ part of all butter.*
- ✓ *Then brush the casserole glass mold with the butter and place 1 Phyllo sheet inside.*
- ✓ *Brush the phyllo sheet with butter and cover it with a second phyllo sheet.*
- ✓ *Blake the dessert filling: heat up milk and add semolina.*
- ✓ *Stir it carefully.*
- ✓ *After this, add the resting softened butter. Erythritol and vanilla extract.*
- ✓ *Bring the mixture to a boil and simmer it for 2 minutes.*
- ✓ *Remove it from the heat and cool to room temperature.*
- ✓ *Then add beaten eggs and mix up well.*
- ✓ *Pour the semolina mixture into the mold over the Phyllo sheets, flatten it if needed.*
- ✓ *When covering the semolina mixture with resting Phyllo sheets and brush with resting melted butter.*
- ✓ *Cut the dessert on the bars.*
- ✓ *Bake galaktoboureko for 1 hour at 365F.*
- ✓ *Then make the syrup: bring lemon juice, honey, and water to a boil and remove the liquid from the heat.*
- ✓ *Pour the syrup over the hot dessert and let it chill well.*

Nutrition Calories 304, Fat 18g, Protein 6g, Carbs 39.5g

1227) Cold Lemon Squares

Ingredients

- *1 cup avocado oil + a drizzle*
- *2 bananas, peeled and chopped*

- *1 tbsp honey*
- *¼ cup lemon juice*
- *A pinch of lemon zest, grated*

Directions: Servings: 4 Preparation time: 0 minutes

✓ *In your food processor, mix the banans with the rest of the ingredients, pulse well, and spread on the bottom of a pan greased with a drizzle of oil.*

✓ *Introduce to the fridge for 30 minutes, slice into squares and serve.*

Nutrition Calories 136, Fat 11.2g, Protein 1.1g, Carbs 0.2g, Fiber 0.2g

1228) Minty Coconut Cream

Ingredients

- *1 banana, peeled*
- *2 cups coconut flesh, shredded*
- *3 tablespoons mint, chopped*
- *1 and ½ cups coconut water*
- *2 tablespoons stevia*
- *½ avocado pitted and peeled*

Directions: Servings: 2 Preparation time: 0 minutes

✓ *In a blender, combine the coconut with the banana and the rest of the ingredients, pulse well, divide into cups and serve cold.*

Nutrition Calories 193, Fat 5.4g, Fiber 3.4g, Carbs 7.6g, Protein 3.4g

1229) Cherry Cream

Ingredients

- *2 cups cherries, pitted and chopped*
- *1 cup almond milk*
- *½ cup whipping cream*
- *3 eggs, whisked*
- *1/3 cup stevia*
- *1 tsp lemon juice*
- *½ tsp vanilla extract*

Directions: Servings: 4 Preparation time: 0 minutes

✓ *In your food processor, combine the cherries with the milk and the rest of the ingredients, pulse well, divide into cups and keep to the fridge for 2 hours before serving.*

Nutrition Calories 200, Fat 4.5g, Protein 3.4g, Carbs 5.6g, Fiber 3.3g

1230) Tiny Orange Cardamom Cookies

Ingredients

- *½ cup whole-wheat flour*
- *½ cup all-purpose flour*
- *1 large egg*
- *1 tablespoon sesame seeds, toasted, optional (salted roasted pistachios, chopped)*
- *1 teaspoon orange zest*
- *1 teaspoon vanilla extract*
- *½ cup butter softened*
- *½ cup sugar*
- *¼ teaspoon ground cardamom*

Directions: Servings: 8 Preparation time: 12 minutes

✓ *Switch on the oven, preheat it setting its temperature to 375F.*

✓ *In a medium container, blend the orange zest and the sugar thoroughly, and then blend to the cardamom. Add the butter and with a mixer, beat until the mixture is flux and light. Beat the egg and the vanilla into the mixture. With the mixer on low speed, mix the flours into the mixture.*

✓ *Line 3 baking sheets with parchment paper. Using a lead teaspoon measure, drop the batter of the cookie mixture onto the sheets. Top each cookie with a pinch of sesame seeds or nuts, if desired, bake for 10-12 minutes or until the cookies are brown at the edges and crisp. When baked, transfer the cookies to a cooling rack and let them cool completely.*

Nutrition Calories 113, Fat 6.5g, Protein 1.4g, Carbs 12g, Fiber 0.3g, Sodium 46mg, Chol 29mg

1231) Sparkling Limoncello

Ingredients

- *4 ounces club soda*
- *1-ounce vodka*
- *1-ounce Limoncello*
- *1 ½ teaspoon simple syrup*
- *Ice, as needed*
- *Lemon peels for garnish*
- *Splash lemon juice*

Directions: Servings: 1 Preparation time: 5 minutes

✓ *Combine the lemon juice, simple syrup, club soda, vodka, and limoncello in a cocktail shaker. Fill the shaker 2/3 full with ice. Stir for about 10 to 15 minutes to chill. Strato the ice into a cocktail glass, garnish with the lemon peel and serve.*

Nutrition Calories 98, Fat 0g, Protein 0g, Carbs 8.4g

1232) Mast-O Khiar (Persian Yogurt)

Ingredients

- *4 cup yogurt, plain Greek*
- *2 teaspoon mint, dried*
- *2 teaspoon dill, dried*
- *¼ teaspoon black pepper, ground*
- *½ teaspoon salt*
- *1 ½ cup Persian cucumbers, diced*

Directions: Servings: 8 Preparation time: 10 minutes

✓ *Combine all the ingredients in a medium-sized container.*

Nutrition Calories 62, Fat 4g, Protein 0.8g, Carbs 7.2g, Sugar 5.5g

1233) Mediterranean Martini

Ingredients

- 4 pieces fresh strawberries
- 30 ml vodka
- 2 pieces fresh gooseberries
- Chilled sparkling wine, to top
- Few pieces of mint leaves
- Splash of lime juice
- Splash of sugar syrup

Directions: Servings: 2 Preparation time: 10 minutes

✓ Put the gooseberries, strawberries, and mint leaves into a mixing glass; muddle the ingredients to release the juices.

✓ Put ice into a mixing glass until full. Add to the lime, sugar, and vodka. Shake and then stir into chilled martini glasses. Top with the sparkling wine and then garnish, serve.

Nutrition Calories 51, Fat 0.1g, Protein 0.3g, Carbs 4.6g, Sugar 1.2g, Fiber 1g

1234) Greek Mountain Tea

Ingredients

- Greek Mountain Tea
- 1 cup water
- Honey or sugar, optional

Directions: Servings: 1 Preparation time: 5 minutes

✓ Get about 1 to 2 Greek Mountain Tea leaves and break them into thirds.

✓ Fill a pot with water. Turn the flame or heat on to medium-high. Put the tea leaves into the pot from the heat and let the tea steep for 7 minutes.

✓ After steeping, pour the tea into a cup over a strainer to catch the tea leaves.

✓ If desired, sweeten with honey and sugar. Enjoy!

Nutrition Calories 3, Fat 0g, Protein 0g, Carbs 0.9g, Sugar 0.7g

1235) Santorini Sunrise

Ingredients

- 2 1/4 cups vodka, unflavored, plus more
- 1 pink grapefruit, sliced
- 1 ounce Campari
- 2 ounce Pink Grapefruit-infused vodka
- 2 slices pink grapefruit, quartered (8 total pieces)
- 2 teaspoons honey (or Greek honey, if available)
- 3 ounces freshly squeezed pink grapefruit juice
- 4 mint leaves, plus more for garnish

DIRECTIONS: Servings: 1 Preparation time: 5 minutes

✓ For the grapefruit-infused vodka:

✓ Put the grapefruit in a sterilized 1-quart glass jar, stuffing them tight. Pour the vodka over the grapefruit.

✓ Add more vodka, if needed, to submerge the grapefruit completely. Seal the jar with tight lit; let sit at room temperature for 3 days. After 3 days, strato the infused vodka through a coffee filter into another sterilized glass jar; store with other spirits for up to 2 months.

✓ For the cocktail:

✓ In a highball glass, muddle 7 pieces of the quartered grapefruit slices with the honey and mint leaves. Add ice until the glass is filled. Add the vodka, Campari, and grapefruit juice. Stir. Garnish with the resting 1 grapefruit slice and mint leaves: serve.

Nutrition Calories 284, Fat 0.6g, Fiber 6.2g, Carbs 38.3g, Sugar 7.3g, Iron 31%, Calcium 12%, Protein 3.3g

1236) Pink Lady Mediterranean Drink

Ingredients

- 1 ½ ounce London Dry gin
- 1 large egg white
- ½ ounce Cointreau
- 1/2 ounce freshly squeezed lemon juice
- ¼ ounce Campari
- ¼ ounce limoncello
- 3-4 lemon zest, thin strips for garnish
- Ice

Directions: Servings: 1 Preparation time: 5 minutes

✓ Except for the ice and garnish, combine all the ingredients in a cocktail shaker; shake well. Add the ice; shake again. Strato the drink into a chilled coupe. Garnish with the strips of lemon zest.

Nutrition Calories 163, Fat 0.2g, Fiber 0g, Carbs 0.5, Sugar 0.5g, Iron 0%, Calcium 1%, Protein 3.7g

1237) Spinach Pancake Cake

Ingredients

- 1 cup heavy cream
- ¼ cup Erythritol
- 1 cup fresh spinach, chopped
- ½ cup skim milk
- 1 teaspoon vanilla extract
- 1 cup all-purpose flour
- ½ cup of rice flour
- 1 teaspoon baking powder
- 1 teaspoon olive oil
- 1 egg, beaten
- ¼ teaspoon ground clove
- 1 teaspoon butter

DIRECTIONS: Servings: 6 Preparation time: 15

minutes

- ✓ Blend the spinach until you set the puree mixture.
- ✓ After this, add skim milk, vanilla extract, all-purpose flour, and rice flour.
- ✓ Add baking powder, egg, and ground clove.
- ✓ Blend the ingredients until you set a smooth and thick batter.
- ✓ Then add olive oil and pulse the batter for 30 seconds more.
- ✓ Heat up the butter into the skillet.
- ✓ Ladle 1 ladle of the crepe batter into the skillet and flatten it to the shape of a crepe.
- ✓ Cook it for 1.5 minutes from one side and then flip it to another side and cook for 20 seconds more.
- ✓ Place the cooked crepe on the plate.
- ✓ Repeat the same steps will all crepe batter.
- ✓ Make the cake filling: whip the heavy cream with Erythritol. Spread every crepe with sweet whipped cream.
- ✓ Store the cake in the fridge for up to 2 days.

Nutrition Calories 228, Fat 10 g, Protein 5.1g, Carbs 38.8g

1238) Fruit Salad With Orange Blossom Water

Ingredients

- 4 oranges, peeled and cut into bite-sized pieces
- 8 dried figs, quartered
- 2 Medjool dates, pitted and chopped
- ½ cup pomegranate seeds
- 2 tablespoons honey
- 2 tablespoons orange blossom water
- 2 bananas, peeled and sliced
- ¼ cup pistachio nuts, shelled and chopped

Directions: Servings: 8 Preparation time: 3 minutes

- ✓ In a large mixing container, toss in all the ingredients except for the pistachio nuts.
- ✓ Let the rest of the fruit in the fridge for at least 8 hours before serving.
- ✓ Garnish with chopped pistachios before serving.

Nutrition Calories 185, Fat 2g, Protein 3g, Carbs 43g

1239) Blueberry Frozen Yogurt

Ingredients

- 1-pint blueberries, fresh
- 2/3 cup honey
- 1 small lemon, juiced and zested
- 2 cups yogurt, chilled

Directions: Servings: 6 Preparation time: 30 minutes

- ✓ In a saucepan, combine the blueberries, honey, lemon juice, and zest.
- ✓ Heat over medium heat and allow to simmer for 15 minutes while stirring constantly.
- ✓ Once the liquid has reduced, transfer the fruits to a container and allow them to cool to the fridge for another 15 minutes.
- ✓ Once chilled, mix together with the chilled yogurt.

Nutrition Calories 233, Fat 2.9g, Protein 3.5g, Carbs 52.2g

1240) Apple Pear Compote

Ingredients

- 4 apples, cored and cubed
- 2 pears, cored and cubed
- 1 cinnamon stick
- 1-star anise
- 2 whole cloves
- 1 orange peel
- 4 cups water
- 2 tablespoons lemon juice

Directions: Servings: 6 Preparation time: 45 minutes

- ✓ Combine all the ingredients in a saucepan.
- ✓ Place over low heat and cook for 25 minutes.
- ✓ Serve the compote chilled.

Nutrition Calories 110, Fat 0.5g, Protein 0.8g, Carbs 28.6g

1241) Cream Cheese Cake

Ingredients

- 2 teaspoons cream cheese
- 1 cup Erythritol
- 2 egg whites
- 1/2 teaspoon lemon juice
- ½ teaspoon vanilla extract
- 2 strawberries, sliced

Directions: Servings: 2 Preparation time: 60 minutes

- ✓ Whisk the egg whites until you get soft peaks.
- ✓ Keep whisking and gradually add Erythritol and lemon juice.
- ✓ Whisk the egg whites till you get a strong peak mass.
- ✓ After this, mix up together cream cheese and vanilla extract.
- ✓ Line the baking tray with baking paper.
- ✓ With the help of the spoon, make egg white nests to the tray. Bake the white egg nests for 60 minutes at 205F.
- ✓ When the 'nests' are cooked, fill them with Vanilla cream cheese and top with sliced strawberries.

Nutrition Cal 36, Fat 1.3g, Protein 3.9g, Carbs 121.4g,

1242) Nutmeg Lemon Pudding

Ingredients

- 2 tablespoons lemon marmalade
- 4 eggs, whisked
- 2 tablespoons stevia
- 3 cups almond milk
- 4 allspice berries, crushed
- ¼ teaspoon nutmeg, grated

Directions: Servings: 6 Preparation time: 20 minutes

✓ In a container, mix the lemon marmalade with the eggs and the other ingredients and whisk well.

✓ Divide the mix into ramekins, introduce to the oven and bake at 350 degrees F for 20 minutes.

✓ Serve cold.

Nutrition Calories 220, Fat 6.6g, Protein 3.4g, Carbs 12.4g, Fiber 3.4g

1243) Yogurt Panna Cotta With Fresh Berries

Ingredients

- 2 cups Greek yogurt
- 1 cup milk
- 1 cup heavy cream
- 2 teaspoons gelatin powder
- 4 tablespoons cold water
- 4 tablespoons honey
- 1 teaspoon vanilla extract
- 1 teaspoon lemon zest
- 1 pinch salt
- 2 cups mixed berries for serving

Directions: Servings: 6 Preparation time: 1 hour

✓ Combine the milk and cream in a saucepan and heat them up.

✓ Bloom the gelatin in cold water for 10 minutes.

✓ Remove the milk off the heat and stir to the gelatin until dissolved.

✓ Add the vanilla, lemon zest, and salt and allow to cool down.

✓ Stir to the yogurt, then pour the mixture into serving glasses.

✓ When set, top with fresh berries and serve.

Nutrition Calories 219, Fat 9.7g, Protein 10.8g, Carbs 22.6g

1244) Flourless Chocolate Cake

Ingredients

- 8 oz. dark chocolate, chopped
- 4 oz. butter, cubed
- 6 eggs, separated
- 1 teaspoon vanilla extract
- 1 pinch salt
- 4 tablespoons white sugar
- Berries for serving

Directions: Servings: 8 Preparation time: 1 hour

✓ Combine the chocolate and butter in a heatproof container and melt them together until smooth.

✓ When smooth, remove off heat and place aside.

✓ Separate the eggs.

✓ Mix the egg yolks with the chocolate mixture.

✓ Whip the egg whites with a pinch of salt until puffed up. Add the sugar and mix for a few more minutes until glossy and stiff.

✓ Fold the meringue into the chocolate mixture, then pour the batter into a 9-inch round cake pan lined with baking paper.

✓ Bake to the preheated oven at 350F for 25 minutes.

✓ See e the cake chilled.

Nutrition Calories 324, Fat 23.2g, Protein 6.4g, Carbs 23.2g

1245) Creamy Mint Strawberry Mix

Ingredients

- Cooking spray
- ¼ cup stevia
- 1 and ½ cup almond flour
- 1 teaspoon baking powder
- 1 cup almond milk
- 1 egg, whisked
- 2 cups strawberries, sliced
- 1 tablespoon mint, chopped
- 1 teaspoon lime zest, grated
- ½ cup whipping cream

Directions:Servings: 6 Preparation Time:30 Minutes

✓ In a container, combine the almond with the strawberries, mint, and the other ingredients except for the cooking spray and whisk well.

✓ Grease 6 ramekins with the cooking spray, pour the strawberry mix inside, introduce to the oven and bake at 350F for 30 minutes.

✓ Cooldown and serve.

Nutrition Calories 200, Fat 6.3g, Protein 8g, Carbs 6.5g

1246) Creamy Pie

Ingredients

- ¼ cup lemon juice
- 1 cup cream
- 4 egg yolks
- 4 tablespoons Erythritol
- 1 tablespoon cornstarch

- *1 teaspoon vanilla extract*
- *3 tablespoons butter*
- *6 oz wheat flour, whole grain*

Directions: Servings: 6 Preparation time: 30 minutes

- ✓ *Mix up together wheat flour and butter and knead the sort dough.*
- ✓ *Put the dough into the round cake mold and flatten it to the shape of pie crust.*
- ✓ *Bake it for 15 minutes at 365F.*
- ✓ *Meanwhile, make the lemon filling: Mix up together cream, egg yolks, and lemon juice. When the liquid is smooth, start to heat it up over medium heat. Stir it constantly.*
- ✓ *When the liquid is hot, add vanilla extract, cornstarch, and Erythritol. Whisk well until smooth.*
- ✓ *Bring the lemon filling to a boil and remove it from the heat. Cool it to room temperature.*
- ✓ *Cook the pie crust to room temperature.*
- ✓ *Pour the lemon filling over the pie crust, flatten it well and leave to cool to the fridge for 25 minutes.*

Nutrition Calories 225, Fat 11.4g, Protein 5.2g, Carbs 34.8g, Fiber 0.8g

1247) Watermelon Ice Cream

Ingredients

- *8 oz watermelon*
- *1 tablespoon gelatin powder*

Directions: Servings: 2 Preparation time: 5 minutes

- ✓ *Make the juice from the watermelon with the help of the fruit juicer.*
- ✓ *Combine together 5 tablespoons of watermelon juice and 1 tablespoon of gelatin powder. Stir it and leave for 5 minutes.*
- ✓ *Then preheat the watermelon juice until warm, add gelatin mixture, and heat it up over medium heat until gelatin is dissolved.*
- ✓ *Then remove the liquid from the heat and pour it into the silicone molds.*
- ✓ *Freeze the jelly for 30 minutes in the freezer or for 4 hours in the fridge.*

Nutrition Calories 46, Fat 0.2g, Protein 3.7g, Carbs 8.5g

1248) Eggless Farina Cake (Namoura)

Ingredients

- *2 cups farina*
- *½ cup semolina*
- *½ cup all-purpose flour*
- *1 TB. baking powder*
- *1 tsp. active dry yeast*
- *½ cup sugar*
- *½ cup plain Greek yogurt*
- *1 cup whole milk*
- *¾ cup butter, melted*
- *1/4 cup water*
- *2 GB. tahini paste*
- *15 almonds*
- *2 cups Simple Syrup*

Directions: Servings: 1 Preparation time: 4 minutes

- ✓ *Combine farina, semolina, all-purpose flour, baking powder, yeast, sugar, Greek yogurt, whole milk, butter, and water in a large container. Set aside for 15 minutes.*
- ✓ *Switch on the oven, preheat it setting its temperature to 375F.*
- ✓ *Spread tahini paste evenly on the bottom of a 9x13-inch baking pan, and pour into the cake batter. Orange almonds on top of the batter, about where each slice will be. Bake for 45 minutes or until golden brown.*
- ✓ *Remove cake from the oven, and using a toothpick, poke holes throughout cake for Simple Syrup to seep into. Pour syrup over the cake, and let the cake sit for 1 hour to absorb the syrup.*
- ✓ *Cool cake completed before cutting and serving.*

Nutrition Calories 122, Protein 3g, Carbs 27g, Fiber 1g

1249) Minty Orange Greek Yogurt

Ingredients

- *6 tablespoons Greek yogurt, fat-free*
- *4 fresh mint leaves, thinly sliced*
- *1 large orange, peeled, quartered, and then sliced crosswise*
- *1 ½ teaspoon honey*

Directions: Servings: 1 Preparation Time: 5 Minutes

- ✓ *Stir together the honey and the yogurt.*
- ✓ *Place the orange slices into a dessert glass. Spoon the honeyed yogurt over the orange slices to the glass and scatter the mint on top of the yogurt.*

Nutrition Calories 171, Protein 11g, Carbs 34g, Fiber 5g

1250) Yogurt Mousse With Sour Cherry Sauce

Ingredients

- *1 ½ cups Greek yogurt*
- *1 teaspoon vanilla extract*
- *4 tablespoons honey*
- *1 ½ cups heavy cream, whipped*
- *2 cups sour cherries*
- *¼ cup white sugar*
- *1 cinnamon stick*

Directions: Servings: 6 Preparation Time: 1 Hour

- ✓ Combine the yogurt with vanilla and honey in a container.
- ✓ Fold to the whipped cream, then spoon the mousse into serving glasses and refrigerate.
- ✓ For the sauce, combine the cherries, sugar, and cinnamon in a saucepan. Allow to rest for 10 minutes, then cook on low heat for 10 minutes.
- ✓ Cool the sauce down, then spoon it over the mousse.
- ✓ Serve right away.

Nutrition Cal 245, Fat 12.1g, Protein 5.8g, Carbs 29.7g

1251) Vanilla Apple Pie

Ingredients

- 3 apples, sliced
- ½ teaspoon ground cinnamon
- 1 teaspoon vanilla extract
- 1 tablespoon Erythritol
- 7 oz yeast roll dough
- 1 egg, beaten

Directions: Servings: 8 Preparation Time: 50 Minutes

- ✓ Roll up the dough and cut it into 2 parts.
- ✓ Line the springform pan with baking paper.
- ✓ Place the first dough part in the springform pan.
- ✓ Then arrange the apples over the dough and sprinkle it with Erythritol, vanilla extract, and ground cinnamon.
- ✓ Then cover the apples with the resting dough and secure the edges of the pie with the help of the fork.
- ✓ Make the small cuts on the surface of the pie.
- ✓ Brush the pie with a beaten egg and bake it for 50 minutes at 375F.
- ✓ Cool the cooked pie well, and then remove it from the springform pan.
- ✓ Cut it on the servings.

Nutrition Calories 139, Fat 3.6g, Protein 2.8g, Carbs 26.1g

1252) Mediterranean Sunset

Ingredients

- 1-ounce ouzo, or more to taste
- 1 tablespoon grenadine
- Orange juice or lemonade or grapefruit juice

Directions: Servings: 1

Preparation Time: 2 Minutes

- ✓ Fill a highball glass with ice cubes. Add all of the ingredients into a shaker: shake to mix. Pour the concoction into the highball class. Enjoy!

Nutrition Calories 47, Fat 0g, Protein 0g, Carbs 12.4g

1253) Mediterranean Bloody Mary

Ingredients

- 4 teaspoons hot sauce
- 3 ounces vodka
- 1 teaspoon Worcestershire sauce
- 2 tablespoons red wine vinegar
- 12 ounces tomato juice
- 1 teaspoon fresh oregano, chopped
- Cubed feta for garnish
- Ice
- Pepperoncini for garnish
- Pitted Kalamata olives for garnish

Directions: Servings: 2 Preparation Time: 5 Minutes

- ✓ Put the tomato juice, vodka, red wine vinegar, hot sauce, Worcestershire sauce, and oregano into a cocktail shaker; shake. Fill 2-pint glasses with ice. Pour the bloody Mary mixture into the glasses. Garnish with olives, feta, and pepperoncini.

Nutrition Calories 139, Fat 0.2g, Fiber 1g, Carbs 9g, Sugar 7.3g, Iron 6%, Calcium 3%

1254) Mixed Berry Sorbet

Ingredients

- 2 cups water
- ½ cup white sugar
- 2 cups mixed berries
- 1 tablespoon lemon juice
- 2 tablespoons honey
- 1 teaspoon lemon zest
- 1 mint spring

Directions: Servings: 8 Preparation Time: 2 ½ Hours

- ✓ Combine the water, sugar, berries, lemon juice, honey, and lemon zest in a saucepan.
- ✓ Bring to a boil and cook on low heat for 5 minutes.
- ✓ Add the mint sprig and remove off heat. Allow infusing for 10 minutes, then remove the mint.
- ✓ Pour the syrup into a blender and puree until smooth and creamy.
- ✓ Pour the smooth syrup into an airtight container and freeze for at least 2 hours.
- ✓ Serve the sorbet chilled.

Nutrition Calories 84, Fat 0.1g, Protein 0.4g, Carbs 21.3g

1255) Lemon And Semolina Cookies

Ingredients

- ½ teaspoon lemon zest, grated
- 4 tablespoons Erythritol
- 4 tablespoons semolina
- 2 tablespoons olive oil
- 8 tablespoons wheat flour, whole grain
- 1 teaspoon vanilla extract

- ½ teaspoon coconut oil
- ½ teaspoon ground clove
- 3 teaspoon baking powder
- ¼ cup of water

Directions: Servings: 6 Preparation Time: 20 Minutes

✓ Make the dough: to the mixing container, combine together lemon zest, semolina, olive oil, wheat flour, vanilla extract, ground clove, coconut oil, and baking powder.

✓ Knead the soft dough.

✓ Make the small cookies in the shape of walnuts and press them gently with the help of the fork.

✓ Line the baking tray with the baking paper.

✓ Place the cookies on the tray and bake them for 20 minutes at 375F.

✓ Meanwhile, bring the water to a boil.

✓ Add Erythritol and simmer the liquid for 2 minutes over medium heat. Cool it.

✓ Pour the cooled sweet water over the hot baked cookies and leave them for 10 minutes.

✓ When the cookies soak all liquid, transfer them to the serving plates.

Nutrition Calories 165, Fat 11.7g, Protein 2g, Carbs 23.7g

1256) Strawberry Sorbet

Ingredients

- 1 cup strawberries, chopped
- 1 tablespoon of liquid honey
- 2 tablespoons water
- 1 tablespoon lemon juice

Directions: Servings: 2 Preparation Time: 20 Minutes

✓ Preheat the water and liquid honey until you they're homogenous liquid.

✓ Blend the strawberries until smooth and combine them with honey liquid and lemon juice.

✓ Transfer the strawberry mixture to the ice cream maker and churn it for 20 minutes or until the sorbet is thick.

✓ Scoop the cooked sorbet into the ice cream cups.

NutritionCalories 57, Fat 0.3g, Protein 0.6g, Carbs 14.3g

1257) Shredded Phyllo And Sweet Cheese Pie

Ingredients

- 1 lb. pkg. shredded phyllo (kataifi dough)
- 1 cup butter, melted
- ½ cup whole milk
- 2 TB. semolina flour
- 1 lb. ricotta cheese, shredded
- 2 TB. sugar
- 1 cup Simple Syrup

Directions: Servings: 1/8 Pie Preparation Time: 30 Minutes

✓ Make 1 cup of Simple Syrup.

✓ In a food processor fitted with a chopping blade, pulse shredded phyllo and butter 10 times. Transfer mixture to a container.

✓ In a small saucepan over low heat, warm whole milk.

✓ Stir in semolina flour, and cook for 1 minute.

✓ Rinse the food processor and add ricotta cheese, mozzarella cheese, sugar, and semolina mixture. Blend for 1 minute.

✓ Switch on the oven, preheat it setting its temperature to 375°F.

✓ In a 9-inch-round baking dish, add 1/2 of shredded phyllo mixture, and press down to compress. Add cheese mixture, and spread out evenly. Add rest of shredded phyllo mixture, spread evenly, and gently press down. Bake for 40 minutes or until golden brown.

✓ Let pie rest for 10 minutes before serving with Simple Sump drizzled over the top.

Nutrition Calories 632, Fat 37g, Carbs 56g, Fiber 1g, Protein 19g

1258) Apple And Walnut Salad

Ingredients

- Juice from ½ orange
- Zest from ½ orange, grated
- 2 tablespoons honey
- 1 tablespoon olive oil
- 4 medium Gala apples, cubed
- 8 dried apricots, chopped
- ¼ cup walnuts, toasted and chopped

Directions: Servings: 6 Preparation Time: 5 Minutes

✓ In a small container, whisk together the orange juice, zest, honey, and olive oil. Set aside.

✓ In a larger container, toss the apples, apricots, and walnuts.

✓ Drizzle with the vinaigrette and toss to coat all ingredients.

✓ Serve chilled.

Nutrition Calories 178, Fat 6g, Protein 1g, Carbs 30g

1259) Almond Citrus Muffins

Ingredients

- 2 eggs, beaten
- 1 ½ cup whole wheat flour
- ½ cup almond meal
- 1 teaspoon vanilla extract
- 1 tablespoon butter, softened

- *1 teaspoon orange zest, grated*
- *1 tablespoon orange juice*
- *¾ cup Erythritol*
- *1 oz orange pulp*
- *1 teaspoon baking powder*
- *½ teaspoon lime zest, grated*
- *Cooking spray*

Directions: Servings: 6 Preparation Time: 30 Minutes

- ✓ *Blake the muffin batter: combine together almond meal, eggs, whole wheat flour, vanilla extract, butter, orange zest, orange juice, and orange pulp.*
- ✓ *Add lime zest and baking powder.*
- ✓ *Then add Erythritol.*
- ✓ *With the help of the hand mixer, mix up the ingredients.*
- ✓ *When the mixture is soft and smooth, it is done.*
- ✓ *Spray the muffin molds with cooking spray from inside and Switch on the oven, preheat it setting its temperature to 365F.*
- ✓ *Fill ½ part of every muffin mold with muffin batter and transfer them to the oven.*
- ✓ *Cook the muffins for 30 minutes.*
- ✓ *Then check if the muffins are cooked by piercing them with a toothpick (if it is dry, the muffins are cooked; if it is not dry, bake the muffins for 5-7 minutes more.)*

Nutrition Cal204, Fat 7.7g, Protein 6.8g, Carbs 57.1g

1260) Poached Cherries

Ingredients

- *1 pound fresh and sweet cherries, rinsed, pitted*
- *3 strips (1x3 inches each) orange zest*
- *3 strips (1x3 inches each) lemon zest*
- *2/3 cup sugar*
- *15 peppercorns*
- *1/4 vanilla bean, split but not scraped*
- *1 3/4 cups water*

Directions: Servings: 5 Preparation time: 10 minutes

- ✓ *In a saucepan, mix the water, citrus zest, sugar, peppercorns, and vanilla bean: bring to a boil, stirring until the sugar is dissolved.*
- ✓ *Add the cherries: simmer for about 10 minutes until the cherries are soft but not falling apart. Skim any foam from the surface and let the poached cherries cool. Refrigerate with the poaching liquid. Before serving, strato the cherries.*

Nutrition Calories 170, Fat 1g, Fiber 2g, Carbs 42g

1261) Watermelon Salad

Ingredients

- *14 oz watermelon*
- *1 oz dark chocolate*
- *3 tablespoons coconut cream*
- *1 teaspoon Erythritol*
- *2 Kiwi, chopped*
- *1 oz Feta cheese, crumbled*

Directions: Servings: 6 Preparation Time: 0 Minutes

- ✓ *Peel the watermelon and remove the seeds from it.*
- ✓ *Chop the fruit and place it in the salad container.*
- ✓ *Add chopped kiwi and crumbled feta. Stir the salad well.*
- ✓ *Then mix up together coconut cream and Erythritol.*
- ✓ *Pour the cream mixture over the salad.*
- ✓ *Then shave the chocolate over the salad with the help of the potato peeler.*
- ✓ *The salad should be served immediately.*

Nutrition Calories 90, Fat 4.4g, Protein 1.9g, Carbs 12.9g

1262) Easy Fruit Compote

Ingredients

- *1-pound fresh fruits of your choice*
- *2 tablespoons maple syrup*
- *A dash of salt*

Directions: Servings: 2 Preparation Time: 15 Minutes

- ✓ *Slice the fruits thinly and place them in a saucepan.*
- ✓ *Add the honey and salt.*
- ✓ *Heat the saucepan over medium-low heat and allow the fruits to simmer for 15 minutes or until the liquid has reduced.*
- ✓ *Make sure that you constantly stir to prevent the fruits from sticking at the bottom of your pan and eventually burning.*
- ✓ *Transfer in a lidded jar.*
- ✓ *Allow cooling.*
- ✓ *Serve with slices of whole wheat bread or vegan ice cream.*

NutritionCal 218, Fat 0.2g, Protein 0.9g, Carbs 56.8g

1263) Papaya Cream

Ingredients

- *1 cup papaya, peeled and chopped*
- *1 cup heavy cream*
- *1 tablespoon stevia*
- *½ teaspoon vanilla extract*

Directions:Servings: 2 Preparation Time: 0 Minutes

- ✓ *In a blender, combine the cream with the papaya and the other ingredients, pulse well, divide into cups and serve cold.*

Nutrition Calories 182, Fat 3.1g, Protein 2g, Carbs 3.5g,

1264) Minty Tart

Ingredients

- ✓ 1 cup tart cherries, pitted
- ✓ 1 cup wheat flour, whole grain
- ✓ 1/3 cup butter, softened
- ✓ ½ teaspoon baking powder
- ✓ 1 tablespoon Erythritol
- ✓ ¼ teaspoon dried mint
- ✓ ¾ teaspoon salt

Directions:Servings: 6 **Preparation Time:30 Minutes**

- ✓ Mix up together wheat flour and cutter.
- ✓ Add baking powder and salt. Knead the soft dough.
- ✓ Then place the dough in the freezer for 10 minutes.
- ✓ When the dough is solid, remove it from the freezer and grate with the help of the grater. Place ¼ part of the grated dough in the freezer.
- ✓ Sprinkle the springform pan with the resting dough and place tart cherries on it.
- ✓ Sprinkle the berries with Erythritol and dried mint and cover with ¼ part of dough from the freezer.
- ✓ Bake the cake for 30 minutes at 365F. The cooked tart will have a golden brown surface.

Nutrition Calories 177, Fat 10.4g, Protein 2.4g, Carbs 21g

1265) Orange-Sesame Almond Tuiles

Ingredients

- ¾ cup unblanched or blanched sliced almonds
- 3 tablespoons orange juice, freshly squeezed
- 3 tablespoons (about 1 1/2 ounce) unsalted or salted butter
- 2 tablespoons white sesame seeds
- 10 tablespoons granulated sugar
- 1/8 cup whole-wheat flour
- 1/8 cup all-purpose flour
- 1 tablespoon toasted sesame oil
- 1 1/2 teaspoons black sesame seeds
- Grated zest of 1 orange, preferably organic

Directions:Servings: 20 **Preparation Time:45 Minutes**

- ✓ In a small-sized saucepan, warm the butter, sesame oil, orange zest, orange juice, and sugar over low heat until the mixture is smooth. Remove from the heat. Stir the flour, almonds, and sesame seeds; let the batter rest for 1 hour at normal room temperature.
- ✓ Switch on the oven, preheat it setting its temperature to 375F. Line 2 pieces baking sheet with parchment paper.
- ✓ Set a rolling pin on a folded dishtowel. Ready a wire rack.
- ✓ Measuring by level tablespoons, drop batter into the prepared baking sheets, place only 4 on each sheet, and evenly spacing them apart.
- ✓ With dampened fingers, slightly flatten the batter. Place one baking sheet in the oven, bake the tiles for about 8 to 9 minutes, rotating the baking sheet halfway through baking until the cookies are evenly browned. Let the cookies cool slightly for 1 minute.
- ✓ Lift each cookie off the baking sheet with a metal spatula and then drape them over the rolling pin. Let them cool to the rolling pin and then transfer to the wire rack. Repeat the process with the resting batter. Serve the tuiles a few hours after baking.

Nutrition Calories 78, Fat 4.7g, Protein 1.1g, Carbs 8.6g, Fiber 0.7g

1266) Strawberry Ice Cream

Ingredients

- 1 pound strawberries, hulled
- 1 cup Greek yogurt
- 1 cup heavy cream
- 3 tablespoons honey
- 1 teaspoon lime zest

Directions:Servings: 6 **Preparation time:1 ¼ minutes**

- ✓ Combine all the ingredients in a blender and pulse until well mixed and smooth.
- ✓ Pour the mixture into your ice cream machine and churn for 1 hour or according to your machine's instructions.
- ✓ Serve the ice cream right away.

NutritionCalories 150, Fat 8.3g, Protein 4.3g, Carbs16.4

1267) Creamy Strawberries

Ingredients

- 6 tablespoons almond butter
- 1 tablespoon Erythritol
- 1 cup milk
- 1 teaspoon vanilla extract
- 1 cup strawberries, sliced

Directions:Servings: 4 **Preparation Time:5 Minutes**

- ✓ Pour milk into the saucepan.
- ✓ Add Erythritol, vanilla extract, and almond butter.
- ✓ With the help of the hand mixer, mix up the liquid until smooth and bring it to a boil.
- ✓ Then remove the mixture from the heat and let it cool.
- ✓ The cooled mixture will be thick.
- ✓ Put the strawberries to the serving glasses and top with the thick almond butter dip.

NutritionCal 192, Fat 14.9g, Protein 7.3g, Carbs 10.4g

1268) Greek Yogurt Pie

Ingredients

- *1 package phyllo dough sheets*
- *4 cups plain yogurt*
- *4 eggs*
- *½ cup white sugar*
- *1 teaspoon vanilla extract*
- *1 teaspoon lemon zest*
- *1 teaspoon orange zest*

***Directions:Servings:** 8 **Preparation Time:** 1 Hour*

- ✓ *Mix the yogurt, eggs, sugar, vanilla, and citrus zest in a container.*
- ✓ *Layer 2 phyllo sheets in a deep dish baking pan, then pour a few tablespoons of yogurt mixture over the dough.*
- ✓ *Continue layering the phyllo dough and yogurt into the pan.*
- ✓ *Bake to the preheated oven at 350F for 40 minutes.*
- ✓ *Allow the pie to cool down before serving.*

Nutrition Calories 175, Fat 3.8g, Protein 9.9g, Carbs 22.7g

1269) Fice Berry Mint Orange Infusion

Ingredients

- *½ cup water*
- *3 orange pekoe tea bags*
- *3 sprigs of mint*
- *1 cup fresh strawberries*
- *1 cup fresh golden raspberries*
- *1 cup fresh raspberries*
- *1 cup blackberries*
- *1 cup fresh blueberries*
- *1 cup pitted fresh cherries*
- *1 bottle Sauvignon Blanc*
- *½ cup pomegranate juice, natural*
- *1 teaspoon vanilla*

***Directions:Servings:** 12 **Preparation Time:** 10 Minutes*

- ✓ *In a saucepan, bring water to a boil over medium heat. Add the tea bags, mint, and stir. Let it stand for 10 minutes.*
- ✓ *In a large container, combine the rest of the ingredients.*
- ✓ *Put to the bridge to chill for at least 3 hours.*

Nutrition Calories 140, Fat 1.5g, Protein 1.2g, Carbs 32.1g

1270) Cocoa Yogurt

Ingredients

- *1 tablespoon cocoa powder*
- *¼ cup strawberries, chopped*
- *¾ cup Greek yogurt*
- *5 drops vanilla stevia*

Directions: Servings: 2 Preparation Time: 0 Minutes

- ✓ *In a container, mix the yogurt with the cocoa, strawberries, and stevia and whisk well.*
- ✓ *Divide the mix into containers and serve.*

Nutrition Calories 200, Fat 8g, Protein 4.3g, Carbs 7.6g

1271) Almond Rice Dessert

Ingredients

- *1 cup white rice*
- *2 cups almond milk*
- *1 cup almonds, chopped*
- *1/2 cup stevia*
- *1 tablespoon cinnamon powder*
- *½ cup pomegranate seeds*

Directions:Servings:** 4 **Preparation Time:20 Minutes

- ✓ *In a pot, mix the rice with the milk and stevia, bring to a simmer and cook for 20 minutes, stirring often.*
- ✓ *Add the rest of the ingredients, stir, divide into containers and serve.*

Nutrition Calories 234, Fat 9.5g, Protein 6.5g, Carbs 12.4g

1272) Frozen Strawberry Greek Yogurt

Ingredients

- *3 cups Greek yogurt, plain, low-fat (2%)*
- *2 teaspoons vanilla*
- *1/8 teaspoon salt*
- *¼ cup freshly squeezed lemon juice*
- *1 cup sugar*
- *1 cup strawberries, sliced*

Directions: Servings: 16 Preparation Time: 15 Minutes

- ✓ *In a medium-sized container, combine the rest of the ingredients, whisking until the mixture is smooth, except for the strawberries.*
- ✓ *Transfer the yogurt into a 1 ½ or 2-quart ice cream maker and freeze according to the manufacturer's direction, adding the strawberry slices for the last minute. Transfer into an airtight container and freeze for about 2-4 hours. Before serving, let stand for 15 minutes at room temperature.*

Nutrition Calories 86, Fat 1g, Protein 4g, Carbs 16g

1273) Almond Peaches Mix

Ingredients

- *1/3 cup almonds, toasted*
- *1/3 cup pistachios, toasted*
- *1 teaspoon mint, chopped*
- *1/2 cup coconut water*

- *1 teaspoon lemon zest, grated*
- *4 peaches, Halved*
- *2 tablespoons stevia*

Directions: Servings: *4* **Preparation Time:** *10 Minutes*

- ✓ *In a pan, combine the peaches with the stevia and the rest of the ingredients, simmer over medium heat for 10 minutes, divide into containers and serve cold.*

Nutrition Calories 135, Fat 4.1g, Protein 2.3g, Carbs 4.1g

1274) Walnuts Cake

Ingredients

- *1/2 pound walnuts, minced*
- *Zest of 1 lemon, grated*
- *1 and ¼ cups stevia*
- *Eggs whisked*
- *1 teaspoon almond extract*
- *1 and 1/2 cup almond flour*
- *1 teaspoon baking soda*

Directions:Servings: *4* **Preparation Time:** *40 Minutes*

- ✓ *In a container, combine the walnuts with the orange zest and the other ingredients, whisk well and pour into a cake pan lined with parchment paper.*
- ✓ *Introduce to the oven at 350 degrees F, bake for 40 minutes, cool down, slice, and serve.*

Nutrition Cal 205, Fat 14.1g, Protein 3.4g, Carbs 9.1g

1275) Spiced Cookies

Ingredients

- *1egg, beaten*
- *1 teaspoon vanilla extract*
- *1/2 teaspoon ground cinnamon*
- *1 teaspoon ground turmeric*
- *1 tablespoon butter, softened*
- *1 cup wheat flour*
- *1 teaspoon baking powder*
- *4 tablespoons pumpkin puree*
- *1 tablespoon Erythritol*

Directions:Servings: *6* **Preparation Time:** *30 Minutes*

- ✓ *Put all ingredients into the mixing container and knead the sort and non-sticky dough.*
- ✓ *After this, line the baking tray with baking paper.*
- ✓ *Make 6 balls from the dough and press them gently with the help of the spoon.*
- ✓ *Arrange the dough balls to the tray.*
- ✓ *Bake the cookies for 30 minutes at 355F.*
- ✓ *Chill the cooked cookies well and store them in the glass jar.*

Nutrition Cal 111, Fat 2.9g, Protein 3.2g, Carbs 20.2g

1276) Delectable Mango Smoothie

Ingredients

- *2 cups diced mango*
- *1 carrot, peeled and sliced roughly*
- *1 orange, peeled and segmented*
- *Fresh mint leaves*

Directions: Servings: *2* **Preparation Time:** *5 Minutes*

- ✓ *Place the mango, carrot, and oranges in a blender.*
- ✓ *Pulse until smooth.*
- ✓ *Pour in a glass container and allow to chill before serving.*
- ✓ *Garnish with mint leaves on top.*

Nutrition Calories 134, Fat 0.7g, Protein 2g, Carbs 33.6g

1277) Blackberries And Pomegranate Parfait

Ingredients

- *1 cup Plain yogurt*
- *1 tablespoon coconut flakes*
- *1 tablespoon liquid honey*
- *4 teaspoons peanuts, chopped*
- *1 cup blackberries*
- *1 tablespoon pomegranate seeds*

Directions:Servings: *4* **Preparation Time:** *20 Minutes*

- ✓ *Mix up together plain yogurt and coconut flakes.*
- ✓ *Put the mixture in the freezer.*
- ✓ *Meanwhile, combine together liquid honey and blackberries.*
- ✓ *Place 1/2 part of the blackberry mixture into the serving glasses.*
- ✓ *Then add 1/4 part of the cooled yogurt mixture.*
- ✓ *Sprinkle the yogurt mixture with all peanuts and cover with ½ part of the resting yogurt mixture.*
- ✓ *Then add resting blackberries and top the dessert with yogurt.*
- ✓ *Garnish the parfait with pomegranate seeds and cool to the fridge for 20 minutes.*

Nutrition Calories 115, Fat 3.1g, Protein 5.1g, Carbs 13g

1278) Yellow Cake With Jam Topping

Ingredients

- *5 large eggs*
- *11/4 cups sugar*
- *1 TB. vanilla extract*
- *2 cups all-purpose flour*
- *2 tsp. baking powder*
- *½ tsp salt*
- *1/2 cup whole milk*
- *1/2 cup butter, melted*

- *2 cups apricot or peach jam*
- *1/4 cup sweetened condensed milk*
- *2 GB. Hot water*

DIRECTIONS: Servings:1 PiecePreparation Time:20 Minutes

- ✓ *Switch on the oven, preheat it setting its temperature to 350F. Lightly coat a 9x13-inch cake pan with cooking spray and dust with about 2 tablespoons of all-purpose flour.*
- ✓ *In a large container and using an electric mixer on medium speed, beat eggs for 3 minutes.*
- ✓ *Add sugar and vanilla extract, and beat for 2 more minutes.*
- ✓ *Add all-purpose flour, baking powder, salt, whole milk, and melted butter, and blend for 1 minute.*
- ✓ *Pour batter into the prepared pan, and bake for 20 minutes or until a toothpick inserted into the center of the cake comes out clean.*
- ✓ *Cool cake completely.*
- ✓ *In a small container, whisk together apricot jam, sweetened condensed milk, and hot water.*
- ✓ *Pour jam icing over the cake, letting it run over the edges, cut, and serve.*

Nutrition Calories 313, Fat 8g, Carbs 57g, Fiber 1g, Protein 5g

1279) Raspberry Tart

Ingredients

- *3 tablespoons butter, softened*
- *1 cup wheat flour, whole wheat*
- *1 teaspoon baking powder*
- *1 egg, beaten*
- *4 tablespoons pistachio paste*
- *2 tablespoons raspberry jam*

Directions:Servings: 6 **Preparation Time:** 20 Minutes

- ✓ *Knead the dough: combine together softened butter, flour, baking powder, and egg. You should set the non-sticky and very soft dough.*
- ✓ *Put the dough into the springform pan and flatten it with the help of the fingertips until you get pie crust.*
- ✓ *Bake it for 10 minutes at 365F.*
- ✓ *After this, spread the pie crust with raspberry jam and then with pistachio paste.*
- ✓ *Bake the tart at 365F for another 10 minutes.*
- ✓ *Cool the cooked tart and cut on the servings.*

Nutrition Calories 311, Fat 11g, Protein 4.5g, Carbs 24.7g

1280) Mango And Honey Cream

Ingredients

- *2 cups coconut cream, chipped*
- *6 teaspoons honey*
- *2 mango, chopped*

Directions:Servings: 6 **Preparation Time:** 30 Minutes

- ✓ *Blend together honey and mango.*
- ✓ *When the mixture is smooth, combine it with whipped cream and stir carefully.*
- ✓ *Put the mango-cream mixture into the serving glasses and refrigerate for 30 minutes.*

NutritionCalories 272, Fat 19.5g, Protein 2.8g, Carbs 27g

1281) Raw Truffles

Ingredients

- *1/2 pound dates, pitted*
- *½ cup water, hot*
- *2 tablespoons raw honey*
- *½ teaspoon vanilla extract*
- *2 tablespoons cocoa powder*
- *1 cup shredded coconut*
- *1 tablespoon chia seeds*
- *1 oz candied orange, diced*
- *Extra cocoa powder for coating*

Directions:Servings: 6 **Preparation Time:** 30 Minutes

- ✓ *Combine the hot water, dates, honey, and vanilla in a food processor and pulse until well mixed.*
- ✓ *Add the rest of the ingredients and mix well.*
- ✓ *Form small balls and roll them through cocoa powder.*
- ✓ *Serve right away.*

Nutrition Cal 196, Fat 4.8g, Protein 1.7g, Carbs 41.3

1282) Baked Peaches

Ingredients

- *4 teaspoons stevia*
- *4 peaches, halved and pitted*
- *1 teaspoon vanilla extract*
- *3 tablespoons honey*

Directions:Servings: 4 **Preparation Time:** 30 Minutes

- ✓ *Arrange the peaches on a baking sheet lined with parchment paper, add the stevia, honey, and vanilla and bake at 350 degrees F for 30 minutes.*
- ✓ *Divide them between plates and serve.*

Nutrition Calories 176, Fat 4.5g, Protein 5g, Carbs 11.5g

1283) Chocolate Baklava

Ingredients

- *24 sheets (14x9-inch) frozen whole-wheat phyllo (filo) dough, thawed*
- *1/8 teaspoon salt*
- *1/3 cup toasted walnuts, chopped coarsely*
- *1/3 cup almonds, blanched toasted, chopped coarsely*
- *1/2 teaspoon ground cinnamon*

- *1/2 cup water*
- *1/2 cup hazelnuts, toasted, chopped coarsely*
- *1/2 cup pistachios, roasted, chopped coarsely*
- *3/4 cup honey*
- *1/2 cup of butter, melted*
- *1 cup chocolate-hazelnut spread (I used Nutella)*
- *1 piece (3-inch) cinnamon stick*
- *Cooling spray*

Directions:Servings: 4 **Preparation Time:** 35 Minutes

- ✓ *Into a medium-sized saucepan, combine the water, honey, and the cinnamon stick; stir until the honey is dissolved. Increase the heat/flame to medium; continue cooking for about 10 minutes without stirring.*
- ✓ *A candy thermometer should read 230F. Remove the saucepan from the heat, and then keep warm. Remove and discard the cinnamon stick.*
- ✓ *Switch on the oven, preheat it setting its temperature to 350F.*
- ✓ *Put the chocolate hazelnut spread into a microwavable container; microwavable the spread for about 30 seconds on HIGH or until the spread is melted.*
- ✓ *Combine the hazelnuts, pistachios, almonds, walnuts, ground cinnamon, and salt in a container.*
- ✓ *Lightly grease with the cooling spray a 9x13-inch ceramic or glass baking dish.*
- ✓ *Put 1 sheet lengthwise into the bottom of the prepared baking dish, extending the ends of the sheet over the edges of the dish. Lightly brush the sheet with the butter. Repeat the process with 5 sheets of phyllo and a light brush of butter. Drizzle 1/3 cup of the melted chocolate hazelnut spread over the buttered phyllo sheets. Sprinkle about 1/3 of the nut mixture (1/2 cup) over the spread. Repeat the process, layering phyllo sheet, a brush of butter, spread and with nut mixture. For the last, nut mixture top layer, top with 6 phyllo sheets, pressing each phyllo gently into the dish and brushing each sheet with butter.*
- ✓ *Slice the layers into 24 portions by making 3 cuts lengthwise and then 5 cuts crosswire with a sharp knife; bake for about 35 minutes at 350F or until the phyllo sheets are golden. Remove the dish from the oven, drizzle the honey sauce over the baklava. Pace the dish on a wire rack and let cool. Cover and store the Baklava at normal room temperature if not serving right away.*

NutritionCalories 238, Fat 13.4g, Protein 4g, Carbs 27.8g, Fiber 1.6g

1284) Apricot Rosemary Muffins

Ingredients

- *2 eggs*
- *1/3 cup white sugar*
- *1 teaspoon vanilla extract*
- *1 cup buttermilk*
- *¼ cup olive oil*
- *1 ½ cups all-purpose flour*
- *¼ teaspoon salt*
- *1 teaspoon baking powder*
- *¼ teaspoon baking soda*
- *4 apricots, pitted and diced*
- *1 teaspoon dried rosemary*

Directions:Servings: 12 **Preparation Time:** 1 Hour

- ✓ *Combine the eggs, sugar, and vanilla in a container and mix until double in volume.*
- ✓ *Stir to the oil and buttermilk and mix well.*
- ✓ *Fold to the flour, salt, baking powder, and baking soda, then add the apricots and rosemary and mix gently.*
- ✓ *Spoon the batter in a muffin tin lined with muffin papers and bake in the preheated oven at 350F for 20-25 minutes or until the muffins pass the toothpick test.*
- ✓ *Serve the muffins chilled*

Nutrition Calories 140, Fat 5.4g, Protein 3.4g, Carbs 20.1g

1285) Blueberry Yogurt Mousse

Ingredients

- *2 cups Greek yogurt*
- *¼ cup stevia*
- *¾ heavy cream*
- *2 cups blueberries*

Directions:Servings: 4 **Preparation Time:** 0 Minutes

- ✓ *In a blender, combine the yogurt with the other ingredients, pulse well, divide into cups and keep in the fridge for 30 minutes before serving*

Nutrition Calories 141, Fat 4.7g, Protein 0.8g, Carbs 8.3g

1286) Pistachio Cheesecake

Ingredients

- *½ cup pistachio, chopped*
- *4 teaspoons butter, softened*
- *4 teaspoon Erythritol*
- *2 cups cream cheese*
- *½ cup cream, whipped*

Directions:Servings: 6 **Preparation Time:** 10 Minute

- ✓ *Mix up together pistachios, butter, and Erythritol.*
- ✓ *Put the mixture into the baking mold and bake for 10 minutes at 355F.*
- ✓ *Meanwhile, whisk together cream cheese and whipped cream.*
- ✓ *When the pistachio mixture is baked, chill it well.*
- ✓ *After this, transfer the pistachio mixture to the round cake mold and flatten it in one layer.*
- ✓ *Then put the cream cheese mixture over the*

pistachio mixture, flatten the surface until smooth.

- ✓ *Cool the cheesecake in the fridge for 1 hour before serving*

NutritionCalories 332, Fat 33g, Protein 7g, Carbs 7.49

1287) Almonds And Oats Pudding

Ingredients

- *1 tablespoon lemon juice*
- *Zest of 1 lime*
- *1 and ½ cups almond milk*
- *1 teaspoon almond extract*
- *½ cup oats*
- *2 tablespoons stevia*
- *½ cup silver almonds, chopped*

Directions:Servings: 4 **Preparation Time:** 15 Minutes

- ✓ *In a pan, combine the almond milk with the lime zest and the other ingredients, whisk, bring to a simmer and cook over medium heat for 15 minutes.*
- ✓ *Divide the mix into containers and serve cold.*

NutritionCalories 174, Fat 12.1g, Carbs 3.9g, Protein 4.8g

1288) Banana And Berries Trifle

Ingredients

- *8 oz biscuits, chopped*
- *¼ cup strawberries, chopped*
- *1 banana, chopped*
- *1 peach, chopped*
- *1/2 mango, chopped*
- *1 cup grapes, chopped*
- *1 tablespoon liquid honey*
- *1 cup of orange juice*
- *1/2 cup Plain yogurt*
- *1/4 cup cream cheese*
- *1 teaspoon coconut flakes*

Directions:Servings: 10 **Preparation Time:** 5 Minutes

- ✓ *Bring the orange juice to a boil and remove it from the heat.*
- ✓ *Add liquid honey and stir until it is dissolved.*
- ✓ *Cool the liquid to room temperature.*
- ✓ *Add chopped banana, peach, mango, grapes, and strawberries. Shake the fruits gently and leave to soak the orange juice for 15 minutes.*
- ✓ *Meanwhile, with the help of the hand mixer, mix up together Plain yogurt and cream cheese.*
- ✓ *Then separate the chopped biscuits, yogurt mixture, and fruits into 4 parts.*
- ✓ *Place the first part of the biscuits to the big-serving glass in one layer.*
- ✓ *Spread it with a yogurt mixture and add fruits.*
- ✓ *Repeat the same steps till you use all ingredients.*
- ✓ *Top the trifle with coconut flakes.*

Nutrition Cal 164, Fat 6.2g, Carbs 24.8g, Protein 3.2g

1289) Banana Kale Smoothie

Ingredients

- *2 cups kale leaves*
- *1 cup almond milk*
- *1/2 cup crushed ice*
- *1 banana, peeled*
- *1 apple, peeled and cored*
- *A dash of cinnamon*

Directions:Servings: 3 **Preparation Time:** 5 Minutes

- ✓ *Place all ingredients in a blender.*
- ✓ *Blend until smooth.*
- ✓ *Pour in a glass container and allow to chill to the fridge for at least 30 minutes.*

Nutrition Calories 165, Fat 4.2g, Carbs 32.1g, Protein 2.3g

1290) Cinnamon Stuffed Peaches

Ingredients

- *4 peaches, pitted, halved*
- *2 tablespoons ricotta cheese*
- *2 tablespoons of liquid honey*
- *3/4 cup of water*
- *1/2 teaspoon vanilla extract*
- *¾ teaspoon ground cinnamon*
- *1 tablespoon almonds, sliced*
- *¾ teaspoon saffron*

Directions:Servings: 4 **Preparation time:5 minutes**

- ✓ *Pour water into the saucepan and bring to a boil*
- ✓ *Add vanilla extract, saffron, ground cinnamon, and liquid honey.*
- ✓ *Cook the liquid until the honey is melted.*
- ✓ *Then remove it from the heat.*
- ✓ *Put the halved peaches into the hot honey liquid.*
- ✓ *Meanwhile, make the filling: mix up together ricotta cheese, vanilla extract, and sliced almonds.*
- ✓ *Remove the peaches from the honey liquid and arrange them on the plate.*
- ✓ *Fill 4 peach halves with ricotta filling and cover them with resting peach halves.*
- ✓ *Sprinkle the cooked dessert with liquid honey mixture gently.*

NutritionCalories 113, Fat 1.8g, Carbs 23.9g, Protein 2.7g

1291) Cinnamon Tea

Ingredients

- *6 cups water*
- *1 (3-in.) cinnamon stick*

- *6 TB. Ahmad Tea, Ceylon tea, or your favorite*
- *3 TB. sugar*

DIRECTIONS: Servings: 1 cup Preparation time: 32 minutes

- ✓ *In a teapot over low heat, bring water and cinnamon stick to a simmer for 3 minutes. Remove cinnamon stick.*
- ✓ *Stir in Ahmad tea and sugar, and simmer for 2 minutes.*
- ✓ *Remove from heat, and let sit for 10 minutes.*
- ✓ *Strain tea into teacups and serve warm.*

Nutrition Calories 39, Carbs 10g

1292) Custard-Filled Pancakes

Ingredients

- *1 cup all-purpose flour*
- *1/2 cup whole-wheat flour*
- *1 cup whole milk*
- *1/2 cup water*
- *1 tsp. active yeast*
- *1 tsp. baking powder*
- *½ tsp salt*
- *2 TB. sugar*
- *2 cups. Ashta Custard*
- *½ cup ground pistachios*
- *1 cup Simple syrup*

DIRECTIONS: Servings:1 pancake Preparation time:15 minutes

- ✓ *Whisk together all-purpose flour, whole-wheat flour, whole milk, water, yeast, baking powder, salt, and sugar in a large container. Set aside for 30 minutes.*
- ✓ *Preheat a nonstick griddle over low heat.*
- ✓ *Spoon 3 tablespoons batter onto the middle and cook the pancake for about 30 seconds or until bubbles form along the entire top of the pancake. Do not flip over pancake. You're only browning the bottom.*
- ✓ *Transfer pancake to a plate, and let cool while cooking the resting pancakes. Do not overlap the pancakes while letting them cool.*
- ✓ *Form pancake into a pocket by folding pancake into a half-moon and pinch together the edges, but only halfway up.*
- ✓ *Spoon Ashta Custard into a piping bag or a zipper-lock plastic bag, snip off the corner, and squeeze about 2 tablespoons custard into each pancake pocket. Sprinkle custard with pistachios.*
- ✓ *Serve pancakes chilled with Simple Syrup drizzled on top.*

Nutrition Calories 216, Carbs 42g, Fat 3g, Protein 3g

1293) Halva

Ingredients

- *11/2 cups honey*
- *11/2 cups tahini paste*
- *1 cup pistachios, coarsely chopped*

DIRECTIONS:Servings: ¼ Cup Preparation Time:10Minutes

- ✓ *Pour honey into a saucepan, set over low heat, and bring to 240F.*
- ✓ *In another saucepan over low heat, bring tahini paste to 120F.*
- ✓ *In a container, whisk together heated honey and tahini paste until smooth. Fold in pistachios.*
- ✓ *Line a loaf pan with parchment paper and spray with cooking spray. Pour tahini mixture into the loaf pan, and refrigerate for 2 days to set.*
- ✓ *Cut halva into bite-size pieces, and serve.*

Nutrition Calories 273, Fat 11g, Protein 2g, Carbs 42g,

1294) Hazelnut Pudding

Ingredients

- *2 and ¼ cups almond flour*
- *3 tablespoons hazelnuts, chopped*
- *5 eggs, whisked*
- *1 cup stevia*
- *1 and 1/3 cups Greek yogurt*
- *1 teaspoon baking powder*
- *1 teaspoon vanilla extract*

Directions:Servings: *8* ***Preparation Time:*** *40 Minutes*

- ✓ *In a container, combine the flour with the hazelnuts and the other ingredients, whisk well and pour into a cake pan lined with parchment paper.*
- ✓ *Introduce to the oven at 350F, bake for 30 minutes, cool down, slice, and serve.*

Nutrition Calories 178, Fat 8.4g, Carbs 11.5g, Protein 1.4g

1295) Line Grapes And Apples

Ingredients

- *1/2 cup red grapes*
- *2 apples*
- *1 teaspoon lime juice*
- *1 teaspoon Erythritol*
- *3 tablespoons water*

Directions:Servings: *2* ***Preparation Time:*** *25 Minutes*

- ✓ *Line the baking tray with baking paper.*
- ✓ *Then cut the apples on the halves and remove the seeds with the help of the cooper.*
- ✓ *Cut the apple halves into 2 more parts.*
- ✓ *Arrange all fruits to the tray in one layer, drizzle with water and bake for 20 minutes at 375F.*
- ✓ *Flip the fruits on another side after 10 minutes of cooking.*

- ✓ Then remove them from the oven and sprinkle with lime juice and Erythritol.
- ✓ Return the fruits back to the oven and bake for 5 minutes more.
- ✓ Serve the cooked dessert hot or warm.

Nutrition Cal 142, Fat 0.4g, Carbs 40.1g, Protein 0.9g

1296) Mediterranean Bread Pudding

Ingredients

- ✓ 8 slices white bread, crust removed
- ✓ 1 cup sugar
- ✓ 1/2 cup water
- ✓ 1 TB. fresh lemon juice
- ✓ 2 cups Simple Syrup
- ✓ 4 cups Ashta Custard
- ✓ 1/2 cup coconut flakes, toasted
- ✓ 1/2 cup pistachios, ground
- ✓ 1 strawberry, sliced

DIRECTIONS: Servings: **1/9 Of Pudding** Preparation Time: **20 Minutes**

- ✓ Turn on the oven, preheat it by setting the temperature to 450F.
- ✓ Place bread slices on a baking sheet and toast for 10 minutes or until bread is golden brown and dry.
- ✓ In a small saucepan over medium-low heat, combine the sugar, water, and lemon juice. Simmer for 5-7 minutes or until sugar reaches a dark golden brown color.
- ✓ Carefully pour the hot dark brown syrup into an 8x8-inch baking dish, moving the dish from side to side to spread the syrup to the bottom of the dish.
- ✓ Place 4 slices of bread on top of the brown syrup. Pour 1 cup simple syrup over bread, spread 2 cups Ashta custard over the bread, and add another layer of 4 bread slices. Pour the remaining 1 cup of simple syrup over the bread and spread the remaining 2 cups of Ashta custard over the bread layer.
- ✓ Cover the dish with plastic wrap and refrigerate for 4 hours.
- ✓ Decorate the top of the dish with toasted coconut, pistachios, and strawberry slices, and serve.

Nutrition Calories 95, Fat 2g, Protein 4g, Carbs 19g, Fiber 2g

1297) Mediterranean Cheesecakes

Ingredients

- 4 cups shredded phyllo (kataifi dough)
- 1/2 cup butter, melted
- 12 oz cream cheese
- 1 cup Greek yogurt
- 3/4 cup confectioners' sugar
- 1 TB. vanilla extract
- 2 TB. orange blossom water
- 1 TB. orange zest
- 2 large eggs
- 1 cup coconut flakes

DIRECTIONS:Servings: 1 Cheesecake **Preparation Time:** 20 Minutes

- ✓ Switch on the oven, preheat it setting its temperature to 450F.
- ✓ In a large container, and using your hands, combine shredded phyllo and melted butter, working the two together and breaking up phyllo shreds as you work.
- ✓ Using a 12-cup muffin tin, add 1/3 cup shredded phyllo mixture to each tin, and press down to form a crust on the bottom of the cup. Bake crusts for 8 minutes, remove them from the oven and set aside.
- ✓ In a large container, blend cream cheese and Greek yogurt with an electric mixer on low speed for 1 minute.
- ✓ Add confectioners' sugar, vanilla extract, orange blossom water, and orange zest and blend for 1 minute.
- ✓ Add eggs, and blend for about 30 seconds or just until eggs are incorporated.
- ✓ Lightly coat the sides of each muffin tin with cooking spray.
- ✓ Pour about 1/3 cup cream cheese mixture over crust in each tin. Do not overflow.
- ✓ Bake for 12 minutes.
- ✓ Spread shredded coconut on a baking sheet and place in the oven with cheesecakes to toast for 4 or 5 minutes or until golden brown. Remove from the oven and set aside.
- ✓ Remove cheesecakes from the oven and cool for 1 hour on the countertop.
- ✓ Place the tin in the fridge and cool for 1 more hour.
- ✓ To serve, dip a sharp knife in warm water and then run it along the sides of cheesecakes to loosen from the tin. Gently remove cheesecakes and place them on a seizing plate.
- ✓ Sprinkle with toasted coconut flakes and serve.

Nutrition Calories 540, Fat 28g, Carbs 14g, Fiber 5g, Sugar 4g, Protein 56g

1298) Olive Oil Cake

Ingredients

- 2 large eggs
- 3/4 cup sugar
- 1/2 cup light olive oil
- 1 cup plain Greek yogurt
- 3 TB. fresh orange juice
- 2 TB. orange zest

- *13/4 cups all-purpose flour*
- *½ tsp salt*
- *2 tsp. baking powder*
- *1/2 tsp. baking soda*
- *3,/4 cup dried cranberries*
- *2 TB. confectioners' sugar*

Directions:Servings: 1 Piece **Preparation Time:** 45 Minutes

- ✓ *Turn on the oven and preheat it by setting the temperature to 350F.*
- ✓ *Lightly coat a 9-inch cake pan or Bundt pan with cooking spray and dust with about 2 tablespoons of all-purpose flour.*
- ✓ *In a large bowl, mix the eggs and sugar with an electric mixer on medium speed for 2 minutes.*
- ✓ *Stir in the light olive oil, Greek yogurt, orange juice, and orange zest for another 2 minutes.*
- ✓ *Add the flour, salt, baking powder, and baking soda and blend for 1 more minute.*
- ✓ *Using a spatula or wooden spoon, fold the blueberries into the batter.*
- ✓ *Pour the batter into the prepared pan and bake for 45 minutes or until a toothpick inserted into the center of the cake comes out clean.*
- ✓ *Cool the cake completely.*
- ✓ *Dust the top of the cake with powdered sugar, cut, and serve.*

Nutrition Calories 241, Fat 12g, Protein 4g, Carbs 31g, Fiber 2g

1299) Phyllo Custard Pockets

Ingredients

- *8 phyllo sheets*
- *1/2 cup butter, melted*
- *21/4 cups Ashta Custard*
- *1 cup Simple syrup*
- *1/2 cup pistachios, ground*

Directions: Servings: 1 pocket **Preparation time:** 10 minutes

- ✓ *Turn on the oven, preheat it by setting the temperature to 450F.*
- ✓ *Roll out one sheet of phyllo dough, brush with butter and overlap another sheet of phyllo dough. Cut sheets into 3 equal-sized columns, each about 3 to 4 inches wide.*
- ✓ *Place 3 tablespoons of Ashta custard at one end of each column and fold the bottom right corner over the custard. Pull up the bottom left corner and repeat the folding of each corner to the opposite corner, forming a triangle as you fold.*
- ✓ *Place the triangle pockets on a baking sheet, brush with butter and bake for 10 minutes or until golden brown.*
- ✓ *Serve warm or cold, drizzled with simple syrup and sprinkled with pistachios.*

Nutrition Cals 393, Carbs 55g, Fat 15g, Protein 8g

1300) Semolina Cake

Ingredients

- *1/2 cup wheat flour, whole grain*
- *1/2 cup semolina*
- *1 teaspoon baking powder*
- *½ cup Plain yogurt*
- *1 teaspoon vanilla extract*
- *4 tablespoons Erythritol*
- *1 teaspoon lemon rind*
- *2 tablespoons olive oil*
- *1 tablespoon almond flakes*
- *4 teaspoons liquid honey*
- *1/2 cup of orange juice*

Directions:Servings: 6 **Preparation Time:** 30 Minutes

- ✓ *Mix wheat flour, semolina, baking powder, plain yogurt, vanilla extract, Erythritol, and olive oil together.*
- ✓ *Then add lemon rind and mix up the ingredients until smooth.*
- ✓ *Transfer the mixture to the non-sticky cake mold, sprinkle with almond flakes and bake for 30 minutes at 365F.*
- ✓ *Meanwhile, bring the orange juice to a boil.*
- ✓ *Add liquid honey and stir until dissolved.*
- ✓ *When the cake is cooked, pour the hot orange juice mixture over it and let it rest for at least 10 minutes.*
- ✓ *Cut the cake into servings.*

Nutrition Calories 179, Fat 6.1g, Carbs 36.3g, Protein 4.5g

1301) White Wine Grapefruit Poached Peaches

Ingredients

- *4 peaches*
- *2 cups white wine*
- *1 grapefruit, peeled and juiced*
- *¼ cup white sugar*
- *1 cinnamon stick*
- *1-star anise*
- *1 cardamom pod*
- *1 cup Greek yogurt for serving*

Directions:Servings: 6 **Preparation Time:** 40 Minutes

- ✓ *Combine the wine, grapefruit, sugar, and spices in a saucepan.*
- ✓ *Bring to a boil, then place the peaches in the hot syrup.*
- ✓ *Lower the heat, then cover it using a lid.*
- ✓ *Cook for 15 minutes. After this, allow to cool down.*

✓ *Carefully peel the peaches and place them in a small serving container.*

✓ *Top with yogurt and serve right away.*
Nutrition Cal 157, Fat 0.9g, Carbs 20.4g, Protein 4.2g

1302) Yogurt Cake

Ingredients

- *1 cup plain Greek yogurt*
- *1 cup sugar*
- *2 large eggs*
- *1 TB. vanilla extract*
- *4 TB. fresh lemon juice*
- *1 TB. lemon zest*
- *1/2 cup light olive oil*
- *13,/4 cups all-purpose flour*
- *2 tsp. baking powder*
- *½ tsp salt*
- *1 cup confectioners' sugar*

DIRECTIONS: Servings: *1 Piece* ***Preparation Time:*** *55 Minutes*

✓ *Switch on the oven, preheat it setting its temperature to 350F. Lightly brush a 9-inch-round cake pan with cooking spray and dust the pan using about 2 tablespoons of all-purpose flour.*

✓ *In a large container, blend Greek yogurt, eggs, sugar, vanilla extract, 2 tablespoons lemon juice, lemon zest, and vegetable oil using an electric mixer on medium speed for about 2 minutes.*

✓ *Add flour, baking powder, and salt and blend for 2 more minutes.*

✓ *Pour batter into the prepared cake pan and bake until a toothpick inserted into the center of the cake comes out clean. Cool cake completely.*

✓ *In a small container, whisk together confectioners' sugar and the resting 2 tablespoons lemon juice to make the glaze.*

✓ *When the cake is cool, pour glaze over the top, cut, and serve.*
Nutrition Calories 88, Fat 6g, Protein 3g, carbs 7g, Fiber 1g

4 Week Meal Plan

Day	Breakfast	Lunch	Dinner	Snacks
1	Fruit de salad recipe	Lamb And Rice	Bulgur Salad	150gr. Greek Yogurt and 100 gr Almond
2	Bacon, Vegetable and Parmesan Combo	Flavors Herb Risotto	Spinach and Grilled Feta Salad	Quinoa Fruit Salad
3	Avocado and Eggs Breakfast Tacos	Cod Potato Soup	Delicious Greek Chicken Pasta	Healthy Blueberry and Coconut Smoothie
4	Cheesy Caprese Style Portobellos Mushrooms	Lamb And Rice	Bulgur Salad	Herbed Panini Fillet O'Fish
5	Bacon Veggies Combo	Roasted Pepper Pasta	A Refreshing Detox Salad	Halibut Sandwiches Mediterranean Style
6	Buttered Thyme Scallops	Bulgur Salad	Grilled Salmon Summer Salad	Quinoa Fruit Salad
7	Delicious Frittata with Brie and Bacon	Grilled Burgers with Mushrooms	Baked Cauliflower Mixed Salad	150gr. Greek Yogurt and 100 gr Almond
8	Baked Avocado Eggs	Sweet and Sour Spinach Salad	Pesto Chicken Pasta	Halibut Sandwiches Mediterranean Style
9	Orzo and Veggie Containers	Sea Bass Crusted with Moroccan Spices	Eggplant and Zucchini Gratin	Healthy Blueberry and Coconut Smoothie
10	Baked Eggs and Asparagus with Parmesan	Cod Potato Soup	Whole-Wheat Fusilli with Chickpea Sauce	150gr. Greek Yogurt and 100 gr Almond

11	Orzo and Veggie Containers	Spinach Cheese Pies	Cheesy Sweet Potato Burgers	Healthy Blueberry and Coconut Smoothie
12	Feta and Pepper Frittata	Veggie-Stuffed Portabello Mushrooms	Hearty Beef Ragu	Quinoa Fruit Salad
13	Poblano Fritatta	Lamb And Rice	Walnut Carrots with Honey Glaze	Halibut Sandwiches Mediterranean Style
14	Delicious Frittata with Brie and Bacon	Grilled Salmon Summer Salad	Carrots and Tomatoes Chicken	Healthy Blueberry and Coconut Smoothie
15	Protein-Packed Blender Pancakes	Paprika Salmon And Green Beans	Coriander and Coconut Chicken	150gr. Greek Yogurt and 100 gr Almond
16	Stuffed Figs	Ground Pork Salad	Almond-Crusted Chicken Tenders with Honey	Halibut Sandwiches Mediterranean Style
17	Poblano Fritatta	Thyme Ginger Garlic Beef	Beef And Dill Mushrooms	Quinoa Fruit Salad
18	Ham Muffins	Salmon and Watermelon Gazpacho	Italian Beef	Healthy Blueberry and Coconut Smoothie
19	Veggie Stuffed Hash Browns	Roasted Pepper Pasta	Creamy Chicken And Mushrooms	150gr. Greek Yogurt and 100 gr Almond
20	Avocado Egg Scramble	Beef Curry	Spinach Cheese Pies	Halibut Sandwiches Mediterranean Style
21	Mediterranean Egg Casserole	Beef And Grape Sauce	Baked Cauliflower Mixed Salad	Healthy Blueberry and Coconut Smoothie
22	Pear Oatmeal	Pork and Prunes Stew	Paprika Salmon And Green Beans	Halibut Sandwiches Mediterranean Style

23	Blueberry and Vanilla Scones	Pesto Chicken Pasta	Beef And Potatoes With Tahini Sauce	Healthy Blueberry and Coconut Smoothie
24	Blueberry and Vanilla Scones	Pork And Sage Couscous	Paprika Salmon And Green Beans	150gr. Greek Yogurt and 100 gr Almond
25	Peas Omelet	Lamb And Rice	Beef And Dill Mushrooms	Healthy Blueberry and Coconut Smoothie
26	Cheesy Thyme Waffles	Flavors Herb Risotto	Cod Potato Soup	Halibut Sandwiches Mediterranean
27	Baked Eggs and Asparagus with Parmesan	Paprika Salmon And Green Beans	Veggie-Stuffed Portabello Mushrooms	150gr. Greek Yogurt and 100 gr Almond
28	Ham Spinach Ballet	Cod Potato Soup	Pork and Prunes Stew	Quinoa Fruit Salad
29	Scrambled Eggs	Beef And Dill Mushrooms	Grilled Burgers with Mushrooms	150gr. Greek Yogurt and 100 gr Almond
30	Cocoa Oatmeal	Pork And Sage Couscous	Baked Cauliflower Mixed Salad	Halibut Sandwiches Mediterranean Style

CONCLUSION

The Mediterranean diet is ideal for connoisseurs. You can choose between delicious dishes.

The Mediterranean diet consists of a mixed diet of fresh fruit and vegetables, lots of fish and little red meat. Olive oil is used for the preparation and one glass of red wine can be drunk a day. However, the diet only has an influence on body weight if attention is paid to the calorie intake. It has not been proven whether the diet has a positive effect on lifespan.

A Mediterranean diet, a diet typical of the Mediterranean region, is one of the healthiest forms of nutrition. These include lots of vegetables, legumes, fruits, nuts, olive oil and fish and little red meat, dairy products and saturated fat.

For everyone who wants to lose weight and do something for their cardiovascular health, the Mediterranean diet is the best choice, because it not only sheds the most pounds, but also minimizes the risk of heart attacks by 30 percent.

Alphabetical Index

A

B

C

D

E

F

G

H

I

J

K

L

M

N

O

P

Q

R

S

T

V

W

Y

Z

Made in United States
Orlando, FL
29 December 2021